307   36
309   55
         67
11
302
304
310
360
383

The Oxford Dictionary of

Political
Quotations

The Oxford Dictionary of

Political Quotations

SECOND EDITION

edited by **Antony Jay**

OXFORD

UNIVERSITY PRESS

OXFORD
UNIVERSITY PRESS

Great Clarendon Street, Oxford OX2 6DP

Oxford University Press is a department of the University of Oxford.
It furthers the University's objective of excellence in research, scholarship,
and education by publishing worldwide in

Oxford New York

Athens Auckland Bangkok Bogotá Buenos Aires Calcutta
Cape Town Chennai Dar es Salaam Delhi Florence Hong Kong Istanbul
Karachi Kuala Lumpur Madrid Melbourne Mexico City Mumbai
Nairobi Paris São Paulo Shanghai Singapore Taipei Tokyo Toronto Warsaw
with associated companies in Berlin Ibadan

Published in the United States
by Oxford University Press Inc., New York

British Library Cataloguing in Publication Data
Data available

Library of Congress Cataloging in Publication Data
Data available
ISBN 0-19-863167-7

10 9 8 7 6 5 4 3 2 1

Designed by Jane Stevenson
Typeset in Photina and Argo
by Inter-active Sciences Ltd
Printed in Great Britain
by T. J. International Ltd
Padstow, Cornwall

Project Team

Managing Editor	Elizabeth Knowles
Associate Editor	Susan Ratcliffe
Index Editor	Christina Malkowska Zaba
Library Research	Ralph Bates Marie G. Diaz
Reading Programme	Helen Rappaport Verity Mason
Data Capture	Muriel Summersgill
Proof-reading	Fabia Claris Penny Trumble

Contents

Preface to the Second Edition

When I worked on a television current affairs programme in the late 1950s we regularly rang Madame Tussaud's at the end of December to find out which new celebrities had entered the hall of fame during the past year, and—regrettably even more interesting—who had been melted down. In editing the first edition of this dictionary I did not see myself as having anything in common with the manager of a waxworks exhibition, but coming to the second edition the similarity is clear. Neither can remain unchanged and continue to be as interesting and useful as they were when they started. New quotations, like new models, demand inclusion, while some old ones can no longer justify the space they take up.

All quotations dictionaries—at least all those drawing on a living culture rather than a dead language—need updating from time to time if they are to continue as a useful work of reference rather than dwindle into a literary curiosity. This is especially true of political quotations. Certainly the past five years have supplied at least their fair share of quotation fodder. The election of the first Labour government for eighteen years led to a prolonged national debate on such profound constitutional issues as devolution and hereditary peerages, and gave London its first mayoral election and the millennium dome. We have seen the war in Kosovo, the Good Friday Agreement in Northern Ireland, and the impeachment of the President of the United States. Issues like the single currency, genetic modification of food, and spin doctors have moved rapidly up the national agenda, and famous figures have left the international stage: Boris Yeltsin, Helmut Kohl, François Mitterrand, Nelson Mandela, Princess Diana.

Accommodating the quotations generated by these new issues and events might have forced some difficult decisions, but fortunately the publishers have found ways of increasing the amount of space available, with the result that the second edition contains over 800 quotations not in the first book. Research has also enabled us to increase the richness of the text with new 'classic' material from sources such as Elizabeth the First, Napoleon, Aristophanes, Hazlitt, and Genghis Khan. And we have improved access to the material with new special categories, including Slogans, Mottoes, Epitaphs, Last Words, Newspaper Headlines and Misquotations.

There is however a further and special value to a second edition when there has not previously been—at least in the UK—a dictionary on a similar theme: it stimulates readers to point out omissions. No quotations dictionary can ever be as comprehensive, exhaustive or definitive as the editor would like, but a first edition on a new topic is particularly likely to have gaps. I am most grateful to all those who sent in suggestions, and would encourage others to do the same with this edition; it seems that the readership of this dictionary is gratifyingly weighted towards the scholarly and well-read. The reviewers, too, often made helpful suggestions. Several of those north of the border complained, not wholly unfairly, about a shortage of Scottish quotations, and I am especially grateful to Magnus Linklater for his help in supplying that particular deficiency. Professor Peter Hennessy also came up with another invaluable batch of recent quotations. And once again I have to acknowledge the debt this second edition owes to the diligence and vigilance of the editors and research staff of the Oxford University Press.

ANTONY JAY

Somerset, August, 2000

Introduction to the First Edition

'The hard pressed writer in turning over these pages may find and note many excellent phrases, whether to give a pleasing touch of erudition or to save the trouble of thinking for himself.' Bernard Darwin's words in his introduction to the first *Oxford Dictionary of Quotations* are as true today as they were fifty-five years ago. But there are more honourable reasons for using quotations, especially in the world of politics. In mobilizing support for a project or a policy it is especially agreeable to be able to call upon the distinguished dead; their distinction adds intellectual weight and moral force to the argument, and their death makes it impossible for them to appear on television later and say that they meant something completely different.

Even more important, perhaps, than the support of the eminent is the wisdom of the ages. New ideas in politics are always suspect, but recourse to quotation can show that your ideas, far from being new and tender shoots, are rooted deep in the history of political society. Those who argue for punishment as deterrent rather than rehabilitation may find themselves out of the fashion, but a quick look at Aeschylus will enable them to demonstrate the two and a half thousand year pedigree of their belief. Those who oppose closer ties with Europe can quote Bagehot, 'Are they [the English people] not above all nations divided from the rest of the world? . . . Are they not out of the current of common European causes and affairs?' from the nineteenth century, and Gibbon, 'The division of Europe into a number of independent states is productive of the most beneficial consequences to the liberty of mankind,' from the eighteenth, to show that there is nothing new in their belief that there is strength and logic in their resistance, while Europhiles can adduce the dictum of the nineteenth century Prime Minister Lord Salisbury: 'We are part of the community of Europe and we must do our duty as such.' Just occasionally, too, quotations can be used not just for intellectual support, but for dramatic effect, as if they carried some magical power. Two Prime Ministers in living memory have felt the force of it. The first was Chamberlain in 1940, when Leo Amery quoted Cromwell's historic words to the Rump Parliament 'You have sat too long for any good you have been doing. Depart, I say, and let us have done with you. In the name of God, go!' Chamberlain went. The second was Macmillan in 1963, when a fellow Conservative, Nigel Birch, quoted just as lethally from Browning's *The Lost Leader*:

> Life's night begins; let him never come back to us!
> There would be doubt, hesitation and pain,
> Forced praise on our part—the glimmer of twilight,
> Never glad confident morning again!

Perhaps Macmillan was doomed anyway, but Birch's quotation made certain of his fall as surely as Brutus' dagger.

This Dictionary, it is hoped, will be of service to those who want to support their arguments and opinions with evidence of their distinguished pedigree and ancient lineage, as well as those looking for no more than a pleasing touch of erudition or the avoidance of thought. It is not, however, simply an anthology of political wit and wisdom. It is, first, foremost, and above all, a work of reference. The primary qualification for an entry is not its antiquity or its profundity but its familiarity. There is a bank of political quotations which are part of the currency of political speeches and writings throughout the English-speaking world. All of them should be in these pages, and if they are not (and I am sure time and alert readers will expose some glaring omissions) then the editor is to blame.

Beyond the central core of universally recognized political quotations there is a much wider circle of entries which, while they are quoted from time to time, are not immediately recognizable to all of those to whom they are addressed. These are subject to editorial judgment, and here the editor might try to defend an omission rather than apologize for it. But in both cases the key question has been 'Should this be in a work of reference?' The two principal users for whom the book is intended are those who have encountered or partly recall a quotation and want to verify or source it, and those who are looking for a quotation on a particular subject or from a given writer.

Many works of reference, however, have an appeal to browsers and grazers as well as hunters, and a dictionary of political quotations must be very close to the top of the list; it offers the delight of discovery as well as confirmation and verification. While this one is not designed as an anthology, it is bound to give the reader most of the pleasure of an anthology, and so in many cases I have tried to supply more contextual information than might be necessary in a work of pure reference. Some quotations (for instance Wellington's 'If you believe that you'll believe anything') make little sense to any but the expert reader, unless accompanied by some indication of the context. Others, while intelligible (like Margaret Thatcher's 'Now it must be business as usual'), can become much more interesting with some knowledge of the circumstances in which they were uttered. For the same reason the Dictionary is organized not by theme but by the name of the speaker or writer. I have never myself been entirely at ease with thematic organization—I always have a niggling suspicion that any thematic entry could legitimately have been included under a different heading, and often under several—whereas entries grouped under the name of the source cannot suffer under this disability, and arrangement by source is just as helpful as arrangement by theme for reference purposes. In a collection of political quotations, this form is particularly advantageous, especially for the random dipper: reading through the citations from one individual—Lloyd George, de Tocqueville, Halifax—gives a quick but vivid sense not only of what he said but also of his quality and individuality. So although this is indeed a work of reference, it is hoped that many people will also use it as an illuminating, if wildly unsystematic, compendium of opinions, ideas, and personalities that have marked our progress towards the political society we live in today.

So what makes a quotation into a political quotation? Often, of course, the answer is obvious. General truths about politics are immediate candidates: Aeschylus's 'Everyone's quick to blame the alien', Bacon's 'All rising to great place is by a winding stair', and Burke's 'To tax and to please, no more than to love and be wise, is not given to men.' Then there are quotations specific to an event or an individual which have passed into the language: Disraeli's 'I have climbed to the top of the greasy pole' or Mary Tudor's 'When I am dead and opened, you shall find "Calais" lying in my heart', even though it is more often misquoted than quoted. Some quotations would not merit inclusion but for the source; if you or I had said 'No woman in my time will be Prime Minister' we would hardly expect to find ourselves in the Dictionary. The fact that Margaret Thatcher said it makes all the difference.

There is however a disputed territory between what is obviously a political quotation and what is obviously not. There is nothing remotely political about the words 'I can't tell a lie, Pa; you know I can't tell a lie. I did cut it with my hatchet,' but because it illuminates Washington's character, and because its frequent quotation testifies to his reputation, there can be no question of leaving it out. But what about the sayings of great men when they are writing fiction and the words come from the mouths of their characters, as in Macaulay's poems or Disraeli's novels. Surely it can not be cheating to include them if exclusion would mean omitting 'A Jacobite's Epitaph'? And the 'Two nations' speech in *Sybil* is currently at the heart of the Conservative Party's internal strife.

Another obscure territorial boundary is that which divides, or fails to divide, political quotations from those which, while having large areas that overlap politics, might more properly be classified under headings such as law, warfare, royalty, or economics. If these subjects had their own Oxford quotation dictionaries, there might have been some debate about where to place Adam Smith's observation that 'people of the same trade seldom meet together, even for merriment and diversion, but the conversation ends in a conspiracy against the public, or in some contrivance to raise prices.' Since there is however (as yet) no Oxford Dictionary of Economics Quotations, there was no argument. There is however an excellent *Oxford Book of Political Anecdotes* and, while some anecdotes are the source of quotation, anecdotes as such are not included. Obviously there were temptations. After losing office in 1964 Iain Macleod was a conspicuous absentee from the opposition front bench, which Wilson knew was a cause of much critical comment among Conservative back-benchers. One day however he did appear, to put a challenging question to the Prime Minister. Wilson rose, paused, and then said 'Do you come here often?' It produced one of the biggest laughs ever heard from a party against one of its own front-benchers. But somehow 'Do you come here often?' did not sound like a political quotation; it belongs only in that anecdote and had to be excluded.

Of course not all political quotations are either by politicians or about politics. Lewis Carroll was certainly not a politician and *Alice Through the Looking Glass* is equally certainly not a political work, but 'Jam tomorrow' and 'when I use a word it means just what I choose it to mean' are regularly quoted in political debate—as witness the quotation from Tony Benn, 'Some of that jam we thought was for tomorrow we have already eaten.' The Dictionary would be failing its readers if it left them out. Politicians may no longer quote poetry as freely as they used to, but students of the politics of the recent past will find many quotations from and references to poets, and even today them may encounter Kipling's 'Paying the Dane-geld', Chesterton's 'The Secret People', and copious allusions to the Vicar of Bray. And there is of course one poet who stands out above all the others for frequency of quotation: it is not just the power and range of Shakespeare's writing that makes him so quotable in a political context, it is the fact that so many of his plays are so intensely political in their themes, characters, and conflicts. If readers feel that he is over-represented here, I can only say that I have been acutely aware of the apparently excessive space he has been given, and that the original section was considerably longer. Much weeding has been done, and the surviving entries represent the editor's judgement of those that could not be omitted without loss.

Shakespeare is not the only writer (though he is the only poet) to occupy what might seem to be a disproportionate amount of space. Four great national leaders—Churchill, Disraeli, Jefferson, and Lincoln—have been endlessly quoted by their contemporaries and successors. Certainly they had the gift of language, but it also seems as if the fame they achieved during their lifetime may have led to their words being more diligently recorded and more frequently repeated than those of their less famous contemporaries. There are however two people who figure prominently in these pages without having achieved the same world wide fame. Burke, though he was indeed a statesman, was not in their class, and Bagehot was never even a member of parliament. Both, however, consistently found a way of expressing ideas and arguments that everyone could remember and no one could improve on. Some of their ideas were original, but even those that were not have proved to be endlessly quotable. They exemplify Pope's definition:

> True wit is Nature to advantage dressed.
> What oft was thought, but ne'er so well expressed.

The editor feels no need to apologize for the amount of space they command.

There is one particular danger which confronts all quotation dictionaries: the danger of including only those quotations which have already appeared in other dictionaries. It is of course inevitable that many of the quotations will be found in others collections, but it is equally important that lexicographers should not be endlessly recycling the same material. If quotations are to refresh and invigorate political communication, they should be drawn from a living stream and not a stagnant pond. So while the starting point for this Dictionary was the existing corpus of political quotations held on the files of the Oxford University Press, it was only the starting point. The principal means of bringing in new material was a team of researchers who combed the daily papers and the periodicals, and listened to radio and television programmes, to record every significant quotation they came across and submit it for consideration. Another important source has been correspondence. A living dictionary of quotations will necessarily include quotations from the living, and many of them have been kind enough not only to verify and source entries attributed to them, but also to supply other of their writings and sayings that they have found being quoted. The living have also interceded for the dead: for example, the first draft selection, like all the quotation dictionaries I have encountered, was disturbingly short of quotation from one of Britain's most distinguished Prime Ministers,

Robert Peel. It was hard to believe that he had left so few quotable remarks behind him, and a letter to the leading authority on Peel, Professor Norman Gash, produced evidence that it was not Peel but the record that was at fault. Peel's entry is now of a respectable length. Equally, one of the most politically astute civil servants of the nineteenth century would have remained unrepresented if Lord Dacre had not directed me to Henry Taylor's *The Statesman.*

This leads to the final aspect of the question 'What is a political quotation?', namely does it have to have been quoted, or is it sufficient for it to be quotable? Once you accept quotability as the criterion, you are on a slippery slope, at the bottom of which lie the broad acres of anthologies and commonplace books. The compilers of the first edition of the *Oxford Dictionary of Quotations* were in no doubt: 'During the whole work of selection a great effort was made to restrict the entries to actual current quotations and not to include phrases which the various editors or contributors believed to be quotable or wanted to be quoted.' Of course they were right. And yet even they said only that a great effort was made, not that it was successful in every case. I must confess to not having been quite so purist. Certainly this is essentially a dictionary of what has been quoted, but here and there I have taken one or two small steps down the slippery slope and included lines that I believed modern readers would like to quote. After all, how can one know that they have not been quoted somewhere at some time? I took the liberty of including Laertes's advice to Ophelia about marriage to the heir to the throne:

> His greatness weighed, his will is not his own
> For he himself is subject to his birth.
> He may not, as unvalued persons do,
> Carve for himself, for on his choice depends
> The sanity and health of the whole state;
> And therefore must his choice be circumscribed
> Unto the voice and yielding of that body
> Whereof he is the head.

I had no record of its being politically quoted anywhere, but in view of the continuing current debate about the divorce and remarriage of the Prince of Wales it seemed to me that many people might like to be reminded of it. It was only after it had been passed for the press that I discovered that Stanley Baldwin had quoted that same speech in the House of Commons, in relation to the abdication of King Edward VIII. So the reader will find here a small number— and an exceedingly small percentage—of entries that I cannot swear have been previously quoted, though equally I cannot swear that they have not. They are also another way of stopping the pool of political quotation from stagnating. And another aspect of this question is, when does a political quotation stop being a political quotation? It would have been easy to decide that Bismarck's observation that the Balkan conflict was 'not worth the healthy bones of a single Pomeranian grenadier' had passed into history's out-tray; but it surfaced again in 1995 in a House of Commons debate on the role of the UN forces in Bosnia.

If I may have taken slight liberties with the quotable as opposed to the quoted, this has not been the case with verification and sourcing. My colleagues at the

Press have been rigorous and scrupulous about the tracing of quotations, and many promising runners fell at this last fence. They include familiar lines like *Pas d'ennemi à gauche* and 'Whoever is in office, the Conservatives are always in power', but among the omissions are a few whose absence I particularly regret. I am sure Bacon said 'Councils to which Time hath not been called, Time will not ratify' (and I am absolutely certain I did not make it up), and I am fairly sure he said 'Great events may have small occasions, but seldom small causes', but no amount of research has been able to track either of them down. I also wish we could have found who it was who said of Gladstone that when making a speech he not only followed every bay and headland along the coastline of his argument, but also insisted on tracking every river to its source. And I believe it was the American scholar Donald Schon who said that government bureaux are memorials to dead problems, but alas I cannot prove it. Another source of regret is the quotations that appeared just too late for inclusion, in particular Shimon Peres's observations 'Television has made dictatorship impossible, but democracy unbearable.' But we were not too late for President Izetbegović's words after signing the Dayton Accord: 'And to my people I say, this may not be a just peace, but it is more just than a continuation of war.'

Perhaps the most problematic of all the quotations are the very recent ones. Ultimately, time is the judge of whether an observation can be accepted as a quotation, and whether 'Tough on crime and tough on the causes of crime' is a full member of the club or merely a short-term visitor, only time will tell. On the other hand, to set an arbitrary limit of ten or twenty years from the first citation as a qualifying period would mean excluding many quotations to which readers would want to refer. I suspect that in any future edition it will be the most topical recent entries that are the least likely to survive.

And what about speech-writers? This is surely a recent problem. It may be that politicians in the past had help from time to time, but it is hard to picture Lincoln or Disraeli or Lloyd George or Churchill asking the boys in the back room to come up with some ideas for the next speech. Today a team of speech writers is part of the standard entourage of an international leader, and on occasions we learn, at least informally, that some famous phrase or other was coined by a hand unconnected to the tongue that uttered it. Should we seek out the names of the writers and give them due recognition? It would be an impossible task, and moreover the reader would look for the phrase under the name of the politician who delivered it. This is also true of quotations that were in circulation some time before a politician gave them national or international currency. Where we can trace the original we attribute it, but it has to be accepted that some of the quotations attributed to politicians were probably not their own coinage. Nevertheless they will always be associated with the words, just as Clark Gable, and not Margaret Mitchell or Sidney Howard, will always be associated with the line 'Frankly, my dear, I don't give a damn' (which would probably be the politician's comment on this question).

The other difficulty presented by the most recent quotations is the possibility that in their original form they reached a national or international audience without ever appearing on a printed page. Radio and television archives are not always accessible, and slow to plough through even when you know exactly what you are looking for; but when you have only an imprecise recollection or reference it can be effectively impossible to locate what would be fairly easy to find in a newspaper or press cuttings library. Of course all the memorable quotations eventually find their way into print, but not always in their original form. The chief whip's famous phrase in Michael Dobbs's *House of Cards*, 'You might very well think that. I couldn't possibly comment', is taken from the television script; it does not appear in the book. Equally, transcripts from radio and television can miss important emphases and nuances: when Neil Kinnock spoke to the Labour Party Conference about Liverpool Council, his stress on 'Labour' in the phrase, 'the grotesque chaos of a Labour council—a *Labour* council—hiring taxis to scuttle round the city handing out redundancy notices to its own workers' did not come through in the press reports as it did in the television news bulletins. And the televising of parliamentary debates has exposed the difference between the semi-incoherence of some members' speeches and the comparative lucidity and logic of the phrasing that appears subsequently in the august pages of Hansard.

Finally I must acknowledge with gratitude the large number of people whose help has been invaluable. Christopher Booker, Simon Heffer, Nigel Rees, and Peter Hennessy all read the whole of the first draft and made numerous comments and suggestions of which many were immediately incorporated. All of them are extremely busy professionals and I was astonished as well as delighted at the amount of time and care they were willing to give to the task. Indeed one of the happiest aspects of an unusually happy assignment has been the willingness of almost everyone I contacted to give up time and take trouble to make the Dictionary as full and accurate as possible. Of those who helped out on specific topics or authors I would like to offer especial thanks to the following: Lord Bauer, Tony Benn, John Biffen, John Blundell, Dr Eamonn Butler, the Bishop of Coventry, Lord Dacre, Lord Deedes, Oliver Everett, Milton Friedman, Norman Gash, Martin Gilbert, Henry Hardy, Lord Healey, Sir Bernard Ingham, Simon Jenkins, Bernard Levin, Kenneth Morgan, Nigel Nicolson, Matthew Parris, Enoch Powell, Stanley Wells, and Chris Wrigley. Above all, I want to thank the editorial team of the Quotations Dictionaries department of the Oxford University Press. Not only have they done the bulk of the work; their knowledge, expertise, and scholarly rigour have contributed immeasurably to the quality of the book.

Any credit for the final result must be shared with all of the above; the blame remains exclusively the editor's.

ANTONY JAY

Somerset, January 1996

How to Use the Dictionary

The sequence of entries is by alphabetical order of author, usually by surname but with occasional exceptions such as imperial or royal titles, or authors known by a pseudonym ('**Saki**'), or a nickname (**Caligula**). In general authors' names are given in the form by which they are best known, so that we have **Harold Macmillan** (not Lord Stockton), **Lord Melbourne** (not William Lamb), **H. G. Wells** (not Herbert George Wells), and **Harold Wilson** (not James Harold Wilson). Collections such as **Anonymous** and the **Bible** are included in the alphabetical sequence.

Author names are followed by dates of birth and death (where known) and brief descriptions; where appropriate, cross references are then given to quotations about that author elsewhere in the text (*on Acheson*: see **Pearson** 200:7). Within each author entry, quotations from speeches are given in date order and appear first; quotations from diaries and letters are included in this chronological sequence, as are quotations from secondary sources to which a date in the author's lifetime can be assigned. Literary and published works, which follow, are arranged by alphabetical order of title, 'a' and 'the' being ignored. Quotations from secondary sources to which no specific date can be assigned come at the end of the entry, and are arranged in alphabetical order of quotation text. Foreign-language text is given where it is felt that the quotation is more familiar in the language of origin ('*L'État c'est moi*').

Where the information is available (the date of a speech, or composition date of a letter or diary) a quotation can be accorded a precise date. Some quotations are dated according to the circumstances with which the remark or comment is associated (Stanton's comment following the assassination of Abraham Lincoln, 'Now he belongs to the ages', dates the quotation as 1865). When the date is uncertain or unknown, and the quotation cannot be related to a particular event, the author's date of death has been used to date the quotation.

Contextual information regarded as essential to a full appreciation of the quotation precedes the relevant text in an italicized note; information seen as providing helpful information follows in an italicized note. Bibliographical information as to the source from which the quotation is taken appears in a marginal note; titles and dates of publication are supplied, but full finding references are not given. Every attempt has been made to trace quotations to citable sources, but where necessary 'attributed' is used to indicate that while attribution to a particular author is popularly made, a specific reference has not been traced. It is felt more helpful to include widely known material with an account of its status, than to omit the item because it is not susceptible of final verification.

Within the alphabetical sequence there are a number of special category entries: **Epitaphs**, **Last words**, **Military sayings**, **Misquotations**, **Mottoes**, **Newspaper headlines and leaders**, **Official advice**, **Proverbs and sayings**, **Slogans**, and **Songs and ballads**. Quotations in these sections are arranged alphabetically according to the first word of the quotation (ignoring 'a' and 'the').

Cross-references are made both to individual quotations (see **Disraeli** 121:1) and to whole entries. References to specific quotations consist of the author's name followed by the page number and the number of the quotation on the page (**Burke** 63:1). Authors who have their own entries are typographically distinguished by the use of bold (epitaph for John **Adams**, of Lord **Halifax**) in context or source notes, or in the author descriptions (son of Joseph **Kennedy**).

The Index

Both the keywords and the entries following each keyword, including those in foreign languages, are in strict alphabetical order. Singular and plural nouns (with their possessive forms) are grouped separately.

The references show the author's name, usually in abbreviated form (SHAK/Shakespeare), followed by the page number and the number of the quotation on that page: 183:8 therefore means quotation 8 on page 183.

Diane Abbott 1953–
British Labour politician

1 Being an MP is the sort of job all working-class parents want for their children—clean, indoors and no heavy lifting.

in Independent 18 January 1994

Bella Abzug 1920–98
American politician

2 Richard Nixon impeached himself. He gave us Gerald Ford as his revenge.

in Rolling Stone; Linda Botts *Loose Talk* (1980)

Accius 170–c.86 BC
Latin poet and dramatist

3 Let them hate, so long as they fear.

Atreus

Dean Acheson 1893–1971 ✓
American statesman
on Acheson: see **Pearson** 285:4

4 I will undoubtedly have to seek what is happily known as gainful employment, which I am glad to say does not describe holding public office.

in Time 22 December 1952

5 Great Britain has lost an empire and has not yet found a role.

speech at the Military Academy, West Point, 5 December 1962

6 The first requirement of a statesman is that he be dull.

in Observer 21 June 1970

7 A memorandum is written not to inform the reader but to protect the writer.

in Wall Street Journal 8 September 1977

of President **Eisenhower***:*
8 I doubt very much if a man whose main literary interests were in works by Mr Zane Grey, admirable as they may be, is particularly equipped to be the chief executive of this country, particularly where Indian Affairs are concerned.

attributed

Lord Acton 1834–1902
British historian

9 Power tends to corrupt and absolute power corrupts absolutely.
often quoted as 'All power corrupts . . . '

letter to Bishop Mandell Creighton, 3 April 1887; see **Pitt** 289:10

10 Great men are almost always bad men, even when they exercise influence and not authority.

letter to Bishop Mandell Creighton, 3 April 1887

Abigail Adams 1744–1818
wife of John **Adams**, 2nd President of the USA, and mother of John Quincy **Adams**

11 In the new code of laws which I suppose it will be necessary for you to make I desire you would remember the ladies, and be more generous and favourable to them than your ancestors. Do not put such unlimited power into the hands of the husbands. Remember all men would be tyrants if they could.

letter to John Adams, 31 March 1776

1 These are times in which a genius would wish to live. It is not in the still calm of life, or the repose of a pacific station, that great characters are formed . . . Great necessities call out great virtues.

letter to John Quincy Adams, 19 January 1780

2 Patriotism in the female sex is the most disinterested of all virtues. Excluded from honours and from offices, we cannot attach ourselves to the State or Government from having held a place of eminence . . . Yet all history and every age exhibit instances of patriotic virtue in the female sex; which considering our situation equals the most heroic of yours.

letter to John Adams, 17 June 1782

Franklin P. Adams 1881–1960 ✓
American journalist and humorist

3 When the political columnists say 'Every thinking man' they mean themselves, and when candidates appeal to 'Every intelligent voter' they mean everybody who is going to vote for them.

Nods and Becks (1944)

4 The trouble with this country is that there are too many politicians who believe, with a conviction based on experience, that you can fool all of the people all of the time.

Nods and Becks (1944)

5 Elections are won by men and women chiefly because most people vote against somebody rather than for somebody.

Nods and Becks (1944)

Gerry Adams 1948–
Northern Irish politician; President of Sinn Féin

6 We want him to be the last British Prime Minister with jurisdiction in Ireland.
   *of Tony **Blair***

in *Irish Times* 18 October 1997

7 Peace cannot be built on exclusion. That has been the price of the past 30 years.

in *Daily Telegraph* 11 April 1998

8 Well done, David.
   at the Sinn Féin annual conference, on hearing that the Ulster Unionist Council had given its support to David Trimble and the Northern Ireland peace agreement

in *Independent on Sunday* 19 April 1998

Henry Brooks Adams 1838–1918 ✓
American man of letters

9 Politics, as a practice, whatever its professions, has always been the systematic organization of hatreds.

The Education of Henry Adams (1907)

10 A friend in power is a friend lost.

The Education of Henry Adams (1907)

11 [Charles] Sumner's mind had reached the calm of water which receives and reflects images without absorbing them; it contained nothing but itself.
   *of the American politician and orator Charles **Sumner***

The Education of Henry Adams (1907)

12 The progress of evolution from President Washington to President Grant was alone evidence to upset Darwin.

The Education of Henry Adams (1907)

13 Practical politics consists in ignoring facts.

The Education of Henry Adams (1907)

John Adams 1735–1826

1st Vice-President of the United States and 2nd President; father of John Quincy **Adams** and husband of Abigail **Adams**
see also **Last words** 214:2

1 The law, in all vicissitudes of government . . . will preserve a steady undeviating course; it will not bend to the uncertain wishes, imaginations, and wanton tempers of men . . . On the one hand it is inexorable to the cries of the prisoners; on the other it is deaf, deaf as an adder to the clamours of the populace.

> argument in defence of the British soldiers in the Boston Massacre Trials, 4 December 1770; see **Sidney** 332:5

2 There is danger from all men. The only maxim of a free government ought to be to trust no man living with power to endanger the public liberty.

> Notes for an Oration at Braintree (Spring 1772)

of the Boston Tea Party:
3 There is a dignity, a majesty, a sublimity, in this last effort of the patriots that I greatly admire. The people should never rise without doing something to be remembered— something notable and striking.

> diary, 17 December 1773

4 A government of laws, and not of men.
   later incorporated in the Massachusetts Constitution (1780)

> in *Boston Gazette* (1774)

5 I agree with you that in politics the middle way is none at all.

> letter to Horatio Gates, 23 March 1776

6 Yesterday, the greatest question was decided which ever was debated in America, and a greater perhaps never was nor will be decided among men. A resolution was passed without one dissenting colony, 'that these United Colonies are, and of right ought to be, free and independent States.'

> letter to Abigail Adams, 3 July 1776

7 I must study politics and war that my sons may have liberty to study mathematics and philosophy.

> letter to Abigail Adams, 12 May 1780

of the vice-presidency:
8 My country has in its wisdom contrived for me the most insignificant office that ever the invention of man contrived or his imagination conceived.

> letter to Abigail Adams, 19 December 1793

9 Democracy never lasts long. It soon wastes, exhausts, and murders itself. There never was a democracy that did not commit suicide.

> letter to John Taylor, 15 April 1814

10 The fundamental article of my political creed is that despotism, or unlimited sovereignty, or absolute power, is the same in a majority of a popular assembly, an aristocratic council, an oligarchical junto, and a single emperor.

> letter to Thomas Jefferson, 13 November 1815

11 The jaws of power are always opened to devour, and her arm is always stretched out, if possible, to destroy the freedom of thinking, speaking, and writing.

> *A Dissertation on the Canon and the Feudal Law* (1765)

12 Liberty cannot be preserved without a general knowledge among the people, who have a right . . . and a desire to know; but besides this, they have a right, an indisputable, unalienable, indefeasible, divine right to that most dreaded and envied kind of knowledge, I mean of the characters and conduct of their rulers.

> *A Dissertation on the Canon and Feudal Law* (1765)

13 The happiness of society is the end of government.

> *Thoughts on Government* (1776)

14 Fear is the foundation of most governments.

> *Thoughts on Government* (1776)

1 The judicial power ought to be distinct from both the legislative and executive, and independent upon both, that so it may be a check upon both, as both should be checks upon that.

Thoughts on Government (1776)

John Quincy Adams 1767–1848

6th President of the USA and son of the 2nd President, John **Adams**, and Abigail **Adams**
see also **Last Words** 214:1

2 Think of your forefathers! Think of your posterity!

Oration at Plymouth 22 December 1802

3 *Fiat justitia, pereat coelum* [Let justice be done, though heaven perish]. My toast would be, may our country be always successful, but whether successful or otherwise, always right.

letter to John Adams, 1 August 1816; see **Decatur** 103:9, **Mansfield** 241:11, **Mottoes** 262:3

4 This house will bear witness to his piety; this town [Braintree, Massachusetts], his birthplace, to his munificence; history to his patriotism; posterity to the depth and compass of his mind.

epitaph for John **Adams**, 1829

Samuel Adams 1722–1803

American revolutionary leader

5 Let us contemplate our forefathers, and posterity, and resolve to maintain the rights bequeathed to us by the former, for the sake of the latter.

speech, 1771

6 What a glorious morning this is.
on hearing gunfire at Lexington, 19 April 1775

J. K. Hosmer *Samuel Adams* (1886); see **Misquotations** 256:1

7 A nation of shopkeepers are very seldom so disinterested.

Oration in Philadelphia 1 August 1776 (the authenticity of this publication is doubtful); see **Napoleon** 265:1, **Smith** 333:8

8 We cannot make events. Our business is wisely to improve them . . . Mankind are governed more by their feelings than by reason. Events which excite those feelings will produce wonderful effects.

J. N. Rakove *The Beginnings of National Politics* (1979)

Frank Ezra Adcock 1886–1968

British classicist and historian of Greece and Rome

9 Rome under Sulla was like a bus, with half the passengers trying to drive, and the rest trying to collect the fare.

lecture at Cambridge in the 1940s

Joseph Addison 1672–1719

English poet, playwright, and essayist; co-founder of *The Spectator*

10 What pity is it
That we can die but once to serve our country!

Cato (1713)

11 From hence, let fierce contending nations know
What dire effects from civil discord flow.

Cato (1713)

Konrad Adenauer 1876–1967

German statesman, first Chancellor of the Federal Republic of Germany, 1949–63

1 It was at the Congress of Vienna, when you so foolishly put Prussia on the Rhine as a safeguard against France and another Napoleon.
identifying England's greatest mistake in its relations with Germany

answering his own question to Noel Annan in 1945; Noel Annan *Changing Enemies: the Defeat and Regeneration of Germany* (1989)

2 A thick skin is a gift from God.

in *New York Times* 30 December 1959

Aeschylus c.525–456 BC

Greek tragedian

3 Do not taint pure laws with mere expediency
Guard well and reverence that form of government
Which will eschew alike licence and slavery.
And from your policy do not wholly banish fear
For what man living, freed from fear, will still be just?

The Eumenides

4 Everyone's quick to blame the alien.

The Suppliant Maidens

Herbert Agar 1897–1980

American poet and writer

5 The truth which makes men free is for the most part the truth which men prefer not to hear.

Time for Greatness (1942)

Spiro T. Agnew 1918–96

American Republican politician, Vice-President 1968–73; he resigned the vice-presidency on 10 October 1973 amid charges of financial wrong-doing while Governor of Maryland

6 I didn't say I wouldn't go into ghetto areas. I've been in many of them and to some extent I would say this: If you've seen one city slum you've seen them all.

in *Detroit Free Press* 19 October 1968

7 A spirit of national masochism prevails, encouraged by an effete corps of impudent snobs who characterize themselves as intellectuals.

speech in New Orleans, 19 October 1969

8 In the United States today, we have more than our share of the nattering nabobs of negativism.

speech in San Diego, 11 September 1970

Bertie Ahern 1951–

Irish Fianna Fáil statesman, Taoiseach since 1997

9 It is a day we should treasure. Today is about the promise of a bright future, a day when we hope a line will be drawn under the bloody past.

in *Guardian* 11 April 1998

10 This is the first time since 1918 in an act of self-determination that everyone on this island, on the one issue, has had the opportunity to pass their verdict.
opening the Fianna Fáil referendum campaign

in *Irish Times* 9 May 1998 'This Week They Said'

Jonathan Aitken 1942–
British Conservative politician

1 If it falls to me to start a fight to cut out the cancer of bent and twisted journalism in our country with the simple sword of truth and the trusty shield of British fair play, so be it.

statement, London, 10 April 1995

Madeleine Albright 1937–
American diplomat

2 Hallelujah . . . Never again will your fates be tossed around like poker chips on a bargaining table.
    accepting the admission papers for Hungary, Poland, and the Czech Republic to become members of Nato

in *Daily Telegraph* 13 March 1999

Alcuin c.735–804
English scholar and theologian

3 And those people should not be listened to who keep saying the voice of the people is the voice of God [*Vox populi, vox Dei*], since the riotousness of the crowd is always very close to madness.

letter 164 in *Works* (1863)

Richard Aldington 1892–1962
English poet, novelist, and biographer

4 Patriotism is a lively sense of collective responsibility. Nationalism is a silly cock crowing on its own dunghill.

The Colonel's Daughter (1931)

Cecil Frances Alexander 1818–95
Irish poet

5 The rich man in his castle,
The poor man at his gate,
God made them, high or lowly,
And ordered their estate.

'All Things Bright and Beautiful' (1848)

Woody Allen 1935–
American film director, writer, and actor

6 I believe there is something out there watching over us. Unfortunately, it's the government.

Peter McWilliams *Ain't Nobody's Business If You Do* (1993); attributed

Joseph Alsop b. 1910
American journalist

7 Gratitude, like love, is never a dependable international emotion.

in *Observer* 30 November 1952

Leo Amery 1873–1955
British Conservative politician

of H. H. **Asquith***:*
8 For twenty years he has held a season-ticket on the line of least resistance and has gone wherever the train of events has carried him, lucidly justifying his position at whatever point he has happened to find himself.

in *Quarterly Review* July 1914

1 Speak for England.

said to Arthur Greenwood in House of Commons, 2 September 1939; see **Boothby** 48:3

2 I will quote certain other words. I do it with great reluctance, because I am speaking of those who are old friends and colleagues of mine, but they are words which, I think, are applicable to the present situation. This is what Cromwell said to the Long Parliament when he thought it was no longer fit to conduct the affairs of the nation: 'You have sat too long here for any good you have been doing. Depart, I say, and let us have done with you. In the name of God, go.'

in the House of Commons, 7 May 1940; see **Cromwell** 98:5

Fisher Ames 1758–1808

American politician

3 A monarchy is a merchantman which sails well, but will sometimes strike on a rock, and go to the bottom; whilst a republic is a raft which would never sink, but then your feet are always in the water.

attributed to Ames, speaking in the House of Representatives, 1795, but not traced in Ames's speeches

Anacharsis

Scythian prince of the sixth century BC

4 Written laws are like spider's webs; they will catch, it is true, the weak and poor, but would be torn in pieces by the rich and powerful.

Plutarch *Parallel Lives* 'Solon'; see **Shenstone** 330:5, **Swift** 350:7

Kofi Annan 1938–

Ghanaian diplomat, Secretary-General of the United Nation

5 You can do a lot with diplomacy, but of course you can do a lot more with diplomacy backed up by fairness and force.
of the agreement reached with Saddam Hussein over weapons inspections, February 1998

in *Mail on Sunday* 1 March 1998 'Quotes of the Week'

Anonymous

6 All the 'isms are wasms.
said to have been the comment of a Foreign Office spokesman on the signing of the Molotov–Ribbentrop Pact in August 1939

Peter Hennessy *Whitehall* (1990)

7 Beneath that extraordinary exterior there is a little pink, quivering Ted trying to get out.
comment of a former Cabinet colleague on Edward **Heath**

in 1993; Peter Hennessy *The Prime Minister: the Office and its Holders since 1945* (2000)

8 The best defence against the atom bomb is not to be there when it goes off.

contributor to *British Army Journal*, in *Observer* 20 February 1949

9 But this is terrible—*they've* elected a Labour Government, and *the country* will never stand for that!
unidentified lady diner in the Savoy Hotel, 26 July 1945

Michael Sissons and Philip French (eds.) *The Age of Austerity 1945–51* (1964)

10 A community in which power, wealth and opportunity are in the hands of the many not the few, where the rights we enjoy reflect the duties we owe . . . in which the enterprise of the market and the rigour of competition are joined with the forces of partnership and cooperation.

new Clause Four of the Labour Party constitution, passed at a special conference 29 April 1995; see **Anonymous** 11:11

1 A Company for carrying on an undertaking of Great Advantage, but no one to know what it is.

Company Prospectus at the time of the South Sea Bubble (1711)

2 Every country has its own constitution; ours is absolutism moderated by assassination.
of Russia

Ernst Friedrich Herbert, Count Münster, quoting 'an intelligent Russian', in *Political Sketches of the State of Europe, 1814–1867* (1868)

3 Expletive deleted.

Submission of Recorded Presidential Conversations to the Committee on the Judiciary of the House of Representatives by President Richard M. Nixon 30 April 1974

4 Exterminate . . . the treacherous English, walk over General French's contemptible little army.
often attributed to Kaiser Wilhelm II, but most probably fabricated by the British; source of the nickname 'the Old Contemptibles'

Annexe to British Expeditionary Force Routine Orders of 24 September 1914; Arthur Ponsonby *Falsehood in Wartime* (1928)

5 The finest brute votes in Europe.
a 'cynical politician' 's view of the parliamentary county members

Walter Bagehot *The English Constitution* (1867) 'The House of Commons'

6 The first and only thing they have to do is to decide how a resigned commission behaves.
unidentified British official in Brussels of the European Commission

in *Daily Telegraph* 18 March 1999

7 For the sake of brevity we have followed the common practice of using the phrase 'Communists' throughout to include Fascists.

Radcliffe Report 'Security Procedures in the Public Service' April 1962

8 Frederick the Great lost the battle of Jena.
*attributing the Prussians' defeat at Jena by **Napoleon** in 1806 to their rigid adherence to the strategy of **Frederick** (who had died in 1786)*

Walter Bagehot *The English Constitution* (1867)

9 Happy is that city which in time of peace thinks of war.
inscription found in the armoury of Venice

Robert Burton *The Anatomy of Melancholy* (1621–51)

10 Hark the herald angels sing
Mrs Simpson's pinched our king.
*contemporary children's rhyme on the abdication of **Edward VIII***

Clement Attlee letter 26 December 1938; Kenneth Harris *Attlee* (1982)

11 Harold wanted to be a combination of the Head of MI5 and News Editor of the *Daily Mirror*.
*Downing Street official shortly after **Wilson**'s resignation*

Peter Hennessy *The Prime Minister: the Office and its Holders since 1945* (2000)

12 Have I said something foolish?

Athenian statesman, on being cheered by the populace

13 Have you heard? The Prime Minister has resigned and Northcliffe has sent for the King.
*a joke (c.1919) suggesting that Lord **Northcliffe**, the press baron and **Lloyd George**'s implacable enemy, would succeed him as Prime Minister*

Hamilton Fyfe *Northcliffe, an Intimate Biography* (1930)

14 Hear ye! Hear ye! All persons are commanded to keep silent, on pain of imprisonment, while the House of Representatives is exhibiting to the Senate of the United States articles of impeachment against William Jefferson Clinton, President of the United States.
formal announcement read by the serjeant-at-arms

in *Guardian* 8 January 1999

1 He may be a minister of the British Government but we are the Walt Disney Corporation and we don't roll over for anyone.
a Disneyland executive commenting on reports that Peter Mandelson might use the theme park's ideas in the Millennium Dome without authorization

in *Sunday Telegraph* 18 January 1998

2 He talked shop like a tenth muse.
*of **Gladstone**'s Budget speech*

G. W. E. Russell *Collections and Recollections* (1898)

3 He who writes the minutes rules the roost.

Civil Service maxim

4 The idea that the PM gets integrated advice is nonsense. You could not see a more *unjoined* system. To say they have imported the White House to No. 10—Washington to Downing Street—is absolutely right.
a senior Whitehall figure on the Blair administration, January 2000

Peter Hennessy *The Prime Minister: the Office and its Holders since 1945* (2000)

5 I like Mr Baldwin: he promises nothing and keeps his word.

unattributed

6 I like my Prime Ministers to be a bit inhumane. The PM has insufficient inhumanity . . . He wants to be liked.
*a senior civil servant, shortly after John **Major** had become Prime Minister*

Peter Hennessy *The Prime Minister: the Office and its Holders since 1945* (2000)

7 I never vote. It only encourages them.

elderly American lady quoted by comedian Jack Parr; William Safire *The New Language of Politics* (1968)

8 The iron lady.
*name given to Margaret **Thatcher**, then Leader of the Opposition, by the Soviet Defence Ministry newspaper* Red Star, *which accused her of trying to revive the cold war*

in *Sunday Times* 25 January 1976

9 It became necessary to destroy the town to save it.
comment by unidentified US Army major on Ben Tre, Vietnam

in Associated Press Report, *New York Times* 8 February 1968

10 It is becoming difficult to find anyone in the Commission who has even the slightest sense of responsibility.

report on the European Commission; in *Guardian* 17 March 1999

11 The King over the Water.
Jacobite toast to the deposed and exiled James II and his heirs

current in the 18th century

12 Liberty is always unfinished business.

title of 36th Annual Report of the American Civil Liberties Union, 1 July 1955–30 June 1956

13 [Like] watching a stream of blood coming from beneath a closed door.
a contemporary expression of the feelings evoked by news of the executions after the Easter Rising

Robert Kee *Ourselves Alone* (1916)

14 Lost is our old simplicity of times,
The world abounds with laws, and teems with crimes.

On the Proceedings Against America (1775)

15 CHILD: Mamma, are Tories born wicked, or do they grow wicked afterwards?
MOTHER: They are born wicked, and grow worse.

G. W. E. Russell *Collections and Recollections* (1898)

16 Men said openly that Christ and His saints slept.
of twelfth-century England during the civil war between Stephen and Matilda

Anglo-Saxon Chronicle for 1137

17 The ministry of all the talents.
name given ironically to William Grenville's coalition of 1806, and also applied to later coalitions

G. W. Cooke *The History of Party* (1837) vol. 3

1 My name is George Nathaniel Curzon,
I am a most superior person.
My face is pink, my hair is sleek,
I dine at Blenheim once a week.
   of Lord **Curzon**

The Masque of Balliol (c.1870), in
W. G. Hiscock *The Balliol Rhymes*
(1939, the last two lines are a later
addition); see **Parris** 284:5

2 The nearest thing to death in life
Is David Patrick Maxwell Fyfe,
Though underneath that gloomy shell
He does himself extremely well.
   of David Maxwell Fyfe, later Lord **Kilmuir**, *and said to have been
   current on the Northern circuit in the late 1930s*

E. Grierson *Confessions of a Country
Magistrate* (1972)

3 Never stand when you could sit, and never miss a chance to
relieve yourself.

advice given by a private secretary
or equerry to **George V** or **George
VI**

4 No man's life, liberty or property are safe while the
legislature is in session.
   view of an unidentified New York State Surrogate Court Judge

in 1866; unattributed

5 Now that the Cabinet's gone to its dinner,
The Secretary stays and gets thinner and thinner,
Racking his brains to record and report
What he thinks they think they ought to have thought.

anonymous verse, undated; S. S.
Wilson *The Cabinet Office* (1975)

6 One Cartwright brought a Slave from Russia, and would
scourge him, for which he was questioned: and it was
resolved, That England was too pure an Air for Slaves to
breathe in.

'In the 11th of Elizabeth' (17
November 1568–16 November
1569); John Rushworth *Historical
Collections* (1680–1722)

7 Order reigns in Warsaw.
   after the brutal suppression of an uprising

the newspaper *Moniteur* reported,
16 September 1831, 'Order and
calm are completely restored in
the capital'; on the same day
Count Sebastiani, minister of
foreign affairs, declared: 'Peace
reigns in Warsaw'

8 A place within the meaning of the Act.

usually taken to be a reference to
the Betting Act 1853, sect. 2,
which banned off-course betting
on horse-races

9 Prudence is the other woman in Gordon's life.
   of Gordon **Brown**

unidentified aide, quoted in BBC
News online (Budget Briefing), 20
March 1998

10 Psychological flaws.
   on which, according to an unnamed source, Gordon **Brown** *needed
   to 'get a grip'*

in *Observer* 18 January 1998;
attributed to Alastair **Campbell** by
Bernard **Ingham** in minutes of the
Parliamentary Select Committee
on Public Administration, 2 June
1998, but denied by Campbell in
evidence to the Committee, 23
June 1998

11 Reorganizing the Civil Service is like drawing a knife
through a bowl of marbles.

unattributed comment

1 A revolution which lacks the anchor of ideology or the compass of principle will founder on the rocks of mere personality.
an unidentified left-winger on the reported feud between New Labour's Gordon Brown and Peter Mandelson

in *The Mail on Sunday* 19 May 1996

2 *Sic transit gloria mundi.*

Thus passes the glory of the world.
said during the coronation of a new Pope, while flax is burned to represent the transitoriness of earthly glory

used at the coronation of Alexander V in Pisa, 7 July 1409, but earlier in origin

3 The silly, flat, dishwatery utterances of the man who has to be pointed out to intelligent observers as the President of the United States.

review of **Lincoln**'s Gettysburg Address, in *Chicago Times* 20 November 1863; see **Everett** 127:8

4 *Tempora mutantur, et nos mutamur in illis.*

Times change, and we change with them.

William Harrison *Description of Britain* (1577); attributed to the Emperor Lothar I (795–855) in the form '*omnia mutantur, nos et mutamur in illis* [all things change, and we change with them]'

5 There is one thing stronger than all the armies in the world; and that is an idea whose time has come.

in *Nation* 15 April 1943; see **Hugo** 178:3

6 There shall be a Scottish parliament.

first clause of the Scotland Act, 1998; see **Dewar** 108:7

*an unnamed Labour MP commenting on the unusually pale eyes of Hugh **Dalton**:*
7 They have a habit of looking at you intently and conveying unfathomable depths of insincerity.
sometimes quoted as 'eyes blazing with insincerity'

Patricia Strauss *Bevin and Co. The Leaders of British Labour* (1941)

annotation to a ministerial brief, said to have been read out inadvertently in the House of Lords:
8 This is a rotten argument, but it should be good enough for their lordships on a hot summer afternoon.

Lord Home *The Way the Wind Blows* (1976)

9 Those on the opposite side are your opponents; your enemies are on your own side.

traditional advice to a new MP

10 Though I yield to no one in my admiration for Mr Coolidge, I do wish he did not look as if he had been weaned on a pickle.
*of President Calvin **Coolidge***

anonymous remark, in Alice Roosevelt Longworth *Crowded Hours* (1933)

11 To secure for the workers by hand or by brain the full fruits of their industry and the most equitable distribution thereof that may be possible upon the basis of the common ownership of the means of production, distribution, and exchange.

Clause Four of the Labour Party's Constitution of 1918 (revised 1929); the commitment to common ownership of services was largely removed in 1995; see **Anonymous** 7:10

12 Under capitalism man exploits man. And under Communism it is just the reverse.
*joke told to J. K. **Galbraith** at a dinner given for him during his lecture tour of Poland by the Polish Economic Society, May 1958*

J. K. Galbraith *A Life in Our Times* (1981)

13 We hold these truths to be self-evident, that all men are created equal, that they are endowed by their Creator with certain unalienable rights, that among these are life, liberty and the pursuit of happiness.

The American Declaration of Independence, 4 July 1776

1 We trained hard . . . but it seemed that every time we were beginning to form up into teams we would be reorganized. I was to learn later in life that we tend to meet any new situation by reorganizing; and a wonderful method it can be for creating the illusion of progress while producing confusion, inefficiency, and demoralization.

modern saying, frequently (and wrongly) attributed to Petronius Arbiter

2 We value excellence as well as fairness, independence as dearly as mateship.

draft preamble to the Australian constitution, made public 23 March 1999

3 We want eight, and we won't wait.
  on the construction of Dreadnoughts

George Wyndham's speech in *The Times* 29 March 1909

4 We wouldn't trust Labour to deliver a pizza—let alone a Parliament.
  view of the Scottish Nationalist Party

unattributed; Brian Taylor *The Scottish Parliament* (1999)

5 What did the President know and when did he know it?

question current at the time of Watergate, associated particularly with Howard Baker, Vice-Chairman of the Senate Watergate Committee

6 When war enters a country
  It produces lies like sand.

epigraph to Arthur Ponsonby *Falsehood in Wartime* (1928)

7 Why is there only one Monopolies Commission?

British graffito; incorporated in the Official Monster Raving Loony Party Manifesto, 1987

8 A willing foe and sea room.
  Naval toast in the time of Nelson

W. N. T. Beckett *A Few Naval Customs, Expressions, Traditions, and Superstitions* (1931) 'Customs'

9 Winston is back.
  Board of Admiralty signal to the Fleet on Winston Churchill's reappointment as First Sea Lord, 3 September 1939

Martin Gilbert *Winston S. Churchill* (1976) vol. 5

Susan Brownell Anthony 1820—1906
American feminist and political activist

10 The men and women of the North are slaveholders, those of the South slaveowners. The guilt rests on the North equally with the South.

Speech on No Union with Slaveholders 1857

11 Join the union, girls, and together say *Equal Pay for Equal Work.*

in *The Revolution* 8 October 1869

12 Here, in the first paragraph of the Declaration [of Independence], is the assertion of the natural right of all to the ballot; for how can 'the consent of the governed' be given, if the right to vote be denied?
  speech in 1873 before her trial for voting

Is It a Crime for a Citizen of the United States to Vote?

John Arbuthnot 1667-1735
Scottish physician and pamphleteer

13 He [the writer] warns the heads of parties against believing their own lies.

The Art of Political Lying (1712)

Mary Archer 1955–

British scientist and wife of the writer and Conservative politician Jeffrey Archer
on Archer: see **Caulfield** 73:1

1 I am cross with Jeffrey, but I have formed the judgement that he is a decent and generous spirited man over 35 years and that will not change over one weekend.
following the revelation that her husband had planned to establish a false alibi in his 1987 libel case; he was forced to withdraw as Conservative candidate for Mayor of London and his political career collapsed

in *Observer* 28 November 1999 'They said what . . . ?'

Hannah Arendt 1906–75

American political philosopher

2 The most radical revolutionary will become a conservative on the day after the revolution.

in *New Yorker* 12 September 1970

3 Under conditions of tyranny it is far easier to act than to think.

W. H. Auden *A Certain World* (1970)

Marquis d'Argenson 1694–1757

French politician and political essayist

4 *Laisser-faire.*
No interference.
term applied to the doctrine of minimum state intervention in economic affairs

Mémoires et Journal Inédit du Marquis d'Argenson; see **Quesnay** 295:7

Aristophanes *c.*450–*c.*385 BC

Athenian comic dramatist

5 How about 'Cloudcuckooland'?
naming the capital city of the Birds

The Birds (414 BC) l. 819

6 You have all the characteristics of a popular politician: a horrible voice, bad breeding and a vulgar manner.

The Knights (424 BC) l. 217

7 Under every stone lurks a politician.

Thesmophoriazusae l. 530

Aristotle 384–322 BC

Greek philosopher

8 Therefore, the good of man must be the objective of the science of politics.

Nicomachean Ethics

9 We make war that we may live in peace.

Nicomachean Ethics

10 Politicians also have no leisure, because they are always aiming at something beyond political life itself, power and glory, or happiness.

Nicomachean Ethics

11 Man is by nature a political animal.

Politics

12 He who is unable to live in society, or who has no need because he is sufficient for himself, must be either a beast or a god.

Politics

13 For that some should rule, and others be ruled, is a thing not only necessary but expedient, for from the hour of their birth some are marked for subjection, others for rule.

Politics

1 Poverty is the parent of revolution and crime.   *Politics*

2 Where some people are very wealthy and others have nothing, the result will be either extreme democracy or absolute oligarchy, or despotism will come from either of those excesses.   *Politics*

3 The most perfect political community is one in which the middle class is in control, and outnumbers both of the other classes.   *Politics*

4 No tyrant need fear till men begin to feel confident in each other.   *Politics*

Robert Armstrong 1927–
British civil servant, Head of the Civil Service, 1981–7

5 It contains a misleading impression, not a lie. It was being economical with the truth.   in *Daily Telegraph* 19 November 1986; see **Burke** 60:1, **Clark** 87:14
   referring to a letter during the 'Spycatcher' trial, Supreme Court, New South Wales, November 1986

William Armstrong 1915–80
British civil servant, Head of the Civil Service 1968–74

6 The business of the Civil Service is the orderly management of decline.   in 1973: Peter Hennessy *Whitehall* (1990)

Matthew Arnold 1822–88
English poet and essayist; son of Thomas **Arnold**

7 Our society distributes itself into Barbarians, Philistines, and Populace; and America is just ourselves, with the Barbarians quite left out, and the Populace nearly.   *Culture and Anarchy* (1869) preface

8 The men of culture are the true apostles of equality.   *Culture and Anarchy* (1869)

9 When I want to distinguish clearly the aristocratic class from the Philistines proper, or middle class, [I] name the former, in my own mind *the Barbarians*.   *Culture and Anarchy* (1869)

10 That vast portion . . . of the working-class which, raw and half-developed, has long lain half-hidden amidst its poverty and squalor, and is now issuing from its hiding-place to assert an Englishman's heaven-born privilege of doing as he likes, and is beginning to perplex us by marching where it likes, meeting where it likes, bawling what it likes, breaking what it likes—to this vast residuum we may with great propriety give the name of Populace.   *Culture and Anarchy* (1869)

Thomas Arnold 1795–1842
English historian; Headmaster of Rugby School from 1828; father of Matthew **Arnold**

11 As for rioting, the old Roman way of dealing with that is always the right one; flog the rank and file, and fling the ringleaders from the Tarpeian rock.   from an unpublished letter written before 1828

Raymond Aron 1905–
French sociologist and political journalist

12 Political thought, in France, is retrospective or utopian.   *L'opium des intellectuels* (1955)

Paddy Ashdown 1941-
British Liberal Democrat politician

1 There can be no place in a 21st-century parliament for
people with 15th-century titles upholding 19th-century
prejudices.

in Independent 24 November 1998

Herbert Henry Asquith 1852-1928
British Liberal statesman; Prime Minister, 1908-16
on Asquith: see **Churchill** 80:6, **Hennessy** 168:6

2 We had better wait and see.
*phrase used repeatedly in speeches in 1910, referring to the
rumour that the House of Lords was to be flooded with new
Liberal peers to ensure the passage of the Finance Bill*

Roy Jenkins *Asquith* (1964)

3 We shall never sheath the sword which we have not lightly
drawn until Belgium recovers in full measure all and more
than all that she has sacrificed, until France is adequately
secured against the menace of aggression, until the rights of
the smaller nationalities of Europe are placed upon an
unassailable foundation, and until the military domination
of Prussia is wholly and finally destroyed.

speech at the Guildhall, London, 9
November 1914

4 There is no more striking illustration of the immobility of
British institutions than the House of Commons.

Fifty Years of Parliament (1926) vol.
2

5 The office of the Prime Minister is what its holder chooses
and is able to make of it.

Fifty Years of Parliament (1926) vol.
2

6 He is a Chimborazo or Everest among the sandhills of the
Baldwin Cabinet.
of Winston **Churchill**

Roy Jenkins *Asquith* (1964)

7 It is fitting that we should have buried the Unknown Prime
Minister [Bonar Law] by the side of the Unknown Soldier.

Robert Blake *The Unknown Prime
Minister* (1955)

8 [The War Office kept three sets of figures:] one to mislead
the public, another to mislead the Cabinet, and the third to
mislead itself.

Alistair Horne *Price of Glory* (1962)

Margot Asquith 1864-1945
British political hostess; wife of Herbert **Asquith**

9 Kitchener is a great poster.

More Memories (1933)

10 There is nothing more popular in the House of Commons
than to blame yourself. 'I have killed my mother. I will
never do it again,' is certain to raise a cheer.

Off the Record (1943)

11 No amount of education will make women first-rate
politicians. Can you see a woman becoming a Prime
Minister? I cannot imagine a greater calamity for these
islands than to be put under the guidance of a woman in 10
Downing Street.

Off the Record (1943)

12 Lord Birkenhead is very clever but sometimes his brains go
to his head.

in *Listener* 11 June 1953 'Margot
Oxford' by Lady Violet Bonham
Carter

13 He can't see a belt without hitting below it.
of **Lloyd George**

in *Listener* 11 June 1953 'Margot
Oxford' by Lady Violet Bonham
Carter

Nancy Astor 1879–1964
American-born British Conservative politician

1 NANCY ASTOR: If I were your wife I would put poison in your coffee.
WINSTON CHURCHILL: And if I were your husband I would drink it.

Consuelo Vanderbilt *Glitter and Gold* (1952)

Brooks Atkinson 1894–1984
American journalist and critic

2 After each war there is a little less democracy to save.

Once Around the Sun (1951) 7 January

3 In every age 'the good old days' were a myth. No one ever thought they were good at the time. For every age had consisted of crises that seemed intolerable to the people who lived through them.

Once Around the Sun (1951) 8 February

4 There is a good deal of solemn cant about the common interests of capital and labour. As matters stand, their only common interest is that of cutting each other's throat.

Once Around the Sun (1951) 7 September

Clement Attlee 1883–1967
British Labour statesman; Prime Minister, 1945–51
on Attlee: see **Churchill** 86:1, 86:9, **Hennessy** 168:6, **Nicolson** 266:9, **Pimlott** 289:5

5 Why does Mosley always speak to us as though he were a feudal landlord abusing tenants who are in arrears with their rent?
at a meeting of the Parliamentary Labour Party, 20 November 1930, a few months before Oswald Mosley was expelled from the Party

Hugh Dalton *Political Diary* (1986) 20 November 1930

6 A monologue is not a decision.
to Winston **Churchill***, who had complained that a matter had been raised several times in Cabinet*

Francis Williams *A Prime Minister Remembers* (1961)

7 The voice we heard was that of Mr Churchill but the mind was that of Lord Beaverbrook.

speech on radio, 5 June 1945

8 A period of silence on your part would be welcome.
in reply to a letter from the Chairman of the Labour Party, Harold **Laski***, asking (for the second time and at length) that Attlee should not form a new government until the Parliamentary Labour Party had had the chance to elect a new leader*

letter to Harold Laski, 20 August 1945

9 If the King asks you to form a Government you say 'Yes' or 'No', not 'I'll let you know later!'

Kenneth Harris *Attlee* (1982)

at a Cabinet Meeting, when Aneurin **Bevan** *as Minister of Housing complained that he could not get enough people for his building programme:*

10 BEVAN: Where are all the people I need for my programme?
ATTLEE: Looking for houses, Nye!

Michael Foot *Aneuran Bevan* (1973) vol. 2

11 I should be a sad subject for any publicity expert. I have none of the qualities which create publicity.

Harold Nicolson diary, 14 January 1949

response to a memorandum from the Ministry of Works saying, 'We have read the Cabinet's proposals':

1 The Cabinet does not propose, it decides. — Tony Benn diary, 20 May 1974

2 I believe that conscience is a still small voice and not a loudspeaker. — attributed, 1955

3 Few thought he was even a starter
There were many who thought themselves smarter
But he ended PM
CH and OM
An earl and a knight of the garter.
   describing himself in a letter to Tom Attlee, 8 April 1956

— Kenneth Harris *Attlee* (1982)

4 [Russian Communism is] the illegitimate child of Karl Marx and Catherine the Great. — speech at Aarhus University, 11 April 1956

5 Generally speaking the Press lives on disaster. — attributed, 1956

6 Democracy means government by discussion, but it is only effective if you can stop people talking. — speech at Oxford, 14 June 1957

7 Often the 'experts' make the worst possible Ministers in their own fields. In this country we prefer rule by amateurs. — speech at Oxford, 14 June 1957

8 It's a good maxim that if you have a good dog you don't bark yourself. I had a very good dog in Mr Ernest Bevin. — attributed, 1960

definition of the art of politics:
9 Judgement which is needed to make important decisions on imperfect knowledge in a limited time. — attributed

10 A lot of clever people have got everything except judgement. — Francis Williams *A Prime Minister Remembers* (1961)

W. H. Auden 1907-73

English poet

11 To save your world you asked this man to die:
Would this man, could he see you now, ask why?

— 'Epitaph for the Unknown Soldier' (1955)

12 He knew human folly like the back of his hand,
And was greatly interested in armies and fleets;
When he laughed, respectable senators burst with laughter,
And when he cried the little children died in the streets.

— 'Epitaph on a Tyrant' (1940); see **Motley** 261:5

13 In the nightmare of the dark
All the dogs of Europe bark,
And the living nations wait,
Each sequestered in its hate.

— 'In Memory of W. B. Yeats' (1940)

14 Private faces in public places
Are wiser and nicer
Than public faces in private places.

— *Orators* (1932) dedication

15 There is no such thing as the State
And no one exists alone;
Hunger allows no choice
To the citizen or the police;
We must love one another or die.

— 'September 1, 1939' (1940)

16 Our researchers into Public Opinion are content
That he held the proper opinions for the time of year;
When there was peace, he was for peace; when there was war, he went.

— 'The Unknown Citizen' (1940)

1 This marble monument was erected by the state.
Was he free? Was he happy? The question is absurd:
Had anything been wrong, we should certainly have heard.

'The Unknown Citizen' (1940)

Augustus 63 BC–AD 14
first Roman emperor
on Augustus: see **Cicero** 87:3

2 Quintilius Varus, give me back my legions.
after the annihilation by the German leader Arminius of three Roman legions under Quintilius Varus

Suetonius *Lives of the Caesars*

3 He could boast that he inherited it brick and left it marble.
of the city of Rome

Suetonius *Lives of the Caesars*

Aung San Suu Kyi 1945–
Burmese political leader

4 It's very different from living in academia in Oxford. We called someone vicious in the *Times Literary Supplement*. We didn't know what vicious was.
on returning to Burma (Myanmar)

in *Observer* 25 September 1988 'Sayings of the Week'

5 In societies where men are truly confident of their own worth, women are not merely tolerated but valued.

videotape speech at NGO Forum on Women, China, early September 1995

Marcus Aurelius AD 121–80
Roman emperor from AD 161

6 Man, you have been a citizen in this world city, what does it matter whether for five years or fifty?

Meditations

Jane Austen 1775–1817
English novelist

7 From politics, it was an easy step to silence.

Northanger Abbey (1818)

Isaac Babel 1894–1940
Russian short-story writer

8 Now a man talks frankly only with his wife, at night, with the blanket over his head.

remark c.1937; Solomon Volkov *St Petersburg* (1996)

9 They didn't let me finish.

to his wife, on the day of his arrest by the NKVD, 16 May 1939

Francis Bacon 1561–1626
English lawyer, courtier, philosopher, and essayist
see also **Last Words** 212:6

10 To worship the people is to be worshipped.

De Dignitate et Augmentis Scientiarum (1623)

11 He is the fountain of honour.

An Essay of a King (1642); attribution doubtful; see **Bagehot** 20:9

12 In civil business; what first? boldness; what second and third? boldness: and yet boldness is a child of ignorance and baseness.

Essays (1625) 'Of Boldness'

1 There be [some] that can pack the cards and yet cannot play well; so there are some that are good in canvasses and factions, that are otherwise weak men.

Essays (1625) 'Of Cunning'

2 Nothing doth more hurt in a state than that cunning men pass for wise.

Essays (1625) 'Of Cunning'

3 There is surely no greater wisdom than well to time the beginnings and endings of things.

Essays (1625) 'Of Delays'

4 The difficulties in princes' business are many and great, but the greatest difficulty is often in their own mind.

Essays (1625) 'Of Empire'

5 Men in great place are thrice servants: servants of the sovereign or state, servants of fame, and servants of business.

Essays (1625) 'Of Great Place'

6 The rising unto place is laborious, and by pains men come to greater pains; and it is sometimes base, and by indignities men come to dignities. The standing is slippery, and the regress is either a downfall, or at least an eclipse.

Essays (1625) 'Of Great Place'

7 Severity breedeth fear, but roughness breedeth hate. Even reproofs from authority ought to be grave, and not taunting.

Essays (1625) 'Of Great Place'

8 All rising to great place is by a winding stair.

Essays (1625) 'Of Great Place'

9 New nobility is but the act of power, but ancient nobility is the act of time.

Essays (1625) 'Of Nobility'

10 Fame is like a river, that beareth up things light and swollen, and drowns things weighty and solid.

Essays (1625) 'Of Praise'

11 So when any of the four pillars of government are mainly shakened or weakened (which are religion, justice, counsel, and treasure) men had need to pray for fair weather.

Essays (1625) 'Of Seditions and Troubles'

12 The surest way to prevent seditions (if the times do bear it) is to take away the matter of them.

Essays (1625) 'Of Seditions and Troubles'

13 Suspicions amongst thoughts are like bats amongst birds, they ever fly by twilight.

Essays (1625) 'Of Suspicion'

14 Neither is money the sinews of war (as it is trivially said).

Essays (1625) 'Of the True Greatness of Kingdoms'

15 Neither will it be, that a people overlaid with taxes should ever become valiant and martial.

Essays (1625) 'Of the True Greatness of Kingdoms'

16 What is truth? said jesting Pilate; and would not stay for an answer.

Essays (1625) 'Of Truth'

17 All colours will agree in the dark.

Essays (1625) 'Of Unity in Religion'

18 In the youth of a state arms do flourish; in the middle age of a state, learning; and then both of them together for a time; in the declining age of a state, mechanical arts and merchandise.

Essays (1625) 'Of Vicissitude of Things'

19 For also knowledge itself is power.

Meditationes Sacrae 1597) 'Of Heresies'

1 It is well to observe the force and virtue and consequence of discoveries, and these are to be seen nowhere more conspicuously than in those three which were unknown to the ancients, and of which the origins, though recent, are obscure and inglorious; namely, printing, gunpowder, and the magnet [Mariner's Needle]. For these three have changed the whole face and state of things throughout the world.

Novum Organum (1620)

2 There be three things which make a nation great and prosperous: a fertile soil, busy workshops, easy conveyance for men and goods from place to place.

attributed; S. Platt (ed.) *Respectfully Quoted* (1989)

Joan Baez 1941–
American singer and songwriter

3 The only thing that's been a worse flop than the organization of non-violence has been the organization of violence.

Daybreak (1970) 'What Would You Do If?'

Walter Bagehot 1826–77
English economist and essayist

4 In happy states, the Conservative party must rule upon the whole a much longer time than their adversaries. In well-framed politics, innovation—great innovation that is—can only be occasional. If you are always altering your house, it is a sign either that you have a bad house, or that you have an excessively restless disposition—there is something wrong somewhere.

'The Chances for a Long Conservative Régime in England' (1874)

5 Capital must be propelled by self-interest; it cannot be enticed by benevolence.

Economic Studies (1880)

6 The mystic reverence, the religious allegiance, which are essential to a true monarchy, are imaginative sentiments that no legislature can manufacture in any people.

The English Constitution (1867) 'The Cabinet'

7 In such constitutions [as England's] there are two parts . . . first, those which excite and preserve the reverence of the population—the *dignified* parts . . . and next, the *efficient* parts—those by which it, in fact, works and rules.

The English Constitution (1867) 'The Cabinet'

8 No orator ever made an impression by appealing to men as to their plainest physical wants, except when he could allege that those wants were caused by some one's tyranny.

The English Constitution (1867) 'The Cabinet'

9 The Crown is, according to the saying, the 'fountain of honour'; but the Treasury is the spring of business.

The English Constitution (1867) 'The Cabinet'; see **Bacon** 18:11

10 A cabinet is a combining committee—a *hyphen* which joins, a *buckle* which fastens, the legislative part of the state to the executive part of the state.

The English Constitution (1867) 'The Cabinet'

11 It has been said that England invented the phrase, 'Her Majesty's Opposition'; that it was the first government which made a criticism of administration as much a part of the polity as administration itself. This critical opposition is the consequence of cabinet government.

The English Constitution (1867) 'The Cabinet'; see **Hobhouse** 174:2

12 *The Times* has made many ministries.

The English Constitution (1867) 'The Cabinet'

1 The great qualities, the imperious will, the rapid energy, the eager nature fit for a great crisis are not required—are impediments—in common times.

The English Constitution (1867) 'The Cabinet'

2 By the structure of the world we often want, at the sudden occurrence of a grave tempest, to change the helmsman—to replace the pilot of the calm by the pilot of the storm.

The English Constitution (1867) 'The Cabinet'

of Queen **Victoria** *and the future* **Edward VII**

3 It is nice to trace how the actions of a retired widow and an unemployed youth become of such importance.

The English Constitution (1867) 'The Monarchy'

4 The best reason why Monarchy is a strong government is, that it is an intelligible government. The mass of mankind understand it, and they hardly anywhere in the world understand any other.

The English Constitution (1867) 'The Monarchy'

5 The characteristic of the English Monarchy is that it retains the feelings by which the heroic kings governed their rude age, and has added the feelings by which the constitutions of later Greece ruled in more refined ages.

The English Constitution (1867) 'The Monarchy'

6 Women—one half the human race at least—care fifty times more for a marriage than a ministry.

The English Constitution (1867) 'The Monarchy'

7 Royalty is a government in which the attention of the nation is concentrated on one person doing interesting actions. A Republic is a government in which that attention is divided between many, who are all doing uninteresting actions. Accordingly, so long as the human heart is strong and the human reason weak, Royalty will be strong because it appeals to diffused feeling, and Republics weak because they appeal to the understanding.

The English Constitution (1867) 'The Monarchy'

8 Throughout the greater part of his life George III was a kind of 'consecrated obstruction'.

The English Constitution (1867) 'The Monarchy'

9 There are arguments for not having a Court, and there are arguments for having a splendid Court; but there are no arguments for having a mean Court.

The English Constitution (1867) 'The Monarchy'

10 The Queen . . . must sign her own death-warrant if the two Houses unanimously send it up to her.

The English Constitution (1867) 'The Monarchy'

11 Above all things our royalty is to be reverenced, and if you begin to poke about it you cannot reverence it . . . Its mystery is its life. We must not let in daylight upon magic.

The English Constitution (1867) 'The Monarchy'

12 The Sovereign has, under a constitutional monarchy such as ours, three rights—the right to be consulted, the right to encourage, the right to warn.

The English Constitution (1867) 'The Monarchy'

13 The only fit material for a constitutional king is a prince who begins early to reign—who in his youth is superior to pleasure—who in his youth is willing to labour—who has by nature a genius for discretion. Such kings are among God's greatest gifts, but they are also among His rarest.

The English Constitution (1867) 'The Monarchy'

14 The order of nobility is of great use, too, not only in what it creates, but in what it prevents. It prevents the rule of wealth—the religion of gold. This is the obvious and natural idol of the Anglo-Saxon.

The English Constitution (1867) 'The House of Lords'

15 A severe though not unfriendly critic of our institutions said that 'the cure for admiring the House of Lords was to go and look at it.'

The English Constitution (1867) 'The House of Lords'

1 If you want to raise a certain cheer in the House of Commons, make a general panegyric on economy; if you want to invite a sure defeat, propose a particular saving.

The English Constitution (1867) 'The House of Lords'

2 Nations touch at their summits.

The English Constitution (1867) 'The House of Lords'

3 The House of Commons lives in a state of perpetual potential choice: at any moment it can choose a ruler and dismiss a ruler. And therefore party is inherent in it, is bone of its bone, and breath of its breath.

The English Constitution (1867) 'The House of Commons'

4 An Opposition, on coming into power, is often like a speculative merchant whose bills become due. Ministers have to make good their promises, and they find a difficulty in so doing.

The English Constitution (1867) 'The House of Commons'

5 It is an inevitable defect, that bureaucrats will care more for routine than for results.

The English Constitution (1867) 'On Changes of Ministry'

6 A bureaucracy is sure to think that its duty is to augment official power, official business, or official members, rather than to leave free the energies of mankind; it overdoes the quantity of government, as well as impairs its quality.

The English Constitution (1867) 'On Changes of Ministry'

7 But would it not have been a miracle if the English people, directing their own policy, and being what they are, had directed a good policy? Are they not above all nations divided from the rest of the world, insular both in situation and in mind, both for good and for evil? Are they not out of the current of common European causes and affairs? Are they not a race contemptuous of others? Are they not a race with no special education or culture as to the modern world, and too often despising such culture? Who could expect such a people to comprehend the new and strange events of foreign places?

The English Constitution (1867) 'On Changes of Ministry'

8 It has been said, not truly, but with a possible approximation to truth, that in 1802 every hereditary monarch was insane.

The English Constitution (1867) 'Its Supposed Checks and Balances'

9 As soon as we see that England is a disguised republic we must see too that the classes for whom the disguise is necessary must be tenderly dealt with.

The English Constitution (1867) 'Its History'

10 The natural impulse of the English people is to resist authority.

The English Constitution (1867) 'Its History'

11 A political country is like an American forest: you only have to cut down the old trees, and immediately new trees come up to replace them; the seeds were waiting in the ground, and they began to grow as soon as the withdrawal of the old ones brought in light and air.

The English Constitution: introduction to the second edition (1872)

12 No real English gentleman, in his secret soul, was ever sorry for the death of a political economist.

Estimates of some Englishmen and Scotchmen (1858)

13 Dullness in matters of government is a good sign, and not a bad one—in particular, dullness in Parliamentary government is a test of its excellence, an indication of its success.

in *Saturday Review* 16 February 1856

14 A constitutional statesman is in general a man of common opinion and uncommon abilities.

in *National Review* July 1856

1 Public opinion is a permeating influence, and it exacts obedience to itself; it requires us to think other men's thoughts, to speak other men's words, to follow other men's habits.

in *National Review* July 1856

2 He believes, with all his heart and soul and strength, that there *is* such a thing as truth; he has the soul of a martyr with the intellect of an advocate.
   of **Gladstone**

in *National Review* July 1860

3 If . . . the country should ever look on the proceedings of Parliament as an intellectual and theatrical exhibition, no merit in our laws, no excellence in our national character, could save our institutions from very serious danger.

in *The Economist* 1861

4 Years of acquiescing in proposals as to which he has not been consulted, of voting for measures which he did not frame, and in the wisdom of which he often did not believe of arguing for proposals from half of which he dissents— usually de-intellectualize a parliamentary statesman before he comes to half his power.

in *National Review* 1861 'William Pitt'

5 There is no method by which men can be both free and equal.

in *The Economist* 5 September 1863

6 Persecute a sect and it holds together, legalize it and it splits and resplits, till its unity is either null or a non-oppressive bond.

in *The Economist* 27 April 1867

7 The highest and most important capacity in the Leader of the Opposition is to be able on special occasions to resist the mistaken wishes of the party which he leads.

in *The Economist* 1874

8 Policies must 'grow'; they cannot be suddenly made.

in *The Economist* 1874

9 A great Premier must add the vivacity of an idle man to the assiduity of a very laborious one.

in *The Economist* 2 January 1875

10 The being without an opinion is so painful to human nature that most people will leap to a hasty opinion rather than undergo it.

in *The Economist* 4 December 1875

11 In every country the extreme party is most irritated against the party which comes nearest to itself, but does not go so far.

in *The Economist* 22 April 1876

12 Good government depends at least as much on an impartial respect for the rights of all as it does on energy in enforcing respect for the authority which protects those rights.

in *The Economist* 27 May 1876

13 The characteristic danger of great nations, like the Romans or the English, which have a long history of continuous creation, is that they may at last fail from not comprehending the great institutions which they have created.

in *Fortnightly Review* 1 November 1876

14 There never was a worse blunder than the supposition that the more states there are to suffer by a sanguinary quarrel, the sooner will the motives prevail for bringing it to a conclusion.

in *The Economist* 17 March 1877

Ewen Bain 1925–89
Scottish cartoonist

15 No son—they're not the same—devolution takes longer.
   father to his son, who is reading a book on evolution

cartoon caption, in *Scots Independent* January 1978

Jacques Bainville 1879–1936

French historian

of the Treaty of Versailles:

1 Written by Bible readers *for* Bible readers.

'Les Consequences Politiques de la Paix' (1920)

Kenneth Baker 1934–

British Conservative politician

2 Why should Scottish and Welsh nationalism be seen as a noble thing, when in England it is seen as something dirty?

in *Sunday Times* 6 January 2000 'Talking Heads'

Michael Bakunin 1814–76

Russian revolutionary and anarchist

3 The urge for destruction is also a creative urge!

in *Jahrbuch für Wissenschaft und Kunst* (1842)

4 We wish, in a word, equality—equality in fact as corollary, or rather, as primordial condition of liberty. From each according to his faculties, to each according to his needs; that is what we wish sincerely and energetically.
    declaration signed by forty-seven anarchists on trial after the failure of their uprising at Lyons in 1870

J. Morrison Davidson *The Old Order and the New* (1890)

James Baldwin 1924–87

American novelist and essayist

5 Freedom is not something that anybody can be given; freedom is something people take and people are as free as they want to be.

Nobody Knows My Name (1961) 'Notes for a Hypothetical Novel'

6 At the root of the American Negro problem is the necessity of the American white man to find a way of living with the Negro in order to be able to live with himself.

in *Harper's Magazine* October 1953 'Stranger in a Village'

7 It comes as a great shock around the age of 5, 6 or 7 to discover that the flag to which you have pledged allegiance, along with everybody else, has not pledged allegiance to you. It comes as a great shock to see Gary Cooper killing off the Indians and, although you are rooting for Gary Cooper, that the Indians are you.
    speaking for the proposition that 'The American Dream is at the expense of the American Negro' at the Cambridge Union, England, 17 February 1965

in *New York Times Magazine* 7 March 1965

8 If they take you in the morning, they will be coming for us that night.

in *New York Review of Books* 7 January 1971 'Open Letter to my Sister, Angela Davis'

Stanley Baldwin 1867–1947

British Conservative statesman; Prime Minister, 1923–4, 1924–9, 1935–7
on Baldwin: see **Beaverbrook** 29:11, **Churchill** 83:11, 84:4, **Curzon** 100:2, **Trevelyan** 363:3; *see also* **Kipling** 207:1

9 They [parliament] are a lot of hard-faced men who look as if they had done very well out of the war.

J. M. Keynes *Economic Consequences of the Peace* (1919)

1 A platitude is simply a truth repeated until people get tired of hearing it.

speech in the House of Commons, 29 May 1924

2 There are three classes which need sanctuary more than others—birds, wild flowers, and Prime Ministers.

in *Observer* 24 May 1925

3 'Safety first' does not mean a smug self-satisfaction with everything as it is. It is a warning to all persons who are going to cross a road in dangerous circumstances.

in *The Times* 21 May 1929

4 Had the employers of past generations all of them dealt fairly with their men there would have been no unions.

speech in Birmingham, 14 January 1931

5 I think it is well also for the man in the street to realize that there is no power on earth that can protect him from being bombed. Whatever people may tell him, the bomber will always get through. The only defence is in offence, which means that you have to kill more women and children more quickly than the enemy if you want to save yourselves.

speech in the House of Commons, 10 November 1932

6 Since the day of the air, the old frontiers are gone. When you think of the defence of England you no longer think of the chalk cliffs of Dover; you think of the Rhine. That is where our frontier lies.

speech in the House of Commons, 30 July 1934

*of his reasons for excluding **Churchill** from the Cabinet:*
7 If there is going to be a war—and no one can say that there is not—we must keep him fresh to be our war Prime Minister.

letter, 17 November 1935

8 I shall be but a short time tonight. I have seldom spoken with greater regret, for my lips are not yet unsealed. Were these troubles over I would make a case, and I guarantee that not a man would go into the lobby against us.

speech in the House of Commons on the Abyssinian crisis, 10 December 1935; see **Misquotations** 255:4

9 Supposing I had gone to the country and said that Germany was rearming and that we must rearm, does anybody think that this pacific democracy would have rallied to that cry at that moment? I cannot think of anything that would have made the loss of the election from my point of view more certain.

speech in the House of Commons, 12 November 1936

10 This House today is a theatre which is being watched by the whole world. Let us conduct ourselves with that dignity which His Majesty is showing in this hour of his trial.

speech, House of Commons, 10 December 1936

11 Once I leave, I leave. I am not going to speak to the man on the bridge, and I am not going to spit on the deck.
on resigning

statement to the Cabinet, 28 May 1937

12 You will find in politics that you are much exposed to the attribution of false motive. Never complain and never explain.

Harold Nicolson *Diary* 21 July 1943

13 Do not run up your nose dead against the Pope or the NUM!

Lord Butler *The Art of Memory* (1982); see **Macmillan** 236:10

14 He spent his whole life in plastering together the true and the false and therefrom manufacturing the plausible.
*of **Lloyd George***

attributed

Arthur James Balfour 1848–1930

British Conservative statesman; Prime Minister, 1902–5; in 1917, as Foreign Secretary, Balfour issued the declaration in favour of a Jewish National Home in Palestine that came to be known as the Balfour Declaration.
on Balfour: see **Churchill** 80:6, 84:14, **Lloyd George** 222:5, 223:5

1 It is unfortunate, considering that enthusiasm moves the world, that so few enthusiasts can be trusted to speak the truth.

letter to Mrs Drew, 19 May 1891

2 I do not come here to preach any doctrines of passive obedience or non-resistance. You have had to fight for your liberties before. I pray God you may never have to fight for them again. I do not believe that you ever will have to fight for them, but I admit that the tyranny of majorities may be as bad as the tyranny of Kings . . . and I do not think that any rational or sober man will say that what is justifiable against a tyrannical King may not under certain circumstances be justifiable against a tyrannical majority.
watching the Belfast march past of Ulster Loyalists in 1893

in *Times* 5 April 1893

3 When it comes I shall not be sorry. Only let us have separation as well as Home Rule: England cannot afford to go on with the Irishmen in her Parliament.

Wilfrid Scawen Blunt *The Land War in Ireland* (1912)

4 His Majesty's Government view with favour the establishment in Palestine of a national home for the Jewish people, and will use their best endeavours to facilitate the achievement of this object, it being clearly understood that nothing shall be done which may prejudice the civil and religious rights of existing non-Jewish communities in Palestine, or the rights and political status enjoyed by Jews in any other country.

letter to Lord Rothschild, 2 November 1917; see **Weizmann** 378:6

5 Zionism, be it right or wrong, good or bad, is rooted in age-long traditions, in present need, in future hopes, of far profounder import than the desires and prejudices of the seven hundred thousand Arabs who now inhabit that ancient land.

in August 1919; Max Egremont *Balfour* (1980)

on being asked what he thought of the behaviour of the German delegation at the signing of the Treaty of Versailles:
6 I make it a rule never to stare at people when they are in obvious distress.

Max Egremont *Balfour* (1980)

replying to Frank Harris, who had claimed that 'all the faults of the age come from Christianity and journalism':
7 Christianity, of course . . . but why journalism?

Margot Asquith *Autobiography* (1920) vol. 1

*on the continuing financial dependence of **Curzon**, who had failed to become Prime Minister in succession to **Bonar Law**, on his second wife Grace Duggan:*
8 He may have lost the hope of glory, but he still retains the means of Grace.

attributed

9 Biography should be written by an acute enemy.

in *Observer* 30 January 1927

of an unwelcome supporter:

1 He pursues us with malignant fidelity.

Winston Churchill *Great Contemporaries* (1937)

2 I am more or less happy when being praised, not very uncomfortable when being abused, but I have moments of uneasiness when being explained.

K. Young *A. J. Balfour* (1963)

3 I never forgive but I always forget.

R. Blake *Conservative Party* (1970)

4 I thought he was a young man of promise, but it appears he is a young man of promises.
   describing Churchill

Winston Churchill *My Early Life* (1930)

E. Digby Baltzell 1915–

5 There is a crisis in American leadership in the middle of the twentieth century that is partly due, I think, to the declining authority of an establishment which is now based on an increasingly castelike White-Anglo Saxon-Protestant (WASP) upper class.

The Protestant Establishment (1964)

Honoré de Balzac 1799–1850

French novelist

6 Despotism accomplishes great things illegally; liberty doesn't even go to the trouble of accomplishing small things legally.

La Peau de Chagrin (1831)

George Bancroft 1800–91

American historian and politician

7 Calvinism [in Switzerland] . . . established a religion without a prelate, a government without a king.

History of the United States (1855 ed.) vol. 3

Lord Bancroft 1922–96

British civil servant; Head of the Civil Service 1978–81

8 Conviction politicians, certainly: conviction civil servants, no.

'Whitehall: Some Personal Reflections', lecture at the London School of Economics 1 December 1983

Imamu Amiri Baraka 1934–

American poet and playwright

9 A man is either free or he is not. There cannot be any apprenticeship for freedom.

in *Kulchur* Spring 1962 'Tokenism'

Ernest Barker 1874–1960

British political scientist

10 Sovereignty is unlimited—unlimited and illimitable.

Principles of Social and Political Theory (1951)

Pat Barker 1943-

English novelist

1 The Somme is like the Holocaust. It revealed things about mankind that we cannot come to terms with and cannot forget. It can never become the past.
   on winning the Booker Prize 1995

in *Athens News* 9 November 1995

Michael Joseph Barry 1817-89

Irish nationalist writer

2 The wild geese—the wild geese,—'tis long since they flew, O'er the billowy ocean's bright bosom of blue.

in *Spirit of the Nation* (Dublin, 1845)

Bernard Baruch 1870-1965

American financier and presidential adviser

3 Let us not be deceived—we are today in the midst of a cold war.

speech to South Carolina Legislature 16 April 1947; the expression 'cold war' was suggested to him by H. B. Swope, former editor of the *New York World*

4 Vote for the man who promises least; he'll be the least disappointing.

Meyer Berger *New York* (1960)

5 You can talk about capitalism and communism and all that sort of thing, but the important thing is the struggle everybody is engaged in to get better living conditions, and they are not interested too much in government.

in *The Times* 20 August 1964

6 A political leader must keep looking over his shoulder all the time to see if the boys are still there. If they aren't still there, he's no longer a political leader.

in *New York Times* 21 June 1965

Lord Bauer 1915-

British economist

7 Foreign aid is a system of taking money from poor people in rich countries and giving it to rich people in poor countries.

attributed; not recollected by Lord Bauer but not repudiated by him.

of foreign aid:
8 With every mouth God sends a pair of hands.

saying taken from a Cambridge Economics Tripos examination question in the 1930s

Claude-Frédéric Bastiat 1801-50

French economist

9 All men's impulses, when motivated by legitimate self-interest, fall into a harmonious social pattern.

Economic Harmonies (1964)

10 Once an abuse exists, everything is arranged on the assumption that it will last indefinitely; and, as more and more people come to depend upon it for their livelihood, and still others depend upon them, a superstructure is erected that soon comprises a formidable edifice.

in *Journal des economistes* 1848

Beverley Baxter 1891–1964
British journalist and Conservative politician

1 Beaverbrook is so pleased to be in the Government that he is like the town tart who has finally married the Mayor!

Henry ('Chips') Channon diary, 12 June 1940

Charles Austin Beard 1874–1948
and **Mary Ritter Beard** 1876–1958

2 At no time, at no place, in solemn convention assembled, through no chosen agents, had the American people officially proclaimed the United States to be a democracy . . . When the Constitution was framed no respectable person called himself or herself a democrat.

America in Midpassage (1939)

Lord Beaverbrook 1879–1964
Canadian-born British newspaper proprietor and Conservative politician
on Beaverbrook: see **Baxter** 29:1, **Lloyd George** 223:14; see also **Kipling** 207:1

3 I hope you will give up the New Party. If you must burn your fingers in public life, go to a bright and big blaze.
*to Harold **Nicolson***

letter, 25 June 1931

4 Our cock won't fight.
*said to Winston **Churchill**, of **Edward VIII**, during the abdication crisis of 1936*

Frances Donaldson *Edward VIII* (1974)

5 The Daily Express declares that Great Britain will not be involved in a European war this year or next year either.

in *Daily Express* 19 September 1938

6 Now who is responsible for this work of development on which so much depends? To whom must the praise be given? To the boys in the back rooms. They do not sit in the limelight. But they are the men who do the work.

in *Listener* 27 March 1941

7 I ran the paper [the *Daily Express*] purely for propaganda and with no other purpose.
evidence to the Royal Commission on the Press, 18 March 1948

A. J. P. Taylor *Beaverbrook* (1972)

8 [Lloyd George] did not seem to care which way he travelled providing he was in the driver's seat.

The Decline and Fall of Lloyd George (1963)

9 Always threatening resignation, he never signed off.
*of Lord **Derby***

Men and Power (1956)

*of Lord **Curzon**, who had been created Viceroy of India at the age of thirty-nine:*
10 For all the rest of his life Curzon was influenced by his sudden journey to heaven at the age of thirty-nine, and then by his return seven years later to earth, for the remainder of his mortal existence.

Men and Power (1956)

11 His conversation turned on the beauty of the mountain rose, and the splendour of hawthorn buds in spring.
*of Stanley **Baldwin***

Men and Power (1956)

12 Often undecided whether to desert a sinking ship for one that might not float, he would make up his mind to sit on the wharf for a day.
*of Lord **Curzon***

Men and Power (1956)

1 With the publication of his Private Papers in 1952, he [Earl   *Men and Power* (1956)
  Haig] committed suicide 25 years after his death.
    of Earl **Haig**

2 Churchill on top of the wave has in him the stuff of which   *Politicians and the War* (1932)
  tyrants are made.

3 British electors will never vote for a man who doesn't wear   Tom Driberg *Ruling Passions* (1997)
  a hat.
    advice to Tom Driberg

  of **Bonar Law** *and* **Churchill**:
4 I have had two masters and one of them betrayed me.   A. J. P. Taylor letter, 16 December
                                                           1973

Margaret Beckett 1943–
British Labour politician

5 Being effective is more important to me than being   in *Independent on Sunday* 2 January
  recognized.   2000

Henry Becque 1837–99
French dramatist and critic

6 What makes equality such a difficult business is that we   *Querelles littéraires* (1890)
  only want it with our superiors.

Brendan Behan 1923–64
Irish playwright

7 PAT: He was an Anglo-Irishman.   *The Hostage* (1958)
  MEG: In the blessed name of God what's that?
  PAT: A Protestant with a horse.

8 When I came back to Dublin, I was courtmartialled in my   *The Hostage* (1958)
  absence and sentenced to death in my absence, so I said
  they could shoot me in my absence.

Lord Belhaven 1656–1708
Scottish politician

9 Good God! What, is this an entire surrender?   speech in the Scottish Parliament,
    culmination of a speech opposing the Union with England   2 November 1706

George Bell 1883–1958
Anglican clergyman, Bishop of Chichester

10 The policy is obliteration, openly acknowledged. This is not   speech, House of Lords, 9 February
  a justifiable act of war.   1944
    of the saturation bombing of Berlin

Martin Bell 1938–
British journalist and Independent politician

11 I knew when Sir Alec Guinness endorsed my campaign that   in *Oxford Mail* 2 May 1997
  the force was with us.
    victory speech on winning the Tatton constituency, 2 May 1997

Francis Bellamy 1856–1931

American clergyman and editor

1 I pledge allegiance to the flag of the United States of America and to the republic for which it stands, one nation under God, indivisible, with liberty and justice for all.

The Pledge of Allegiance to the Flag (1892)

Hilaire Belloc 1870–1953

British poet, essayist, historian, novelist, and Liberal politician

2 Sir! you have disappointed us!
We had intended you to be
The next Prime Minister but three:
The stocks were sold; the Press was squared;
The Middle Class was quite prepared.
But as it is! . . . My language fails!
Go out and govern New South Wales!

Cautionary Tales (1907) 'Lord Lundy'

3 Here richly, with ridiculous display,
The Politician's corpse was laid away.
While all of his acquaintance sneered and slanged
I wept: for I had longed to see him hanged.

'Epitaph on the Politician Himself' (1923)

4 Whatever happens we have got
The Maxim Gun, and they have not.

The Modern Traveller (1898)

5 The accursed power which stands on Privilege
(And goes with Women, and Champagne, and Bridge)
Broke—and Democracy resumed her reign:
(Which goes with Bridge, and Women and Champagne).

'On a Great Election' (1923)

6 Gentlemen, I am a Catholic . . . If you reject me on account of my religion, I shall thank God that He has spared me the indignity of being your representative.

speech to voters of South Salford, 1906

Julien Benda 1867–1956

French philosopher and novelist

7 *La trahison des clercs.*
The treachery of the intellectuals.

title of book, 1927

Ruth Fulton Benedict 1887–1948

American anthropologist

8 The tough-minded . . . respect difference. Their goal is a world made safe for differences, where the United States may be American to the hilt without threatening the peace of the world, and France may be France, and Japan may be Japan on the same conditions.

The Chrysanthemum and the Sword (1946)

Ernest Benn 1875–1954

English publisher and economist

9 Politics is the art of looking for trouble, finding it whether it exists or not, diagnosing it incorrectly, and applying the wrong remedy.

attributed

Tony Benn 1925–

British Labour politician and sometime Viscount Stansgate, who campaigned for the change in the law that made it possible to renounce a hereditary peerage
on Benn: see **Levin** 217:1

1 Not a reluctant peer but a persistent commoner.

at a Press Conference, 23 November 1960

2 Some of the jam we thought was for tomorrow, we've already eaten.

attributed, 1969

3 In developing our industrial strategy for the period ahead, we have the benefit of much experience. Almost everything has been tried at least once.

speech in House of Commons, 13 March 1974

on seeing Harold **Wilson**, *who had resigned as Prime Minister in March, looking 'absolutely shrunk':*
4 Office is something that builds up a man only if he is somebody in his own right.

diary, 12 April 1976

5 Marxism is now a world faith and must be allowed to enter into a continuous dialogue with other world faiths, including religious faiths.

Karl Marx lecture, 16 March 1982

of the influence of Parliament:
6 Through talk, we tamed kings, restrained tyrants, averted revolution.

Anthony Sampson *The Changing Anatomy of Britain* (1982)

7 I did not enter the Labour Party forty-seven years ago to have our manifesto written by Dr Mori, Dr Gallup and Mr Harris.

in *Guardian* 13 June 1988

8 A faith is something you die for; a doctrine is something you kill for: there is all the difference in the world.

in *Observer* 16 April 1989 'Sayings of the Week'

questions habitually asked by Tony Benn on meeting somebody in power:
9 What power have you got? Where did you get it from? In whose interests do you exercise it? To whom are you accountable? How do we get rid of you?

'The Independent Mind', lecture at Nottingham, 18 June 1993

10 The Civil Service is a bit like a rusty weathercock. It moves with opinion then it stays where it is until another wind moves it in a different directions.

briefing for 'Cabinet and Premiership' course (Queen Mary and Westfield College), held at the House of Commons 1 March 1995

11 When you get to No. 10, you've climbed there on a little ladder called 'the status quo'. And, when you're there, the status quo looks very good.

at the House of Commons 1 March 1995

12 We should put the spin-doctors in spin clinics, where they can meet other spin patients and be treated by spin consultants. The rest of us can get on with the proper democratic process.

in *Independent* 25 October 1997 'Quote Unquote'

13 When I think of Cool Britannia, I think of old people dying of hypothermia.
   at the Labour Party Conference

in *Daily Star* 30 September 1998

Alan Bennett 1934–

English actor and playwright

14 The office of Prince of Wales is not a position, it is a predicament.

The Madness of George III

Arnold Bennett 1867–1931
English novelist

1 Seventy minutes had passed before Mr Lloyd George arrived at his proper theme. He spoke for a hundred and seventeen minutes, in which period he was detected only once in the use of an argument.

Things that have Interested Me (1921) 'After the March Offensive'

2 Examine the Honours List and you can instantly tell how the Government feels in its inside. When the Honours List is full of rascals, millionaires, and—er—chumps, you may be quite sure that the Government is dangerously ill.

The Title (1918)

3 Literature's always a good card to play for Honours. It makes people think that Cabinet ministers are educated.

The Title (1918)

A. C. Benson 1862–1925
English writer

4 Land of Hope and Glory, Mother of the Free,
How shall we extol thee who are born of thee?
Wider still and wider shall thy bounds be set;
God who made thee mighty, make thee mightier yet.

'Land of Hope and Glory' written to be sung as the Finale to Elgar's *Coronation Ode* (1902)

Jeremy Bentham 1748–1832
English philosopher

5 Right . . . is the child of law: from real laws come real rights; but from imaginary laws, from laws of nature, fancied and invented by poets, rhetoricians, and dealers in moral and intellectual poisons, come imaginary rights, a bastard brood of monsters.

Anarchical Fallacies (1843)

6 Natural rights is simple nonsense: natural and imprescriptible rights, rhetorical nonsense—nonsense upon stilts.

Anarchical Fallacies (1843)

7 The greatest happiness of the greatest number is the foundation of morals and legislation.
Bentham claims to have acquired the 'sacred truth' either from Joseph Priestley (1733–1804) or Cesare Beccaria (1738–94)

The Commonplace Book (1843)

8 Every law is contrary to liberty.

Principles of the Civil Code (1843)

9 He rather hated the ruling few than loved the suffering many.
of James Mill

H. N. Pym (ed.) *Memories of Old Friends, being Extracts from the Journals and Letters of Caroline Fox* (1882)

Edmund Clerihew Bentley 1875–1956
English writer

10 When their lordships asked Bacon
How many bribes he had taken
He had at least the grace
To get very red in the face.

Baseless Biography (1939) 'Bacon'

11 George the Third
Ought never to have occurred.
One can only wonder
At so grotesque a blunder.

More Biography (1929) 'George the Third'

Lloyd Bentsen 1921–

American Democratic politician

*responding to Dan Quayle's claim to have 'as much experience in the
Congress as Jack **Kennedy** had when he sought the presidency':*

1 Senator, I served with Jack Kennedy. I knew Jack Kennedy.
Jack Kennedy was a friend of mine. Senator, you're no Jack
Kennedy.

in the vice-presidential debate, 5
October 1988

Peter Berger

political scientist

2 Capitalism, as an institutional arrangement, has been
singularly devoid of plausible myths. By contrast, socialism,
its major alternative under modern conditions, has been
singularly blessed with myth-generating potency.

in 1986; Anthony Sampson *The
Company Man* (1995)

George Berkeley 1685–1753

Irish philosopher and Anglican bishop

3 Westward the course of empire takes its way;
The first four acts already past,
A fifth shall close the drama with the day:
Time's noblest offspring is the last.

'On the Prospect of Planting Arts
and Learning in America' (1752);
see John Quincy Adams *Oration at
Plymouth* (1802): 'Westward the
star of empire takes its way'

Irving Berlin 1888–1989

American songwriter

4 God bless America,
Land that I love,
Stand beside her and guide her
Thru the night with a light from above.
From the mountains to the prairies,
To the oceans white with foam,
God bless America,
My home sweet home.

'God Bless America' (1939)

Isaiah Berlin 1909–97

British philosopher

5 The fundamental sense of freedom is freedom from chains,
from imprisonment, from enslavement by others. The rest is
extension of this sense, or else metaphor.

Four Essays on Liberty (1969);
introduction

6 Injustice, poverty, slavery, ignorance—these may be cured
by reform or revolution. But men do not live only by
fighting evils. They live by positive goals, individual and
collective, a vast variety of them, seldom predictable, at
times incompatible.

Four Essays on Liberty (1969)

7 Those who have ever valued liberty for its own sake believed
that to be free to choose, and not be chosen for, is an
inalienable ingredient in what makes human beings human.

Four Essays on Liberty (1969)

8 Liberty is liberty, not equality or fairness or justice or
human happiness or a quiet conscience.

Two Concepts of Liberty (1958)

1 It is this—the 'positive' conception of liberty: not freedom from, but freedom to—which the adherents of the 'negative' notion represent as being, at times, no better than a specious disguise for brutal tyranny.

Two Concepts of Liberty (1958)

2 Few new truths have ever won their way against the resistance of established ideas save by being overstated.

Vico and Herder (1976)

J. D. Bernal 1901–71
Irish-born physicist

3 Men will not be content to manufacture life: they will want to improve on it.

The World, the Flesh and the Devil (1929)

Carl Bernstein 1944–
American journalist

4 This convention, they got the show business right. They got their message out. They got their candidate to look exactly like they wanted him to look. Great achievement.
   of the 2000 Republican convention

on *Larry King Live* (CNN) 4 August 2000

Carl Bernstein 1944–
and **Bob Woodward** 1943–
American journalists

5 All the President's men.

title of book (1974) on the Watergate scandal

Daniel Berrigan
US anti-Vietnam War activist

6 This is a war run to show the world, and particularly the Third World, where exactly it stands in relation to our technology.

attributed, 1973

Theobald von Bethmann Hollweg
1856–1921
Chancellor of Germany, 1909–17

7 Just for a word 'neutrality'—a word which in wartime has so often been disregarded—just for a scrap of paper, Great Britain is going to make war on a kindred nation who desires nothing better than to be friends with her.

summary of a report by E. Goschen to Edward Grey in *British Documents on Origins of the War 1898–1914* (1926) vol. 11

Mary McLeod Bethune 1875–1955
American educator

8 If we accept and acquiesce in the face of discrimination, we accept the responsibility ourselves and allow those responsible to salve their conscience by believing that they have our acceptance and concurrence.

Rayford W. Logan (ed.) *What the Negro Wants* (1944) 'Certain Inalienable Rights'

John Betjeman 1906–84
English poet

1 Think of what our Nation stands for,
Books from Boots' and country lanes,
Free speech, free passes, class distinction,
Democracy and proper drains.
Lord, put beneath Thy special care
One-eighty-nine Cadogan Square.

'In Westminster Abbey' (1940)

Aneurin Bevan 1897–1960
British Labour politician

2 This island is made mainly of coal and surrounded by fish. Only an organizing genius could produce a shortage of coal and fish at the same time.

speech at Blackpool 24 May 1945

3 No amount of cajolery, and no attempts at ethical or social seduction, can eradicate from my heart a deep burning hatred for the Tory Party . . . So far as I am concerned they are lower than vermin.

speech at Manchester, 4 July 1948

4 The language of priorities is the religion of Socialism.

speech at Labour Party Conference in Blackpool, 8 June 1949

5 Why read the crystal when he can read the book?
*referring to Robert **Boothby** during a debate on the Sterling Exchange Rate*

in the House of Commons, 29 September 1949

6 [Winston Churchill] does not talk the language of the 20th century but that of the 18th. He is still fighting Blenheim all over again. His only answer to a difficult situation is send a gun-boat.

speech at Labour Party Conference, Scarborough, 2 October 1951

7 The Tories, every election, must have a bogy man. If you haven't got a programme, a bogy man will do. In 1945 it was Harold Laski, in 1951 it is me.

speech in the general election campaign at Stonehouse, Gloucester, 13 October 1951

8 We know what happens to people who stay in the middle of the road. They get run down.

in *Observer* 6 December 1953

9 Damn it all, you can't have the crown of thorns *and* the thirty pieces of silver.
on his position in the Labour Party, c.1956

Michael Foot *Aneurin Bevan* vol. 2 (1973)

10 I am not going to spend any time whatsoever in attacking the Foreign Secretary . . . If we complain about the tune, there is no reason to attack the monkey when the organ grinder is present.
during a debate on the Suez crisis

in the House of Commons, 16 May 1957

11 If you carry this resolution you will send Britain's Foreign Secretary naked into the conference chamber.
speaking against a motion proposing unilateral nuclear disarmament by the United Kingdom

speech at Labour Party Conference in Brighton, 3 October 1957

12 You call that statesmanship? I call it an emotional spasm.
speaking against a motion proposing unilateral nuclear disarmament by the United Kingdom

speech at Labour Party Conference in Brighton, 3 October 1957

1 I know that the right kind of leader for the Labour Party is a desiccated calculating machine who must not in any way permit himself to be swayed by indignation. If he sees suffering, privation or injustice he must not allow it to move him, for that would be evidence of the lack of proper education or of absence of self-control. He must speak in calm and objective accents and talk about a dying child in the same way as he would about the pieces inside an internal combustion engine.

> *frequently taken as referring to Hugh* **Gaitskell**, *although Bevan specifically denied it in an interview with Robin Day on 28 April 1959*

Michael Foot *Aneurin Bevan* vol. 2 (1973)

2 The conquest of the commanding heights of the economy.

> *recalling his own earlier use of the phrase (possibly originated by Lenin)*

at the Labour Party Conference, November 1959

3 The Prime Minister has an absolute genius for putting flamboyant labels on empty luggage.

> *of Harold* **Macmillan**

in the House of Commons, 3 November 1959

4 I read the newspapers avidly. It is my one form of continuous fiction.

in *The Times* 29 March 1960

5 Discontent arises from a knowledge of the possible, as contrasted with the actual.

In Place of Fear (1952)

6 In one sense the Commons is the most unrepresentative of representative assemblies. It is an elaborate conspiracy to prevent the real clash of opinion which exists outside from finding an appropriate echo within its walls. It is a social shock absorber placed between privilege and the pressure of popular discontent.

In Place of Fear (1952)

of his handling of the consultants during the establishment of the National Health Service:

7 I stuffed their mouths with gold.

Brian Abel-Smith *The Hospitals 1800–1948* (1964)

8 Listening to a speech by Chamberlain is like paying a visit to Woolworth's: everything in its place and nothing above sixpence.

Michael Foot *Aneurin Bevan* vol. 1 (1962)

9 There are only two ways of getting into the Cabinet. One way is to crawl up the staircase of preferment on your belly; the other way is to kick them in the teeth.

Richard Crossman *Inside View* (1972)

Albert Jeremiah Beveridge 1862–1927

American Republican politician and member of the Senate, who in 1912 chaired the convention that organized the Progressive party and nominated Theodore **Roosevelt** for President

10 This party comes from the grass roots. It has grown from the soil of the people's hard necessities.

address at the Bull Moose Convention in Chicago, 5 August 1912

William Henry Beveridge 1879–1963

British economist

11 Ignorance is an evil weed, which dictators may cultivate among their dupes, but which no democracy can afford among its citizens.

Full Employment in a Free Society (1944)

1 The object of government in peace and in war is not the glory of rulers or of races, but the happiness of the common man.

Social Insurance and Allied Services (1942)

2 Want is one only of five giants on the road of reconstruction . . . the others are Disease, Ignorance, Squalor and Idleness.

Social Insurance and Allied Services (1942)

3 The state is or can be master of money, but in a free society it is master of very little else.

Voluntary Action (1948)

Ernest Bevin 1881–1951
British Labour politician and trade unionist

4 The most conservative man in this world is the British Trade Unionist when you want to change him.

speech, 8 September 1927

5 I hope you will carry no resolution of an emergency character telling a man with a conscience like Lansbury what he ought to do . . . It is placing the Executive in an absolutely wrong position to be taking your conscience round from body to body to be told what you ought to do with it.

in *Labour Party Conference Report* (1935); see **Misquotations** 254:8

6 I am not one of those who decry Eton and Harrow. I was very glad of them in the Battle of Britain.

speech at Blackpool, 1945

7 There never has been a war yet which, if the facts had been put calmly before the ordinary folk, could not have been prevented . . . The common man, I think, is the great protection against war.

in the House of Commons, 23 November 1945

as Minister of Labour to his Civil Servants:
8 You've just given me twenty reasons why I can't do this; I'm sure that clever chaps like you can go away and produce twenty good reasons why I can.

oral tradition; Peter Hennessy *Whitehall* (1990)

9 My [foreign] policy is to be able to take a ticket at Victoria Station and go anywhere I damn well please.

in *Spectator* 20 April 1951

10 I didn't ought never to have done it. It was you, Willie, what put me up to it.
    to Lord Strang, after officially recognizing Communist China

C. Parrott *Serpent and Nightingale* (1977)

11 If you open that Pandora's Box, you never know what Trojan 'orses will jump out.
    on the Council of Europe

Roderick Barclay *Ernest Bevin and the Foreign Office* (1975)

*someone had remarked that Aneurin **Bevan** was his own worst enemy:*
12 Not while I'm alive 'e ain't.
    *also attributed to Bevin of Herbert **Morrison***

Roderick Barclay *Ernest Bevin and the Foreign Office* (1975)

Benazir Bhutto 1953–
Pakistani stateswoman

13 Every dictator uses religion as a prop to keep himself in power.

interview on *60 Minutes*, CBS-TV, 8 August 1986

14 You can't be fuelled by bitterness. It can eat you up, but it cannot drive you.

Daughter of Destiny (1989)

The Bible (Authorized Version)

1 Let my people go. Exodus

2 Let them live; but let them be hewers of wood and drawers of water unto all the congregation. Joshua

3 He smote them hip and thigh. Judges

4 And she named the child I-chabod, saying, The glory is departed from Israel. I Samuel

5 And Saul said, God hath delivered him into mine hand. I Samuel

6 He shall know that there is a prophet in Israel. II Kings

7 Had Zimri peace, who slew his master? II Kings

8 Thus shall it be done to the man whom the king delighteth to honour. Esther

9 Great men are not always wise. Job

10 Where there is no vision, the people perish. Proverbs

11 The race is not to the swift, nor the battle to the strong. Ecclesiastes

12 Woe to thee, O land, when thy king is a child. Ecclesiastes

13 They shall beat their swords into plowshares, and their spears into pruninghooks: nation shall not lift up sword against nation, neither shall they learn war any more. Isaiah; see **Rendall** 300:8

14 Of the increase of his government and peace there shall be no end. Isaiah

15 Now, O king, establish the decree, and sign the writing, that it be not changed, according to the law of the Medes and Persians, which altereth not. Daniel

16 They have sown the wind, and they shall reap the whirlwind. Hosea

17 Let us now praise famous men, and our fathers that begat us. Ecclesiasticus

18 Judge not, that ye be not judged. St Matthew

19 I came not to send peace, but a sword. St Matthew

20 He that is not with me is against me. St Matthew; St Luke

21 Render therefore unto Caesar the things which are Caesar's; and unto God the things that are God's. St Matthew

22 Ye shall hear of wars and rumours of wars: see that ye be not troubled: for all these things must come to pass but the end is not yet. St Matthew

23 For nation shall rise against nation, and kingdom against kingdom. St Matthew, St John

24 Those that have turned the world upside down are come hither also. Acts of the Apostles

25 But Paul said, I am a man which am a Jew of Tarsus, a city in Cilicia, a citizen of no mean city. Acts of the Apostles

26 Hast thou appealed unto Caesar? unto Caesar shalt thou go. Acts of the Apostles

27 For where no law is, there is no transgression. Romans

Georges Bidault 1899–1983

French statesman; Prime Minister, 1946, 1949–50

1 The weak have one weapon: the errors of those who think they are strong.

in Observer 15 July 1962 'Sayings of the Week'

Ambrose Bierce 1842–c.1914

American writer

2 BATTLE, *n.* A method of untying with the teeth a political knot that would not yield to the tongue.

The Cynic's Word Book (1906)

3 CONSERVATIVE, *n.* A statesman who is enamoured of existing evils, as distinguished from the Liberal, who wishes to replace them with others.

The Cynic's Word Book (1906)

4 PEACE, *n.* In international affairs, a period of cheating between two periods of fighting.

The Devil's Dictionary (1911)

John Biffen 1930–

British Conservative politician

of Margaret **Thatcher** *as Prime Minister:*
5 She was a tigress surrounded by hamsters.

in Observer 9 December 1990

6 In politics I think it is wiser to leave five minutes too soon than to continue for five years too long.
  resignation letter

in Daily Telegraph 5 January 1995

John Biggs-Davison 1918–88

British Conservative politician

7 I have never conceived it my duty as a Member of Parliament to seek to amend the Ten Commandments.

speech at Chelmsford, 7 November 1976

Steve Biko 1946–77

South African anti-apartheid campaigner

8 The most potent weapon in the hands of the oppressor is the mind of the oppressed.

statement as witness, 3 May 1976

Josh Billings 1818–85

American humorist

9 It is better to know nothing than to know what ain't so.

Proverb (1874)

Nigel Birch 1906–81

British Conservative politician

on hearing of the resignation of Hugh **Dalton**, *Chancellor of the Exchequer in the Labour Government, 13 November 1947:*
10 My God! They've shot our fox!

Harold Macmillan *Tides of Fortune* (1969)

11 For the second time the Prime Minister has got rid of a Chancellor of the Exchequer who tried to get expenditure under control. Once is more than enough.
  after Harold **Macmillan***'s dismissal of Selwyn Lloyd in favour of Reginald Maudling*

letter to *The Times*, 14 July 1962

1 On the question of competence and good sense I cannot think that the verdict can be favourable.
> *of Harold **Macmillan** and his handling of the Profumo affair; Birch's peroration for this speech was from Browning's 'The Lost Leader': 'Let him never come back to us . . . never glad confident morning again'*

in the House of Commons, 17 June 1963

2 No one could accuse himself of courage more often than the Prime Minister.
> *of Harold **Wilson***

in the House of Commons, 2 August 1965

Lord Birkenhead see **F. E. Smith**

Augustine Birrell 1850–1933
British essayist and politician

at a dinner in Trinity College, Cambridge, in 1902, the Master in proposing the health of the college pointed out that at that moment the Sovereign and the Prime Minister were both Trinity men:
3 The Master should have added that he can go further, for it is obvious that the affairs of the world are built upon the momentous fact that God also is a Trinity man.

Harold Laski letter, 4 December 1926

Otto von Bismarck 1815–98 ✓
German statesman, and the driving force behind the unification of Germany; Chancellor of the new German Empire 1871–90
*on Bismarck: see **Taylor** 353:16, **Tenniel** 355:3*

4 If the Princess can leave the Englishwoman at home and become a Prussian, then she may be a blessing to the country.
> *on the marriage of Victoria, Princess Royal, to Prince Frederick William of Prussia*

letter, c.1857

5 The secret of politics? Make a good treaty with Russia.
> *in 1863, when first in power*

A. J. P. Taylor Bismarck (1955)

6 Politics is not an exact science.

speech to the Prussian legislature, 18 December 1863

7 Politics is the art of the possible.

*in conversation with Meyer von Waldeck, 11 August 1867; see **Galbraith** 140:13*

8 Let us . . . put Germany in the saddle! She will know well enough how to ride!

in 1867; Alan Palmer Bismarck (1976)

9 The politician has not to revenge what has happened but to ensure that it does not happen again.
> *c.1871, following public criticism of courtesy shown to the defeated Napoleon III after the battle of Sedan*

A. J. P. Taylor Bismarck (1955)

10 We will not go to Canossa.
> *during his quarrel with Pope Pius IX regarding papal authority over German subjects, in allusion to the Emperor Henry IV's submission to Pope Gregory VII at Canossa in Modena in 1077*

speech to the Reichstag, 14 May 1872

11 Whoever speaks of Europe is wrong, [it is] a geographical concept.

*marginal note on a letter from the Russian Chancellor Gorchakov, November 1876; see **Metternich** 249:3*

1 I have always found the word Europe on the lips of those politicians who wanted something from other Powers which they dared not demand in their own names.
   to the Russian Chancellor Gorchakov, who had urged that a rising in Bosnia in 1878 was a European, rather than a German or Russian, question

A. J. P. Taylor *Bismarck* (1955)

2 I do not regard the procuring of peace as a matter in which we should play the role of arbiter between different opinions . . . more that of an honest broker who really wants to press the business forward.
   before the Congress of Berlin

speech to the Reichstag, 19 February 1878

3 A lath of wood painted to look like iron.
   *of Lord **Salisbury** at the Congress of Berlin in 1878*

attributed, but vigorously denied by Sidney Whitman in *Personal Reminiscences of Prince Bismarck* (1902)

4 The old Jew! That is the man.
   *of **Disraeli** at the Congress of Berlin*

attributed

5 Place in the hands of the King of Prussia the strongest possible military power, then he will be able to carry out the policy you wish; this policy cannot succeed through speeches, and shooting-matches, and songs; it can only be carried out through blood and iron.

in the Prussian House of Deputies, 28 January 1886; in a speech on 30 September 1862, Bismarck had used the form 'iron and blood'

6 I am bored; the great things are done. The German *Reich* is made.

A. J. P. Taylor *Bismarck* (1955)

7 Jena came twenty years after the death of Frederick the Great; the crash will come twenty years after my departure if things go on like this.
   *to Kaiser **Wilhelm II** at their last meeting in 1895*

A. J. P. Taylor *Bismarck* (1955)

8 If there is ever another war in Europe, it will come out of some damned silly thing in the Balkans.

reported by the shipping magnate Herr Ballen as being said by Bismarck in his later years; quoted in the House of Commons, 16 August 1945

9 Man cannot create the current of events. He can only float with it and steer.

A. J. P. Taylor *Bismarck* (1955)

of possible German involvement in the Balkans:
10 Not worth the healthy bones of a single Pomeranian grenadier.

George O. Kent *Bismarck and his Times* (1978); see **Harris** 162:9

11 A statesman . . . must wait until he hears the steps of God sounding through events; then leap up and grasp the hem of his garment.

A. J. P. Taylor *Bismarck* (1955)

12 There is a a providence that protects idiots, drunkards, children, and the United States of America.

attributed, perhaps apocryphal

13 The tongue in the balance.
   of Germany's position in relation to other European states

A. J. P. Taylor *Bismarck* (1955)

14 When a man says he approves of something in principle, it means he hasn't the slightest intention of putting it into practice.

attributed

Hugo La Fayette Black 1886–1971 ✓

American judge

1 The First Amendment has erected a wall between church and state. That wall must be kept high and impregnable. We could not approve the slightest breach.

in Emerson v. Board of Education 1947

2 In revealing the workings of government that led to the Vietnam War, the newspapers nobly did precisely that which the Founders hoped and trusted they would do.

concurring opinion on the publication of the Pentagon Papers, 1971

William Blackstone 1723–80

English jurist

3 The king never dies.

Commentaries on the Laws of England (1765)

4 The royal navy of England hath ever been its greatest defence and ornament; it is its ancient and natural strength; the floating bulwark of the island.

Commentaries on the Laws of England (1765)

5 That the king can do no wrong, is a necessary and fundamental principle of the English constitution.

Commentaries on the Laws of England (1765)

6 In all tyrannical governments the supreme magistracy, or the right both of making and of enforcing the laws, is vested in one and the same man, or one and the same body of men; and wherever these two powers are united together, there can be no public liberty.

Commentaries on the Laws of England (1765)

7 Herein indeed consists the excellence of the English government, that all parts of it form a mutual check upon each other.

Commentaries on the Laws of England (1765)

Tony Blair 1953– ✓

British Labour statesman; Prime Minister since 1997
on Blair: see **Mandelson** 241:5, **Newspaper headlines** 267:6, **Thatcher** 358:8

8 Labour is the party of law and order in Britain today. Tough on crime and tough on the causes of crime.
as Shadow Home Secretary

speech at the Labour Party Conference, 30 September 1993

9 Those who seriously believe we cannot improve on words written for the world of 1918 when we are now in 1995 are not learning from our history but living it.
on the proposed revision of Clause IV

in *Independent* 11 January 1995

10 Ask me my three main priorities for Government, and I tell you: education, education and education.

speech at the Labour Party Conference, 1 October 1996; see **Michelet** 249:10

11 We are not the masters. The people are the masters. We are the servants of the people . . . What the electorate gives, the electorate can take away.
addressing Labour MPs on the first day of the new Parliament, 7 May 1997

in *Guardian* 8 May 1997; see **Burke** 60:9

12 Those who governed in London at the time failed their people through standing by while a crop failure turned into a massive human tragedy. We must not forget such a dreadful event. It is also right that we should pay tribute to the ways in which the Irish people have triumphed in the face of this catastrophe.

official statement, 1 June 1997, read at the Famine commemoration at Millstreet, County Cork.

1 She was the People's Princess, and that is how she will stay . . . in our hearts and in our memories forever.
on hearing of the death of **Diana**, *Princess of Wales, 31 August 1997*

in *Times* 1 September 1997

2 I am from the Disraeli school of Prime Ministers in their relations with the Monarch.
at the Queen's golden wedding celebration, 20 November 1997; see **Elizabeth II** 125:9

in *Daily Telegraph* 21 November 1997

3 This is not a time for soundbites. We've left them at home. I feel the hand of history upon our shoulders . . . I'm here to try.
arriving in Belfast for the final stage of the Northern Irish negotiations, 8 April 1998

in *Irish Times* 11 April 1998 'This Week They Said'

4 In future, welfare will be a hand-up not a hand-out.

lecture, London, 18 March 1999

5 Arrayed against us: the forces of conservatism, the cynics, the elites, the establishment. On our side, the forces of modernity and justice.

speech to Labour Party Conference, 28 September 1999

6 Mr Hague may be good at telling jokes, but every time you come to a critical question of judgement like this, he gets it wrong.
on William Hague's endorsement of Jeffrey Archer as mayoral candidate for London

in *Daily Telegraph* 23 November 1999

7 After all the fun and games down at the Assembly are over.
during Prime Minister's Question Time, as the news broke that Alun Michael had resigned as First Secretary for Wales

in the House of Commons, 9 February 2000

8 We need two or three eye-catching initiatives . . . I should be personally associated with as much of this as possible.

leaked memorandum, 29 April 2000; in *Times* 18 July 2000

William Blake 1757–1827

English poet

9 The strongest poison ever known
Came from Caesar's laurel crown.

'Auguries of Innocence' (c.1803)

10 The whore and gambler by the State
Licensed build that nation's fate
The harlot's cry from street to street
Shall weave old England's winding sheet.

'Auguries of Innocence' (c.1803)

11 He who would do good to another, must do it in minute particulars
General good is the plea of the scoundrel, hypocrite and flatterer.

Jerusalem (1815) 'Chapter 3' (plate 55, l. 60)

12 And was Jerusalem builded here
Among these dark Satanic mills?

Milton (1804–10) preface 'And did those feet in ancient time'

13 I will not cease from mental fight,
Nor shall my sword sleep in my hand,
Till we have built Jerusalem,
In England's green and pleasant land.

Milton (1804–10) preface 'And did those feet in ancient time'

David Blunkett 1947–

British Labour politician, Minister for Education

14 Let me say this very slowly indeed. Watch my lips: no selection by examination or interview under a Labour government.

in *Daily Telegraph* (electronic edition) 5 October 1995

1 I was parodying George Bush . . . Watch my lips was a joke.
If I were doing it again I would say 'no more selection'.

in Sunday Telegraph 12 March 2000

Alfred Blunt, Bishop of Bradford

1879–1957

English clergyman

2 The benefit of the King's Coronation depends, under God,
upon two elements: First on the faith, prayer, and self-
dedication of the King himself, and on that it would be
improper for me to say anything except to commend him,
and ask you to commend him, to God's grace, which he will
so abundantly need . . . if he is to do his duty faithfully. We
hope that he is aware of his need. Some of us wish that he
gave more positive signs of his awareness.
  *it was this speech that broke the story of **Edward VIII** and Mrs
  Simpson which the media had been voluntarily suppressing until
  then*

speech to Bradford Diocesan
Conference, 1 December 1936

David Boaz 1953–

American foundation executive

3 Alcohol didn't cause the high crime rates of the '20s and
'30s, Prohibition did. Drugs don't cause today's alarming
crime rates, but drug prohibition does.

'The Legalization of Drugs' 27 April
1988

4 Trying to wage war on 23 million Americans who are
obviously very committed to certain recreational activities is
not going to be any more successful than Prohibition was.

'The Legalization of Drugs' 27 April
1988

Allan Boesak 1945–

South African politician and clergyman, anti-apartheid
campaigner

5 My humanity is not dependent on the acceptance of white
people.
  *after losing in Western Cape, April 1994, as an African National
  Congress candidate*

in *The New York Review of Books* 20
October 1994 'The Election
Mandela Lost'

Ivan Boesky 1937–

American financier, imprisoned in 1987 for insider dealing

6 Greed is all right . . . Greed is healthy. You can be greedy
and still feel good about yourself.

commencement address at the
University of California, Berkeley,
18 May 1986; see **Weiser** 378:5

Vernon Bogdanor 1943–

British academic

7 You are giving people a weapon—and if you give a child a
weapon you shouldn't be surprised if he shoots you.
  on devolution and central government

in *Independent on Sunday* 13
February 2000

Curtis Bok 1897–1962

American federal judge

8 It has been said that a judge is a member of the Bar who
once knew a Governor.

The Backbone of the Herring (1941)

Alan Bold 1943–
Scottish poet

1 Scotland, land of the omnipotent No.

'A Memory of Death' (1969)

Henry St John, Lord Bolingbroke
1678–1751
English statesman

2 The great mistake is that of looking upon men as virtuous, or thinking that they can be made so by laws.

comment (c.1728) in Joseph Spence *Observations, Anecdotes, and Characters* (1820)

3 The greatest art of a politician is to render vice serviceable to the cause of virtue.

comment (c.1728) in Joseph Spence *Observations, Anecdotes, and Characters* (1820)

4 Nations, like men, have their infancy.

On the Study of History letter 5, in *Works* (1809) vol. 3

Simón Bolívar 1783–1830
Venezuelan patriot and statesman

5 Those who have served the cause of the revolution have ploughed the sea.

attributed

Robert Bolt 1924–95
English playwright

6 THOMAS MORE: This country's planted thick with laws from coast to coast—Man's laws, not God's—and if you cut them down—and you're just the man to do it—d'you really think you could stand upright in the winds that would blow then?

A Man for All Seasons (1960)

Andrew Bonar Law 1858–1923
Canadian-born British Conservative statesman, Prime Minister 1922–3
on Bonar Law: see **Asquith** 15:7, **Beaverbrook** 30:4

7 If, therefore, war should ever come between these two countries [Great Britain and Germany], which Heaven forbid! it will not, I think, be due to irresistible natural laws, it will be due to want of human wisdom.

in the House of Commons, 27 November 1911

8 There are things stronger than parliamentary majorities. I can imagine no length of resistance to which Ulster will not go, in which I shall not be ready to support them.
at a Unionist meeting at Blenheim in 1912

Robert Blake *The Unknown Prime Minister* (1955)

9 In war it is necessary not only to be active but to seem active.

letter to **Asquith**, 1916; Robert Blake *The Unknown Prime Minister* (1955)

10 We cannot alone act as the policemen of the world.

letter to *Times*, 7 October 1922

11 If I am a great man, then all great men are frauds.

Lord Beaverbrook *Politicians and the War* (1932)

Violet Bonham Carter 1887–1969

British Liberal politician

1 HOW DARE YOU BECOME PRIME MINISTER WHEN I'M AWAY GREAT LOVE CONSTANT THOUGHT VIOLET.
  telegram to her father, H. H. Asquith, 7 April 1908

Mark Bonham Carter and Mark Pottle (eds.) *Lantern Slides* (1996)

Dietrich Bonhoeffer 1906–45

German Lutheran theologian and pastor

2 It is the nature, and the advantage, of strong people that they can bring out the crucial questions and form a clear opinion about them. The weak always have to decide between alternatives that are not their own.

Widerstand und Ergebung (1951)

Bono 1960–

Irish rock star, member of U2

3 They didn't have Kalashnikovs but U2 tickets in their hands.
  of the audience at the U2 concert in Sarajevo, 24 September 1997

in *Daily Telegraph* 25 September 1997

The Book of Common Prayer 1662

4 The Bishop of Rome hath no jurisdiction in this Realm of England.

Articles of Religion (1562) no. 37

Christopher Booker 1937–

English author and journalist

5 In the life of any government, however safe its majority, there comes a moment when the social movements of which it had once been the expression turn inexorably against it . . . After that moment, every mistake it makes becomes magnified; indeed blunders multiply as if feeding on themselves; and both outwardly and inwardly the Government appears to be at the mercy of every wind.

The Neophiliacs (1969)

6 It is a familiar pattern of history that, on the eve of revolutionary crises, the established order veers erratically between liberal concessions and recklessly reactionary steps which seem calculated to cast it in the most unfavourable light and to hasten its own destruction.

The Neophiliacs (1969)

7 Our government has recently unleashed the greatest avalanche of regulations in peacetime history; and wherever we examine their working we see that they are using a sledgehammer to miss a nut.

speech, 1995

Christopher Booker 1937–
and Richard North 1946–

8 Castle of lies: why Britain must get out of Europe.

title of book (1996) on Britain's membership of the European Union

Daniel J. Boorstin 1914–
American writer

1 A pseudo event . . . comes about because someone has planned, planted, or incited it. Typically, it is not a train wreck or an earthquake, but an interview.

The Image (1962)

John Wilkes Booth 1838–65
American assassin

2 *Sic semper tyrannis!* The South is avenged.
  *having shot President **Lincoln**, 14 April 1865*

in *New York Times* 15 April 1865; the second part of the statement does not appear in any contemporary source, and is possibly apocryphal; see **Mottoes** 262:8

Robert Boothby 1900–86
British Conservative politician

3 *You* speak for Britain!
  *to Arthur Greenwood, acting Leader of the Labour Party, after Neville **Chamberlain** had failed to announce an ultimatum to Germany; perhaps taking up an appeal already voiced by Leo **Amery***

Harold Nicolson diary, 2 September 1939; see **Amery** 7:1

Betty Boothroyd 1929–
Labour politician; Speaker of the House of Commons, 1992–2000

4 My desire to get here [Parliament] was like miners' coal dust, it was under my fingers and I couldn't scrub it out.

Glenys Kinnock and Fiona Millar (eds.) *By Faith and Daring* (1993)

5 Be happy for me.
  announcing her retirement as Speaker

in the House of Commons, 12 July 2000

6 The level of cynicism about Parliament and the accompanying alienation of many of the young from the democratic process is troubling. Let's make a start by remembering that the function of Parliament is to hold the executive to account.
  in her valedictory statement as Speaker

in the House of Commons, 26 July 2000

7 Time's up!
  concluding her valedictory statement

in the House of Commons, 26 July 2000

James H. Boren 1925–
American bureaucrat

8 Guidelines for bureaucrats: (1) When in charge, ponder. (2) When in trouble, delegate. (3) When in doubt, mumble.

in *New York Times* 8 November 1970

Jorge Luis Borges 1899–1986
Argentinian writer

9 The Falklands thing was a fight between two bald men over a comb.

application of a proverbial phrase; in *Time* 14 February 1983

Cesare Borgia see **Mottoes** 262:1

Robert H. Bork 1927–
American judge and educationalist

1 One of the uses of history is to free us of a falsely imagined past. The less we know of how ideas actually took root and grew, the more apt we are to accept them unquestioningly, as inevitable features of the world in which we move.

The Antitrust Paradox (1978)

George Borrow 1803–81
English writer

2 I am invariably of the politics of the people at whose table I sit, or beneath whose roof I sleep.

The Bible in Spain (1843)

James Boswell 1740–95
Scottish lawyer; biographer of Samuel Johnson

3 We [Boswell and Johnson] are both *Tories*; both convinced of the utility of monarchical power, and both lovers of that reverence and affection for a sovereign which constitute loyalty, a principle which I take to be absolutely extinguished in Britain.

Journal of a Tour to the Hebrides 13 September 1773

Antoine Boulay de la Meurthe 1761–1840
French statesman

on hearing of the execution of the Duc d'Enghien, 1804:
4 It is worse than a crime, it is a blunder.

C.-A. Sainte-Beuve *Nouveaux Lundis* (1870) vol. 12

Pierre Boulez 1925–
French conductor and composer

5 Revolutions are celebrated when they are no longer dangerous.

in *Guardian* 13 January 1989

Lord Bowen 1835–94
British judge

6 The man on the Clapham omnibus.
  the average man

in *Law Reports* (1903); attributed

Omar Bradley 1893–1981
American general

7 The way to win an atomic war is to make certain it never starts.

speech to Boston Chamber of Commerce, 10 November 1948

8 We have grasped the mystery of the atom and rejected the Sermon on the Mount.

speech on Armistice Day, 1948

9 The world has achieved brilliance without wisdom, power without conscience. Ours is a world of nuclear giants and ethical infants.

speech on Armistice Day, 1948

10 In war there is no second prize for the runner-up.

in *Military Review* February 1950

1 This strategy would involve us in the wrong war, at the wrong place, at the wrong time, and with the wrong enemy.
on General Macarthur's wish to extend the Korean War into China

in *US Congressional Senate Committee on Armed Service* (1951) vol. 2

John Bradshaw 1602–59
English judge at the trial of Charles I

2 Rebellion to tyrants is obedience to God.

suppositious epitaph; Henry S. Randall *Life of Thomas Jefferson* (1865) vol. 3; see **Mottoes** 262:6

Edward Stuyvesant Bragg 1827–1912
American politician

3 They love him most for the enemies he has made.
seconding the presidential nomination of Grover **Cleveland**

speech, 9 July 1884

Louis D. Brandeis 1856–1941
Justice of the US Supreme Court

4 Fear of serious injury cannot alone justify suppression of free speech and assembly. Men feared witches and burned women. It is the function of speech to free men from the bondage of irrational fears.

in *Whitney v. California* (1927)

5 They [the makers of the Constitution] conferred, as against the Government, the right to be let alone—the most comprehensive of rights and the right most valued by civilized men.

in *Olmstead v. United States* (1928)

6 The greatest dangers to liberty lurk in insidious encroachment by men of zeal, well-meaning but without understanding.

dissenting opinion in *Olmstead v. United States* (1928)

William Cowper Brann 1855–98

7 No man can be a patriot on an empty stomach.

The Iconoclast, Old Glory 4 July 1893

Bertolt Brecht 1898–1956
German playwright

8 ANDREA: Unhappy the land that has no heroes! . . .
GALILEO: No. Unhappy the land that needs heroes.

Life of Galileo (1939)

9 One observes, they have gone too long without a war here. Where is morality to come from in such a case, I ask? Peace is nothing but slovenliness, only war creates order.

Mother Courage (1939)

10 The finest plans are always ruined by the littleness of those who ought to carry them out, for the Emperors can actually do nothing.

Mother Courage (1939)

11 War always finds a way.

Mother Courage (1939)

12 Don't tell me peace has broken out, when I've just bought some new supplies.

Mother Courage (1939)

1 Would it not be easier
In that case for the government
To dissolve the people
And elect another?
  *on the uprising against the Soviet occupying forces in East
  Germany in 1953*

'The Solution' (1953)

William Joseph Brennan Jr. 1906–
American judge

2 Debate on public issues should be uninhibited, robust, and wide open, and that . . . may well include vehement, caustic, and sometimes unpleasantly sharp attacks on government and public officials.

in *New York Times Co. v. Sullivan* (1964)

Aristide Briand 1862–1932
French statesman

3 The high contracting powers solemnly declare . . . that they condemn recourse to war and renounce it . . . as an instrument of their national policy towards each other . . . The settlement or the solution of all disputes or conflicts of whatever nature or of whatever origin they may be which may arise . . . shall never be sought by either side except by pacific means.

draft, 20 June 1927, later incorporated into the Kellogg Pact, 1928

Edward Bridges 1892–1969
British Cabinet Secretary and Head of the Civil Service

4 I confidently expect that we [civil servants] shall continue to be grouped with mothers-in-law and Wigan Pier as one of the recognized objects of ridicule.

Portrait of a Profession (1950)

John Bright 1811–89
English Liberal politician and reformer

5 The angel of death has been abroad throughout the land; you may almost hear the beating of his wings.
  on the effects of the war in the Crimea

in the House of Commons, 23 February 1855

of British foreign policy:
6 A gigantic system of outdoor relief for the aristocracy of Great Britain.

speech at Birmingham, 29 October 1858

7 I am for 'Peace, retrenchment, and reform', the watchword of the great Liberal party 30 years ago.

speech at Birmingham, 28 April 1859; the phrase quoted may be found in Samuel Warren's novel *Ten Thousand a Year* (1841)

8 England is the mother of Parliaments.

speech at Birmingham, 18 January 1865

of Robert Lowe, leader of the dissident Whigs opposed to the Reform Bill of 1866:
9 The right hon Gentleman . . . has retired into what may be called his political Cave of Adullam—and he has called about him every one that was in distress and every one that was discontented.

in the House of Commons, 13 March 1866; see I Samuel ch. 22

of Robert Lowe and Edward Horsman:

1 This party of two is like the Scotch terrier that was so covered with hair that you could not tell which was the head and which was the tail.

in the House of Commons, 13 March 1866

2 Force is not a remedy.

speech to the Birmingham Junior Liberal Club, 16 November 1880

Vera Brittain 1893–1970
English writer

3 Politics are usually the executive expression of human immaturity.

Rebel Passion (1964)

Russell Brockbank 1913–
British cartoonist

4 Fog in Channel—Continent isolated.

newspaper placard in cartoon, *Round the Bend with Brockbank* (1948); the phrase 'Continent isolated' was quoted as already current by John Gunther *Inside Europe* (1938)

Fenner Brockway 1888–1988
British Labour politician

5 I have spent three years in prison and three years in Parliament, and I saw character deteriorate more in Parliament than in prison.

Inside the Left (1942)

David Broder 1929– ✓
American columnist

6 Anybody that wants the presidency so much that he'll spend two years organizing and campaigning for it is not to be trusted with the office.

in *Washington Post* 18 July 1973

D. W. Brogan 1900–74
Scottish historian

7 A people that has licked a more formidable enemy than Germany or Japan, primitive North America . . . a country whose national motto has been 'root, hog, or die.'

The American Character (1944)

8 Any well-established village in New England or the northern Middle West could afford a town drunkard, a town atheist, and a few Democrats.

The American Character (1944)

Henry Brooke 1703–83
Irish poet and playwright

9 For righteous monarchs,
Justly to judge, with their own eyes should see;
To rule o'er freemen, should themselves be free.

Earl of Essex (performed 1750, published 1761)

Robert Barnabas Brough 1828–60

English satirical writer

1 My Lord Tomnoddy is thirty-four;
  The Earl can last but a few years more.
  My Lord in the Peers will take his place:
  Her Majesty's councils his words will grace.
  Office he'll hold and patronage sway;
  Fortunes and lives he will vote away;
  And what are his qualifications?—ONE!
  He's the Earl of Fitzdotterel's eldest son.

Songs of the Governing Classes
(1855) 'My Lord Tomnoddy'

Lord Brougham 1778–1868

Scottish lawyer and politician; Lord Chancellor 1830–4
on Brougham: see **Melbourne** 247:3, 247:4

2 In my mind, he was guilty of no error—he was chargeable
  with no exaggeration—he was betrayed by his fancy into no
  metaphor, who once said, that all we see about us, King,
  Lords, and Commons, the whole machinery of the State, all
  the apparatus of the system, and its varied workings, end in
  simply bringing twelve good men into a box.

in the House of Commons, 7
February 1828

3 Education makes a people easy to lead, but difficult to drive;
  easy to govern, but impossible to enslave.

attributed

Heywood Broun 1888–1939

American journalist

4 Just as every conviction begins as a whim so does every
  emancipator serve his apprenticeship as a crank. A fanatic is
  a great leader who is just entering the room.

in *New York World* 6 February 1928

5 Appeasers believe that if you keep on throwing steaks to a
  tiger, the tiger will turn vegetarian.

attributed

Gordon Brown 1951–

British Labour politician
on Brown: see **Anonymous** 10:9, 10:10

6 Socialism is an ideology more often successfully caricatured
  by our enemies than defined by our friends.

in *Independent* 25 June 1994

7 Ideas which stress the growing importance of international
  cooperation and new theories of economic sovereignty
  across a wide range of areas—macroeconomics, the
  environment, the growth of post neo-classical endogenous
  growth theory and the symbiotic relationships between
  growth and investment in people and infrastructure.

New Labour Economics speech,
September 1994, 'winner' of the
ironic Plain English No Nonsense
Award for 1994

8 It is about time we had an end to the old Britain, where all
  that matters is the privileges you were born with, rather
  than the potential you actually have.

speech, 25 May 2000

*before the Treasury Select Committee, answering the question 'Do
you want to be Prime Minister?':*

9 It would be dishonest to say I'd rule out indefinitely the
  office you refer to.

in *Sunday Times* 30 July 2000

H. Rap Brown 1943–
American Black Power leader

1 I say violence is necessary. It is as American as cherry pie.   speech at Washington, 27 July 1967

John Brown 1800–59
American abolitionist
on Brown: see **Songs** *342:5; see also* **Last words** *213:3*

2 I am yet too young to understand that God is any respecter   on 2 November 1859
of persons.
   last speech to the court at his trial

3 If it is deemed necessary that I should forfeit my life for the   on 2 November 1859
furtherance of the ends of justice, and mingle my blood
further with the blood of my children, and with the blood of
millions in this slave country whose rights are disregarded
by wicked, cruel, and most unjust enactments, I submit: so
let it be done!
   last speech to the court at his trial

Joseph Brown 1821–94
American politician; Confederate Governor of Georgia during the
Civil War

refusing to accept the Confederate President Jefferson **Davis***'s call for
a day of national fasting:*
4 I entered into this Revolution to contribute my mite to   in 1863; Geoffrey C. Ward *The Civil
sustain the rights of states and prevent the consolidation of   War* (1991)
the Government, and I am *still* a rebel . . . no matter who
may be in power.

William Browne 1692–1774
English physician and writer

5 The King to Oxford sent a troop of horse,   reply to Trapp's epigram, in J.
For Tories own no argument but force: Nichols *Literary Anecdotes* vol. 3;
With equal skill to Cambridge books he sent,   see **Trapp** 362:8
For Whigs admit no force but argument.

Frederick 'Boy' Browning 1896–1965
British soldier and courtier; husband of Daphne du Maurier

*expressing reservations about the Arnhem 'Market Garden'
operation to Field Marshal Montgomery on 10 September 1944:*
6 I think we might be going a bridge too far.   R. E. Urquhart *Arnhem* (1958)

Robert Browning 1812–89
English poet

7 Just for a handful of silver he left us,   'The Lost Leader' (1845)
Just for a riband to stick in his coat.
   of **Wordsworth***'s implied abandonment of radical principles by his
   acceptance of the Laureateship*

8 Life's night begins: let him never come back to us!   'The Lost Leader' (1845); see **Birch**
There would be doubt, hesitation and pain,   41:1
Forced praise on our part—the glimmer of twilight,
Never glad confident morning again!

Cathal Brugha 1874–1922

Irish nationalist
on Brugha: see **Collins** 93:2

1 Don't you realize that, if you sign this thing, you will split
Ireland from top to bottom?
    to **de Valera**, December 1921, on the Treaty

Jim Ring Erskine Childers (1996)

Gro Harlem Brundtland 1939–

Norwegian stateswoman; Prime Minister 1981, 1986–89, and
1990–96

2 I do not know of any environmental group in any country
that does not view its government as an adversary.

in Time 25 September 1989

John Bruton 1947–

Irish Fine Gael statesman

3 Ministers are behaving like sheep scattered in a fog on a
mountainside.

in 1994, criticizing the Fianna Fáil
administration

4 The strategy of the ballot box in one hand and the gun in
the other was . . . originated by the Nazis.

in Irish Times 10 October 1996

William Jennings Bryan 1860–1925

American Democratic politician; a fervent proponent of
bimetallism as an alternative to the gold standard

5 The humblest citizen of all the land, when clad in the
armour of a righteous cause, is stronger than all the hosts of
error.

speech at the Democratic National
Convention, Chicago, 1896

6 Destroy our farms and the grass will grow in the streets of
every city in the country.

speech at the Democratic National
Convention, Chicago 1896; see
Hoover 176:6

7 You shall not press down upon the brow of labour this
crown of thorns, you shall not crucify mankind upon a
cross of gold.

speech at the Democratic National
Convention, Chicago, 1896; see
Slogans 335:16

Zbigniew Brzezinski 1928–

US Secretary of State and National Security Advisor

8 Russia can be an empire or a democracy, but it cannot be
both.

in Foreign Affairs March/April 1994
'The Premature Partnership'

Frank Buchman 1878–1961

American evangelist; founder of the Moral Re-Armament
movement

9 I thank heaven for a man like Adolf Hitler, who built a front
line of defence against the anti-Christ of Communism.

in New York World-Telegram 26
August 1936

Gerald Bullett
British writer

1 My Lord Archbishop, what a scold you are!
And when your man is down how bold you are!
Of charity how oddly scant you are!
How Lang, O Lord, how full of Cantuar!
on the role of Cosmo Gordon Lang, Archbishop of Canterbury, in the abdication of Edward VIII

in 1936

Ivor Bulmer-Thomas 1905–93
British Conservative politician

of Harold **Wilson**:
2 If he ever went to school without any boots it was because he was too big for them.

speech at the Conservative Party Conference, in *Manchester Guardian* 13 October 1949

Prince Bernhard von Bülow 1849–1929
Chancellor of Germany, 1900–9

3 In a word, we desire to throw no one into the shade [in East Asia], but we also demand our own place in the sun.

speech in the Reichstag, 6 December 1897; see **Wilhelm II** 383:7

Edward George Bulwer-Lytton 1803–73
British novelist and politician

4 Here Stanley meets,—how Stanley scorns, the glance!
The brilliant chief, irregularly great,
Frank, haughty, rash,—the Rupert of Debate!
on Edward Stanley, 14th Earl of **Derby**

The New Timon (1846); see **Disraeli** 111:6

Samuel Dickinson Burchard 1812–91
American Presbyterian minister

5 We are Republicans and don't propose to leave our party and identify ourselves with the party whose antecedents are rum, Romanism, and rebellion.

speech at the Fifth Avenue Hotel, New York, 29 October 1884

Anthony Burgess 1917–93
English novelist and critic

6 The US presidency is a Tudor monarchy plus telephones.

George Plimpton (ed.) *Writers at Work* (4th Series, 1977)

Edmund Burke 1729–97
Irish-born Whig politician and man of letters
on Burke: see **Gibbon** 145:14, **Johnson** 191:19, **O'Brien** 272:4, **Paine** 279:13, 279:14; *see also* **Misquotations** 255:2

7 Those who have been once intoxicated with power, and have derived any kind of emolument from it, even though for but one year, can never willingly abandon it.

Letter to a Member of the National Assembly (1791)

8 Tyrants seldom want pretexts.

Letter to a Member of the National Assembly (1791)

1 You can never plan the future by the past.

Letter to a Member of the National Assembly (1791)

2 Men are qualified for civil liberty, in exact proportion to their disposition to put moral chains upon their own appetites.

Letter to a Member of the National Assembly (1791)

3 The king, and his faithful subjects, the lords and commons of this realm,—the triple cord, which no man can break.

A Letter to a Noble Lord (1796)

4 To innovate is not to reform.

A Letter to a Noble Lord (1796)

5 Bodies tied together by so unnatural a bond of union as mutual hatred are only connected to their ruin.

Letter to the Sheriffs of Bristol (1777)

6 I was persuaded that government was a practical thing made for the happiness of mankind, and not to furnish out a spectacle of uniformity to gratify the schemes of visionary politicians.

Letter to the Sheriffs of Bristol (1777)

7 Among a people generally corrupt, liberty cannot long exist.

Letter to the Sheriffs of Bristol (1777)

8 It is a general popular error to imagine the loudest complainers for the public to be the most anxious for its welfare.

Observations on a late Publication on the Present State of the Nation (2nd ed., 1769)

9 There is, however, a limit at which forbearance ceases to be a virtue.

Observations on a late Publication on the Present State of the Nation (2nd ed., 1769)

10 It is the nature of all greatness not to be exact; and great trade will always be attended with considerable abuses.

On American Taxation (1775)

11 To tax and to please, no more than to love and to be wise, is not given to men.

On American Taxation (1775)

12 I have in general no very exalted opinion of the virtue of paper government.

On Conciliation with America (1775)

13 The concessions of the weak are the concessions of fear.

On Conciliation with America (1775)

14 When we speak of the commerce with our colonies, fiction lags after truth, invention is unfruitful, and imagination cold and barren.

On Conciliation with America (1775)

15 The use of force alone is but *temporary*. It may subdue for a moment; but it does not remove the necessity of subduing again; and a nation is not governed, which is perpetually to be conquered.

On Conciliation with America (1775)

16 Nothing less will content me, than *whole America*.

On Conciliation with America (1775)

17 I do not know the method of drawing up an indictment against an whole people.

On Conciliation with America (1775)

18 It is not, what a lawyer tells me I *may* do; but what humanity, reason, and justice, tells me I ought to do.

On Conciliation with America (1775)

19 Freedom and not servitude is the cure of anarchy; as religion, and not atheism, is the true remedy for superstition.

On Conciliation with America (1775)

20 Instead of a standing revenue, you will have therefore a perpetual quarrel.

On Conciliation with America (1775)

21 Parties must ever exist in a free country.

On Conciliation with America (1775)

22 Slavery they can have anywhere. It is a weed that grows in every soil.

On Conciliation with America (1775)

1 Deny them this participation of freedom, and you break that sole bond, which originally made, and must still preserve the unity of the empire.

On Conciliation with America (1775)

2 It is the love of the people; it is their attachment to their government, from the sense of the deep stake they have in such a glorious institution, which gives you your army and your navy, and infuses into both that liberal obedience, without which your army would be a base rabble, and your navy nothing but rotten timber.

On Conciliation with America (1775)

3 Magnanimity in politics is not seldom the truest wisdom; and a great empire and little minds go ill together.

On Conciliation with America (1775)

4 By adverting to the dignity of this high calling, our ancestors have turned a savage wilderness into a glorious empire: and have made the most extensive, and the only honourable conquests; not by destroying, but by promoting the wealth, the number, the happiness of the human race.

On Conciliation with America (1775)

5 I flatter myself that I love a manly, moral, regulated liberty as well as any gentleman.

Reflections on the Revolution in France (1790)

6 Whenever our neighbour's house is on fire, it cannot be amiss for the engines to play a little on our own.

Reflections on the Revolution in France (1790)

7 A state without the means of some change is without the means of its conservation.

Reflections on the Revolution in France (1790)

8 Make the Revolution a parent of settlement, and not a nursery of future revolutions.

Reflections on the Revolution in France (1790)

9 People will not look forward to posterity, who never look backward to their ancestors.

Reflections on the Revolution in France (1790)

10 Those who attempt to level never equalize.

Reflections on the Revolution in France (1790)

11 Government is a contrivance of human wisdom to provide for human *wants*. Men have a right that these wants should be provided for by this wisdom.

Reflections on the Revolution in France (1790)

12 Flattery corrupts both the receiver and the giver.

Reflections on the Revolution in France (1790)

*of **Marie-Antoinette**:*

13 I thought ten thousand swords must have leapt from their scabbards to avenge even a look that threatened her with insult.

Reflections on the Revolution in France (1790)

14 The age of chivalry is gone.—That of sophisters, economists, and calculators, has succeeded; and the glory of Europe is extinguished for ever.

Reflections on the Revolution in France (1790)

15 This barbarous philosophy, which is the offspring of cold hearts and muddy understandings.

Reflections on the Revolution in France (1790)

16 In the groves of *their* academy, at the end of every vista, you see nothing but the gallows.

Reflections on the Revolution in France (1790)

17 Kings will be tyrants from policy when subjects are rebels from principle.

Reflections on the Revolution in France (1790)

18 Because half a dozen grasshoppers under a fern make the field ring with their importunate chink, whilst thousands of great cattle, reposed beneath the shadow of the British oak, chew the cud and are silent, pray do not imagine that those who make the noise are the only inhabitants of the field.

Reflections on the Revolution in France (1790)

1 Society is indeed a contract . . . it becomes a partnership not only between those who are living, but between those who are living, those who are dead, and those who are to be born.

Reflections on the Revolution in France (1790)

2 Nobility is a graceful ornament to the civil order. It is the Corinthian capital of polished society.

Reflections on the Revolution in France (1790)

3 By hating vices too much, they come to love men too little.

Reflections on the Revolution in France (1790)

4 We begin our public affections in our families. No cold relation is a zealous citizen.

Reflections on the Revolution in France (1790)

5 Good order is the foundation of all good things.

Reflections on the Revolution in France (1790)

6 Nothing turns out to be so oppressive and unjust as a feeble government.

Reflections on the Revolution in France (1790)

7 Ambition can creep as well as soar.

Third Letter . . . on the Proposals for Peace with the Regicide Directory (1797)

8 And having looked to government for bread, on the very first scarcity they will turn and bite the hand that fed them.

Thoughts and Details on Scarcity (1800)

9 To complain of the age we live in, to murmur at the present possessors of power, to lament the past, to conceive extravagant hopes of the future, are the common dispositions of the greatest part of mankind.

Thoughts on the Cause of the Present Discontents (1770)

10 I am not one of those who think that the people are never in the wrong. They have been so, frequently and outrageously, both in other countries and in this. But I do say, that in all disputes between them and their rulers, the presumption is at least upon a par in favour of the people.

Thoughts on the Cause of the Present Discontents (1770)

11 The power of the crown, almost dead and rotten as Prerogative, has grown up anew, with much more strength, and far less odium, under the name of Influence.

Thoughts on the Cause of the Present Discontents (1770)

12 We must soften into a credulity below the milkiness of infancy to think all men virtuous. We must be tainted with a malignity truly diabolical, to believe all the world to be equally wicked and corrupt.

Thoughts on the Cause of the Present Discontents (1770)

13 When . . . [people] imagine that their food is only a cover for poison, and when they neither love nor trust the hand that serves it, it is not the name of the roast beef of old England that will persuade them to sit down to the table that is spread for them.

Thoughts on the Cause of the Present Discontents (1770)

14 When bad men combine, the good must associate; else they will fall, one by one, an unpitied sacrifice in a contemptible struggle.

Thoughts on the Cause of the Present Discontents (1770); see **Misquotations** 255:2

15 Of this stamp is the cant of *Not men, but measures*; a sort of charm by which many people get loose from every honourable engagement.

Thoughts on the Cause of the Present Discontents (1770); see **Canning** 69:1

16 Laws, like houses, lean on one another.

A Tract on the Popery Laws (planned c.1765)

17 In all forms of Government the people is the true legislator.

A Tract on the Popery Laws (planned c.1765)

1 Falsehood and delusion are allowed in no case whatsoever: But, as in the exercise of all the virtues, there is an economy of truth.

Two Letters on the Proposals for Peace with the Regicide Directory (9th ed., 1796); see **Armstrong** 14:5

2 All men that are ruined are ruined on the side of their natural propensities.

Two Letters on the Proposals for Peace with the Regicide Directory (9th ed., 1796)

3 If ever there was in all the proceedings of government a rule that is fundamental, universal, invariable it is this: that you ought never to attempt a measure of authority you are not morally sure you can go through with.

in the House of Commons, 9 May 1770

4 The greater the power, the more dangerous the abuse.

speech on the Middlesex Election, 7 February 1771

5 Your representative owes you, not his industry only, but his judgement; and he betrays, instead of serving you, if he sacrifices it to your opinion.

speech, 3 November 1774, in *Speeches at his Arrival at Bristol* (1774)

6 People crushed by law have no hopes but from power. If laws are their enemies, they will be enemies to laws; and those, who have much to hope and nothing to lose, will always be dangerous, more or less.

letter to Charles James Fox, 8 October 1777

7 It is the interest of the commercial world that wealth should be found everywhere.

letter to Samuel Span, 23 April 1778

8 Bad laws are the worst sort of tyranny.

Speech at Bristol, previous to the Late Election (1780)

9 The people are the masters.

in the House of Commons, 11 February 1780; see **Blair** 43:10

*of the younger **Pitt**'s maiden speech, February 1781:*
10 Not merely a chip of the old 'block', but the old block itself.

N. W. Wraxall *Historical Memoirs of My Own Time* (1904 ed.)

11 I feel an insuperable reluctance in giving my hand to destroy any established institution of government, upon a theory, however plausible it may be.

in the House of Commons on Fox's East India Bill, 1 December 1783

12 The people never give up their liberties but under some delusion.

speech at County Meeting of Buckinghamshire, 1784, attributed in E. Latham *Famous Sayings* (1904), with 'except' substituted for 'but'

13 You strike at the whole corps, if you strike at the head.

opening speech, impeachment of Warren Hastings, House of Commons 13 February 1788

14 An event has happened, upon which it is difficult to speak, and impossible to be silent.

speech, 5 May 1789; E. A. Bond (ed.) *Speeches . . . in the Trial of Warren Hastings* (1859) vol. 2

15 At last dying in the last dyke of prevarication.

speech, 7 May 1789; E. A. Bond (ed.) *Speeches . . . in the Trial of Warren Hastings* (1859) vol. 2

16 Somebody has said, that a king may make a nobleman but he cannot make a gentleman.

letter to William Smith, 29 January 1795

George **Burns** 1896–1996

American comedian

1 Too bad all the people who know how to run the country are busy driving taxi cabs and cutting hair.

in *Daily Mail* 30 September 1997

John **Burns** 1858–1943

British Labour politician

2 I have seen the Mississippi. That is muddy water. I have seen the St Lawrence. That is crystal water. But the Thames is liquid history.

in *Daily Mail* 25 January 1943

Robert **Burns** 1759–96

Scottish poet

3 The rank is but the guinea's stamp,
The man's the gowd for a' that!

'For a' that and a' that' (1790)

4 A fig for those by law protected!
LIBERTY's a glorious feast!
Courts for cowards were erected,
Churches built to please the PRIEST.

'The Jolly Beggars' (1799)

5 Liberty's in every blow!
Let us do—or die!!!

'Robert Bruce's March to Bannockburn' (1799)

6 We labour soon, we labour late,
To feed the titled knave, man;
And a' the comfort we're to get,
Is that ayont the grave, man.

'The Tree of Liberty' (1838)

Burnum **Burnum** 1936–97

Australian political activist

7 We wish no harm to England's native people. We are here to bring you good manners, refinement and an opportunity to make a *Koompartoo*, a fresh start.
in 1988, the year of Australia's bicentenary, on planting an Aboriginal flag on the white cliffs of Dover and 'claiming' England for the Aboriginal people

on 26 January 1988; in obituary, *Independent* 20 August 1997

Aaron **Burr** 1756–1836

American politician

8 Law is whatever is boldly asserted and plausibly maintained.

James Parton *The Life and Times of Aaron Burr* (1857); attributed

Barbara **Bush** 1925–

wife of George **Bush**; First Lady 1989–93

9 Somewhere out in this audience may even be someone who will one day follow in my footsteps, and preside over the White House as the President's spouse. I wish him well!

at Wellesley College Commencement, 1 June 1990

10 Remember, they only name things after you when you're dead or really old.
at the naming ceremony for the George Bush Centre for Intelligence

at Wellesley College Commencement, 1 June 1990

George Bush 1924–

American Republican statesman; 41st President of the US, 1989–93

1 Is that man crazy? He thinks there's a bug behind all the pictures.
   *as Director of the CIA, having visited Harold **Wilson** during Wilson's last premiership*

Peter Hennessy *The Prime Minister: the Office and its Holders since 1945* (2000)

2 I'm President of the United States, and I'm not going to eat any more broccoli!

in *New York Times* 23 March 1990

3 Oh, the vision thing.
   responding to the suggestion that he turn his attention from short-term campaign objectives and look to the longer term.

in *Time* 26 January 1987

4 What's wrong with being a boring kind of guy?

during the campaign for the Republican nomination; in *Daily Telegraph* 28 April 1988

5 We are a nation of communities, of tens and tens of thousands of ethnic, religious, social, business, labour union, neighbourhood, regional and other organizations, all of them varied, voluntary, and unique . . . a brilliant diversity spread like stars, like a thousand points of light in a broad and peaceful sky.

acceptance speech at the Republican National Convention in New Orleans, 18 August 1988

6 Read my lips: no new taxes.
   accepting the Republican nomination

in *New York Times* 19 August 1988; see **Blunkett** 45:1

7 And now, we can see a new world coming into view. A world in which there is the very real prospect of a new world order.

speech, in *New York Times* 7 March 1991

8 What I see emerging is that the old guy drove the choice. That is absolutely inaccurate.
   of his son's selection of Dick Cheney as a running mate

in *Newsweek* 7 August 2000 'Perspectives'

George W. Bush 1946–

American Republican statesman; 43rd President of the US from 2001; son of George **Bush**

9 New Hampshire has long been known as the bump in the road for front runners—and this year is no exception.
   after being defeated in the New Hampshire primary

in *Sunday Times* 6 February 2000

10 It's no sign of weakness to talk to your dad.
   denying that he is too much under his father's influence

in *Sunday Telegraph* 30 July 2000

11 It is the office of Lincoln's conscience and Teddy Roosevelt's energy and Harry Truman's integrity and Ronald Reagan's optimism.
   accepting his party's presidential nomination

in *Seattle Times* 4 August 2000

Laura Bush 1946–

wife of George W. **Bush**, First Lady from 2001

of parents and grandparents encountered on the campaign trail:
12 They hold out pictures of their children and they say to George, 'I'm counting on you. I want my son or daughter to respect the president of the United States of America.'

speech at the Republican Convention, 1 August 2000

David Butler 1924–

British political scientist

1 Has he got a resignation in him?
  *of James **Callaghan**, to Hugh **Dalton***

Hugh Dalton *Political Diary* (1986) 13 July 1960

Lord Butler of Brockwell 1938–

British Civil Servant; Cabinet Secretary 1988–97

2 We do have a system in which very great power is given to people if they have a large parliamentary majority as well . . . The deal is that you give people very considerable power for five years, then they can be thrown out. And, in the meantime, if things get bad enough there are ways of getting rid of them. That is the deal of our constitution.

in 1998; Peter Hennessy *The Prime Minister: The Office and its Holders since 1945* (2000)

R. A. ('Rab') Butler 1902–82

British Conservative politician
*on Butler: see **Hennessy** 168:8*

*on hearing of the appointment of Winston **Churchill** as Prime Minister in succession to Neville **Chamberlain**:*
3 The good clean tradition of English politics, that of Pitt as opposed to Fox, has been sold to the greatest adventurer of modern political history.

John Colville diary, 10 May 1940

4 REPORTER: Mr Butler, would you say that this [Anthony Eden] is the best Prime Minister we have?
  R. A. BUTLER: Yes.
  interview at London Airport, 8 January 1956

R. A. Butler *The Art of the Possible* (1971)

5 The Civil Service is a bit like a Rolls-Royce—you know it's the best machine in the world, but you're not quite sure what to do with it.

Anthony Sampson *Anatomy of Britain* (1962)

6 I think a Prime Minister has to be a butcher and know the joints. That is perhaps where I have not been quite competent, in knowing all the ways that you can cut up a carcass.

in *Listener* 28 June 1966

7 In politics you must always keep running with the pack. The moment that you falter and they sense that you are injured, the rest will turn on you like wolves.

Dennis Walters *Not Always with the Pack* (1989)

Isaac Butt 1813–79

Irish nationalist politician

8 The people of this country are not idle. Let no man tell me this, when I see a peasant from Connaught going over to reap the harvest in England.

speech in defence of Thomas F. Meagher, 1848

9 I am not responsible for the member for Meath and cannot control him. I have, however, a duty to discharge to the great nation of Ireland and I think I should discharge it best when I say I disapprove entirely of the conduct of the honourable member for Meath.
  *of the parliamentary delaying tactics instigated by **Parnell***

in the House of Commons, 12 April 1877

John Byrom 1692–1763

English poet

1 God bless the King, I mean the Faith's Defender;
God bless—no harm in blessing—the Pretender;
But who Pretender is, or who is King,
God bless us all—that's quite another thing.

'To an Officer in the Army,
Extempore, Intended to allay the
Violence of Party-Spirit' (1773)

Lord Byron 1788–1824 ✓

English poet

2 For what were all these country patriots born?
To hunt, and vote, and raise the price of corn?

'The Age of Bronze' (1823)

3 Year after year they voted cent per cent
Blood, sweat, and tear-wrung millions—why? for rent!

'The Age of Bronze' (1823)

4 So he has cut his throat at last!—He! Who?
The man who cut his country's long ago.
on Castlereagh's suicide, c.1822

'Epigram on Lord Castlereagh'

5 The Cincinnatus of the West.
of George **Washington**

'Ode to Napoleon Bonaparte'
(1814)

6 The arbiter of others' fate
A suppliant for his own!

'Ode to Napoleon Bonaparte'
(1814)

7 I have no consistency, except in politics; and *that* probably
arises from my indifference on the subject altogether.

letter, 16 January 1814

Michael Bywater

8 The American dream is that any citizen can rise to the
highest office in the land. The British dream is that the
Queen drops in for tea.

in *Independent* 20 October 1997

Julius Caesar 100–44 BC ✓

Roman general and statesman

9 *Gallia est omnis divisa in partes tres.*
Gaul as a whole is divided into three parts.

De Bello Gallico

10 Men are nearly always willing to believe what they wish.

De Bello Gallico

11 Caesar's wife must be above suspicion.

oral tradition, based on Plutarch
Parallel Lives 'Julius Caesar'

12 Caesar had rather be first in a village than second at Rome.

Francis Bacon *The Advancement of
Learning* (based on Plutarch *Parallel
Lives* 'Julius Caesar')

13 *Iacta alea est.*
The die is cast.
at the crossing of the Rubicon

Suetonius *Lives of the Caesars*
'Divus Julius' (often quoted in Latin
'*Iacta alea est*' but originally
spoken in Greek)

1 *Veni, vidi, vici.*
I came, I saw, I conquered.

inscription displayed in Caesar's Pontic triumph, according to Suetonius *Lives of the Caesars* 'Divus Julius'; or, according to Plutarch *Parallel Lives* 'Julius Caesar', written in a letter by Caesar, announcing the victory of Zela which concluded the Pontic campaign

2 *Et tu, Brute?*
You too, Brutus?

traditional rendering of Suetonius *Lives of the Caesars* 'Divus Julius': 'Some have written that when Marcus Brutus rushed at him, he said in Greek, "You too, my child?" '

Joseph Cairns 1920-
British industrialist and politician

3 The betrayal of Ulster, the cynical and entirely undemocratic banishment of its properly elected Parliament and a relegation to the status of a fuzzy wuzzy colony is, I hope, a last betrayal contemplated by Downing Street because it is the last that Ulster will countenance.
speech on retiring as Lord Mayor of Belfast, 31 May 1972

in *Daily Telegraph* 1 June 1972

John Caldwell Calhoun 1782-1850
American politician
on Calhoun: see **Jackson** 183:7

4 The very essence of a free government consists in considering offices as public trusts, bestowed for the good of the country, and not for the benefit of an individual or party.

speech 13 February 1835

5 The surrender of life is nothing to sinking down into acknowledgement of inferiority.

speech in the Senate, 19 February 1847

Caligula (Gaius Julius Caesar Germanicus) AD 12-41
Roman emperor from AD 37

6 Would that the Roman people had but one neck!

Suetonius *Lives of the Caesars* 'Gaius Caligula'

James Callaghan 1912-
British Labour statesman; Prime Minister 1976-9
on Callaghan: see **Butler** 63:1, **Jenkins** 188:4; see also
Misquotations 254:4

7 Leaking is what you do; briefing is what *I* do.
when giving evidence to the Franks Committee on Official Secrecy in 1971

Franks Report (1972); oral evidence

8 We say that what Britain needs is a new social contract. That is what this document [*Labour's Programme for Britain*] is about.

speech at Labour Party Annual Conference, 2 October 1972

9 You cannot now, if you ever could, spend your way out of a recession.

speech at Labour Party Conference, 28 September 1976

1 You never reach the promised land. You can march towards it.

in a television interview, 20 July 1978

2 I had known it was going to be a 'winter of discontent'.

television interview, 8 February 1979; see **Newspaper headlines** 268:5

3 It's the first time in recorded history that turkeys have been known to vote for an early Christmas.
   in the debate resulting in the fall of the Labour government, when the pact between Labour and the Liberals had collapsed, and the Nationalists also withdrew their support in the wake of the failure of the devolution bills

in the House of Commons, 28 March 1979

4 I doubt if you accumulate much intellectual weight whilst you're in the office [of Prime Minister] . . . I think you rather spend your intellectual capital whilst you're in the office so it's important to take some baggage in.
   to his Principal Private Secretary, towards the end of the 'Winter of Discontent', 1979

in conversation with Michael Cockerell, 1996; Peter Hennessy *The Prime Minister: the Office and its Holders* (2000)

5 I let the country down.
   to his Principal Private Secretary, towards the end of the 'Winter of Discontent', 1979

Kenneth O. Morgan *Callaghan, A Life* (1997)

6 There are times, perhaps once every thirty years, when there is a sea-change in politics. It then does not matter what you say or what you do. There is a shift in what the public wants and what it approves of. I suspect there is now such a sea-change—and it is for Mrs Thatcher.
   during the election campaign of 1979

Kenneth O. Morgan *Callaghan* (1997)

of the popularity of Mrs **Thatcher***:*
7 The further you got from Britain, the more admired you found she was.

in *Spectator* 1 December 1990

8 It's never a misfortune to become Prime Minister. It's always the greatest thing in your life. It's absolute heaven— I enjoyed every moment of it until those last few months of the 'Winter of Discontent'.

interview on *Analysis*, BBC Radio 4, 20 June 1991

9 Well, it works, doesn't it? So I think that's the answer, even if it is on the back of an envelope and doesn't have a written constitution with every comma and every semi-colon in place. Because sometimes they can make for difficulties that common sense can overcome.

Peter Hennessy and Simon Coates *The Back of the Envelope* (1991)

10 I certainly didn't go down on one knee. I think she said it's about time we got married.
   on his diamond wedding day, remembering his proposal

in *Daily Telegraph* 29 July 1998

Italo Calvino 1923–85
Italian novelist and short-story writer

11 Revolutionaries are more formalistic than conservatives.

Il Barone Rampante (1957)

Helder Camara 1909–99
Brazilian priest

12 When I give food to the poor they call me a saint. When I ask why the poor have no food they call me a communist.

attributed, 1992

Lord Camden 1714–94

British Whig politician; Lord Chancellor, 1766–70

1 Taxation and representation are inseparable . . . whatever is a man's own, is absolutely his own; no man hath a right to take it from him without his consent either expressed by himself or representative; whoever attempts to do it, attempts an injury; whoever does it, commits a robbery; he throws down and destroys the distinction between liberty and slavery.
on the taxation of Americans by the British parliament

in the House of Lords, 10 February 1766

Simon Cameron 1799–1889

American politician

2 An honest politician is one who when he's bought stays bought.

attributed

Alastair Campbell 1957–

British journalist, Press Secretary to the Prime Minister from 1997
see also **Anonymous** 10:10

3 Live media is where it's at. Broadcasters are following the newspapers and broadcasters should be more confident in using live voices.

in *Guardian* 10 February 1999

4 Labour spin doctors aren't supposed to like Tory MPs. But Alan Clark was an exceptional man.

in *Mirror* 8 September 1999

5 I have no intention of getting into a war of words with the WI.
*after Tony **Blair** was heckled at the Women's Institute's annual conference for making what was regarded as a party political speech*

in *Guardian* 8 June 2000

Lord Campbell of Eskan 1912–

British industrialist

6 The only justification of the [House of] Lords is its irrationality: once you try to make it rational, you satisfy no one.

Anthony Sampson *The Changing Anatomy of Britain* (1982)

Thomas Campbell 1777–1844

Scottish poet

7 What millions died—that Caesar might be great!

Pleasures of Hope (1799)

Timothy Campbell 1840–1904

American politician

8 What's the Constitution between friends?
*reported response to President **Cleveland**'s refusing to support a bill on the grounds of its being unconstitutional*

attributed, *c.*1885

Henry Campbell-Bannerman 1836–1908

British Liberal statesman, Prime Minister 1905–8
on Campbell-Bannerman: see **Cecil** 73:8

1 There is a phrase which seems in itself somewhat self-
evident, which is often used to account for a good deal—
that 'war is war' But when you come to ask about it, then
you are told that the war now going on is not war.
[Laughter] When is a war not a war? When it is carried on
by methods of barbarism in South Africa.

speech to National Reform Union,
14 June 1901

2 Good government could never be a substitute for
government by the people themselves.

speech at Stirling, 23 November
1905

Albert Camus 1913–60

French novelist, playwright, and essayist

3 Politics and the fate of mankind are formed by men without
ideals and without greatness. Those who have greatness
within them do not go in for politics.

Carnets, 1935–42 (1962)

4 What is a rebel? A man who says no.

The Rebel (1951)

5 All modern revolutions have ended in a reinforcement of the
State.

The Rebel (1951)

6 Every revolutionary ends as an oppressor or a heretic.

The Rebel (1951)

Dennis Canavan 1942–

Scottish labour politician

7 Members of Parliament are representatives of the people, we
are not party puppets sent down to Westminster to vote
simply the way the whips instruct us to.
*having failed to be selected as an official Labour candidate for the
Scottish assembly*

in *Scotsman* 12 November 1998

George Canning 1770–1827

British Tory statesman; Prime Minister, 1827

8 A steady patriot of the world alone,
The friend of every country but his own.
on the Jacobin

'New Morality' (1821)

9 And finds, with keen discriminating sight,
Black's not so black;—nor white so very white.

'New Morality' (1821)

10 Give me the avowed, erect and manly foe;
Firm I can meet, perhaps return the blow;
But of all plagues, good Heaven, thy wrath can send,
Save me, oh, save me, from the candid friend.
the last two lines were quoted by **Peel** *to* **Disraeli** *in the House of
Commons; Disraeli's reply rested on the view that Peel had
treated Canning shabbily*

'New Morality' (1821)

11 Pitt is to Addington
As London is to Paddington.

'The Oracle' (c.1803)

1 Away with the cant of 'Measures not men'!—the idle supposition that it is the harness and not the horses that draw the chariot along. If the comparison must be made, if the distinction must be taken, men are everything, measures comparatively nothing.
  speech on the Army estimates, 8 December 1802

Speeches of . . . Canning (1828) vol. 2; the phrase 'measures not men' may be found as early as 1742 (in a letter from Chesterfield to Dr Chevenix, 6 March); also in Goldsmith *The Good Natured Man* (1768), 'Measures not men, have always been my mark'; see **Burke** 59:15

2 In matters of commerce the fault of the Dutch
Is offering too little and asking too much.
The French are with equal advantage content,
So we clap on Dutch bottoms just twenty per cent.

dispatch, in cipher, to the English ambassador at the Hague, 31 January 1826

3 I called the New World into existence, to redress the balance of the Old.
  speech on the affairs of Portugal

in the House of Commons, 12 December 1826

4 [The Whip's duty is] to make a House, and keep a House, and cheer the minister.

J. E. Ritchie *Modern Statesmen* (1861)

Al Capone 1899–1947
Italian-born American gangster, notorious for his domination of organized crime in Chicago in the 1920s

5 Don't you get the idea I'm one of these goddam radicals. Don't get the idea I'm knocking the American system.

interview, c.1929; Claud Cockburn *In Time of Trouble* (1956)

Benjamin Nathan Cardozo 1870–1938
American judge

6 [The Constitution] was framed upon the theory that the peoples of the several states must sink or swim together, and that in the long run prosperity and salvation are in union and not division.

in *Baldwin v. Seelig* (1935)

Thomas Carlyle 1795–1881
Scottish historian and political philosopher

7 A witty statesman said, you might prove anything by figures.

Chartism (1839)

8 Surely of all 'rights of man', this right of the ignorant man to be guided by the wiser, to be, gently or forcibly, held in the true course by him, is the indisputablest.

Chartism (1839)

9 In epochs when cash payment has become the sole nexus of man to man.

Chartism (1839)

10 To the very last he [Napoleon] had a kind of idea; that, namely, of *La carrière ouverte aux talents*, The tools to him that can handle them.

Critical and Miscellaneous Essays (1838) 'Sir Walter Scott'

11 The three great elements of modern civilization, Gunpowder, Printing, and the Protestant Religion.

Critical and Miscellaneous Essays (1838) 'The State of German Literature'

12 Two centuries; hardly less; before Democracy go through its due, most baleful, stages of *Quackocracy*.

History of the French Revolution (1837) vol. 1

13 The seagreen Incorruptible.
  *describing **Robespierre***

History of the French Revolution (1837) vol. 2

1   France was long a despotism tempered by epigrams.   *History of the French Revolution* (1837) vol. 3

2   Aristocracy of the Moneybag.   *History of the French Revolution* (1837) vol. 3

3   A Parliament speaking through reporters to Buncombe and the twenty-seven millions mostly fools.   *Latter-Day Pamphlets* (1850) 'Parliaments'; see **Walker** 372:14

of political economy:
4   The Dismal Science.   *Latter-Day Pamphlets* (1850) 'The Present Time'

of himself:
5   Little other than a redtape talking-machine, and unhappy bag of parliamentary eloquence.   *Latter-Day Pamphlets* (1850) 'The Present Time'

6   A Hell in England—the Hell of not making money.   *Past and Present* (1843)

7   Despotism is essential in most enterprises.   *Past and Present* (1843)

8   Councillors of state sit plotting, and playing their high chess-game, whereof the pawns are men.   *Sartor Resartus* (1858)

*of **Disraeli**:*
9   A superlative Hebrew conjuror.   *Shooting Niagara: and After?* (1867)

10   Democracy, which means despair of finding any heroes to govern you.   attributed

11   Vote by ballot is the dyspepsia of the society.   Simon Heffer *Moral Desperado* (1995)

Stokely Carmichael 1941–98
and Charles Vernon Hamilton 1929–

12   Black power . . . is a call for black people in this country to unite, to recognize their heritage, to build a sense of community.   *Black Power* (1967)

13   Before a group can enter the open society, it must first close ranks.   *Black Power* (1967)

Lewis Carroll 1832–98
English writer and logician

14   The rule is, jam to-morrow and jam yesterday—but never jam today.   *Through the Looking-Glass* (1872)

15   'When *I* use a word,' Humpty Dumpty said in a rather scornful tone, 'it means just what I choose it to mean— neither more nor less.'   *Through the Looking-Glass* (1872); see **Shawcross** 329:1

Edward Carson 1854–1935
British lawyer and politician, Ulster leader and Unionist

16   I now enter into compact with you, and with the help of God you and I joined together . . . will yet defeat the most nefarious conspiracy that has ever been hatched against a free people . . . We must be prepared . . . the morning Home Rule passes, ourselves to become responsible for the government of the Protestant Province of Ulster.   speech at Craigavon, 23 September 1911

17   My one affection left me is my love for Ireland.   Montgomery Hyde *Carson* (1953)
     after the death of his wife in 1913

1 We do not want a sentence of death with a stay of execution for six years.
   rejecting the suggestion that the Home Rule Bill should allow the temporary exclusion of Ulster for six years

speech, March 1914

2 From the day I first entered parliament up to the present, devotion to the union has been the guiding star of my political life.

in *Dictionary of National Biography* (1917-)

3 My only great qualification for being put at the head of the Navy is that I am very much at sea.

Ian Colvin *Life of Lord Carson* (1936) vol. 3

Jimmy Carter 1924-

American Democratic statesman, 39th President of the US,1977-81

4 We should live our lives as though Christ were coming this afternoon.
   to a Bible class at Plains, Georgia, March 1976

in *Boston Sunday Herald Advertiser* 11 April 1976

5 I've looked on a lot of women with lust. I've committed adultery in my heart many times. This is something that God recognizes I will do—and I have done it—and God forgives me for it.

in *Playboy* November 1976

John Cartwright 1740-1824

English political reformer

6 One man shall have one vote.

The People's Barrier Against Undue Influence (1780) 'Principles, maxims, and primary rules of politics' no. 68

Thomas Nixon Carver

American conservative, who had previously given the course In agricultural economics at Harvard taken over by Galbraith in 1934

7 The trouble with radicals is that they only read radical literature, and the trouble with conservatives is that they don't read anything.

'Carver's Law'; J. K. Galbraith *A Life in Our Times* (1981)

Roger Casement 1864-1916

Irish nationalist; executed for treason in 1916

8 Self-government is our right, a thing born in us at birth, a thing no more to be doled out to us, or withheld from us, by another people than the right to life itself—than the right to feel the sun, or smell the flowers, or to love our kind.

statement at the conclusion of his trial, the Old Bailey, London, 29 June 1916

9 Where all your rights become only an accumulated wrong; where men must beg with bated breath for leave to subsist in their own land, to think their own thoughts, to sing their own songs, to garner the fruits of their own labours . . . then surely it is a braver, a saner and truer thing, to be a rebel in act and deed against such circumstances as these than tamely to accept it as the natural lot of men.

statement from prison, 29 June 1916

Barbara Castle 1910–
British Labour politician

1 She is so clearly the best man among them.
*of Margaret **Thatcher***

diary, 11 February 1975

2 Dogs make you walk. Politics make you think. Only boredom makes you old.

Lynda Lee-Potter in *Daily Mail*; in *The Week* 11 January 1997

3 I will fight for what I believe in until I drop dead. And that's what keeps you alive.

in *Guardian* 14 January 1998

Ted Castle 1907–79
British journalist

4 In place of strife.

title of Labour Government White Paper, 17 January 1969; suggested by Castle to his wife, Barbara **Castle**, then Secretary of State for Employment

Fidel Castro 1927–
Cuban statesman, Prime Minister 1959–76 and President since 1976
on Castro: see **Ceaușescu** 73:6

5 Capitalism is using its money; we socialists throw it away.

in *Observer* 8 November 1964

Willa Cather 1873–1947
American novelist

6 Oh, the Germans classify, but the French arrange!

Death Comes For the Archbishop (1927))

Catherine the Great 1729–96
Empress of Russia from 1762

7 I shall be an autocrat: that's my trade. And the good Lord will forgive me: that's his.

attributed

Wyn Catlin

8 Diplomacy is saying 'Nice doggie' until you find a rock.

Laurence J. Peter (ed.) *Quotations for our Time* (1977)

Cato the Elder (or 'the Censor') 234–149 BC
Roman statesman, orator, and writer

9 *Delenda est Carthago.*
Carthage must be destroyed.
words concluding every speech Cato made in the Senate

Pliny the Elder *Naturalis Historia*

Carrie Chapman Catt 1859–1947
American feminist

10 When a just cause reaches its flood-tide . . . whatever stands in the way must fall before its overwhelming power.

speech at Stockholm, *Is Woman Suffrage Progressing?* (1911)

Mr Justice Caulfield 1914–

British lawyer

1 Remember Mary Archer in the witness box. Your vision of her will probably never disappear. Has she elegance? Has she fragrance? Would she have—without the strain of this trial—a radiance?

summing up of court case between Jeffrey Archer and the *Star*, July 1987, in *The Times* 24 July 1987

Constantine Cavafy 1863–1933

Greek poet

2 What are we waiting for, gathered in the market-place? The barbarians are to arrive today.

'Waiting for the Barbarians' (1904)

3 And now, what will become of us without the barbarians? Those people were a kind of solution.

'Waiting for the Barbarians' (1904)

Edith Cavell 1865–1915

English nurse

4 Patriotism is not enough. I must have no hatred or bitterness towards anyone.
   on the eve of her execution by the Germans for assisting in the escape of British soldiers from occupied Belgium

in *The Times* 23 October 1915

Count Cavour 1810–61

Italian statesman

5 We are ready to proclaim throughout Italy this great principle: a free church in a free state.

speech, 27 March 1861

Nicolae Ceauşescu 1918–89

Romanian Communist statesman, first President of the Socialist Republic of Romania 1974–89

6 Fidel Castro is right. You do not quieten your enemy by talking with him like a priest, but by burning him.
   at a Communist Party meeting 17 December 1989

in *Guardian* 11 January 1990

Lord Edward Cecil 1867–1918

British soldier and civil servant; chief British adviser in the Egyptian government

definition of a compromise:
7 An agreement between two men to do what both agree is wrong.

letter 3 September 1911

Lord Hugh Cecil 1869–1956

British Conservative politician and Provost of Eton

8 There is no more ungraceful figure than that of a humanitarian with an eye to the main chance.
   dismissal of a manoeuvre by **Campbell-Bannerman**

in *The Times* 24 June 1901

9 The socialist believes that it is better to be rich than poor, the Christian that it is better to be poor than rich.

Conservatism (1912)

Robert Cecil 1563–1612

English courtier and statesman, son of William Cecil, Lord Burghley

1 Rest content, and give heed to one that hath sorrowed in the bright lustre of a court, and gone heavily even on the best-seeming fair ground . . . I know it bringeth little comfort on earth; and he is, I reckon, no wise man that looketh this way to Heaven.

letter to Sir John Harington; Algernon Cecil *A Life of Robert Cecil* (1915)

Paul Celan 1920–70

German poet

2 *Der Tod ist ein Meister aus Deutschland.*
Death is a master from Germany.

'Deathfugue' (written 1944)

3 There's nothing in the world for which a poet will give up writing, not even when he is a Jew and the language of his poems is German.

letter to relatives, 2 August 1948

Joseph Chamberlain 1836–1914

British Liberal politician; father of Neville **Chamberlain**

4 In politics, there is no use looking beyond the next fortnight.

A. J. Balfour letter to Lord Salisbury, 24 March 1886; see **Wilson** 385:3

5 It is not to your interest to arouse the prejudices of the society in which you hope one day again to take your place . . . Therefore my advice is: Be as Radical as you like. Be Home Ruler if you must. But be a little Jingo if you can.
   to his friend Charles Dilke, who was hoping to make a political comeback

Roy Jenkins *Sir Charles Dilke* (1958)

6 Provided that the City of London remains, as it is at present, the clearing-house of the world, any other nation may be its workshop.

speech at the Guildhall, 19 January 1904

7 Learn to think Imperially.
   *with reference to Alexander **Hamilton**'s advice to the newly independent United States*

speech at the Guildhall, 19 January 1904; see **Hamilton** 160:11

8 The day of small nations has long passed away. The day of Empires has come.

speech at Birmingham, 12 May 1904

9 We are not downhearted. The only trouble is we cannot understand what is happening to our neighbours.
   referring to a constituency which had remained unaffected by an electoral landslide

speech at Smethwick, 18 January 1906

Neville Chamberlain 1869–1940

British Conservative statesman; Prime Minister, 1937–40; son of Joseph **Chamberlain**
on Chamberlain: see **Bevan** 37:8, **Churchill** 81:7, **Lloyd George** 223:8, **Roberts** 302:8

10 How horrible, fantastic, incredible it is that we should be digging trenches and trying on gas-masks here because of a quarrel in a far away country between people of whom we know nothing.
   on Germany's annexation of the Sudetenland

radio broadcast, 27 September 1938

1 This morning I had another talk with the German Chancellor, Herr Hitler, and here is the paper which bears his name upon it as well as mine . . . 'We regard the agreement signed last night and the Anglo-German Naval Agreement, as symbolic of the desire of our two peoples never to go to war with one another again.'

speech at Heston Airport, 30 September 1938

2 This is the second time in our history that there has come back from Germany to Downing Street peace with honour. I believe it is peace for our time.
  speech from the window of 10 Downing Street, 30 September 1938

in The Times 1 October 1938; see **Disraeli** 113:5

the British Ambassador in Berlin had handed the German government a final note stating that unless the British government had heard by eleven o'clock that Germany was prepared to withdraw her troops from Poland, a state of war would exist between the two countries:

3 I have to tell you now that no such undertaking has been received, and that consequently this country is at war with Germany.

radio broadcast, 3 September 1939

4 Whatever may be the reason—whether it was that Hitler thought he might get away with what he had got without fighting for it, or whether it was that after all the preparations were not sufficiently complete—however, one thing is certain—he missed the bus.

speech at Central Hall, Westminster, 4 April 1940

Henry ('Chips') Channon 1897-1958

American-born British Conservative MP and diarist

5 I personally think . . . that there will be an unheaval, that the Throne will sway a little, but that it will survive and that the King will get away with it. We are working up to something terrific. What is history unfolding?
  during the Abdication crisis of 1936

diary, 22 November 1936

6 There is nowhere in the world where sleep is so deep as in the libraries of the House of Commons.

diary, 17 December 1937

7 I gather it has now been decided not to embrace the Russian bear, but to hold out a hand and accept its paw gingerly. No more. The worst of both worlds.

diary, 16 May 1939

Charles I 1600-49

King of England, Scotland, and Ireland from 1625
on Charles I: see **Marvell** 244:1

8 Never make a defence or apology before you be accused.

letter to Lord Wentworth, 3 September 1636

9 I see all the birds are flown.
  after attempting to arrest the Five Members

in the House of Commons, 4 January 1642

10 Sweet-heart, now they will cut off thy father's head. Mark, child, what I say: they will cut off my head, and perhaps make thee a king. But mark what I say: you must not be a king, so long as your brothers Charles and James do live.
  said to Prince Henry

in Reliquiae Sacrae Carolinae (1650)

1 You manifestly wrong even the poorest ploughman, if you demand not his free consent.
  rejecting the jurisdiction of the High Court of Justice, 21 January 1649

S. R. Gardiner *Constitutional Documents of the Puritan Revolution* (1906 ed.)

2 As to the King, the laws of the land will clearly instruct you for that . . . For the people; and truly I desire their liberty and freedom, as much as any body: but I must tell you, that their liberty and freedom consists in having the government of those laws, by which their life and their goods may be most their own; 'tis not for having share in government [sirs] that is nothing pertaining to 'em. A subject and a sovereign are clean different things . . . If I would have given way to an arbitrary way, for to have all laws changed according to the power of the sword, I needed not to have come here; and therefore I tell you (and I pray God it be not laid to your charge) that I am the martyr of the people.
  speech on the scaffold, 30 January 1649

J. Rushworth *Historical Collections* vol. 2 (1701)

3 I die a Christian, according to the profession of the Church of England, as I found it left me by my father.

J. Rushworth *Historical Collections* vol. 2 (1701)

Charles II 1630–85

King of England, Scotland and Ireland from 1660
on Charles II: see **Rochester** 304:2

4 It is upon the navy under the good Providence of God that the safety, honour, and welfare of this realm do chiefly depend.

'Articles of War' preamble (probably a popular paraphrase); Geoffrey Callender *The Naval Side of British History* (1952)

5 This is very true: for my words are my own, and my actions are my ministers'.
  reply to Lord **Rochester**'s *epitaph on him*

in *Thomas Hearne: Remarks and Collections* (1885–1921) 17 November 1706; see **Epitaphs** 128:3

6 Better than a play.
  on the debates in the House of Lords on Lord Ross's Divorce Bill

A. Bryant *King Charles II* (1931)

7 I am sure no man in England will take away my life to make you King.
  to his brother James, afterwards James II

William King *Political & Literary Anecdotes* (1818)

8 I am weary of travelling and am resolved to go abroad no more. But when I am dead and gone I know not what my brother will do: I am much afraid that when he comes to wear the crown he will be obliged to travel again.
  on the difference between himself and his brother

attributed

9 I, who will never use arbitrary government myself, am resolved not to suffer it in others.
  to the Whigs

attributed

10 Not a religion for gentlemen.
  of Presbyterianism

Gilbert Burnet *History of My Own Time* (1724) vol. 1

11 He had been, he said, an unconscionable time dying; but he hoped that they would excuse it.

Lord Macaulay *History of England* (1849) vol. 1

Salmon Portland Chase 1808–73

American lawyer and politician

12 The Constitution, in all its provisions, looks to an indestructible Union composed of indestructible States.

decision in Texas v. White, 1868

Mary Chesnut 1823–86
American diarist and Confederate supporter

1 The Confederacy has been done to death by politicians.

in 1863; Ken Burns The Civil War (documentary, 1989) episode 4

2 Atlanta is gone. That agony is over. There is no hope but we will try to have no fear.
   after the fall of Atlanta to Sherman's army in 1864

Geoffrey C. Ward The Civil War (1991)

Lord Chesterfield 1694–1773
English writer and politician
on Chesterfield: see **Johnson** 191:2, **Walpole** 373:5

3 Women, then, are only children of a larger growth: they have an entertaining tattle, and sometimes wit; but for solid, reasoning good sense, I never knew in my life one that had it, or who reasoned or acted consequentially for four and twenty hours together.

letter, 5 September 1748

4 Politicians neither love nor hate. Interest, not sentiment, directs them.

Letters 1748

5 I . . . could not help reflecting in my way upon the singular ill-luck of this my dear country, which, as long as ever I remember it, and as far back as I have read, has always been governed by the only two or three people, out of two or three millions, totally incapable of governing, and unfit to be trusted.

in The World 7 October 1756

G. K. Chesterton 1874–1936
English essayist, novelist, and poet

6 'My country, right or wrong' is a thing no patriot would ever think of saying except in a desperate case. It is like saying, 'My mother, drunk or sober.'

The Defendant (1901)

7 Tradition means giving votes to the most obscure of all classes, our ancestors. It is the democracy of the dead.

Orthodoxy (1908)

8 Democrats object to men being disqualified by the accident of birth; tradition objects to their being disqualified by the accident of death. Tradition refuses to submit to the small and arrogant oligarchy of those who merely happen to be walking around.

Orthodoxy (1908)

9 All conservatism is based upon the idea that if you leave things alone you leave them as they are. But you do not. If you leave a thing alone you leave it to a torrent of change.

Orthodoxy (1908)

10 Talk about the pews and steeples
   And the Cash that goes therewith!
   But the souls of Christian peoples . . .
   Chuck it, Smith!
   satirizing F. E. **Smith***'s response to the Welsh Disestablishment Bill*

'Antichrist' (1912)

11 They died to save their country and they only saved the world.

'English Graves' (1922)

12 Smile at us, pay us, pass us; but do not quite forget.
   For we are the people of England, that never have spoken yet.

'The Secret People' (1915)

1 We only know the last sad squires ride slowly towards the   'The Secret People' (1915)
   sea,
   And a new people takes the land: and still it is not we.

2 They have given us into the hand of new unhappy lords,   'The Secret People' (1915)
   Lords without anger and honour, who dare not carry their
       swords.
   They fight us by shuffling papers; they have bright dead
       alien eyes;
   And they look at our labour and laughter as a tired man
       looks at flies.
   And the load of their loveless pity is worse than the ancient
       wrongs,
   Their doors are shut in the evening; And they know no
       songs.

3 Lancashire merchants whenever they like   'Songs of Education: II Geography'
   Can water the beer of a man in Klondike   (1922)
   Or poison the meat of a man in Bombay;
   And that is the meaning of Empire Day.

4 Democracy means government by the uneducated, while   in New York Times 1 February 1931
   aristocracy means government by the badly educated.

Lydia Maria Child 1802–80
American abolitionist and suffragist

5 We first crush people to the earth, and then claim the right   An Appeal on Behalf of That Class of
   of trampling on them forever, because they are prostrate.   Americans Called Africans (1833)

6 Woman stock is rising in the market. I shall not live to see   letter to Sarah Shaw, 3 August
   women vote, but I'll come and rap at the ballot box.   1856

Erskine Childers see Last words 212:3

Lawton Chiles 1930–
American politician

7 You are misunderstood, maligned, viewed by the press as a   in St Petersburg (Florida) Times 6
   Pulitzer Prize ready to be won.   March 1991
   on the problems of investigative journalism for politicians

Jaques Chirac 1932–
French statesman, Prime Minister 1974–6 and 1986–8, President
since 1995

8 For its part, France wants you to take part in this great   speech to both Houses of
   undertaking.   Parliament, 15 May 1996
   on European Monetary Union

Rufus Choate 1799–1859
American lawyer and politician

9 We join ourselves to no party that does not carry the flag   letter to the Whig Convention,
   and keep step to the music of the Union.   Worcester, Massachusetts, 1
       October 1855

10 Its constitution the glittering and sounding generalities of   letter to the Maine Whig State
   natural right which make up the Declaration of   Central Committee, 9 August 1856
   Independence.

Frank Chodorov 1887–1966
American economist and writer

1 [When people] say 'let's do something about it,' they mean 'let's get hold of the political machinery so that we can do something to somebody else.' And that somebody is invariably you.

'Freedom is Better' (1949)

2 The only way to a world society is through free trade.

'One Worldism' (1950)

Duc de Choiseul 1719–85
French politician

3 A minister who moves about in society is in a position to read the signs of the times even in a festive gathering, but one who remains shut up in his office learns nothing.

Jack F. Bernard *Talleyrand* (1973)

David Christy 1802–c.68

4 Cotton is King; or, the economical relations of slavery.

title of book, 1855

Clementine Churchill 1885–1977
wife of Winston **Churchill**

5 Winston . . . has the supreme quality which I venture to say very few of your present or future Cabinet possess, the power, the imagination, the deadliness to fight Germany.
   *letter to **Asquith** on Winston **Churchill**'s dismissal from the Admiralty, May 1915*

Martin Gilbert *In Search of Churchill* (1994)

Lord Randolph Churchill 1849–94
British Conservative politician; father of Winston **Churchill**
on Churchill: see **Gladstone** 148:7

6 To tell the truth I don't know myself what Tory Democracy is. But I believe it is principally opportunism.
   having urged Wilfrid Scawen Blunt in 1885 to stand for Parliament as a Tory Democrat

Elizabeth Longford *A Pilgrimage of Passion* (1979)

7 For the purposes of recreation he [Gladstone] has selected the felling of trees, and we may usefully remark that his amusements, like his politics, are essentially destructive . . . The forest laments in order that Mr Gladstone may perspire.

speech on Financial Reform, delivered in Blackpool, 24 January 1884

8 I decided some time ago that if the G.O.M. [Gladstone] went for Home Rule, the Orange card would be the one to play. Please God it may turn out the ace of trumps and not the two.
   *often quoted as 'Play the Orange card'; see **Shapiro** 327:11*

letter to Lord Justice FitzGibbon, 16 February 1886

9 Ulster will fight; Ulster will be right.

public letter, 7 May 1886

10 An old man in a hurry.
   *of **Gladstone***

in an address to the electors of South Paddington, 19 June 1886

11 All great men make mistakes. Napoleon forgot Blücher, I forgot Goschen.
   *when Lord Randolph suddenly resigned the position of Chancellor of the Exchequer in 1886, **Goschen** had been appointed in his place*

in *Leaves from the Notebooks of Lady Dorothy Nevill* (1907)

12 I never could make out what those damned dots meant.
   of decimal points

Winston Churchill *Lord Randolph Churchill* (1906) vol. 2

1 I have tried all forms of excitement, from tip-cat to tiger-shooting; all degrees of gambling, from beggar-my-neighbour to Monte Carlo; but have found no gambling like politics, and no excitement like a big division in the House of Commons.

Robert Rhodes James *An Introduction to the House of Commons* (1961)

Winston Churchill 1874–1965

British Conservative statesman; Prime Minister, 1940–5, 1951–5
on Churchill: see **Asquith** 15:6, **Baldwin** 25:7, **Balfour** 27:4, **Bevan** 36:6, **Butler** 63:3, **Laski** 211:2, **Lloyd George** 223:10, 223:18, **Nicolson** 266:9, **Webb** 376:8

2 A labour contract into which men enter voluntarily for a limited and for a brief period, under which they are paid wages which they consider adequate . . . may not be a healthy or proper contract, but it cannot in the opinion of His Majesty's Government be classified as slavery in the extreme acceptance of the word without some risk of terminological inexactitude.

in the House of Commons, 22 February 1906

3 He is one of those orators of whom it was well said, 'Before they get up, they do not know what they are going to say; when they are speaking, they do not know what they are saying; and when they have sat down, they do not know what they have said.'
of Lord Charles Beresford

in the House of Commons, 20 December 1912

4 Business carried on as usual during alterations on the map of Europe.
on the self-adopted 'motto' of the British people

speech at Guildhall, 9 November 1914

5 A drizzle of Empires . . . falling through the air.
of the Austro-Hungarian and Ottoman empires in 1918

Martin Gilbert *In Search of Churchill* (1994)

comparing H. H. **Asquith** *with Arthur* **Balfour***:*
6 The difference between him and Arthur is that Arthur is wicked and moral, Asquith is good and immoral.

E. T. Raymond *Mr Balfour* (1920)

7 The whole map of Europe has been changed . . . but as the deluge subsides and the waters fall short we see the dreary steeples of Fermanagh and Tyrone emerging once again.

in the House of Commons, 16 February 1922

8 Anyone can rat, but it takes a certain amount of ingenuity to re-rat.
on rejoining the Conservatives twenty years after leaving them for the Liberals, c.1924

Kay Halle *Irrepressible Churchill* (1966)

of a meeting in 1926 with **Lloyd George***, by then out of office:*
9 Within five minutes the old relationship between us was completely re-established. The relationship between Master and Servant. And I was the Servant.

Lord Boothby *Recollections of a Rebel* (1978)

10 I decline utterly to be impartial as between the fire brigade and the fire.
replying to complaints of his bias in editing the British Gazette *during the General Strike*

in the House of Commons, 7 July 1926

11 Cultured people are merely the glittering scum which floats upon the deep river of production.
on hearing his son Randolph criticize the lack of culture of the Calgary oil magnates, probably c.1929

Martin Gilbert *In Search of Churchill* (1994)

1 I remember, when I was a child, being taken to the celebrated Barnum's circus, which contained an exhibition of freaks and monstrosities, but the exhibit on the programme which I most desired to see was the one described as 'The Boneless Wonder'. My parents judged that that spectacle would be too revolting and demoralizing for my youthful eyes, and I have waited 50 years to see the boneless wonder sitting on the Treasury Bench.

*of Ramsay **MacDonald***

speech in the House of Commons, 28 January 1931

2 There is not much collective security in a flock of sheep on the way to the butcher.

speech at the New Commonwealth Society luncheon, Dorchester Hotel, 25 November 1936

3 [The Government] go on in strange paradox, decided only to be undecided, resolved to be irresolute, adamant for drift, solid for fluidity, all-powerful to be impotent.

in the House of Commons, 12 November 1936

4 Dictators ride to and fro upon tigers which they dare not dismount. And the tigers are getting hungry.

letter, 11 November 1937

5 The utmost he [Neville Chamberlain] has been able to gain for Czechoslovakia and in the matters which were in dispute has been that the German dictator, instead of snatching his victuals from the table, has been content to have them served to him course by course.

in the House of Commons, 5 October 1938

6 I cannot forecast to you the action of Russia. It is a riddle wrapped in a mystery inside an enigma.

radio broadcast, 1 October 1939

*on being asked where to set the podium from which Neville **Chamberlain** was to give an address to local Conservatives:*

7 It doesn't matter where you put it as long as he has the sun in his eyes and the wind in his teeth.

Martin Gilbert *In Search of Churchill* (1994)

8 An appeaser is one who feeds a crocodile hoping it will eat him last.

in the House of Commons, January 1940

as Prime Minister:

9 [I was] conscious of a profound source of relief. I felt as if I was walking with destiny, and that all my past life had been but a preparation for this hour and this trial.

on 10 May 1940

10 I have nothing to offer but blood, toil, tears and sweat.

speech in the House of Commons, 13 May 1940

11 What is our policy? . . . to wage war against a monstrous tyranny, never surpassed in the dark, lamentable catalogue of human crime.

speech in the House of Commons, 13 May 1940

12 We shall not flag or fail. We shall go on to the end. We shall fight in France, we shall fight on the seas and oceans, we shall fight with growing confidence and growing strength in the air, we shall defend our island, whatever the cost may be. We shall fight on the beaches, we shall fight on the landing grounds, we shall fight in the fields and in the streets, we shall fight in the hills; we shall never surrender.

speech in the House of Commons, 4 June 1940

13 Let us therefore brace ourselves to our duty, and so bear ourselves that, if the British Empire and its Commonwealth lasts for a thousand years, men will still say, 'This was their finest hour.'

speech in the House of Commons, 18 June 1940

14 Never in the field of human conflict was so much owed by so many to so few.

on the skill and courage of British airmen

speech in the House of Commons, 20 August 1940

1 Death and sorrow will be the companions of our journey; hardship our garment; constancy and valour our only shield. We must be united, we must be undaunted, we must be inflexible.

speech in the House of Commons, 8 October 1940

comment allegedly made on a long-winded report submitted by Anthony Eden on his tour of the Near East:
2 As far as I can see you have used every cliché except 'God is Love' and 'Please adjust your dress before leaving.'

in Life December 1940

3 What I want is for you to keep the flies off the meat. It becomes bad if they are allowed to settle even for a moment. I am the meat and you must show me the warning light when troubles arise in the Parliamentary and political scene.
to his newly appointed Parliamentary Private Secretary, c.1941

Andrew Roberts Eminent Churchillians (1994)

4 It becomes still more difficult to reconcile Japanese action with prudence or even with sanity. What kind of a people do they think we are?

speech to US Congress, 26 December 1941

5 The British nation is unique in this respect. They are the only people who like to be told how bad things are, who like to be told the worst.

speech in the House of Commons, 10 June 1941

6 The people of London with one voice would say to Hitler: 'You have committed every crime under the sun . . . We will have no truce or parley with you, or the grisly gang who work your wicked will. You do your worst—and we will do our best.'

speech at County Hall, London, 14 July 1941

7 Here is the answer which I will give to President Roosevelt . . . Give us the tools and we will finish the job.

radio broadcast 9 February 1941

8 When I warned them [the French Government] that Britain would fight on alone whatever they did, their generals told their Prime Minister and his divided Cabinet, 'In three weeks England will have her neck wrung like a chicken.' Some chicken! Some neck!

speech to Canadian Parliament, 30 December 1941

9 A medal glitters, but it also casts a shadow.
a reference to the envy caused by the award of honours

in 1941; Kenneth Rose King George V (1983)

10 I have not become the King's First Minister in order to preside over the liquidation of the British Empire.

speech in London, 10 November 1942

11 Now this is not the end. It is not even the beginning of the end. But it is, perhaps, the end of the beginning.
on British success in the North African campaign

speech at the Mansion House, London, 10 November 1942

12 We make this wide encircling movement in the Mediterranean, having for its primary object the recovery of the command of that vital sea, but also having for its object the exposure of the under-belly of the Axis, especially Italy, to heavy attack.

speech in the House of Commons, 11 November 1942; see **Misquotations** 255:6

13 National compulsory insurance for all classes for all purposes from the cradle to the grave.

radio broadcast 21 March 1943

14 There is no finer investment for any community than putting milk into babies.

radio broadcast, 21 March 1943

15 The empires of the future are the empires of the mind.

speech at Harvard, 6 September 1943

on rebuilding the Houses of Parliament:

1 We shape our dwellings, and afterwards our dwellings shape us.

speech in the House of Commons, 28 October 1944

2 I do not see any other way of realizing our hopes about World Organization in five or six days. Even the Almighty took seven.
*to Franklin **Roosevelt** on the likely duration of the Yalta conference with **Stalin** in 1945*

The Second World War (1954) vol. 6

3 He devised the extraordinary measure of assistance called Lend-Lease, which will stand forth as the most unselfish and unsordid financial act of any country in all history.
*of President **Roosevelt***

speech in the House of Commons, 17 April 1945

after the General Election of 1945:

4 Why should I accept the Order of the Garter from His Majesty when the people have just given me the order of the boot?

D. Bardens *Churchill in Parliament* (1967)

*of Aneurin **Bevan**:*

5 Unless the right hon. gentleman changes his policy and methods and moves without the slightest delay, he will be as great a curse to this country in time of peace, as he was a squalid nuisance in time of war.

speech in the House of Commons, 6 December 1945

6 The Prime Minister has nothing to hide from the President of the United States
*on stepping from his bath in the presence of a startled President **Roosevelt***

as recalled by Roosevelt's son in *Churchill* (BBC television series presented by Martin Gilbert, 1992) pt. 3

7 From Stettin in the Baltic to Trieste in the Adriatic an iron curtain has descended across the Continent.
the expression 'iron curtain' previously had been applied by others to the Soviet Union or her sphere of influence, e.g. Ethel Snowden Through Bolshevik Russia (1920), Dr Goebbels Das Reich, 25 February 1945, and by Churchill himself in a cable to President Truman, 4 June 1945

speech at Westminster College, Fulton, Missouri, 5 March 1946

8 The first step in the re-creation of the European family must be a partnership between France and Germany. In this way only can France recover the moral leadership of Europe. There can be no revival of Europe without a spiritually great France and a spiritually great Germany.

speech in Zurich, 19 September 1946

9 Time may be short . . . The fighting has stopped; but the dangers have not stopped. If we are to form the United States of Europe or whatever name or form it may take, we must begin now.
speaking of the threat posed by the atom bomb

speech in Zurich, 19 September 1946

after the Nuremberg war trials:

10 From now on I shall have to take care not to lose wars.

attributed

11 I wish Stanley Baldwin no ill, but it would have been much better if he had never lived.
*on being asked to send **Baldwin** an 80th birthday tribute*

Martin Gilbert *In Search of Churchill* (1994)

12 It would be a great reform in politics if wisdom could be made to spread as easily and as rapidly as folly.

speech at the Guildhall, London, 10 September 1947

13 Democracy is the worst form of Government except all those other forms that have been tried from time to time.

speech in the House of Commons, 11 November 1947

1 When I am abroad I always make it a rule never to criticize or attack the Government of my country. I make up for lost time when I am at home.

speech in the House of Commons, 18 April 1947

2 This is the sort of English up with which I will not put.
after an official had gone through one of his papers moving prepositions away from the ends of sentences

Ernest Gowers *Plain Words* (1948) 'Troubles with Prepositions'

3 Naval tradition? Monstrous. Nothing but rum, sodomy, prayers, and the lash.
often quoted as, 'rum, sodomy, and the lash', as in Peter Gretton Former Naval Person *(1968)*

Harold Nicolson diary, 17 August 1950

4 The candle in that great turnip has gone out.
*in reply to the comment 'One never hears of **Baldwin** nowadays—he might as well be dead'*

Harold Nicolson diary, 17 August 1950

5 The object of Parliament is to substitute argument for fisticuffs.

speech in the House of Commons, 6 June 1951

6 When the English history of the first quarter of the twentieth century is written, it will be seen that the greater part of our fortunes in peace and in war were shaped by this one man.
*of **Lloyd George***

in *Evening Standard* 4 October 1951

7 It is an error to believe that the world began when any particular party or statesman got into office. It has all been going on quite a long time.

speech at the Guildhall, London, 9 November 1951

8 A modest man who has much to be modest about.
*of Clement **Attlee***

in *Chicago Sunday Tribune Magazine of Books* 27 June 1954

9 I am prepared to meet my Maker. Whether my Maker is prepared for the great ordeal of meeting me is another matter.

at a news conference in Washington in 1954

10 To jaw-jaw is always better than to war-war.

speech at the White House, 26 June 1954

11 It was the nation and the race dwelling all round the globe that had the lion's heart. I had the luck to be called upon to give the roar.

speech at Westminster Hall, 30 November 1954

12 I still have the ideas, Walter, but I can't find the words to clothe them.
to Walter Monckton

Tony Benn diary, 15 December 1956

*of Lord **Montgomery**:*
13 In defeat unbeatable: in victory unbearable.

Edward Marsh *Ambrosia and Small Beer* (1964)

*of **Balfour**'s moving from **Asquith**'s Cabinet to that of **Lloyd George**:*
14 Like a powerful graceful cat walking delicately and unsoiled across a rather muddy street.

Great Contemporaries (1937)

*of the career of Lord **Curzon**:*
15 The morning had been golden; the noontide was bronze; and the evening lead. But all were solid, and each was polished till it shone after its fashion.

Great Contemporaries (1937)

16 No part of the education of a politician is more indispensable than the fighting of elections.

Great Contemporaries (1937)

when taking the entrance examination for Harrow, Churchill's answer paper consisted of his own name and a bracketed figure 1 for the first question:

1 It was from these slender indications of scholarship that Mr Welldon drew the conclusion that I was worthy to pass into Harrow. It is very much to his credit.

My Early Life (1930)

2 Headmasters have powers at their disposal with which Prime Ministers have never yet been invested.

My Early Life (1930)

3 I am biased in favour of boys learning English. I would make them all learn English: and then I would let the clever ones learn Latin as an honour, and Greek as a treat.

My Early Life (1930)

4 Mr Gladstone read Homer for fun, which I thought served him right.

My Early Life (1930)

5 It may be that vengeance is sweet, and that the gods forbade vengeance to men because they reserved for themselves so delicious and intoxicating a drink. But no one should drain the cup to the bottom. The dregs are often filthy-tasting.

The River War (1899)

6 In war: resolution. In defeat: defiance. In victory: magnanimity. In peace: goodwill.

The Second World War vol. 1 (1948) epigraph, which according to Edward Marsh in *A Number of People* (1939), occurred to Churchill shortly after the conclusion of the First World War

7 The loyalties which centre upon number one are enormous. If he trips he must be sustained. If he makes mistakes they must be covered. If he sleeps he must not be wantonly disturbed. If he is no good he must be pole-axed. But this last extreme process cannot be carried out every day; and certainly not in the days just after he has been chosen.

The Second World War vol. 2 (1949)

8 It may almost be said, 'Before Alamein we never had a victory. After Alamein we never had a defeat.'

The Second World War (1951) vol. 4

9 I did not suffer from any desire to be relieved of my responsibilities. All I wanted was compliance with my wishes after reasonable discussion.

The Second World War (1951) vol. 4

10 I do not like elections, but it is in my many elections that I have learnt to know and honour the people of this island. They are good through and through.

Thoughts and Adventures (1932)

of the General Election of 1922:
11 In the twinkling of an eye I found myself without an office, without a seat, without a party, and without an appendix.

Thoughts and Adventures (1932)

of the qualifications desirable in a prospective politician:
12 The ability to foretell what is going to happen tomorrow, next week, next month, and next year. And to have the ability afterwards to explain why it didn't happen.

B. Adler *Churchill Wit* (1965)

13 As to freedom of the press, why should any man be allowed to buy a printing press and disseminate pernicious opinions calculated to embarrass the government?

Piers Brendon *Winston Churchill* (1984)

of his recurring depression:
14 Black dog is back again.

attributed

15 An empty taxi arrived at 10 Downing Street, and when the door was opened Attlee got out.
    attributed to Churchill, but strongly repudiated by him

Kenneth Harris *Attlee* (1982)

1 Feed a bee on royal jelly, and it becomes a queen.   attributed
   on Attlee's showing unexpected authority as Prime Minister

   *of Stanley **Baldwin**:*
2 He occasionally stumbled over the truth, but hastily picked   attributed
   himself up and hurried on as if nothing had happened.

3 I am fond of pigs. Dogs look up to us. Cats look down on us.   Martin Gilbert *Never Despair*
   Pigs treat us as equals.   (1988); attributed

4 I have taken more out of alcohol than alcohol has taken out   Quentin Reynolds *By Quentin*
   of me.   *Reynolds* (1964)

5 I know of no case where a man added to his dignity by   attributed
   standing on it.

6 If you have ten thousand regulations you destroy all respect   attributed
   for the law.

7 In the course of my life I have often had to eat my words,   W. Manchester *The Caged Lion*
   and I must confess that I have always found it a wholesome   (1988)
   diet.

8 Most wars in history have been avoided simply by   J. K. Galbraith *A Life in Our Times*
   postponing them.   (1981)

9 A sheep in sheep's clothing.   Lord Home *The Way the Wind*
   *of Clement **Attlee***   *Blows* (1976)

10 Take away that pudding—it has no theme.   Lord Home *The Way the Wind*
          Blows (1976)

11 There but for the grace of God, goes God.   P. Brendon *Churchill* (1984)
   of Stafford Cripps

   of Alfred Bossom:
12 Who is this man whose name is neither one thing nor the   attributed
   other?

Count Galeazzo Ciano 1903–44
Italian fascist politician; son-in-law of Mussolini

13 Victory has a hundred fathers, but defeat is an orphan.   diary, 9 September 1942 (literally
          'no-one wants to recognise defeat
          as his own')

Cicero (Marcus Tullius Cicero) 106–43 BC
Roman orator and statesman
on Cicero: see **Plutarch** 291:4, **Stevenson** 347:9

14 For he delivers his opinions as though he were living in   *Ad Atticum*
   Plato's Republic rather than among the dregs of Romulus.
   of M. Porcius Cato, the Younger

15 *Salus populi suprema est lex.*   *De Legibus*; see **Selden** 317:5
   The good of the people is the chief law.

16 Let war yield to peace, laurels to paeans.   *De Officiis*

17 In men of the highest character and noblest genius there is   *De Officis*
   to be found an insatiable desire for honour, command,
   power, and glory.

18 The sinews of war, unlimited money.   *Fifth Philippic*

19 *O tempora, O mores!*   *In Catilinam*
   Oh, the times! Oh, the manners!

1 *Civis Romanus sum.*
  I am a Roman citizen.

In Verrem

2 Laws are silent in time of war.

Pro Milone

3 The young man should be praised, decorated, and got rid of.
  of Octavian, the future Emperor **Augustus**

referred to in a letter from
Decimus Brutus to Cicero; *Epistulae
ad Familiares*

Edward Hyde, Lord Clarendon 1609–74

English statesman and historian

4 Without question, when he first drew the sword, he threw
  away the scabbard.
  of John Hampden

The History of the Rebellion (1703)
vol. 3

5 He had a head to contrive, a tongue to persuade, and a
  hand to execute any mischief.
  of Hampden

The History of the Rebellion (1703)
vol. 3

6 He . . . would, with a shrill and sad accent, ingeminate the
  word *Peace*, *Peace*.
  of **Falkland**

The History of the Rebellion (1703)
vol. 3

7 So enamoured on peace that he would have been glad the
  King should have bought it at any price.
  of **Falkland**

The History of the Rebellion (1703)
vol. 3

8 He will be looked upon by posterity as a brave bad man.
  of **Cromwell**

The History of the Rebellion (1703)
vol. 6

Alan Clark 1928–99

British Conservative politician
on Clark: see **Campbell** 67:4, **Parris** 284:4

9 In the end we are all sacked and it's always awful. It is as
  inevitable as death following life. If you are elevated there
  comes a day when you are demoted. Even Prime Ministers.

diary, 21 June 1983

10 Give a civil servant a good case and he'll wreck it with
  clichés, bad punctuation, double negatives and convoluted
  apology.

diary, 22 July 1983

11 Like most Chief Whips he knew who the shits were.
  of Michael Jopling

diary, 17 June 1987

12 There's nothing so improves the mood of the Party as the
  imminent execution of a senior colleague.

diary, 13 July 1990

13 There are no true friends in politics. We are all sharks
  circling, and waiting, for traces of blood to appear in the
  water.

diary, 30 November 1990

14 Our old friend economical . . . with the *actualité*.
  *under cross-examination at the Old Bailey during the Matrix
  Churchill case*

in *Independent* 10 November 1992;
see **Armstrong** 14:5

15 Safe is spelled D-U-L-L. Politics has got to be a fun activity.
  *on being selected as parliamentary candidate for Kensington and
  Chelsea, 24 January 1997*

in *Daily Telegraph* 25 January 1997

16 If I can comport myself with the dignity and competence of
  Ms Mo Mowlam, I shall be very satisfied.
  after surgery for a brain tumour

in *Sunday Times* 6 June 1999
'Talking Heads'

1 Alan died suddenly at Saltwood on Sunday 5th September. He said he would like it to be stated that he regarded himself as having gone to join Tom and the other dogs.

announcement in The Times 8 September 1999

Kenneth Clarke 1940–
British Conservative politician

2 Tell your kids to get their scooters off my lawn.
   allegedly said to the Party Chairman, Brian Mawhinney; see **Wilson** 385:6

in Guardian 7 December 1996

3 The Government doesn't have a hostile attitude to the single currency. It was a slip of the tongue.
   in response to a statement by fellow Conservative Malcolm Rifkind, 19 February 1997

in Guardian 20 February 1997

4 I do not wear a bleeper. I can't speak in soundbites. I refuse to repeat slogans. . . . I hate focus groups. I absolutely hate image consultants.

in New Statesman 12 February 1999

Karl von Clausewitz 1780–1831
Prussian soldier and military theorist

5 War is nothing but a continuation of politics with the admixture of other means.
   commonly rendered 'War is the continuation of politics by other means'

On War (1832–4)

Henry Clay 1777–1852
American politician
on Clay: see **Glascock** 149:3, **Jackson** 183:7

6 I am for resistance by the *sword*. No man in the nation desires peace more than I. But I prefer the troubled ocean of war . . . to the tranquil, putrescent pool of ignominious peace.

speech in the US Senate on the Macon Bill, 22 February 1810

7 If you wish to avoid foreign collision, you had better abandon the ocean.

in the House of Representatives, 22 January 1812

8 The gentleman [Josiah Quincy] can not have forgotten his own sentiment, uttered even on the floor of this House, 'peaceably if we can, forcibly if we must'.

speech in Congress, 8 January 1813

9 [Andrew Jackson] is ignorant, passionate, hypocritical, corrupt, and easily swayed by the basest men who surround him.

letter to Francis T. Brooke, 2 August 1833

10 The arts of power and its minions are the same in all countries and in all ages. It marks a victim; denounces it; and excites the public odium and the public hatred, to conceal its own abuses and encroachments.

speech in the Senate, 14 March 1834

11 It has been my invariable rule to do all for the Union. If any man wants the key of my heart, let him take the key of the Union, and that is the key to my heart.

speech in Norfolk, 22 April 1844

12 I had rather be right than be President.

to Senator Preston of South Carolina, 1839

13 I have heard something said about allegiance to the South. I know no South, no North, no East, no West, to which I owe any allegiance . . . The Union, sir, is my country.

speech in the US Senate, 1848

Philip 'Tubby' Clayton 1885–1972

Australian-born British clergyman, founder of Toc H

1 CHAIRMAN: What is service?
   CANDIDATE: The rent we pay for our room on earth.
   *admission ceremony of Toc H, a society founded after the First
   World War to provide Christian fellowship and social service*

Tresham Lever *Clayton of Toc H*
(1971)

Eldridge Cleaver 1935–98

American political activist

2 What we're saying today is that you're either part of the
  solution or you're part of the problem.

speech in San Francisco, 1968; R.
Scheer *Eldridge Cleaver, Post Prison
Writings and Speeches* (1969)

John Cleese 1939–
and Connie Booth

British comedy writer and actor; British comedy actress

3 They're Germans. Don't mention the war.

Fawlty Towers 'The Germans' (BBC
TV programme, 1975)

Sarah Norcliffe Cleghorn 1876–1959

4 The golf-links lie so near the mill
  That almost every day
  The labouring children can look out
  And watch the men at play.

'For Some Must Watch, While—'
(1914)

Georges Clemenceau 1841–1929

French statesman; Prime Minister of France, 1906–9, 1917–20
on Clemenceau: see **Keynes** 200:7, **Lloyd George** 223:3

5 My home policy: I wage war; my foreign policy: I wage war.
  All the time I wage war.

speech to French Chamber of
Deputies, 8 March 1918

  *to André Tardieu, on being asked why he always gave in to Lloyd
  George at the Paris Peace Conference, 1918*
6 What do you expect when I'm between two men of whom
  one [Lloyd George] thinks he is Napoleon and the other
  [Woodrow Wilson] thinks he is Jesus Christ?

Harold Nicolson letter, 20 May
1919

7 It is easier to make war than to make peace.

speech at Verdun, 20 July 1919

8 War is too serious a matter to entrust to military men.

attributed to Clemenceau, but also
to Briand and Talleyrand; see also
de Gaulle 105:5

  on seeing a pretty girl on his eightieth birthday:
9 Oh, to be seventy again!

James Agate diary, 19 April 1938;
has also been attributed to Oliver
Wendell **Holmes** Jr.

Grover Cleveland 1837–1908

American Democratic statesman, 22nd and 24th President of the
US, 1885–9 and 1893–7
on Cleveland: see **Bragg** 50:3

1 Your every voter, as surely as your chief magistrate, exercises a public trust.

'public office is a public trust' was used as the motto of the Cleveland administration

inaugural address, 4 March 1885

2 I have considered the pension list of the republic a roll of honour.

veto of Dependent Pension Bill, 5 July 1888

3 The lessons of paternalism ought to be unlearned and the better lesson taught that, while the people should patriotically and cheerfully support their government, its functions do not include the support of the people.

inaugural address, 4 March 1893

Harlan Cleveland 1918–

American government official

4 The revolution of rising expectations.

phrase coined, 1950; see Arthur Schlesinger *A Thousand Days* (1965)

Hillary Rodham Clinton 1947– ⌐

American Democratic politician, wife of Bill **Clinton**,
First Lady of the US, 1993–2001

5 I am not standing by my man, like Tammy Wynette. I am sitting here because I love him, I respect him, and I honour what he's been through and what we've been through together.

interview on *60 Minutes*, CBS-TV, 27 January 1992

6 I could have stayed home and baked cookies and had teas. But what I decided was to fulfil my profession, which I entered before my husband was in public life.

comment on questions raised by rival Democratic contender Edmund G. Brown Jr.; in *Albany Times-Union* 17 March 1992

7 The great story here . . . is this vast right-wing conspiracy that has been conspiring against my husband since the day he announced for president.

interview on *Today* (NBC television), 27 January 1998

8 A hard dog to keep on the porch.
   on her husband

in *Guardian* 2 August 1999

William Jefferson ('Bill') Clinton 1946– ⌐

American Democratic statesman; 42nd President of the US,
1993–2001
on Clinton: see **Jackson** 183:11

9 I experimented with marijuana a time or two. And I didn't like it, and I didn't inhale.

in *Washington Post* 30 March 1992

10 The comeback kid!
   description of himself after coming second in the New Hampshire primary in the 1992 presidential election (since 1952, no presidential candidate had won the election without first winning in New Hampshire)

Michael Barone and Grant Ujifusa *The Almanac of American Politics* 1994

11 The urgent question of our time is whether we can make change our friend and not our enemy.

inaugural address, 1993

1 I did not have sexual relations with that woman.

in a television interview, Daily Telegraph (electronic edition) 27 January 1998

2 Peace is no longer a dream. It is a reality.
  of the Northern Ireland referendum on the Good Friday agreement

in Sunday Times 24 May 1998

3 I did have a relationship with Ms Lewinsky that was not appropriate. In fact, it was wrong.
  broadcast to the American people, 18 August 1998

in Times 19 August 1998

4 It depends on what the meaning of 'is' is.
  videotaped evidence to the grand jury; tapes broadcast 21 September 1998

in Guardian 22 September 1998

5 I believe any person who asks for forgiveness has to be prepared to give it.

statement after being acquitted by the Senate, 12 February 1999

6 Today we are learning the language in which God created life.
  on the deciphering of 90% of the human genome

in Independent 27 June 2000

Lord Clive 1725-74

British general; Governor of Bengal

7 By God, Mr Chairman, at this moment I stand astonished at my own moderation!
  reply during Parliamentary cross-examination, 1773

G. R. Gleig The Life of Robert, First Lord Clive (1848)

while attempting to take his own life, his pistol twice failed to fire:
8 I feel that I am reserved for some end or other.

G. R. Gleig The Life of Robert, First Lord Clive (1848)

Thomas W. Cobb

American politician

9 If you persist, the Union will be dissolved. You have kindled a fire which all the waters of the ocean cannot put out, which seas of blood can only extinguish.
  to James Tallmadge, on his amendment to the bill to admit Missouri to the Union as a slave state in 1820

Robert V. Remini Henry Clay (1991)

William Cobbett 1762-1835

English political reformer and radical journalist

10 Nouns of number, or multitude, such as Mob, Parliament, Rabble, House of Commons, Regiment, Court of King's Bench, Den of Thieves, and the like.

English Grammar (1817) letter 17 'Syntax as Relating to Pronouns'

11 From a very early age, I had imbibed the opinion, that it was every man's duty to do all that lay in his power to leave his country as good as he had found it.

Political Register 22 December 1832

12 But what is to be the fate of the great wen of all? The monster, called . . . 'the metropolis of the empire'?
  of London

Rural Rides: The Kentish Journal 5 January 1822

Claud Cockburn 1904–81

British left-wing journalist

1 I am prepared to believe that a lot of the people I had cast as principal figures were really mere cat's-paws. But then a cat's-paw is a cat's-paw and must expect to be treated as part of the cat.

    of his writing about the 'Cliveden Set'

Crossing the Line (1958)

2 Believe nothing until it has been officially denied.

    advice frequently given to the young Claud Cockburn

In Time of Trouble (1956)

George M. Cohan 1878–1942

American actor-manager and dramatist

3 Over there, over there,
Send the word, send the word over there
That the Yanks are coming, the Yanks are coming,
The drums rum-tumming everywhere.
So prepare, say a prayer,
Send the word, send the word to beware.
We'll be over, we're coming over
And we won't come back till it's over, over there.

'Over There' (1917 song)

Edward Coke 1552–1634

English jurist

4 Magna Charta is such a fellow, that he will have no sovereign.

    on the Lords' Amendment to the Petition of Right, 17 May 1628

J. Rushworth *Historical Collections* (1659) vol. 1

Samuel Taylor Coleridge 1772–1834

English poet, critic, and philosopher

5 State policy, a cyclops with one eye, and that in the back of the head!

On the Constitution of the Church and State (1839)

6 In politics, what begins in fear usually ends in folly.

Table Talk (1835) 5 October 1830

Michael Collins 1890–1922

Irish nationalist leader and politician; on the death of Arthur **Griffith** in 1922, he became head of state, but was shot in an ambush ten days later

7 That volley which we have just heard is the only speech which it is proper to make over the grave of a dead Fenian.

    at the funeral of Thomas Ashe, who had died in prison while on hunger strike

at Glasnevin cemetery, 30th September 1917

8 Think—what I have got for Ireland? Something which she has wanted these past seven hundred years. Will anyone be satisfied at the bargain? Will anyone? I tell you this—early this morning I signed my death warrant. I thought at the time how odd, how ridiculous—a bullet may just as well have done the job five years ago.

    on signing the treaty establishing the Irish Free State; he was shot from ambush in the following year

letter, 6 December 1921

on arriving at Dublin Castle for the handover by British forces on 16
January 1922, and being told that he was seven minutes late:
1 We've been waiting 700 years, you can have the seven
minutes.

Tim Pat Coogan *Michael Collins*
(1990); attributed

2 Because of his sincerity, I would forgive him anything.
*after the death of Cathal **Brugha**, July 1922*

Robert Kee *Ourselves Alone* (1976)

3 My own fellow-countrymen won't kill me.
before leaving for Cork where he was ambushed and killed, 20
August 1922

James Mackay *Michael Collins*
(1996)

John Robert Colombo 1936–

Canadian writer

4 Canada could have enjoyed:
English government,
French culture,
and American know-how.

Instead it ended up with:
English know-how,
French government,
and American culture.

'O Canada' (1965)

Henry Steele Commager 1902–

American historian

5 It was observed half a century ago that what is a stone wall
to a layman, to a corporate lawyer is a triumphant arch.
Much the same might be said of civil rights and freedoms.
To the layman the Bill of Rights seems to be a stone wall
against the misuse of power. But in the hands of a
congressional committee, or often enough of a judge, it
turns out to be so full of exceptions and qualifications that it
might be a whole series of arches.

'The Right to Dissent' in *Current
History* October 1955; see below

> A law, Hinnissey, that might look like a wall to you or me
> wud look like a triumphal arch to th'expeeryenced eye iv
> a lawyer.

Peter Finley Dunne (1867–1936)
'Mr Dooley on the Power of the
Press' in *American Magazine* 1906

Barber B. Conable Jr. 1922–

American Republican politician and banker

6 I guess we have found the smoking pistol, haven't we?
*on hearing a tape of President **Nixon**'s discussion with H. R.*
***Haldeman**, on 23 June 1972, as to how the FBI's investigation*
of the Watergate burglary could be limited

Nigel Rees *Brewer's Quotations*
(1994)

Gerry Conlon 1954–

first member of the Guildford Four to be released from prison

7 The life sentence goes on. It's like a runaway train that you
can't just get off.
of life after his conviction was quashed by the Court of Appeal

in *Irish Post* 13 September 1997

James M. Connell see Songs and ballads 343:1

Sean Connery 1930–
Scottish actor

1 It is Scotland's rightful heritage that its people should create a modern Parliament . . . This entire issue is above and beyond any political party.
of Scottish devolution, in the Referendum campaign

speech in Edinburgh, 7 September 1997; in *Scottish Daily Record* 8 September 1997

2 We have waited nearly 300 years. My hope is that it will evolve with dignity and integrity and it will truly reflect the new voice of Scotland. My position on Scotland has never changed in 30-odd years. Scotland should be nothing less than an equal of other nations of the world.

in *Daily Telegraph* 27 April 1999

Cyril Connolly 1903–74
English writer

3 M is for Marx
And Movement of Masses
And Massing of Arses.
And Clashing of Classes.

'Where Engels Fears to Tread'

James Connolly 1868–1916
Irish labour leader; executed after the Easter Rising, 1916

4 Apostles of freedom are ever idolised when dead, but crucified when alive.

in *Workers' Republic* August 1898

5 The worker is the slave of capitalist society, the female worker is the slave of that slave.

The Re-conquest of Ireland (1915)

6 The time for Ireland's battle is NOW, the place for Ireland's battle is HERE.

in *The Workers' Republic* 22 January 1916

7 I can always guarantee that the Irish Citizen Army will fight, but I cannot guarantee that it will be on time.

Diana Norman *Terrible Beauty* (1987)

8 The man who is bubbling over with love and affection for 'Ireland' and can pass unmoved through our streets and witness all the sorrow and suffering . . . without burning to end it, is a fraud and a liar in his heart, no matter how much he loves that combination of chemical elements he is pleased to call 'Ireland'.

Desmond Ryan *James Connolly* (1924)

Joseph Conrad 1857–1924
Polish-born English novelist

9 The terrorist and the policeman both come from the same basket.

The Secret Agent (1907)

10 The scrupulous and the just, the noble, humane, and devoted natures; the unselfish and the intelligent may begin a movement—but it passes away from them. They are not the leaders of a revolution. They are its victims.

Under Western Eyes (1911)

Constitution of the United States 1787

the first ten amendments are known as the Bill of Rights

1 Congress shall make no law respecting an establishment of religion, or prohibiting the free exercise thereof; or abridging the freedom of speech, or of the press; or the right of the people peaceably to assemble, and to petition the government for a redress of grievances.

First Amendment (1791)

2 A well-regulated militia, being necessary to the security of a free State, the right of the people to keep and bear arms, shall not be infringed.

Constitution of the United States (Second Amendment, 1791)

3 Excessive bail shall not be required, nor excessive fines imposed, nor cruel and unusual punishment inflicted.

Eighth Amendment (1791)

A. J. Cook 1885–1931

English labour leader; Secretary of the Miners' Federation of Great Britain, 1924–31

4 Not a penny off the pay, not a second on the day.
   often quoted with 'minute' substituted for 'second'

speech at York, 3 April 1926

Peter Cook 1937–95

British satirist and performer

*sketch satirizing the Prime Minister, Harold **Macmillan**:*
5 I have recently been travelling round the world—on your behalf, and at your expense—visiting some of the chaps with whom I hope to be shaping your future. I went first to Germany, and there I spoke with the German Foreign Minister, Herr . . . Herr and there, and we exchanged many frank words in our respective languages.

Beyond the Fringe (1961)

Robin Cook 1946–

British Labour politician, Foreign Secretary from 1997

6 Our foreign policy must have an ethical dimension and must support the demands of other people for the democratic rights on which we insist for ourselves.
   mission statement by the new Foreign Secretary, 12 May 1997

in *Times* 13 May 1997

Calvin Coolidge 1872–1933

American Republican statesman, 30th President of the US 1923–9
*on Coolidge: see **Anonymous** 11:10, **Mencken** 248:13, **Parker** 282:9*

7 There is no right to strike against the public safety by anybody, anywhere, any time.

telegram to Samuel Gompers, 14 September 1919

8 Civilization and profits go hand in hand.

speech in New York, 27 November 1920

9 The chief business of the American people is business.

speech in Washington, 17 January 1925

10 They hired the money, didn't they?
   on the subject of war debts incurred by England and others

John H. McKee *Coolidge: Wit and Wisdom* (1933)

account (probably apocryphal) supposedly given by Coolidge to his wife of what a preacher had said about sin:

1 He was against it.

John H. McKee *Coolidge: Wit and Wisdom* (1933)

2 Nothing is easier than spending the public money. It does not appear to belong to anybody. The temptation is overwhelming to bestow it on somebody.

attributed

Francis M. Cornford 1874–1943
English classical scholar

3 Every public action, which is not customary, either is wrong, or, if it is right, is a dangerous precedent. It follows that nothing should ever be done for the first time.

Microcosmographia Academica (1908)

of propaganda:
4 That branch of the art of lying which consists in very nearly deceiving your friends without quite deceiving your enemies.

Microcosmographia Academica (1922 ed.)

Coronation Service

5 We present you with this Book, the most valuable thing that this world affords. Here is wisdom; this is the royal Law; these are the lively Oracles of God.

'The Presenting of the Holy Bible'; L. G. Wickham Legge *English Coronation Records* (1901)

Thomas Coventry 1578–1640
English judge

6 The dominion of the sea, as it is an ancient and undoubted right of the crown of England, so it is the best security of the land . . . The wooden walls are the best walls of this kingdom.

speech to the Judges, 17 June 1635

Lord Cranborne 1946–
British Conservative peer, former Leader in the Lords

7 [I was sacked for] running in like an ill-trained spaniel.
 of his independent negotiation with the government on Lords reform, and subsequent dismissal by William Hague

in *Daily Telegraph* 3 December 1998

8 There was this odd mixture of misery and the limpet—the miserable limpet if you like—which was a great inhibition to his premiership.

on *The Major Years* pt 3, BBC1, 25 October 1999

Crazy Horse (Ta-Sunko-Witko) c.1849–77
Oglala Sioux leader

9 One does not sell the earth upon which the people walk.

Dee Brown *Bury My Heart at Wounded Knee* (1970) ch. 12

Edith Cresson 1934–
French politician and European Commissioner

10 *Je ne regrette rien.*
 I have no regrets.
 on the inquiry into fraud at the European Commission

in an interview, 16 March 1999; 'Non, je ne regrette rien' was the title of a song (1960) by Michel Vaucaire, sung by Edith Piaf

1 Perhaps I have been a little careless.

after the appearance of the report into fraud at the European Commission

in an interview, 16 March 1999

Michel Guillaume Jean de Crèvecoeur

1735–1813

French-born immigrant to America

2 What then is the American, this new man? He is either a European, or the descendant of a European, hence that strange mixture of blood, which you will find in no other country . . . Here individuals of all nations are melted into a new race of men, whose labours and posterity will one day cause great changes in the world.

Letters from an American Farmer (1782)

Ivor Crewe 1945–

British political scientist

3 The British public has always displayed a healthy cynicism of MPs. They have taken it for granted that MPs are self-serving impostors and hypocrites who put party before country and self before party.

addressing the Nolan inquiry into standards in public life

in *Guardian* 18 January 1995

George Washington Crile 1864–1943

American surgeon and physiologist

4 France . . . a nation of forty millions with a deep-rooted grievance and an iron curtain at its frontier.

A Mechanistic View of War and Peace (1915)

Julian Critchley 1930–2000

British Conservative politician and journalist

5 He could not see a parapet without ducking beneath it.

of Michael **Heseltine**

Heseltine (1987)

6 The only safe pleasure for a parliamentarian is a bag of boiled sweets.

in *Listener* 10 June 1982

7 She cannot see an institution without hitting it with her handbag.

of Margaret **Thatcher**

in *The Times* 21 June 1982

8 Disloyalty is the secret weapon of the Tory Party.

in *Observer* 11 November 1990; see **Kilmuir** 202:11

Oliver Cromwell 1599–1658

English soldier, politician, and general; Lord Protector from 1653 *see also* **Last words** 213:5, **Misquotations** 255:8

on being asked by Lord **Falkland** *what he would have done if the Grand Remonstrance of 1641 against the King had not passed:*

9 I would have sold all I had the next morning, and never have seen England more.

Clarendon *History of the Rebellion* (1826)

10 A few honest men are better than numbers.

letter to William Spring, September 1643

11 I would rather have a plain russet-coated captain that knows what he fights for, and loves what he knows, than that which you call 'a gentleman' and is nothing else.

letter to William Spring, September 1643

1 Cruel necessity.
   on the execution of **Charles I**

Joseph Spence *Anecdotes* (1820)

2 For that which you mention concerning liberty of
   conscience, I meddle not with any man's conscience.
   letter to the Governor of Ross in Ireland, 19 October 1649

W. C. Abbott *Writings and Speeches of Oliver Cromwell* (1939) vol. 3

3 I beseech you, in the bowels of Christ, think it possible you
   may be mistaken.

letter to the General Assembly of the Kirk of Scotland, 3 August 1650

4 The dimensions of this mercy are above my thoughts. It is,
   for aught I know, a crowning mercy.

letter to William **Lenthall**, Speaker of the Parliament of England, 4 September 1651

5 You have sat too long here for any good you have been
   doing. Depart, I say, and let us have done with you. In the
   name of God, go!
   *addressing the Rump Parliament, 20 April 1653 (oral tradition;
   quoted by Leo* **Amery** *to Neville* **Chamberlain** *in the House of
   Commons, 7 May 1940)*

Bulstrode Whitelock *Memorials of the English Affairs* (1732 ed.)

6 Take away that fool's bauble, the mace.
   at the dismissal of the Rump Parliament, 20 April 1653

Bulstrode Whitelock *Memorials of the English Affairs* (1732 ed.); see **Misquotations** 255:8

7 It's a maxim not to be despised, 'Though peace be made, yet
   it's interest that keeps peace.'

speech to Parliament, 4 September 1654

8 Necessity hath no law. Feigned necessities, imaginary
   necessities . . . are the greatest cozenage that men can put
   upon the Providence of God, and make pretences to break
   known rules by.

speech to Parliament, 12 September 1654

9 Your poor army, those poor contemptible men, came up
   hither.

speech to Parliament, 21 April 1657

10 You have accounted yourselves happy on being environed
   with a great ditch from all the world besides.

speech to Parliament, 25 January 1658

11 Hell or Connaught.
   *summary of the choice offered to the Catholic population of
   Ireland, transported to the western counties to make room for
   settlers*

traditionally attributed

12 None climbs so high as he who knows not whither he is
   going.

attributed

13 There is no one I am more at a loss how to manage than
   that Marcus Tullius Cicero, the little man with three names.
   of Anthony Ashley Cooper, Lord **Shaftesbury**

B. Martyn and Dr Kippis *The Life of the First Earl of Shaftesbury* (1836)

Anthony Crosland 1918–77

British Labour politician; Foreign Secretary 1976–7

14 Total abstinence and a good filing system are not now the
   right signposts to the socialist Utopia; or at least, if they are,
   some of us will fall by the wayside.

The Future of Socialism (1956)

15 Harold knows best. Harold is a bastard, but he is a genius.
   He's like Odysseus. Odysseus was a bastard, but he managed
   to steer the ship between Scylla and Charybdis.
   on Harold **Wilson**

Susan Crosland *Tony Crosland* (1982)

1 If it's the last thing I do, I'm going to destroy every fucking grammar school in England. And Wales, and Northern Ireland.
  c.1965, while Secretary of State for Education and Science

Susan Crosland *Tony Crosland* (1982)

2 The party's over.
  cutting back central government's support for rates, as Minister of the Environment in the 1970's

Anthony Sampson *The Changing Anatomy of Britain* (1982)

3 In the blood of the socialist there should always run a trace of the anarchist and the libertarian, and not too much of the prig and the prude.

Susan Crosland *Tony Crosland* (1982)

Richard Crossman 1907–74

British Labour politician
on Crossman: see **Dalton** 100:8

4 While there is death there is hope.
  on the death of Hugh **Gaitskell** *in 1963*

Tam Dalyell *Dick Crossman* (1989)

5 The Civil Service is profoundly deferential—'Yes, Minister! No, Minister! If you wish it, Minister!'

Diaries of a Cabinet Minister vol. 1 (1975) 22 October 1964

6 [To strip away] the thick masses of foliage which we call the myth of democracy.

introduction to *Diaries of a Cabinet Minister* vol. 1 (1975)

e. e. cummings 1894–1962

American poet

7 a politician is an arse upon
which everyone has sat except a man.

1 x 1 (1944) no. 10

Mario Cuomo 1932–

American Democratic politician, former Governor of New York

8 You campaign in poetry. You govern in prose.

in *New Republic*, Washington, DC, 8 April 1985

John Philpot Curran 1750–1817

Irish judge

9 The condition upon which God hath given liberty to man is eternal vigilance; which condition if he break, servitude is at once the consequence of his crime, and the punishment of his guilt.

speech on the right of election of the Lord Mayor of Dublin, 10 July 1790; see **Demosthenes** 106:1

of Robert **Peel**'s *smile:*
10 Like the silver plate on a coffin.

quoted by Daniel **O'Connell** in the House of Commons, 26 February 1835

Lord Curzon 1859–1925

British Conservative politician; Viceroy of India 1898–1905
on Curzon: **Anonymous** 10:1, **Beaverbrook** 29:10, 29:12; **Churchill** 84:15, **Nehru** 265:12

11 Other countries have but one capital—Paris, Berlin, Madrid. Great Britain has a series of capitals all over the world, from Ottawa to Shanghai.

notebook, 1887; Kenneth Rose *Superior Person* (1969)

1 When a group of Cabinet Ministers begins to meet separately and to discuss independent action, the death-tick is audible in the rafters.

in November 1922, shortly before the fall of **Lloyd George**'s *Coalition Government*

David Gilmour *Curzon* (1994)

2 Not even a public figure. A man of no experience. And of the utmost insignificance.

of Stanley **Baldwin**, *appointed Prime Minister in 1923 in succession to* **Bonar Law**

Harold Nicolson *Curzon: the Last Phase* (1934)

3 Gentlemen do not take soup at luncheon.

E. L. Woodward *Short Journey* (1942)

4 I never knew that the lower classes had such white skins.

supposedly said when watching troops bathing during the First World War

Kenneth Rose *Superior Person* (1969)

Astolphe Louis Léonard, Marquis de Custine 1790–1857

French author and traveller

5 This empire, vast as it is, is only a prison to which the emperor holds the key.

of Russia

La Russie en 1839; at Peterhof, 23 July 1839

6 Whoever has really seen Russia will find himself content to live anywhere else. It is always good to know that a society exists where no happiness is possible because, by a law of nature, man cannot be happy unless he is free.

La Russie en 1839; at Peterhof, 23 July 1839; conclusion

Richard J. Daley 1902–76

American Democratic politician and Mayor of Chicago

7 The policeman isn't there to create disorder; the policeman is there to preserve disorder.

to the press, on the riots during the Democratic Convention in 1968

Milton N. Rakove *Don't Make No Waves: Don't Back No Losers* (1975)

Hugh Dalton 1887–1962

British Labour politician
on Dalton: see **Anonymous** 11:7, **Birch** 40:10

8 I view this able and energetic man with some detachment. He is loyal to his own career but only incidentally to anything or anyone else.

of Richard **Crossman**

diary, 17 September 1941

Tam Dalyell 1932–

Scottish-born Labour politician

9 Under the new Bill, shall I still be able to vote on many matters in relation to West Bromwich but not West Lothian, as I was under the last Bill, and will my right hon. Friend [James Callaghan, MP for Cardiff] be able to vote on many matters in relation to Carlisle but not Cardiff?

formulation of the 'West Lothian question', identifying the constitutional anomaly that would arise if devolved assemblies were established for Scotland and for Wales but not for England

in the House of Commons, 3 November 1977

1 The West-Lothian-West-Bromwich problem pinpoints a basic design fault in the steering of the devolutionary coach which will cause it to crash into the side of the road.

in the House of Commons, 14 November 1977

2 I make no apology for returning yet again to the subject of the sinking of the *Belgrano*.
on the question of whether the Argentine cruiser Belgrano *had been a legitimate target in the Falklands War*

in the House of Commons, 13 May 1983

George Dangerfield 1904–86
British historian

3 To reform the House of Lords [in 1910] meant to set down in writing a Constitution which for centuries had remained happily unwritten, to conjure a great ghost into the narrow and corruptible flesh of a code.

The Strange Death of Liberal England (1936)

Samuel Daniel 1563–1619
English poet and playwright

4   Princes in this case
Do hate the traitor, though they love the treason.

The Tragedy of Cleopatra (1594)

Georges Jacques Danton 1759–94
French revolutionary

5 *De l'audace, et encore de l'audace, et toujours de l'audace!*
Boldness, and again boldness, and always boldness!

speech to the Legislative Committee of General Defence, 2 September 1792

6 Thou wilt show my head to the people: it is worth showing.
to his executioner, 5 April 1794

Thomas Carlyle History of the French Revolution (1837) vol. 3

Bill Darnell
Canadian environmentalist

7 Make it a *green* peace.
at a meeting of the Don't Make a Wave Committee, which preceded the formation of Greenpeace

in Vancouver, 1970; Robert Hunter The Greenpeace Chronicle (1979); see **Hunter** 179:7

Clarence Darrow 1857–1938
American lawyer

8 When I was a boy I was told that anybody could become President. I'm beginning to believe it.

Irving Stone Clarence Darrow for the Defence (1941)

Harry Daugherty 1860–1941
American Republican supporter

9 Some twelve or fifteen men, worn out and bleary-eyed for lack of sleep, will sit down about two o'clock in the morning around a table in a smoke-filled room in some hotel and decide the nomination.
the way in which the Republican Party's presidential candidate for the 1920 would be selected if (as in fact happened) no clear nomination emerged from the convention; see **Simpson** 332:9

attributed (although subsequently denied by Daugherty); William Safire The New Language of Politics (1968)

Charles D'Avenant 1656–1714
English playwright and political economist

1 Custom, that unwritten law,
By which the people keep even kings in awe.

Circe (1677)

Ian Davidson 1950–
Scottish Labour politician

2 Anyone in the Labour Party hierarchy who believes that
new Labour is popular in Scotland should get out more.
*after Labour was beaten into third place in the Ayr by-election for
the Scottish Parliament*

in *Scotsman* 18 March 2000

Robertson Davies 1913–95
Canadian novelist

3 I see Canada as a country torn between a very northern,
rather extraordinary, mystical spirit which it fears and its
desire to present itself to the world as a Scotch banker.

The Enthusiasms of Robertson Davies
(1990)

Ron Davies 1946–
British Labour politician

4 It was a moment of madness for which I have subsequently
paid a very, very heavy price.
*of the episode on Clapham Common leading to his resignation as
Welsh Secretary*

interview with BBC Wales and HTV,
30 October 1998

5 We are what we are. We are all different, the products of
both our genes and our experiences.

personal statement to the House
of Commons, 2 November 1998

Jefferson Davis 1808–89
American statesman; President of the Confederate states 1861–5
on Davis: see **Yancey** 389:3

6 If the Confederacy fails, there should be written on its
tombstone: *Died of a Theory.*

in 1865; Geoffrey C. Ward *The Civil
War* (1991)

Thomas Davis 1814–45
Irish poet and nationalist

7 But the land of their heart's hope they never saw more,
For in far, foreign fields, from Dunkirk to Belgrade
Lie the soldiers and chiefs of the Irish Brigade.

'The Battle-Eve of the Brigade'
(1845)

8 Viva la the New Brigade!
Viva la the Old One, too!
Viva la, the Rose shall fade,
And the shamrock shine for ever new.

'Clare's Dragoons' (1845)

9 And then I prayed I yet might see
Our fetters rent in twain,
And Ireland, long a province, be
A Nation once again.

'A Nation Once Again' (1846)

10 But—hark!—some voice like thunder spake:
The West's awake! the West's awake!

'The West's Asleep' (1845); see
Robinson 303:13

11 The Wild Geese fly where others walk;
The Wild Geese do what others talk.

'When South Winds Blow' (1845)

1 If we live influenced by wind, and sun, and tree, and not by the passions and deeds of the past, we are a thriftless and hopeless people.

Literary and Historical Essays (1846)

Michael Davitt 1846–1905

Irish nationalist

2 An Englishman of the strongest type moulded for an Irish purpose.
   of Charles Stewart **Parnell**

The Fall of Feudalism in Ireland (1906)

Lord Dawson of Penn 1864–1945

British doctor; physician to King **George V**

3 The King's life is moving peacefully towards its close.
   bulletin, drafted on a menu card at Buckingham Palace on the eve of the king's death, 20 January 1936

Kenneth Rose *King George V* (1983)

John Dean 1938–

American lawyer and White House counsel during the Watergate affair

4 We have a cancer within, close to the Presidency, that is growing.

from the [Nixon] Presidential Transcripts, 21 March 1973

5 The White House is another world. Expediency is everything.

in *New York Post* 18 June 1973

Régis Debray 1940–

French Marxist theorist

6 International life is right-wing, like nature. The social contract is left-wing, like humanity.

Charles de Gaulle (1994)

Eugene Victor Debs 1855–1926

founder of the Socialist party of America

7 When great changes occur in history, when great principles are involved, as a rule the majority are wrong. The minority are right.
   speech at his trial for sedition in Cleveland, Ohio, 11 September 1918

Speeches (1928)

8 While there is a lower class, I am in it; while there is a criminal element, I am of it; while there is a soul in prison, I am not free.
   speech at his trial for sedition in Cleveland, Ohio, 11 September 1918

in *Liberator* November 1918

Stephen Decatur 1779–1820

American naval officer

9 Our country! In her intercourse with foreign nations, may she always be in the right; but our country, right or wrong.
   Decatur's toast at Norfolk, Virginia, April 1816

A. S. Mackenzie *Life of Stephen Decatur* (1846); see **Adams** 4:3

John de Chastelain 1937–

Canadian soldier and diplomat

1 The pike in the thatch is not quite the same as the surface-to-air missile in the thatch.
  on decommissioning in Northern Ireland

interview in *Daily Telegraph* 11 June 1999

Declaration of Arbroath

2 So long as there shall but one hundred of us remain alive, we will never subject ourselves to the dominion of the English. For it is not glory, it is not riches, neither is it honour, but it is freedom alone that we fight and contend for, which no honest man will lose but with his life.

letter sent by the Scottish Parliament, 6 April 1320, to the pope, asserting the independence of Scotland.

W. F. Deedes 1913–

Conservative politician and journalist

3 The millennium is going to present us with a very sharp portrait of ourselves: drinking is to continue all night and religious observance, as far as possible, is to be kept at bay.

in *Sunday Times* 15 August 1999

4 One golden rule for people who want to get on in politics is to keep their traps shut in August.

in *Mail on Sunday* 22 August 1999

5 The man who said nobody ever lost money by underrating public taste has been proved wrong.
  on the Millennium Dome

in *Mail on Sunday* 4 June 2000

Daniel Defoe 1660–1731

English novelist and journalist

6 Nature has left this tincture in the blood,
  That all men would be tyrants if they could.

The History of the Kentish Petition (1712–13)

7 Fools out of favour grudge at knaves in place.

The True-Born Englishman (1701) introduction

8 From this amphibious ill-born mob began
  That vain, ill-natured thing, an Englishman.

The True-Born Englishman (1701)

9 Your Roman-Saxon-Danish-Norman English.

The True-Born Englishman (1701)

10 His lazy, long, lascivious reign.
  *of **Charles II***

The True-Born Englishman (1701)

11 Great families of yesterday we show,
  And lords whose parents were the Lord knows who.

The True-Born Englishman (1701)

12 And of all plagues with which mankind are curst,
  Ecclesiastic tyranny's the worst.

The True-Born Englishman (1701)

13 When kings the sword of justice first lay down,
  They are no kings, though they possess the crown.
  Titles are shadows, crowns are empty things,
  The good of subjects is the end of kings.

The True-Born Englishman (1701)

Charles de Gaulle 1890–1970
French general; President of France, 1959–69

1 France has lost a battle. But France has not lost the war!
proclamation, 18 June 1940

2 Faced by the bewilderment of my countrymen, by the disintegration of a government in thrall to the enemy, by the fact that the institutions of my country are incapable, at the moment, of functioning, I General de Gaulle, a French soldier and military leader, realize that I now speak for France.
speech in London, 19 June 1940

3 Since they whose duty it was to wield the sword of France have let it fall shattered to the ground, I have taken up the broken blade.
speech, 13 July 1940

4 Yes, it is Europe, from the Atlantic to the Urals, it is Europe, it is the whole of Europe, that will decide the fate of the world.
speech to the people of Strasbourg, 23 November 1959

5 Politics are too serious a matter to be left to the politicians.
  *replying to Clement **Attlee**'s remark that 'De Gaulle is a very good soldier and a very bad politician'*
Clement Attlee *A Prime Minister Remembers* (1961)

6 How can you govern a country which has 246 varieties of cheese?
Ernest Mignon *Les Mots du Général* (1962)

7 Since a politician never believes what he says, he is quite surprised to be taken at his word.
Ernest Mignon *Les Mots du Général* (1962)

8 *Europe des patries.*
  A Europe of nations.
c.1962; widely associated with De Gaulle and taken as encapsulating his views, although perhaps not coined by him; J. Lacouture *De Gaulle: the Ruler* (1991)

9 Treaties, you see, are like girls and roses: they last while they last.
speech at Elysée Palace, 2 July 1963

10 *Vive Le Québec Libre.*
  Long Live Free Quebec.
    quoting the slogan of the separatist movement for an independent Quebec
speech in Montreal, 24 July 1967

11 Authority doesn't work without prestige, or prestige without distance.
Le Fil de l'épée (1932) 'Du caractère'

12 The sword is the axis of the world and its power is absolute.
Vers l'armée de métier (1934) 'Comment?' Commandement 3

on the death of his daughter, who had been born with Down's Syndrome:
13 And now she is like everyone else.
in 1948; Jean Lacouture *De Gaulle* (1965)

14 The EEC is a horse and carriage: Germany is the horse and France is the coachman.
attributed; Bernard Connolly *The Rotten Heart of Europe* (1995)

15 One does not put Voltaire in the Bastille.
  *when asked to arrest **Sartre**, in the 1960s*
in *Encounter* June 1975

Vine Victor Deloria Jr. 1933–
Standing Rock Sioux

16 This country was a lot better off when the Indians were running it.
in *New York Times Magazine* 3 March 1970

Demosthenes c.384–c.322 BC

Athenian orator and statesman

1 There is one safeguard known generally to the wise, which is an advantage and security to all, but especially to democracies against despots—suspicion.

Philippic; see **Curran** 99:9

2 When asked what was first in oratory, [he] replied to his questioner, 'action,' what second, 'action,' and again third, 'action'.

Cicero *Brutus* ch. 37, sect. 142

Jack Dempsey 1895–1983

American boxer

3 Honey, I just forgot to duck.
  *to his wife, on losing the World Heavyweight title, 23 September 1926; after a failed attempt on his life in 1981, Ronald **Reagan** quipped to his wife 'Honey, I forgot to duck'*

J. and B. P. Dempsey *Dempsey* (1977)

Deng Xiaoping 1904–97

Chinese Communist statesman, Vice-Premier 1973–6 and 1977–80; Vice-Chairman of the Central Committee of the Chinese Communist Party 1977–80, and from that period paramount leader of China

4 The colour of the cat doesn't matter as long as it catches the mice.

proverbial expression; in *Financial Times* 18 December 1986

5 I should love to be around in 1997 to see with my own eyes Hong Kong's return to China.

in 1984; in *Daily Telegraph* 20 February 1997, obituary

Lord Denning 1899–99

British judge

6 The Treaty [of Rome] is like an incoming tide. It flows into the estuaries and up the rivers. It cannot be held back.

in 1975; Anthony Sampson *The Essential Anatomy of Britain* (1992)

7 To every subject of this land, however powerful, I would use Thomas Fuller's words over three hundred years ago, 'Be ye never so high, the law is above you.'

in a High Court ruling against the Attorney-General, January 1977

8 The keystone of the rule of law in England has been the independence of judges. It is the only respect in which we make any real separation of powers.

The Family Story (1981)

9 We shouldn't have all these campaigns to get the Birmingham Six released if they'd been hanged. They'd have been forgotten and the whole community would be satisfied.

in *Spectator* 18 August 1990

10 Properly exercised the new powers of the executive lead to the welfare state; but abused they lead to the totalitarian state.

Anthony Sampson *The Changing Anatomy of Britain* (1982)

Edward Stanley, 14th Earl of Derby

1799–1869

British Conservative statesman; Prime Minister, 1852, 1858–9, 1866–8
on Derby: see **Bulwer-Lytton** 56:4; **Disraeli** 111:6

1 The duty of an Opposition [is] very simple . . . to oppose everything, and propose nothing.

quoting 'Mr Tierney, a great Whig authority', in the House of Commons, 4 June 1841

2 Meddle and muddle.
summarizing Lord John **Russell***'s foreign policy*

speech on the Address, in the House of Lords 4 February 1864

Proinsias de Rossa

Irish politician

3 If the Three Wise Men arrived here tonight, the likelihood is that they would be deported.
advocating an amnesty for asylum-seekers

in *Irish Times* 20 December 1997 'This Week They Said'

Camille Desmoulins 1760–94

French revolutionary

4 My age is that of the *bon Sansculotte Jésus*; an age fatal to Revolutionists.
reply given at his trial

Thomas Carlyle *History of the French Revolution* (1837)

Eamonn de Valera 1882–1975

American-born Irish statesman, Taoiseach 1937–48, 1951–4, and 1957–9, and President of the Republic of Ireland 1959–73
on de Valera: see **Lloyd George** 224:1

5 I am against this Treaty, not because I am a man of war, but because I am a man of peace.

in 1921

6 Whenever I wanted to know what the Irish people wanted, I had only to examine my own heart and it told me straight off what the Irish people wanted.

speech in Dáil Éireann, 6 January 1922

7 Further sacrifice of life would now be in vain . . . Military victory must be allowed to rest for the moment with those who have destroyed the Republic.

message to the Republican armed forces, 24 May 1923

8 I signed it the same way as I signed an autograph for a newspaper.
on taking the oath of allegiance to the King before entering Dáil Éireann

in 1932, attributed

9 If I were told tomorrow, 'You can have a united Ireland if you give up the idea of restoring the national language to be the spoken language of the majority of the people,' I would for myself say no.

speech in the Dáil, 1939

1 That Ireland which we dreamed of would be the home of a people who valued material wealth only as a basis of right living, of a people who were satisfied with frugal comfort and devoted their leisure to the things of the spirit; a land whose countryside would be bright with cosy homesteads, whose fields and villages would be joyous with sounds of industry, the romping of sturdy children, the contests of athletic youths, the laughter of comely maidens; whose firesides would be the forums of the wisdom of serene old age.

St Patrick's Day broadcast, 17 March 1943

2 Mr Churchill is proud of Britain's stand alone, after France had fallen, and before America had entered the war. Could he not find in his heart the generosity to acknowledge that there is a small nation that stood alone, not for one year or two, but for several hundred years, against aggression; that endured spoliation, famines, massacres in endless succession; that was clubbed many times into insensibility but each time, on returning consciousness, took up the fight anew; a small nation that could never be got to accept defeat and has never surrendered her soul?

radio broadcast, 16 May 1945

3 I sometimes admit that when I think of television and radio and their immense power, I feel somewhat afraid.

at the inauguration of Telefís Éireann in 1961

4 Whoever misunderstood Madame, the poor did not.
   of Constance **Markievicz**

Diana Norman *Terrible Beauty* (1987)

5 Women are at once the boldest and most unmanageable revolutionaries.

in conversation, c.1975

Donald Dewar 1937–2000
Scottish Labour politician; First Minister for Scotland from 1999

6 He could start a party in an empty room—and often did— filling it with good cheer, Gaelic songs, and argument.
   of John **Smith**

at John Smith's funeral service, 19 May 1994

7 'There shall be a Scottish parliament.' Through long years, those words were first a hope, then a belief, then a promise. Now they are a reality.
   at the official opening of the Scottish Parliament

speech, 1 July 1999; see **Anonymous** 11:6

8 We look forward to the time when this moment will be seen as a turning point: the day when democracy was renewed in Scotland, when we revitalised our place in this our United Kingdom.
   at the official opening of the Scottish Parliament

speech, 1 July 1999

9 This is about more than our politics and our laws. This is about who we are, how we carry ourselves.
   at the official opening of the Scottish Parliament

speech, 1 July 1999

Thomas E. Dewey 1902–71
American politician and presidential candidate
on Dewey: see **Newspaper headlines** 267:2

10 That's why it's time for a change!
   phrase used extensively in campaigns of 1944, 1948, and 1952

campaign speech in San Francisco, 21 September 1944

Diana, Princess of Wales 1961–97

1 I'd like to be a queen in people's hearts but I don't see myself being Queen of this country.

interview on *Panorama*, BBC1 TV, 20 November 1995

2 I'm not a political figure . . . I'm a humanitarian figure. I always have been and I always will be.
   on taking part in the campaign against landmines

in *Daily Telegraph* 17 January 1997

3 The press is ferocious. It forgives nothing, it only hunts for mistakes . . . In my position anyone sane would have left a long time ago.
   contrasting British and foreign press

in *Le Monde* 27 August 1997

Porfirio Diaz 1830–1915

President of Mexico, 1877–80, 1884–1911

4 Poor Mexico, so far from God and so close to the United States.

attributed

A. V. Dicey 1835–1922

British jurist

5 The beneficial effect of state intervention, especially in the form of legislation, is direct, immediate, and, so to speak, visible, while its evil effects are gradual and indirect, and lie out of sight . . . Hence the majority of mankind must almost of necessity look with undue favour upon government intervention.

Lectures on the Relation between Law and Public Opinion (1914)

Charles Dickens 1812–70

English novelist

6 O let us love our occupations,
Bless the squire and his relations,
Live upon our daily rations,
And always know our proper stations.

The Chimes (1844) 'The Second Quarter'

7 Annual income twenty pounds, annual expenditure nineteen nineteen six, result happiness. Annual income twenty pounds, annual expenditure twenty pounds ought and six, result misery.

David Copperfield (1850)

8 'It's always best on these occasions to do what the mob do.' 'But suppose there are two mobs?' suggested Mr Snodgrass. 'Shout with the largest,' replied Mr Pickwick.

Pickwick Papers (1837)

9 It was the best of times, it was the worst of times, it was the age of wisdom, it was the age of foolishness, it was the epoch of belief, it was the epoch of incredulity, it was the season of Light, it was the season of Darkness, it was the spring of hope, it was the winter of despair, we had everything before us, we had nothing before us, we were all going direct to Heaven, we were all going direct the other way.
   of the French Revolution

A Tale of Two Cities (1859)

10 'It is possible—that it may not come, during our lives . . . We shall not see the triumph.' 'We shall have helped it,' returned madame.

A Tale of Two Cities (1859)

1 Detestation of the high is the involuntary homage of the low.

A Tale of Two Cities (1859)

2 My faith in the people governing is, on the whole, infinitesimal; my faith in The People governed is, on the whole, illimitable.

speech at Birmingham and Midland Institute, 27 September 1869

John Dickinson 1732–1808

American politician

3 We have counted the cost of this contest, and find nothing so dreadful as voluntary slavery . . . Our cause is just, our union is perfect.
declaration of reasons for taking up arms against England, presented to Congress, 8 July 1775

C. J. Stillé *The Life and Times of John Dickinson* (1891)

4 Then join hand in hand, brave Americans all,—
By uniting we stand, by dividing we fall.

'The Liberty Song' (1768)

Denis Diderot 1713–84

French philosopher and man of letters

5 And [with] the guts of the last priest
Let's shake the neck of the last king.

Dithrambe sur fete de rois; see **Meslier** 249:2

Joan Didion 1934–

American writer

6 When we start deceiving ourselves into thinking not that we want something or need something, not that it is a pragmatic necessity for us to have it, but that it is a *moral imperative* that we have it, then is when we join the fashionable madmen, and then is when the thin whine of hysteria is heard in the land, and then is when we are in bad trouble.

Slouching towards Bethlehem (1968) 'On Morality'

John Dillon 1851–1927

Irish nationalist politician

7 Women's suffrage will, I believe, be the ruin of our Western civilisation. It will destroy the home, challenging the headship of men laid down by God. It may come in your time—I hope not in mine.
c.1912, to a deputation led by Hanna Sheehy Skeffington

Diana Norman *Terrible Beauty* (1987)

8 I say I am proud of their courage and if you were not so dense and stupid, as some of you English people are, you could have had these men fighting for you . . . It is not murderers who are being executed; it is insurgents who have fought a clean fight, however misguided, and it would have been a damned good thing for you if your soldiers were able to put up as good a fight as did those men in Dublin.
of those executed after the Easter Rising

speech in the British House of Commons, 11 May 1916

Benjamin Disraeli 1804–81

British Tory statesman, Prime Minister 1868 and 1874–80
on Disraeli: see **Bismarck** 42:4, **Carlyle** 70:9, **Foot** 134:1,
Palmerston 281:10; see also **Last words** 213:6

1 Between ourselves I could floor them all. This *entre nous*. I
was never more confident of anything than that I could
carry everything before me in that House. The time will
come.
four years before he entered Parliament

letter, 7 February 1833

2 In the 'Town' yesterday, I am told 'some one asked Disraeli,
in offering himself for Marylebone, on what he intended *to
stand*. "On my head," was the reply.'

letter, 8 April 1833

3 Though I sit down now, the time will come when you will
hear me.
maiden speech

in the House of Commons, 7
December 1837

4 The Continent will [not] suffer England to be the workshop
of the world.

in the House of Commons, 15
March 1838

5 Thus you have a starving population, an absentee
aristocracy, and an alien Church, and in addition the
weakest executive in the world. That is the Irish Question.

in the House of Commons, 16
February 1844

6 The noble Lord is the Prince Rupert of Parliamentary
discussion.
*of Lord Stanley, later the 14th Earl of **Derby***

in the House of Commons, 24 April
1844; see **Bulwer-Lytton** 56:4

7 The right hon. Gentleman caught the Whigs bathing, and
walked away with their clothes.
*on Robert **Peel**'s abandoning protection in favour of free trade,
traditionally the policy of the [Whig] Opposition*

in the House of Commons, 28
February 1845

8 Protection is not a principle, but an expedient.

in the House of Commons, 17
March 1845

9 A Conservative Government is an organized hypocrisy.

in the House of Commons, 17
March 1845; (Bagehot, quoting
Disraeli in *The English Constitution*
(1867) 'The House of Lords',
elaborated on the theme with the
words 'so much did the ideas of its
"head" differ from the sensations
of its "tail" ')

10 He traces the steam-engine always back to the tea-kettle.
*of Robert **Peel***

in the House of Commons, 11 April
1845

11 Justice is truth in action.

In the House of Commons, 11
February 1851

12 I read this morning an awful, though monotonous,
manifesto in the great organ of public opinion, which
always makes me tremble: Olympian bolts; and yet I could
not help fancying amid their rumbling terrors I heard the
plaintive treble of the Treasury Bench.

in the House of Commons, 13
February 1851

13 These wretched colonies will all be independent, too, in a
few years, and are a millstone round our necks.

letter to Lord Malmesbury, 13
August 1852

14 England does not love coalitions.

in the House of Commons, 16
December 1852

1 Finality is not the language of politics.

in the House of Commons, 28 February 1859

2 It is, I say, in the noble Lord's power to come to some really cordial understanding . . . between this country and France . . . and to put an end to these bloated armaments which only involve states in financial embarrassment.

in the House of Commons, 8 May 1862

3 Colonies do not cease to be colonies because they are independent.

in the House of Commons, 5 February 1863

4 You are not going, I hope, to leave the destinies of the British Empire to prigs and pedants.

in the House of Commons, 5 February 1863

5 Party is organized opinion.

speech at Oxford, 25 November 1864

6 I hold that the characteristic of the present age is craving credulity.

speech at Oxford, 25 November 1864

7 Is man an ape or an angel? Now I am on the side of the angels.

speech at Oxford, 25 November 1864

8 Assassination has never changed the history of the world.

in the House of Commons, 1 May 1865

9 I had to prepare the mind of the country, and . . . to educate our party.

speech at Edinburgh, 29 October 1867

10 Change is inevitable in a progressive country. Change is constant.

speech at Edinburgh, 29 October 1867

11 There can be no economy where there is no efficiency.

address to his Constituents, 1 October 1868

to Queen Victoria after the publication of Leaves from the Journal of our Life in the Highlands *in 1868:*
12 We authors, Ma'am.

Elizabeth Longford *Victoria R.I.* (1964)

13 We have legalized confiscation, consecrated sacrilege, and condoned high treason.
  on **Gladstone**'s *Irish policy*

in the House of Commons, 27 February 1871

14 I look upon Parliamentary Government as the noblest government in the world.

speech at Manchester, 3 April 1872

15 I believe that without party Parliamentary government is impossible.

speech at Manchester, 3 April 1872

16 You behold a range of exhausted volcanoes.
  of the Liberal Government

speech at Manchester, 3 April 1872

17 Increased means and increased leisure are the two civilizers of man.

speech at Manchester, 3 April 1872

18 The very phrase 'foreign affairs' makes an Englishman convinced that I am about to treat of subjects with which he has no concern.

speech at Manchester, 3 April 1872

19 A University should be a place of light, of liberty, and of learning.

in the House of Commons, 11 March 1873

20 An author who speaks about his own books is almost as bad as a mother who talks about her own children.
  at a banquet given in Glasgow on his installation as Lord Rector, 19 November 1873

in *The Times* 20 November 1873

21 Upon the education of the people of this country the fate of this country depends.

in the House of Commons, 15 June 1874

1 He is a great master of gibes and flouts and jeers.
*of Lord **Salisbury***

in the House of Commons, 5 August 1874

2 Mr Gladstone not only appeared but rushed into the debate ... The new Members trembled and fluttered like small birds when a hawk is in the air.

letter to Queen Victoria, March 1875, after an election in which **Gladstone**'s party had lost office;

3 Coffee house babble.
on the Bulgarian Atrocities, 1876

R. W. Seton-Watson *Britain in Europe 1789–1914* (1955)

4 Cosmopolitan critics, men who are the friends of every country save their own.

speech at Guildhall, 9 November 1877

5 Lord Salisbury and myself have brought you back peace— but a peace I hope with honour.
speech on returning from the Congress of Berlin, 16 July 1878

in *The Times* 17 July 1878; see **Chamberlain** 75:2, **Russell** 311:10

6 A series of congratulatory regrets.
of Lord Harrington's Resolution on the Berlin Treaty

at a banquet, Knightsbridge, 27 July 1878

7 A sophistical rhetorician, inebriated with the exuberance of his own verbosity.
*of **Gladstone***

in *The Times* 29 July 1878

8 I admit that there is gossip ... But the government of the world is carried on by sovereigns and statesmen, and not by anonymous paragraph writers ... or by the hare-brained chatter of irresponsible frivolity.

speech at Guildhall, London, 9 November 1878

9 One of the greatest of Romans, when asked what were his politics, replied, *Imperium et Libertas*. That would not make a bad programme for a British Ministry.

Here the two great interests Imperium & Libertas, res olim insociabiles (saith Tacitus), began to incounter each other.

speech at Mansion House, London, 10 November 1879

Winston Churchill (c.1620–88) *Divi Britannici* (1675); see **Tacitus** 351:3

10 Take away that emblem of mortality.
on being offered an air cushion to sit on, 1881

Robert Blake *Disraeli* (1966)

11 I will not go down to posterity talking bad grammar.
while correcting proofs of his last Parliamentary speech, 31 March 1881

Robert Blake *Disraeli* (1966)

12 The House of Commons is absolute. It is the State. 'L'État c'est moi.'

Coningsby (1844)

13 What by way of jest they call the Lower House.
of the House of Commons

Coningsby (1844)

14 A government of statesmen or of clerks? Of Humbug or Humdrum?

Coningsby (1844)

15 We owe the English peerage to three sources: the spoliation of the Church; the open and flagrant sale of honours by the elder Stuarts; and the borough-mongering of our own time.

Coningsby (1844)

16 Conservatism discards Prescription, shrinks from Principle, disavows Progress; having rejected all respect for antiquity, it offers no redress for the present, and makes no preparation for the future.

Coningsby (1844)

17 'A sound Conservative government,' said Taper, musingly. 'I understand: 'Tory men and Whig measures.'

Coningsby (1844)

18 Youth is a blunder; Manhood a struggle; Old Age a regret.

Coningsby (1844)

19 It seems to me a barren thing this Conservatism—an unhappy cross-breed, the mule of politics that engenders nothing.

Coningsby (1844); see **Donnelly** 117:2, **Power** 294:4

1 The depositary of power is always unpopular. *Coningsby* (1844)

2 Where can we find faith in a nation of sectaries? *Coningsby* (1844)

3 No Government can be long secure without a formidable Opposition. *Coningsby* (1844)

4 Read no history: nothing but biography, for that is life without theory. *Contarini Fleming* (1832)

5 The practice of politics in the East may be defined by one word—dissimulation. *Contarini Fleming* (1832)

6 The transient and embarrassed phantom of Lord Goderich. *Endymion* (1880)
  of Lord Goderich as Prime Minister

7 An insular country, subject to fogs, and with a powerful middle class, requires grave statesmen. *Endymion* (1880)

8 As for our majority . . . one is enough. *Endymion* (1880)

9 The greatest opportunity that can be offfered to an Englishman—a seat in the House of Commons. *Endymion* (1880)

10 The sweet simplicity of the three per cents. *Endymion* (1880); see **Stowell** 349:1

11 I believe they went out, like all good things, with the Stuarts. *Endymion* (1880)

12 What we anticipate seldom occurs; what we least expected generally happens. *Henrietta Temple* (1837)

13 An aristocracy is rather apt to exaggerate the qualities and magnify the importance of a plebeian leader. *Lord George Bentinck* (1852)

of Robert **Peel***:*
14 Wanting imagination he lacked prescience . . . His judgement was faultless provided he had not to deal with the future. *Lord George Bentinck* (1852)

15 'Two nations; between whom there is no intercourse and no sympathy; who are as ignorant of each other's habits, thoughts, and feelings, as if they were dwellers in different zones, or inhabitants of different planets; who are formed by a different breeding, are fed by a different food, are ordered by different manners, and are not governed by the same laws.' 'You speak of—' said Egremont, hesitatingly, 'THE RICH AND THE POOR.' *Sybil* (1845)

16 Pretending that people can be better off than they are is radicalism and nothing else. *Sybil* (1845)

17 'Frank and explicit'—that is the right line to take when you wish to conceal your own mind and to confuse the minds of others. *Sybil* (1845)

18 The Youth of a Nation are the trustees of Posterity. *Sybil* (1845)

19 That fatal drollery called a representative government. *Tancred* (1847)

20 A majority is always the best repartee. *Tancred* (1847)

21 Progress to what and from where . . . The European talks of progress because by an ingenious application of some scientific acquirements he has established a society which has mistaken comfort for civilization. *Tancred* (1847)

22 London is a modern Babylon. *Tancred* (1847)

1 We should never lose an occasion. Opportunity is more powerful even than conquerors and prophets.

Tancred (1847)

2 The grovelling tyranny of self-government.

Tancred (1847)

3 There is no act of treachery or meanness of which a political party is not capable; for in politics there is no honour.

Vivian Grey (1826)

4 Experience is the child of thought and thought is the child of action. We cannot learn men from books.

Vivian Grey (1826)

5 I repeat . . . that all power is a trust—that we are accountable for its exercise—that, from the people, and for the people, all springs, and all must exist.

Vivian Grey (1826)

6 Damn your principles! Stick to your party.

attributed to Disraeli and believed to have been said to Edward **Bulwer-Lytton**; E. Latham *Famous Sayings and their Authors* (1904)

7 Everyone likes flattery; and when you come to Royalty you should lay it on with a trowel.

to Matthew **Arnold**, in G. W. E. Russell *Collections and Recollections* (1898) ch. 23

8 I have climbed to the top of the greasy pole.
on becoming Prime Minister

W. Monypenny and G. Buckle *Life of Benjamin Disraeli* vol. 4 (1916)

9 I am dead; dead, but in the Elysian fields.
to a peer, on his elevation to the House of Lords

W. Monypenny and G. Buckle *Life of Benjamin Disraeli* vol. 5 (1920)

10 I never deny; I never contradict; I sometimes forget.
said to Lord Esher of his relations with Queen Victoria

Elizabeth Longford *Victoria R. I* (1964)

11 Never complain and never explain.

J. Morley *Life of William Ewart Gladstone* (1903) vol. 1; see **Fisher** 132:2

12 The palace is not safe when the cottage is not happy.

Robert Blake *Disraeli* (1966)

13 Palmerston is now seventy. If he could prove evidence of his potency in his electoral address he'd sweep the country.
to the suggestion that capital could be made from one of Palmerston's affairs

Hesketh Pearson *Dizzy* (1951); attributed, probably apocryphal

14 Posterity will do justice to that unprincipled maniac Gladstone—extraordinary mixture of envy, vindictiveness, hypocrisy and superstition; and with one commanding characteristic—whether Prime Minister or Leader of the Opposition, whether preaching, praying, speechifying or scribbling—never a gentleman.

W. Monypenny and G. Buckle *Life of Benjamin Disraeli* vol. 6 (1920)

15 Pray remember, Mr Dean, no dogma, no Dean.

W. Monypenny and G. Buckle *Life of Benjamin Disraeli* vol. 4 (1916)

16 Protection is not only dead, but damned.

W. Monypenny and G. Buckle *Life of Benjamin Disraeli* vol. 3 (1914)

17 The school of Manchester.
*of the free trade politics of Cobden and **Bright***

Robert Blake *Disraeli* (1966)

18 There are three kinds of lies: lies, damned lies and statistics.

attributed to Disraeli in Mark Twain *Autobiography* (1924) vol. 1

19 We came here for fame.
*to John **Bright**, in the House of Commons*

Robert Blake *Disraeli* (1966)

20 When Gentlemen cease to be returned to Parliament this Empire will perish.

W. Fraser *Disraeli and His Day* (1891)

1 When I want to read a novel, I write one.

W. Monypenny and G. Buckle *Life of Benjamin Disraeli* vol. 6 (1920)

2 You will find as you grow older that courage is the rarest of all qualities to be found in public life.
  to Lady Gwendolen Cecil, telling her that her father Lord
  Salisbury *was the only man of real courage with whom Disraeli had worked*

Lady Gwendolen Cecil *Life of Robert Marquis of Salisbury* (1931)

Milovan Djilas 1911–

political writer and former member of the Yugoslav Communist Party (from which he resigned in April 1954)

3 The Party line is that there is no Party line.
  comment on reforms of the Yugoslavian Communist Party, November 1952

Fitzroy Maclean *Disputed Barricade* (1957)

Michael Dobbs 1948–

British writer

4 You might very well think that. I couldn't possibly comment.
  the Chief Whip's habitual response to questioning

House of Cards (as dramatised for television, 1990)

Frank Dobson 1940–

British Labour politician

5 I trudge the streets rather than trade the soundbite. I . . . would not know a focus group if I met one. I am unspun.

in *Sunday Times* 27 February 2000

6 The ego has landed.
  *of Ken **Livingstone**'s independent candidacy for Mayor of London*

in *Times* 7 March 2000

Bubb Dodington 1691–1762

English politician

7 Love thy country, wish it well,
  Not with too intense a care,
  'Tis enough, that when it fell,
  Thou its ruin didst not share.

'Ode' (written 1761) in Joseph Spence *Anecdotes* (1820)

Elizabeth Dole 1936–

American Republican presidential candidate, wife of Robert ('Bob') **Dole**

8 From what I've seen, the answer is yes.
  on being asked if the country is ready for its first woman President

in *Sunday Telegraph* 14 March 1999

9 I'm not a politician and, frankly, I think that's a plus today.

in *Sunday Times* 14 March 1999

Robert Dole 1923–

American Republican politician

announcing his decision to relinquish his Senate seat and step down as majority leader:

10 I will seek the presidency with nothing to fall back on but the judgement of the people and with nowhere to go but the White House or home.

on Capitol Hill, 15 May 1996

1 It's a lot more fun winning. It hurts to lose.
conceding the US presidential election

in *Daily Telegraph* 7 November 1996

Ignatius Donnelly 1831–1901
American politician

2 The Democratic Party is like a mule—without pride of ancestry or hope of posterity.

attributed; see **Disraeli** 113:19, **Power** 294:4

John Dos Passos 1896–1970
American novelist, noted for his collage-like portrayal of the energy and diversity of American life in the first decades of the 20th century

3 America our nation has been beaten by strangers who have bought the laws and fenced off the meadows and cut down the woods for pulp and turned our pleasant cities into slums and sweated the wealth out of our people and when they want to they hire the executioner to throw the switch.

The Big Money (1936)

William O. Douglas 1898–1980
US Justice of the Supreme Court

4 The Fifth Amendment is an old friend and a good friend. It is one of the great landmarks in man's struggle to be free of tyranny, to be decent and civilized.

An Almanac of Liberty (1954)

5 The search . . . for ways and means to make the machine— and the vast bureaucracy of the corporation state and of government that runs that machine—the servant of man. That is the revolution that is coming.

in 1970; Anthony Sampson *The Company Man* (1995)

Alec Douglas-Home see Home

Frederick Douglass c.1818–1895
American former slave and Civil Rights campaigner

6 Every tone [of the songs of the slaves] was a testimony against slavery, and a prayer to God for deliverance from chains.

Narrative of the Life of Frederick Douglass (1845) ch. 2

7 What, to the American slave, is your Fourth of July? I answer: A day that reveals to him, more than all other days in the year, the gross injustice and cruelty to which he is the constant victim. To him your celebration is a sham.

speech at Rochester, New York, 4 July 1852

8 In all the relations of life and death, we are met by the colour line.

speech at the Convention of Coloured Men, Louisville, Kentucky, 24 September 1883

9 No man can put a chain about the ankle of his fellow man without at last finding the other end fastened about his own neck.

speech at Civil Rights Mass Meeting, Washington, DC, 22 October 1883

Maureen Dowd 1925–
American journalist

10 These are not grounds for impeachment. These are grounds for divorce.
on the Lewinsky affair.

in *Guardian* 14 September 1998

Margaret Drabble 1939–
English novelist

1 England's not a bad country . . . It's just a mean, cold, ugly,   *A Natural Curiosity* (1989)
divided, tired, clapped-out, post-imperial, post-industrial
slag-heap covered in polystyrene hamburger cartons.

Francis Drake c.1540–96
English sailor and explorer

2 The singeing of the King of Spain's Beard.   Francis Bacon *Considerations*
on the expedition to Cadiz, 1587   *touching a War with Spain* (1629)

3 There is plenty of time to win this game, and to thrash the   attributed, in *Dictionary of National*
Spaniards too.   *Biography* (1917–) vol. 5

Joseph Rodman Drake 1795–1820
American poet

4 Forever float that standard sheet!   'The American Flag' in *New York*
Where breathes the foe but falls before us,   *Evening Post*, 29 May 1819 (also
With Freedom's soil beneath our feet,   attributed to Fitz-Greene Halleck)
And Freedom's banner streaming o'er us?

William Driver 1803–86
American sailor

5 I name thee Old Glory.   attributed
*as the flag was hoisted to the masthead of his ship (Driver was
captain of the* Charles Doggett, *the ship on which the Bounty
mutineers were returned from Tahiti to Pitcairn, and was
presented with a large American flag by a band of women in
recognition of this)*

John Dryden 1631–1700
English poet, critic, and playwright

6 Plots, true or false, are necessary things,   *Absalom and Achitophel* (1681)
To raise up commonwealths and ruin kings.

7 Of these the false Achitophel was first,   *Absalom and Achitophel* (1681)
A name to all succeeding ages curst.
For close designs and crooked counsels fit,
Sagacious, bold, and turbulent of wit,
Restless, unfixed in principles and place,
In power unpleased, impatient of disgrace.
*in Dryden's political satire relating to the Protestant succession
'Achitophel' represented* **Shaftesbury**, *and 'Absalom' the Duke of*
Monmouth

8 A daring pilot in extremity;   *Absalom and Achitophel* (1681)
Pleased with the danger, when the waves went high
He sought the storms; but for a calm unfit,
Would steer too nigh the sands to boast his wit.

9 In friendship false, implacable in hate: *Absalom and Achitophel* (1681)
Resolved to ruin or to rule the state.

10 The people's prayer, the glad diviner's theme,   *Absalom and Achitophel* (1681)
The young men's vision and the old men's dream!

1 All empire is no more than power in trust.

Absalom and Achitophel (1681)

2 Better one suffer, than a nation grieve.

Absalom and Achitophel (1681)

3 For who can be secure of private right,
If sovereign sway may be dissolved by might?
Nor is the people's judgement always true:
The most may err as grossly as the few.

Absalom and Achitophel (1681)

4 Never was patriot yet, but was a fool.

Absalom and Achitophel (1681)

5 Reason to rule, but mercy to forgive:
The first is law, the last prerogative.

The Hind and the Panther (1687)

6 Either be wholly slaves or wholly free.

The Hind and the Panther (1687)

7 T'abhor the makers, and their laws approve,
Is to hate traitors and the treason love.

The Hind and the Panther (1687)

8 War is the trade of kings.

King Àrthur (1691)

9 But treason is not owned when 'tis descried;
Successful crimes alone are justified.

The Medal (1682)

10 But 'tis the talent of our English nation,
Still to be plotting some new reformation.

'The Prologue at Oxford, 1680'
(prologue to Nathaniel Lee
Sophonisba, 2nd ed., 1681)

11 Freedom which in no other land will thrive,
Freedom an English subject's sole prerogative.

Threnodia Augustalis (1685)

12 If by the people you understand the multitude, the *hoi polloi*,
'tis no matter what they think; they are sometimes in the
right, sometimes in the wrong: their judgement is a mere
lottery.

An Essay of Dramatic Poesy (1668)

Alexander Dubček 1921–92
Czechoslovak statesman, First Secretary of the Czechoslovak
Communist Party 1968–9

13 In the service of the people we followed such a policy that
socialism would not lose its human face.

in *Rudé Právo* 19 July 1968

Joachim Du Bellay 1522–60
French poet

14 France, mother of arts, of warfare, and of laws.

Les Regrets (1558) Sonnet no. 9

W. E. B. Du Bois 1868–1963
American social reformer and political activist

15 The cost of liberty is less than the price of repression.

John Brown (1909)

16 The problem of the twentieth century is the problem of the
colour line—the relation of the darker to the lighter races of
men in Asia and Africa, in America and the islands of the
sea.

The Souls of Black Folk (1905)

John Foster Dulles 1888–1959
American international lawyer and politician

17 If . . . the European Defence Community should not become
effective; if France and Germany remain apart . . . That
would compel an agonizing reappraisal of basic United
States policy.

speech to NATO Council in Paris, 14
December 1953

1 The ability to get to the verge without getting into the war is the necessary art. If you cannot master it, you inevitably get into war. If you try to run away from it, if you are scared to go to the brink, you are lost. We've had to look it square in the face—on the question of enlarging the Korean war, on the question of getting into the Indochina war, on the question of Formosa. We walked to the brink and we looked it in the face.

this policy became known as 'brinkmanship'

in *Life* 16 January 1956; see **Stevenson** 00:00

Henry Dundas 1742–1811

Scottish-born politician

2 When it is said that no alternative is left to the New Englanders but to starve or rebel, this is not the fact, for there is another way, to submit.

the word 'starvation' was said to have been coined in relation to this speech, and Dundas became known as 'Starvation Dundas'

in the House of Commons, 1775

John Dunning, Lord Ashburton 1731–83

English lawyer and politician

3 The influence of the Crown has increased, is increasing, and ought to be diminished.

resolution passed in the House of Commons, 6 April 1780

Ray Durem 1915–63

American poet

4 Some of my best friends are white boys.
when I meet 'em
I treat 'em
just the same as if they was people.

'Broadminded' (written 1951)

John George Lambton, Lord Durham

1792–1840

English Whig politician

5 £40,000 a year a moderate income—such a one as a man *might jog on with*.

Thomas Creevey, letter to Elizabeth Ord, 13 September 1821

6 I expected to find a contest between a government and a people: I found two nations warring in the bosom of a single state.

Report of the Affairs of British North America (1839)

Esther Dyson

American businesswoman

7 Crime is crime, but that doesn't mean you can have a law making everyone keep their curtains up to help the police.
on the British government's Regulation of Investigatory Powers bill

in *Times* 6 July 2000

8 It is cute to have the British pound, it is quaint. But Britain has more hope if it joins them and fights for what it want.
on why Britain should join the euro

in *Times* 6 July 2000

Stephen T. Early 1889–1951

1 Don't Worry Me—I am an 8 Ulcer Man on 4 Ulcer Pay.
card received by Harry Truman

William Hillman *Mr President: the First Publication from the Personal Diaries, Private Letters, Papers and Revealing Interviews of Harry S. Truman* (1952)

Abba Eban 1915–

Israeli diplomat

2 History teaches us that men and nations behave wisely once they have exhausted all other alternatives.

speech in London, 16 December 1970

of the British Foreign Office:
3 A hotbed of cold feet.

in conversation with Antony Jay

Anthony Eden 1897–1977

British Conservative statesman, Prime Minister 1955–7
on Eden: see **Butler** 63:4, **Muggeridge** 263:2, **Newspaper headlines** 267:11, **Roberts** 302:7

4 Everyone is always in favour of general economy and particular expenditure.

in *Observer* 17 June 1956

5 We are in an armed conflict; that is the phrase I have used. There has been no declaration of war.
on the Suez crisis

in the House of Commons, 1 November 1956

6 Long experience has taught me that to be criticized is not always to be wrong.
during the Suez crisis

speech at Lord Mayor's Guildhall banquet; in *Daily Herald* 10 November 1956

Clarissa Eden 1920–

wife of Anthony **Eden**

7 For the past few weeks I have really felt as if the Suez Canal was flowing through my drawing room.

speech at Gateshead, 20 November 1956

Edward VII 1841–1910

King of the United Kingdom from 1901

8 The last King of England.
introducing his son, the future George V, to Lord Haldane, expressing his pessimism for the survival of the British monarchy

Andrew Roberts *Eminent Churchillians* (1994)

Edward VIII 1894–1972

King of the United Kingdom, 1936; afterwards Duke of Windsor
on Edward VIII: see **George V** 144:1, **Thomas** 359:3

9 These works brought all these people here. Something should be done to get them at work again.
speaking at the derelict Dowlais Iron and Steel Works, 18 November 1936

in *Western Mail* 19 November 1936; see **Misquotations** 255:7

10 At long last I am able to say a few words of my own . . . you must believe me when I tell you that I have found it impossible to carry the heavy burden of responsibility and to discharge my duties as King as I would wish to do without the help and support of the woman I love.
radio broadcast following his abdication, 11 December 1936

in *The Times* 12 December 1936

John Ehrlichman 1925–99 ˅

Presidential assistant to Richard Nixon

1 I think we ought to let him hang there. Let him twist
slowly, slowly in the wind.
    *speaking of Patrick Gray (regarding his nomination as director of
    the FBI) in a telephone conversation with John Dean*

in Washington Post 27 July 1973

Albert Einstein 1879–1955   ✓

German-born American theoretical physicist, founder of the
theory of relativity

2 The prestige of government has undoubtedly been lowered
considerably by the Prohibition laws. For nothing is more
destructive of respect for the government and the law of the
land than passing laws which cannot be enforced.

*after visiting America in 1921; The
World As I See It (1935)*

3 Nationalism is an infantile sickness. It is the measles of the
human race.

*Helen Dukas and Banesh Hoffman
Albert Einstein, the Human Side
(1979)*

4 One must divide one's time between politics and equations.
But our equations are much more important to me.

*C. P. Snow 'Einstein' in M.
Goldsmith et al. (eds.) Einstein
(1980)*

Dwight D. Eisenhower 1890–1969

American general and Republican statesman, 34th President of
the US, 1953–61
on Eisenhower: see **Acheson** 1:8, **Truman** 366:7

5 People of Western Europe: A landing was made this
morning on the coast of France by troops of the Allied
Expeditionary Force. This landing is part of the concerted
United Nations plan for the liberation of Europe, made in
conjunction with our great Russian allies . . . I call upon all
who love freedom to stand with us now. Together we shall
achieve victory.

broadcast on D-Day, 6 June 1944

6 Every gun that is made, every warship launched, every
rocket fired signifies, in the final sense, a theft from those
who hunger and are not fed, those who are cold and are not
clothed. This world in arms is not spending money alone. It
is spending the sweat of its labourers, the genius of its
scientists, the hopes of its children.

*speech in Washington, 16 April
1953*

7 You have broader considerations that might follow what
you might call the 'falling domino' principle. You have a
row of dominoes set up. You knock over the first one, and
what will happen to the last one is that it will go over very
quickly. So you have the beginning of a disintegration that
would have the most profound influences.

*speech at press conference, 7 April
1954*

8 Governments are far more stupid than their people.

attributed, 1958

9 I think that people want peace so much that one of these
days governments had better get out of the way and let
them have it.

*broadcast discussion, 31 August
1959*

1 In the councils of government, we must guard against the acquisition of unwarranted influence, whether sought or unsought, by the military-industrial complex. The potential for the disastrous rise of misplaced power exists and will persist.
farewell broadcast, 17 January 1961

in New York Times 18 January 1961

2 No *easy* problems ever come to the president of the United States. If they are easy to solve, someone else has solved them.

quoted by John F. Kennedy, in Parade 8 April 1962

George Eliot 1819–80

English novelist

3 An election is coming. Universal peace is declared, and the foxes have a sincere interest in prolonging the lives of the poultry.

Felix Holt (1866)

T. S. Eliot 1888–1965

Anglo-American poet, critic, and playwright

4 This is the way the world ends
Not with a bang but a whimper.

'The Hollow Men' (1925)

Queen Elisabeth of Belgium 1876–1965

German-born consort of King Albert of the Belgians

5 Between them [Germany] and me there is now a bloody curtain which has descended forever.
on Germany's invasion of Belgium in 1914

attributed

Elizabeth I 1533–1603

Queen of England and Ireland from 1558
see also **Last words** 212:1, **Mottoes** 262:7

6 This judgement I have of you that you will not be corrupted by any manner of gift and that you will be faithful to the state; and that without respect of my private will you will give me that counsel which you think best.
to William Cecil, appointing him her Secretary of State in 1558

Conyers Read *Mr Secretary Cecil and Queen Elizabeth* (1955)

7 The queen of Scots is this day leichter of a fair son, and I am but a barren stock.

to her ladies, June 1566, in Sir James Melville *Memoirs of His Own Life* (1827 ed.)

8 I am your anointed Queen. I will never be by violence constrained to do anything. I thank God that I am endued with such qualities that if I were turned out of the Realm in my petticoat, I were able to live in any place in Christome.

speech to Members of Parliament, 5 November 1566

9 I know what it is to be a subject, what to be a Sovereign, what to have good neighbours, and sometimes meet evil-willers.

speech to a Parliamentary deputation at Richmond, 12 November 1586; J. E. Neale *Elizabeth I and her Parliaments 1584–1601* (1957), from a report 'which the Queen herself heavily amended in her own hand'; see **Misquotations** 255:1

1 I will make you shorter by the head.
to the leaders of her Council, who were opposing her course towards **Mary** *Queen of Scots*

F. Chamberlin *Sayings of Queen Elizabeth* (1923)

2 I know I have the body of a weak and feeble woman, but I have the heart and stomach of a king, and of a king of England too; and think foul scorn that Parma or Spain, or any prince of Europe, should dare to invade the borders of my realm.
speech to the troops at Tilbury on the approach of the Armada, 1588

Lord Somers *A Third Collection of Scarce and Valuable Tracts* (1751)

3 The daughter of debate, that eke discord doth sow.
on **Mary** *Queen of Scots*

George Puttenham (ed.) *The Art of English Poesie* (1589)

4 I will have here but one Mistress, and no Master.
reproving the presumption of the Earl of Leicester

Robert Naunton *Fragmenta Regalia* (1641)

5 My lord, we make use of you, not for your bad legs, but for your good head.
to William **Cecil**, *who suffered from gout*

F. Chamberlin *Sayings of Queen Elizabeth* (1923)

6 I do entreat heaven daily for your longer life, else will my people and myself stand in need of cordials too. My comfort hath been in my people's happiness and their happiness in thy discretion.
to William **Cecil** *on his death-bed*

F. Chamberlin *Sayings of Queen Elizabeth* (1923)

7 Though God hath raised me high, yet this I count the glory of my crown: that I have reigned with your loves.
the Golden Speech, 1601

in *The Journals of All the Parliaments . . . Collected by Sir Simonds D'Ewes* (1682)

8 God may pardon you, but I never can.
to the dying Countess of Nottingham, February 1603, *for her part in the death of the Earl of* **Essex**; *the story is almost certainly apocryphal*

David Hume *The History of England under the House of Tudor* (1759) vol. 2

9 Must! Is *must* a word to be addressed to princes? Little man, little man! thy father, if he had been alive, durst not have used that word.
to Robert **Cecil**, *on his saying in her last illness that she must go to bed*

J. R. Green *A Short History of the English People* (1874); *Dodd's Church History of England* vol. 3 (ed. M. A. Tierney, 1840) adds, 'but thou knowest I must die, and that maketh thee so presumptuous'

10 If thy heart fails thee, climb not at all.
lines after Walter **Ralegh**, *written on a window-pane*

Thomas Fuller *Worthies of England* vol. 1; see **Ralegh** 298:3

11 I think that, at the worst, God has not yet ordained that England shall perish.

F. Chamberlin *Sayings of Queen Elizabeth* (1923)

12 I would not open windows into men's souls.

oral tradition, in J. B. Black *Reign of Elizabeth 1558–1603* (1936) (the words very possibly originating in a letter drafted by Bacon)

13 Like strawberry wives, that laid two or three great strawberries at the mouth of their pot, and all the rest were little ones.
describing the tactics of the Commission of Sales, in their dealings with her

Francis Bacon *Apophthegms New and Old* (1625)

1 Madam I may not call you; mistress I am ashamed to call you; and so I know not what to call you; but howsoever, I thank you.
  to the wife of the Archbishop of Canterbury, the Queen disapproving of marriage among the clergy

John Harington *A Brief View of the State of the Church of England* (1653)

welcoming Edward de Vere, Earl of Oxford, on his return from seven years self-imposed exile, occasioned by the acute embarrassment to himself of breaking wind in the presence of the Queen:
2 My Lord, I had forgot the fart.

John Aubrey *Brief Lives* 'Edward de Vere'

on being asked her opinion of Christ's presence in the Sacrament:
3 'Twas God the word that spake it,
He took the bread and brake it;
And what the word did make it;
That I believe, and take it.

S. Clarke *The Marrow of Ecclesiastical History* (1675) 'The Life of Queen Elizabeth'

Elizabeth II 1926–

Queen of the United Kingdom from 1952

4 I declare before you all that my whole life, whether it be long or short, shall be devoted to your service and the service of our great Imperial family to which we all belong.
  broadcast speech, as Princess Elizabeth, to the Commonwealth from Cape Town, 21 April 1947

in *The Times* 22 April 1947

speech at Guildhall, London, on her 25th wedding anniversary:
5 I think everybody really will concede that on this, of all days, I should begin my speech with the words 'My husband and I'.

in *The Times* 21 November 1972

6 In the words of one of my more sympathetic correspondents, it has turned out to be an 'annus horribilis'.

speech at Guildhall, London, 24 November 1992

7 The British Constitution has always been puzzling and always will be.

Peter Hennessy *The Hidden Wiring* (1995)

8 I for one believe that there are lessons to be drawn from her life and from the extraordinary and moving reaction to her death.
  *broadcast from Buckingham Palace on the evening before the funeral of **Diana**, Princess of Wales, 5 September 1997*

in *The Times* 6 September 1997

9 Please don't be too effusive.
  adjuration to the Prime Minister on the speech he was to make to celebrate her golden wedding, 18 November 1997

in *Daily Telegraph* 21 November 1997; see **Blair** 44:2

Queen Elizabeth, the Queen Mother

1900–

Queen Consort of **George VI** and mother of **Elizabeth II**

10 I'm glad we've been bombed. It makes me feel I can look the East End in the face.
  to a London policeman, 13 September 1940

John Wheeler-Bennett *King George VI* (1958)

on the suggestion that the royal family be evacuated during the Blitz:
11 The Princesses would never leave without me and I couldn't leave without the King, and the King will never leave.

Penelope Mortimer *Queen Elizabeth* (1986)

Ebenezer Elliott 1781–1849
English poet known as the 'Corn Law Rhymer'

1 What is a communist? One who hath yearnings
For equal division of unequal earnings.

'Epigram' (1850)

Thomas Edward Ellis 1859–99
British Liberal politician and Welsh nationalist

2 Over and above all, we shall work for a Legislature, elected
by the manhood and womanhood of Wales.

speech at Bala, 1890

Ben Elton 1959–
British writer and performer

3 I did not vote Labour because they've heard of Oasis and
nobody is going to vote Tory because William Hague has
got a baseball cap.

in Radio Times 18 April 1998

Ralph Waldo Emerson 1803–82
American philosopher and poet

4 The two parties which divide the state, the party of
Conservatism and that of Innovation, are very old, and have
disputed the possession of the world ever since it was made.

'The Conservative' (lecture, 1841)

5 The louder he talked of his honour, the faster we counted
our spoons.

The Conduct of Life (1860)
'Worship'

6 When you strike at a king, you must kill him.

attributed to Emerson by Oliver
Wendell **Holmes** Jr.; Max Lerner
The Mind and Faith of Justice Holmes
(1943)

Robert Emmet 1778–1803
Irish nationalist

7 Let no man write my epitaph . . . When my country takes
her place among the nations of the earth, *then*, and *not till
then*, let my epitaph be written.

speech from the dock when
condemned to death, 19
September 1803

Friedrich Engels 1820–95
German socialist; founder, with Karl Marx, of modern
Communism

8 The State is not 'abolished', *it withers away.*

Anti-Dühring (1878)

9 Naturally, the workers are perfectly free; the manufacturer
does not force them to take his materials and his cards, but
he says to them . . . 'If you don't like to be frizzled in my
frying-pan, you can take a walk into the fire'.

The Condition of the Working Class
in England in 1844 (1892)

Friedrich Engels see also **Marx** and **Engels**

Ennius 239–169 BC
Roman writer

10 *Moribus antiquis res stat Romana virisque.*
The Roman state survives by its ancient customs and its
manhood.

Annals

1 *Unus homo nobis cunctando restituit rem.*   *Annals*

One man by delaying put the state to rights for us.
  referring to the Roman general Fabius Cunctator ('The Delayer')

■ **Epitaphs** *see box overleaf*

Erasmus *c.*1469–1536
Dutch Christian humanist

2 In the country of the blind the one-eyed man is king.   *Adages*

Ludwig Erhard 1897–1977
German statesman, Chancellor of West Germany (1963–6)

3 Without Britain Europe would remain only a torso.   remark on W. German television,
27 May 1962; in *The Times* 28 May
1962

Dudley Erwin 1917–84
Australian politician

*claiming that the 'political manoeuvre' which had cost him his job in
the reshuffled Government was actually the Prime Minister's
secretary:*

4 It wiggles, it's shapely and its name is Ainsley Gotto.   in *The Times* 14 November 1969

Lord Esher 1913–
English architect and planner

5 When politicians and civil servants hear the word 'culture'   speech, House of Lords, 2 March
they feel for their blue pencils.   1960; see **Johst** 16300:0013

Robert Devereux, Lord Essex 1566–1601
English soldier and courtier, executed for treason

6 Reasons are not like garments, the worse for wearing.   letter to Lord Willoughby, 4
January 1599

William Maxwell Evarts 1818–83
American politician and lawyer

7 The pious ones of Plymouth, who, reaching the Rock, first   in *Louisville Courier-Journal* 4 July
fell upon their own knees and then upon the aboriginees.   1913; a pun which has been
variously attributed

Edward Everett 1794–1865
American orator and politician

8 I should be glad if I could flatter myself that I came as near   letter to Lincoln, 20 November
the central idea of the occasion in two hours as you did in   1863; see **Anonymous** 11:3
two minutes.
  *to Abraham **Lincoln** on the Gettysburg address, which had been
  publicly criticized while Everett's two hour speech had received
  adulatory attention in the press*

Epitaphs

1 Free at last, free at last
Thank God almighty
We are free at last.
epitaph of Martin Luther **King** (*1929–68*), *Atlanta, Georgia*

anonymous spiritual; see **King** 203:6

2 Go, tell the Spartans, thou who passest by,
That here obedient to their laws we lie.
epitaph for the 300 Spartans killed at Thermopylae, 480 BC

attributed to **Simonides**; Herodotus *Histories* bk. 7, ch. 228

3 Here lies a great and mighty king
Whose promise none relies on;
He never said a foolish thing,
Nor ever did a wise one.
of **Charles II** (*1630–85*); *an alternative first line reads: 'Here lies our sovereign lord the King'*

John Wilmot, Earl of **Rochester** 'The King's Epitaph'; in C. E. Doble et al. *Thomas Hearne: Remarks and Collections* (1885–1921) 17 November 1706; see **Charles II** 76:5

4 Here lies a valiant warrior
Who never drew a sword;
Here lies a noble courtier
Who never kept his word;
Here lies the Earl of Leicester
Who governed the estates
Whom the earth could never living love,
And the just heaven now hates.
of Robert Dudley, Earl of Leicester (*c.1532–88*)

attributed to Ben **Jonson** in Silvester Tissington *A Collection of Epitaphs and Monumental Inscriptions* (1857)

5 Here lies Fred,
Who was alive and is dead:
Had it been his father,
I had much rather;
Had it been his brother,
Still better than another;
Had it been his sister,
No one would have missed her;
Had it been the whole generation,
Still better for the nation:
But since 'tis only Fred,
Who was alive and is dead,—
There's no more to be said.
of Frederick Louis, Prince of Wales (*1707–1751*), *son of* **George II** *and* **Caroline** *of Ansbach*

in Horace Walpole *Memoirs of George II* (1847) vol. 1

6 Here lies he who neither feared nor flattered any flesh.
of John **Knox**, *said as he was buried, 26 November 1572*

Earl of Morton (c.1516–81); George R. Preedy *The Life of John Knox* (1940)

7 Here lies wise and valiant dust,
Huddled up, 'twixt fit and just:
Strafford, who was hurried hence
'Twixt treason and convenience.
He spent his time here in a mist,
A Papist, yet a Calvinist . . .
Riddles lie here, or in a word,
Here lies blood; and let it lie
Speechless still, and never cry.

John Cleveland (1613–58) 'Epitaph on the Earl of **Strafford**' (1647)

8 I will return. And I will be millions.

inscription on the tomb of Eva **Perón**, Buenos Aires

Epitaphs *continued*

1 Rest in peace. The mistake shall not be repeated.

inscription on the cenotaph at Hiroshima, Japan

2 A soldier of the Great War known unto God.
standard epitaph for the unidentified dead of World War One

adopted by the War Graves Commission

3 Their name liveth for evermore.
*standard inscription on the Stone of Sacrifice in each military cemetery of World War One, proposed by Rudyard **Kipling** as a member of the War Graves Commission*

Charles Carrington *Rudyard Kipling* (rev. ed. 1978)

4 When you go home, tell them of us and say,
'For your tomorrow we gave our today.'

Kohima memorial to the Burma campaign of the Second World War; in recent years used at Remembrance Day parades in the UK

When you go home, tell them of us and say,
'For your tomorrows these gave their today.'

John Maxwell Edmonds (1875-1958) *Inscriptions Suggested for War Memorials* (1919)

William Norman Ewer 1885–1976

British writer

5 I gave my life for freedom—This I know:
For those who bade me fight had told me so.

'Five Souls' (1917)

Winifred Ewing 1929–

Scottish Nationalist politician

6 As I took my seat it was said by political pundits that 'a chill ran along the Labour back benches looking for a spine to run up.'
of her arrival at Westminster after winning the Hamilton by-election in 1967; use of a general political expression

in 1988, attributed; Angela Cran and James Robertson *Dictionary of Scottish Quotations* (1996)

7 The Scottish Parliament which adjourned on 25 March in the year 1707 is hereby reconvened.
opening speech, as oldest member of the new Parliament

in *Scottish Parliament* 12 May 1999

8 I am an expert in being a minority. I was alone in the House of Commons for three years and alone in the European Parliament for nineteen years, but we are all minorities now.
opening speech, as oldest member of the new Parliament

in *Scottish Parliament* 12 May 1999

Quintus Fabius Maximus *c.*275–203 BC

Roman politician and general

9 To be turned from one's course by men's opinions, by blame, and by misrepresentation shows a man unfit to hold an office.

Plutarch *Parallel Lives* 'Fabius Maximus'

Émile Faguet 1847–1916

French writer and critic

*commenting on **Rousseau**'s 'Man was born free, and everywhere he is in chains':*

1 It would be equally correct to say that sheep are born carnivorous, and everywhere they nibble grass.

paraphrasing Joseph de Maistre; *Politiques et Moralistes du Dix-Neuvième Siècle* (1899)

Thomas Fairfax 1621–71

English Parliamentary general, appointed commander of the New Model Army in 1645, and replaced in 1650 by Oliver **Cromwell** for refusing to march against the Scots, who had proclaimed the future **Charles II** king

2 Human probabilities are not sufficient grounds to make war upon a neighbour nation.
    to the proposal in 1650 that the expected attack by the Scots should be anticipated by the invasion of Scotland

in *Dictionary of National Biography*

Lucius Cary, Lord Falkland 1610–43

English royalist politician

3 When it is not necessary to change, it is necessary not to change.

Discourses of Infallibility (1660) 'A Speech concerning Episcopacy' delivered in 1641

Frantz Fanon 1925–61

French West Indian psychoanalyst and writer

4 The shape of Africa resembles a revolver, and Zaire is the trigger.

attributed

Michael Faraday 1791–1867

English chemist and physicist

*to **Gladstone**, when asked about the usefulness of electricity:*

5 Why sir, there is every possibility that you will soon be able to tax it!

W. E. H. Lecky *Democracy and Liberty* (1899 ed.)

James A. Farley 1888–1976

American Democratic politician

6 As Maine goes, so goes Vermont.
    *after predicting correctly that Franklin **Roosevelt** would carry all but two states in the election of 1936*

statement to the press, 4 November 1936; see **Proverbs and sayings** 296:2

Farouk 1920–65

King of Egypt, 1936–52

7 The whole world is in revolt. Soon there will be only five Kings left—the King of England, the King of Spades, the King of Clubs, the King of Hearts and the King of Diamonds.

Lord Boyd-Orr *As I Recall* (1966), addressed to the author at a conference in Cairo, 1948

Guy Fawkes 1570–1606
conspirator in the Gunpowder Plot, 1605

1 A desperate disease requires a dangerous remedy.

on 6 November 1605, in *Dictionary of National Biography* (1917–) vol. 6

Dianne Feinstein 1933–
American Democratic politician, Mayor of San Francisco

2 Toughness doesn't have to come in a pinstripe suit.

in *Time* 4 June 1984

3 There was a time when you could say the least government was the best—but not in the nation's most populous state.

campaign speech, 15 March 1990

Ferdinand I see Mottoes 262:3

Paul Feyerabend 1924–94
Austrian philosopher

4 The time is overdue for adding the separation of state and science to the by now customary separation of state and church. Science is only *one* of the many instruments man has invented to cope with his surroundings. It is not the only one, it is not infallible, and it has become too powerful, too pushy, and too dangerous to be left on its own.

Against Method (1975)

L'Abbé Edgeworth de Firmont 1745–1807
Irish-born confessor to Louis XVI

5 Son of Saint Louis, ascend to heaven.
   to Louis XVI as he mounted the steps of the guillotine, 1793

attributed

H. A. L. Fisher 1856–1940
English historian

6 Men wiser and more learned than I have discerned in history a plot, a rhythm, a predetermined pattern. These harmonies are concealed from me. I can see only one emergency following upon another as wave follows upon wave, only one great fact with respect to which, since it is unique, there can be no generalizations, only one safe rule for the historian: that he should recognize in the development of human destinies the play of the contingent and the unforeseen.

A History of Europe (1935)

7 Purity of race does not exist. Europe is a continent of energetic mongrels.

A History of Europe (1935)

8 Nothing commends a radical change to an Englishman more than the belief that it is really conservative.

A History of Europe (1935)

John Arbuthnot Fisher 1841–1920
British admiral

1 Sack the lot!
   on overmanning and overspending within government
   departments

letter to *The Times*, 2 September
1919

2 Never contradict
   Never explain
   Never apologize.

letter to *The Times*, 5 September
1919; see **Disraeli** 115:11

John Fiske 1842–1901

3 The United States—bounded on the north by the Aurora
   Borealis, on the south by the precession of the equinoxes, on
   the east by the primeval chaos, and on the west by the Day
   of Judgement.

Bounding the United States

Gerry Fitt 1926–
Northern Irish politician

4 People [in Northern Ireland] don't march as an alternative
   to jogging. They do it to assert their supremacy. It is pure
   tribalism, the cause of troubles all over the world.

in *The Times* 5 August 1994

5 The people have spoken and the politicians have had to
   listen.
   on the outcome of the referendum on the Good Friday agreement

in *Sunday Telegraph* 24 May 1998

F. Scott Fitzgerald 1896–1940
American novelist

6 See that little stream—we could walk to it in two minutes. It
   took the British a month to walk it—a whole empire
   walking very slowly, dying in front and pushing forward
   behind. And another empire walked very slowly backward a
   few inches a day, leaving the dead like a million bloody
   rugs.

Tender is the Night (1934)

Garret Fitzgerald 1926–
Irish Fine Gael statesman

7 Living in history is a bit like finding oneself in a shuttered
   mansion to which one has been brought blindfold, and
   trying to imagine what it might look like from the outside.

in *Irish Times* 9 May 1998

Robert, Marquis de Flers 1872–1927
and Arman de Caillavet 1869–1915
French playwrights

8 Democracy is the name we give the people whenever we
   need them.

L'habit vert, in *La petite illustration*
série théâtre 31 May 1913

Andrew Fletcher of Saltoun 1655–1716
Scottish patriot and anti-Unionist
see also **Last words** 213:3

1 I knew a very wise man so much of Sir Chr—'s sentiment, that he believed if a man were permitted to make all the ballads, he need not care who should make the laws of a nation.

'An Account of a Conversation concerning a Right Regulation of Government for the Good of Mankind. In a Letter to the Marquis of Montrose' (1704)

2 The Scots deserve no pity, if they voluntarily surrender their united and separate interests to the mercy of an united Parliament, where the English have so vast a majority . . . their 45 Scots members may dance round to all eternity, in this trap of their own making.

State of the Controversy betwixt United and Separate Parliaments (1706)

Paul Flynn 1935–
British Labour politician

3 He is hard on soft drugs and soft on hard drugs.
on Jack **Straw** *as Home Secretary and the dangers of alcohol*

in *Sunday Times* 16 April 2000 'Talking Heads'

Dario Fo 1926–
Italian dramatist

4 *Non si paga, non si paga.*
We won't pay, we won't pay.

title of play (1975; translated by Lino Pertile in 1978 as 'We Can't Pay? We Won't Pay!' and performed in London in 1981 as 'Can't Pay? Won't Pay!'); see **Slogans** 334:11

Ferdinand Foch 1851–1929
French general

5 My centre is giving way, my right is retreating, situation excellent, I am attacking.
message sent during the first Battle of the Marne, September 1914

R. Recouly *Foch* (1919)

6 This is not a peace treaty, it is an armistice for twenty years.
at the signing of the Treaty of Versailles, 1919

Paul Reynaud *Mémoires* (1963) vol. 2

Ken Follett 1949–
British writer

7 They are the rent boys of politics.
of those who give off-the-record briefing against ministers

in *Observer* 2 July 2000

8 The polite fiction that the Prime Minister's advisers are responsible is absurd. Control-freak Tony doesn't let Alastair Campbell and Peter Mandelson go around saying anything they like . . . Peter isn't the Prince of Darkness, though he may be Lady Macbeth.

in *Observer* 2 July 2000

Michael Foot 1913–
British Labour politician

9 Think of it! A second Chamber selected by the Whips. A seraglio of eunuchs.

in the House of Commons, 3 February 1969

1 Disraeli was my favourite Tory. He was an adventurer pure and simple, or impure and complex. I'm glad to say Gladstone got the better of him.

in Observer 16 March 1975 'Sayings of the Week'

2 It is not necessary that every time he rises he should give his famous imitation of a semi-house-trained polecat.
   of Norman **Tebbit**

in the House of Commons, 2 March 1978

of David **Steel**, *Leader of the Liberal Party:*
3 He's passed from rising hope to elder statesman without any intervening period whatsoever.

in the House of Commons, 28 March 1979

4 A speech from Ernest Bevin on a major occasion had all the horrific fascination of a public execution. If the mind was left immune, eyes and ears and emotions were riveted.

Aneurin Bevan (1962) vol. 1

Gerald Ford 1909–
American Republican statesman, 38th President of the US 1974–7
on Ford: see **Abzug** 1:2, **Johnson** 190:9, **Morton** 261:3

5 If the Government is big enough to give you everything you want, it is big enough to take away everything you have.

John F. Parker *If Elected* (1960); a similar remark has been attributed to Barry **Goldwater**

6 I am a Ford, not a Lincoln.
   on taking the vice-presidential oath, 6 December 1973

in Washington Post 7 December 1973

7 Our long national nightmare is over. Our Constitution works; our great Republic is a Government of laws and not of men.
   on being sworn in as President in succession to Richard **Nixon**

speech on 9 August 1974

8 I believe that truth is the glue that holds Government together, not only our Government, but civilization itself.
   on being sworn in as President

speech on 9 August 1974

Howell Forgy 1908–83
American naval chaplain

9 Praise the Lord and pass the ammunition.
   at Pearl Harbor, 7 December 1941, as Forgy moved along a line of sailors passing ammunition by hand to the deck (later the title of a song by Frank Loesser, 1942)

in New York Times 1 November 1942

E. M. Forster 1879–1970
English novelist

10 If I had to choose between betraying my country and betraying my friend, I hope I should have the guts to betray my country.

Two Cheers for Democracy (1951) 'What I Believe'

11 So Two cheers for Democracy: one because it admits variety and two because it permits criticism. Two cheers are quite enough: there is no occasion to give three. Only Love the Beloved Republic deserves that.

Two Cheers for Democracy (1951) 'What I Believe' ('Love, the beloved republic' borrowed from Swinburne's poem 'Hertha')

Frederick Forsyth 1938–
English thriller writer

12 If a man cannot keep a measly affair secret, what is he doing in charge of the Intelligence Service.
   on the Foreign Secretary Robin Cook and the news coverage surrounding the break-up of his marriage

in Guardian 14 January 1998

Harry Emerson Fosdick 1878–1969
American Baptist minister

1 I renounce war for its consequences, for the lies it lives on and propagates, for the undying hatred it arouses, for the dictatorships it puts in the place of democracy, for the starvation that stalks after it.

Armistice Day Sermon in New York, 1933, in *The Secret of Victorious Living* (1934)

Charles Foster 1828–1904
American politician

2 Isn't this a billion dollar country?
at the 51st Congress, responding to a Democratic gibe about a 'million dollar Congress'

also attributed to Thomas B. Reed, who reported the exchange in *North American Review* March 1892, vol. 154

George Foster 1847–1931
Canadian politician

3 In these somewhat troublesome days when the great Mother Empire stands splendidly isolated in Europe.

in *Official Report of the Debates of the House of Commons of the Dominion of Canada* (1896) vol. 41, for 16 January 1896; on 22 January 1896; see **Newspaper headlines** 267:14

Charles Fourier 1772–1837
French social theorist

4 The extension of women's rights is the basic principle of all social progress.

Théorie des Quatre Mouvements (1808) vol. 2

Norman Fowler 1938–
British Conservative politician

5 I have a young family and for the next few years I should like to devote more time to them.
often quoted as 'spend more time with my family'

resignation letter to the Prime Minister, in *Guardian* 4 January 1990; see **Thatcher** 357:15

Caroline Fox d. 1774
wife of Henry Fox, Lord **Holland**, and mother of Charles James **Fox**

6 That little boy will be a thorn in Charles's side as long as he lives.
*seeing in the young William **Pitt** a prospective rival for her son Charles James **Fox***

attributed

Charles James Fox 1749–1806
English Whig politician, son of Henry Fox, Lord **Holland** and Caroline **Fox**
on Fox: see **Gibbon** 145:15, **Holland** 175:1, **Johnson** 192:1, **Shaw-Lefevre** 329:3; see also **Last words** 212:9

7 He [Pitt the Younger] was uniformly of an opinion which, though not a popular one, he was ready to aver, that the right of governing was not property but a trust.
*on **Pitt**'s scheme of Parliamentary Reform, 1785*

J. L. Hammond *Charles James Fox* (1903)

1 How much the greatest event it is that ever happened in the world! and how much the best!
   on the fall of the Bastille

letter to Richard Fitzpatrick, 30 July 1789

In the last year of his life Fox's friends suggested that he should accept a peerage:

2 I will not close my politics in that foolish way.

in *Dictionary of National Biography* (1917–)

Henry Fox see Holland

Anatole France 1844–1924
French novelist and man of letters

3 In every well-governed state, wealth is a sacred thing; in democracies it is the only sacred thing.

L'Île des pingouins (1908)

4 They [the poor] have to labour in the face of the majestic equality of the law, which forbids the rich as well as the poor to sleep under bridges, to beg in the streets, and to steal bread.

Le Lys rouge (1894)

Francis I 1494–1547
King of France from 1515

5 Of all I had, only honour and life have been spared.
   letter to his mother following his defeat at Pavia, 1525, usually quoted as 'All is lost, save honour'

in *Collection des Documents Inédits sur l'Histoire de France* (1847) vol. 1; see **Misquotations** 254:1

Anne Frank 1929–45
German-born Jewish diarist

6 I want to go on living even after death!

diary, 4 April 1944

Felix Frankfurter 1882–1965
American judge

7 It is a fair summary of history to say that the safeguards of liberty have been forged in controversies involving not very nice people.

dissenting opinion in *United States v. Rabinowitz* (1950)

Benjamin Franklin 1706–90
American politician, inventor, and scientist
on Franklin: see **Turgot** 367:7

8 Idleness and pride tax with a heavier hand than kings and parliaments. If we can get rid of the former, we may easily bear the latter.
   on the Stamp Act

letter 11 July 1765

9 We must indeed all hang together, or, most assuredly, we shall all hang separately.
   at the signing of the Declaration of Independence, 4 July 1776 (possibly not original)

P. M. Zall *Ben Franklin* (1980)

10 There never was a good war, or a bad peace.

letter to Josiah Quincy, 11 September 1783

1 I wish the bald eagle had not been chosen as the representative of our country; he is a bird of bad moral character . . . like those among men who live by sharping and robbing, he is generally poor, and often very lousy.
   The turkey . . . is a much more respectable bird, and withal a true original native of America.

on being asked, 'have we got a republic or a monarchy?':
2 A republic, if you can keep it.

3 In this world nothing can be said to be certain, except death and taxes.

4 George Washington, Commander of the American Armies, who, like Joshua of old, commanded the sun and the moon to stand still, and they obeyed him.
   *toast given at a dinner at Versailles, when the British minister had proposed a toast to **George III**, likening him to the sun, and the French minister had likened **Louis XVI** to the moon*

5 They that can give up essential liberty to obtain a little temporary safety deserve neither liberty nor safety.

6 No nation was ever ruined by trade.

	letter to Sarah Bache, 26 January 1784
	in conversation, 18 September 1787
	letter to Jean Baptiste Le Roy, 13 November 1789; see Daniel Defoe *History of the Devil* (1726) 'Things as certain as death and taxes, can be more firmly believed'
	attributed
	Historical Review of Pennsylvania (1759)
	Thoughts on Commercial Subjects

Lord Franks 1905–92
British philosopher and administrator

7 The Pentagon, that immense monument to modern man's subservience to the desk.

on the composition of such bodies as royal commissions and committees of inquiry:
8 There is a fashion in these things and when you are in fashion you are asked to do a lot.

9 A secret in the Oxford sense: you may tell it to only one person at a time.

	in *Observer* 30 November 1952
	in conversation, 24 January 1977; Peter Hennessy *Whitehall* (1990)
	in *Sunday Telegraph* 30 January 1977

Michael Frayn 1933–
British writer

10 To be absolutely honest, what I feel really bad about is that I don't feel worse. That's the ineffectual liberal's problem in a nutshell.

in *Observer* 8 August 1965

Frederick the Great 1712–86
King of Prussia from 1740

11 Drive out prejudices through the door, and they will return through the window.

12 My people and I have come to an agreement which satisfies us both. They are to say what they please, and I am to do what I please.
   his interpretation of benevolent despotism

13 Rascals, would you live for ever?
   to hesitant Guards at Kolin, 18 June 1757

	letter to Voltaire, 19 March 1771
	attributed
	attributed

E. A. Freeman 1823–92
English historian

1 History is past politics, and politics is present history.

Methods of Historical Study (1886)

John Freeth c.1731–1808
English poet

2 The loss of America what can repay?
New colonies seek for at Botany Bay.

'Botany Bay' in *New London Magazine* (1786)

Milton Friedman 1912–
American economist and exponent of monetarism; policy adviser to President Reagan 1981–9

3 There is an invisible hand in politics that operates in the opposite direction to the invisible hand in the market. In politics, individuals who seek to promote only the public good are led by an invisible hand to promote special interests that it was no part of their intention to promote.

Bright Promises, Dismal Performance: An Economist's Protest (1983)

4 Few trends could so thoroughly undermine the very foundations of our free society as the acceptance by corporate officials of a social responsibility other than to make as much money for their stockholders as possible.

Capitalism and Freedom (1962)

5 A society that puts equality—in the sense of equality of outcome—ahead of freedom will end up with neither equality nor freedom.

Free to Choose (1980)

6 The high rate of unemployment among teenagers, and especially black teenagers, is both a scandal and a serious source of social unrest. Yet it is largely a result of minimum wage laws . . . We regard the minimum wage law as one of the most, if not the most, antiblack laws on the statute books.

Free to Choose (1980)

7 There's only one place where inflation is made: that's in Washington.

in 1977; attributed

8 Thank heavens we do not get all of the government that we are made to pay for.

attributed; quoted by Lord Harris in the House of Lords, 24 November 1994

Robert Frost 1874–1963
American poet

9 I never dared be radical when young
For fear it would make me conservative when old.

'Desert Places' (1936)

10 My apple trees will never get across
And eat the cones under his pines, I tell him.
He only says, 'Good fences make good neighbours.'

'Mending Wall' (1914)

Francis Fukuyama 1952–
American historian

11 What we may be witnessing is not just the end of the Cold War but the end of history as such: that is, the end point of man's ideological evolution and the universalism of Western liberal democracy.

in *Independent* 20 September 1989

J. William Fulbright 1905-95
American Senator

1 The Soviet Union has indeed been our greatest menace, not so much because of what it has done, but because of the excuses it has provided us for our failures.

in Observer 21 December 1958 'Sayings of the Year'

2 A policy that can be accurately, though perhaps not prudently, defined as one of 'peaceful coexistence'.

speech in the US Senate, 27 March 1964

3 We must dare to think 'unthinkable' thoughts. We must learn to explore all the options and possibilities that confront us in a complex and rapidly changing world. We must learn to welcome and not to fear the voices of dissent. We must dare to think about 'unthinkable things' because when things become unthinkable, thinking stops and action becomes mindless.

speech in the US Senate, 27 March 1964

Alfred Funke b. 1869
German writer

4 *Gott strafe England!*
God punish England!

Sword and Myrtle (1914)

David Maxwell Fyfe see Kilmuir

Hugh Gaitskell 1906-63
British Labour politician; Leader of the Labour Party from 1955
on Gaitskell: see **Bevan** 37:1, **Crossman** 99:4

5 The subtle terrorism of words.
in a warning given to his Party, c.1957

Harry Hopkins *The New Look* (1963); attributed

6 There are some of us . . . who will fight and fight and fight again to save the Party we love.
opposing the vote in favour of unilateral disarmament

speech at Labour Party Conference, 5 October 1960

7 It means the end of a thousand years of history.
on a European federation

speech at Labour Party Conference, 3 October 1962

John Kenneth Galbraith 1908-
Canadian-born American economist, noted for his criticism of a perceived preoccupation in Western society with economic growth for its own sake; US Ambassador to India 1961-3

8 The affluent society.

title of book (1958)

9 The conventional wisdom.
ironic term for 'the beliefs that are at any time assiduously, solemnly and mindlessly traded between the conventionally wise'

The Affluent Society (1958)

10 It is a far, far better thing to have a firm anchor in nonsense than to put out on the troubled seas of thought.

The Affluent Society (1958)

11 In a community where public services have failed to keep abreast of private consumption things are very different. Here, in an atmosphere of private opulence and public squalor, the private goods have full sway.

The Affluent Society (1958)

12 The greater the wealth, the thicker will be the dirt.

The Affluent Society (1958)

13 It is not necessary to advertise food to hungry people, fuel to cold people, or houses to the homeless.

American Capitalism (1952)

1 Trickle-down theory—the less than elegant metaphor that if   *The Culture of Contentment* (1992)
one feeds the horse enough oats, some will pass through to
the road for the sparrows.

2 You cannot know the intentions of a government that   *A Life in Our Times* (1981)
doesn't know them itself.
    'Galbraith's First Law of Intelligence', formulated in early 1960s

3 The reduction of politics to a spectator sport . . . has been   *A Life in Our Times* (1981)
one of the more malign accomplishments of television.
Television newsmen are breathless on how the game is
being played, largely silent on what the game is all about.

4 The experience of being disastrously wrong is salutary; no   *A Life in Our Times* (1981)
economist should be denied it, and not many are.

5 In public administration good sense would seem to require   *A Life in Our Times* (1981)
the public expectation be kept at the lowest possible level in
order to minimize eventual disappointment.

6 After a lifetime in public office, self-censorship becomes not   *A Life in Our Times* (1981)
only automatic but a part of one's personality.

7 Nothing is so firmly established in Puritan and Presbyterian   *A Life in Our Times* (1981)
belief as that people cannot be suffering very much if they
are out in healthy fresh air—and also safely out of sight.
    of the public view of rural as opposed to urban poverty

8 Of all the races on earth, the Indians have the most nearly   *A Life in Our Times* (1981)
inexhaustible appetite for oratory.

9 One of the recurrent and dangerous influences on our   *A Life in Our Times* (1981)
foreign policy—fear of the political consequences of doing
the sensible thing, which in many cases is nothing much at
all.

10 One of the little-celebrated powers of Presidents (and other   *A Life in Our Times* (1981)
high government officials) is to listen to their critics with
just enough sympathy to ensure their silence.

of the defeat of Germany in World War Two:
11 That they were defeated is conclusive testimony to the   in *Fortune* December 1945
inherent inefficiencies of dictatorship, the inherent
efficiencies of freedom.

12 [Intellectual torpor is] the disease of opposition parties, for   letter to Adlai Stevenson,
initiative and imagination ordinarily lie with responsibility   September 1953
for action.

13 Politics is not the art of the possible. It consists in choosing   letter to President **Kennedy**, 2
between the disastrous and the unpalatable.   March 1962; see **Bismarck** 41:7

14 There are times in politics when you must be on the right   attributed, 1968
side and lose.

15 Galbraith's law states that anyone who says he won't resign   attributed, 1973
four times, will.

Indira Gandhi 1917–84

Indian stateswoman and daughter of Jawaharlal **Nehru**, Prime
Minister of India 1966–77 and 1980–4

16 Politics is the art of acquiring, holding, and wielding power.   attributed, 1975

Mahatma Gandhi 1869–1948

Indian nationalist and spiritual leader
on Gandhi: see **Naidu** 263:11, **Nehru** 265:6

1 What difference does it make to the dead, the orphans and the homeless, whether the mad destruction is wrought under the name of totalitarianism or the holy name of liberty or democracy?

Non-Violence in Peace and War (1942) vol. 1

2 The moment the slave resolves that he will no longer be a slave, his fetters fall. He frees himself and shows the way to others. Freedom and slavery are mental states.

Non-Violence in Peace and War (1949) vol. 2

3 Non-violence is the first article of my faith. It is also the last article of my creed.
    speech at Shahi Bag, 18 March 1922, on a charge of sedition

in *Young India* 23 March 1922

4 Please go on. It is my day of silence.
    note passed to the British Cabinet Mission at a meeting in 1942

Peter Hennessy *Never Again* (1992)

on being asked what he thought of modern civilization:
5 That would be a good idea.
    while visiting England in 1930

E. F. Schumacher *Good Work* (1979)

James A. Garfield 1831–81

American Republican statesman, 20th President of the US, who was assassinated within months of taking presidential office

6 Fellow-citizens: God reigns, and the Government at Washington lives!
    *speech on the assassination of President **Lincoln**, 1865*

in *Death of President Garfield* (1881)

7 I am not willing that this discussion should close without any mention of the value of a true teacher. Give me a log hut, with only a simple bench, Mark Hopkins [president of Williams College] on one end and I on the other, and you may have all the buildings, apparatus and libraries without him.

address to Williams College Alumni, New York, 28 December 1871

Giuseppe Garibaldi 1807–82

Italian patriot and military leader

8 Men, I'm getting out of Rome. Anyone who wants to carry on the war against the outsiders, come with me. I can offer you neither honours nor wages; I offer you hunger, thirst, forced marches, battles and death. Anyone who loves his country, follow me.

Giuseppe Guerzoni *Garibaldi* (1882) vol. 1 (not a verbatim record)

John Nance Garner 1868–1967

American politician

9 The vice-presidency isn't worth a pitcher of warm piss.

O. C. Fisher *Cactus Jack* (1978)

William Lloyd Garrison 1805–79

American anti-slavery campaigner

10 I am in earnest—I will not equivocate—I will not excuse—I will not retreat a single inch—and I will be heard!

in *The Liberator* 1 January 1831 'Salutatory Address'

11 The compact which exists between the North and the South is 'a covenant with death and an agreement with hell'.

resolution adopted by the Massachusetts Anti-Slavery Society, 27 January 1843

James Louis Garvin 1868–1947
British journalist and editor of the *Observer*

1 He spoke for an hour and put the house in his pocket.
  of F. E. **Smith***'s maiden speech in the House of Commons, 12 May 1906*

attributed

Eric Geddes 1875–1937
British politician and administrator

2 The Germans, if this Government is returned, are going to pay every penny; they are going to be squeezed as a lemon is squeezed—until the pips squeak.

speech at Cambridge, 10 December 1918

Martha Gellhorn 1908–98
American journalist

of the defeat of the Spanish Republic:
3 I daresay we all became more competent press tourists because of it, since we never again cared so much. You can only love one war; afterward, I suppose, you do your duty.

The Honeyed Peace (1953)

Jean Genet 1910–86
French novelist, poet, and dramatist

4 What we need is hatred. From it our ideas are born.

The Blacks (1959); epigraph

5 Are you there . . . Africa of the millions of royal slaves, deported Africa, drifting continent, are you there? Slowly you vanish, you withdraw into the past, into the tales of castaways, colonial museums, the works of scholars.

The Blacks (1959)

Genghis Khan (Temujin) 1162–1227
founder of the Mongol empire, who took the name Genghis Khan ('ruler of all') in 1206 after uniting the nomadic tribes

6 Happiness lies in conquering one's enemies, in driving them in front of oneself, in taking their property, in savouring their despair, in outraging their wives and daughters.

Witold Rodzinski *The Walled Kingdom: A History of China* (1979)

Máire Geoghegan-Quinn 1950–
Irish politician and writer

7 I've kept political diaries ever since I went into politics . . . I'd love to do a political memoir, but a lot of people will have to be dead first.

in *Irish Times* 6 November 1997

George III 1738–1820
King of Great Britain and Ireland from 1760
on George III: see **Walpole** 373:10

8 Born and educated in this country, I glory in the name of Briton.

The King's Speech on Opening the Session 18 November 1760

9 When he has wearied me for two hours he looks at his watch, to see if he may not tire me for an hour more.
  of George **Grenville**

in 1765; Horace Walpole *The Reign of George III* (1845)

of America:
1 Knavery seems to be so much the striking feature of its
  inhabitants that it may not in the end be an evil that they
  become aliens to this kingdom.

draft of letter to Lord Shelburne,
10 November 1782

George IV 1762–1830
King of Great Britain and Ireland from 1820

2 PRINCE OF WALES: True blue and Mrs Crewe.
  MRS CREWE: Buff and blue and all of you.
    toast proposed by George IV when Prince of Wales to Mrs Crewe,
    in honour of her support for the Whigs and Charles James Fox in
    the Westminster election of 1784 (buff and blue were the Whig
    colours)

at a dinner at Carlton House, May
1784; Amanda Foreman *Georgiana
Duchess of Devonshire* (1998)

George V 1865–1936
King of Great Britain and Ireland from 1910
see also **Last words** 212:8

3 I venture to allude to the impression which seemed
  generally to prevail among their brethren across the seas,
  that the Old Country must wake up if she intends to
  maintain her old position of pre-eminence in her Colonial
  trade against foreign competitors.

speech at Guildhall, 5 December
1901 (the speech was reprinted in
1911 with the title 'Wake up,
England')

4 I pray that my coming to Ireland today may prove to be the
  first step towards an end of strife among her people,
  whatever their race or creed. In that hope I appeal to all
  Irishmen to pause, to stretch out the hand of forbearance
  and conciliation, to forgive and forget, and to join with me
  in making for the land they love a new era of peace,
  contentment and goodwill.

speech to the new Ulster
Parliament at Stormont, 22 June
1921; Kenneth Rose *King George V*
(1983)

5 I have many times asked myself whether there can be more
  potent advocates of peace upon earth through the years to
  come than this massed multitude of silent witnesses to the
  desolation of war.
    message read at Terlincthun Cemetery, Boulogne, 13 May 1922

in *The Times* 15 May 1922

6 You have kept up the dignity of the office without using it to
  give you dignity.
    to the outgoing Prime Minister, Ramsay **MacDonald**

Ramsay MacDonald diary 7 June
1934

7 The complex forms and balanced spirit of our constitution
  were not the discovery of a single era, still less of a single
  party or of a single person. They are the slow accretion of
  centuries, the outcome of patience, tradition and experience.
    the words of G. M. Trevelyan in the King's Silver Jubilee address
    to Parliament, 1935

David Cannadine *G. M. Trevelyan: a
Life in History* (1992)

8 I will not have another war. *I will not.* The last one was
  none of my doing and if there is another one and we are
  threatened with being brought into it, I will go to Trafalgar
  Square and wave a red flag myself sooner than allow this
  country to be brought in.

c.1935, in Andrew Roberts *Eminent
Churchillians* (1994)

in conversation with Anthony **Eden**, *23 December 1935, following*
Samuel Hoare's resignation as Foreign Secretary:
9 I said to your predecessor: 'You know what they're all
  saying, no more coals to Newcastle, no more Hoares to
  Paris.' The fellow didn't even laugh.

Earl of Avon *Facing the Dictators*
(1962)

1 After I am dead, the boy will ruin himself in twelve months.
on his son, the future Edward VIII

Keith Middlemas and John Barnes *Baldwin* (1969)

on H. G. Wells's comment on 'an alien and uninspiring court':
2 I may be uninspiring, but I'll be damned if I'm an alien!

Sarah Bradford *George VI* (1989); attributed

3 My father was frightened of his mother; I was frightened of my father, and I am damned well going to see to it that my children are frightened of me.

attributed in Randolph S. Churchill *Lord Derby* (1959), but almost certainly apocryphal; see Kenneth Rose *George V* (1983)

George VI 1895–1952
King of Great Britain and Northern Ireland from 1936

4 Personally I feel happier now that we have no allies to be polite to and to pamper.
to Queen Mary, 27 June 1940

John Wheeler-Bennett *King George VI* (1958)

5 ATTLEE: I've won the election.
GEORGE VI: I know. I heard it on the Six O'Clock News.
first exchange between the King and his newly elected Labour Prime Minister, 26 July 1945; perhaps apocryphal

Peter Hennessy *Never Again* (1992)

6 Well the Prime Minister has had a very difficult time, I'm sure. What I say is 'Thank God for the Civil Service.'
shortly after Labour's election victory

Hugh Dalton *Political Diary* (1986) 28 July 1945

7 HARRY TRUMAN: You've had a revolution.
GEORGE VI: Oh no! we don't have those here.
*during President **Truman**'s visit to Britain just after Labour's election victory.*

Hugh Dalton *Political Diary* (1986) 28 July 1945

8 Everything is going nowadays. Before long, I shall have to go myself.
on hearing, c.1949, that the Sackville-West family home, Knole Park, was to be sold to the National Trust

Andrew Roberts *Eminent Churchillians* (1994)

Geronimo c.1829–1909
Apache leader

9 Once I moved about like the wind. Now I surrender to you and that is all.

surrendering to General Crook, 25 March 1886; Dee Brown *Bury My Heart at Wounded Knee* (1970) ch. 17

Edward Gibbon 1737–94
English historian

10 The division of Europe into a number of independent states connected, however, with each other, by the general resemblance of religion, language, and manners, is productive of the most beneficial consequences to the liberty of mankind.

The Decline and Fall of the Roman Empire (1776–88)

11 In elective monarchies, the vacancy of the throne is a moment big with danger and mischief.

The Decline and Fall of the Roman Empire (1776–88)

12 The various modes of worship, which prevailed in the Roman world, were all considered by the people as equally true; by the philosopher, as equally false; and by the magistrate, as equally useful. And thus toleration produced not only mutual indulgence, but even religious concord.

The Decline and Fall of the Roman Empire (1776–88)

1 The principles of a free constitution are irrecoverably lost, when the legislative power is nominated by the executive.

The Decline and Fall of the Roman Empire (1776–88)

2 The ascent to greatness, however steep and dangerous, may entertain an active spirit with the consciousness and exercise of its own powers; but the possession of a throne could never yet afford a lasting satisfaction to an ambitious mind.

The Decline and Fall of the Roman Empire (1776–88)

3 History . . . is, indeed, little more than the register of the crimes, follies, and misfortunes of mankind.

The Decline and Fall of the Roman Empire (1776–88); see **Voltaire** 372:4

4 In every age and country, the wiser, or at least the stronger, of the two sexes, has usurped the powers of the state, and confined the other to the cares and pleasures of domestic life.

The Decline and Fall of the Roman Empire (1776–88)

5 According to the reasoning of tyrants, those who have been esteemed worthy of the throne deserve death, and those who deliberate have already rebelled.

The Decline and Fall of the Roman Empire (1776–88)

6 All taxes must, at last, fall upon agriculture.

quoting Artaxerxes, in *The Decline and Fall of the Roman Empire* (1776–88) ch. 8

7 Whenever the offence inspires less horror than the punishment, the rigour of penal law is obliged to give way to the common feelings of mankind.

The Decline and Fall of the Roman Empire (1776–88) ch. 14

8 Corruption, the most infallible symptom of constitutional liberty.

The Decline and Fall of the Roman Empire (1776–88)

9 In every deed of mischief he had a heart to resolve, a head to contrive, and a hand to execute.
   of Comnenus

The Decline and Fall of the Roman Empire (1776–88)

10 Our sympathy is cold to the relation of distant misery.

The Decline and Fall of the Roman Empire (1776–88)

11 Persuasion is the resource of the feeble; and the feeble can seldom persuade.

The Decline and Fall of the Roman Empire (1776–88)

12 All that is human must retrograde if it does not advance.

The Decline and Fall of the Roman Empire (1776–88)

13 The satirist may laugh, the philosopher may preach, but Reason herself will respect the prejudices and habits which have been consecrated by the experience of mankind.

Memoirs of My Life (1796)

14 I admire his eloquence, I approve his politics, I adore his chivalry, and I can even forgive his superstition.
   of Edmund **Burke**

letter to Lord Sheffield, 5 February 1791

15 Let him do what he will I must love the dog.
   of Charles James **Fox**

letter to Lord Sheffield, 6 January 1793

Kahlil Gibran 1883–1931

Syrian writer and painter

16 Are you a politician who says to himself: 'I will use my country for my own benefit'? . . . Or are you a devoted patriot, who whispers in the ear of his inner self: 'I love to serve my country as a faithful servant.'

The New Frontier (1931); see **Kennedy** 198:8

W. S. Gilbert 1836–1911

English writer of comic and satirical verse

1 All shall equal be.
The Earl, the Marquis, and the Dook,
The Groom, the Butler, and the Cook,
The Aristocrat who banks with Coutts,
The Aristocrat who cleans the boots.

The Gondoliers (1889)

2 When every one is somebodee,
Then no one's anybody.

The Gondoliers (1889) act 2

3 I always voted at my party's call,
And I never thought of thinking for myself at all.

HMS Pinafore (1878)

4 I often think it's comical
How Nature always does contrive
That every boy and every gal,
That's born into the world alive,
Is either a little Liberal,
Or else a little Conservative!

Iolanthe (1882)

5 The House of Peers, throughout the war,
Did nothing in particular,
And did it very well.

Iolanthe (1882)

6 When in that House MPs divide,
If they've a brain and cerebellum too,
They have to leave that brain outside,
And vote just as their leaders tell 'em to.

Iolanthe (1882)

7 The prospect of a lot
Of dull MPs in close proximity,
All thinking for themselves is what
No man can face with equanimity.

Iolanthe (1882)

8 The idiot who praises, with enthusiastic tone,
All centuries but this, and every country but his own.

The Mikado (1885)

9 No Englishman unmoved that statement hears,
Because, with all our faults, we love our House of Peers.

The Pirates of Penzance (1879)

Ian Gilmour 1926–

British Conservative politician

10 Unfortunately monetarism, like Marxism, suffered the only
fate that for a theory is worse than death: it was put into
practice.

Dancing with Dogma (1992)

Newton Gingrich 1943–

American Republican politician

11 No society can survive, no civilization can survive, with
12-year-olds having babies, with 15-year-olds killing each
other, with 17-year-olds dying of Aids, with 18-year-olds
getting diplomas they can't read.
in December 1994, after the Republican electoral victory

in *The Times* 9 February 1995

12 One of the greatest intellectual failures of the welfare state is
the penchant for sacrifice, so long as the only people being
asked to sacrifice are working, tax-paying Americans.

in *USA Today* 16 January 1995

George Gipp d. 1920
American footballer

1 Win just one for the Gipper.

catch-phrase later associated with Ronald **Reagan**, who uttered the immortal words in the 1940 film *Knute Rockne, All American*

Rudy Giuliani 1944–
American Republican politician, Mayor of New York

2 Freedom is about the willingness of every single human being to cede to lawful authority a great deal of discretion about what you do, and how you do it.

attributed, in *Independent* 10 July 1999

3 Politics comes at least second, maybe third, maybe fourth, somewhere else. It'll all work itself out some way politically.
   announcing that he and his wife were separating

in *Observer* 14 May 2000

Catherine Gladstone 1812–1900
wife of William Ewart **Gladstone**

to her husband:
4 Oh, William dear, if you weren't such a great man you would be a terrible bore.

Roy Jenkins *Gladstone* (1995)

William Ewart Gladstone 1809–98
British Liberal statesman; Prime Minister, 1868–74, 1880–5, 1886, 1892–4
on Gladstone: see **Bagehot** 23:2, **Churchill** 79:7, 79:10, **Churchill** 85:4, **Disraeli** 113:2, 113:7, **Foot** 134:1, **Hennessy** 168:6, **Labouchere** 208:9, **Macaulay** 229:9, **Salisbury** 313:4, **Victoria** 370:9, 371:3

5 Ireland, Ireland! that cloud in the west, that coming storm.

letter to his wife, 12 October 1845

6 This is the negation of God erected into a system of Government.

A Letter to the Earl of Aberdeen on the State Prosecutions of the Neapolitan Government (1851)

7 Finance is, as it were, the stomach of the country, from which all the other organs take their tone.

article on finance, 1858, in H. C. G. Matthew *Gladstone 1809–1874* (1986)

8 Your business is not to govern the country but it is, if you think fit, to call to account those who do govern it.

speech to the House of Commons, 29 January 1869

9 I am come among you 'unmuzzled'.
   after his parliamentary defeat at Oxford University

speech in Manchester, 18 July 1865

10 You cannot fight against the future. Time is on our side.
   on the Reform Bill

speech, House of Commons, 27 April 1866

11 My mission is to pacify Ireland.
   on receiving the news that he was to form his first cabinet, 1 December 1868

H. C. G. Matthew *Gladstone 1809–1874* (1986)

12 Swimming for his life, a man does not see much of the country through which the river winds.

diary, 31 December 1868

13 We have been borne down in a torrent of gin and beer.

letter to his brother, 6 February 1874

1 Human justice is ever lagging after wrong, as the prayers in Homer came limping after sin.

in Contemporary Review December 1876

2 The love of freedom itself is hardly stronger in England than the love of aristocracy.

in Nineteenth Century 1877

3 Let the Turks now carry away their abuses in the only possible manner, namely by carrying off themselves . . . one and all, bag and baggage, shall I hope clear out from the province they have desolated and profaned.

Bulgarian Horrors and the Question of the East (1876)

4 [The British Constitution] presumes more boldly than any other the good sense and the good faith of those who work it.

Gleanings of Past Years (1879) vol. 1

5 [An] Established Clergy will always be a Tory Corps d'Armée.

letter to Bishop Goodwin, 8 September 1881

6 To the actual, as distinct from the reported, strength of the Empire, India adds nothing. She immensely adds to the responsibility of Government.

H. C. G. Matthew *Gladstone 1875–1898* (1995)

7 There never was a Churchill from John of Marlborough down that had either morals or principles.

in conversation in 1882, recorded by Captain R. V. Briscoe; R. F. Foster *Lord Randolph Churchill* (1981)

8 I would tell them of my own intention to keep my counsel . . . and I will venture to recommend them, as an old Parliamentary hand, to do the same.

in the House of Commons, 21 January 1886

9 This, if I understand it, is one of those golden moments of our history, one of those opportunities which may come and may go, but which rarely returns.
on the Second Reading of the Home Rule Bill

in the House of Commons, 7 June 1886

10 I will venture to say, that upon the one great class of subjects, the largest and the most weighty of them all, where the leading and determining considerations that ought to lead to a conclusion are truth, justice, and humanity—upon these, gentlemen, all the world over, I will back the masses against the classes.

speech in Liverpool, 28 June 1886

11 One prayer absorbs all others: Ireland, Ireland, Ireland.

diary, 10 April 1887

12 Welsh nationality is as great a reality as English nationality.

speech at Swansea, 4 June 1887

13 The blubbering Cabinet.
of the colleagues who wept at his final Cabinet meeting

diary, 1 March 1894; note

14 What that Sicilian mule was to me, I have been to the Queen.
of a mule on which Gladstone rode, which he 'could neither love nor like', although it had rendered him 'much valuable service'

memorandum, 20 March 1894

15 Former Prime Ministers are like great rafts floating untethered in a harbour.

Roy Jenkins *Gladstone* (1995)

16 I absorb the vapour and return it as a flood.
on public speaking

Lord Riddell *Some Things That Matter* (1927 ed.)

17 I am sorry to say that I have a long speech fermenting in me, and I feel as a loaf might in the oven.

Roy Jenkins *Gladstone* (1995)

18 It is not a Life at all. It is a Reticence, in three volumes.
on J. W. Cross's Life of George Eliot

E. F. Benson *As We Were* (1930)

19 [Money should] fructify in the pockets of the people.

H. G. C. Matthew *Gladstone 1809–1874* (1986)

1 There is scarcely a single moral action of a single man of which other men can have such a knowledge, in its ultimate grounds, its surrounding incidents, and the real determining cause of its merits, as to warrant their pronouncing a conclusive judgement upon it.

H. C. G. Matthew *Gladstone 1875–1898* (1995)

2 We are bound to lose Ireland in consequence of years of cruelty, stupidity and misgovernment and I would rather lose her as a friend than as a foe.

Margot Asquith *More Memories* (1933)

Thomas Glascock

US Senator

*when General Thomas Glascock of Georgia took his seat in the US Senate, a mutual friend expressed the wish to introduce him to Henry **Clay** of Virginia:*

3 No, sir! I am his adversary, and choose not to subject myself to his fascination.

Robert V. Remini *Henry Clay* (1991)

David Glencross 1936–

British television executive

4 It is unlikely that the government reaches for a revolver when it hears the word culture. The more likely response is to search for a dictionary.

Royal Television Society conference on the future of television, 26–27 November 1988; see **Johst** 192:5

Joseph Goebbels 1897–1945

German Nazi leader

5 We can manage without butter but not, for example, without guns. If we are attacked we can only defend ourselves with guns not with butter.

speech in Berlin, 17 January 1936; see **Goering** 149:7

6 Making noise is an effective means of opposition.

Ernest K. Bramsted *Goebbels and National Socialist Propaganda 1925–45* (1965)

Hermann Goering 1893–1946

German Nazi leader

7 We have no butter . . . but I ask you—would you rather have butter or guns? . . . preparedness makes us powerful. Butter merely makes us fat.

speech at Hamburg, 1936; W. Frischauer *Goering* (1951); see **Goebbels** 149:5

8 I herewith commission you to carry out all preparations with regard to . . . a *total solution* of the Jewish question in those territories of Europe which are under German influence.
  instructions to Heydrich, 31 July 1941

W. L. Shirer *The Rise and Fall of the Third Reich* (1962)

Nikolai Gogol 1809–52

Russian writer

9 [Are not] you too, Russia, speeding along like a spirited *troika* that nothing can overtake? . . . Everything on earth is flying past, and looking askance, other nations and states draw aside and make way.

Dead Souls (1842)

Isaac Goldberg 1887–1938

1 Diplomacy is to do and say
  The nastiest thing in the nicest way.

The Reflex October 1927

Ludwig Max Goldberger 1848–1913

2 America, the land of unlimited possibilities.

Land of Unlimited Possibilities: Observations on Economic Life in the United States of America (1903)

Emma Goldman 1869–1940

American anarchist

3 Anarchism, then, really, stands for the liberation of the human mind from the dominion of religion; the liberation of the human body from the dominion of property; liberation from the shackles and restraints of government.

Anarchism and Other Essays (1910)

Oliver Goldsmith 1728–74

Anglo-Irish writer, poet, and playwright

4 Ill fares the land, to hast'ning ills a prey,
  Where wealth accumulates, and men decay;
  Princes and lords may flourish, or may fade;
  A breath can make them, as a breath has made;
  But a bold peasantry, their country's pride,
  When once destroyed, can never be supplied.
  A time there was, ere England's griefs began,
  When every rood of ground maintained its man;
  For him light labour spread her wholesome store,
  Just gave what life required, but gave no more;
  His best companions, innocence and health;
  And his best riches, ignorance of wealth.

The Deserted Village (1770)

5   How wide the limits stand
  Between a splendid and a happy land.

The Deserted Village (1770)

6 Such is the patriot's boast, where'er we roam,
  His first, best country ever is, at home.

The Traveller (1764)

7 Laws grind the poor, and rich men rule the law.

The Traveller (1764)

8 How small, of all that human hearts endure,
  That part which laws or kings can cause or cure!

The Traveller (1764); see **Johnson** 190:16

Barry Goldwater 1909–98

American Republican politician

9 I would remind you that extremism in the defence of liberty is no vice! And let me remind you also that moderation in the pursuit of justice is no virtue!
  speech accepting the presidential nomination, 16 July 1964

in *New York Times* 17 July 1964

Maud Gonne 1867–1953

Irish nationalist

10 The Famine Queen.
  of Queen Victoria

in *L'Irlande Libre* 1900

Amy Goodman 1957–

American journalist

1 Go to where the silence is and say something.
   *accepting an award from Columbia University for her coverage of
   the 1991 massacre in East Timor by Indonesian troops*

in *Columbia Journalism Review*
March/April 1994

Richard Goodwin

2 People come to Washington believing it's the centre of
power. I know I did. It was only much later that I learned
that Washington is a steering wheel that's not connected to
the engine.

Peter McWilliams *Ain't Nobody's
Business If You Do* (1993)

Mikhail Sergeevich Gorbachev 1931–

Soviet politician, General Secretary of the Communist Party of
the USSR 1985–91 and President 1988–91
on Gorbachev: see **Gromyko** 155:10, **Thatcher** 357:6

3 The guilt of Stalin and his immediate entourage before the
Party and the people for the mass repressions and
lawlessness they committed is enormous and unforgivable.

speech on the seventieth
anniversary of the Russian
Revolution, 2 November 1987

4 The idea of restructuring [*perestroika*] . . . combines
continuity and innovation, the historical experience of
Bolshevism and the contemporaneity of socialism.

speech on the seventieth
anniversary of the Russian
Revolution, 2 November 1987

5 After leaving the Kremlin . . . my conscience was clear. The
promise I gave to the people when I started the process of
perestroika was kept: I gave them freedom.

Memoirs (1995)

Albert Gore Jnr. 1948–

American Democratic politician, Vice-President, 1993–2001;
presidential candidate 2000

6 That year, we voted with our hearts to make history by
tearing down a mighty wall of division. We made history
. . . We will tear down an old wall of division once again.
   comparing the Democrats' selection of the Catholic John F.
   Kennedy *in the presidential campaign of 1960 with his own
   choice of Joseph* **Lieberman**, *an Orthodox Jew, as his running
   mate*

in *Seattle Times* 9 August 2000

Pauline LaFon Gore

mother of Albert **Gore** Jnr
see also **Slogans** 336:4

of her husband, Senator Albert Gore Sr., and her son as politicians:
7 I trained them both, and I did a better job on my son.
   in 1976, campaigning for her son's first Congressional seat

attributed; in *Time* 21 August 2000

Maxim Gorky 1868–1936

Russian writer and revolutionary

8 The proletarian state must bring up thousands of excellent
'mechanics of culture', 'engineers of the soul'.

speech at the Writers' Congress
1934; see **Kennedy** 199:7, **Stalin**
345:3

George Joachim, Lord Goschen 1831–1907

British Liberal Unionist politician, appointed Chancellor of the Exchequer in 1886 on the sudden resignation of Lord Randolph **Churchill**
on Goschen: see **Churchill** 79:11

1 I have the courage of my opinions, but I have not the temerity to give a political blank cheque to Lord Salisbury.

in the House of Commons, 19 February 1884

Philip Gould 1950–

British Labour Party strategist

2 The New Labour brand has been badly contaminated. It is the object of constant criticism and, even worse, ridicule.

internal memo, May 2000, leaked to the press in July; text printed in *Guardian* 20 July 2000

Ernest Gowers 1880–1966

British public servant

3 It is not easy nowadays to remember anything so contrary to all appearances as that officials are the servants of the public; and the official must try not to foster the illusion that it is the other way round.

Plain Words (1948)

D. M. Graham 1911–99

4 That this House will in no circumstances fight for its King and Country.
motion for a debate at the Oxford Union, 9 February 1933 (passed by 275 votes to 153)

motion worded by Graham when Librarian of the Oxford Union

James Graham see Montrose

Phil Gramm 1942–

American Republican politician

5 Balancing the budget is like going to heaven. Everybody wants to do it, but nobody wants to do what you have to do to get there.

in a television interview, 16 September 1990

6 I did not come to Washington to be loved, and I have not been disappointed.

Michael Barone and Grant Ujifusa *The American Political Almanac* 1994

Bernie Grant 1944–2000

British Labour politician

7 The police were to blame for what happened on Sunday night and what they got was a bloody good hiding.
after the Broadwater Farm riots in which a policeman was killed

as leader of Haringey Council outside Tottenham Town Hall, 8 October 1985

Ulysses S. Grant 1822–85

American Union general and 18th President of the US
on Grant: see **Sherman** 331:3

1 I purpose to fight it out on this line, if it takes all summer.
dispatch to Washington, from headquarters in the field, 11 May 1864

P. C. Headley *The Life and Campaigns of General U. S. Grant* (1869)

2 The war is over—the rebels are our countrymen again.
preventing his men from cheering after **Lee***'s surrender at Appomattox*

on 9 April 1865

3 Let us have peace.
letter to General Joseph R. Hawkey, 29 May 1868, accepting the presidential nomination

P. C. Headley *The Life and Campaigns of General U. S. Grant* (1869)

4 I know no method to secure the repeal of bad or obnoxious laws so effective as their stringent execution.

inaugural address, 4 March 1869

5 Leave the matter of religion to the family altar, the church, and the private school, supported entirely by private contributions. Keep the church and state forever separate.

speech at Des Moines, Iowa, 1875

6 Labour disgraces no man; unfortunately you occasionally find men disgrace labour.

speech at Midland International Arbitration Union, Birmingham, England, 1877

Henry Grattan 1746–1820

Irish nationalist leader

7 The thing he proposes to buy is what cannot be sold—liberty.
speech in the Irish Parliament against the proposed union, 16 January 1800

in Dictionary of National Biography

John Chipman Gray 1839–1915

American lawyer

8 Dirt is only matter out of place; and what is a blot on the escutcheon of the Common Law may be a jewel in the crown of the Social Republic.

Restraints on the Alienation of Property (2nd ed., 1895) preface

Muriel Gray 1959–

Scottish writer and broadcaster

9 Of course I want political autonomy but not cultural autonomy. You just have to watch the Scottish Baftas to want to kill yourself.
explaining her preference for devolution rather than full independence

in Scotland on Sunday 14 January 1996

Patrick, Lord Gray d. 1612

10 A dead woman bites not.
oral tradition, Gray being said to have pressed hard for the execution of **Mary** *Queen of Scots in 1587, with the words 'Mortua non mordet [Being dead, she will bite no more]'*

A. Darcy's 1625 translation of William Camden's *Annals of the Reign of Queen Elizabeth* (1615) vol. 1

Thomas Gray 1716–71

English poet

1 The boast of heraldry, the pomp of pow'r,
And all that beauty, all that wealth e'er gave,
Awaits alike th' inevitable hour,
The paths of glory lead but to the grave.

Elegy Written in a Country Churchyard (1751)

2 Some village-Hampden, that with dauntless breast
The little tyrant of his fields withstood;
Some mute inglorious Milton here may rest,
Some Cromwell guiltless of his country's blood.

Elegy Written in a Country Churchyard (1751)

Th'applause of list'ning senates to command
The threats of pain and ruin to despise,
To scatter plenty o'er a smiling land,
And read their history in a nations eyes,

Their lot forbad: nor circumscribed alone
Their growing virtues, but their crimes confined;
Forbad to wade through slaughter to a throne,
And shut the gates of mercy on mankind.

Horace Greeley 1811–72

American editor and politician

3 The illusion that times that were are better than those that are, has probably pervaded all ages.

The American Conflict (1864-6)

4 I never said all Democrats were saloon keepers. What I said was that all saloon keepers were Democrats.

attributed

Pauline Green 1948–

British socialist politician, leader of the Socialist Group in the European Parliament

5 The Commission has an established culture that is secretive and authoritarian.

in *Daily Mail* 17 March 1999

Dick Gregory 1932–

American comedian

6 You gotta say this for the white race—its self-confidence knows no bounds. Who else could go to a small island in the South Pacific where there's no poverty, no crime, no unemployment, no war and no worry—and call it a 'primitive society'?

From the Back of the Bus (1962)

Pope Gregory VII see Last words 212:12

George Grenville 1712–70

British Whig statesman; Prime Minister 1763–5
on Grenville: see **George III** 142:9, **Walpole** 373:9

7 A wise government knows how to enforce with temper, or to conciliate with dignity.
speaking against the expulsion of John **Wilkes**

in the House of Commons, 3 February 1769

Lord Grey of Fallodon 1862–1933
British Liberal politician

1 The lamps are going out all over Europe; we shall not see them lit again in our lifetime.
   on the eve of the First World War

25 Years (1925) vol. 2

Arthur Griffith 1871–1922
Irish statesman

2 What I have signed I will stand by, in the belief that the end of the conflict of centuries is at hand.

statement to Dáil Éireann before the debate on the Treaty, December 1921

3 We have brought back the flag; we have brought back the evacuation of Ireland after 700 years by British troops and the formation of an Irish army. We have brought back to Ireland her full rights.

when moving acceptance of the Treaty in the Dáil, December 1921

Roy Griffiths

4 If Florence Nightingale were carrying her lamp through the corridors of the NHS today she would almost certainly be searching for the people in charge.

in *Report of the NHS Management Inquiry*, DHSS, 1983

John Grigg 1924–
British writer and journalist

5 The personality conveyed by the utterances which are put into her mouth is that of a priggish schoolgirl, captain of the hockey team, a prefect, and a recent candidate for confirmation. It is not thus that she will be able to come into her own as an independent and distinctive character.
   *of Queen **Elizabeth II***

in *National and English Review* August 1958

6 Lloyd George would have a better rating in British mythology if he had shared the fate of Abraham Lincoln.

attributed, 1963

7 Politicians are exiles from the normal, private world.

attributed, 1964

Joseph ('Jo') Grimond 1913–93
British Liberal politician, Leader of the Liberal Party (1956–67)

8 In bygone days, commanders were taught that when in doubt, they should march their troops towards the sound of gunfire. I intend to march my troops towards the sound of gunfire.

speech to the Liberal Party Assembly, 14 September 1963

on the chance of a pact with the Labour Government:
9 Our teeth are in the real meat.

speech to the Liberal Party Assembly, 1965

Andrei Gromyko 1909–89
Soviet statesman, President of the USSR 1985–8

10 Comrades, this man has a nice smile, but he's got iron teeth.
   *of Mikhail **Gorbachev***

speech to Soviet Communist Party Central Committee, 11 March 1985

Philip Guedalla 1889–1944

British historian and biographer

of the Admiralty committee to examine inventions:
1 There they sit, like inverted Micawbers, waiting for something to turn down.

in a speech at the Oxford Union, 1912; a similar commented has also been attributed to Winston Churchill of Treasury staff (Anthony Sampson *The Anatomy of Britain Today*)

Ernesto ('Che') Guevara 1928–67

Argentinian revolutionary and guerrilla leader

2 The Revolution is made by man, but man must forge his revolutionary spirit from day to day.

Socialism and Man in Cuba (1968)

Nell Gwyn 1650–87

English actress and courtesan

3 Pray, good people, be civil. I am the Protestant whore.
   at Oxford, during the Popish Terror, 1681

B. Bevan *Nell Gwyn* (1969)

William Hague 1961–

British Conservative politician, Leader of the Conservative Party since 1997
on Hague: see **Heseltine** 171:6, **Kinnock** 204:12

4 It was inevitable the Titanic was going to set sail, but that doesn't mean it was a good idea to be on it.
   on his opposition to joining the single currency

in *Mail on Sunday* 11 January 1998 'Quotes of the Week'

5 Feather-bedding, pocket-lining, money-grabbing cronies.
   during the debate on lobbyists' influence and 'cronyism'

in the House of Commons, 8 July 1998

6 This is a candidate of probity and integrity—I am going to back him to the full.
   of Jeffrey Archer

at the Conservative party conference, October 1999

7 On Monday you gave the French the third way and today they gave you the two fingers.
   to the Prime Minister on the government's handling of the beef war

in *Sunday Times* 14 November 1999 'Talking Heads'

8 People work hard and save hard to own a car. They do not want to be told that they cannot drive it by a Deputy Prime Minister whose idea of a park and ride scheme is to park one Jaguar and drive away in another.

in House of Commons debate on the Queen's Speech, 17 November 1999

9 Why does he [Tony Blair] not split the job of mayor of London? The former health secretary [Frank Dobson] can run as his 'day mayor' and Ken Livingstone can run as his 'night mayor'.

speech, House of Commons, 17 November 1999

Earl Haig 1861–1928

Commander of British armies in France, 1915–18

1 A very weak-minded fellow I am afraid, and, like the feather pillow, bears the marks of the last person who has sat on him!

describing the 17th Earl of Derby, in a letter to Lady Haig, 14 January 1918

R. Blake *Private Papers of Douglas Haig* (1952)

2 Every position must be held to the last man: there must be no retirement. With our backs to the wall, and believing in the justice of our cause, each one of us must fight on to the end.

order to British troops, 12 April 1918

A. Duff Cooper *Haig* (1936) vol. 2

Lord Hailsham 1907–

British Conservative politician

3 A great party is not to be brought down because of a squalid affair between a woman of easy virtue and a proved liar.

on the Profumo affair

in a television interview, 13 June 1963; in *The Times* 14 June 1963

4 I believe there is a golden thread which alone gives meaning to the political history of the West, from Marathon to Alamein, from Solon to Winston Churchill and after. This I chose to call the doctrine of liberty under the law.

in 1975; Anthony Sampson *The Changing Anatomy of Britain* (1982)

5 The elective dictatorship.

of the British Constitution

title of the Dimbleby Lecture, 19 October 1976

6 In a confrontation with the politics of power, the soft centre has always melted away.

in October 1981; Anthony Sampson *The Changing Anatomy of Britain* (1982)

*of Denis **Healey**:*
7 A piratical old bruiser with a first-class mind and very bad manners.

interview in *The Times* 2 June 1987

8 The English and, more latterly, the British, have the habit of acquiring their institutions by chance or inadvertence, and shedding them in a fit of absent-mindedness.

'The Granada Guildhall Lecture 1987' 10 November 1987; see **Seeley** 317:2

9 Conservatives do not believe that the political struggle is the most important thing in life . . . The simplest of them prefer fox-hunting—the wisest religion.

The Case for Conservatism (1947)

10 We are a democratically governed republic with a wholly admirable head of state.

Values: Collapse and Cure (1994)

11 I've known every Prime Minister to a greater or lesser extent since Balfour, and most of them have died unhappy.

attributed, 1997

Richard Burdon Haldane 1856–1928

British politician, lawyer, and philosopher

12 We have come to the conclusion . . . that in the sphere of civil government the duty of investigation and thought, as preliminary to action, might with great advantage be more definitely added.

Peter Hennessy *Whitehall* (1990)

H. R. Haldeman 1929–93
Presidential assistant to Richard **Nixon**

1 Once the toothpaste is out of the tube, it is awfully hard to get it back in.
on the Watergate affair, to John Dean, 8 April 1973

in *Hearings Before the Select Committee on Presidential Campaign Activities of US Senate: Watergate and Related Activities* (1973) vol. 4

Edward Everett Hale 1822–1909
American clergyman

2 'Do you pray for the senators, Dr Hale?' 'No, I look at the senators and I pray for the country.'

Van Wyck Brooks *New England Indian Summer* (1940)

Matthew Hale 1609–76
English judge

3 Christianity is part of the laws of England.

William Blackstone's summary of Hale's words (Taylor's case, 1676) in *Commentaries* (1769) vol. 4; the origin of the expression has been traced to Sir John Prisot (d. 1460)

Nathan Hale 1755–76 see **Last words** 212:13

Lord Halifax ('the Trimmer') 1633–95
English politician and essayist

4 This innocent word *Trimmer* signifieth no more than this, that if men are together in a boat, and one part of the company would weigh it down on one side, another would make it lean as much to the contrary.

Character of a Trimmer (1685, printed 1688)

5 Men in business are in as much danger from those that work under them, as from those that work against them.

Political, Moral, and Miscellaneous Thoughts and Reflections (1750) 'Instruments of State Ministers'

6 The best way to suppose what may come, is to remember what is past.

Political, Moral, and Miscellaneous Thoughts and Reflections (1750) 'Miscellaneous: Experience'

7 A known liar should be outlawed in a well-ordered government.

Political, Moral, and Miscellaneous Thoughts and Reflections (1750) 'Miscellaneous: Lying'

8 After a revolution, you see the same men in the drawing-room, and within a week the same flatterers.

Political, Moral, and Miscellaneous Thoughts and Reflections (1750) 'Of Courts'

9 Most men make little other use of their speech than to give evidence against their own understanding.

Political, Moral, and Miscellaneous Thoughts and Reflections (1750) 'Of Folly and Fools'

10 There is . . . no fundamental, but that *every supreme power must be arbitrary.*

Political, Moral, and Miscellaneous Thoughts and Reflections (1750) 'Of Fundamentals'

11 The people are never so perfectly backed, but that they will kick and fling if not stroked at seasonable times.

Political, Moral, and Miscellaneous Thoughts and Reflections (1750) 'Of Fundamentals'

1 In corrupted governments the place is given for the sake of the man; in good ones the man is chosen for the sake of the place.

Political, Moral, and Miscellaneous Thoughts and Reflections (1750) 'Of Fundamentals'

2 It is in a disorderly government as in a river, the lightest things swim at the top.

Political, Moral, and Miscellaneous Thoughts and Reflections (1750) 'Of Government'

3 The best definition of the best government is, that it has no inconveniences but such as are supportable; but inconveniences there must be.

Political, Moral, and Miscellaneous Thoughts and Reflections (1750) 'Of Government'

4 If the laws could speak for themselves, they would complain of the lawyers in the first place.

Political, Moral, and Miscellaneous Thoughts and Reflections (1750) 'Of Laws'

5 Malice is of a low stature, but it hath very long arms.

Political, Moral, and Miscellaneous Thoughts and Reflections (1750) 'Of Malice and Envy'

6 In parliaments, men wrangle in behalf of liberty, that do as little care for it, as they deserve it.

Political, Moral, and Miscellaneous Thoughts and Reflections (1750) 'Of Parliaments'

7 The best party is but a kind of conspiracy against the rest of the nation.

Political, Moral, and Miscellaneous Thoughts and Reflections (1750) 'Of Parties'

8 There are men who shine in a faction, and make a figure by opposition, who would stand in a worse light, if they had the preferments they struggle for.

Political, Moral, and Miscellaneous Thoughts and Reflections (1750) 'Of Parties'

9 Party is little less than an inquisition, where men are under such a discipline in carrying on the common cause, as leaves no liberty of private opinion.

Political, Moral, and Miscellaneous Thoughts and Reflections (1750) 'Of Parties'

10 When the people contend for their liberty, they seldom get anything by their victory but new masters.

Political, Moral, and Miscellaneous Thoughts and Reflections (1750) 'Of Prerogative, Power and Liberty'

11 Power is so apt to be insolent and Liberty to be saucy, that they are very seldom upon good terms.

Political, Moral, and Miscellaneous Thoughts and Reflections (1750) 'Of Prerogative, Power and Liberty'

12 If none were to have liberty but those who understand what it is, there would not be many freed men in the world.

Political, Moral, and Miscellaneous Thoughts and Reflections (1750) 'Of Prerogative, Power and Liberty'

13 Men are not hanged for stealing horses, but that horses may not be stolen.

Political, Moral, and Miscellaneous Thoughts and Reflections (1750) 'Of Punishment'

14 Wherever a knave is not punished, an honest man is laughed at.

Political, Moral, and Miscellaneous Thoughts and Reflections (1750) 'Of Punishment'

15 State business is a cruel trade; good nature is a bungler in it.

Political, Moral, and Miscellaneous Thoughts and Reflections (1750) 'Wicked Ministers'

16 To the question, What shall we do to be saved in this World? there is no other answer but this, Look to your Moat.

A Rough Draft of a New Model at Sea (1694)

1 Lord Rochester was made Lord president: which being a post superior in rank, but much inferior both in advantage and credit to that he held formerly, drew a jest from Lord Halifax . . . he had heard of many kicked down stairs, but never of any that was kicked up stairs before.

Gilbert Burnet *History of My Own Time* (written 1683–6) vol. 1 (1724)

Lord Halifax 1881–1959
British Conservative politician and Foreign Secretary

on being asked immediately after the Munich crisis if he were not worn out by the late nights:

2 No, not exactly. But it spoils one's eye for the high birds.

attributed

W. F. ('Bull') Halsey 1882–1959
American admiral

3 The Third Fleet's sunken and damaged ships have been salvaged and are retiring at high speed toward the enemy.
  on hearing claims that the Japanese had virtually annihilated the US fleet

report, 14 October 1944; E. B. Potter *Bull Halsey* (1985)

Margaret Halsey 1910–
American writer

4 The English never smash in a face. They merely refrain from asking it to dinner.

With Malice Toward Some (1938)

Alexander Hamilton c.1755–1804
American Federalist politician, killed in a duel by Aaron **Burr**
on Hamilton: see **Webster** 377:11

5 A national debt, if it is not excessive, will be to us a national blessing.

letter to Robert Morris, 30 April 1781

6 I believe the British government forms the best model the world ever produced . . . This government has for its object public strength and individual security.

in *Debates of the Federal Convention* 18 June 1787

7 We are now forming a republican government. Real liberty is neither found in despotism or the extremes of democracy, but in moderate government.

in *Debates of the Federal Convention* 26 June 1787

8 Let Americans disdain to be the instruments of European greatness. Let the thirteen States, bound together in a strict and indissoluble Union, concur in erecting one great American system, superior to the control of all transatlantic force or influence, and able to dictate the terms of the connection between the old and the new world!

in *The Federalist* (1787–8) no. 11

9 Why has government been instituted at all? Because the passions of men will not conform to the dictates of reason and justice, without constraint.

in *The Federalist* (1787–8) no. 15

10 To admit foreigners indiscriminately to the rights of citizens . . . would be nothing less than to admit the Grecian horse into the citadel of our liberty and sovereignty.

Works (1886) vol.7

11 Learn to think continentally.
  advice to the newly independent United States

attributed; see **Chamberlain** 74:7

Mark Hanna 1837–1904

American politician and businessman

*on Theodore **Roosevelt**'s acceding to the Presidency on the
assassination of William McKinley*
1 Now look, that damned cowboy is President of the United
States.

in September 1901

Brian Hanrahan 1949–

British journalist

2 I counted them all out and I counted them all back.
*on the number of British aeroplanes joining the raid on Port
Stanley*

BBC broadcast report, 1 May 1982

William Harcourt 1827–1904

British Liberal politician; Chancellor of the Exchequer

3 We are all socialists now.
*during the passage of Lord **Goschen**'s 1888 budget, noted for the
reduction of the national debt*

G. B. Shaw (ed.) *Fabian Essays in
Socialism* (1889)

4 The value of the political heads of departments is to tell the
permanent officials what the public will not stand.

A. G. Gardiner *The Life of Sir
William Harcourt* (1923) vol. 2

Keir Hardie 1856–1915

Scottish Labour politician, first Leader of the Independent Labour
Party (1893) and the Labour Party (1906)

5 From his childhood onward this boy [the future Edward
VIII] will be surrounded by sycophants and flatterers by the
score—[*Cries of* 'Oh, oh!']—and will be taught to believe
himself as of a superior creation. [*Cries of* 'Oh, oh!'] A line
will be drawn between him and the people whom he is to be
called upon some day to reign over. In due course, following
the precedent which has already been set, he will be sent on
a tour round the world, and probably rumours of a
morganatic alliance will follow—[*Loud cries of* 'Oh, oh!' *and*
'Order!']—and the end of it all will be that the country will
be called upon to pay the bill. [*Cries of* Divide!]

in the House of Commons, 28 June
1894

6 Woman, even more than the working class, is the great
unknown quantity of the race.

speech at Bradford, 11 April 1914

Warren G. Harding 1865–1923

American Republican statesman, 29th President of the US 1921–3

7 In the great fulfillment we must have a citizenship less
concerned about what the government can do for it and
more anxious about what it can do for the nation.

speech at the Republican National
Convention, 7 June 1916

8 America's present need is not heroics, but healing; not
nostrums but normalcy; not revolution, but restoration.

speech at Boston, 14 May 1920

Thomas Hardy 1840–1928
English novelist and poet

1 A local thing called Christianity.

The Dynasts (1904) pt. 1, act 1, sc. 6

2 War makes rattling good history; but Peace is poor reading.

The Dynasts (1904) pt. 1, act 2, sc. 5

3 'Peace upon earth!' was said. We sing it,
And pay a million priests to bring it.
After two thousand years of mass
We've got as far as poison-gas.

'Christmas: 1924' (1928)

4 The offhand decision of some commonplace mind high in office at a critical moment influences the course of events for a hundred years.

Florence Hardy *The Early Life of Thomas Hardy 1840–91* (1928)

John Harington 1561–1612
English writer and courtier

5 Treason doth never prosper, what's the reason?
For if it prosper, none dare call it treason.

Epigrams (1618)

Lord Harlech 1918–85
British Ambassador to Washington, 1961–5

6 Britain will be honoured by historians more for the way she disposed of an empire than for the way in which she acquired it.

in *New York Times* 28 October 1962

Mary Harney 1953–
Irish politician

7 If you want to push something in politics, you're accused of being aggressive, and that's not supposed to be a good thing for a woman. If you get upset and show it, you're accused of being emotional.

1990s, attributed

Harold II c.1019–66
King of England, 1066

8 He will give him seven feet of English ground, or as much more as he may be taller than other men.
his offer to Harald Hardrada of Norway, invading England, before the battle of Stamford Bridge

Snorri Sturluson *King Harald's Saga* (c.1260)

Arthur Harris 1892–1984
British Air Force Marshal

9 I would not regard the whole of the remaining cities of Germany as worth the bones of one British Grenadier.
supporting the continued strategic bombing of German cities

letter to Norman Bottomley, deputy Chief of Air Staff, 29 March 1945; see **Bismarck** 42:10

Robert Harris 1957–
British political journalist

10 The only leaders Labour loves are dead ones.

in *Sunday Times* 11 August 1996

William Henry Harrison 1773-1841

American Whig statesman and soldier, noted for his victory at
the battle of Tippecanoe in 1811, and 9th President of the US,
1841, who died of pneumonia one month after his inauguration
on Harrison: see **Slogans** 336:7, **Songs** 342:4

1 We admit of no government by divine right . . . the only
legitimate right to govern is an express grant of power from
the governed.

inaugural address, 4 March 1841

2 A decent and manly examination of the acts of government
should be not only tolerated, but encouraged.

inaugural address, 4 March 1841

Minnie Louise Haskins 1875-1957

English teacher and writer

3 And I said to the man who stood at the gate of the year:
'Give me a light that I may tread safely into the unknown.'
    And he replied:
    'Go out into the darkness and put your hand into the
Hand of God. That shall be to you better than light and safer
than a known way.'
    quoted by King **George VI** *in his Christmas broadcast, 25*
December 1939

Desert (1908) 'God Knows'

Roy Hattersley 1932-

British Labour politician

4 Opposition is four or five years' humiliation in which there
is no escape from the indignity of no longer controlling
events.

in *Independent* 25 March 1995
'Quote Unquote'

5 Politicians are entitled to change their minds. But when
they adjust their principles some explanation is necessary.

in *Observer* 21 March 1999

Charles Haughey 1925-

Irish Fianna Fáil statesman; Taoiseach 1979-81, 1982, and
1987-92
on Haughey: see **O'Brien** 272:5

6 Every TD, from the youngest or newest in the House,
dreams of being Taoiseach.

in *Irish Times* 23 May 1970 'This
Week They Said'

7 It was a bizarre happening, an unprecedented situation, a
grotesque situation, an almost unbelievable mischance.
    on the series of events leading to the resignation of the Attorney
    General; the acronym GUBU *was subsequently coined by Conor*
    Cruise **O'Brien** *to describe Haughey's style of government*

at a press conference in 1982; T.
Ryle Dwyer *Charlie: the Political*
Biography of Charles Haughey
(1987) ch. 12

Václav Havel 1936-

Czech dramatist; President of Czechoslovakia 1989-92 and of the
Czech Republic since 1993

8 A spectre is haunting eastern Europe: the spectre of what in
the West is called 'dissent'.

The Power of the Powerless (1978)

9 I see a renewed focus of politics on real people as something
far more profound than merely returning to the everyday
mechanisms of western (or if you like bourgeois) democracy.

Václav Havel et al. *The Power of the*
Powerless (1985)

1 To respond to evil by committing another evil does not eliminate evil but allows it to go on forever.

letter 5 November 1989

R. S. Hawker 1803–75
English clergyman and poet

2 And have they fixed the where and when?
And shall Trelawny die?
Here's twenty thousand Cornish men
Will know the reason why!
  the last three lines are taken from a traditional rhyme dating from
  the imprisonment by James II, in 1688, of the seven Bishops,
  including Trelawny, Bishop of Bristol

'The Song of the Western Men'

Ian Hay 1876–1952
Scottish novelist and dramatist

3 War is hell, and all that, but it has a good deal to recommend it. It wipes out all the small nuisances of peacetime.

The First Hundred Thousand (1915)

John Milton Hay 1838–1905
American politician

4 It has been a splendid little war, begun with the highest motives, carried on with magnificent intelligence and spirit, favoured by that fortune which loves the brave.
  on the Spanish-American War of 1898

letter to Theodore Roosevelt, 27 July 1898

5 The open door.
  on the completion of the trade policy he had negotiated with China

letter to the Cabinet, 2 January 1900

Bill Hayden 1933–
Australian Labor politician

Hayden had resigned as Opposition leader in 1983 as Malcolm Fraser was in the process of calling the election, but remained convinced that he would have won:
6 I am not convinced the Labor Party could not win under my leadership. I believe a drover's dog could lead the Labor Party to victory the way the country is.

John Stubbs *Hayden* (1989)

Friedrich August von Hayek 1899–1992
Austrian-born economist

7 I am certain that nothing has done so much to destroy the juridical safeguards of individual freedom as the striving after this miracle of social justice.

Economic Freedom and Representative Government (1973)

8 The system of private property is the most important guarantee of freedom, not only for those who own property, but scarcely less for those who do not.

The Road to Serfdom (1944)

9 Probably nothing has done so much harm to the liberal cause as the wooden insistence of some liberals on certain rough rules of thumb, above all the principle of *laissez-faire*.

The Road to Serfdom (1944)

10 We need good principles rather than good people. We need fixed rules, not fixers.

Studies in Philosophy, Politics and Economics (1967)

1 One cannot help a country to maintain its standard of life by assisting people to consume more than they produce.

in Daily Telegraph 26 August 1976

Alfred Hayes 1911–85

American songwriter

2 I dreamed I saw Joe Hill last night
Alive as you and me.
Says I, 'But Joe, you're ten years dead.'
'I never died,' says he.

'I Dreamed I Saw Joe Hill Last Night' (1936 song)

William Hazlitt 1778–1830

English essayist

3 Talk of mobs! Is there any body of people that has this character in a more consummate degree than the House of Commons? Is there any set of men that determines more by acclamation, and less by deliberation and individual conviction?

'On the Difference between Writing and Speaking'; in *London Magazine* July 1820

4 The greatest test of courage I can conceive is to speak the truth in the House of Commons.

'On the Difference between Writing and Speaking'; in *London Magazine* July 1820

Cuthbert Morley Headlam 1876–1964

British Conservative politician

5 This Parliament is enough to discourage anyone from entering political life—a vast untutored majority with a helpless minority and an extremely uninteresting Government.

diary 27 March 1933

6 We ought to have made up more to the political leaders and their wives—the latter are an unattractive lot, but their influence is greater than one supposes.

diary 28 July 1933

7 Better to break your party on a matter of principle than to let it fall to pieces because you cannot yourself make up your mind what you want to do.

diary 2 April 1934

Denis Healey 1917–

British Labour politician

8 There are going to be howls of anguish from the 80,000 people who are rich enough to pay over 75% [tax] on the last slice of their income.

speech at the Labour Party Conference, 1 October 1973

9 It's no good ceasing to become the world's policeman in order to become the world's parson instead.

at a meeting of the Cabinet at Chequers, 17 November 1974; Peter Hennessy *Whitehall* (1990)

*of being criticized by Geoffrey **Howe** in the House of Commons:*
10 Like being savaged by a dead sheep.

in the House of Commons, 14 June 1978

*of Margaret **Thatcher**:*
11 And who is the Mephistopheles behind this shabby Faust [the Foreign Secretary, Geoffrey Howe]? . . . To quote her own backbenchers, the Great She-elephant, She-Who-Must-Be-Obeyed, the Catherine the Great of Finchley, the Prime Minister herself.

in the House of Commons, 27 February 1984

1 The Fabians . . . found socialism wandering aimlessly in Cloud-cuckoo-land and set it working on the gas and water problems of the nearest town or village.
of the parochialism of the Fabians

New Fabian Essays (1952)

2 La Passionaria of middle-class privilege.
*of Margaret **Thatcher***

Kenneth Minogue and Michael Biddiss *Thatcherism* (1987)

3 Healey's first law of politics: when you're in a hole, stop digging.

attributed

Edna Healey 1918–
British writer, wife of Denis **Healey**

4 She has no hinterland; in particular she has no sense of history.
*of Margaret **Thatcher***

Denis Healey *The Time of My Life* (1989)

Timothy Michael Healy 1855–1931
Irish nationalist politician

5 REDMOND: Gladstone is now master of the Party!
HEALY: Who is to be mistress of the Party?
*at the meeting of the Irish Parliamentary Party on 6 December 1890, when the Party split over **Parnell**'s involvement in the O'Shea divorce; Healy's reference to Katherine O'Shea was particularly damaging to Parnell*

Robert Kee *The Laurel and the Ivy* (1993)

6 I am for doing business and making peace.

letter to Beaverbrook, 1920; Frank Callanan *T. M. Healy* (1996)

7 The Sinns won in three years what we did not win in forty. You cannot make revolutions with rosewater, or omelettes without breaking eggs.

letter to his brother; Frank Callanan *T. M. Healy* (1996); see **Proverbs** 296:16

8 There is the noble Marquis. Like a pike at the bottom of a pool.
of Lord Hartington, apparently asleep on the Opposition bench

Herbert Gladstone *After Thirty Years* (1928)

Seamus Heaney 1939–
Irish poet

9 Don't be surprised
If I demur, for, be advised
My passport's green.
No glass of ours was ever raised
To toast *The Queen.*
rebuking the editors of The Penguin Book of Contemporary British Poetry *for including him among its authors*

Open Letter (1983)

10 Who would connive
in civilised outrage
yet understand the exact
and tribal, intimate revenge.

'Punishment' (1975)

11 My heart besieged by anger, my mind a gap of danger,
I walked among their old haunts, the home ground where they bled;
And in the dirt lay justice like an acorn in the winter
Till its oak would sprout in Derry where the thirteen men lay dead.
of Bloody Sunday, Londonderry, 30 January 1972

'The Road to Derry'

1   The famous
Northern reticence, the tight gag of place
And times: yes, yes. Of the 'wee six' I sing
Where to be saved you only must save face
And whatever you say, you say nothing.

'Whatever You Say Say Nothing'
(1975)

William Randolph Hearst 1863–1951

American newspaper publisher and tycoon

2 You furnish the pictures and I'll furnish the war.
*message to the artist Frederic Remington in Havana, Cuba,
during the Spanish-American War of 1898*

attributed

Edward Heath 1916–

British Conservative statesman; Prime Minister 1970–4
on Heath: see **Anonymous** 7:8, **Hennessy** 168:6, **Jenkins** 188:2,
Margach 242:8, **Thatcher** 356:4

3 Music means everything to me when I'm here alone. And
it's the best way of getting that bloody man Wilson out of
my hair.
after playing Chopin and Liszt for a visiting journalist, late 1960s

James Margach The Abuse of Power
(1978)

4 This would, at a stroke, reduce the rise in prices, increase
productivity and reduce unemployment.
*press release, never actually spoken by Heath, on proposed tax
cuts and a freeze on prices in nationalized industries*

from Conservative Central Office,
16 June 1970

5 The unpleasant and unacceptable face of capitalism.
on the Lonrho affair

in the House of Commons, 15 May
1973

6 If politicians lived on praise and thanks they'd be forced into
some other line of business.

attributed, 1973

7 Rejoice, rejoice, rejoice.
*telephone call to his office on hearing of Margaret **Thatcher**'s fall
from power in 1990*

attributed; in Daily Telegraph 24
September 1998 (online edition)

8 It was not totally inconceivable that she could have joined
me as my wife at No. 10.
of the starlet Jayne Mansfield

in Sunday Times 6 February 2000
'Talking Heads'

G. W. F. Hegel 1770–1831

German idealist philosopher

9 What experience and history teach is this—that nations and
governments have never learned anything from history, or
acted upon any lessons they might have drawn from it.

Lectures on the Philosophy of World
History: Introduction (1830); see
Marx 244:7

Heinrich Heine 1797–96

German poet

10 Wherever books will be burned, men also, in the end, are
burned.

Almansor (1823)

Joseph Heller 1923–

American novelist

11 If I'm going to be trivial, inconsequential, and deceitful . . .
then I might as well be in government.

Closing Time (1994)

Lillian Hellman 1905–84
American playwright

1 I cannot and will not cut my conscience to fit this year's fashions.

letter to John S. Wood, 19 May 1952

Leona Helmsley c.1920–
American hotelier

2 Only the little people pay taxes.
   reported at her trial for tax evasion

to her housekeeper; in New York Times 12 July 1983

Arthur Henderson 1863–1935
British Labour politician and from 1931 Party Leader

*to critics in his own party, when as adviser on labour matters he was made minister without portfolio in **Lloyd George**'s War Cabinet (December 1916):*
3 I am not here either to please myself or you; I am here to see the war through.

in Dictionary of National Biography (1917–)

4 The first forty-eight hours decide whether a Minister is going to run his office or whether his office is going to run him.

Susan Crosland Tony Crosland (1982)

Leon Henderson 1895–1956
American economist; appointed by Roosevelt to the National Defense Advisory Commission in 1940

5 Having a little inflation is like being a little pregnant.

J. K. Galbraith A Life in Our Times (1981)

Peter Hennessy 1947–
English historian and writer

6 The model of a modern Prime Minister would be a kind of grotesque composite freak—someone with the dedication to duty of a Peel, the physical energy of a Gladstone, the detachment of a Salisbury, the brains of an Asquith, the balls of a Lloyd George, the word-power of a Churchill, the administrative gifts of an Attlee, the style of a Macmillan, the managerialism of a Heath, and the sleep requirements of a Thatcher. Human beings do not come like that.

The Hidden Wiring (1995)

7 MI5 is a job creation scheme for muscular underachievers from the ancient universities.

in The Times 1981, profile of Roger Hollis

*of Rab **Butler** in his last years:*
8 He seemed like a benign and decent beached whale washed up on the harder shores of modern Conservatism.

in Independent 8 May 1987

Henri IV (of Navarre) 1553–1610
King of France from 1589

9 I want there to be no peasant in my kingdom so poor that he is unable to have a chicken in his pot every Sunday.

*In Hardouin de Péréfixe Histoire de Henry le Grand (1681); see **Hoover** 176:5*

1 Hang yourself, brave Crillon; we fought at Arques and you were not there.

traditional form given by Voltaire to a letter from Henri to Crillon, 20 September 1597; Henri's actual words were: 'My good man, Crillon, hang yourself for not having been at my side last Monday at the greatest event that's ever been seen and perhaps ever will be seen'

2 Paris is well worth a mass.
when told that, though a Protestant, he must hear mass at Notre-Dame Cathedral to be consecrated king

attributed to Henri IV; alternatively to his minister Sully, in conversation with Henri

3 The wisest fool in Christendom.
*of **James I** of England*

attributed both to Henri IV and **Sully**

Henry II 1133–89

King of England from 1154

4 Will no one rid me of this turbulent priest?
of Thomas Becket, Archbishop of Canterbury, murdered in Canterbury Cathedral, December 1170

oral tradition, conflating a number of variant forms, including G. Lyttelton *History of the Life of King Henry the Second* (1769): 'so many cowardly and ungrateful men in his court, none of whom would revenge him of the injuries he sustained from one turbulent priest'

Henry VIII 1491–1547

King of England from 1509

5 This man hath the right sow by the ear.
of Thomas Cranmer, June 1529

in *Acts and Monuments of John Foxe* ['Foxe's Book of Martyrs'] (1570)

6 The King found her [Anne of Cleves] so different from her picture . . . that . . . he swore they had brought him a Flanders mare.

Tobias Smollett *A Complete History of England* (3rd ed., 1759)

Patrick Henry 1736–99

American statesman

7 Caesar had his Brutus—Charles the First, his Cromwell—and George the Third—('Treason,' cried the Speaker) . . . *may profit by their example.* If *this* be treason, make the most of it.

speech in the Virginia assembly, May 1765

8 I am not a Virginian, but an American.

in [John Adams's] Notes of Debates in the Continental Congress, Philadelphia, 6 September 1774

9 I know not what course others may take; but as for me, give me liberty, or give me death!

speech in Virginia Convention, 23 March 1775

10 We are not weak if we make a proper use of those means which the God of Nature has placed in our power . . . The battle, sir, is not to the strong alone; it is to the vigilant, the active, the brave.

speech in Virginia Convention, Richmond, 23 March 1775

1 Guard with jealous attention the public liberty. Suspect everyone who approaches that jewel. Unfortunately, nothing will preserve it but downright force. Whenever you give up that force, you are inevitably ruined.

attributed

A. P. Herbert 1890–1971
English writer and humorist

2 This high official, all allow,
Is grossly overpaid;
There wasn't any Board, and now
There isn't any Trade.

'The President of the Board of Trade' (1922)

3 Testators would do well to provide some indication of the particular Liberal Party which they have in mind, such as a telephone number or a Christian name.

Misleading Cases (1935)

4 People must not do things for fun. We are not here for fun. There is no reference to fun in any Act of Parliament.

Uncommon Law (1935) 'Is it a Free Country?'

5 The Common Law of England has been laboriously built about a mythical figure—the figure of 'The Reasonable Man'.

Uncommon Law (1935) 'The Reasonable Man'

Frank Herbert 1920–86
American writer of science fiction

6 If you think of yourselves as helpless and ineffectual, it is certain that you will create a despotic government to be your master. The wise despot, therefore, maintains among his subjects a popular sense that they are helpless and ineffectual.

The Dosadi Experiment (1978)

Herodotus c.485–c.425
Greek historian

7 In peace, children bury their parents; war violates the order of nature and causes parents to bury their children.

Histories

8 The most hateful torment for men is to have knowledge of everything but power over nothing.

Histories

Lord Hervey 1696–1743
English politician and writer

9 Whoever would lie usefully should lie seldom.

Memoirs of the Reign of George II (ed. J. W. Croker, 1848) vol. 1

10 I am fit for nothing but to carry candles and set chairs all my life.

letter to Sir Robert Walpole, 1737

Alexander Ivanovich Herzen 1812–70
Russian author and revolutionary

11 Communism is a Russian autocracy turned upside down.

The Development of Revolutionary Ideas in Russia (1851)

12 Russia's future will be a great danger for Europe and a great misfortune for Russia if there is no emancipation of the individual. One more century of present despotism will destroy all the good qualities of the Russian people.

The Development of Revolutionary Ideas in Russia (1851)

Michael Heseltine 1933–

British Conservative politician
on Heseltine: see **Critchley** 97:5

1 I knew that, 'He who wields the knife never wears the crown.'

in *New Society* 14 February 1986

2 The market has no morality.

on *Panorama* BBC1 27 June 1988

3 Polluted rivers, filthy streets, bodies bedded down in doorways are no advertisement for a prosperous or caring society.

speech at Conservative Party Conference 10 October 1989

4 The Tory recognizes the contrast between laissez-faire and noblesse oblige.

in *Observer* 18 March 1990 'Sayings of the Week'

5 You can't wield a handbag from an empty chair.

at the launch of Britain in Europe, 14 October 1999

6 It's only when Michael Portillo comes back in the House of Commons that William will have to watch his back.
   of William Hague

in *Guardian* 15 June 1999

7 Just keep telling everyone this: keep smiling and keep waving.
   on how to deal with critics of the Dome

in *Independent* on 22 January 2000 'Quotes of the Week'

Gordon Hewart 1870–1943

British lawyer and politician

8 A long line of cases shows that it is not merely of some importance, but is of fundamental importance that justice should not only be done, but should manifestly and undoubtedly be seen to be done.

in *Rex v Sussex Justices* 9 November 1923

John Hewitt 1907–87

Nothern Irish poet

9 I fear their creed as we have always feared
   The lifted hand between the mind and truth.

'The Glens' (1948)

10 Kelt, Briton, Roman, Saxon, Dane, and Scot,
   time and this island tied a crazy knot.

'Ulsterman' (*Collected Poems*, 1991)

11 I'm an Ulsterman, of planter stock. I was born in the island of Ireland, so secondarily I'm an Irishman. I was born in the British archipelago and English is my native tongue, so I am British. The British archipelago consists of offshore islands to the continent of Europe, so I'm European. This is my hierarchy of values and so far as I am concerned, anyone who omits one step in that sequence of values is falsifying the situation.

in *The Irish Times* 4 July 1974

Reinhard Heydrich 1904–42

German Nazi leader

12 Now the rough work has been done we begin the period of finer work. We need to work in harmony with the civil administration. We count on you gentlemen as far as the final solution is concerned.
   on the planned mass murder of eleven million European Jews

speech in Wannsee, 20 January 1942; see **Goering** 149:8

J. R. Hicks 1904–89
British economist

1 The best of all monopoly profits is a quiet life.

Econometrica (1935) 'The Theory of Monopoly'

Jim Hightower
American politician

2 There's nothing in the middle of the road but yellow stripes and dead armadillos.

attributed, 1984

Charles Hill 1904–89
British Conservative politician, doctor, and broadcaster

3 It does not do to appear clever. Advancement in this man's party is due entirely to alcoholic stupidity.
*advice given in 1959 to the newly elected MP, Julian **Critchley**, whom he had seen reading in the Smoking Room of the House of Commons*

Julian Critchley *A Bag of Boiled Sweets* (1994)

Joe Hill 1879–1915
American labour leader and songwriter
see also **Last words** 213:2

4 You will eat, bye and bye,
In that glorious land above the sky;
Work and pray, live on hay,
You'll get pie in the sky when you die.

'Preacher and the Slave' in *Songs of the Workers* (Industrial Workers of the World, 1911)

Paul von Hindenburg 1847–1934
German Field Marshal and statesman, President of the Weimar Republic 1925–34

5 That man for a Chancellor? I'll make him a postmaster and he can lick the stamps with my head on them.
*on **Hitler***

to Meissner, 13 August 1932; J. W. Wheeler-Bennett *Hindenburg: the Wooden Titan* (1936)

Emperor Hirohito 1901–89
Emperor of Japan 1926–89

6 The war situation has developed not necessarily to Japan's advantage.
announcing Japan's surrender, in a broadcast to his people after atom bombs had destroyed Hiroshima and Nagasaki

on 15 August 1945

7 Certainly things happened during the Second World War for which I feel personally sorry.

attributed, 1971

Adolf Hitler 1889–1945
German dictator

8 The broad mass of a nation . . . will more easily fall victim to a big lie than to a small one.

Mein Kampf (1925) vol. 1

9 The night of the long knives.
*applied to the massacre of Ernst Roehm and his associates by Hitler on 29–30 June 1934, though taken from an early Nazi marching song; the phrase was subsequently associated with Harold **Macmillan**'s Cabinet dismissals of 13 July 1962*

speech in the Reichstag, 13 July 1934

1 I go the way that Providence dictates with the assurance of a sleepwalker.

speech in Munich, 15 March 1936

2 It is the last territorial claim which I have to make in Europe, but it is the claim from which I will not recede and which, God-willing, I will make good.
  on the Sudetenland

speech at Berlin Sportpalast, 26 September 1938

3 With regard to the problem of the Sudeten Germans, my patience is now at an end!

speech at Berlin Sportpalast, 26 September 1938

to Mussolini, having spent nine hours intermittently in Franco's company:

4 Rather than go through that again, I would prefer to have three or four teeth taken out.

Paul Preston Franco (1993)

Thomas Hobbes 1588-1679

English philosopher

5 By art is created that great Leviathan, called a commonwealth or state, (in Latin *civitas*) which is but an artificial man . . . and in which, the sovereignty is an artificial soul.

Leviathan (1651); introduction

6 I put for a general inclination of all mankind, a perpetual and restless desire of power after power, that ceaseth only in death.

Leviathan (1651)

7 They that approve a private opinion, call it opinion; but they that mislike it, heresy: and yet heresy signifies no more than private opinion.

Leviathan (1651)

8 During the time men live without a common power to keep them all in awe, they are in that condition which is called war; and such a war as is of every man against every man.

Leviathan (1651)

9 For as the nature of foul weather, lieth not in a shower or two of rain; but in an inclination thereto of many days together: so the nature of war consisteth not in actual fighting, but in the known disposition thereto during all the time there is no assurance to the contrary.

Leviathan (1651)

10 No arts; no letters; no society; and which is worst of all, continual fear and danger of violent death; and the life of man, solitary, poor, nasty, brutish, and short.

Leviathan (1651)

11 Force, and fraud, are in war the two cardinal virtues.

Leviathan (1651)

12 Liberties . . . depend on the silence of the law.

Leviathan (1651)

13 The obligation of subjects to the sovereign, is understood to last as long, and no longer, than the power lasteth, by which he is able to protect them.

Leviathan (1651)

14 I put down for one of the most effectual seeds of the death of any state, that the conquerors require not only a submission of men's actions to them for the future, but also an approbation of all their actions past.

Leviathan (1651)

15 They that are discontented under *monarchy*, call it *tyranny*; and they that are displeased with *aristocracy*, call it *oligarchy*: so also, they which find themselves grieved under a *democracy*, call it *anarchy*, which signifies the want of government; and yet I think no man believes, that want of government, is any new kind of government.

Leviathan (1651)

1 The papacy is not other than the ghost of the deceased Roman Empire, sitting crowned upon the grave thereof.

Leviathan (1651)

John Cam Hobhouse 1786–1869
English politician

2 When I invented the phrase 'His Majesty's Opposition' [Canning] paid me a compliment on the fortunate hit.

Recollections of a Long Life (1865) vol. 2, ch. 12; see below; see **Bagehot** 20:11

It is said to be very hard on his majesty's ministers to raise objections to this proposition. For my own part, I think it is more hard on his majesty's opposition (a laugh) to compel them to take this course.

speech, House of Commons, 10 April 1826

Eric Hobsbawm 1917–
British historian

3 This was the kind of war which existed in order to produce victory parades.
   of the Falklands War

in *Marxism Today* January 1983

August Heinrich Hoffman 1798–1874
German poet

4 *Deutschland über alles.*
   Germany above all.

Title of poem (1841)

Lancelot Hogben 1895–1975
English scientist

5 This is not the age of pamphleteers. It is the age of the engineers. The spark-gap is mightier than the pen. Democracy will not be salvaged by men who talk fluently, debate forcefully and quote aptly.

Science for the Citizen (1938) epilogue

Sarah Hogg 1946–
former head of John Major's policy unit

6 Ministers say one of two things in Cabinet. Some say, 'Look, Daddy, no hands.' Others say, 'Look, Daddy, me too.'
   unidentified senior official to Sarah Hogg on her arrival to take over the Prime Minister's policy unit

in *Sunday Times* 9 April 1995

Simon Hoggart 1946–
British journalist

7 Peter Mandelson is someone who can skulk in broad daylight.

in *Guardian* 10 July 1998

Patrick Holden 1937–
British businessman: director of the Soil Association

8 Tony Blair and his ministers are operating on a 'pollute now, pay later' policy. Farm-scale trial plots are rather like letting a rat with bubonic plague out into the environment and then seeing what happens.
   on GM foods

in *Independent* 18 June 1999

Henry Fox, Lord Holland 1705–74

English Whig politician, father of Charles James **Fox**
on Holland: see **Walpole** 374:8

1 Let nothing be done to break his spirit. The world will do
that business fast enough.
of his son Charles James **Fox** *as a child*

      attributed

2 If Mr Selwyn calls again, shew him up: if I am alive I shall
be delighted to see him; and if I am dead he would like to
see me.
during his last illness

      J. H. Jesse *George Selwyn and his
Contemporaries* (1844) vol. 3

Oliver Wendell Holmes Jr. 1841–1935

Justice of the US Supreme Court

3 The most stringent protection of free speech would not
protect a man falsely shouting fire in a theatre and causing
a panic.
sometimes quoted as, 'shouting fire in a crowded theatre'

      in *Schenck v. United States* (1919)

4 Men must turn square corners when they deal with the
Government.

      in *Rock Island, Arkansas & Louisiana
Ry. v. United States* (1920)

5 I pay my tax bills more readily than any others—for
whether the money is well or ill spent I get civilized society
for it.

      letter to Harold Laski, 12 May 1930

6 A second-class intellect. But a first-class temperament!
of Franklin **Roosevelt**

      on 8 March 1933

7 The mind of a bigot is like the pupil of the eye; the more
light you pour upon it, the more it will contract.

      attributed

Alec Douglas-Home, Lord Home 1903–95

British Conservative statesman; Prime Minister, 1963–4
on Home: see **Peyton** 288:3

8 Oh, they must find someone else, once they get away from
this Blackpool hot-house. Even if they can't agree on Rab or
Quintin there must be someone else. But please, please, not
me!
*to James Margach during the Conservative Party Conference,
October 1963*

      James Margach *The Abuse of Power*
(1978)

9 When I have to read economic documents I have to have a
box of matches and start moving them into position to
simplify and illustrate the points to myself.

      in *Observer* 16 September 1962

10 As far as the fourteenth earl is concerned, I suppose Mr
Wilson, when you come to think of it, is the fourteenth Mr
Wilson.
replying to Harold **Wilson**'s *remark (on Home's becoming leader
of the Conservative party) that* 'the whole [democratic] process
has ground to a halt with a fourteenth Earl'

      in *Daily Telegraph* 22 October 1963

11 There are two problems in my life. The political ones are
insoluble and the economic ones are incomprehensible.

      attributed, 1964

12 Had a letter from your father [Sir Roy Harrod, the
economist] today about inflation . . . or deflation—or
something.
to Dominic Harrod at a Downing Street party

      Peter Hennessy *The Prime Minister:
the Office and its Holders since 1945*
(2000)

Richard Hooker c.1554–1600
English theologian

1 He that goeth about to persuade a multitude, that they are
not so well governed as they ought to be, shall never want
attentive and favourable hearers.

Of the Laws of Ecclesiastical Polity
(1593)

2 Alteration though it be from worse to better hath in it
inconveniences, and those weighty.

Of the Laws of Ecclesiastical Polity
(1593)

Herbert Hoover 1874–1964
American Republican statesman; 31st President of the US
1929–33

3 Our country has deliberately undertaken a great social and
economic experiment, noble in motive and far-reaching in
purpose.
   *on the Eighteenth Amendment enacting Prohibition, often referred
   to as 'the noble experiment'*

letter to Senator W. H. Borah, 23
February 1928

4 The American system of rugged individualism.

speech in New York City, 22
October 1928

5 The slogan of progress is changing from the full dinner pail
to the full garage.
   *sometimes paraphrased as, 'a car in every garage and a chicken in
   every pot'*

speech in New York, 22 October
1928; see **Henri IV** 168:9

6 The grass will grow in the streets of a hundred cities, a
thousand towns.
   *on proposals 'to reduce the protective tariff to a competitive tariff
   for revenue'*

speech, 31 October 1932; see
Bryan 55:6

7 Older men declare war. But it is youth who must fight and
die.

speech at the Republican National
Convention, Chicago, 27 June 1944

Bob Hope 1903–
American comedian

8 I must say the Senator's victory in Wisconsin was a triumph
for democracy. It proves that a millionaire has just as good a
chance as anybody else.
   *of John Fitzgerald **Kennedy**'s electoral victory*

in 1960; William Robert Faith *Bob
Hope* (1983)

Horace 65–8 BC
Roman poet

9 O citizens, first acquire wealth; you can practise virtue
afterwards.

Epistles; see **Pope** 292:6

Samuel Horsley 1733–1806
English bishop

10 In this country . . . the individual subject . . . 'has nothing to
do with the laws but to obey them.'
   defending a maxim he had used earlier in committee

in the House of Lords, 13
November 1795

John Hoskyns 1927–

British businessman; head of the Prime Minister's Policy Unit
1979–82

1 The House of Commons is the greatest closed shop of all . . .
For the purposes of government, a country of 55 million
people is forced to depend on a talent pool which could not
sustain a single multinational company.

'Conservatism is Not Enough'
(Institute of Directors Annual
Lecture) 25 September 1983

2 The Tory party never panics, except in a crisis.

in *Sunday Times* 19 February 1989

Samuel Houston 1793–1863

American politician and military leader who led the struggle to
win control of Texas (1834–6) and make it part of the US

3 The North is determined to preserve this Union. They are
not a fiery, impulsive people as you are, for they live in
colder climates. But when they begin to move in a given
direction . . . they move with the steady momentum and
perseverance of a mighty avalanche.
  in 1861, warning the people of Texas against secession

Geoffrey C. Ward *The Civil War*
(1991)

Geoffrey Howe 1926–

British Conservative politician; Foreign Secretary
on Howe: see **Healey** 165:10

4 It is rather like sending your opening batsmen to the crease
only for them to find, the moment the first balls are bowled,
that their bats have been broken before the game by the
team captain.
  resignation speech which precipitated the fall of Margaret
  Thatcher

in the House of Commons, 13
November 1990

5 The time has come for others to consider their own response
to the tragic conflict of loyalties with which I have myself
wrestled for perhaps too long.
  resignation speech

in the House of Commons, 13
November 1990

Julia Ward Howe 1819–1910

American Unitarian lay preacher

6 Mine eyes have seen the glory of the coming of the Lord:
He is trampling out the vintage where the grapes of wrath
    are stored;
He hath loosed the fateful lightning of his terrible swift
    sword:
His truth is marching on.

'Battle Hymn of the Republic'
(1862)

7 As He died to make men holy, let us die to make men free.

'Battle Hymn of the Republic'
(1862)

Louis McHenry Howe 1871–1936

American Democratic politician

8 You can't adopt politics as a profession, and remain honest.

speech, 17 January 1933

Langston Hughes 1902–67

American writer and poet

1 I, too, sing America.   '*I, Too*' (1925)
I am the darker brother.
They send me to eat in the kitchen
When company comes.

2 'It's powerful,' he said.   *Simple Takes a Wife* (1953)
'What?'
'That one drop of Negro blood—because just *one* drop of
  black blood makes a man coloured. *One* drop—you are a
  Negro!'

Victor Hugo 1802–85

French poet, novelist, and playwright

3 A stand can be made against invasion by an army; no stand   *Histoire d'un Crime* (written
can be made against invasion by an idea.   1851–2, published 1877); see
                                                                 Anonymous 11:5

4 Take away *time is money*, and what is left of England? take *Les Misérables* (1862)
away *cotton is king*, and what is left of America?

David Hume 1711–76

Scottish philosopher

5 Money . . . is none of the wheels of trade: it is the oil which *Essays: Moral and Political* (1741–2)
renders the motion of the wheels more smooth and easy.   'Of Money'

6 That policy is violent, which aggrandizes the public by the   *Essays: Moral and Political* (1741–2)
poverty of individuals.   'Of Money'

7 Should it be said, that, by living under the dominion of a   'Of the Original Contract' (1748)
prince, which one might leave, every individual has given a
tacit assent to his authority . . . We may as well assert, that
a man by remaining in a vessel, freely consents to the
dominion of the master; though he was carried on board
while asleep, and must leap into the ocean, and perish, the
moment he leaves her.

8 In all ages of the world, priests have been enemies of liberty.   'Of the Parties of Great Britain'
                                                                       (1741–2)

9 It is a just political maxim, that every man must be   *Political Discourses* (1751)
supposed a knave.

John Hume 1937–

Northern Irish politician

10 There's a very thin line between dying for Ireland and   in 1994, attributed
killing for Ireland.

Mick Hume

British journalist

11 It is a fitting national symbol, a wonderful structure that   in *Independent on Sunday* 9 January
stands for nothing, a stunning shell with a hole where its   2000
heart should be.
the editor of Living Marxism *on the Millennium Dome*

Hubert Humphrey 1911–78
American Democratic politician

1 There are not enough jails, not enough policemen, not enough courts to enforce a law not supported by the people.

speech at Williamsburg, 1 May 1965

2 The right to be heard does not automatically include the right to be taken seriously.

speech to National Student Association at Madison, 23 August 1965

3 Here we are the way politics ought to be in America, the politics of happiness, the politics of purpose and the politics of joy.

speech in Washington, 27 April 1968

4 Compassion is not weakness, and concern for the unfortunate is not socialism.

attributed

Barry Humphries 1934–
Australian entertainer and writer

5 The prigs who attack Jeffrey Archer should bear in mind that we all, to some extent, reinvent ourselves. Jeffrey has just gone to a bit more trouble.

in Observer *on 19 December 1999 'They said what . . . ?'*

G. W. Hunt see Songs 343:5

Lord Hunt of Tanworth 1919–
British civil servant; Secretary of the Cabinet 1973–9

of British Cabinet government, described as 'a shambles':
6 It has got to be, so far as possible, a democratic and accountable shambles.

at a seminar at the Institute of Historical Research, 20 October 1993

Robert Hunter 1941–

7 The word *Greenpeace* had a ring to it—it conjured images of Eden; it said ecology and antiwar in two syllables; it fit easily into even a one-column headline.

Warriors of the Rainbow *(1979); see* **Darnell** 101:7

Douglas Hurd 1930–
British conservative politician; Foreign Secretary

8 Lord Rothschild roamed like a condottiere through Whitehall, laying an ambush here, there breaching some crumbling fortress which had outlived its usefulness . . . He respected persons occasionally but rarely policies.
   *of Lord **Rothschild** as first Director of the Central Policy Review Staff*

An End to Promises *(1979)*

9 If President Clinton decides to accelerate the run-down in US forces in Europe—and by implication the priority Washington attaches to Nato—that wedge will be removed. With it will go one of the principal props which have allowed Britain to punch above its weight in the world.

speech at Chatham House; in Financial Times *4 February 1993*

10 People in the forefront of environmental causes are destroying experimental crops. That's not logical. That's Luddite.

in Sunday Times *19 September 1999*

Saddam Hussein 1937–
President of Iraq from 1979

1 The mother of battles.
popular interpretation of his description of the approaching Gulf War, given in a speech in Baghdad, 6 January 1991

in *The Times* 7 January 1991 it was reported that Saddam had no intention of relinquishing Kuwait and was ready for the 'mother of all wars'

Aldous Huxley 1894–1963
English novelist

2 So long as men worship the Caesars and Napoleons, Caesars and Napoleons will duly arise and make them miserable.

Ends and Means (1937)

3 Idealism is the noble toga that political gentlemen drape over their will to power.

in *New York Herald Tribune* 25 November 1963

4 The propagandist's purpose is to make one set of people forget that certain other sets of people are human.

attributed

T. H. Huxley 1825–95
English biologist

5 Why, put him in the middle of a moor, with nothing in the world but his shirt, and you could not prevent him being anything he liked.
*of **Gladstone***

Roy Jenkins *Gladstone* (1995)

Douglas Hyde 1860–1949
Irish nationalist

6 The devouring demon of Anglicization in Ireland . . . with its foul jaws has devoured, one after another, everything that was hereditary, national, instructive, ancient, intellectual and noble in our race, our language, our music, our songs, our industries, our dances, and our pastimes—I know, I say, that you will plant your feet firmly, and say with us, 'Back, Demon, back!'

speaking on behalf of the Gaelic League in America, 1904

Henry Hyde 1924–
American Republican politician, leader of the prosecution for the impeachment of President Clinton

7 We hoped that the public would move from its total indifference to concern. That hope was unrequited.

in *Times* 13 February 1999

Dolores Ibarruri ('La Pasionaria') 1895–1989
Spanish Communist leader

8 *No pasarán.*
They shall not pass.

radio broadcast, Madrid, 19 July 1936; see **Military sayings** 251:3

9 It is better to die on your feet than to live on your knees.

speech in Paris, 3 September 1936; also attributed to Emiliano Zapata; see **Roosevelt** 306:4

Henrik Ibsen 1828–1906

Norwegian playwright

1 The majority never has right on its side. Never I say! That is one of the social lies that a free, thinking man is bound to rebel against. Who makes up the majority in any given country? Is it the wise men or the fools? I think we must agree that the fools are in a terrible overwhelming majority, all the wide world over. But, damn it, it can surely never be right that the stupid should rule over the clever!

An Enemy of the People (1882)

2 You should never have your best trousers on when you go out to fight for freedom and truth.

An Enemy of the People (1882)

Harold L. Ickes 1874–1952

American lawyer and administrator

3 The trouble with Senator Long . . . is that he's suffering from halitosis of the intellect. That's presuming Emperor Long has an intellect.

speech, 1935; G. Wolfskill and J. A. Hudson *All But the People: Franklin D. Roosevelt and his Critics, 1933–39* (1969)

4 Dewey threw his diaper into the ring.
on the Republican candidate for the presidency

in *New York Times* 12 December 1939

5 I am against government by crony.
on resigning as secretary of the interior

in February 1946

Ivan Illich 1926–

American sociologist

6 In a consumer society there are inevitably two kinds of slaves: the prisoners of addiction and the prisoners of envy.

Tools for Conviviality (1973)

William Ralph Inge 1860–1954

English writer; Dean of St. Paul's, 1911–34

7 The enemies of Freedom do not argue; they shout and they shoot.

End of an Age (1948)

8 The effect of boredom on a large scale in history is underestimated. It is a main cause of revolutions, and would soon bring to an end all the static Utopias and the farmyard civilization of the Fabians.

End of an Age (1948)

9 It takes in reality only one to make a quarrel. It is useless for the sheep to pass resolutions in favour of vegetarianism, while the wolf remains of a different opinion.

Outspoken Essays: First Series (1919)

10 The nations which have put mankind and posterity most in their debt have been small states—Israel, Athens, Florence, Elizabethan England.

Outspoken Essays: Second Series (1922) 'State, visible and invisible'

11 A man may build himself a throne of bayonets, but he cannot sit on it.
*a similar image was used by Boris **Yeltsin** at the time of the failed military coup in Russia, August 1991*

Philosophy of Plotinus (1923) vol. 2

Bernard Ingham 1932–

British journalist and public relations specialist, Chief Press
Secretary to the Prime Minister, 1979–90

1 Blood sport is brought to its ultimate refinement in the
gossip columns.

speech, 5 February 1986

2 The media . . . is like an oil painting. Close up, it looks like
nothing on earth. Stand back and you get the drift.

speech to the Parliamentary Press
Gallery, February 1990

*at a meeting of the Parliamentary Lobby, noticing that he had a spot
of blood on his shirt:*
3 My God, I've been stabbed in the front.

recalled in a letter to Antony Jay,
January 1995

Eugène Ionesco 1912–94

French playwright

4 A civil servant doesn't make jokes.

The Killer (1958)

Hastings Lionel ('Pug') Ismay 1887–1965

British general and Secretary to the Committee of Imperial
Defence; first Secretary-General of NATO

5 NATO exists for three reasons—to keep the Russians out,
the Americans in and the Germans down.
to a group of British Conservative backbenchers in 1949

Peter Hennessy *Never Again*
(1992); oral tradition

Molly Ivins 1944–
and Lou Dubose

American journalists

6 Young political reporters are always told there are three
ways to judge a politician. The first is to look at the record.
The second is to look at the record. And third, look at the
record.

Molly Ivins and Lou Dubose *Shrub*
(2000)

7 If you think his daddy had trouble with 'the vision thing',
wait till you meet this one.
of presidential candidate George W. Bush

Molly Ivins and Lou Dubose *Shrub*
(2000)

Alija Izetbegović 1925–

Bosnian statesman; President of Bosnia and Herzegovina since
1990

8 And to my people I say, this may not be a just peace, but it
is more just than a continuation of war.
*after signing the Dayton accord with representatives of Serbia and
Croatia*

in Dayton, Ohio, 21 November
1995

Andrew Jackson 1767–1845

American general and Democratic statesman, 7th President of the US 1829–37
on Jackson: see **Clay** 88:9

1 The individual who refuses to defend his rights when called by his Government, deserves to be a slave, and must be punished as an enemy of his country and friend to her foe.

proclamation to the people of Louisiana from Mobile, 21 September 1814

2 The brave man inattentive to his duty, is worth little more to his country, than the coward who deserts her in the hour of danger.
to troops who had abandoned their lines during the battle of New Orleans, 8 January 1815

attributed

3 Our Federal Union: it must be preserved.
toast given on the Jefferson Birthday Celebration, 13 April 1830

Thomas Hart Benton *Thirty Years' View* (1856) vol. 1

4 There are no necessary evils in government. Its evils exist only in its abuses.

veto of the Bank Bill, 10 July 1832

5 You are uneasy; you never sailed with *me* before, I see.

James Parton *Life of Jackson* (1860) vol. 3

6 One man with courage makes a majority.

attributed

shortly before his death, Jackson was asked if he had left anything undone:
7 I didn't shoot Henry Clay, and I didn't hang John C. Calhoun.

Robert V. Remini *Henry Clay* (1991); attributed

Glenda Jackson 1936–

British Labour politician and actress

8 If I am one of Blair's babes, well I've been called a damn sight worse.

in Independent on Sunday 8 August 1999

Jesse Jackson 1941–

American Democratic politician and clergyman

9 My right and my privilege to stand here before you has been won—won in my lifetime—by the blood and the sweat of the innocent.

speech at Democratic National Convention, Atlanta, 19 July 1988

10 When I look out at this convention, I see the face of America, red, yellow, brown, black, and white. We are all precious in God's sight—the real rainbow coalition.

speech at Democratic National Convention, Atlanta, 19 July 1988

11 You can't keep on running from labour, running from blacks, running from cities and expect to inspire them to vote.
on President **Clinton**, *after the results of the 1994 election*

in Guardian 28 November 1994

Robert H. Jackson 1892–1954

American lawyer and judge

12 That four great nations, flushed with victory and stung with injury, stay the hands of vengeance and voluntarily submit their captive enemies to the judgement of the law, is one of the most significant tributes that Power has ever paid to Reason.
opening statement for the prosecution at Nuremberg

before the International Military Tribunal in Nuremberg, 21 November 1945

James I (James VI of Scotland) 1566–1625
King of Scotland from 1567 and of England from 1603

1 No bishop, no King.
   *to a deputation of Presbyterians from the Church of Scotland,
   seeking religious tolerance in England*

W. Barlow *Sum and Substance of
the Conference* (1604)

2 The state of monarchy is the supremest thing upon earth;
   for kings are not only God's lieutenants upon earth, and sit
   upon God's throne, but even by God himself they are called
   gods.

speech to Parliament, 21 March
1610

3 The king is truly *parens patriae*, the polite father of his
   people.

speech to Parliament, 21 March
1610

4 That which concerns the mystery of the king's power is not
   lawful to be disputed; for that is to wade into the weakness
   of Princes and to take away the mystical reverence, that
   belongs unto them that sit in the throne of God.

'A Speech in the Star Chamber'
[speech to the judges] 20 June
1616

5 I will govern according to the common weal, but not
   according to the common will.

in December, 1621; J. R. Green
History of the English People vol. 3
(1879)

James V 1512–42
King of Scotland from 1513

*of the crown of Scotland (which had come to the Stuarts through the
female line), on learning of the birth of **Mary** Queen of Scots,
December 1542:*
6 It came with a lass, and it will pass with a lass.

Robert Lindsay of Pitscottie
(*c.*1500–65) *History of Scotland*
(1728)

Antony Jay see **Lynn** and **Jay**

Douglas Jay 1907–96
British Labour politician
see also **Slogans** 334:14

7 In the case of nutrition and health, just as in the case of
   education, the gentleman in Whitehall really does know
   better what is good for people than the people know
   themselves.

The Socialist Case (1939)

8 He never used one syllable where none would do.
   *of **Attlee***

Peter Hennessy *Muddling Through*
(1996)

Margaret Jay 1939–
British Labour politician, daughter of James **Callaghan**

9 We're simply saying that what may have been right 800 or
   even 200 years ago is not right now.
   on the abolition of the hereditary right to sit in the House of Lords

in *Guardian* 12 November 1999

10 I never aim to be unpredictable.

in *Observer* 20 February 2000 'They
Said What . . . ?'

11 Any proposal totally to elect the second chamber under the
   mistaken view that it would increase the democratic base of
   parliament would in fact undermine democracy.

in the House of Lords, 7 March
2000

Thomas Jefferson 1743–1826

American Democratic Republican statesman, 3rd President of the US 1801–9
on Jefferson: see **Kennedy** 199:2, **Last words** 214:2; *see also* **Last words** 213:14, **Mottoes** 262:6

1 We hold these truths to be sacred and undeniable; that all men are created equal and independent, that from that equal creation they derive rights inherent and inalienable, among which are the preservation of life, and liberty, and the pursuit of happiness.

'Rough Draft' of the American Declaration of Independence; J. P. Boyd et al. *Papers of Thomas Jefferson* vol. 1 (1950)

2 Were it left to me to decide whether we should have a government without newspapers or newspapers without a government, I should not hesitate for a moment to prefer the latter.

letter to Colonel Edward Carrington, 16 January 1787

3 Experience declares that man is the only animal which devours its own kind, for I can apply no milder term to the governments of Europe, and to the general prey of the rich on the poor.

letter to Colonel Edward Carrington, 16 January 1787

4 A little rebellion now and then is a good thing.

letter to James Madison, 30 January 1787

5 The tree of liberty must be refreshed from time to time with the blood of patriots and tyrants. It is its natural manure.

letter to W. S. Smith, 13 November 1787

6 The natural progress of things is for liberty to yield and governments to gain ground.

letter to Colonel Edward Carrington, 27 May 1788

7 If I could not go to Heaven but with a party, I would not go there at all.

letter to Francis Hopkinson, 13 March 1789

8 The republican is the only form of government which is not eternally at open or secret war with the rights of mankind.

letter to William Hunter, 11 March 1790

9 No government ought to be without censors: and where the press is free, no one ever will.

letter to George Washington, 9 September 1792

10 The second office of government is honourable and easy, the first is but a splendid misery.

letter to Elbridge Gerry, 13 May 1797

11 Offices are acceptable here as elsewhere, and whenever a man has cast a longing eye on them [official positions], a rottenness begins in his conduct.

letter to Tench Coxe, 21 May 1799

12 What an augmentation of the field for jobbing, speculating, plundering, office-building and office-hunting would be produced by an assumption of all the state powers into the hands of the general government.

letter, 13 August 1800

13 If the principle were to prevail, of a common law [i.e. a single government] being in force in the U.S. . . . . it would become the most corrupt government on the earth.

letter to Gideon Granger, 13 August 1800

14 A wise and frugal government, which shall restrain men from injuring one another, which shall leave them otherwise free to regulate their own pursuits of industry and improvement, and shall not take from the mouth of labour the bread it has earned. This is the sum of good government, and this is necessary to close the circle of our felicities.

first inaugural address, 4 March 1801

1 All, too, will bear in mind this sacred principle, that though the will of the majority is in all cases to prevail, that will to be rightful must be reasonable; that the minority possess their equal rights, which equal law must protect, and to violate would be oppression.

first inaugural address, 4 March 1801

2 Would the honest patriot, in the full tide of successful experiment, abandon a government which has so far kept us free and firm?

first inaugural address, 4 March 1801

3 Peace, commerce, and honest friendship with all nations— entangling alliances with none.

first inaugural address, 4 March 1801

4 Freedom of religion; freedom of the press, and freedom of person under the protection of *habeas corpus*, and trial by juries impartially selected. These principles form the bright constellation which has gone before us, and guided our steps through an age of revolution and reformation.

first inaugural address, 4 March 1801

5 I have learned to expect that it will rarely fall to the lot of imperfect man to retire from this station with the reputation and the favour which bring him into it.

first inaugural address, March 1801

6 If a due participation of office is a matter of right, how are vacancies to be obtained? Those by death are few; by resignation none.

letter to E. Shipman and others, 12 July 1801; see **Misquotations** 254:6

7 If we can prevent the government from wasting the labours of the people, under the pretence of taking care of them, they must become happy.

letter to Thomas Cooper, 29 November 1802

8 When a man assumes a public trust, he should consider himself as public property.
  to Baron von Humboldt, 1807

B. L. Rayner *Life of Jefferson* (1834)

9 The care of human life and happiness, and not their destruction, is the first and only legitimate object of good government.

to the Republican Citizens of Washington County, Maryland, 31 March 1809

10 Politics, like religion, hold up the torches of martyrdom to the reformers of error.

letter to James Ogilvie, 4 August 1811

11 I agree with you that there is a natural aristocracy among men. The grounds of this are virtue and talents.

letter to John Adams, 28 October 1813

12 Merchants have no country. The mere spot they stand on does not constitute so strong an attachment as that from which they draw their gains.

letter to Horatio G. Spafford, 17 March 1814

13 If a nation expects to be ignorant and free, in a state of civilization, it expects what never was and never will be.

letter to Colonel Charles Yancey, 6 January 1816

14 But this momentous question [the Missouri Compromise], like a firebell in the night awakened and filled me with terror. I considered it the knell of the Union.

letter to John Holmes, 22 April 1820

15 We have the wolf by the ears; and we can neither hold him, nor safely let him go. Justice is in one scale, and self-preservation in the other.
  on slavery

letter to John Holmes, 22 April 1820

16 I know no safe depository of the ultimate powers of the society but the people themselves; and if we think them not enlightened enough to exercise their control with a wholesome discretion, the remedy is not to take it from them, but to inform their discretion by education.

letter to William Charles Jarvis, 28 September 1820

1 That one hundred and fifty lawyers should do business together ought not to be expected.
    on the United States Congress

Autobiography 6 January 1821

2 To attain all this [universal republicanism], however, rivers of blood must yet flow, and years of desolation pass over; yet the object is worth rivers of blood, and years of desolation.

letter to John Adams, 4 September 1823

3 Were we directed from Washington when to sow, and when to reap, we should soon want bread.

Autobiography

4 Millions of innocent men, women, and children, since the introduction of Christianity, have been burnt, tortured, fined, imprisoned; yet we have not advanced one inch towards uniformity [of opinion]. What has been the effect of coercion? To make one half the world fools, and the other half hypocrites.

Notes on the State of Virginia (1781–5)

5 Indeed I tremble for my country when I reflect that God is just.

Notes on the State of Virginia (1781–5)

6 To the press alone, chequered as it is with abuses, the world is indebted for all the triumphs which have been gained by reason and humanity over error and oppression.

Virginia and Kentucky Resolutions (1799)

7 No duty the Executive had to perform was so trying as to put the right man in the right place.

J. B. MacMaster *History of the People of the United States* (1883–1913) vol. 2

8 The legitimate powers of government extend to such acts only as are injurious to others. But it does me no injury for my neighbour to say there are twenty gods, or no God. It neither picks my pocket nor breaks my leg.

attributed

9 The policy of the American government is to leave their citizens free, neither restraining nor aiding them in their pursuits.

attributed

Patrick Jenkin 1926–
British Conservative politician

10 People can clean their teeth in the dark, use the top of the stove instead of the oven, all sorts of savings, but they must use less electricity.
    as Minister for Energy, asking the public to save electricity as a miners' strike reduced supplies; often summarized as, 'clean your teeth in the dark'

radio broadcast, 15 January 1974

Roy Jenkins 1920–
British politician; co-founder of the Social Democratic Party, 1981

11 The politics of the left and centre of this country are frozen in an out-of-date mould which is bad for the political and economic health of Britain and increasingly inhibiting for those who live within the mould. Can it be broken?

speech to Parliamentary Press Gallery, 9 June 1980

*of Margaret **Thatcher**:*
12 A First Minister whose self-righteous stubbornness has not been equalled, save briefly by Neville Chamberlain, since Lord North.

in *Observer* 11 March 1990

1 The record does not provide much sustenance for the view   *in Guardian* 14 April 1990
that limpet-like Prime Ministers can be easily disposed of by
their parties.

of Edward **Heath**:

2 A great lighthouse which stands there, flashing out beams   *in Independent* 22 September 1990
of light, indifferent to the waves which beat against him.

3 Nearly all Prime Ministers are dissatisfied with their   *Gladstone* (1995)
successors, perhaps even more so if they come from their
own party.

4 There is nobody in politics I can remember and no case I   Richard Crossman diary, 5
can think of in history where a man combined such a   September 1969
powerful political personality with so little intelligence.
of James **Callaghan**

W. Stanley Jevons 1835–82

English economist

5 All classes of society are trades unionists at heart, and differ   *The State in Relation to Labour*
chiefly in the boldness, ability, and secrecy with which they   (1882)
pursue their respective interests.

John XXIII 1881–1963

Pope from 1958

6 If civil authorities legislate for or allow anything that is   *Pacem in Terris* (1963)
contrary to that order and therefore contrary to the will of
God, neither the laws made or the authorizations granted
can be binding on the consciences of the citizens, since God
has more right to be obeyed than man.

7 The social progress, order, security and peace of each   *Pacem in Terris* (1963)
country are necessarily connected with the social progress,
order, security and peace of all other countries.

8 [In the universal *Declaration of Human Rights* (December,   *Pacem in Terris* (1963)
1948)] in most solemn form, the dignity of a person is
acknowledged to all human beings; and as a consequence
there is proclaimed, as a fundamental right, the right of free
movement in search for truth and in the attainment of
moral good and of justice, and also the right to a dignified
life.

Elton John 1947–
and Bernie Taupin 1950–

English pop singer and songwriter; songwriter

9 Goodbye England's rose;   'Candle in the Wind' (song, revised
May you ever grow in our hearts.   version, 1997)
rewritten for and sung at the funeral of **Diana**, *Princess of Wales,*
7 September 1997

1 And it seems to me you lived your life
  Like a candle in the wind:
  Never fading with the sunset
  When the rain set in.
  And your footsteps will always fall here
  On England's greenest hills;
  Your candle's burned out long before
  Your legend ever will.

'Candle in the Wind' (song, revised version, 1997)

John Paul II 1920–

Polish cleric, Pope since 1978

2 It would be simplistic to say that Divine Providence caused the fall of communism. It fell by itself as a consequence of its own mistakes and abuses. It fell by itself because of its own inherent weaknesses.
  when asked by the Italian writer Vittorio Missori if the fall of the USSR could be ascribed to God

Carl Bernstein and Marco Politi *His Holiness: John Paul II and the Hidden History of our Time* (1996)

Lyndon Baines Johnson 1908–73

American Democratic statesman, 36th President of the US 1963–9
on Johnson: see **White** 381:6

to a reporter who had queried his embracing Richard **Nixon** *on the vice-president's return from a controversial tour of South America in 1958:*

3 Son, in politics you've got to learn that overnight chicken shit can turn to chicken salad.

Fawn Brodie *Richard Nixon* (1983)

4 I am a free man, an American, a United States Senator, and a Democrat, in that order.

in *Texas Quarterly* Winter 1958

5 I'll tell you what's at the bottom of it. If you can convince the lowest white man that he's better than the best coloured man, he won't notice you're picking his pocket. Hell, give him someone to look down on and he'll empty his pockets for you.
  during the 1960 Presidential campaign, to Bill Moyers

Robert Dallek *Lone Star Rising* (1991)

6 All I have I would have given gladly not to be standing here today.
  following the assassination of J. F. **Kennedy**

first speech to Congress as President, 27 November 1963

7 We have talked long enough in this country about equal rights. We have talked for a hundred years or more. It is time now to write the next chapter, and to write it in the books of law.

speech to Congress, 27 November 1963

8 This administration, here and now declares unconditional war on poverty in America.

State of the Union address to Congress, 8 January 1964

9 For the first time in our history, it is possible to conquer poverty.

speech to Congress, 16 March 1964

10 In your time we have the opportunity to move not only toward the rich society and the powerful society, but upward to the Great Society.

speech at University of Michigan, 22 May 1964

11 We Americans know, although others appear to forget, the risks of spreading conflict. We still seek no wider war.

speech on radio and television, 4 August 1964

1 We are not about to send American boys 9 or 10,000 miles away from home to do what Asian boys ought to be doing for themselves.

speech at Akron University, 21 October 1964

2 Extremism in the pursuit of the Presidency is an unpardonable vice. Moderation in the affairs of the nation is the highest virtue.

speech in New York, 31 October 1964

3 A President's hardest task is not to *do* what is right, but to *know* what is right.

State of the Union address to Congress, 4 January 1965

4 It is not enough to open the gates of opportunity. All of our citizens must have the ability to walk through those gates.
speech at Harvard in 1965

Paul L. Fisher and Ralph L. Lavenstein (eds.) *Race and the News Media* (1967)

5 Better to have him inside the tent pissing out, than outside pissing in.
of J. Edgar Hoover

David Halberstam *The Best and the Brightest* (1972)

6 Come now, let us reason together.

habitual saying

7 Did you ever think that making a speech on economics is a lot like pissing down your leg? It seems hot to you, but it never does to anyone else.
*to J. K. **Galbraith***

J. K. Galbraith *A Life in Our Times* (1981)

8 I don't want loyalty. I want *loyalty*. I want him to kiss my ass in Macy's window at high noon and tell me it smells like roses. I want his pecker in my pocket.
discussing a prospective assistant

David Halberstam *The Best and the Brightest* (1972)

9 So dumb he can't fart and chew gum at the same time.
*of Gerald **Ford***

Richard Reeves *A Ford, not a Lincoln* (1975)

Philander Chase Johnson 1866–1939
American journalist

10 Politics is the art of turning influence into affluence.

Senator Sorghum's Primer of Politics (1906)

Samuel Johnson 1709–84
English poet, critic, and lexicographer

11 Liberty is, to the lowest rank of every nation, little more than the choice of working or starving.

'The Bravery of the English Common Soldier' in *The British Magazine* January 1760

12 If the changes we fear be thus irresistible, what remains but to acquiesce with silence, as in the other insurmountable distresses of humanity? It remains that we retard what we cannot repel, that we palliate what we cannot cure.

A Dictionary of the English Language (1755) preface

13 *Pension.* Pay given to a state hireling for treason to his country.

A Dictionary of the English Language (1755)

14 Among the calamities of war may be jointly numbered the diminution of the love of truth, by the falsehoods which interest dictates and credulity encourages.

The Idler 11 November 1758; see **Proverbs** 297:5

15 How is it that we hear the loudest yelps for liberty among the drivers of negroes?

Taxation No Tyranny (1775)

16 How small of all that human hearts endure,
That part which laws or kings can cause or cure.

lines added to Oliver Goldsmith's *The Traveller* (1764); see **Goldsmith** 150:8

1 I do not much like to see a Whig in any dress; but I hate to
see a Whig in a parson's gown.

James Boswell *Journal of a Tour to
the Hebrides* (1785) 24 September
1773

2 This man [Lord Chesterfield] I thought had been a Lord
among wits; but, I find, he is only a wit among Lords.

James Boswell *Life of Samuel
Johnson* (1791) 1754

3 Your levellers wish to level *down* as far as themselves; but
they cannot bear levelling *up* to themselves.

James Boswell *Life of Samuel
Johnson* (1791) 21 July 1763

4 A woman's preaching is like a dog's walking on his hinder
legs. It is not done well; but you are surprised to find it done
at all.

James Boswell *Life of Samuel
Johnson* (1791) 31 July 1763

5 BOSWELL: So, Sir, you laugh at schemes of political
improvement.
JOHNSON: Why, Sir, most schemes of political improvement
are very laughable things.

James Boswell *Life of Samuel
Johnson* (1791) 26 October 1769

6 So many objections may be made to everything, that
nothing can overcome them but the necessity of doing
something.

James Boswell *Life of Samuel
Johnson* (1791) 1770

7 A decent provision for the poor, is the true test of
civilization.

James Boswell *Life of Samuel
Johnson* (1791) 1770

8 I would not give half a guinea to live under one form of
government rather than another. It is of no moment to the
happiness of an individual.

James Boswell *Life of Samuel
Johnson* (1791) 31 March 1772

9 Sir, I perceive you are a vile Whig.
to Sir Adam Fergusson

James Boswell *Life of Samuel
Johnson* (1791) 31 March 1772

10 There are few ways in which a man can be more innocently
employed than in getting money.

James Boswell *Life of Samuel
Johnson* (1791) 27 March 1775

11 George the First knew nothing, and desired to know
nothing; did nothing, and desired to do nothing; and the
only good thing that is told of him is, that he wished to
restore the crown to its hereditary successor.

James Boswell *Life of Samuel
Johnson* (1791) 6 April 1775

12 Patriotism is the last refuge of a scoundrel.

James Boswell *Life of Samuel
Johnson* (1791) 7 April 1775

13 Politics are now nothing more than means of rising in the
world.

James Boswell *Life of Samuel
Johnson* (1791) 18 April 1775

14 Every man who attacks my belief, diminishes in some degree
my confidence in it, and therefore makes me uneasy; and I
am angry with him who makes me uneasy.

James Boswell *Life of Samuel
Johnson* (1791) 3 April 1776

15 It is better that some should be unhappy than that none
should be happy, which would be the case in a general state
of equality.

James Boswell *Life of Samuel
Johnson* (1791) 7 April 1776

16 Though we cannot out-vote them we will out-argue them.

James Boswell *Life of Samuel
Johnson* (1791) 3 April 1778

17 I have always said, the first Whig was the Devil.

James Boswell *Life of Samuel
Johnson* (1791) 28 April 1778

18 A wise Tory and a wise Whig, I believe, will agree. Their
principles are the same, though their modes of thinking are
different.

James Boswell *Life of Samuel
Johnson* (1791) May 1781; written
statement given to Boswell

19 If a man were to go by chance at the same time with Burke
under a shed, to shun a shower, he would say—'this is an
extraordinary man.'
on Edmund **Burke**

James Boswell *Life of Samuel
Johnson* (1791) 15 May 1784

1 Fox divided the kingdom with Caesar; so that it was a doubt whether the nation should be ruled by the sceptre of George III or the tongue of Fox.
   on the Parliamentary defeat of Charles James **Fox**, *and the subsequent dissolution, in 1784*

in *Dictionary of National Biography* (1917–)

2 Mankind are happier in a state of inequality and subordination. Were they to be in this pretty state of equality, they would soon degenerate into brutes.

attributed

Tom Johnston 1881–1965
Scottish Labour politician

3 I have become . . . uneasy lest we should get political power without our first having, or at least simultaneously having, an adequate economy to administer. What purport would there be in our getting a Scots parliament in Edinburgh if it has to administer an emigration system, a glorified Poor Law, and a graveyard!

Memories (1952)

4 They have barred us by barbed wire fences from the bens and glens: the peasant has been ruthlessly swept aside to make room for the pheasant, and the mountain hare now brings forth her young on the hearthstone of the Gael!

Our Scots Noble Families (1909)

Hanns Johst 1890–1978
German playwright

5 Whenever I hear the word culture . . . I release the safety-catch of my Browning!
   often quoted as: '*Whenever I hear the word culture, I reach for my pistol!*', *and attributed to Hermann* **Goering**

Schlageter (1933); see **Glencross** 149:4

John Paul Jones 1747–92
American admiral

6 I have not yet begun to fight.
   as his ship was sinking, 23 September 1779, having been asked whether he had lowered his flag

Mrs Reginald De Koven *Life and Letters of John Paul Jones* (1914) vol. 1

Mary Harris 'Mother' Jones 1830–1930
Irish-born American labour activist

7 Pray for the dead and fight like hell for the living!

The Autobiography of Mother Jones (1925)

Steve Jones 1944–
English geneticist

8 The greenest political party there has ever been was the Nazi party. The Nazis were great believers in purity, that nature should not be interfered with.

in *Times Higher Education Supplement* 27 August 1999

9 Students accept astonishing things happening in human genetics without turning a hair but worry about GM soya beans.

in *Times Higher Education Supplement* 27 August 1999

William Jones 1746–94

English jurist

1 My opinion is, that power should always be distrusted, in whatever hands it is placed.

letter to Lord Althorpe, 5 October 1782

Ben Jonson c.1573–1637

English playwright and poet

2 PEOPLE: The Voice of Cato is the voice of Rome.
CATO: The voice of Rome is the consent of heaven!

Catiline his Conspiracy (1611)

Janis Joplin 1943–70

American singer

3 Fourteen heart attacks and he had to die in my week. In MY week.
when ex-President **Eisenhower***'s death prevented her photograph appearing on the cover of* Newsweek

in *New Musical Express* 12 April 1969

Barbara Jordan

American Democratic politician

4 The Bill of Rights was not ordained by nature or God. It's very human, very fragile.

in *New York Times Magazine* 21 October 1990

Thomas Jordan c.1612–85

English poet and playwright

5 They plucked communion tables down
And broke our painted glasses;
They threw our altars to the ground
And tumbled down the crosses.
They set up Cromwell and his heir—
The Lord and Lady Claypole—
Because they hated Common Prayer,
The organ and the maypole.

'How the War began' (1664)

Chief Joseph (Hinmaton-Yalaktit) c.1840–1904

Nez Percé leader

6 From where the sun now stands I will fight no more forever.

speech at the end of the Nez Percé war in 1877; Dee Brown *Bury My Heart at Wounded Knee* (1970) ch. 13

7 Good words do not last long unless they amount to something. Words do not pay for my dead people.

on a visit to Washington in 1879; Chester Anders Fee *Chief Joseph* (1936)

Keith Joseph 1918–94

British Conservative politician

8 Problems reproduce themselves from generation to generation . . . I refer to this as a 'cycle of deprivation'.

speech in London to the Pre-School Playgroups Association, 29 June 1972

1 The balance of our population, our human stock, is
  threatened . . . a high and rising proportion of children are
  being born to mothers least fitted to bring children into the
  world and bring them up.

speech in Birmingham, 19 October 1974

2 If we are to be prosperous we need more millionaires and
  more bankrupts.

maiden speech in the House of Lords, 19 February 1988

3 There are no illegitimate children, only illegitimate parents.
  *in Kiss Hollywood Good-Bye (1978), Anita Loos attributes an
  earlier coinage of this statement to the American philanthropist
  Edna Gladney*

speech to National Children's Home, 6 November 1991

Lionel Jospin 1937–
French statesman, Prime Minister of France

4 Yes to the market economy, No to the market society.

in Independent 16 September 1998

Joseph Joubert 1754–1824
French essayist and moralist

5 One of the surest ways of killing a tree is to lay bare its
  roots. It is the same with institutions. We must not be too
  ready to disinter the origins of those we wish to preserve. All
  beginnings are small.

Pensées (1842)

6 It's better to debate a question without settling it than to
  settle a question without debating it.

attributed

Tessa Jowell 1947–
British Labour politician

7 In the last Parliament, the House of Commons had more
  MPs called John than all the women MPs put together.

in Independent on Sunday 14 March 1999 'Quotes'

James Joyce 1882–1941
Irish novelist

8 Poor Parnell! he cried loudly. My dead king!

A Portrait of the Artist as a Young Man (1916) ch. 1

William Joyce ('Lord Haw-Haw') 1906–46
Fascist supporter and wartime broadcaster from Nazi Germany;
executed for treason in 1946

9 Germany calling! Germany calling!
  habitual introduction to propaganda broadcast

broadcasts from Germany to Britain during the Second World War

Juan Carlos I 1938–
King of Spain from 1975

10 The Crown, the symbol of the permanence and unity of
   Spain, cannot tolerate any actions by people attempting to
   disrupt by force the democratic process.
   on the occasion of the attempted coup in 1981

television broadcast at 1.15 a.m., 24 February 1981

11 I will neither abdicate the Crown nor leave Spain. Whoever
   rebels will provoke a new civil war and will be responsible.
   on the occasion of the attempted coup

television broadcast, 24 February 1981

'Junius'

18th-century pseudonymous writer, probably Philip Francis
(1740–1818)

1 The right of election is the very essence of the constitution.

in Public Advertiser 24 April 1769, letter 11

2 Is this the wisdom of a great minister? or is it the ominous vibration of a pendulum?

in Public Advertiser 30 May 1769, letter 12

3 There is a holy mistaken zeal in politics as well as in religion. By persuading others, we convince ourselves.

in Public Advertiser 19 December 1769, letter 35

4 However distinguished by rank or property, in the rights of freedom we are all equal.

in Public Advertiser 19 March 1770, letter 37

5 The injustice done to an individual is sometimes of service to the public.

in Public Advertiser 14 November 1770, letter 41

6 As for Mr Wedderburne, there is something about him, which even treachery cannot trust.

in Public Advertiser 22 June 1771, letter 49

7 The liberty of the press is the *Palladium* of all the civil, political, and religious rights of an Englishman.

The Letters of Junius (1772 ed.) 'Dedication to the English Nation'

John Junor 1919–97

British journalist

8 Such a graceful exit. And then he had to go and do this on the doorstep.
  *on Harold **Wilson**'s 'Lavender List', the honours list he drew up on resigning the British premiership in 1976*

in Observer 23 January 1990

Juvenal AD 483–565

Roman satirist

9 *Quis tulerit Gracchos de seditione querentes?*
  Who would put up with the Gracchi complaining about subversion?
  referring to the Roman tribune Tiberius Sempronius Gracchus (163–133 BC) and his brother Gaius Sempronius Gracchus (c.153–121 BC), who were responsible for radical social and economic legislation, passed against the wishes of the senatorial class

Satires

10   *Sed quis custodiet ipsos Custodes?*
  But who is to guard the guards themselves?

Satires

11 . . . *Verbosa et grandis epistula venit A Capreis.*
  A huge wordy letter came from Capri.
  on the Emperor Tiberius's letter to the Senate, which caused the downfall of Sejanus in AD 31

Satires

12 . . . *Duas tantum res anxius optat, Panem et circenses.*
  Only two things does he [the modern citizen] anxiously wish for—bread and circuses.

Satires

Franz Kafka 1883–1924
Czech novelist

1 It's often better to be in chains than to be free.

The Trial (1925)

Immanuel Kant 1724–1804
German philosopher

2 There is, therefore, only one categorical imperative. It is: Act only according to that maxim by which you can at the same time will that it should become a universal law.

Fundamental Principles of the Metaphysics of Ethics (1785)

3 Out of the crooked timber of humanity no straight thing was ever made.

Idee zu einer allgemeinen Geschichte in weltbürgerliche Absicht (1784)

Gerald Kaufman 1930–
British Labour politician

4 The longest suicide note in history.
   on the Labour Party's New Hope for Britain (*1983*)

Denis Healey *The Time of My Life* (1989)

5 We would prefer to see the House run by a philistine with the requisite financial acumen than by the succession of opera and ballet lovers who have brought a great and valuable institution to its knees.

report of the Commons' Culture, Media and Sport Select Committee on Covent Garden, 3 December 1997

6 Cabinet minutes are studied in Government Departments with the reverence generally reserved for sacred texts, and can be triumphantly produced conclusively to settle any arguments.

How to be a Minister (1980)

John Keane 1949–
Australian political scientist

7 Sovereign state power is an indispensable condition of the democratization of civil society . . . a more democratic order cannot be built *through* state power, it cannot be built *without* state power.

Democracy and Civil Society (1988)

Paul Keating 1944–
Australian Labor statesman; Prime Minister 1991–6

8 You look like an Easter Island statue with an arse full of razor blades.
   in the Australian Parliament to the then Prime Minister, Malcolm Fraser

Michael Gordon *A Question of Leadership* (1993)

9 Even as it [Great Britain] walked out on you and joined the Common Market, you were still looking for your MBEs and your knighthoods, and all the rest of the regalia that comes with it. You would take Australia right back down the time tunnel to the cultural cringe where you have always come from.
   addressing Australian Conservative supporters of Great Britain in the Australian Parliament, 27 February 1992

in *House of Representatives Weekly Hansard* [Australia] (1992) no. 1

1 These are the same old fogies who doffed their lids and tugged the forelock to the British establishment.
of Australian Conservative supporters of Great Britain, 27 February 1992

in *House of Representatives Weekly Hansard* [Australia] (1992) no. 1

2 I'm a bastard. But I'm a bastard who gets the mail through. And they appreciate that.
in 1994, to a senior colleague

in *Sunday Telegraph* 20 November 1994

3 Leadership is not about being nice. It's about being right and being strong.

in *Time* 9 January 1995

John Keegan 1934–

British military historian

4 It now does look as if air power has prevailed in the Balkans and that the time to redefine how victory in war may be won has come.

in *Daily Telegraph* 4 June 1999

Christine Keeler 1942–

English model and showgirl

5 Being in the public eye, as Monica Lewinsky will be for the rest of her life, is like being the lady with the moustache at the circus. You're a curiosity—and you will never stop being one.

attributed, in *The Times* 13 March 1999

Brian Keenan 1950–

Irish writer and teacher

6 Politics can only be a small part of what we are. It's a *way* of seeing, it's not all-seeing in itself.

An Evil Cradling (1992)

Garrison Keillor 1942–

American writer

7 Ronald Reagan, the President who never told bad news to the American people.

We Are Still Married (1989), introduction

8 My ancestors were Puritans from England. They arrived here in 1648 in the hope of finding greater restrictions than were permissible under English law at that time.

attributed, 1993

George F. Kennan 1904–

American diplomat and historian

9 Government . . . is simply not the channel through which men's noblest impulses are to be realized. Its task, on the contrary, is largely to see to it that the ignoble ones are kept under restraint and not permitted to go too far.

Around the Cragged Hill (1993)

10 A war regarded as inevitable or even probable, and therefore much prepared for, has a very good chance of being eventually fought.

The Cloud of Danger (1977)

John F. Kennedy 1917–63

American Democratic statesman, 35th President of the US
1961–3, son of Joseph and Rose **Kennedy** and brother of Robert
Kennedy
on Kennedy: see **Bentsen** 34:1, **Hope** 176:8, **Kennedy** 199:12,
Stevenson 347:9

1 Don't buy a single vote more than necessary. I'll be damned
if I'm going to pay for a landslide.
  *telegraphed message from his father, read at a Gridiron dinner in
  Washington, 15 March 1958, and almost certainly JFK's
  invention*

J. F. Cutler *Honey Fitz* (1962)

2 We stand today on the edge of a new frontier . . . But the
New Frontier of which I speak is not a set of promises—it is
a set of challenges. It sums up not what I intend to offer the
American people, but what I intend to ask of them.
  accepting the Democratic nomination

speech in Los Angeles, 15 July
1960; see **Schlossberg** 316:1

3 Let the word go forth from this time and place, to friend and
foe alike, that the torch has been passed to a new
generation of Americans—born in this century, tempered by
war, disciplined by a hard and bitter peace, proud of our
ancient heritage—and unwilling to witness or permit the
slow undoing of those human rights to which this nation
has always been committed, and to which we are
committed today at home and around the world.

inaugural address, 20 January
1961

4 Let every nation know, whether it wishes us well or ill, that
we shall pay any price, bear any burden, meet any
hardship, support any friend, oppose any foe to assure the
survival and the success of liberty.

inaugural address, 20 January
1961

5 If a free society cannot help the many who are poor, it
cannot save the few who are rich.

inaugural address, 20 January
1961

6 Let us never negotiate out of fear. But let us never fear to
negotiate.

inaugural address, 20 January
1961

7 All this will not be finished in the first 100 days. Nor will it
be finished in the first 1,000 days, nor in the life of this
Administration, nor even perhaps in our lifetime on this
planet. But let us begin.

inaugural address, 20 January
1961

8 And so, my fellow Americans: ask not what your country
can do for you—ask what you can do for your country. My
fellow citizens of the world: ask not what America will do
for you, but what together we can do for the freedom of
man.

inaugural address, 20 January
1961; Oliver Wendell **Holmes** Jr.,
speaking at Keene, New
Hampshire, 30 May 1884 said: 'We
pause to . . . recall what our
country has done for each of us
and to ask ourselves what we can
do for our country in return' (see
also **Gibran** 145:16)

9 I believe that this Nation should commit itself to achieving
the goal, before this decade is out, of landing a man on the
Moon and returning him safely to earth.

supplementary State of the Union
message to Congress, 25 May
1961

10 When we got into office, the thing that surprised me most
was to find that things were just as bad as we'd been saying
they were.

speech at the White House, 27
May 1961

11 Mankind must put an end to war or war will put an end to
mankind

speech to United Nations General
Assembly, 25 September 1961

1 Those who make peaceful revolution impossible will make violent revolution inevitable.

speech at the White House, 13 March 1962

2 Probably the greatest concentration of talent and genius in this house except for perhaps those times when Thomas Jefferson ate alone.
  of a dinner for the Nobel prizewinners at the White House

in *New York Times* 30 April 1962

3 If we cannot end now our differences, at least we can help make the world safe for diversity.

address at American University, Washington, DC, 10 June 1963

4 No one has been barred on account of his race from fighting or dying for America—there are no 'white' or 'coloured' signs on the foxholes or graveyards of battle.

message to Congress on proposed Civil Rights Bill, 19 June 1963

5 All free men, wherever they may live, are citizens of Berlin, and therefore, as a free man, I take pride in the words *Ich bin ein Berliner* [I am a Berliner].
  speaking in the newly divided city of Berlin, and expressing the USA's commitment to the support and defence of West Berlin

speech in West Berlin, 26 June 1963

6 When power leads man toward arrogance, poetry reminds him of his limitations. When power narrows the areas of man's concern, poetry reminds him of the richness and diversity of his existence. When power corrupts, poetry cleanses. For art establishes the basic human truths which must serve as the touchstone of our judgement.

speech at Amherst College, Massachusetts, 26 October 1963

7 In free society art is not a weapon . . . Artists are not engineers of the soul.

speech at Amherst College, Massachusetts, 26 October 1963; see **Gorky** 151:8, **Stalin** 345:3

on being asked how he became a war hero:
8 It was involuntary. They sank my boat.

Arthur M. Schlesinger Jr. *A Thousand Days* (1965)

9 Washington is a city of southern efficiency and northern charm.

Arthur M. Schlesinger Jr. *A Thousand Days* (1965)

10 I'm an idealist without illusions.

attributed; see **Macleod** 234:9

Joseph P. Kennedy 1888–1969

American financier and diplomat; father of John Fitzgerald **Kennedy** and Robert **Kennedy**; husband of Rose **Kennedy**
see also **Proverbs** 297:4

11 This is a hell of a long way from East Boston.
  to his wife Rose, on a visit to Windsor Castle two weeks after his arrival as Ambassador

in *The Times* 24 January 1995 (obituary of Rose **Kennedy**)

12 We're going to sell Jack like soapflakes.
  *when his son John F. **Kennedy** made his bid for the Presidency*

John H. Davis *The Kennedy Clan* (1984)

Robert F. Kennedy 1925–68

American democratic politician; son of Joseph and Rose **Kennedy** and brother of John Fitzgerald **Kennedy**

13 About one-fifth of the people are against everything all the time.

speech at University of Pennsylvania, 6 May 1964

14 What is objectionable, what is dangerous about extremists is not that they are extreme but that they are intolerant.

The Pursuit of Justice (1964)

1 Every society gets the kind of criminal it deserves. What is
equally true is that every community gets the kind of law
enforcement it insists on.

The Pursuit of Justice (1964)

Rose Kennedy 1890–1995
wife of Joseph **Kennedy**, mother of John Fitzgerald and Robert
Kennedy

2 It's our money, and we're free to spend it any way we
please . . . If you have money you spend it, and win.
   in response to criticism of overlavish funding of her son Robert
   Kennedy's 1968 presidential campaign

in *Daily Telegraph* 24 January 1995
(obituary)

3 Now Teddy must run.
   to her daughter, on hearing of the assassination of Robert
   Kennedy

in *The Times* 24 January 1995
(obituary); attributed, perhaps
apocryphal

Jomo Kenyatta 1891–1978
Kenyan statesman, Prime Minister of Kenya 1963 and President
1964–78

4 The African is conditioned, by the cultural and social
institutions of centuries, to a freedom of which Europe has
little conception, and it is not in his nature to accept
serfdom forever. He realizes that he must fight unceasingly
for his own emancipation; for without this he is doomed to
remain the prey of rival imperialisms.

Facing Mount Kenya (1938);
conclusion

Francis Scott Key 1779–1843
American lawyer and verse-writer

5 'Tis the star-spangled banner; O long may it wave
O'er the land of the free, and the home of the brave!

'The Star-Spangled Banner' (1814)

John Maynard Keynes 1883–1946
English economist

6 I work for a Government I despise for ends I think criminal.

letter to Duncan Grant, 15
December 1917

of **Clemenceau***:*
7 He felt about France what Pericles felt of Athens—unique
value in her, nothing else mattering; but his theory of
politics was Bismarck's. He had one illusion—France; and
one disillusion—mankind, including Frenchmen, and his
colleagues not least.

*The Economic Consequences of the
Peace* (1919)

8 Like Odysseus, the President looked wiser when he was
seated.
   of Woodrow **Wilson**

*The Economic Consequences of the
Peace* (1919)

9 Lenin was right. There is no subtler, no surer means of
overturning the existing basis of society than to debauch the
currency. The process engages all the hidden forces of
economic law on the side of destruction, and does it in a
manner which not one man in a million is able to diagnose.

*The Economic Consequences of the
Peace* (1919)

10 Capitalism, wisely managed, can probably be made more
efficient for attaining economic ends than any alternative
system yet in sight, but . . . in itself it is in many ways
extremely objectionable.

The End of Laissez-Faire (1926)

1 Marxian Socialism must always remain a portent to the historians of Opinion—how a doctrine so illogical and so dull can have exercised so powerful and enduring an influence over the minds of men, and, through them, the events of history.

The End of Laissez-Faire (1926)

2 I do not know which makes a man more conservative—to know nothing but the present, or nothing but the past.

The End of Laissez-Faire (1926)

3 The important thing for Government is not to do things which individuals are doing already, and to do them a little better or a little worse; but to do those things which at present are not done at all.

The End of Laissez-Faire (1926)

of Lloyd George:
4 This extraordinary figure of our time, this syren, this goat-footed bard, this half-human visitor to our age from the hag-ridden magic and enchanted woods of Celtic antiquity.

Essays in Biography (1933) 'Mr Lloyd George'

of Lloyd George:
5 Who shall paint the chameleon, who can tether a broomstick?

Essays in Biography (1933) 'Mr Lloyd George'

6 It is better that a man should tyrannize over his bank balance than over his fellow-citizens.

General Theory (1936)

7 We take it as a fundamental psychological rule of any modern community that, when its real income is increased, it will not increase its consumption by an equal *absolute* amount.

General Theory (1936)

8 The ideas of economists and political philosophers, both when they are right and when they are wrong, are more powerful than is commonly understood . . . Practical men, who believe themselves to be quite exempt from any intellectual influences, are usually the slaves of some defunct economist. Madmen in authority, who hear voices in the air, are distilling their frenzy from some academic scribbler of a few years back.

General Theory (1947 ed.)

9 But this *long run* is a misleading guide to current affairs. *In the long run* we are all dead.

A Tract on Monetary Reform (1923)

10 I evidently knew more about economics than my examiners.
explaining why he performed badly in the Civil Service examinations

Roy Harrod *Life of John Maynard Keynes* (1951)

11 We threw good housekeeping to the winds. But we saved ourselves and helped save the world.
of Britain in the Second World War

A. J. P. Taylor *English History, 1914–1945* (1965)

12 LADY VIOLET BONHAM CARTER: What do you think happens to Mr Lloyd George when he is alone in the room?
MAYNARD KEYNES: When he is alone in the room there is nobody there.

Lady Violet Bonham Carter *The Impact of Personality in Politics* (Romanes Lecture, 1963)

Ayatollah Ruhollah Khomeini 1900–89

Iranian Shiite Muslim leader, who returned to Iran from exile in 1979 to lead an Islamic revolution which overthrew the Shah

13 If laws are needed, Islam has established them all.There is no need . . . after establishing a government, to sit down and draw up laws.

Islam and Revolution: Writings and Declarations of Imam Khomeini (1981) ' Islamic Government'

Nikita Khrushchev 1894–1971

Soviet statesman; Premier, 1958–64

1 If anyone believes that our smiles involve abandonment of the teaching of Marx, Engels and Lenin he deceives himself. Those who wait for that must wait until a shrimp learns to whistle.

speech in Moscow, 17 September 1955

2 We must abolish the cult of the individual decisively, once and for all.

speech to secret session of the 20th Congress of the Communist Party, 25 February 1956

3 We say this not only for the socialist states, who are more akin to us. We base ourselves on the idea that we must peacefully co-exist. About the capitalist States, it doesn't depend on you whether or not we exist. If you don't like us, don't accept our invitations and don't invite us to come to see you. Whether you like it or not, history is on our side. We will bury you.

speech to Western diplomats at reception in Moscow for Polish leader Mr Gomulka, 18 November 1956; 'We will bury you' in this context means 'we will outlive you'

in The Times 19 November 1956

4 If one cannot catch the bird of paradise, better take a wet hen.

in Time 6 January 1958

5 Politicians are the same all over. They promise to build a bridge where there is no river.

at a press conference in New York, October 1960

6 We are going to make the imperialists dance like fishes in a saucepan, even without war.

in Vienna, 2 July 1960

7 If you start throwing hedgehogs under me, I shall throw a couple of porcupines under you.

in New York Times 7 November 1963

8 Anyone who believes that the worker can be lulled by fine revolutionary phrases is mistaken . . . If no concern is shown for the growth of material and spiritual riches, the people will listen today, they will listen tomorrow, and then they may say: 'Why do you promise us everything for the future? You are talking, so to speak, about life beyond the grave. The priest has already told us about this.'

speech at World Youth Forum, 19 September 1964

Peter Kilfoyle 1946–

British Labour politician

9 There is now a recognition that we cannot expect people to vote for us just on our say-so.

in Times 6 May 2000

David Maxwell Fyfe, Lord Kilmuir 1900–67

British Conservative politician and lawyer
on Kilmuir: see **Anonymous** 10:2

10 Gratitude is not a normal feature of political life.

Political Adventure (1964)

11 Loyalty is the Tory's secret weapon.

Anthony Sampson *Anatomy of Britain* (1962); see **Critchley** 97:8

Anthony King 1934–

British political scientist

1 It is an asteroid hitting the planet and destroying practically all life on earth.

asserting that the word 'landslide' was too weak to describe the scale of Labour's victory

on 'Election Night' (BBC1) 2 May 1997

Martin Luther King 1929–68

American civil rights leader
see also **Epitaphs** 128:1

2 I want to be the white man's brother, not his brother-in-law.

in *New York Journal-American* 10 September 1962

3 Injustice anywhere is a threat to justice everywhere.

letter from Birmingham Jail, Alabama, 16 April 1963

4 I submit to you that if a man hasn't discovered something he will die for, he isn't fit to live.

speech in Detroit, 23 June 1963

5 I have a dream that one day on the red hills of Georgia the sons of former slaves and the sons of former slave owners will be able to sit down together at the table of brotherhood . . .

I have a dream that my four little children will one day live in a nation where they will not be judged by the colour of their skin but by the content of their character.

speech at Civil Rights March in Washington, 28 August 1963

6 When we let freedom ring, when we let it ring from every village and every hamlet, from every state and every city, we will be able to speed up that day when all of God's children, black men and white men, Jews and Gentiles, Protestants and Catholics, will be able to join hands and sing in the words of the old Negro spiritual, 'Free at last! Free at last! Thank God Almighty, we are free at last!'

speech at Civil Rights March in Washington, 28 August 1963

7 We must learn to live together as brothers or perish together as fools.

speech at St Louis, 22 March 1964

8 I just want to do God's will. And he's allowed me to go up to the mountain. And I've looked over, and I've seen the promised land . . . So I'm happy tonight. I'm not worried about anything. I'm not fearing any man.

speech in Memphis, 3 April 1968, the day before his assassination

in *New York Times* 4 April 1968

9 If we assume that mankind has a right to survive, then we must find an alternative to war and destruction. In our day of space vehicles and guided ballistic missiles, the choice is either nonviolence or nonexistence.

Strength to Love (1963)

10 Nothing in all the world is more dangerous than sincere ignorance and conscientious stupidity.

Strength to Love (1963)

11 The ultimate measure of a man is not where he stands in moments of comfort and convenience, but where he stands at times of challenge and controversy.

Strength to Love (1963)

12 The means by which we live have outdistanced the ends for which we live. Our scientific power has outrun our spiritual power. We have guided missiles and misguided men.

Strength to Love (1963)

13 A riot is at bottom the language of the unheard.

Where Do We Go From Here? (1967)

William Lyon Mackenzie King 1874–1950
Canadian statesman

1 If some countries have too much history, we have too much geography.

speech on Canada as an international power, 18 June 1936

2 Not necessarily conscription, but conscription if necessary.

speech, Canadian House of Commons, 7 July 1942

Hugh Kingsmill 1889–1949
English man of letters

3 A nation is only at peace when it's at war.

attributed

Neil Kinnock 1942–
British Labour politician; Leader of the Labour Party 1983–92
see also **Newspaper headlines** 267:5

4 Loyalty is a fine quality but in excess it fills political graveyards.
   in June 1976, in opposition to Conference decisions on devolution

G. M. F. Drower *Neil Kinnock* (1984)

*of servicemen in the Falklands War, when replying to a heckler who said that Mrs **Thatcher** 'showed guts':*
5 It's a pity others had to leave theirs on the ground at Goose Green to prove it.

television interview, 6 June 1983

6 If Margaret Thatcher wins on Thursday, I warn you not to be ordinary, I warn you not to be young, I warn you not to fall ill, and I warn you not to grow old.
   on the prospect of a Conservative re-election

speech at Bridgend, 7 June 1983

7 The grotesque chaos of a Labour council hiring taxis to scuttle round the city handing out redundancy notices to its own workers.
   of the actions of the Labour city council in Liverpool

speech at the Labour Party Conference, 1 October 1985

8 I would die for my country but I could never let my country die for me.

speech at Labour Party Conference, 30 September 1986

9 Why am I the first Kinnock in a thousand generations to be able to get to university?
   later plagiarized by the American politician Joe Biden

speech at Llandudno, 15 May 1987

10 There are lots of ways to get socialism, but I think trying to fracture the Labour party by incessant contest cannot be one of them.

in *Guardian* 29 January 1988

11 I don't think anyone could accuse someone who has been leader of the Labour party for more than seven years of being impulsive.

in *Sunday Times* 5 August 1990

12 I have a lot of sympathy with him. I too was once a young, bald Leader of the Opposition.
   *on William **Hague***

in *Independent* on 3 October 1999

Rudyard Kipling 1865–1936

English writer and poet, cousin of Stanley **Baldwin**

1 Oh, East is East, and West is West, and never the twain
   shall meet.

'The Ballad of East and West'
(1892)

2 All Power, each Tyrant, every Mob
Whose head has grown too large,
Ends by destroying its own job
And works its own discharge.

'The Benefactors' (1919)

3 Winds of the World, give answer! They are whimpering to
   and fro—
And what should they know of England who only England
   know?—
The poor little street-bred people that vapour and fume and
   brag.

'The English Flag' (1892)

4 I could not dig: I dared not rob:
Therefore I lied to please the mob.
Now all my lies are proved untrue
And I must face the men I slew.
What tale shall serve me here among
Mine angry and defrauded young?

'Epitaphs of the War: A Dead
Statesman' (1919)

5 As it will be in the future, it was at the birth of Man—
There are only four things certain since Social Progress
   began:—
That the Dog returns to his Vomit and the Sow returns to
   her Mire,
And the burnt Fool's bandaged finger goes wabbling back to
   the Fire.

'The Gods of the Copybook
Headings' (1927)

6 And that after this is accomplished, and the brave new
   world begins
When all men are paid for existing, and no man must pay
   for his sins,
As surely as Water will wet us, as surely as Fire will burn,
The Gods of the Copybook Headings with terror and
   slaughter return!

'The Gods of the Copybook
Headings' (1927)

7 If you can keep your head when all about you
Are losing theirs and blaming it on you;
If you can trust yourself when all men doubt you,
But make allowance for their doubting too;
If you can wait and not be tired by waiting,
Or being lied about, don't deal in lies,
Or being hated, don't give way to hating,
And yet don't look too good, nor talk too wise;
If you can dream—and not make dreams your master;
If you can think—and not make thoughts your aim,
If you can meet with triumph and disaster
And treat those two impostors just the same . . .

'If—' (1910)

8 If you can talk with crowds and keep your virtue,
Or walk with Kings—nor lose the common touch.

'If—' (1910)

9 Now this is the Law of the Jungle—as old and as true as the
   sky;
And the Wolf that shall keep it may prosper, but the Wolf
   that shall break it must die.

'The Law of the Jungle' (1895)

1 Ship me somewheres east of Suez, where the best is like the worst,
Where there aren't no Ten Commandments an' a man can raise a thirst.

'Mandalay' (1892)

2 A Nation spoke to a Nation,
A Throne sent word to a Throne:
'Daughter am I in my mother's house,
But mistress in my own.
The gates are mine to open,
As the gates are mine to close,
And I abide by my Mother's House.'
Said our Lady of the Snows.

'Our Lady of the Snows' (1898)

3 God of our fathers, known of old,
Lord of our far-flung battle-line,
Beneath whose awful Hand we hold
Dominion over palm and pine—
Lord God of Hosts, be with us yet,
Lest we forget—lest we forget!

The tumult and the shouting dies—
The captains and the kings depart—
Still stands Thine ancient Sacrifice,
An humble and a contrite heart.

'Recessional' (1897)

4 Far-called our navies melt away—
On dune and headland sinks the fire—
Lo, all our pomp of yesterday
Is one with Nineveh, and Tyre!

'Recessional' (1897)

5 Such boasting as the Gentiles use,
Or lesser breeds without the Law.

'Recessional' (1897)

6 We have fed our sea for a thousand years
And she calls us, still unfed,
Though there's never a wave of all her waves
But marks our English dead:
We have strawed our best to the weed's unrest
To the shark and sheering gull.
If blood be the price of admiralty,
Lord God, we ha' paid in full!

'The Song of the Dead' (1896)

7 It is always a temptation to a rich and lazy nation,
To puff and look important and to say:-
'Though we know we should defeat you, we have not the time to meet you,
We will therefore pay you cash to go away.'

And that is called paying the Dane-geld;
But we've proved it again and again,
That if once you have paid him the Dane-geld
You never get rid of the Dane.

'What Dane-geld means' (1911)

8 Take up the White Man's burden—
Send forth the best ye breed—
Go, bind your sons to exile
To serve your captives' need.

'The White Man's Burden' (1899)

9 He was the greatest, as he was the hugest, of the war correspondents . . . and he always opened his conversation with the news that there would be trouble in the Balkans in the spring.

The Light that Failed (1891) ch. 4

1 Power without responsibility: the prerogative of the harlot throughout the ages.

summing up Lord **Beaverbrook**'s *political standpoint vis-à-vis the Daily Express, after he had said to Kipling, 'What I want is power. Kiss 'em one day and kick 'em the next'; Stanley* **Baldwin**, *Kipling's cousin, subsequently obtained permission to use the phrase in a speech in London on 18 March 1931*

in *Kipling Journal* December 1971

Henry Kissinger 1923–
American politician

2 There cannot be a crisis next week. My schedule is already full.

in *New York Times Magazine* 1 June 1969

3 Power is the great aphrodisiac.

in *New York Times* 19 January 1971

4 The illegal we do immediately. The unconstitutional takes a little longer.

in *Washington Post* 20 January 1977; attributed

5 Ninety percent of the politicians give the other ten percent a bad name.

in 1978, attributed

6 History has so far shown us only two roads to international stability: domination and equilibrium.

in *The Times* 12 March 1991

7 The management of a balance of power is a permanent undertaking, not an exertion that has a foreseeable end.

White House Years (1979)

8 We are the President's men and we must behave accordingly.

M. and B. Kalb *Kissinger* (1974)

9 For other nations, Utopia is a blessed past never to be recovered; for Americans it is just beyond the horizon.

attributed

10 The main advantage of being famous is that when you bore people at dinner parties they think it is their fault.

James Naughtie in *Spectator* 1 April 1995; attributed

Lord Kitchener 1850–1916
British soldier and politician
on Kitchener: see **Asquith** 15:9

11 You are ordered abroad as a soldier of the King to help our French comrades against the invasion of a common enemy . . . In this new experience you may find temptations both in wine and women. You must entirely resist both temptations, and, while treating all women with perfect courtesy, you should avoid any intimacy. Do your duty bravely. Fear God. Honour the King.

message to soldiers of the British Expeditionary Force (1914)

in *The Times* 19 August 1914

12 I don't mind your being killed, but I object to your being taken prisoner.

to the Prince of Wales (later **Edward VIII**) *on his asking to be allowed to the Front during the First World War*

in *Journals and Letters of Reginald Viscount Esher* vol. 3 (1938) 18 December 1914

John Knox c.1505–72
Scottish Protestant reformer
on Knox: see **Epitaphs** 128:6

13 The first blast of the trumpet against the monstrous regiment of women.

regiment here means 'rule'

title of pamphlet (1558)

1 *Un homme avec Dieu est toujours dans la majorité.*
   A man with God is always in the majority.

inscription on the Reformation Monument, Geneva; see **Proverbs** 296:14

Philander C. Knox 1853–1921
US Attorney-General

*Theodore **Roosevelt** had requested a legal justification for his acquisition of the Panama Canal:*

2 Oh, Mr. President, do not let so great an achievement suffer from any taint of legality.

Tyler Dennett *John Hay: From Poetry to Politics* (1933)

Helmut Kohl 1930–
Chancellor of West Germany (1982–90) and first postwar Chancellor of united Germany (1990–8)

3 I have been underestimated for decades. I have done very well that way.

in *New York Times* 25 January 1987

4 My goal, when the historical hour allows it, is the unity of the nation.
   to crowds in Dresden on the occasion of his first official visit to East Germany, 19 December 1989

in *The Times* 20 December 1989

5 We Germans now have the historic chance to realize the unity of our fatherland.

in *Guardian* 15 February 1990

6 The policy of European integration is in reality a question of war and peace in the 21st century.

speech at Louvain University, 2 February 1996

Paul Kruger 1825–1904
South African soldier and statesman

7 A bill of indemnity . . . for raid by Dr Jameson and the British South Africa Company's troops. The amount falls under two heads—first, material damage, total of claim, £677,938 3s. 3d.—second, moral or intellectual damage, total of claim, £1,000,000.
   *telegram from the South African Republic, communicated to the House of Commons by Joseph **Chamberlain***

in the House of Commons 18 February 1897

Stanley Kubrick 1928–99
American film director and screenwriter

8 The great nations have always acted like gangsters, and the small nations like prostitutes.

in *Guardian* 5 June 1963

Henry Labouchere 1831–1912
British politician

9 I do not object to the old man always having a card up his sleeve, but I do object to his insinuating that the Almighty has placed it there.
   *on **Gladstone**'s 'frequent appeals to a higher power'*

Earl Curzon *Modern Parliamentary Eloquence* (1913)

Jean de la Bruyère 1645–96
French satiric moralist

10 When the populace is excited, one cannot conceive how calm can be restored; and when it is peaceful, one cannot see how calm can be disturbed.

Characters (1688) 'Of the Sovereign and the State'

Fiorello La Guardia 1882–1947

American politician, mayor of New York City

1 When I make a mistake, it's a beaut!
  on the appointment of Herbert O'Brien as a judge in 1936

William Manners *Patience and Fortitude* (1976)

2 There is no Democratic or Republican way of cleaning the streets.

Charles Garrett *The La Guardia Years, Machine and Reform Politics in New York City* (1961)

John Lambert 1619–83

English soldier and Parliamentary supporter

3 The quarrel is now between light and darkness, not who shall rule, but whether we shall live or be preserved or no. Good words will not do with the cavaliers.
  speech in the Parliament of 1656 supporting the rule of the major-generals

in *Dictionary of National Biography*

John George Lambton see John George Lambton, Lord Durham

Norman Lamont 1942–

British Conservative politician

4 A price worth paying.
  as Chancellor, responding to criticism on the rise in unemployment

in the House of Commons, 16 May 1991

5 The turn of the tide is sometimes difficult to discern. What we are seeing is the return of that vital ingredient— confidence. The green shoots of economic spring are appearing once again.

speech at the Conservative Party Conference, 9 October 1991; see **Misquotations** 254:7

6 We give the impression of being in office but not in power.
  'in office, but not in power' had earlier been used by A. J. P. **Taylor** *of Ramsay* **Macdonald**'s *minority government of 1924*

speech in House of Commons, 9 June 1993

Giuseppe di Lampedusa 1896–1957

Italian novelist

7 If we want things to stay as they are, things will have to change.

The Leopard (1957)

Bert Lance 1931–

American government official

8 If it ain't broke, don't fix it.

in *Nation's Business* May 1977

Walter Savage Landor 1775–1864

English poet

9 The wise become as the unwise in the enchanted chambers of Power, whose lamps make every face the same colour.

Imaginary Conversations (1824–9)

1 George the First was always reckoned
  Vile, but viler George the Second;
  And what mortal ever heard
  Any good of George the Third?
  When from earth the Fourth descended
  God be praised the Georges ended!

epigram in The Atlas, *28 April 1855*

Andrew Lang 1844–1912
Scottish man of letters

2 He uses statistics as a drunken man uses lampposts—for
  support rather than illumination.

Alan L. Mackay *Harvest of a Quiet Eye* (1977); attributed

William Langland c.1330–c.1400
English poet

3 Brewesters and baksters, bochiers and cokes—
  For thise are men on this molde that moost harm wercheth
  To the povere peple.
  *in an alternative text, 'As bakeres and breweres, bocheres and
  cokes; / For thyse men don most harm to the mene peple'*

The Vision of Piers Plowman

Lao-tzu c.604–c.531 BC
Chinese philosopher; founder of Taoism

4 The best [rulers] are those whose existence is [merely]
    known by the people.
  The next best are those who are loved and praised.
  The next are those who are feared.
  And the next are those who are reviled . . .
  [The great rulers] accomplish their task; they complete their
    work.
  Nevertheless their people say that they simply follow
    Nature.

Tao-te Ching ch. 17

James Larkin 1867–1947
Irish labour leader

5 Our fathers died that we might be free men. Are we going to
  allow their sacrifices to be as naught? Or are we going to
  follow in their footsteps at the Rising of the Moon?

in Irish Worker *July 1914*

6 Hell has no terror for me. I have lived there. Thirty six years
  of hunger and poverty have been my portion. They cannot
  terrify me with hell. Better to be in hell with Dante and
  Davitt than to be in heaven with Carson and Murphy.
  in 1913, during the 'Dublin lockout' labour dispute

Ulick O'Connor *The Troubles* (rev. ed., 1996)

Duc de la Rochefoucauld-Liancourt
1747–1827
French social reformer

7 LOUIS XVI: It is a big revolt.
  LA ROCHEFOUCAULD-LIANCOURT: No, Sire, a big revolution.
    on a report reaching Versailles of the Fall of the Bastille, 1789

F. Dreyfus *La Rochefoucauld-Liancourt* (1903)

Harold Laski 1893–1950
British Labour politician and academic

1 I respect fidelity to colleagues even though they are fit for the hangman.

letter to Oliver Wendell **Holmes** Jr., 4 December 1926

2 He searched always to end a sentence with a climax. He looked for antithesis like a monkey looking for fleas.
of Winston Churchill at a dinner at the London School of Economics

letter to Oliver Wendell **Holmes** Jr., 7 May 1927

■ **Last words** *see box overleaf*

Hugh Latimer see **Last words** 212:2

William L. Laurence 1888–1977
American journalist

3 At first it was a giant column that soon took the shape of a supramundane mushroom.

on the first atomic explosion in New Mexico, 16 July 1945

Wilfrid Laurier 1841–1919
Canadian politician

4 The nineteenth century was the century of the United States. I think we can claim that it is Canada that shall fill the twentieth century.

speech in Ottawa, 18 January 1904; see **Trudeau** 365:14

T. E. Lawrence 1888–1935
English soldier and writer

5 Poets hope too much, and their politics . . . usually stink after twenty years.

letter to Cecil Day Lewis, November 1934

6 The trouble with Communism is that it accepts too much of today's furniture. I hate furniture.

letter to Cecil Day Lewis, 20 December 1934

Mark Lawson 1962–
British writer and journalist

7 Office tends to confer a dreadful plausibility on even the most negligible of those who hold it.

Joe Queenan *Imperial Caddy* (1992); introduction

Nigel Lawson 1932–
British Conservative politician; Chancellor of the Exchequer 1983–9

8 The Conservative Party has never believed that the business of government is the government of business.

in the House of Commons, 10 November 1981

9 Teenage scribblers.
of the financial press

in *Financial Times* 28 September 1985

10 It represented the tip of a singularly ill-concealed iceberg, with all the destructive potential that icebergs possess.
of an article by Alan Walters, the Prime Minister's economic adviser, criticizing the Exchange Rate Mechanism

in the House of Commons following his resignation as Chancellor, 31 October 1989

11 When I was a minister I always looked forward to the Cabinet meeting immensely because it was, apart from the summer holidays, the only period of real rest I got in what was a very heavy job.

'Cabinet Government in the Thatcher Years' (1994)

Last words

1 All my possessions for a moment of time.
   Queen **Elizabeth I** (*1533–1603*)

attributed, but almost certainly apocryphal

2 Be of good comfort Master Ridley, and play the man. We shall this day light such a candle by God's grace in England, as (I trust) shall never be put out.
   Hugh **Latimer** (*c.1485–1555*), *prior to being burned for heresy, 16 October 1555*

John Foxe *Actes and Monuments* (1570 ed.)

3 Come closer, boys. It will be easier for you.
   Erskine **Childers** (*1870–1922*) *to the firing squad at his execution*

Burke Wilkinson *The Zeal of the Convert* (1976) ch. 26

4 Die, my dear Doctor, that's the last thing I shall do!
   Lord **Palmerston** (*1784–1865*)

E. Latham *Famous Sayings and their Authors* (1904)

5 An emperor ought to die standing.
   Vespasian (AD *9–79*)

Suetonius *Lives of the Caesars* 'Vespasian'

6 For my name and memory, I leave it to men's charitable speeches, and to foreign nations, and the next ages.
   Francis **Bacon** (*1561–1626*)

his last will, 19 December 1625

7 God save Ireland!
   called out from the dock by the Manchester Martyrs, William Allen (*d. 1867*), *Michael Larkin* (*d. 1867*), *and William O'Brien* (*d. 1867*)

Robert Kee *The Bold Fenian Men* (1989); see **Sullivan** 349:9

8 How's the Empire?
   said by King **George V** (*1865–1936*) *to his private secretary on the morning of his death, probably prompted by an article in* The Times, *which he held open at the imperial and foreign page; Lord Wigram in a memorandum of 20 January 1936 also recorded that the King had said, 'Gentlemen, I am so sorry for keeping you waiting like this. I am unable to concentrate.' The (probably apocryphal) response 'Bugger Bognor' to the suggestion, 'Cheer up, your Majesty, you will soon be at Bognor again', has also been attributed to an earlier illness in 1929*

letter from Lord Wigram, 31 January 1936, in J. E. Wrench *Geoffrey Dawson and Our Times* (1955).

9 I die happy.
   Charles James **Fox** (*1749–1806*)

Lord John Russell *Life and Times of C. J. Fox* vol. 3 (1860) ch. 69

10 I find, then, I am but a bad anatomist.
   Wolfe Tone (*1763–98*), *who in trying to cut his throat in prison severed his windpipe instead of his jugular, and lingered for several days*

Oliver Knox *Rebels and Informers* (1998)

11 I have a long journey to take, and must bid the company farewell.
   Walter **Ralegh** (*c.1552–1618*), *parting words*

E. Thompson *Sir Walter Raleigh* (1935)

12 I have loved justice and hated iniquity: therefore I die in exile.
   Pope Gregory VII (*c.1020–85*) *at Salerno, following his conflict with the Emperor Henry IV*

J. W. Bowden *The Life and Pontificate of Gregory VII* (1840) vol. 2

13 I only regret that I have but one life to lose for my country.
   Nathan Hale (*1755–76*), *prior to his execution by the British for spying, 22 September 1776*

Henry Phelps Johnston *Nathan Hale, 1776* (1914)

Last words *continued*

1 It is well, I die hard, but I am not afraid to go.
   George **Washington** (*1732–99*)

on 14 December 1799

2 I will die like a true-blue rebel. Don't waste any time in mourning—organize.
   Joe **Hill** (*1879–1915*) *before his death by firing squad*

farewell telegram to Bill Haywood, 18 November 1915, in *Salt Lake* (Utah) *Tribune* 19 November 1915

3 Lord have mercy on my poor country that is so barbarously oppressed.
   Andrew Fletcher of Saltoun, *Scottish patriot and anti-Unionist*

September 1716

4 Lord, open the King of England's eyes!
   William **Tyndale** (*c.*1494–1536), *at the stake*

John Foxe *Actes and Monuments* (1570)

5 My design is to make what haste I can to be gone.
   Oliver **Cromwell** (*1599–1658*)

John Morley *Oliver Cromwell* (1900)

on his death-bed, declining a proposed visit from Queen Victoria:
6 No it is better not. She would only ask me to take a message to Albert.
   Benjamin **Disraeli** (*1804–81*)

Robert Blake *Disraeli* (1966)

7 Ô liberté! Ô liberté! que de crimes on commet en ton nom!
   O liberty! O liberty! what crimes are committed in thy name!
   Mme **Roland** (*1754–93*), *before being guillotined*

A. de Lamartine *Histoire des Girondins* (1847)

8 Oh, my country! how I leave my country!
   William **Pitt** (*1759–1806*); *also variously reported as 'How I love my country'; and 'My country! oh, my country!'*

Earl Stanhope *Life of the Rt. Hon. William Pitt* vol. 3 (1879); Earl Stanhope *Life of the Rt. Hon. William Pitt* (1st ed.), vol. 4 (1862); and G. Rose *Diaries and Correspondence* (1860) 23 January 1806; oral tradition reports:

   I think I could eat one of Bellamy's veal pies.

attributed

9 Put out the light.
   Theodore **Roosevelt** (*1858–1919*)

on 6 January 1919

10 So little done, so much to do.
   Cecil **Rhodes** (*1853–1902*), *on the day of his death*

Lewis Michell *Life of Rhodes* (1910)

11 Strike the tent.
   Robert E. **Lee** (*1807–70*), *12 October 1870*

attributed

12 This hath not offended the king.
   Thomas **More** (*1478–1535*), *lifting his beard aside after laying his head on the block*

Francis Bacon *Apophthegms New and Old* (1625) no. 22

13 This *is* a beautiful country!
   John **Brown** (*1800–59*) *as he rode to the gallows, seated on his coffin*

at his execution on 2 December 1859

14 This is the Fourth?
   Thomas **Jefferson** (*1743–1826*)

on 4 July 1826

Last words *continued*

1 This, this is the end of earth. I am content.
*John Quincy **Adams** (1767–1848) on collapsing in the Senate,*
21 February 1848 (he died two days later)

William H. Seward *Eulogy of John Quincy Adams to Legislature of New York* 1848

2 Thomas—Jefferson—still surv—
*in fact Thomas **Jefferson** died on the same day*

John **Adams**, 4 July 1826

3 Would to God this wound had been for Ireland.
Patrick Sarsfield (c.1655–93) on being mortally wounded at the battle of Landen, 19 August 1693, while fighting for France

attributed

Emma Lazarus 1849–87

American poet

4 Give me your tired, your poor,
Your huddled masses yearning to breathe free,
The wretched refuse of your teeming shore,
Send these, the homeless, tempest-tossed, to me:
I lift my lamp beside the golden door.
inscription on the Statue of Liberty, New York

'The New Colossus' (1883)

Alexandre Auguste Ledru-Rollin 1807–74

French politician

5 Ah well! I am their leader, I really had to follow them!

E. de Mirecourt *Les Contemporains* vol. 14 (1857) 'Ledru-Rollin'

Charles Lee 1731–82

American soldier

6 Beware that your Northern laurels do not change to Southern willows.
to General Horatio Gates after the surrender of Burgoyne at Saratoga

on 17 October 1777

Henry ('Light-Horse Harry') Lee 1756–1818

American soldier and politician

7 A citizen, first in war, first in peace, and first in the hearts of his countrymen.
*of George **Washington***

Funeral Oration on the death of General Washington (1800)

Richard Henry Lee 1732–94

American politician

8 That these united colonies are, and of right ought to be, free and independent states; that they are absolved from all allegiance to the British crown; and that all political connection between them and the State of Great Britain is, and ought to be, totally dissolved.

resolution moved at the Continental Congress on 7 June 1776; adopted 2 July 1776

Robert E. Lee 1807–70
American Confederate general
see also **Last words** 213:11

1 It is well that war is so terrible. We should grow too fond of it.
  after the battle of Fredericksburg, December 1862

attributed

2 There is nothing left for me to do but to go and see General Grant and I would rather die a thousand deaths.
  just before the Confederate surrender at Appomattox in 1865

Geoffrey C. Ward *The Civil War* (1991)

3 I have fought against the people of the North because I believed they were seeking to wrest from the South its dearest rights. But I have never cherished toward them bitter or vindictive feelings, and I have never seen the day when I did not pray for them.

Geoffrey C. Ward *The Civil War* (1991)

Curtis E. LeMay 1906–90
US air-force officer

4 They've got to draw in their horns and stop their aggression, or we're going to bomb them back into the Stone Age.
  on the North Vietnamese

Mission with LeMay (1965)

Lenin 1870–1924
Russian revolutionary, first Premier (Chairman of the Council of People's Commissars) of the Soviet Union 1918–24
see also **Misquotations** 254:3

5 Imperialism is the monopoly stage of capitalism.

Imperialism as the Last Stage of Capitalism (1916) 'Briefest possible definition of imperialism'

6 One step forward two steps back

title of book 1904

7 No, Democracy is *not* identical with majority rule. Democracy is a *State* which recognizes the subjection of the minority to the majority, that is, an organization for the systematic use of *force* by one class against the other, by one part of the population against another.

State and Revolution (1919)

8 While the State exists, there can be no freedom. When there is freedom there will be no State.

State and Revolution (1919)

9 What is to be done?

title of pamphlet (1902); originally the title of a novel (1863) by N. G. Chernyshevsky

10 We must now set about building a proletarian socialist state in Russia.

speech in Petrograd, 7 November 1917

11 Communism equals Soviet power plus the electrification of the whole country.

report to 8th Congress, 1920

12 Who? Whom?
  definition of political science, meaning 'Who will outstrip whom?'

in *Polnoe Sobranie Sochinenii* (1970) 17 October 1921

13 An end to bossing.

Neil Harding *Lenin's Political Thought* (1981) vol.2

14 A good man fallen among Fabians.
  of George Bernard **Shaw**

Arthur Ransome *Six Weeks in Russia in 1919* (1919) 'Notes of Conversations with Lenin'

1 Liberty is precious—so precious that it must be rationed.

Sidney and Beatrice Webb *Soviet Communism* (1935) vol. 2

William Lenthall 1591–1662
Speaker of the House of Commons

2 I have neither eye to see, nor tongue to speak here, but as the House is pleased to direct me.
  to Charles I, 4 January 1642, on being asked if he had seen any of the five MPs whom the King had ordered to be arrested

John Rushworth *Historical Collections. The Third Part* vol. 2 (1692)

Alan Jay Lerner 1918–86

3 Don't let it be forgot
That once there was a spot
For one brief shining moment that was known
As Camelot.
  particularly associated with the Kennedy White House

'Camelot' (1960 song); see **Onassis** 274:9

Doris Lessing 1919–
British novelist and short-story writer, brought up in Rhodesia

4 When old settlers say 'One has to understand the country,' what they mean is, 'You have to get used to our ideas about the native.'

The Grass is Singing (1950)

5 When a white man in Africa by accident looks into the eyes of a native and sees the human being (which it is his chief preoccupation to avoid), his sense of guilt, which he denies, fumes up in resentment and he brings down the whip.

The Grass is Singing (1950)

Leslie Lever 1905–77
British Labour politician

6 Generosity is part of my character, and I therefore hasten to assure this Government that I will never make an allegation of dishonesty against it wherever a simple explanation of stupidity will suffice.

Leon Harris *The Fine Art of Political Wit* (1964)

Primo Levi 1919–87
Italian novelist and poet

7 Our language lacks words to express this offence, the demolition of a man.
  of a year spent in Auschwitz

If This is a Man (1958)

Bernard Levin 1928–
British journalist

8 Since when was fastidiousness a quality useful for political advancement?

If You Want My Opinion (1992)

9 Harold Macmillan, whose elevation was achieved by a brutality, cunning and greed for power normally met only in the conclaves of Mafia *capi*, said, after he had climbed the greasy pole and pushed all his rivals off (*takes out handkerchief containing concealed onion*) that the whole thing was Dead Sea Fruit.

If You Want My Opinion (1992); see **Macmillan** 236:8

1 [Tony] Benn flung himself into the Sixties technology with the enthusiasm (not to say language) of a newly enrolled Boy Scout demonstrating knot-tying to his indulgent parents.

The Pendulum Years (1970)

*of Harold **Macmillan** and Harold **Wilson***:
2 Between them, then, Walrus and Carpenter, they divided up the Sixties.

The Pendulum Years (1970)

3 Whom the mad would destroy, they first make gods.
   *of **Mao** Zedong in 1967*

in *The Times* 21 September 1987

4 Once, when a British Minister sneezed, men half a world away would blow their noses. Now when a British Prime Minister sneezes nobody else will even say, 'Bless You.'

in *The Times* 1976

5 What has happened to architecture since the second world war that the only passers-by who can contemplate it without pain are those equipped with a white stick and a dog?

in *The Times* 1983

6 The less the power, the greater the desire to exercise it.

in *The Times* 21 September 1993

7 I have more than once pointed out that no organization with 'Liberation' in its title has ever, or ever will, liberate anyone or anything.

in *The Times* 14 April 1995

Duc de Lévis 1764–1830
French soldier and writer

8 *Gouverner, c'est choisir.*
   To govern is to choose.

Maximes et Réflexions (1812 ed.)
'Politique: Maximes de Politique'

Willmott Lewis 1877–1950
British journalist and *Times* correspondent in Washington

9 Every government will do as much harm as it can and as much good as it must.
   *to Claud **Cockburn***

Claud Cockburn *In Time of Trouble* (1957)

Joseph Lieberman 1942
American Democratic politician and vice-presidential candidate in 2000

10 His wrongdoing in this sordid saga does not justify making him the first president to be ousted from office in our history.
   *voting to acquit President **Clinton***

at the trial for impeachment, 11 February 1999

*to the suggestion that he and George W. **Bush** share a stance on issues:*
11 That's like saying the veterinarian and the taxidermist are in the same business because either way you get your dog back.

speech in Nashville, Tennessee, 8 August 2000

Abbott Joseph Liebling 1904–63

12 Freedom of the press is guaranteed only to those who own one.

in *New Yorker* 14 May 1960

Charles-Joseph, Prince de Ligne 1735–1814
Belgian soldier

1 *Le congrès ne marche pas, il danse.*

The Congress makes no progress; it dances.
   of the Congress of Vienna

Auguste de la Garde-Chambonas
Souvenirs du Congrès de Vienne
(1820)

Abraham Lincoln 1809–65
American Republican statesman, 16th President of the US 1861–5
on Lincoln: see **Stanton** 345:8, **Whitman** 382:2

2 Prohibition . . . goes beyond the bounds of reason in that it attempts to control a man's appetite by legislation, and makes a crime out of things that are not crimes. A Prohibition law strikes a blow at the very principles upon which our government was founded.

speech in the Illinois House of Representatives, 18 December 1840

3 Any people anywhere, being inclined and having the power, have the *right* to rise up, and shake off the existing government, and form a new one that suits them better.

in the House of Representatives, 12 January 1848

4 No man is good enough to govern another man without that other's consent.

speech at Peoria, Illinois, 16 October 1854

5 To give victory to the right, not bloody bullets, but peaceful ballots only, are necessary.

speech, 18 May 1858; see **Misquotations** 254:2

6 'A house divided against itself cannot stand.' I believe this government cannot endure permanently, half slave and half free.

speech, 16 June 1858

7 As I would not be a *slave*, so I would not be a *master*. This expresses my idea of democracy. Whatever differs from this, to the extent of the difference, is no democracy.

fragment, 1 August 1858?

8 I have no purpose to introduce political and social equality between the white and black races. There is a physical difference between the two which, in my judgement, will probably for ever forbid their living together upon the footing of perfect equality; and inasmuch as it becomes a necessity that there must be a difference, I . . . am in favour of the race to which I belong having the superior position.

speech, 21 August 1858

9 When . . . you have succeeded in dehumanizing the Negro, when you have put him down and made it forever impossible for him to be but as the beasts of the field; when you have extinguished his soul and placed him where the ray of hope is blown out in darkness like that which broods over the spirits of the damned, are you quite sure that the demon you have roused will not turn and rend you?

speech at Edwardsville, Illinois, 11 September 1858

10 What is conservatism? Is it not adherence to the old and tried, against the new and untried?

speech, 27 February 1860

11 If we do not make common cause to save the good old ship of the Union on this voyage, nobody will have a chance to pilot her on another voyage.

address at Cleveland, Ohio, 15 February 1861

12 It is safe to assert that no government proper ever had a provision in its organic law for its own termination.

first inaugural address, 4 March 1861

13 I take the official oath to-day with no mental reservations, and with no purpose to construe the Constitution or laws by any hypercritical rules.

first inaugural address, 4 March 1861

1 This country, with its institutions, belongs to the people who inhabit it. Whenever they shall grow weary of the existing government, they can exercise their constitutional right of amending it, or their revolutionary right to dismember or overthrow it.

first inaugural address, 4 March 1861

2 The mystic chords of memory, stretching from every battlefield and patriot grave to every living heart and heartstone all over this broad land, will yet swell the chorus of the Union when again touched, as surely they will be, by the better angels of our nature.

first inaugural address, 4 March 1861

3 I think the necessity of being *ready* increases. Look to it.

the whole of a letter to Governor Andrew Curtin of Pennsylvania, 8 April 1861

4 My paramount object in this struggle is to save the Union . . . If I could save the Union without freeing any slave, I would do it; and if I could save it by freeing all the slaves, I would do it; and if I could save it by freeing some and leaving others alone, I would also do that . . . I have here stated my purpose according to my views of official duty and I intend no modification of my oft-expressed personal wish that all men everywhere could be free.

letter to Horace **Greeley**, 22 August 1862

5 On the first day of January in the year of our Lord, one thousand eight hundred and sixty-three, all persons held as slaves within any state, or designated part of a state, the people whereof shall then be in rebellion against the United States shall be then, thenceforward, and forever free.

Preliminary Emancipation Proclamation, 22 September 1862

when asked how he felt about the New York elections:
6 Somewhat like the boy in Kentucky who stubbed his toe while running to see his sweetheart. The boy said he was too big to cry, and far too badly hurt to laugh.

in *Frank Leslie's Illustrated Weekly* 22 November 1862

7 Fellow citizens, we cannot escape history . . . No personal significance or insignificance can spare one or another of us. The fiery trial through which we pass will light us down in honour or dishonour to the last generation.

annual message to Congress, 1 December 1862

8 In giving freedom to the slave, we assure freedom to the free—honourable alike in what we give and what we preserve. We shall nobly save, or meanly lose, the last, best hope of earth.

annual message to Congress, 1 December 1862

9 Fourscore and seven years ago our fathers brought forth upon this continent a new nation, conceived in liberty, and dedicated to the proposition that all men are created equal . . . In a larger sense we cannot dedicate, we cannot consecrate, we cannot hallow this ground. The brave men, living and these dead, who struggled here, have consecrated it far above our power to add or detract. The world will little note, nor long remember, what we say here, but it can never forget what they did here. It is for us, the living, rather to be dedicated here to the unfinished work which they who fought here have thus far so nobly advanced . . . we here highly resolve that the dead shall not have died in vain, that this nation, under God, shall have a new birth of freedom; and that government of the people, by the people, and for the people, shall not perish from the earth.

address at the Dedication of the National Cemetery at Gettysburg, 19 November 1863, as reported the following day; the Lincoln Memorial inscription reads 'by the people, for the people'; see **Anonymous** 11:3, **Everett** 127:8, **Webster** 377:7

1 The President tonight has a dream:—He was in a party of plain people, and, as it became known who he was, they began to comment on his appearance. One of them said:— 'He is a very common-looking man.' The President replied:—'The Lord prefers common-looking people. That is the reason he makes so many of them.'

John Hay *Letters of John Hay and Extracts from Diary* (1908) vol 1, 23 December 1863

2 Only those generals who gain success can set up dictators. What I ask of you is military success, and I will risk the dictatorship.
letter appointing Joseph Hooker to command of the Army of the Potomac in 1863

Shelby Foote *The Civil War: Fredericksburg to Meridian* (1991)

3 I claim not to have controlled events, but confess plainly that events have controlled me.

letter to A. G. Hodges, 4 April 1864

4 It is not best to swap horses when crossing streams.

reply to National Union League, 9 June 1864

5 I desire so to conduct the affairs of this administration that if at the end, when I come to lay down the reins of power, I have lost every other friend on earth, I shall at least have one friend left, and that friend shall be down inside me.

reply to the Missouri Committee of Seventy, 1864

6 Fondly do we hope, fervently do we pray, that this mighty scourge of war may speedily pass away. Yet, if God wills that it continue until all the wealth piled by the bond-man's two hundred and fifty years of unrequited toil shall be sunk, and until every drop of blood drawn with the lash shall be paid by another drawn with the sword, as was said three thousand years ago, so still it must be said, 'The judgements of the Lord are true and righteous altogether.'

second inaugural address, 4 March 1865

7 With malice toward none; with charity for all; with firmness in the right, as God gives us to see the right, let us strive on to finish the work we are in: to bind up the nation's wounds; to care for him who shall have borne the battle, and for his widow and his orphan, to do all which may achieve and cherish a just and lasting peace among ourselves, and with all nations.

second inaugural address, 4 March 1865

8 Whenever I hear anyone arguing for slavery, I feel a strong impulse to see it tried on him personally.

address to an Indiana Regiment, 17 March 1865

9 As President, I have no eyes but constitutional eyes; I cannot see you.
reply to the South Carolina Commissioners

attributed

10 People who like this sort of thing will find this the sort of thing they like.
judgement of a book

G. W. E. Russell *Collections and Recollections* (1898)

11 So you're the little woman who wrote the book that made this great war!
on meeting Harriet Beecher Stowe, author of Uncle Tom's Cabin (1852)

Carl Sandburg *Abraham Lincoln: The War Years* (1936) vol. 2

12 You cannot help the poor by destroying the rich. You cannot lift the wage earner by pulling down the wage payer.

attributed, but probably apocryphal

13 You may fool all the people some of the time; you can even fool some of the people all the time; but you can't fool all of the people all the time.

Alexander K. McClure *Lincoln's Yarns and Stories* (1904); also attributed to Phineas Barnum; see **Thurber** 360:4

Eric Linklater 1899–1974
Scottish novelist

1 'There won't be any revolution in America,' said Isadore. Nikitin agreed. 'The people are all too clean. They spend all their time changing their shirts and washing themselves. You can't feel fierce and revolutionary in a bathroom.'

Juan in America (1931)

Walter Lippmann 1889–1974
American journalist

2 Private property was the original source of freedom. It still is its main bulwark.

The Good Society (1937)

3 Mr Coolidge's genius for inactivity is developed to a very high point. It is far from being an indolent activity. It is a grim, determined, alert inactivity which keeps Mr Coolidge occupied constantly. Nobody has ever worked harder at inactivity, with such force of character, with such unremitting attention to detail, with such conscientious devotion to the task.

Men of Destiny (1927)

4 The final test of a leader is that he leaves behind him in other men the conviction and the will to carry on.

in *New York Herald Tribune* 14 April 1945

5 A free press is not a privilege but an organic necessity in a great society.

address at the International Press Institute Assembly in London, 27 May 1965

6 The will to be free is perpetually renewed in every individual who uses his faculties and affirms his manhood.

Arthur Seldon *The State is Rolling Back* (1994)

Maxim Litvinov 1876–1951
Soviet diplomat

7 Peace is indivisible.
note to the Allies, 25 February 1920

A. U. Pope *Maxim Litvinoff* (1943)

Ken Livingstone 1945–
British Labour politician

8 If voting changed anything, they'd abolish it.

title of book, 1987; recorded earlier as a saying

9 The problem is that many MPs never see the London that exists beyond the wine bars and brothels of Westminster.

in *The Times* 19 February 1987

10 Politics is a marathon, not a sprint.

in *New Statesman* 10 October 1997

11 I feel like Galileo going before the Inquisition to explain that the sun doesn't revolve around the earth. I hope I have more success.
at Millbank, prior to appearing before the Labour Party's selection panel for the Mayor of London

in *Guardian* 17 November 1999

12 I've met serial killers and professional assassins and nobody scared me as much as Mrs T.
*on Margaret **Thatcher***

in *Observer* 23 January 2000 'They Said What . . . ?'

13 I have been forced to choose between the party I love and have given 31 years of my life to, and upholding the democratic rights of Londoners.
announcing his independent candidacy for Mayor of London

in *Times* 7 March 2000

1 When Mr Blair invited me down to Chequers two weeks ago to discuss what I would do if I was elected mayor, we had a very pleasant 50 minutes, whilst my nephew and niece wandered around the grounds and did a bit of vandalism.

in *Observer* 12 March 2000 'They Said What . . . ?'

2 Every year the international finance system kills more people than the Second World War. But at least Hitler was mad, you know.

in *Sunday Times* 16 April 2000 'Talking Heads'

Livy 59 BC–AD 17
Roman historian

3 *Vae victis.*

Down with the defeated!
>   *cry (already proverbial) of the Gallic King, Brennus, on capturing Rome in 390 BC*

Ab Urbe Condita

4 *Pugna magna victi sumus.*

We have been defeated in a great battle.
>   *the announcement of disaster for the Romans in Hannibal's ambush at Lake Trasimene in 217 BC*

Ab Urbe Condita

David Lloyd George 1863–1945
British Liberal politician; Prime Minister, 1916–22
on Lloyd George: see **Asquith** 15:13, **Baldwin** 25:14, **Bennett** 33:1, **Churchill** 84:6, **Clemenceau** 89:6, **Grigg** 155:6, **Keynes** 201:4, 201:5, **Taylor** 353:4

5 The leal and trusty mastiff which is to watch over our interests, but which runs away at the first snarl of the trade unions . . . A mastiff? It is the right hon. Gentleman's poodle.
>   *on the House of Lords and Arthur **Balfour** respectively*

in the House of Commons, 26 June 1907

6 I have no nest-eggs. I am looking for someone else's hen-roost to rob next year.
>   *in 1908, as Chancellor*

Frank Owen *Tempestuous Journey* (1954)

7 A fully-equipped duke costs as much to keep up as two Dreadnoughts; and dukes are just as great a terror and they last longer.

speech at Newcastle, 9 October 1909

8 The great peaks of honour we had forgotten—Duty, Patriotism, and—clad in glittering white—the great pinnacle of Sacrifice, pointing like a rugged finger to Heaven.

speech at Queen's Hall, London, 19 September 1914

of the House of Lords, c.1911:
9 A body of five hundred men chosen at random from amongst the unemployed.

speech at Newcastle, 9 October 1909

10 I would as soon go for a sunny evening stroll round Walton Heath with a grasshopper, as try to work with Northcliffe.
>   *of Lord **Northcliffe**, c.1916*

Frank Owen *Tempestuous Journey* (1954)

11 At eleven o'clock this morning came to an end the cruellest and most terrible war that has ever scourged mankind. I hope we may say that thus, this fateful morning, came to an end all wars.

in the House of Commons, 11 November 1918; see **Wells** 380:4

12 What is our task? To make Britain a fit country for heroes to live in.

speech at Wolverhampton, 23 November 1918

1 Wild men screaming through the keyholes.
   of the Versailles Peace Conference

in the House of Commons, 16 April 1919

2 If you want to succeed in politics, you must keep your conscience well under control.

Lord Riddell diary, 23 April 1919

3 M. Clemenceau . . . is one of the greatest living orators, but he knows that the finest eloquence is that which gets things done and the worst is that which delays them.
   speech at Paris Peace Conference, 18 January 1919

in *The Times* 20 January 1919

4 Unless I am mistaken, by the steps we have taken [in Ireland] we have murder by the throat.

speech at the Mansion House, 9 November 1920

   *of Arthur **Balfour**'s impact on history:*
5 No more than the whiff of scent on a lady's pocket handkerchief.

Thomas Jones, diary, 9 June 1922

6 The world is becoming like a lunatic asylum run by lunatics.

in *Observer* 8 January 1933

7 A politician was a person with whose politics you did not agree. When you did agree, he was a statesman.

speech at Central Hall, Westminster, 2 July 1935

8 Neville has a retail mind in a wholesale business.
   *of Neville **Chamberlain***

in 1935; David Dilks *Neville Chamberlain* (1984)

   *after meeting **Hitler** in 1936:*
9 Führer is the proper name for him. He is a great and wonderful leader.

Frank Owen *Tempestuous Journey* (1954)

10 Winston would go up to his Creator and say that he would very much like to meet His Son, of Whom he had heard a great deal and, if possible, would like to call on the Holy Ghost. Winston *loves* meeting people.
   *of Winston **Churchill***

A. J. Sylvester diary, 2 January 1937

11 The Prime Minister should give an example of sacrifice, because there is nothing which can contribute more to victory than that he should sacrifice the seals of office.
   *of Neville **Chamberlain***

in the House of Commons, 7 May 1940

12 Truth against the world.
   Welsh proverb; motto taken on becoming Earl Lloyd-George of Dwyfor, January 1945

Donald McCormick *The Mask of Merlin* (1963)

13 Of all the bigotries that savage the human temper there is none so stupid as the anti-Semitic.

Is It Peace? 1923

   *on being told by Lord **Beaverbrook**'s butler that, 'The Lord is out walking':*
14 Ah, on the water, I presume.

Lord Cudlipp letter in *Daily Telegraph* 13 September 1993

15 Brilliant—to the top of his boots.
   of Earl Haig

attributed

16 Death is the most convenient time to tax rich people.

in *Lord Riddell's Intimate Diary of the Peace Conference and After, 1918–23* (1933)

17 He has sat on the fence so long the iron has entered into his soul.
   of John Simon

attributed

18 He would make a drum out of the skin of his mother in order to sound his own praises.
   *of Winston **Churchill***

Peter Rowland *Lloyd George* (1975)

1 Negotiating with de Valera . . . is like trying to pick up mercury with a fork.
   *to which **de Valera** replied, 'Why doesn't he use a spoon?'*

M. J. MacManus *Eamon de Valera* (1944)

2 Sufficient conscience to bother him, but not sufficient to keep him straight.
   *of Ramsay **MacDonald***

A. J. Sylvester *Life with Lloyd George* (1975)

3 There is no friendship at the top.

habitual remark, said to be quoting **Gladstone**; A. J. P. Taylor *Lloyd George, Rise and Fall* (1961)

of the 1905 Tory Government:
4 They died with their drawn salaries in their hands.

attributed

John Locke 1632–1704
English philosopher

5 Man . . . hath by nature a power . . . to preserve his property—that is, his life, liberty, and estate—against the injuries and attempts of other men.

Second Treatise of Civil Government (1690)

6 Man being . . . by nature all free, equal, and independent, no one can be put out of this estate, and subjected to the political power of another, without his own consent.

Second Treatise of Civil Government (1690)

7 The great and chief end, therefore, of men's uniting into commonwealths, and putting themselves under government, is the preservation of their property.

Second Treatise of Civil Government (1690)

8 The only way by which any one divests himself of his natural liberty and puts on the bonds of civil society is by agreeing with other men to join and unite into a community.

Second Treatise of Civil Government (1690)

9 This power to act according to discretion for the public good, without the prescription of the law, and sometimes even against it, is that which is called prerogative.

Second Treatise of Civil Government (1690)

Henry Cabot Lodge Jr. 1902–85
American Republican politician

10 It was those damned tea parties that beat me!
   attributing the loss of his 1952 senatorial campaign, against the national Republican trend, to the tea parties given by Rose Kennedy on behalf of her son, the Democratic candidate John F. Kennedy

in obituary of Rose **Kennedy** in *Guardian* 24 January 1995

Huey Long 1893–1935
American Democratic politician; Governor of Louisiana

11 For the present you can just call me the Kingfish.

Every Man a King (1933)

answering his opponent's supporters, who said their candidate had gone barefoot as a boy:
12 I can go Mr Wilson one better; I was born barefoot.

T. Harry Williams *Huey Long* (1969)

13 Oh hell, say that I am *sui generis* and let it go at that.
   to journalists attempting to analyse his political personality

T. Harry Williams *Huey Long* (1969)

14 The time has come for all good men to rise above principle.

attributed

Lord Longford 1905–
British Labour politician and philanthropist

1 You would get second raters, people who could not get into the Commons or the European Parliament or even into the Scottish or Welsh Parliaments. You would get the dregs.
opposing an elected second chamber

in *Observer* 12 March 2000 'They Said What...?'

Alice Roosevelt Longworth 1884–1980
daughter of Theodore **Roosevelt**

2 Harding was not a bad man. He was just a slob.
of US President Warren G. Harding

Crowded Hours (1933)

Louis XIV (the 'Sun King') 1638–1715
King of France from 1643

3 *L'État c'est moi.*
I am the State.
before the Parlement de Paris, 13 April 1655 (probably apocryphal)

J. A. Dulaure *Histoire de Paris* (1834) vol. 6

4 *Il n'y a plus de Pyrénées.*
The Pyrenees are no more.
on the accession of his grandson to the throne of Spain, 1700

attributed to Louis by Voltaire in *Siècle de Louis XIV* (1753), but to the Spanish Ambassador to France in the *Mercure Galant* (Paris) November 1700

5 I was nearly kept waiting.

attribution queried, among others, by E. Fournier in *L'Esprit dans l'Histoire* (1857)

6 Every time I create an appointment, I create a hundred malcontents and one ingrate.

Voltaire *Siècle de Louis XIV* (1768 ed.) vol. 2

Louis XVI 1754–93
King of France from 1774; deposed in 1789 on the outbreak of the French Revolution and executed in 1793

diary entry for 14 July 1789, the day of the storming of the Bastille:

7 *Rien.*
Nothing.

Simon Schama *Citizens* (1989)

Louis XVIII 1755–1824
King of France from 1814; titular king from 1795

8 Remember that there is not one of you who does not carry in his cartridge-pouch the marshal's baton of the duke of Reggio; it is up to you to bring it forth.
speech to Saint-Cyr cadets, 9 August 1819

in *Moniteur Universel* 10 August 1819

9 *L'exactitude est la politesse des rois.*
Punctuality is the politeness of kings.

in *Souvenirs de J. Lafitte* (1844), attributed

Louis Philippe 1773–1850
King of France 1830–48

10 Died, has he? Now I wonder what he meant by that?
of Talleyrand

attributed, perhaps apocryphal

David Low 1891–1963

British political cartoonist and creator of 'Colonel Blimp',
proponent of reactionary establishment opinions

1 I have never met anyone who wasn't against war. Even
Hitler and Mussolini were, according to themselves.

in *New York Times Magazine* 10
February 1946

Robert Lowe, Viscount Sherbrooke 1811–92

British Liberal politician

2 I believe it will be absolutely necessary that you should
prevail on our future masters to learn their letters.
on the passing of the 2nd Reform Bill

in the House of Commons, 15 July
1867; see **Misquotations** 255:11

3 The Chancellor of the Exchequer is a man whose duties
make him more or less of a taxing machine. He is intrusted
with a certain amount of misery which it is his duty to
distribute as fairly as he can.

in the House of Commons, 11 April
1870

James Russell Lowell 1819–91

American poet

4 We've a war, an' a debt, an' a flag; an' ef this
Ain't to be inderpendunt, why, wut on airth is?

The Biglow Papers (Second Series,
1867) no. 4 'A Message of Jeff.
Davis in Secret Session'

5 Once to every man and nation comes the moment to decide,
In the strife of Truth with Falsehood, for the good or evil
side.

'The Present Crisis' (1845)

6 Truth forever on the scaffold, Wrong forever on the
throne,—
Yet that scaffold sways the future, and, behind the dim
unknown,
Standeth God within the shadow, keeping watch above his
own.

'The Present Crisis' (1845)

Lucan AD 39–65

Roman poet

7   *Quis iustius induit arma*
Scire nefas, magno se iudice quisque tuetur:
Victrix causa deis placuit, sed victa Catoni.

It is not granted to know which man took up arms with
more right on his side. Each pleads his cause before a great
judge: the winning cause pleased the gods, but the losing
one pleased Cato.

Pharsalia

8 *Stat magni nominis umbra.*

There stands the ghost of a great name.
of Pompey

Pharsalia

9 *Nil actum credens, dum quid superesset agendum.*

Thinking nothing done while anything remained to be done.

Pharsalia

Clare Booth Luce 1903–

American diplomat, politician, and writer

10 Much of . . . his global thinking is, no matter how you slice
it, still globaloney.

speech to the House of
Representatives, February 1943

Martin Luther 1483–1546
German Protestant theologian

1 Here stand I. I can do no other. God help me. Amen.

speech at the Diet of Worms, 18 April 1521; attributed

2 If I had heard that as many devils would set on me in Worms as there are tiles on the roofs, I should none the less have ridden there.

to the Princes of Saxony, 21 August 1524

Rosa Luxemburg 1871–1919
German revolutionary

3 Freedom is always and exclusively freedom for the one who thinks differently.

Die Russische Revolution (1918)

Jack Lynch 1917–
Irish statesman, Taoiseach 1966–73, 1977–9

4 I have never and never will accept the right of a minority who happen to be a majority in a small part of the country to opt out of a nation.

in *Irish Times* 14 November 1970 'This Week They Said'

Robert Lynd 1879–1949
Anglo-Irish essayist and journalist

5 The belief in the possibility of a short decisive war appears to be one of the most ancient and dangerous of human illusions.

attributed

Jonathan Lynn 1943–
and **Antony Jay** 1930–

6 'Opposition's about asking awkward questions.' 'Yes . . . and government's about not answering them.'

Yes Minister vol. 1 (1981)

7 The PM—whose motto is . . . 'In Defeat, Malice—in Victory, Revenge!'

Yes Minister vol. 1 (1981)

8 If you wish to describe a proposal in a way that guarantees that a Minister will reject it, describe it as *courageous*.

Yes Minister vol. 1 (1981)

9 The Official Secrets Act is not to protect secrets but to protect officials.

Yes Minister vol. 1 (1981)

10 Diplomacy is about surviving till the next century—politics is about surviving till Friday afternoon.

Yes Prime Minister vol. 1 (1986)

what is known to the Civil Service as the Politicians' Syllogism:
11 Step One: We must do something.
Step Two: This is something.
Step Three: Therefore we must do it.

Yes Prime Minister vol. 2 (1987)

Mary McAleese 1951–
Irish stateswoman; President from 1997

12 I sense a mood among the people that they want a president who can speak to them from above politics. It will look at an Ireland where people are not pigeon-holed any more.
after being selected as Fianna Fáil candidate

in *Irish Times* 20 September 1997

1 Apart from the shamrock, the President should not wear emblems or symbols of any kind.

in *Guardian* 6 November 1997

> *deciding not to wear a poppy at her inauguration on 11 November 1997*

2 People ask me what does the Celtic Tiger look like; it looks like this place.

in *Irish Times* 13 April 1998

> *visiting Clonaslee in Co. Laois*

3 The day of the dinosaurs is over. The future belongs to the bridge-builders, not the wreckers.

in *Irish Times* 27 June 1998

> *on the election to the Northern Ireland Assembly*

4 Those whom we commemorate . . . fell victim to a war against oppression in Europe. Their memory, too, fell victim to a war for independence at home in Ireland . . . Respect for the memory of one set of heroes was often at the expense of respect for the memory of another.

in *Irish Times* 14 November 1998 'This Week They Said'

> *at the Armistice Day commemorations in Belgium*

Bernadette Devlin McAliskey 1947–
Irish nationalist

5 Expectation of good news from the British government is never something I have lived with easily. And yet I have it and I appreciate it. Maybe I should have more faith.

in *Irish Times* 14 March 1998 'This Week They Said'

> *on the decision by the British Government not to extradite her daughter, Róisín, to Germany*

Dorothy Macardle 1889–1958
Irish nationalist

6 He knew Ireland too little, and the English House of Commons too well.

Diana Norman *Terrible Beauty* (1987)

> *of John* **Redmond**

Douglas MacArthur 1880–1964
American general

7 I came through and I shall return.

in *New York Times* 21 March 1942

> *on reaching Australia, 20 March 1942, having broken through Japanese lines en route from Corregidor*

8 In war, indeed, there can be no substitute for victory.

in *Congressional Record* 19 April 1951, vol. 97

9 I still remember the refrain of one of the most popular barracks ballads of that day, which proclaimed most proudly that old soldiers never die; they just fade away. I now close my military career and just fade away.

address to a Joint Meeting of Congress, 19 April 1951

Lord Macaulay 1800–59
English Whig politician, historian, and poet
on Macaulay: see **Melbourne** 247:7, **Smith** 339:5

10 In order that he might rob a neighbour whom he had promised to defend, black men fought on the coast of Coromandel, and red men scalped each other by the Great Lakes of North America.

Biographical Essays (1857) 'Frederic the Great'

11 The gallery in which the reporters sit has become a fourth estate of the realm.

Essays Contributed to the Edinburgh Review (1843) vol. 1 'Hallam'

1 He knew that the essence of war is violence, and that moderation in war is imbecility.

Essays Contributed to the Edinburgh Review (1843) vol. 1 'John Hampden'

*of Niccolò **Machiavelli**:*
2 Out of his surname they have coined an epithet for a knave, and out of his Christian name a synonym for the Devil.

Essays Contributed to the Edinburgh Review (1843) vol. 1 'Machiavelli'

3 Many politicians of our time are in the habit of laying it down as a self-evident proposition, that no people ought to be free till they are fit to use their freedom. The maxim is worthy of the fool in the old story, who resolved not to go into the water till he had learnt to swim. If men are to wait for liberty till they become wise and good in slavery, they may indeed wait for ever.

Essays Contributed to the Edinburgh Review (1843) vol. 1 'Milton'

4 On the rich and the eloquent, on nobles and priests, they [the Puritans] looked down with contempt: for they esteemed themselves rich in a more precious treasure, and eloquent in a more sublime language, nobles by the right of an earlier creation, and priests by the imposition of a mightier hand.

Essays Contributed to the Edinburgh Review (1843) vol. 1 'Milton'

5 We know no spectacle so ridiculous as the British public in one of its periodical fits of morality.

Essays Contributed to the Edinburgh Review (1843) vol. 1 'Moore's *Life of Lord Byron*'

6 We have heard it said that five per cent is the natural interest of money.

Essays Contributed to the Edinburgh Review (1843) vol. 1 'Southey's Colloquies'

7 With the dead there is no rivalry. In the dead there is no change. Plato is never sullen. Cervantes is never petulant. Demosthenes never comes unseasonably. Dante never stays too long. No difference of political opinion can alienate Cicero. No heresy can excite the horror of Bossuet.

Essays Contributed to the Edinburgh Review (1843) vol. 2 'Lord Bacon'

8 An acre in Middlesex is better than a principality in Utopia.

Essays Contributed to the Edinburgh Review (1843) vol. 2 'Lord Bacon'

9 The rising hope of those stern and unbending Tories.
   *of **Gladstone***

Essays Contributed to the Edinburgh Review (1843) vol. 2 'Gladstone on Church and State'

10 The history of England is emphatically the history of progress.

Essays Contributed to the Edinburgh Review (1843) vol. 2 'Sir James Mackintosh'

11 On the day of the accession of George the Third, the ascendancy of the Whig party terminated; and on that day the purification of the Whig party began.

Essays Contributed to the Edinburgh Review (1843) vol. 2 'William Pitt, Earl of Chatham'

12 The reluctant obedience of distant provinces generally costs more than it [the territory] is worth.

Essays Contributed to the Edinburgh Review (1843) vol. 2 'The War of Succession in Spain'

13 Every schoolboy knows who imprisoned Montezuma, and who strangled Atahualpa.

Essays Contributed to the Edinburgh Review (1843) vol. 3 'Lord Clive'

14 The Chief Justice was rich, quiet, and infamous.

Essays Contributed to the Edinburgh Review (1843) vol. 3 'Warren Hastings'

15 Thus our democracy was, from an early period, the most aristocratic, and our aristocracy the most democratic in the world.

History of England vol. 1 (1849)

1 Persecution produced its natural effect on them [Puritans and Calvinists]. It found them a sect; it made them a faction.

History of England vol. 1 (1849)

2 [Louis XIV] had shown, in an eminent degree, two talents invaluable to a prince, the talent of choosing his servants well, and the talent of appropriating to himself the chief part of the credit of their acts.

History of England vol. 1 (1849)

3 No man is fit to govern great societies who hesitates about disobliging the few who have access to him for the sake of the many he will never see.

History of England vol. 1 (1849)

4 It was a crime in a child to read by the bedside of a sick parent one of those beautiful collects which had soothed the griefs of forty generations of Christians.

History of England vol. 1 (1849)

5 The Puritan hated bear-baiting, not because it gave pain to the bear, but because it gave pleasure to the spectators.

History of England vol. 1 (1849)

6 It has often been found that profuse expenditure, heavy taxation, absurd commercial restrictions, corrupt tribunals, disastrous wars, seditions, persecutions, conflagrations, inundations, have not been able to destroy capital so fast as the exertions of private citizens have been able to create it.

History of England vol. 1 (1849)

7 Obadiah Bind-their-kings-in-chains-and-their-nobles-with-links-of-iron.

'The Battle of Naseby' (1824)
fictitious author's name

8 Oh, wherefore come ye forth in triumph from the north,
With your hands, and your feet, and your raiment all red?
And wherefore doth your rout send forth a joyous shout?
And whence be the grapes of the wine-press which ye tread?

'The Battle of Naseby' (1824)

9 And the Man of Blood was there, with his long essenced hair,
And Astley, and Sir Marmaduke, and Rupert of the Rhine.

'The Battle of Naseby' (1824)

10 To my true king I offered free from stain
Courage and faith; vain faith, and courage vain.

'A Jacobite's Epitaph' (1845)

11 By those white cliffs I never more must see,
By that dear language which I spake like thee,
Forget all feuds, and shed one English tear
O'er English dust. A broken heart lies here.

'A Jacobite's Epitaph' (1845)

12 Then none was for a party;
Then all were for the state;
Then the great man helped the poor,
And the poor man loved the great:
Then lands were fairly portioned;
Then spoils were fairly sold:
The Romans were like brothers
In the brave days of old.

Lays of Ancient Rome (1842)
'Horatius'

13 Thank you, madam, the agony is abated.
  aged four, having had hot coffee spilt over his legs

G. O. Trevelyan *Life and Letters of Lord Macaulay* (1876)

14 The object of oratory alone is not truth, but persuasion.

'Essay on Athenian Orators' in *Knight's Quarterly Magazine* August 1824

15 Nothing is so galling to a people not broken in from the birth as a paternal, or in other words a meddling government, a government which tells them what to read and say and eat and drink and wear.

in *Edinburgh Review* January 1830

1 He has one eminent merit—that of being an enthusiastic admirer of mine—so that I may be the Hero of a novel yet, under the name of Delamere or Mortimer. Only think what an honour.
   of the novelist and politician **Bulwer Lytton**

letter, 5 August 1831

2 I detest him more than cold boiled veal.
   of the Tory essayist and politician John Wilson Croker

letter, 5 August 1831

3 We must at present do our best to form a class who may be interpreters between us and the millions whom we govern; a class of persons, Indian in blood and colour, but English in taste, in opinions, in morals, and in intellect.

minute, as Member of Supreme Council of India, 2 February 1835

John McCain 1936-

American Republican politician and presidential candidate

4 I will not take the low road to the highest office in the land. I want the presidency in the best way, not the worst way.
   conceding victory in the South Carolina primary to George W. **Bush**

in *Guardian* 24 February 2000

Eugene McCarthy 1916-

American Democratic politician

5 Being in politics is like being a football coach. You have to be smart enough to understand the game, and dumb enough to think it's important.
   while campaigning for the presidency

in an interview, 1968

Joseph McCarthy 1908-57

American politician and anti-Communist agitator

6 I have here in my hand a list of two hundred and five [people] that were known to the Secretary of State as being members of the Communist Party and who nevertheless are still working and shaping the policy of the State Department.

speech at Wheeling, West Virginia, 9 February 1950

7 McCarthyism is Americanism with its sleeves rolled.

speech in Wisconsin, 1952; Richard Rovere *Senator Joe McCarthy* (1973)

Mary McCarthy 1912-89

American writer

8 Bureaucracy, the rule of no one, has become the modern form of despotism.

in *New Yorker* 18 October 1958

George B. McClellan 1826-85

American soldier and politician

9 All quiet along the Potomac.
   said at the time of the American Civil War

attributed

Colonel McCormick

of the *Chicago Tribune*

10 The British are no longer important enough for me to dislike.
   explaining his willingness to give an interview to the British journalist Woodrow Wyatt

J. K. Galbraith *A Life in Our Times* (1981)

John McCrae 1872–1918

Canadian poet and military physician

1 To you from failing hands we throw
   The torch; be yours to hold it high.
   If ye break faith with us who die
   We shall not sleep, though poppies grow
   In Flanders Fields.

'In Flanders Fields' (1915)

Hugh MacDiarmid 1892–1978

Scottish poet and nationalist

2 The rose of all the world is not for me.
   I want for my part
   Only the little white rose of Scotland
   That smells sharp and sweet—and breaks the heart.

'The Little White Rose' (1934)

3 Scotland small? Our multiform, our infinite Scotland *small*?
   Only as a patch of hillside may be a cliché corner
   To a fool who cries 'Nothing but heather!' . . .

Direadh 1 (1974)

Dwight Macdonald 1906–82

American writer and film critic

4 Götterdämmerung without the gods.
   of the use of atomic bombs against the Japanese

in *Politics* September 1945 'The Bomb'

Ramsay MacDonald 1866–1937

British Labour statesman, Prime Minister 1924, 1929–31, and 1931–5
on MacDonald: see **Churchill** 81:1, **George V** 143:6, **Lloyd George** 224:2, **Nicolson** 266:8; see also **Lamont** 209:6

5 Wars are popular. Contractors make profits; the aristocracy glean honour.

in *Labour Leader* 11 March 1915

6 A terror decreed by a Secret Committee is child's play compared with a terror instituted by 'lawful authority'.

in *Socialist Review* January–March 1921

7 We hear war called murder. It is not: it is suicide.

in *Observer* 4 May 1930

8 Tomorrow every Duchess in London will be wanting to kiss me!
   after forming the National Government, 25 August 1931

Viscount Snowden *An Autobiography* (1934) vol. 2

9 A body representing the citizenship of the whole nation is charged with so much that it can do nothing swiftly and well.

Carl Cohen *Parliament and Democracy* (1962)

George McGovern 1922–

American Democratic politician, presidential candidate in 1972

10 Sometimes, when they say you're ahead of your time, it's just a polite way of saying you have a real bad sense of timing.

in *Observer* 18 March 1990 'Sayings of the Week'

Lord McGregor 1921–

British sociologist

1 An odious exhibition of journalists dabbling their fingers in the stuff of other people's souls.

on press coverage of the marriage of the Prince and Princess of Wales, speaking as Chairman of the Press Complaints Commission

in *The Times* 9 June 1992

Ian McEwan 1948–

English novelist

2 The committee divided between the theorists, who had done all their thinking long ago, or had had it done for them, and the pragmatists, who hoped to discover what it was they thought in the process of saying it.

The Child in Time (1987)

3 No human society, from the hunter-gatherer to the postindustrial, has come to the attention of anthropologists that did not have its leaders and the led; and no emergency was ever dealt with effectively by democratic process.

Enduring Love (1987)

Niccolò Machiavelli 1469–1527

Florentine statesman and political philosopher

4 And if, to be sure, sometimes you need to conceal a fact with words, do it in such a way that it does not become known, or, if it does become known, that you have a ready and quick defence.

'Advice to Raffaello Girolami when he went as Ambassador to the Emperor' (October 1522)

5 It is necessary for him who lays out a state and arranges laws for it to presuppose that all men are evil and that they are always going to act according to the wickedness of their spirits whenever they have free scope.

Discourses on the First Ten Books of Livy (1513–17)

6 Success or failure lies in conforming to the times.

Discourses on the First Ten Books of Livy (1513–17)

7 Wars begin when you will, but they do not end when you please.

History of Florence (1521–4)

8 Men should be either treated generously or destroyed, because they take revenge for slight injuries—for heavy ones they cannot.

The Prince (1513)

9 This leads to a debate: is it better to be loved than feared, or the reverse? The answer is that it is desirable to be both, but because it is difficult to join them together, it is much safer for a prince to be feared than loved, if he is to fail in one of the two.

The Prince (1513)

10 Let no one oppose this belief of mine with that well-worn proverb: 'He who builds on the people builds on mud.'

The Prince (1513)

11 Since, then, a prince is necessitated to play the animal well, he chooses among the beasts the fox and the lion, because the lion does not protect himself from traps; the fox does not protect himself from wolves. The prince must be a fox, therefore, to recognize the traps and a lion to frighten the wolves.

The Prince (1513)

12 So long as the great majority of men are not deprived of either property or honour, they are satisfied.

The Prince (1513)

1 There is no other way for securing yourself against flatteries   *The Prince* (1513)
except that men understand that they do not offend you by
telling you the truth; but when everybody can tell you the
truth, you fail to get respect.

2 In seizing a state, the usurper ought to examine closely into   *The Prince* (1513)
all those injuries which it is necessary for him to inflict, and
to do them all at one stroke, so as not to have to repeat
them daily; and thus by not unsettling men he will be able
to reassure them, and win them to himself by benefits. He
who does otherwise, either from timidity or evil advice, is
always compelled to keep the knife in his hand.

3 Princes ought to leave affairs of reproach to the   *The Prince* (1513)
management of others, and keep those of grace in their own
hands.

James Mackintosh 1765–1832

Scottish philosopher and historian

4 Men are never so good or so bad as their opinions.   *Dissertation on the Progress of
Ethical Philosophy* (1830) 'Jeremy
Bentham'

5 The Commons, faithful to their system, remained in a wise   *Vindiciae Gallicae* (1791)
and masterly inactivity.
of the French Commons

Iain Macleod 1913–70

British Conservative politician
on Macleod: see **Salisbury** 313:8

6 To have a debate on the National Health Service without   in the House of Commons, 27
the right hon. Gentleman [Aneurin Bevan] would be like   March 1952
putting on Hamlet with no one in the part of the First
Gravedigger.

7 It is some measure of the tightness of the magic circle on   in *The Spectator* 17 January 1964
this occasion that neither the Chancellor of the Exchequer
nor the Leader of the House of Commons had any inkling of
what was happening.
of the 'evolvement' of Alec **Douglas-Home** *as Conservative leader
after the resignation of Harold* **Macmillan**

8 The Conservative Party always in time forgives those who   in *The Spectator* 21 February 1964
were wrong. Indeed often, in time, they forgive those who
were right.

9 John Fitzgerald Kennedy described himself, in a brilliant   in the House of Commons, 1
phrase, as an idealist without illusions. I would describe the   March 1966; see **Kennedy** 199:10
Prime Minister as an illusionist without ideals.

10 In Parliament it should not only be the duty but the   in *The Spectator* 26 August 1966
pleasure of the Opposition to oppose whenever they
reasonably can.

11 I cannot help it if every time the Opposition are asked to   in *Dictionary of National Biography*
name their weapons they pick boomerangs.   (1917–)

Marshall McLuhan 1911–80

Canadian communications scholar

1 Television brought the brutality of war into the comfort of
the living room. Vietnam was lost in the living rooms of
America—not the battlefields of Vietnam.

in Montreal Gazette 16 May 1975

Comte de Macmahon 1808–93

French military commander; President of the Third Republic,
1873–9

2 *J'y suis, j'y reste.*
Here I am, and here I stay.
   *at the taking of the Malakoff fortress during the Crimean War, 8
   September 1855*

G. Hanotaux *Histoire de la France
Contemporaine* (1903–8) vol. 2

William McMahon 1908–88

Australian statesman, Prime Minister 1971–2

3 Politics is trying to get into office.

L. Oakes and D. Solomon *The
Making of an Australian Prime
Minister* (1973)

Harold Macmillan 1894–1986

British Conservative statesman, Prime Minister 1957–63
on Macmillan: see **Bevan** 37:3, **Birch** 40:11, 41:1, **Hennessy**
168:6, **Levin** 216:9, 217:2, **Macleod** 234:7, **Stockton** 348:5,
Thorpe 360:2

4 Toryism has always been a form of paternal socialism.
   in 1936

Anthony Sampson *Macmillan*
(1967)

5 We . . . are Greeks in this American empire . . . We must
run the Allied Forces HQ as the Greeks ran the operations of
the Emperor Claudius.
   to Richard **Crossman** *in 1944, after French North Africa had
   become an American sphere of influence, with* **Eisenhower** *as
   Supreme Allied Commander*

in Sunday Telegraph 9 February
1964

6 The Whips want the safe men . . . I reminded Winston again
that it took Hitler to make him PM and me an under-
secretary. The Tory Party would do neither.

diary, 13 October 1954

7 There ain't gonna be no war.
   *at a London press conference, 24 July 1955, following the Geneva
   summit*

in News Chronicle 25 July 1955

8 Forever poised between a cliché and an indiscretion.
   on the life of a Foreign Secretary

in Newsweek 30 April 1956

9 Let us be frank about it: most of our people have never had
it so good. Go around the country, go to the industrial
towns, go to the farms, and you'll see a state of prosperity
such as we have never had in my lifetime—nor indeed ever
in the history of this country. What is beginning to worry
some of us is 'Is it too good to be true?' or perhaps I should
say 'Is it too good to last?'

speech at Bedford, 20 July 1957;
see **Slogans** 337:1

1 I thought the best thing to do was to settle up these little local difficulties, and then turn to the wider vision of the Commonwealth.
statement at London airport on leaving for a Commonwealth tour, 7 January 1958, following the resignation of the Chancellor of the Exchequer and others

in *The Times* 8 January 1958

2 The wind of change is blowing through this continent, and, whether we like it or not, this growth of [African] national consciousness is a political fact.

speech at Cape Town, 3 February 1960

3 Can we say that with fifteen representatives, Ambassadors or Ministers, in Nato acting in unanimity, the deterrent would continue to be credible? There might be one finger on the trigger. There would be fifteen fingers on the safety catch.

attributed, 1960

4 As usual the Liberals offer a mixture of sound and original ideas. Unfortunately none of the sound ideas is original and none of the original ideas is sound.

speech to London Conservatives, 7 March 1961

5 He [Aneurin Bevan] enjoys prophesying the imminent fall of the capitalist system and is prepared to play a part, any part, in its burial, except that of mute.

Michael Foot *Aneurin Bevan* (1962)

6 I was determined that no British government should be brought down by the action of two tarts.
comment on the Profumo affair, July 1963

Anthony Sampson *Macmillan* (1967)

7 It is thinking about themselves that is really the curse of the younger generation—they appear to have no other subject which interests them at all.

the 'Tuesday memorandum', a draft of a letter to the Queen, advising on his successor but not sent, 1963; D. R. Thorpe *Alec Douglas-Home* (1996)

8 Power? It's like a Dead Sea fruit. When you achieve it, there is nothing there.

Anthony Sampson *The New Anatomy of Britain* (1971); see **Levin** 216:9

9 Churchill was fundamentally what the English call unstable—by which they mean anybody who has that touch of genius which is inconvenient in normal times.

attributed, 1975

10 There are three bodies no sensible man directly challenges: the Roman Catholic Church, the Brigade of Guards and the National Union of Mineworkers.

in *Observer* 22 February 1981; see **Baldwin** 25:13

11 First of all the Georgian silver goes, and then all that nice furniture that used to be in the saloon. Then the Canalettos go.
on privatization

speech to the Tory Reform Group, 8 November 1985, in *The Times* 9 November 1985; see **Misquotations** 255:5

12 It has always seemed to me more artistic, when the curtain falls on the last performance, to accept the inevitable *E finita la commedia*. It is tempting, perhaps, but unrewarding to hang about the greenroom after final retirement from the stage.

At the End of the Day (1973)

of the office of Prime Minister:
13 Sometimes the strain is awful, you have to resort to Jane Austen.

in the Butler Papers; Peter Hennessy *The Hidden Wiring* (1995)

Robert McNamara 1916–

American Democratic politician, Secretary of Defense during the Vietnam War

1 I don't object to it's being called 'McNamara's War' . . . It is a very important war and I am pleased to be identified with it and do whatever I can to win it.

in New York Times 25 April 1964

2 We . . . acted according to what we thought were the principles and traditions of this nation. We were wrong. We were terribly wrong.
   *of the conduct of the Vietnam War by the **Kennedy** and **Johnson** administrations*

speaking in Washington, just before the twentieth anniversary of the American withdrawal from Vietnam; in Daily Telegraph (electronic edition) 10 April 1995

Eoin MacNeill 1867–1945

Irish nationalist

3 What we call our country is not a poetical abstraction . . . There is no such person as Caitlin Ni Uallachain or Roisin Dubh or the Sean-bhean Bhocht, who is calling on us to save her.

in February, 1916; Robert Kee The Bold Fenian Men (1989)

4 I wish it then to be clearly understood that under present conditions I am definitely opposed to any proposal that may come forward involving insurrection.

memorandum to Irish Volunteers, February 1916

Salvador de Madariaga 1886–1978

Spanish writer and diplomat

5 Since, in the main, it is not armaments that cause wars but wars (or the fears thereof) that cause armaments, it follows that every nation will at every moment strive to keep its armament in an efficient state as required by its fear, otherwise styled security.

Morning Without Noon (1974) pt. 1, ch. 9

James Madison 1751–1836

American Democratic Republican statesman, 4th President of the US 1809–17

6 Liberty is to faction what air is to fire, an aliment without which it instantly expires. But it could not be less folly to abolish liberty, which is essential to political life, because it nourishes faction than it would be to wish the annihilation of air, which is essential to animal life, because it imparts to fire its destructive agency.

The Federalist (1787)

7 The diversity in the faculties of men, from which the rights of property originate, is not less an insuperable obstacle to a uniformity of interests. The protection of these faculties is the first object of government. From the protection of different and unequal faculties of acquiring property, the possession of different degrees and kinds of property immediately results.

The Federalist (1787)

8 The accumulation of all powers, legislative, executive, and judiciary, in the same hands, whether of one, a few, or many, and whether hereditary, self-appointed, or elective, may justly be pronounced the very definition of tyranny.

The Federalist (1787)

1 In framing a government, which is to be administered by   attributed
men over men, the great difficulty lies in this: you must first
enable the government to control the governed, and in the
next place oblige it to control itself.

John Maffey 1877–1969
British diplomat

as British Ambassador to Dublin:
2 Phrases make history here.   letter, 21 May 1945

Magna Carta
Political charter signed by King John at Runnymede, 1215

3 That the English Church shall be free.   Clause 1

4 No free man shall be taken or imprisoned or dispossessed, or Clause 39
outlawed or exiled, or in any way destroyed, nor will we go
upon him, nor will we send against him except by the
lawful judgement of his peers or by the law of the land.

5 To no man will we sell, or deny, or delay, right or justice. Clause 40

Alfred T. Mahan 1840–1914
American naval officer and historian

6 Those far distant, storm-beaten ships, upon which the   *The Influence of Sea Power upon the*
Grand Army never looked, stood between it and the   *French Revolution and Empire*
dominion of the world.   *1793–1812* (1892) vol. 2

Norman Mailer 1923–
American novelist and essayist

7 All the security around the American President is just to   in *Sunday Telegraph* 4 March 1990
make sure the man who shoots him gets caught.

Henry Sumner Maine 1822–88
British jurist

8 War appears to be as old as mankind, but peace is a modern   *International Law* (Whewell
invention.   Lectures, 1887)

Joseph de Maistre 1753–1821
French writer and diplomat

9 *Toute nation a le gouvernement qu'elle mérite.*   letter, 15 August 1811
Every country has the government it deserves.

John Major 1943–
British Conservative statesman, Prime Minister 1990–7
on Major: see **Anonymous** 9:6, **Cranborne** 96:8, **Shephard**
330:6, **Thatcher** 358:4, **Waldegrave** 372:12

10 The first requirement of politics is not intellect or stamina in *Daily Express* 25 July 1989
but patience. Politics is a very long-run game and the
tortoise will usually beat the hare.

11 If the policy isn't hurting, it isn't working.   speech in Northampton, 27
October 1989; see **Slogans** 336:13

1 Society needs to condemn a little more and understand a little less.

interview with *Mail on Sunday* 21 February 1993

2 Fifty years on from now, Britain will still be the country of long shadows on county [cricket] grounds, warm beer, invincible green suburbs, dog lovers, and—as George Orwell said—old maids bicycling to Holy Communion through the morning mist.

speech to the Conservative Group for Europe, 22 April 1993; see **Orwell** 275:12

3 It is time to get back to basics: to self-discipline and respect for the law, to consideration for others, to accepting responsibility for yourself and your family, and not shuffling it off on the state.

speech to the Conservative Party Conference, 8 October 1993

4 So right. OK. We lost.
on election night

in *Guardian* 3 May 1997

5 When the final curtain comes down, it's time to get off the stage.
outside 10 Downing Street on 2 May, leaving office as Prime Minister and announcing that he would resign as Party Leader

in *Guardian* 3 May 1997

6 In retrospect, I think her behaviour was intolerable, and I hope none of my successors are treated in that way.
of Margaret Thatcher

in *Daily Telegraph* 11 August 1999

7 Margaret had been at her happiest confronting political dragons: I chose consensus.
contrasting himself with Margaret Thatcher

John Major *The Autobiography* (1999)

Bernard Malamud 1914–86
American novelist and short-story writer

8 There's no such thing as an unpolitical man, especially a Jew.

The Fixer (1966)

Malcolm X 1925–65
American civil rights campaigner

9 If you're born in America with a black skin, you're born in prison.

in an interview, June 1963

10 We are not fighting for integration, nor are we fighting for separation. We are fighting for recognition as human beings. We are fighting for . . . human rights.

Black Revolution, speech in New York, 1964

11 You can't separate peace from freedom because no one can be at peace unless he has his freedom.

speech in New York, 7 January 1965

Seamus Mallon 1936–
Northern Irish politician

12 A pint of Guinness, or a large whisky, or maybe two.
when asked how he proposed to celebrate the agreement on Northern Ireland

in *Times* 11 April 1998

13 Sunningdale for slow learners.
comparing the earlier stages of the Northern Irish talks with the 1973 negotiations towards a power-sharing executive held at Sunningdale College, Berkshire

in *Daily Telegraph* 6 April 1998

Thomas Robert Malthus 1766–1834
English political economist

1 Population, when unchecked, increases in a geometrical ratio. Subsistence only increases in an arithmetical ratio.
Essay on the Principle of Population (1798)

2 The perpetual struggle for room and food.
Essay on the Principle of Population (1798)

3 A man who is born into a world already possessed, if he cannot get subsistence from his parents on whom he has a just demand, and if the society do not want his labour, has no claim of *right* to the smallest portion of food, and, in fact, has no business to be where he is. At Nature's mighty feast there is no vacant cover for him.
Essay on the Principle of Population (1803 ed.)

Earl of Manchester 1602–71
politician and Parliamentary commander in the Civil War

4 If we beat the King ninety-nine times, yet he is king still and so will his posterity be after him; but if the king beat us once we shall all be hanged, and our posterity made slaves.
at a Parliamentary Council-of-War, 10 November 1644
in *Calendar of State Papers, Domestic* 1644-5

Lord Mancroft 1914–87
British Conservative politician

5 Cricket—a game which the English, not being a spiritual people, have invented in order to give themselves some conception of eternity.
Bees in Some Bonnets (1979)

Nelson Mandela 1918–
South African statesman and African National Congress activist; President since 1994

6 I have dedicated my life to this struggle of the African people. I have fought against white domination, and I have fought against black domination. I have cherished the ideal of a democratic and free society in which all persons live together in harmony with equal opportunities. It is an ideal which I hope to live for and to achieve. But if needs be, it is an ideal for which I am prepared to die.
speech at his trial in Pretoria, 20 April 1964

7 I stand here before you not as a prophet but as a humble servant of you, the people. Your tireless and heroic sacrifices have made it possible for me to be here today. I therefore place the remaining years of my life in your hands.
speech in Cape Town, 11 February 1990

8 Through its imperialist system Britain brought about untold suffering of millions of people. And this is an historical fact. To be able to admit this would increase the respect, you know, which we have for British institutions.
in *Guardian* 2 April 1990

9 True reconciliation does not consist in merely forgetting the past.
on healing the bitterness caused by apartheid
speech, 7 January 1996

10 No one is born hating another person because of the colour of his skin, or his background, or his religion. People must learn to hate, and if they can learn to hate, they can be taught to love, for love comes more naturally to the human heart than its opposite.
Long Walk to Freedom (1994)

1 We close the century with most people still languishing in poverty, subjected to hunger, preventable disease, illiteracy and insufficient shelter.
   speaking at a ceremony at his former prison cell on Robben Island

in *Observer* on 2 January 2000

2 One of the things I learnt when I was negotiating was that until I changed myself I could not change others.

in *Sunday Times* 16 April 2000

Winnie Madikizela-Mandela 1934–
South African political activist

3 With that stick of matches, with our necklace, we shall liberate this country.
   speech in black townships, 14 April 1986; a 'necklace' was a tyre soaked or filled with petrol, placed around a victim's neck, and set alight

in *Guardian* 15 April 1986

4 Maybe there is no rainbow nation after all because it does not have the colour black.
   at the funeral of a black child reportedly shot dead by a white farmer

in *Irish Times* 25 April 1998 'Quotes of the Week'

Peter Mandelson 1953–
Labour politician

5 Few politicians are good at taking the high ground and throwing themselves off it.
   *of Tony **Blair** and the revision of Clause Four; see **Blair** 43:9*

in *New Yorker* 5 February 1996

6 I can have a big say because I am the owner, the sole shareholder. I don't get involved in half measures.
   on the £750 million Millennium Dome project

in *Observer* 6 July 1997 'Soundbites'

7 You'll say I'm in charge of a Mickey Mouse project.
   refusing to be photographed holding a balloon at Disney World

in *Daily Telegraph* 5 January 1998

8 [It's] not huge but it's nice, in a good street with smashing neighbours and I will miss it.
   putting his Notting Hill house on the market, after publicity surrounding the personal loan with which he had bought it, and his resignation from the Department of Trade and Industry

in *Daily Telegraph* 29 January 1999

9 Every politician is allowed the occasional gaffe, if only to remind the public that they are still human.
   apologising for referring to the Guards as 'chinless wonders' in recollections of seeing them as a child

in *Mail on Sunday* 19 March 2000

John Manners, Duke of Rutland 1818–1906
English Tory politician and writer

10 Let wealth and commerce, laws and learning die,
   But leave us still our old nobility!

England's Trust (1841)

Lord Mansfield 1705–93
Scottish lawyer and politician

11 The constitution does not allow reasons of state to influence our judgements: God forbid it should! We must not regard political consequences; however formidable soever they might be: if rebellion was the certain consequence, we are bound to say '*fiat justitia, ruat caelum*'.

Rex v. Wilkes, 8 June 1768, in *The English Reports* (1909) vol. 98; see **Adams** 4:3

1 Consider what you think justice requires, and decide accordingly. But never give your reasons; for your judgement will probably be right, but your reasons will certainly be wrong.
　advice to a newly appointed colonial governor ignorant in the law

Lord Campbell *The Lives of the Chief Justices of England* (1849) vol. 2

Mao Zedong 1893–1976

Chinese statesman, chairman of the Communist Party of the Chinese People's Republic 1949–76 and head of state 1949–59

2 Politics is war without bloodshed while war is politics with bloodshed.

lecture, 1938

3 Every Communist must grasp the truth, 'Political power grows out of the barrel of a gun'.

speech, 6 November 1938

4 The atom bomb is a paper tiger which the United States reactionaries use to scare people. It looks terrible, but in fact it isn't . . . All reactionaries are paper tigers.

interview, 1946

5 Letting a hundred flowers blossom and a hundred schools of thought contend is the policy for promoting progress in the arts and the sciences and a flourishing socialist culture in our land.

speech in Peking, 27 February 1957

6 People of the world, unite and defeat the US aggressors and all their running dogs!

'Statement Supporting the People of the Congo against US Aggression' 28 November 1964

John Marchi 1948–

American Republican politician

7 We ought not to permit a cottage industry in the God business.
　on hearing that British scientists had successfully cloned a lamb (Dolly)

in *Guardian* 28 February 1997

James Margach d. 1979

British journalist

8 Power, which has the ability to mellow some of those who achieve it . . . in Heath's case changed his personality overnight. When Prime Minister he became authoritarian and intolerant.

The Abuse of Power (1978)

Marie-Antoinette 1755–93

Queen consort of Louis XVI

9 Let them eat cake.
　on being told that her people had no bread

attributed; in *Confessions* (1740) Rousseau refers to a similar remark being a well-known saying; in *Relation d'un Voyage à Bruxelles et à Coblentz en 1791* (1823), Louis XVIII attributes 'Why don't they eat pastry?' to Marie-Thérèse (1638–83), wife of Louis XIV

Constance Markievicz 1868–1927

Irish nationalist
on Markievicz: see **de Valera** 108:4

1 A good Nationalist should look upon slugs in the garden in much the same way as she looks on the English in Ireland.

in Bean na hÉireann November 1908

2 I wish you had the decency to shoot me.
on hearing of the commutation of her death sentence

Diana Norman *Terrible Beauty* (1987)

3 I have seen the stars, and I am not going to follow a flickering will o' the wisp.
rejecting the Treaty in the Dáil debate, 1921

Diana Norman *Terrible Beauty* (1987)

4 How could I ever meet Paddy Pearse or Jim Connolly in the hereafter if I took an oath to a British king?
in 1926, on her refusal to take the oath which would allow her to enter the Dáil

Diana Norman *Terrible Beauty* (1987)

George C. Marshall 1880–1959

American general and statesman, who as US Secretary of State (1947–9) initiated the programme of economic aid to European countries known as the Marshall Plan

5 If man does find the solution for world peace it will be the most revolutionary reversal of his record we have ever known.

biennial report of the Chief of Staff, United States Army, 1 September 1945

6 Our policy is directed not against any country or doctrine but against hunger, poverty, desperation and chaos. Its purpose should be the revival of a working economy in the world so as to permit the emergence of political and social conditions in which free institutions can exist.
announcing the Marshall Plan

address at Harvard, 5 June 1947

John Marshall 1755–1835

American jurist

7 The power to tax involves the power to destroy.

in McCulloch v. Maryland (1819)

8 The people made the Constitution, and the people can unmake it. It is the creature of their own will, and lives only by their will.

in Cohens v. Virginia (1821)

Thomas R. Marshall 1854–1925

American politician

9 What this country needs is a really good 5-cent cigar.

in New York Tribune 4 January 1920

Thurgood Marshall 1908–93

American Supreme Court judge

10 We must never forget that the only real source of power that we as judges can tap is the respect of the people.

in Chicago Tribune 15 August 1981

Andrew Marvell 1621–78

English poet

11 Choosing each stone, and poising every weight,
Trying the measures of the breadth and height;
Here pulling down, and there erecting new,
Founding a firm state by proportions true.

'The First Anniversary of the Government under His Highness the Lord Protector, 1655'

1 *He* nothing common did or mean
Upon that memorable scene:
But with his keener eye
The axe's edge did try:
Nor called the gods with vulgar spite
To vindicate his helpless right,
But bowed his comely head,
Down as upon a bed.
on the execution of **Charles I**

'An Horatian Ode upon Cromwell's Return from Ireland' (written 1650)

2 And now the Irish are ashamed
To see themselves in one year tamed:
So much one man can do,
That does both act and know.

'An Horatian Ode upon Cromwell's Return from Ireland' (written 1650)

Karl Marx 1818–83

German political philosopher; founder of modern Communism

3 Religion . . . is the opium of the people.

A Contribution to the Critique of Hegel's Philosophy of Right (1843–4) introduction

4 Mankind always sets itself only such problems as it can solve; since, looking at the matter more closely, it will always be found that the task itself arises only when the material conditions for its solution already exist or are at least in the process of formation.

A Contribution to the Critique of Political Economy (1859) preface

5 It is not the consciousness of men that determines their being, but, on the contrary, their social being that determines their consciousness.

A Contribution to the Critique of Political Economy (1859) preface

6 From each according to his abilities, to each according to his needs.

Critique of the Gotha Programme (written 1875, but of earlier origin); see Morelly *Code de la nature* (1755) , and J. J. L. Blanc *Organisation du travail* (1839) (who, in quoting Saint-Simon, rejects the notion) for possible sources

7 Hegel says somewhere that all great events and personalities in world history reappear in one fashion or another. He forgot to add: the first time as tragedy, the second as farce.

The Eighteenth Brumaire of Louis Bonaparte (1852); the origin of the Hegel reference is uncertain, but see **Hegel** 167:9

8 It is the ultimate aim of this work, to lay bare the economic law of motion of modern society.

Das Kapital (1st German ed., 1867) preface (25 July 1865)

9 The philosophers have only interpreted the world in various ways; the point is to change it.

Theses on Feuerbach (written 1845)

10 What I did that was new was to prove . . . that the class struggle necessarily leads to the dictatorship of the proletariat.
the phrase 'dictatorship of the proletariat' had been used earlier in the Constitution of the World Society of Revolutionary Communists (1850), signed by Marx and others

letter to Georg Weydemeyer 5 March 1852; Marx claimed that the phrase had been coined by Auguste Blanqui (1805–81), but it has not been found in this form in Blanqui's work

11 All I know is that I am not a Marxist.

attributed in a letter from Friedrich Engels to Conrad Schmidt, 5 August 1890

Karl Marx 1818–83
and **Friedrich Engels** 1820–95
Co-founders of modern Communism

1 A spectre is haunting Europe—the spectre of Communism.

The Communist Manifesto (1848) opening words

2 The history of all hitherto existing society is the history of class struggles.

The Communist Manifesto (1848)

3 In place of the old bourgeois society, with its classes and class antagonists, we shall have an association, in which the free development of each is the free development of all.

The Communist Manifesto (1848)

4 The proletarians have nothing to lose but their chains. They have a world to win. WORKING MEN OF ALL COUNTRIES, UNITE!
   often quoted as 'Workers of the world, unite!'

The Communist Manifesto (1848) *ad fin.*

Queen Mary 1867–1953
Queen Consort of George V

5 *This* is a pretty kettle of fish!
   *to the Prime Minister, Stanley **Baldwin**, after **Edward VIII** had told her that he was prepared to give up the throne to marry Mrs Simpson*

James Pope-Hennessy *Life of Queen Mary* (1959)

6 All *this* thrown away for *that.*
   *on returning home to Marlborough House, London after the abdication of her son, King **Edward VIII**, December 1936*

David Duff *George and Elizabeth* (1983)

7 I do not think you have ever realised the shock, which the attitude you took up caused your family and the whole nation. It seemed inconceivable to those who had made such sacrifices during the war that you, as their King, refused a lesser sacrifice.

letter to the Duke of Windsor, the former **Edward VIII**, July 1938

Mary, Queen of Scots 1542–87
Queen of Scotland, 1542–67

8 Look to your consciences and remember that the theatre of the world is wider than the realm of England.
   to the commissioners appointed to try her at Fotheringhay, 13 October 1586

Antonia Fraser *Mary Queen of Scots* (1969) ch. 25

9 *En ma fin git mon commencement.*
   In my end is my beginning.
   motto embroidered with an emblem of her mother, Mary of Guise

quoted in a letter from William Drummond of Hawthornden to Ben Jonson in 1619

Mary Tudor 1516–58
Queen of England from 1553

10 When I am dead and opened, you shall find 'Calais' lying in my heart.

in *Holinshed's Chronicles* vol. 4 (1808)

Philip Massinger 1583–1640
English playwright

11 Ambition, in a private man a vice,
   Is in a prince the virtue.

The Bashful Lover (licensed 1636, published 1655)

1   Greatness, with private men
Esteemed a blessing, is to me a curse;
And we, whom, for our high births, they conclude
The only freemen, are the only slaves.
Happy the golden mean!

The Great Duke of Florence (licensed 1627, printed 1635)

W. Somerset Maugham 1874–1965
British novelist, short-story writer, and dramatist

2 The geniality of the politician who for years has gone out of his way to be cordial with everyone he meets.

A Writer's Notebook (1949) written in 1938

James Maxton 1885–1946
British Labour politician

3 All I say is, if you cannot ride two horses you have no right in the circus.
    opposing disaffiliation of the Scottish Independent Labour Party from the Labour Party, often quoted as 'no right in the bloody circus'

in *Daily Herald* 12 January 1931

Horace Maybray-King 1901–86
British Labour politician; Speaker of the House of Commons

4 One of the myths of the British Parliament is that there are three parties there. I can assure you from bitter personal experience there are 629.

in *Observer* 9 October 1966 'Sayings of the Week'

Jonathan Mayhew 1720–66
American divine

5 Rulers have no authority from God to do mischief.

A Discourse Concerning Unlimited Submission and Non-Resistance to the Higher Powers (1750)

6 As soon as the prince sets himself up above the law, he loses the king in the tyrant; he does to all intents and purpose unking himself . . . And in such cases, has no more right to be obeyed, than any inferior officer who acts beyond his commission.

A Discourse Concerning Unlimited Submission and Non-Resistance to the Higher Powers (1750)

Catherine de' Medici 1518–89
Queen Consort of France, wife of Henri II

7 A false report, if believed during three days, may be of great service to a government.

Isaac D'Israeli *Curiosities of Literature* 2nd series (1849) vol. 2; perhaps apocryphal

Robert Megarry 1910–

8 Whereas in England all is permitted that is not expressly prohibited, it has been said that in Germany all is prohibited unless expressly permitted and in France all is permitted that is expressly prohibited. In the European Common Market (as it then was) no-one knows what is permitted and it all costs more.

'Law and Lawyers in a Permissive Society' (5th Riddell Lecture delivered in Lincoln's Inn Hall 22 March 1972)

Golda Meir 1898–1978

Israeli stateswoman, Prime Minister 1969–74

1 Those that perished in Hitler's gas chambers were the last
Jews to die without standing up to defend themselves.

speech to United Jewish Appeal
Rally, New York, 11 June 1967

Lord Melbourne 1779–1848

British Whig politician; Prime Minister 1834, 1835–41

2 I have always thought complaints of ill-usage contemptible,
whether from a seduced disappointed girl or a turned-out
Prime Minister.
on being dismissed by William IV

Emily Eden, letter to Mrs Lister, 23
November 1834

3 If left out he would be dangerous, but if taken in, he would
be simply destructive.
*when forming his second administration in 1835, Melbourne
omitted the former Lord Chancellor,* **Brougham**

Lord David Cecil *Lord M* (1954)

4 You domineered too much, you interfered too much with
other departments, you encroached upon the provinces of
the Prime Minister, you worked, as I believe, with the Press
in a manner unbecoming to the dignity of your station.
letter to the former Lord Chancellor, **Brougham***, explaining why
he had been omitted from Melbourne's second administration*

Lord David Cecil *Lord M* (1954)

5 Damn it! Another Bishop dead! I believe they die to vex me.

Lord David Cecil *Lord M* (1954)

6 God help the Minister that meddles with art!

Lord David Cecil *Lord M* (1954)

7 I wish I was as cocksure of anything as Tom Macaulay is of
everything.

Earl Cowper *Preface to Lord
Melbourne's Papers* (1889)

8 Nobody ever did anything very foolish except from some
strong principle.

Lord David Cecil *The Young
Melbourne* (1939)

9 Now, is it to lower the price of corn, or isn't it? It is not
much matter which we say, but mind, we must all say *the
same.*
*at the end of a Cabinet meeting to agree a fixed tariff for corn;
Melbourne is said to have put his back to the door and opened it
only when they agreed*

Walter Bagehot *The English
Constitution* (1867)

10 Things have come to a pretty pass when religion is allowed
to invade the sphere of private life.
on hearing an evangelical sermon

G. W. E. Russell *Collections and
Recollections* (1898)

11 This damned morality will undo us all.
*of Prince Albert's wish to establish the Royal Family as a
national icon of domestic life*

Samuel Weintraub *Albert* (1997)

12 What all the wise men promised has not happened, and
what all the d—d fools said would happen has come to pass.
of the Catholic Emancipation Act (1829)

H. Dunckley *Lord Melbourne* (1890)

13 What I want is men who will support me when I am in the
wrong.
*replying to a politician who said 'I will support you as long as you
are in the right'*

Lord David Cecil *Lord M* (1954)

14 When in doubt what should be done, do nothing.

Lord David Cecil *Lord M* (1954)

15 The whole duty of government is to prevent crime and to
preserve contracts.

Lord David Cecil *Lord M* (1954)

Lord Melchett 1948–
British peer, executive director of Greenpeace

1 The menu could not guarantee GM-free food but I ate
vegetarian shepherd's pie.
on his two days in prison after leading a raid to destroy GM crops

in Sunday Times 1 August 1999
'Talking Heads'

David Mellor 1949–
British Conservative politician

2 I do believe the popular press is drinking in the last chance
saloon.

interview on *Hard News* (Channel
4), 21 December 1989

H. L. Mencken 1880–1956
American journalist and literary critic

3 Nothing is so abject and pathetic as a politician who has lost
his job, save only a retired stud-horse.

Chrestomathy (1949)

4 Puritanism. The haunting fear that someone, somewhere,
may be happy.

Chrestomathy (1949)

5 The whole aim of practical politics is to keep the populace
alarmed (and hence clamorous to be led to safety) by
menacing it with an endless series of hobgoblins, all of them
imaginary.

In Defence of Women (1923)

6 Democracy is the theory that the common people know
what they want, and deserve to get it good and hard.

A Little Book in C major (1916)

7 A government can never be the impersonal thing described
in text-books. It is simply a group of men like any other. In
every 100 of the men composing it there are two who are
honest and intelligent, ten obvious scoundrels, and 88 poor
fish.

Minority Report (1956)

8 Under democracy one party always devotes its chief energies
to trying to prove that the other party is unfit to rule—and
both commonly succeed, and are right.

Minority Report (1956)

9 The worst government is often the most moral. One
composed of cynics is often very tolerant and humane. But
when fanatics are on top there is no limit to oppression.

Minority Report (1956)

10 A good politician is quite as unthinkable as an honest
burglar.

Prejudices 4th series (1925)

11 No one in this world, so far as I know—and I have searched
the records for years, and employed agents to help me—has
ever lost money by underestimating the intelligence of the
great masses of the plain people.

in *Chicago Tribune* 19 September
1926

12 The saddest life is that of a political aspirant under
democracy. His failure is ignominious and his success is
disgraceful.

in *Baltimore Evening Sun* 9
December 1929

13 He [Calvin Coolidge] slept more than any other President,
whether by day or by night. Nero fiddled, but Coolidge only
snored.

in *American Mercury* April 1933

14 If there had been any formidable body of cannibals in the
country he would have promised to provide them with free
missionaries fattened at the taxpayer's expense.
*of Harry **Truman**'s success in the 1948 presidential campaign*

in *Baltimore Sun* 7 November 1948

Robert Gordon Menzies 1894–1978
Australian Liberal statesman, Prime Minister 1939–41 and
1949–66

1 What Great Britain calls the Far East is to us the near north.

in *Sydney Morning Herald* 27 April
1939

Jean Meslier c.1664–1733
French priest

2 I remember, on this matter, the wish made once by an
ignorant, uneducated man . . . He said he wished . . . that
all the great men in the world and all the nobility could be
hanged, and strangled with the guts of priests. For myself
. . . I wish I could have the strength of Hercules to purge the
world of all vice and sin, and to have the pleasure of
destroying all those monsters of error and sin [priests] who
make all the peoples of the world groan so pitiably.
*often quoted as, 'I should like . . . the last king to be strangled
with the guts of the last priest'*

Testament (1864); see **Diderot**
110:5, **Nairn** 264:1

Prince Metternich 1773–1859
Austrian statesman

3 Italy is a geographical expression.
*discussing the Italian question with **Palmerston** in 1847*

*Mémoires, Documents, etc. de
Metternich publiés par son fils*
(1883) vol. 7; see **Bismarck** 41:11

of his own downfall:
4 I feel obliged to call to the supporters of the social uprising:
Citizens of a dream-world, nothing is altered. On 14 March
1848, there was merely one man fewer.

*Aus Metternich's Nachgelassenen
Papieren* (ed. A. von Klinkowström,
1880) vol. 8

5 Error has never approached my spirit.
addressed to Guizot in 1848

François Pierre G. Guizot *Mémoires*
(1858–67) vol. 4

6 The Emperor is everything, Vienna is nothing.

letter to Count Bombelles, 5 June
1848

7 The greatest gift of any statesman rests not in knowing
what concessions to make, but recognising when to make
them.

Concessionen und Nichtconcessionen
(1852)

8 The word 'freedom' means for me not a point of departure
but a genuine point of arrival. The point of departure is
defined by the word 'order'. Freedom cannot exist without
the concept of order.

Mein Politisches Testament

Anthony Meyer 1920–
British Conservative politician

9 I question the right of that great Moloch, national
sovereignty, to burn its children to save its pride.
speaking against the Falklands War, 1982

in *Listener* 27 September 1990

Jules Michelet 1798–1874
French historian

10 What is the first part of politics? Education. The second?
Education. And the third? Education.

Le Peuple (1846); see **Blair** 43:11

William Porcher Miles 1822–96

1 'Vote early and vote often,' the advice openly displayed on the election banners in one of our northern cities.

in the House of Representatives, 31 March 1858

■ **Military sayings** *see box opposite*

John Stuart Mill 1806–73
English philosopher and economist

2 No great improvements in the lot of mankind are possible, until a great change takes place in the fundamental constitution of their modes of thought.

Autobiography (1873)

3 The Conservatives . . . being by the law of their existence the stupidest party.

Considerations on Representative Government (1861)

4 It is but a small portion of the public business of a country which can be well done, or safely attempted, by the central authorities.

Considerations on Representative Government (1861)

5 When society requires to be rebuilt, there is no use in attempting to rebuild it on the old plan.

Dissertations and Discussions vol. 1 (1859) 'Essay on Coleridge'

6 The sole end for which mankind are warranted, individually or collectively, in interfering with the liberty of action of any of their number, is self-protection.

On Liberty (1859)

7 The only freedom worth the name, is that of pursuing our own good in our own way.

On Liberty (1859)

8 The only purpose for which power can be rightfully exercised over any member of a civilized community, against his will, is to prevent harm to others. His own good, either physical or moral, is not a sufficient warrant.

On Liberty (1859)

9 If all mankind minus one were of one opinion, and only one person were of the contrary opinion, mankind would be no more justified in silencing that one person, than he, if he had the power, would be justified in silencing mankind.

On Liberty (1859)

10 A party of order or stability, and a party of progress or reform, are both necessary elements of a healthy state of political life.

On Liberty (1859)

11 The liberty of the individual must be thus far limited; he must not make himself a nuisance to other people.

On Liberty (1859)

12 I am not aware that any community has a right to force another to be civilized.

On Liberty (1859)

13 Liberty consists in doing what one desires.

On Liberty (1859)

14 A State which dwarfs its men, in order that they may be more docile instruments in its hands even for beneficial purposes, will find that with small men no great thing can really be accomplished.

On Liberty (1859)

15 The principle which regulates the existing social relations between the two sexes—the legal subordination of one sex to the other—is wrong in itself, and now one of the chief hindrances to human improvement.

The Subjection of Women (1869)

continued

Military sayings

1 Action this day.

annotation as used by Winston Churchill at the Admiralty in 1940

2 Daddy, what did you do in the Great War?

daughter to father in First World War recruiting poster

3 *Ils ne passeront pas.*
  They shall not pass.
  slogan used by French army defence at Verdun in 1916

variously attributed to Marshal Pétain and to General Robert Nivelle; see **Ibarruri** 180:8

4 Lions led by donkeys.
  associated with British soldiers during the First World War

attributed to Max Hoffman (1869-1927) in Alan Clark *The Donkeys* (1961); this attribution has not been traced elsewhere, and the phrase is of much earlier origin:

  Unceasingly they had drummed into them the utterance of *The Times*: 'You are lions led by packasses.'
  of French troops defeated by Prussians

Francisque Sarcey *Paris during the Siege* (1871)

5 Your King and Country need you.

recruitment slogan for First World War, coined by Eric Field, July 1914; *Advertising* (1959); see **Songs** 342:8

John Stuart Mill *continued*

6 Everyone who desires power, desires it most over those who are nearest to him, with whom his life is passed, with whom he has most concerns in common, and in whom any independence of his authority is oftenest likely to interfere with his individual preferences.

The Subjection of Women (1869)

Edna St Vincent Millay 1892–1950

American poet

7 Justice denied in Massachusetts.
  *relating to the trial of Sacco and **Vanzetti** and their execution on 22 August 1927*

title of poem (1928)

8 The sun that warmed our stooping backs and withered the
    weeds uprooted—
  We shall not feel it again.
  We shall die in darkness, and be buried in the rain.

'Justice Denied in Massachusetts' (1928)

Alice Duer Miller 1874–1942

American writer

9 I am American bred,
  I have seen much to hate here—much to forgive,
  But in a world where England is finished and dead,
  I do not wish to live.

The White Cliffs (1940)

Arthur Miller 1915–

American dramatist

1 The ultimate human mystery may not be anything more than the claims on us of clan and race, which may yet turn out to have the power, because they defy the rational mind, to kill the world.

Timebends (1987)

2 A good newspaper, I suppose, is a nation talking to itself.

in *Observer* 26 November 1961

3 A theatre where no-one is allowed to walk out and everyone is forced to applause.
describing Eastern Europe

Omnibus (BBC TV) 30 October 1987; in *Independent* 31 October 1987

Charles Wright Mills 1916–62

American sociologist

4 By the power elite, we refer to those political, economic, and military circles which as an intricate set of overlapping cliques share decisions having at least national conseqences. In so far as national events are decided, the power elite are those who decide them.

The Power Elite (1956)

Lord Milner 1854–1925

British colonial administrator

5 If we believe a thing to be bad, and if we have a right to prevent it, it is our duty to try to prevent it and to damn the consequences.

speech in Glasgow, 26 November 1909

John Milton 1608–74

English poet, who became a politically active Parliamentarian during the Civil War, publishing the *Areopagitica* (1644) which demanded a free press, and writing a defence of republicanism on the eve of the Restoration (1660)

6 Cromwell, our chief of men.

'To the Lord General Cromwell' (written 1652)

7 . . . Peace hath her victories
No less renowned than war.

'To the Lord General Cromwell' (written 1652)

8 They also serve who only stand and wait.

'When I consider how my light is spent' (1673)

9 I cannot praise a fugitive and cloistered virtue, unexercised and unbreathed, that never sallies out and sees her adversary, but slinks out of the race, where that immortal garland is to be run for, not without dust and heat.

Areopagitica (1644)

10 Here the great art lies, to discern in what the law is to be to restraint and punishment, and in what things persuasion only is to work.

Areopagitica (1644)

11 Let not England forget her precedence of teaching nations how to live.

The Doctrine and Discipline of Divorce (1643) 'To the Parliament of England'

12 What I have spoken, is the language of that which is not called amiss *The good old Cause*.

The Ready and Easy Way to Establish a Free Commonwealth (2nd ed., 1660)

1 The land had once enfranchised herself from this impertinent yoke of prelaty, under whose inquisitorious and tyrannical duncery no free and splendid wit can flourish.

The Reason of Church Government (1642) bk. 2, introduction

2 None can love freedom heartily, but good men; the rest love not freedom, but licence.

The Tenure of Kings and Magistrates (1649)

3 No man who knows aught, can be so stupid to deny that all men naturally were born free.

The Tenure of Kings and Magistrates (1649)

Comte de Mirabeau 1749–91
French revolutionary

4 War is the national industry of Prussia.

attributed to Mirabeau by Albert Sorel (1842–1906), based on Mirabeau's introduction to *De la monarchie prussienne sous Frédéric le Grand* (1788)

■ Misquotations *see box overleaf*

John Mitchel 1815–75
Irish nationalist

5 Families, when all was eaten and no hope left, took their last look at the sun, built up their cottage doors, that none might see them die nor hear their groans, and were found weeks afterwards, skeletons on their own hearth.
   of the Irish Famine

Jail Journal (1854)

6 I am ready for my fourteen years' ordeal, and for whatsoever the same may bring me—toil, sickness, ignominy, death. Fate, thou art defied.

Jail Journal (1854)

7 Next to the British government, the worst enemy Ireland ever had—or rather the most fatal friend.
   of Daniel O'Connell

The Last Conquest of Ireland (Perhaps) (1861)

Austin Mitchell 1934–
British Labour politician

8 Welcome to Britain's New Political Order. No passion . . . No Right. No Left. Just multi-hued blancmange.

in *Observer* 11 April 1999 'Sayings of the Week'

George Mitchell 1933–
American politician

9 Although he is regularly asked to do so, God does not take sides in American politics.

comment during the hearing of the Senate Select Committee on the Iran-Contra affair, July 1987

10 Nobody ever said it would be easy—and that was an understatement.
   on the peace talks

in *Times* 19 February 1998

continued

Misquotations

1 All is lost save honour.

    Of all I had, only honour and life have been spared.

popular summary of the words of **Francis I** of France:

letter to his mother following his defeat at Pavia, 1525; see **Francis I** 136:5

2 The ballot is stronger than the bullet.

popular version of a speech by **Lincoln**, 18 May 1858; see **Lincoln** 218:5

3 The capitalists will sell us the rope with which to hang them.

attributed to **Lenin**, but not found in his published works; I. U. Annenkov, in 'Remembrances of Lenin' includes a manuscript note attributed to Lenin:

    They [capitalists] will furnish credits which will serve us for the support of the Communist Party in their countries and, by supplying us materials and technical equipment which we lack, will restore our military industry necessary for our future attacks against our suppliers. To put it in other words, they will work on the preparation of their own suicide.

in *Novyi Zhurnal/New Review* September 1961

4 Crisis? What Crisis?

Sun headline, 11 January 1979, summarizing James **Callaghan**'s remark; see **Newspaper headlines** 267:1

    I don't think other people in the world would share the view there is mounting chaos.

interview at London Airport, 10 January 1979

5 England and America are two countries divided by a common language.

attributed in this and other forms to George Bernard **Shaw**, but not found in Shaw's published writings; see **Wilde** 383:4

6 Few die and none resign.

popular summary of a letter of Thomas **Jefferson**, 1801; see **Jefferson** 186:6

7 The green shoots of recovery.

popular misquotation of Norman **Lamont**'s upbeat assessment of the economic situation, 9 October 1991; see **Lamont** 209:5

8 Hawking his conscience round the Chancelleries of Europe.

popular version of Ernest **Bevin**'s description of Lansbury, 1935; see **Bevin** 38:5

9 I disapprove of what you say, but I will defend to the death your right to say it.
    *to **Helvétius**, following the burning of* De l'esprit *in 1759*

attributed to **Voltaire**, but in fact a later summary of his attitude by S. G. Tallentyre in *The Friends of Voltaire* (1907); see **Voltaire** 372:10

Misquotations *continued*

1 In trust I have found treason.

traditional concluding words of a speech by **Elizabeth I** to a Parliamentary deputation at Richmond, 12 November 1586; see **Elizabeth I** 123:9

2 It is necessary only for the good man to do nothing for evil to triumph.

attributed (in a number of forms) to **Burke**, but not found in his writings; see **Burke** 59:14

3 Just a heart-beat away from the Presidency of the United States.

popular version of Adlai **Stevenson**'s description of the Vice-Presidency, 23 October 1952; see **Stevenson** 347:4

4 My lips are sealed.

popular version of **Baldwin**'s speech on the Abyssinian crisis, 10 December 1935; see **Baldwin** 25:8

5 Selling off the family silver.

popular summary of Harold **Macmillan**'s attack on privatization, 8 November 1985; see **Macmillan** 236:11

6 The soft underbelly of Europe.

popular version of **Churchill**'s words in the House of Commons, 11 November 1942; see **Churchill** 82:12

7 Something must be done.

popular version of **Edward VIII**'s words at the derelict Dowlais Iron and Steel Works, 18 November 1936; see **Edward VIII** 121:9

8 Take away these baubles.

popular version of **Cromwell's** words at the dismissal of the Rump Parliament, 20 April 1653; see **Cromwell** 98:6

9 Warts and all.

popular summary of **Cromwell**'s instructions to the court painter Lely:

Mr Lely, I desire you would use all your skill to paint my picture truly like me, and not flatter me at all; but remark all these roughnesses, pimples, warts, and everything as you see me; otherwise I will never pay a farthing for it.

Horace Walpole *Anecdotes of Painting in England* vol. 3 (1763) ch. 1

10 We are the masters now.

popular misquotation of Hartley **Shawcross**'s speech in the House of Commons, 2 April 1946; see **Shawcross** 329:1

11 We must educate our masters.

popular version of Robert **Lowe**'s comment on the passing of the Reform Bill, 1867; see **Lowe** 226:2

Misquotations *continued*

1 What a glorious morning for America.

popular version of the words of **Samuel Adams** on hearing gunfire at Lexington, 19 April 1775; see **Adams** 4:6

2 The white heat of technology.

popular version of Harold **Wilson**'s speech at the Labour Party Conference, 1 October 1963; see **Wilson** 384:9

George Mitchell *continued*

3 I am pleased to announce that the two governments and the political parties in Northern Ireland have reached agreement.
announcing the Good Friday agreement

in *Times* 11 April 1998

4 I have that bittersweet feeling that comes in life. I am dying to leave but I hate to go.
after the signing of the Good Friday agreement

in *Times* 11 April 1998

5 Peace, political stability and reconciliation are not too much to ask for. They are the minimum that a decent society provides.

in *Irish Post* 18 April 1998

John Mitchell 1785–1859

English soldier

6 The most important political question on which modern times have to decide is the policy that must now be pursued, in order to maintain the security of Western Europe against the overgrown power of Russia.

Thoughts on Tactics (1838)

Joni Mitchell 1943–

Canadian singer and songwriter

7 Lord, there's danger in this land.
You get witch-hunts and wars when church and state hold hands.

attributed; Peter McWilliams *Ain't Nobody's Business If You Do* (1993)

François Mitterrand 1916–96

French socialist politician; President of France 1981–95

8 She has the eyes of Caligula, but the mouth of Marilyn Monroe.
*of Margaret **Thatcher**, briefing his new European Minister Roland Dumas*

in *Observer* 25 November 1990

George Monbiot 1963–

British environmentalist

9 I saw how hard it is for our own society ever to become wise while old people are ostracized.

No Man's Land (1994)

Walter Mondale 1928–

American Democratic politician and Vice-President

1 When I hear your new ideas I'm reminded of that ad, 'Where's the beef?'
   alluding to an advertising slogan which made an unfavourable comparison between the relative sizes of a small hamburger and a large bun

   in a televised debate with Gary Hart, 11 March 1984

2 Political image is like mixing cement. When it's wet, you can move it around and shape it, but at some point it hardens and there's almost nothing you can do to reshape it.

   in *Independent on Sunday* 12 May 1991

Duke of Monmouth 1649–85

illegitimate son of Charles II; focus of the supporters of the Protestant succession in the Exclusion crisis of 1681 (see **Dryden**) and leader of the failed Monmouth rebellion against James II

3 Do not hack me as you did my Lord Russell.
   words addressed to his executioner; according to a contemporary account five blows were needed

   T. B. Macaulay *History of England* vol. 1 (1849)

Jean Monnet 1888–1979

French economist and diplomat; founder of the European Community

4 Europe has never existed. It is not the addition of national sovereignties in a conclave which creates an entity. One must genuinely *create* Europe.

   Anthony Sampson *The New Europeans* (1968)

5 The common market is a process, not a product.

   Anthony Sampson *The New Europeans* (1968)

6 I did not understand the politics of Versailles, only the economics.
   of the Treaty of Versailles

   in an interview in 1971; François Duchêne *Jean Monnet* (1994)

7 A great statesman is one who can work for long-term goals which eventually suit situations as yet unforeseen.

   Memoirs (1978)

8 Each man begins the world afresh. Only institutions grow wiser; they store up the collective experience; and, from this experience and wisdom, men subject to the same laws will gradually find, not that their natures change but that their experience does.
   a favourite sentiment ascribed by Monnet to the nineteenth-century Genevese diarist Henri Frédéric Amiel

   François Duchêne *Jean Monnet* (1994)

9 Institutions govern relationships between people. They are the real pillars of civilization.

   François Duchêne *Jean Monnet* (1994)

10 We should not create a nation Europe instead of a nation France.

   François Duchêne *Jean Monnet* (1994)

James Monroe 1758–1831

American Democratic Republican statesman, 5th President of the
US 1817–25, who in 1803 negotiated the Louisiana Purchase, and
who formulated the Monroe Doctrine

1 We owe it . . . to the amicable relations existing between the
United States and those [European] powers to declare that
we should consider any attempt on their part to extend their
system to any portion of this hemisphere as dangerous to
our peace and safety.
principle that became known as the 'Monroe Doctrine'

annual message to Congress, 2
December 1823

Montaigne 1533–92

French moralist and essayist

2 There is scarcely any less bother in the running of a family
than in that of an entire state. And domestic business is no
less importunate for being less important.

Essais (1580)

3 Fame and tranquillity can never be bedfellows.

Essais (1580)

4 On the highest throne in the world, we still sit only on our
own bottom.

Essais (1580)

Montesquieu 1689–1755

French political philosopher

5 Ever since the invention of gunpowder . . . I continually
tremble lest men should, in the end, uncover some secret
which would provide a short way of abolishing mankind, of
annihilating peoples and nations in their entirety.

Lettres Persanes (1721)

6 Just as the sea, which seems to want to cover the whole
earth, is checked by the grasses and the smallest bits of
gravel on the shore, so monarchs, whose power seems
boundless, are checked by the slightest obstacles and submit
their natural pride to supplication and prayer.

The Spirit of the Laws (1748)

7 Republics end in luxury; monarchies, in poverty.

The Spirit of the Laws (1748)

8 The corruption of each government almost always begins
with that of its principles.

The Spirit of the Laws (1748)

9 The principle of democracy is corrupted not only when the
spirit of equality is lost but also when the spirit of extreme
equality is taken up and each one wants to be the equal of
those chosen to command.

The Spirit of the Laws (1748)

10 If a republic is small, it is destroyed by a foreign force; if it is
large, it is destroyed by an internal vice.

The Spirit of the Laws (1748)

11 Liberty is the right to do everything the laws permit.

The Spirit of the Laws (1748)

12 It has eternally been observed that any man who has power
is led to abuse it.

The Spirit of the Laws (1748)

13 The English have taken their idea of political government
from the Germans. This fine system was found in the forests.

The Spirit of the Laws (1748)

14 This state [England] will perish when legislative power is
more corrupt than executive power.

The Spirit of the Laws (1748)

15 Royal authority is a great spring that should move easily
and noiselessly.

The Spirit of the Laws (1748)

1 In moderate states, there is a compensation for heavy taxes; it is liberty. In despotic states, there is an equivalent for liberty; it is the modest taxes.

The Spirit of the Laws (1748)

2 Lands produce less by reason of their fertility than by reason of the liberty of their inhabitants.

Alexis de Tocqueville *The Ancien Régime* (1856); attributed

Lord Montgomery 1887–1976
British field marshal

3 War is a very rough game, but I think that politics is worse.

attributed, 1956

4 Rule 1, on page 1 of the book of war, is: 'Do not march on Moscow' . . . [Rule 2] is: 'Do not go fighting with your land armies in China.'

in the House of Lords, 30 May 1962

James Graham, Marquess of Montrose
1612–50
Scottish royalist general and poet

5 Great, Good and Just, could I but rate
My grief to thy too rigid fate!

'Epitaph on King Charles I'

6 Let them bestow on every airth a limb;
Then open all my veins, that I may swim
To thee, my Maker! in that crimson lake;
Then place my parboiled head upon a stake—
Scatter my ashes—strew them in the air;—
Lord! since thou know'st where all these atoms are,
I'm hopeful thou'lt recover once my dust,
And confident thou'lt raise me with the just.

'Lines written on the Window of his Jail the Night before his Execution'

Thomas More 1478–1535
English scholar and saint; Lord Chancellor of England, 1529–32
on More: see **Whittington** 382:10; *see also* **Last words** 213:12

7 Your sheep, that were wont to be so meek and tame, and so small eaters, now, as I hear say, be become so great devourers, and so wild, that they eat up and swallow down the very men themselves.

Utopia (1516); following the marginal précis 'The Disaster Produced by Standing Military Garrisons'

8 If the parties will at my hands call for justice, then, all were it my father stood on the one side, and the Devil on the other, his cause being good, the Devil should have right.

William Roper *Life of Sir Thomas More*

9 'By god's body, master More, *Indignatio principis mors est* [The anger of the sovereign is death].' 'Is that all, my Lord?' quoth he [to the Duke of Norfolk]. 'Then in good faith is there no more difference between your grace and me, but that I shall die to-day, and you to-morrow.'

William Roper *Life of Sir Thomas More*

10 Is not this house [the Tower of London] as nigh heaven as my own?

William Roper *Life of Sir Thomas More*

11 I pray you, master Lieutenant, see me safe up, and my coming down let me shift for my self.
on mounting the scaffold

William Roper *Life of Sir Thomas More*

Rhodri Morgan 1939–
British Labour politician

1 I thought you were the original professor of rotational medicine.

to Bernard Ingham, who was appearing before the Commons public administration select committee

in *Mail on Sunday* 7 June 1998 'Quotes of the Week'

2 Nice try, but no deal.

on his party's suggestion that he should stand as deputy to Alun Michael as leader of the new Welsh assembly

in *Mirror* 6 November 1998

3 We cannot allow the culling of First Secretaries to become Wales's own annual blood sport. My number one target as First Secretary is to survive until the half-term recess at the end of this week.

on succeeding Alun Michael as First Secretary for Wales

in *Observer* 20 February 2000 'They Said What . . . ?'

John Morley 1838–1923
British Liberal politician and writer

4 The golden Gospel of Silence is effectively compressed in thirty fine volumes.

on Carlyle's History of Frederick the Great *(1858–65), Carlyle having written of his subject as 'that strong, silent man'*

Critical Miscellanies (1886) 'Carlyle'

5 Simplicity of character is no hindrance to subtlety of intellect.

Life of Gladstone (1903)

6 You have not converted a man, because you have silenced him.

On Compromise (1874)

of parliamentary life:

7 Having the singular peculiarity of being neither business nor rest.

Recollections (1917) vol. 1

8 The proper memory for a politician is one that knows what to remember and what to forget.

Recollections (1917)

9 Although in Cabinet all its members stand on an equal footing, speak with equal voices and, on the rare occasions when a division is taken, are counted on the fraternal principle of one man, one vote, yet the head of the Cabinet is *primus inter pares,* and occupies a position which, so long as it lasts, is one of exceptional and peculiar authority.

Walpole (1889)

William Morris 1834–96
English writer, artist, and designer

10 What is this, the sound and rumour? What is this that all men hear,
Like the wind in hollow valleys when the storm is drawing near,
Like the rolling on of ocean in the eventide of fear?
'Tis the people marching on.

Chants for Socialists (1885) 'The March of the Workers'

Herbert Morrison 1888–1965
British Labour politician

11 Work is the call. Work at war speed. Good-night—and go to it.

broadcast as Minister of Supply, 22 May 1940

Dwight D. Morrow 1873–1931
American lawyer, banker, and diplomat

1 Any party which takes credit for the rain must not be surprised if its opponents blame it for the drought.

attributed; William Safire *Safire's New Political Dictionary* (1993)

Owen Morshead 1893–1977
English Royal Librarian

2 The House of Hanover, like ducks, produce bad parents— they trample on their young.
*in conversation with Harold **Nicolson**, biographer of **George V***

Harold Nicolson, letter to Vita Sackville-West, 7 January 1949

Rogers Morton 1914–79
American public relations officer

3 I'm not going to rearrange the furniture on the deck of the Titanic.
*having lost five of the last six primaries as President **Ford**'s campaign manager*

in *Washington Post* 16 May 1976

Oswald Mosley 1896–1980
English politician and Fascist leader
on Mosley: see **Attlee** 16:5

4 I am not, and never have been, a man of the right. My position was on the left and is now in the centre of politics.

letter to *The Times* 26 April 1968

John Lothrop Motley 1814–77
American historian

5 As long as he lived, he was the guiding-star of a whole brave nation, and when he died the little children cried in the streets.
of William the Silent, Prince of Orange (1533–84)

The Rise of the Dutch Republic (1856); see **Auden** 17:12

■ Mottoes *see box overleaf*

Lord Mountbatten 1900–79
British sailor, soldier, and statesman

6 Right, now I understand people think you're the Forgotten Army on the Forgotten Front. I've come here to tell you you're quite wrong. You're not the Forgotten Army on the Forgotten Front. No, make no mistake about it. Nobody's ever *heard* of you.
encouragement to troops when taking over as Supreme Allied Commander South-East Asia in late 1943

R. Hough *Mountbatten* (1980)

7 The nuclear arms race has no military purpose. Wars cannot be fought with nuclear weapons. Their existence only adds to our perils.

speech at Strasbourg, 11 May 1979

Marjorie ('Mo') Mowlam 1949–
British Labour politician

8 It takes courage to push things forward.
on her decision to visit Loyalist prisoners in The Maze

in *Guardian* 8 January 1998

9 You can't switch on peace like a light.

in *Independent* 6 September 1999

continued

Mottoes

1 *Aut Caesar, aut nihil.*
Caesar or nothing.

motto inscribed on the sword of Cesare Borgia (1476–1507)

2 The buck stops here.

motto on the desk of Harry S **Truman**

3 *Fiat justitia et pereat mundus.*
Let justice be done, though the world perish.

motto of Ferdinand I (1503–64), Holy Roman Emperor; Johannes Manlius *Locorum Communium Collectanea* (1563) vol. 2 'De Lege: Octatum Praeceptum'; see **Adams** 4:3, **Watson** 375:11

4 *Honi soit qui mal y pense.*
Evil be to him who evil thinks.

motto of the Order of the Garter, originated by Edward III (1312–77), probably on 23 April of 1348 or 1349

5 *Nemo me impune lacessit.*
No one provokes me with impunity.

motto of the Crown of Scotland and of all Scottish regiments

6 Rebellion to tyrants is obedience to God.

motto of Thomas **Jefferson**, from John **Bradshaw**; see **Bradshaw** 50:2

7 *Semper eadem.*
Ever the same.

motto of **Elizabeth I**

8 *Sic semper tyrannis.*
Thus always to tyrants.

motto of the State of Virginia; see **Booth** 48:2

Marjorie ('Mo') Mowlam *continued*

9 Ian Paisley said he pitied my husband having to put up with 'the sinner', which is what he often called me.

in *Sunday Times* 16 April 2000

Daniel P. Moynihan 1927–

American Democratic politician

10 Welfare became a term of opprobrium—a contentious, often vindictive area of political conflict in which liberals and conservatives clashed and children were lost sight of.

in *The Washington Post* 25 November 1994

Robert Mugabe 1924–

Zimbabwean statesman; Prime Minister of Zimbabwe, 1980–7, President since 1987

11 Cricket civilizes people and creates good gentlemen. I want everyone to play cricket in Zimbabwe; I want ours to be a nation of gentlemen.

in *Sunday Times* 26 February 1984

12 Our present state of mind is that you are now our enemies.
  to white farmers in Zimbabwe

television broadcast, 18 April 2000

Malcolm Muggeridge 1903–90
British journalist

1 To succeed pre-eminently in English public life it is necessary to conform either to the popular image of a bookie or of a clergyman; Churchill being a perfect example of the former, Halifax of the latter.

The Infernal Grove (1973)

2 He was not only a bore; he bored for England.
of Anthony **Eden**

Tread Softly (1966)

Rupert Murdoch 1931–
Australian-born American publisher and media entrepreneur

3 I have heard cynics who say he's a very political old monk shuffling around in Gucci shoes.
on the Dalai Lama

in *Daily Telegraph* 7 September 1999

Ed Murrow 1908–65
American broadcaster and journalist

4 I admired your history, doubted your future.
of Britain in the 1930s

radio broadcast; in *Listener* 28 February 1946

5 Future generations who bother to read the official record of proceedings in the House of Commons will discover that British armies retreated from many places, but that there was no retreat from the principles for which your ancestors fought.

radio broadcast; in *Listener* 28 February 1946

6 No one can terrorize a whole nation, unless we are all his accomplices.
of Joseph **McCarthy**

'See It Now', broadcast, 7 March 1954

of **Winston Churchill**:
7 He mobilized the English language and sent it into battle to steady his fellow countrymen and hearten those Europeans upon whom the long dark night of tyranny had descended.

broadcast, 30 November 1954; *In Search of Light* (1967)

8 When the politicians complain that TV turns their proceedings into a circus, it should be made plain that the circus was already there, and that TV has merely demonstrated that not all the performers are well trained.

attributed, 1959

9 Anyone who isn't confused doesn't really understand the situation.
on the Vietnam War

Walter Bryan *The Improbable Irish* (1969)

Benito Mussolini 1883–1945
Italian Fascist statesman, Prime Minister 1922–43

10 We must leave exactly on time . . . From now on everything must function to perfection.
to a stationmaster

Giorgio Pini *Mussolini* (1939) vol. 2

Sarojini Naidu 1879–1949
Indian politician

11 If only Bapu [Gandhi] knew the cost of setting him up in poverty!

A. Campbell-Johnson *Mission with Mountbatten* (1951)

Tom Nairn
Scottish writer

1 As far as I am concerned, Scotland will be reborn when the last minister is strangled with the last copy of the *Sunday Post*.

'The Dreams of Scottish Nationalism'; Karl Miller (ed.) *Memoirs of a Modern Scotland* (1970); see **Meslier** 249:2

Lewis Namier 1888–1960
Polish-born British historian

2 What matters most about political ideas is the underlying emotions, the music, to which ideas are a mere libretto, often of very inferior quality.

Personalities and Powers (1955)

3 No number of atrocities however horrible can deprive a nation of its right to independence, nor justify its being put under the heel of its worst enemies and persecutors.

in 1919; Julia Namier *Lewis Namier* (1971)

Napoleon I 1769–1821 ✓
Emperor of France, 1804–15

4 Think of it, soldiers; from the summit of these pyramids, forty centuries look down upon you.
   speech to the Army of Egypt on 21 July 1798, before the Battle of the Pyramids

Gaspard Gourgaud *Mémoires* (1823) vol. 2 'Égypte—Bataille des Pyramides'

5 It [the Channel] is a mere ditch, and will be crossed as soon as someone has the courage to attempt it.

letter to Consul Cambacérès, 16 November 1803

6 A prince who gets a reputation for good nature in the first year of his reign, is laughed at in the second.

letter to the King of Holland, 4 April 1807

7 It is easier to put up with unpleasantness from a man of one's own way of thinking than from one who takes an entirely different point of view.

letter to J. Finckenstein, 14 April 1807

8 I want the whole of Europe to have one currency; it will make trading much easier.

letter to his brother Louis, 6 May 1807

9 It is a matter of great interest what sovereigns are doing; but as to what Grand Duchesses are doing—Who cares?

letter 17 December 1811

10 There is only one step from the sublime to the ridiculous.
   to De Pradt, Polish ambassador, after the retreat from Moscow in 1812

D. G. De Pradt *Histoire de l'Ambassade dans le grand-duché de Varsovie en 1812* (1815)

11 As to moral courage, I have very rarely met with two o'clock in the morning courage: I mean instantaneous courage.

E. A. de Las Cases *Mémorial de Ste-Hélène* (1823) vol. 1, 4–5 December 1815

12 An army marches on its stomach.

attributed, but probably condensed from a long passage in E. A. de Las Cases *Mémorial de Ste-Hélène* (1823) vol. 4, 14 November 1816; also attributed to **Frederick the Great**

   when asked how to deal with the Pope:
13 As though he had 200,000 men.

J. M. Robinson *Cardinal Consalvi* (1987)

14 The career open to the talents.

Barry E. O'Meara *Napoleon in Exile* (1822) vol. 1

1 England is a nation of shopkeepers.

Barry E. O'Meara *Napoleon in Exile* (1822) vol. 2; see **Adams** 4:7, **Smith** 333:8

2 Nothing is more contrary to the organization of the mind, of the memory, and of the imagination . . . The new system of weights and measures will be a stumbling block and the source of difficulties for several generations . . . It's just tormenting the people with trivia!!!
   on the introduction of the metric system

Mémoires . . . écrits à Ste-Hélène (1823–5)

3 Not tonight, Josephine.

attributed, but probably apocryphal; R. H. Horne *The History of Napoleon* (1841) vol. 2 describes the circumstances in which the affront may have occurred

*of **Talleyrand**:*
4 A pile of shit in a silk stocking.

attributed

Jawaharlal Nehru 1889–1964

Indian statesman, Prime Minister 1947–64

5 At the stroke of the midnight hour, while the world sleeps, India will awake to life and freedom.
   immediately prior to Independence

speech to the Indian Constituent Assembly, 14 August 1947

6 The light has gone out of our lives and there is darkness everywhere.
   *broadcast, 30 January 1948, following **Gandhi**'s assassination*

Richard J. Walsh *Nehru on Gandhi* (1948)

7 I may lose many things including my temper, but I do not lose my nerve.

at a press conference in Delhi, 4 June 1958

8 Democracy and socialism are means to an end, not the end itself.

'Basic Approach'; written for private circulation and reprinted in Vincent Shean *Nehru: the Years of Power* (1960)

9 Normally speaking, it may be said that the forces of a capitalist society, if left unchecked, tend to make the rich richer and the poor poorer and thus increase the gap between them.

'Basic Approach' in Vincent Shean *Nehru . . .* (1960)

10 History is almost always written by the victors and conquerors and gives their viewpoint.

The Discovery of India (1946)

11 There is no easy walk-over to freedom anywhere, and many of us will have to pass through the valley of the shadow again and again before we reach the mountain-tops of our desire.

'From Lucknow to Tripuri' (1939)

12 After every other Viceroy has been forgotten, Curzon will be remembered because he restored all that was beautiful in India.
   in conversation with Lord Swinton

Kenneth Rose *Superior Person* (1969)

13 I shall be the last Englishman to rule in India.

J. K. Galbraith *A Life in Our Times* (1981)

Allan Nevins 1890–1971
American historian

1 The former Allies had blundered in the past by offering Germany too little, and offering even that too late, until finally Nazi Germany had become a menace to all mankind.

in Current History (New York) May 1935

■ Newspaper headlines and leaders
see box opposite

Huey Newton 1942–
American political activist

2 I suggested [in 1966] that we use the panther as our symbol and call our political vehicle the Black Panther Party. The panther is a fierce animal, but he will not attack until he is backed into a corner; then he will strike out.

Revolutionary Suicide (1973)

Nicholas I 1796–1855
Russian emperor from 1825

3 Turkey is a dying man. We may endeavour to keep him alive, but we shall not succeed. He will, he must die.
origin of the expression 'the sick man of Europe' referring to Ottoman Turkey

F. Max Müller (ed.) Memoirs of Baron Stockmar (1873)

4 Russia has two generals in whom she can confide— Generals Janvier [January] and Février [February].

attributed; in Punch 10 March 1855

Nicias c.470–413 BC
Athenian politician and general

5 For a city consists in men, and not in walls nor in ships empty of men.
speech to the defeated Athenian army at Syracuse, 413 BC

Thucydides History of the Peloponnesian Wars

Harold Nicolson 1886–1968
English diplomat, politician, and writer; father of Nigel **Nicolson**

6 Ponderous and uncertain is that relation between pressure and resistance which constitutes the balance of power. The arch of peace is morticed by no iron tendons . . . One night a handful of dust will patter from the vaulting: the bats will squeak and wheel in sudden panic: nor can the fragile fingers of man then stay the rush and rumble of destruction.

Public Faces (1932)

7 We shall have to walk and live a Woolworth life hereafter.
anticipating the aftermath of the Second World War

diary, 4 June 1941

8 I am haunted by mental decay such as I saw creeping over Ramsay MacDonald. A gradual dimming of the lights.

diary, 28 April 1947

*comparing **Attlee** as a public speaker with Winston **Churchill**:*
9 Like a village fiddler after Paganini.

diary, 10 November 1947

10 I do not think it is quite fair to say that the British businessman has trampled on the faces of the poor. But he has sometimes not been very careful where he put his feet.
replying to a heckler in the North Croydon by-election, 1948

Nigel Nicolson (ed.) Diaries and Letters of Harold Nicolson 1945–1962 vol. 3 (1968)

continued

Newspaper headlines and leaders

1 Crisis? What crisis?
*summarizing an interview with James **Callaghan***

headline in *Sun*, 11 January 1979; see **Misquotations** 254:4

2 Dewey defeats Truman.
*anticipating the result of the Presidential election, which **Truman** won against expectation*

in *Chicago Tribune* 3 November 1948

3 GOTCHA!
on the sinking of the General Belgrano

headline in *Sun* 4 May 1982

4 Go West, young man, go West!

editorial in *Terre Haute* [Indiana] *Express* (1851), by John L. B. Soule (1815–91)

5 If Kinnock wins today will the last person to leave Britain please turn out the lights.
on election day, showing Neil Kinnock's head inside a light bulb

headline in *Sun* 9 April 1992

6 Is THIS the most dangerous man in Britain?
*headline beside a picture of Tony **Blair**, attacking his perceived sympathy for the euro*

in *The Sun* 25 June 1998

7 It *is* a moral issue.
leader following the resignation of Profumo

in *The Times* 11 June 1963, written by William Haley (1901–87)

8 It's that man again . . . ! At the head of a cavalcade of seven black motor cars Hitler swept out of his Berlin Chancellery last night on a mystery journey.

headline in *Daily Express* 2 May 1939; the acronym ITMA became the title of a BBC radio show, from September 1939

9 It's The Sun wot won it.
following the 1992 general election

headline in *Sun* 11 April 1992

10 King's Moll Reno'd in Wolsey's Home Town.
US newspaper headline on the divorce proceedings of Wallis Simpson (later Duchess of Windsor) in Ipswich

Frances Donaldson *Edward VIII* (1974)

11 Most Conservatives, and almost certainly some of the wiser Trade Union leaders, are waiting to feel the *smack of firm government.*
on the government of Anthony Eden

editorial comment in *Sunday Telegraph* 3 January 1956, written by Donald McLachlan

12 Only a sentence, but what a sentence!
on Prince Charles' speech referring to the Falklands

in *La Nación* (Buenos Aires) 11 March 1999

13 Outside the G.O.P.'s big tent, hoping he's let back in.
of the former Republican Robert C. Smith, whose independent campaign for the presidential nomination had failed; G.O.P. = 'Grand Old Party'

headline in *New York Times* 1 November 1999; see **Slogans** 334:7

14 Splendid isolation.

headline in *The Times* 22 January 1896, referring to George **Foster**'s speech in the Canadian House of Commons; see **Foster** 135:3

15 The Sun backs Blair.
the day after the announcement of the general election

headline in *Sun* 18 March 1997

Newspaper headlines and leaders *continued*

1 Unless the people—the people everywhere—come forward and petition, ay, thunder for reform.
   leader on the Reform Bill, possibly written by Edward Sterling (1773–1847), resulting in the nickname 'The Thunderer'

in *The Times* 29 January 1831; the phrase 'we thundered out' had been used earlier, 11 February 1829

2 Wall St. lays an egg.

crash headline, *Variety* 30 October 1929

3 We shall not pretend that there is nothing in his long career which those who respect and admire him would wish otherwise.
   on Edward VII's accession to the throne

in *The Times* 23 January 1901, leading article

4 Whose finger do you want on the trigger?
   headline alluding to the atom bomb, apropos the failure of both the Labour and Conservative parties to purge their leaders of proven failures

in *Daily Mirror* 21 September 1951

5 Winter of discontent.

headline in *Sun* 30 April 1979; see below; see **Callaghan** 66:2

   Now is the winter of our discontent
   Made glorious summer by this sun of York.

William Shakespeare (1564–1616) *Richard III* (1591)

Harold Nicolson *continued*

6 For seventeen years he did nothing at all but kill animals and stick in stamps.
   of **George V** *as a subject for biography*

letter to Vita Sackville-West, 17 August 1949

7 Suez—a smash and grab raid that was all smash and no grab.

in conversation with Antony Jay, November 1956; see also letter to Vita Sackville-West, 8 November 1956, 'Our smash-and-grab raid got stuck at the smash'

Nigel Nicolson 1917–

British Conservative politician and writer; son of Harold **Nicolson**

8 There is no place where a man can occupy himself more intensively or usefully, and no place where he can hold down his job by doing so little.
   of the House of Commons

People and Parliament (1958)

9 One final tip to rebels: always have a second profession in reserve.
   reflecting on the vote on the Maastricht Treaty in the House of Commons, in the light of having abstained from voting with the Government on the Suez Crisis in 1956 and subsequently lost his seat

in *The Spectator* 7 November 1992

Reinhold Niebuhr 1892–1971

American theologian

10 Man's capacity for justice makes democracy possible, but man's inclination to injustice makes democracy necessary.

Children of Light and Children of Darkness (1944) foreword

Martin Niemöller 1892-1984
German theologian

1 When Hitler attacked the Jews I was not a Jew, therefore, I
was not concerned. And when Hitler attacked the Catholics,
I was not a Catholic, and therefore, I was not concerned.
And when Hitler attacked the unions and the industrialists,
I was not a member of the unions and I was not concerned.
Then, Hitler attacked me and the Protestant church—and
there was nobody left to be concerned.
> *often quoted in the form 'In Germany they came first for the*
> *Communists, and I didn't speak up because I wasn't a Communist*
> *. . .' and so on*

in Congressional Record 14 October 1968

Friedrich Nietzsche 1844-1900 ✓
German philosopher and writer

2 I teach you the superman. Man is something to be
surpassed.

Also Sprach Zarathustra (1883) prologue

3 Morality is the herd-instinct in the individual.

Die fröhliche Wissenschaft (1882)

4 Master-morality and slave-morality.

Jenseits von Gut und Böse (1886)

5 At the base of all these aristocratic races the predator is not
to be mistaken, the splendorous *blond beast*, avidly rampant
for plunder and victory.

Zur Genealogie der Moral (1887)

Richard Milhous Nixon 1913-94 ✓
American Republican statesman, 37th President of the US
1969–74; re-elected for a second term in November 1972, it soon
became clear that he was implicated in the Watergate scandal,
and in 1974 he became the first President to resign from office
on Nixon: see **Abzug** 1:2, **Anonymous** 8:3, **Conable** 93:6,
Johnson 189:3, **Roosevelt** 305:2, **Stevenson** 347:13, **Ziegler**
391:3

6 Pat and I have the satisfaction that every dime that we've
got is honestly ours . . . Pat doesn't have a mink coat. But
she does have a respectable Republican cloth coat. And I
always tell her that she'd look good in anything.
> *having been elected as Vice-President in 1952, in response to*
> *criticisms of his electoral campaign*

speech on television, 23 September 1952

of the post-election gift of a cocker spaniel, named Checkers by his
small daughter:

7 One other thing I probably should tell you, because if I don't
they'll probably be saying this about me too, we did get
something—a gift—after the election . . . It was a little
cocker-spaniel dog . . . The kids love that dog and I just
want to say this right now, that regardless of what they say
about it, we're going to keep it.

speech on television, 23 September 1952

8 There is no such thing as a nonpolitical speech by a
politician.

address to Radio-Television Executives Society, New York City, 14 September 1955

9 You won't have Nixon to kick around any more.
> *at a press conference after losing the election for Governor of*
> *California, 5 November 1962*

in New York Times 8 November 1962

1 There is nothing wrong with this country which a good election can't fix.
   at a campaign meeting during the Presidential election

in Syracuse, New York, 29 October 1968

2 Let us begin by committing ourselves to the truth, to see it like it is and tell it like it is, to find the truth, to speak the truth and to live the truth. That's what we will do.
   nomination acceptance speech in Miami, 1968

in *New York Times* 9 August 1968

3 This is the greatest week in the history of the world since the Creation.
   welcoming the return of the first men to land on the moon

speech, 24 July 1969

4 The great silent majority.

broadcast, 3 November 1969

5 In our own lives, let each of us ask—not just what government will do for me, but what can I do for myself?

second inaugural address, 20 January 1973

6 There can be no whitewash at the White House.

television speech on Watergate, 30 April 1973

7 I made my mistakes, but in all my years of public life, I have never profited, never profited from public service. I've earned every cent. And in all of my years in public life I have never obstructed justice . . . I welcome this kind of examination because people have got to know whether or not their President is a crook. Well, I'm not a crook.

speech at press conference, 17 November 1973

8 This country needs good farmers, good businessmen, good plumbers, good carpenters.
   farewell address at White House, 9 August 1974

in *New York Times* 10 August 1974

9 My own view is that taping of conversations for historical purposes was a bad decision.

attributed, 1974

10 I brought myself down. I gave them a sword. And they stuck it in.

television interview, 19 May 1977; David Frost *I Gave Them a Sword* (1978)

11 Foreign aid is the most unpopular damn thing in the world. It is a loser politically.

in *Observer* 21 April 1985 'Sayings of the Week'

12 I played by the rules of politics as I found them. Not taking a higher road than my predecessors and my adversaries was my central mistake.

In the Arena (1990)

13 Defeat doesn't finish a man—quit does. A man is not finished when he's defeated. He's finished when he quits.
   on Edward Kennedy and Chappaquiddick

William Safire *Before the Fall* (1975)

14 When the President does it, that means that it is not illegal.

in conversation; David Frost *I Gave Them a Sword* (1978)

Kwame Nkrumah 1900–72

Ghanaian statesman, Prime Minister 1957–60, President 1960–6

15 Freedom is not something that one people can bestow on another as a gift. They claim it as their own and none can keep it from them.

speech in Accra, 10 July 1953

16 We face neither East nor West: we face forward.

conference speech, Accra, 7 April 1960; *Axioms of Kwame Nkrumah* (1967)

Peggy Noonan 1950–
American writer, speechwriter for Ronald Reagan

1 The battle for the mind of Ronald Reagan was like the trench warfare of World War I. Never have so many fought so hard for such barren terrain.

What I Saw at the Revolution (1990)

Steven Norris 1945–
British Conservative politician

2 You have your own company, your own temperature control, your own music—and don't have to put up with dreadful human beings sitting alongside you.
   on cars compared to public transport

comment to Commons Environment Select Committee, in *Daily Telegraph* 9 February 1995

Christopher North 1785–1854
Scottish literary critic

3 His Majesty's dominions, on which the sun never sets.

in *Blackwood's Magazine* (April 1829) 'Noctes Ambrosianae'

4 Laws were made to be broken.

in *Blackwood's Magazine* (May 1830) 'Noctes Ambrosianae'

5 I cannot sit still, James, and hear you abuse the shopocracy.

in *Blackwood's Magazine* (February 1835) 'Noctes Ambrosianae'

Lord North 1732–92
British statesman and Prime Minister

6 His Majesty has thought proper to order a new Commission of the Treasury to be made out, in which I do not see your name.

letter dismissing Charles James **Fox** from office, 1774

7 Oh God! It is all over!
   on receiving the news of Cornwallis's surrender at Yorktown, 19 October 1781

in *Dictionary of National Biography* (1917–)

Lord Northcliffe 1865–1922
British newspaper proprietor

8 The power of the press is very great, but not so great as the power of suppress.
   office message, Daily Mail *1918*

Reginald Rose and Geoffrey Harmsworth *Northcliffe* (1959)

9 When I want a peerage, I shall buy it like an honest man.

Tom Driberg *Swaff* (1974)

Sam Nunn 1938–
American Democratic politician

10 Don't ask, don't tell.
   summary of the **Clinton** *administration's compromise policy on homosexuals serving in the armed forces*

in *New York Times* 12 May 1993

Julius Nyerere 1922–99
Tanzanian statesman, President of Tanganyika 1962–4 and of Tanzania 1964–85

11 Should we really let our people starve so we can pay our debts?

in *Guardian* 21 March 1985

1 We are a poor country and we opted for socialist policies, but to build a socialist society you have to have a developed society.

in *Observer* 28 July 1985 'Sayings of the Week'

Michael Oakeshott 1901–91

British academic

2 A plan to resist all planning may be better than its opposite, but it belongs to the same style of politics.
   of **Hayek**'s The Road to Serfdom

Rationalism in Politics (1962)

Conor Cruise O'Brien 1917–

Irish politician, writer, and journalist

3 The strength of these men was that each of them could look a Pearsean ghost in the eye . . . Each of them, in their youth, had done the thing the ghost asked them to do, in 1916 or 1919—21 or both. That was it; from now on they would do what seemed reasonable to themselves in the interests of the actual people inhabiting the island of Ireland and not of a personified abstraction, or of a disembodied voice, or of a ghost.
   of Sean Lemass (1899–1971) and other senior Irish politicians in the 1960s; see **Pearse** 285:2

Ancestral Voices (1994)

4 The first great act of intellectual resistance to the first great experiment in totalitarian innovation.
   of **Burke**'s *writings on the French Revolution*

The Great Melody (1992)

5 If I saw Mr Haughey buried at midnight at a crossroads, with a stake driven through his heart—politically speaking—I should continue to wear a clove of garlic round my neck, just in case.

in *Observer* 10 October 1982

Daniel O'Connell 1775–1847

Irish nationalist leader and social reformer, elected to Parliament in 1828

6 I shall be as brief as I can upon this subject, for it is quite clear, that no man ever yet rose to address a more unwilling audience.
   introducing a motion for the Repeal of the Union

speech in the House of Commons, 22 April 1834

7 A NATION is starving.

in 1846; Charles Chevenix Trench *The Great Dan* (1984)

8 He speaks of '98! Their struggle was of blood and defeated in blood. The means they adopted weakened Ireland and enabled England to carry the Union.
   in a debate with the Young Irelander, John **Mitchel**, *13 July 1846*

Charles Chevenix Trench *The Great Dan* (1984)

9 I have given my advice to my countrymen, and whenever I feel it necessary I shall continue to do so, careless whether it pleases or displeases this house or any mad person out of it.

in *Dictionary of National Biography* (1917–)

10 There is a moral electricity in the continuous expression of public opinion concentrated on a single point.

R. F. Foster *Modern Ireland* (1988)

Bernard O'Donoghue 1945–

Irish poet and academic

1 We were terribly lucky to catch
The Ceauşescus' execution, being
By sheer chance that Christmas Day
In the only house for twenty miles
With satellite TV. We sat,
Cradling brandies, by the fire
Watching those two small, cranky autocrats
Lying in snow against a blood-spattered wall,
Hardly able to believe our good fortune.

'Carolling' (1995)

2 The reporter told us how
The cross woman's peasant origins
Came out at the last, shouting
At her executioners 'I have been
A mother to you and this is how
You thank me for it.'

'Carolling' (1995)

Jeremiah O'Donovan Rossa 1831–1915

Irish nationalist

3 I don't believe the Saxon will ever relax his grip except by
the persuasion of cold lead and steel.

Robert Kee *The Bold Fenian Men*
(1989)

■ Official advice *see box overleaf*

James Ogilvy, Lord Seafield 1664–1730

Lord Chancellor of Scotland

4 Now there's ane end of ane old song.
as he signed the engrossed exemplification of the Act of Union,
1706

in *The Lockhart Papers* (1817)

Kevin O'Higgins 1892–1927

Irish nationalist politician

5 We had an opportunity of building up a worthy State that
would attract and, in time, absorb and assimilate the
[Unionist] elements. We preferred to burn our own houses,
blow up our own bridges, rob our own banks . . . Generally
we preferred to practise upon ourselves worse iniquities
than the British had practised on us since Cromwell and
Mountjoy, and now we wonder why the Orangemen are not
hopping like so many fleas across the Border in their anxiety
to come within our fold.

Robert Kee *The Green Flag* (1972)

Abraham Okpik

Canadian Inuit spokesman

6 There are very few Eskimos, but millions of Whites, just like
mosquitoes. It is something very special and wonderful to be
an Eskimo—they are like the snow geese. If an Eskimo
forgets his language and Eskimo ways, he will be nothing
but just another mosquito.

attributed, 1966

Official advice

1 Careless talk costs lives.	Second World War security poster
2 Dig for Victory.	Second World War slogan; see below:
Let 'Dig for Victory' be the motto of every one with a garden and of every able-bodied man and woman capable of digging an allotment in their spare time.	Reginald Dorman-Smith (1899–1977) radio broadcast, 3 October 1939, in *The Times* 4 October 1939
3 Don't die of ignorance.	Aids publicity campaign, 1987
4 Is your journey *really* necessary?	slogan coined to discourage Civil Servants from going home for Christmas, 1939
5 Make do and mend.	wartime slogan, 1940s
6 Smoking can seriously damage your health. *government health warning now required by British law to be printed on cigarette packets*	from early 1970s, in form 'Smoking can damage your health'
7 *Taisez-vous! Méfiez-vous! Les oreilles ennemies vous écoutent.* Keep your mouth shut! Be on your guard! Enemy ears are listening to you.	official notice in France, 1915

Jacqueline Kennedy Onassis 1929–94

wife of John Fitzgerald **Kennedy**, First Lady of the US 1961–3

8 The one thing I do not want to be called is First Lady. It sounds like a saddle horse.

Peter Colier and David Horowitz *The Kennedys* (1984)

9 There'll be great Presidents again—and the Johnsons are wonderful, they've been wonderful to me—but there'll never be another Camelot again.

in *Life* 6 December 1963; see **Lerner** 216:3

Thomas ('Tip') O'Neill 1912–94

American Democratic politician; Speaker of the House of Representatives 1977–87

10 All politics is local.

in *New York Review of Books* 13 March 1989

Lord Onslow 1938–

British peer

11 I will be sad if I either look up or down after my death and don't see my son fast asleep on the same benches on which I have slept.

in *Times* 31 October 1998 'Quotes of the Week'

J. Robert Oppenheimer 1904–67

American physicist

12 I remembered the line from the Hindu scripture, the *Bhagavad Gita* . . . 'I am become death, the destroyer of worlds.'
on the explosion of the first atomic bomb near Alamogordo, New Mexico, 16 July 1945

Len Giovannitti and Fred Freed *The Decision to Drop the Bomb* (1965)

1 When you see something that is technically sweet, you go ahead and do it and you argue about what to do about it only after you have had your technical success. That is the way it was with the atomic bomb.

in In the Matter of J. Robert Oppenheimer, USAEC Transcript of Hearing Before Personnel Security Board (1954)

P. J. O'Rourke 1947–
American humorous writer and journalist

2 Giving money and power to government is like giving whisky and car keys to teenage boys.

Parliament of Whores (1991)

3 Whatever it is that the government does, sensible Americans would prefer that the government does it to somebody else. This is the idea behind foreign policy.

Parliament of Whores (1991)

4 Every government is a parliament of whores. The trouble is, in a democracy the whores are us.

Parliament of Whores (1991)

George Orwell 1903–50
English novelist

5 Man is the only creature that consumes without producing.

Animal Farm (1945)

6 Four legs good, two legs bad.

Animal Farm (1945)

7 All animals are equal but some animals are more equal than others.

Animal Farm (1945)

8 Down here it was still the England I had known in my childhood: the railway cuttings smothered in wild flowers . . . the red buses, the blue policemen—all sleeping the deep, deep sleep of England, from which I sometimes fear that we shall never wake till we are jerked out of it by the roar of bombs.

Homage to Catalonia (1938)

9 Most revolutionaries are potential Tories, because they imagine that everything can be put right by altering the *shape* of society; once that change is effected, as it sometimes is, they see no need for any other.

Inside the Whale (1940) 'Charles Dickens'

10 England . . . resembles a family, a rather stuffy Victorian family, with not many black sheep in it but with all its cupboards bursting with skeletons. It has rich relations who have to be kowtowed to and poor relations who are horribly sat upon, and there is a deep conspiracy of silence about the source of the family income. It is a family in which the young are generally thwarted and most of the power is in the hands of irresponsible uncles and bed-ridden aunts. Still, it is a family. It has its private language and its common memories, and at the approach of an enemy it closes its ranks. A family with the wrong members in control.

The Lion and the Unicorn (1941) pt. 1 'England Your England'

11 Probably the battle of Waterloo *was* won on the playing-fields of Eton, but the opening battles of all subsequent wars have been lost there.

The Lion and the Unicorn (1941) pt. 1 'England Your England'; see **Wellington** 379:11

12 Old maids biking to Holy Communion through the mists of the autumn mornings . . . these are not only fragments, but *characteristic* fragments, of the English scene.

The Lion and the Unicorn (1941) pt. 1 'England Your England'; see **Major** 239:2

13 BIG BROTHER IS WATCHING YOU.

Nineteen Eighty-Four (1949)

14 War is peace. Freedom is slavery. Ignorance is strength.

Nineteen Eighty-Four (1949)

1 Who controls the past controls the future: who controls the present controls the past.

Nineteen Eighty-Four (1949)

2 Don't you see that the whole aim of Newspeak is to narrow the range of thought? In the end we shall make thoughtcrime literally impossible, because there will be no words in which to express it.

Nineteen Eighty-Four (1949)

3 Freedom is the freedom to say that two plus two make four. If that is granted, all else follows.

Nineteen Eighty-Four (1949)

4 Syme was not only dead, he was abolished, an un-person.

Nineteen Eighty-Four (1949)

5 *Doublethink* means the power of holding two contradictory beliefs in one's mind simultaneously, and accepting both of them.

Nineteen Eighty-Four (1949)

6 Power is not a means, it is an end. One does not establish a dictatorship in order to safeguard a revolution; one makes the revolution in order to establish the dictatorship.

Nineteen Eighty-Four (1949)

7 If you want a picture of the future, imagine a boot stamping on a human face—for ever.

Nineteen Eighty-Four (1949)

8 In a Lancashire cotton-town you could probably go for months on end without once hearing an 'educated' accent, whereas there can hardly be a town in the South of England where you could throw a brick without hitting the niece of a bishop.

The Road to Wigan Pier (1937)

9 The typical Socialist is . . . a prim little man with a white-collar job, usually a secret teetotaller and often with vegetarian leanings, with a history of Nonconformity behind him, and, above all, with a social position which he has no intention of forfeiting.

The Road to Wigan Pier (1937)

10 To the ordinary working man, the sort you would meet in any pub on Saturday night, Socialism does not mean much more than better wages and shorter hours and nobody bossing you about.

The Road to Wigan Pier (1937)

11 We of the sinking middle class . . . may sink without further struggles into the working class where we belong, and probably when we get there it will not be so dreadful as we feared, for, after all, we have nothing to lose but our aitches.

The Road to Wigan Pier (1937)

12 The great enemy of clear language is insincerity. When there is a gap between one's real and one's declared aims, one turns as it were instinctively to long words and exhausted idioms, like a cuttlefish squirting out ink.

Shooting an Elephant (1950)
'Politics and the English Language'

13 In our time, political speech and writing are largely the defence of the indefensible.

Shooting an Elephant (1950)
'Politics and the English Language'

14 Political language . . . is designed to make lies sound truthful and murder respectable, and to give an appearance of solidity to pure wind.

Shooting an Elephant (1950)
'Politics and the English Language'

15 The Catholic and the Communist are alike in assuming that an opponent cannot be both honest and intelligent.

in *Polemic* January 1946 'The Prevention of Literature'

16 The quickest way of ending a war is to lose it.

in *Polemic* May 1946 'Second Thoughts on James Burnham'

John Osborne 1929–94

English playwright

1 There aren't any good, brave causes left. If the big bang does come, and we all get killed off, it won't be in aid of the old-fashioned, grand design. It'll just be for the Brave New-nothing-very-much-thank-you. About as pointless and inglorious as stepping in front of a bus.

Look Back in Anger (1956)

2 Royalty . . . is the gold filling in a mouthful of decay.

'They call it cricket'; T. Maschler (ed.) *Declaration* (1957)

3 This is a letter of hate. It is for you my countrymen, I mean those men of my country who have defiled it. The men with manic fingers leading the sightless, feeble, betrayed body of my country to its death . . . damn you England.

in *Tribune* 18 August 1961

Arthur O'Shaughnessy 1844–81

English poet

4 One man with a dream, at pleasure
Shall go forth and conquer a crown;
And three with a new song's measure
Can trample an empire down.

'Ode' (1874)

5 For each age is a dream that is dying,
Or one that is coming to birth.

'Ode' (1874)

John L. O'Sullivan 1813–95

American journalist and diplomat

6 Understood as a central consolidated power, managing and directing the various general interests of the society, all government is evil, and the parent of evil . . . The best government is that which governs least.

in *United States Magazine and Democratic Review* (1837) introduction; see **Thoreau** 359:8

7 A spirit of hostile interference against us . . . checking the fulfilment of our manifest destiny to overspread the continent allotted by Providence for the free development of our yearly multiplying millions.
   on opposition to the annexation of Texas

in *United States Magazine and Democratic Review* (1845) vol. 17

James Otis 1725–83

American politician

8 Taxation without representation is tyranny.
   watchword (c.1761) of the American Revolution

in *Dictionary of American Biography*

9 Where liberty is, there is my country.

motto used by James Otis; also attributed to Benjamin **Franklin**; see **Paine** 281:1

Ovid 43 BC–AD c.17

Roman poet

10 *Video meliora, proboque;*
   Deteriora sequor.
   I see the better things, and approve; I follow the worse.

Metamorphoses

1 *Teque, rebellatrix, tandem, Germania, magni*   *Tristia*
  Triste caput pedibus supposuisse ducis!

How you, rebellious Germany, laid your wretched head
beneath the feet of the great general.

Robert Owen 1771–1858
Welsh-born socialist and philanthropist

2 All the world is queer save thee and me, and even thou art a   attributed
little queer.
   to his partner W. Allen, on severing business relations at New
   Lanark, 1828

David Owen 1938–
British Social Democratic politician

3 The price of championing human rights is a little   speech, House of Commons, 30
inconsistency at times.   March 1977

4 We are fed up with fudging and mudging, with mush and   speech to his supporters at Labour
slush. We need courage, conviction, and hard work.   Party Conference in Blackpool, 2
   October 1980

Count Oxenstierna 1583–1654
Swedish statesman

5 Dost thou not know, my son, with how little wisdom the   letter to his son, 1648; John
world is governed?   Selden, in *Table Talk* (1689) 'Pope',
   quotes 'a certain Pope' (possibly
   Julius III) saying 'Thou little
   thinkest what *a little foolery*
   governs the whole world!'

William Tyler Page 1868–1942

6 I believe in the United States of America as a government of   *American's Creed* (prize-winning
the people, by the people, for the people, whose just powers   competition entry, 1918) in
are derived from the consent of the governed; a democracy   *Congressional Record* vol. 56
in a republic; a sovereign Nation of many sovereign States;
a perfect Union, one and inseparable, established upon those
principles of freedom, equality, justice, and humanity for
which American patriots sacrificed their lives and fortunes. I
therefore believe it is my duty to my country to love it, to
support its Constitution, to obey its laws, to respect its flag,
and to defend it against all enemies.

Thomas Paine 1737–1809
English political theorist

7 It is necessary to the happiness of man that he be mentally   *The Age of Reason* pt. 1 (1794)
faithful to himself. Infidelity does not consist in believing, or
in disbelieving, it consists in professing to believe what one
does not believe.

8 Though we have been wise enough to shut and lock a door   *Common Sense* (1776)
against absolute Monarchy, we at the same time have been
foolish enough to put the crown in possession of the key.

1 Government, even in its best state, is but a necessary evil; in   *Common Sense* (1776)
   its worst state, an intolerable one. Government, like dress, is
   the badge of lost innocence; the palaces of kings are built
   upon the ruins of the bowers of paradise.

2 Monarchy and succession have laid . . . the world in blood   *Common Sense* (1776)
   and ashes.

3 Of more worth is one honest man to society, and in the sight   *Common Sense* (1776)
   of God, than all the crowned ruffians that ever lived.

4 'Tis not the affair of a city, a county, a province, or a   *Common Sense* (1776)
   kingdom; but of a continent—of at least one eighth part of
   the habitable globe. 'Tis not the concern of a day, a year, or
   an age; posterity are virtually involved in the contest. Now
   is the seed-time of continental union.

5 Any submission to, or dependence on, Great Britain, tends   *Common Sense* (1776)
   directly to involve this continent in European wars and
   quarrels, and set us at variance with nations who would
   otherwise seek our friendship, and against whom we have
   neither anger nor complaint.

   to America:
6 Freedom hath been hunted round the globe. Asia and Africa   *Common Sense* (1776)
   have long expelled her. Europe regards her like a stranger,
   and England hath given her warning to depart. O! receive
   the fugitive, and prepare in time an asylum for mankind.

7 We have it in our power to begin the world over again.   *Common Sense* (1776)

8 As to religion, I hold it to be the indispensable duty of   *Common Sense* (1776)
   government to protect all conscientious professors thereof,
   and I know of no other business which government hath to
   do therewith.

9 These are the times that try men's souls. The summer   *The Crisis* (December 1776)
   soldier and the sunshine patriot will, in this crisis, shrink   introduction
   from the service of their country; but he that stands it *now*,
   deserves the love and thanks of men and women.

10 What we obtain too cheap, we esteem too lightly.   *The Crisis* (December 1776)
    introduction

11 The religion of humanity.   *Letter . . . on the Invasion of England*
    (1804)

12 A total reformation is wanted in England. She wants an   *Letter to the Abbé Raynal* (1782)
    expanded mind—a heart which embraces the universe.
    Instead of shutting herself up in an island, and quarrelling
    with the world, she would derive more lasting happiness,
    and acquire more real riches, by generously mixing with it,
    and bravely saying, I am the enemy of none.

13 As he rose like a rocket, he fell like the stick.   *Letter to the Addressers on the late*
    *on Edmund **Burke**'s losing the parliamentary debate on the French*   *Proclamation* (1792)
    *Revolution to Charles James **Fox***

14 [Edmund Burke] is not affected by the reality of distress   *The Rights of Man* (1791)
    touching his heart, but by the showy resemblance of it
    striking his imagination. He pities the plumage, but forgets
    the dying bird.
    *on **Burke**'s* Reflections on the Revolution in France, *1790*

1 Lay then the axe to the root, and teach governments
humanity. It is their sanguinary punishments which
corrupt mankind.

The Rights of Man (1791)

2 [In France] all that class of equivocal generation, which in
some countries is called *aristocracy*, and in others *nobility*, is
done away, and the peer is exalted into MAN.

The Rights of Man (1791)

3 Titles are but nick-names, and every nick-name is a title.

The Rights of Man (1791)

4 The idea of hereditary legislators is as inconsistent as that of
hereditary judges, or hereditary juries; and as absurd as an
hereditary mathematician, or an hereditary wise man; and
as ridiculous as an hereditary poet laureate.

The Rights of Man (1791)

5 Persecution is not an original feature of *any* religion; but it
is always the strongly marked feature of all law-religions, or
religions established by law.

The Rights of Man (1791)

6 All hereditary government is in its nature tyranny . . . To
inherit a government, is to inherit the people, as if they
were flocks and herds.

The Rights of Man pt. 2 (1792)

7 With respect to the two Houses, of which the English
Parliament is composed, they appear to be effectually
influenced into one, and as a legislature, to have no temper
of its own. The Minister, whoever he at any time may be,
touches it as with an opium wand, and it sleeps obedience.

The Rights of Man pt. 2 (1792)

8 The candidates were not men but principles.

The Rights of Man (1791)

9 What were formerly called revolutions were little more than
a change of persons . . . what we now see in the world, from
the revolutions of America and France, is a renovation of
the natural order of things.

The Rights of Man (1791)

10 The instant formal government is abolished, society begins
to act. A general association takes place, and common
interest produces common security.

The Rights of Man pt. 2 (1792)

of monarchy:
11 I compare it to something kept behind a curtain, about
which there is a great deal of bustle and fuss, and a
wonderful air of seeming solemnity; but when, by any
accident, the curtain happens to be open, and the company
see what it is, they burst into laughter.

The Rights of Man pt. 2 (1792)

12 When, in countries that are called civilized, we see age
going to the workhouse and youth to the gallows,
something must be wrong in the system of government.

The Rights of Man pt. 2 (1792)

13 My country is the world, and my religion is to do good.

The Rights of Man pt. 2 (1792)

14 I do not believe that any two men, on what are called
doctrinal points, think alike who think at all. It is only those
who have not thought that appear to agree.

The Rights of Man pt. 2 (1792)

15 To elect, and to reject, is the prerogative of a free people.

in *National Intelligencer* 29
November 1802

16 When moral principles, rather than persons, are candidates
for power, to vote is to perform a moral duty, and not to
vote is to neglect a duty.

in *Trenton True-American* April 1803

17 A share in two revolutions is living to some purpose.

Eric Foner *Tom Paine and
Revolutionary America* (1976)

1 Where Liberty is not, there is my country.   ·   John Keane *Tom Paine* (1995); see
Otis 277:9

2 When it shall be said in any country in the world, 'My poor   John Keane *Tom Paine* (1995)
are happy; neither ignorance nor distress is to be found
among them; my jails are empty of prisoners, my streets of
beggars; the aged are not in want, the taxes are not
oppressive; the rational world is my friend, because I am the
friend of its happiness': when these things can be said, then
may that country boast of its constitution and its
government.

Ian Paisley 1926–

Northern Irish politician and Presbyterian minister

3 Trusting in the God of our fathers and confident that our   in *Guardian* 21 August 1968
cause is just, we will never surrender our heritage.

4 I will walk on no grave of Ulster's honoured dead to do a   in *Irish Times* 6 December 1997
deal with the IRA or the British government.   'This Week They Said'
speech at the annual conference of the Democratic Unionist Party

5 The mother of all treachery.   in *Times* 16 April 1998
on the Good Friday agreement

6 They have graduated from the devil's school. They have   in *Irish Times* 16 May 1998 'This
destroyed the Act of Union and given the title deeds of Ulster   Week They Said'
to Dublin on a plate.
on those Unionists who support the Belfast Agreement

7 She has become a parrot.   in *Daily Telegraph* 27 May 1998
*on the perceived readiness of the Queen to repeat the views of her
Prime Minister*

Lord Palmerston 1784–1865

British Whig statesman, Prime Minister 1855–8 and 1859–65
see also Last words 212:4

8 We have no eternal allies and we have no perpetual   in the House of Commons, 1
enemies. Our interests are eternal and perpetual, and those   March 1848
interests it is our duty to follow.

9 I therefore fearlessly challenge the verdict which this House   in the House of Commons, 25 June
... is to give ... whether, as the Roman, in days of old, held   1850
himself free from indignity, when he could say *Civis
Romanus sum*; so also a British subject, in whatever land he
may be, shall feel confident that the watchful eye and the
strong arm of England will protect him against injustice and
wrong.
*speech in the debate on the protection afforded to the Greek trader
David Pacifico (1784–1854), who had been born a British
subject at Gibraltar*

10 You may call it combination, you may call it the accidental   in the House of Commons, 5
and fortuitous concurrence of atoms.   March 1857
*on a projected coalition with **Disraeli***

11 The function of a government is to calm, rather than to   P. Guedalla *Gladstone and
excite agitation.   Palmerston* (1928)

1 Lord Palmerston, with characteristic levity had once said that only three men in Europe had ever understood [the Schleswig-Holstein question], and of these the Prince Consort was dead, a Danish statesman (unnamed) was in an asylum, and he himself had forgotten it.

R. W. Seton-Watson *Britain in Europe 1789–1914* (1937)

2 What is merit? The opinion one man entertains of another.

T. Carlyle *Shooting Niagara: and After?* (1867)

on being told that English has no word equivalent to sensibilité:
3 Yes we have. Humbug.

attributed

Christabel Pankhurst 1880–1958

English suffragette; daughter of Emmeline **Pankhurst**

4 Never lose your temper with the Press or the public is a major rule of political life.

Unshackled (1959)

5 We are here to claim our right as women, not only to be free, but to fight for freedom. That it is our right as well as our duty.

in *Votes for Women* 31 March 1911

Emmeline Pankhurst 1858–1928

English suffragette leader; founder of the Women's Social and Political Union, 1903

6 There is something that Governments care far more for than human life, and that is the security of property, and so it is through property that we shall strike the enemy . . . I say to the Government: You have not dared to take the leaders of Ulster for their incitement to rebellion. Take me if you dare.

speech at Albert Hall, 17 October 1912

7 The argument of the broken window pane is the most valuable argument in modern politics.

George Dangerfield *The Strange Death of Liberal England* (1936)

Boris Pankin 1931–

Russian diplomat

8 Recession is when you have to tighten the belt. Depression is when there is no belt to tighten. We are probably in the next degree of collapse when there are no trousers as such.
 of Russia

in *Independent* 25 July 1992

Dorothy Parker 1893–1967

American critic and humorist

*on being told that Calvin **Coolidge** was dead:*
9 How do they know?

Malcolm Cowley *Writers at Work* 1st Series (1958)

Martin Parker d. c.1656

English balladmonger

10 But all's to no end, for the times will not mend
 Till the King enjoys his own again.

'Upon Defacing of Whitehall' (1671)

Henry Parkes 1815-95
English-born Australian statesman

1 The crimson thread of kinship runs through us all.
on Australian federation

speech at banquet in Melbourne 6 February 1890; The Federal Government of Australasia (1890)

C. Northcote Parkinson 1909-
English writer

2 Expenditure rises to meet income.

Parkinson's Law (1958)

3 Work expands so as to fill the time available for its completion.

Parkinson's Law (1958)

4 A committee is organic rather than mechanical in its nature: it is not a structure but a plant. It takes root and grows, it flowers, wilts, and dies, scattering the seed from which other committees will bloom in their turn.

Parkinson's Law (1958)

5 Time spent on any item of the agenda will be in inverse proportion to the sum involved.

Parkinson's Law (1958)

6 The man who is denied the opportunity of taking decisions of importance begins to regard as important the decisions he is allowed to take.

Parkinson's Law (1958)

7 Men enter local politics solely as a result of being unhappily married.

Parkinson's Law (1958)

Rosa Parks 1913-
American civil rights activist

8 Our mistreatment was just not right, and I was tired of it.
of her refusal, in December 1955, to surrender her seat on a segregated bus in Alabama to a white man

Quiet Strength (1994)

Charles Stewart Parnell 1846-91
Irish nationalist leader
on Parnell: see **Joyce** 194:8, **Yeats** 390:2

9 Why should Ireland be treated as a geographical fragment of England . . . Ireland is not a geographical fragment, but a nation.

In the House of Commons, 26 April 1875

10 I do not believe, and I never shall believe, that any murder was committed at Manchester.
objecting to the expression 'the Manchester murders' in alluding to the escape of the Fenians, Kelly and Deasy, in 1867

in the House of Commons, June 1876

11 My policy is not a policy of conciliation, but a policy of retaliation.
in 1877, on his parliamentary tactics in the House of Commons as leader of the Irish party

in Dictionary of National Biography (1917-)

12 None of us, whether we are in America or Ireland, or wherever we may be, will be satisfied until we have destroyed the last link which keeps Ireland bound to England.

speech at Cincinnati, 20 February 1880

13 No man has a right to fix the boundary of the march of a nation; no man has a right to say to his country—thus far shalt thou go and no further.

speech at Cork, 21 January 1885

1 Get the advice of everybody whose advice is worth having—
they are very few—and then do what you think best
yourself.

Conor Cruise O'Brien *Parnell*

Matthew Parris 1949–
British journalist and former Conservative politician

*of Lady **Thatcher** in the House of Lords:*
2 A big cat detained briefly in a poodle parlour, sharpening
her claws on the velvet.

Look Behind You! (1993)

3 Being an MP feeds your vanity and starves your self-respect.

in *The Times* 9 February 1994

4 Why waste it on some vanilla-flavoured pixie. Bring on the
fruitcakes, we want a fruitcake for an unlosable seat. They
enliven the Commons.
*the day before the Kensington and Chelsea association chose Alan
Clark as their parliamentary candidate*

in *Mail on Sunday* 26 January 1997

5 My name is Mandy: Peter B.,
I'm back in charge—don't mess with me.
My cheeks are drawn, my face is bony,
The line I take comes straight from Tony.
on Peter Mandelson's return to government

in *Times* 21 October 1999; see
Anonymous 10:1

Tony Parsons 1953–
English critic and writer

6 I never saw a beggar yet who would recognise guilt if it bit
him on his unwashed ass.

*Dispatches from the Front Line of
Popular Culture* (1994)

Blaise Pascal 1623–62
French mathematician, physicist, and moralist

7 Had Cleopatra's nose been shorter, the whole face of the
world would have changed.

Pensées (1909)

Sadashiv Kanoji Patil
Indian politician; Minister for Food and Agriculture in **Nehru**'s
government

8 The Prime Minister is like the great banyan tree. Thousands
shelter beneath it, but nothing grows.
*when asked in an interview who would be **Nehru**'s successor*

J. K. Galbraith *A Life in Our Times*
(1981)

Chris Patten 1944–
British Conservative politician

9 Attacking the Liberals is a difficult business, involving all
the hazards of wrestling with a greased pig at a village fair,
and then insulting the vicar.

attributed, 1996

Jeremy Paxman 1950–
British journalist

10 No government in history has been as obsessed with public
relations as this one . . . Speaking for myself, if there is a
message I want to be off it.
after criticism from Alastair Campbell of interviewing tactics in
The World at One *and* Newsnight

in *Daily Telegraph* 3 July 1998

Patrick Pearse 1879–1916

Irish nationalist leader; executed after the Easter Rising
on Pearse: see **Yeats** 389:5

1 The fools, the fools, the fools, they have left us our Fenian
dead, and while Ireland holds these graves Ireland unfree
shall never be at peace.

oration over the grave of the
Fenian Jeremiah O'Donovan Rossa,
1 August 1915

2 Here be ghosts that I have raised this Christmastide, ghosts
of dead men that have bequeathed a trust to us living men.
Ghosts are troublesome things in a house or in a family, as
we knew even before Ibsen taught us. There is only one way
to appease a ghost. You must do the thing it asks you. The
ghosts of a nation sometimes ask very big things and they
must be appeased, whatever the cost.

on Christmas Day, 1915; Conor
Cruise O'Brien *Ancestral Voices*
(1994); see **O'Brien** 272:3

Lester Pearson 1897–1972

Canadian diplomat and Liberal statesman, Prime Minister 1963–8

3 The grim fact is that we prepare for war like precocious
giants and for peace like retarded pygmies.

speech in Toronto, 14 March 1955

4 Not only did he not suffer fools gladly, he did not suffer them
at all.
of Dean **Acheson**

in *Time* 25 October 1971

5 The chief distinction of a diplomat is that he can say no in
such a way that it sounds like yes.

Geoffrey Pearson *Seize the Day*
(1993)

Robert Peel 1788–1850

British Conservative statesman, Prime Minister 1834–5 and
1841–6
on Peel: see **Curran** 99:10, **Disraeli** 111:7, 111:10, 114:14,
Hennessy 168:6, **Wellington** 379:13

6 What is right must unavoidably be politic.

to Goulburn, 23 September 1822

7 There is no appetite for truth in Ireland.

to Leveson Gower in 1828

8 As minister of the Crown . . . I reserve to myself, distinctly
and unequivocally, the right of adapting my conduct to the
exigency of the moment, and to the wants of the country.

in the House of Commons, 30
March 1829

9 All my experience in public life is in favour of the
employment of what the world would call young men
instead of old ones.

to Wellington in 1829

10 The longer I live, the more clearly do I see the folly of
yielding a rash and precipitate assent to any political
measure.

in the House of Commons, 1830

11 Men, if in office, seemed really to be like the Indians—they
inherited all the qualities of those enemies they killed.

in the House of Commons,1831

12 We are here to consult the interests and not to obey the will
of the people, if we honestly believe that that will conflicts
with those interests.

in the House of Commons, 1831

13 No man attached to his country could always acquiesce in
the opinions of the majority.

in the House of Commons, 1831

14 No government can exist which does not control and
restrain the popular sentiments.

in the House of Commons, 1832

1 There will always be found a permanent fund of discontent and dissatisfaction in every country.

in the House of Commons, 1832

2 The hasty inordinate demand for peace might be just as dangerous as the clamour for war.

in the House of Commons, 1832

3 I see no dignity in persevering in error.

in the House of Commons, 1833

*of Robert **Walpole**:*
4 So far as the great majority of his audience was concerned, he had blocks to cut, and he chose a fitter instrument than a razor to cut them with.

to Mahon in 1833

5 I am not sure that those who clamour most, suffer most.

in the House of Commons, 1834

6 Of all vulgar arts of government, that of solving every difficulty which might arise by thrusting the hand into the public purse is the most delusory and contemptible.

in the House of Commons, 1834

7 The distinction of being without an honour is becoming a rare and valuable one and should not become extinct.

to Graham in 1841

8 A cordial and good understanding between France and England is essential to the peace and welfare of Europe.

in the House of Commons, 1841

9 Speaking with that caution with which I am sometimes taunted but which I find a great convenience.

in the House of Commons, 1842

10 There are those who seem to have nothing else to do but to suggest modes of taxation to men in office.

in the House of Commons, 1842

11 The great art of government is to work by such instruments as the world supplies.

in Cabinet, 1844

12 There are many parties in Ireland who desire to have a grievance and prefer the grievance to the remedy.

to the Queen, 1844

13 Philosophers are very regardless of expense when the public has to bear it.

to Haddington in 1844

14 Priests are not above sublunary considerations. Priests have nephews.

to Graham, 13 August 1845

15 An Irishman has no sense of the ridiculous when office is in question.

to Graham, 28 December 1845

16 There seem to me very few facts, at least ascertainable facts, in politics.

*to Lord **Brougham** in 1846*

17 Great public measures cannot be carried by the influence of mere reason.

to Lord Radnor in 1846

Charles Péguy 1873–1914
French poet and essayist

18 Tyranny is always better organized than freedom.

Basic Verities (1943) 'War and Peace'

Henry Herbert, Lord Pembroke
c.1534–1601

19 A parliament can do any thing but make a man a woman, and a woman a man.

quoted by his son, the 4th Earl, in a speech on 11 April 1648, proving himself Chancellor of Oxford

William Penn 1644–1718
English Quaker; founder of Pennsylvania

1 It is a reproach to religion and government to suffer so much poverty and excess.
Some Fruits of Solitude (1693)

2 The taking of a bribe or gratuity, should be punished with as severe penalties as the defrauding of the State.
Some Fruits of Solitude (1693)

Samuel Pepys 1633–1703
English diarist

3 I went out to Charing Cross, to see Major-general Harrison hanged, drawn, and quartered; which was done there, he looking as cheerful as any man could do in that condition.
diary, 13 October 1660

4 But methought it lessened my esteem of a king, that he should not be able to command the rain.
diary, 19 July 1662

5 I see it is impossible for the King to have things done as cheap as other men.
diary, 21 July 1662

6 While we were talking came by several poor creatures carried by, by constables, for being at a conventicle . . . I would to God they would either conform, or be more wise, and not be catched!
diary, 7 August 1664

7 Pretty witty Nell.
of Nell Gwyn
diary 3 April 1665

Shimon Peres 1923–
Israeli statesman

8 Television has made dictatorship impossible, but democracy unbearable.
at a Davos meeting, in *Financial Times* 31 January 1995

Pericles c.495–429 BC
Athenian statesman

9 For famous men have the whole earth as their memorial.
Thucydides *History of the Peloponnesian War*

Eva Perón 1919–52
wife of Juan **Perón**
on Perón: see **Epitaphs** 128:8

10 Keeping books on charity is capitalist nonsense! I just use the money for the poor. I can't stop to count it.
Fleur Cowles *Bloody Precedent: the Peron Story* (1952)

Juan Perón 1895–1974
Argentinian soldier and statesman, President 1946–55 and 1973–4

11 If I had not been born Perón, I would have liked to be Perón.
in *Observer* 21 February 1960

Henri Philippe Pétain 1856–1951
French general and statesman, head of state 1940–2

12 To write one's memoirs is to speak ill of everybody except oneself.
in *Observer* 26 May 1946

Mike Peters
American cartoonist

1 When I go into the voting booth, do I vote for the person who is the best President? Or the slime bucket who will make my life as a cartoonist wonderful?

in *Wall Street Journal* 20 January 1993

Roger Peyrefitte 1907–
French writer

2 The ideal civil servant should always be colourless, odourless and tasteless.

Diplomatic Diversions (1953)

Lord Peyton 1919–
British Conservative politician

3 The great thing about Alec Home is that he was not media driven. He would have had some difficulty in spelling the word 'image'.
    of Lord **Home**

in conversation, 1997; Peter Hennessy *The Prime Minister: the Office and its Holders since 1945* (2000)

Edward John Phelps 1822–1900
American lawyer and diplomat

4 The man who makes no mistakes does not usually make anything.

speech at the Mansion House, London, 24 January 1889

Kim Philby 1912–88
British intelligence officer and Soviet spy

5 To betray, you must first belong.

in *Sunday Times* 17 December 1967

Prince Philip 1921–
husband of **Elizabeth II**

6 Just at this moment we are suffering a national defeat comparable to any lost military campaign, and what is more it is self-inflicted . . . I think it is about time we pulled our finger out.

speech to businessmen, 17 October 1961

Morgan Phillips 1902–63
British Labour politician

7 The Labour Party owes more to Methodism than to Marxism.

James Callaghan *Time and Chance* (1987)

Wendell Phillips 1811–84
American abolitionist and orator

8 Revolutions are not made; they come. A revolution is as natural a growth as an oak. It comes out of the past. Its foundations are laid far back.

speech 8 January 1852

9 The best use of laws is to teach men to trample bad laws under their feet.

speech, 12 April 1852

10 One on God's side is a majority.

speech, 1 November 1859

1 Truth is one forever absolute, but opinion is truth filtered through the moods, the blood, the disposition of the spectator.

in *Idols* 4 October 1859

Phocion c.402–317 BC
Athenian soldier

2 DEMOSTHENES: The Athenians will kill thee, Phocion, should they go crazy.
PHOCION: But they will kill thee, should they come to their senses.

Plutarch *Parallel Lives* 'Phocion'

John Pilger 1939–
Australian journalist

3 I used to see Vietnam as a war, rather than a country.

in *Sunday Times* 1 December 1996

Ben Pimlott 1945–
English historian and royal biographer

4 If you have a Royal Family you have to make the best of whatever personalities the genetic lottery comes up with.

in *Independent* 13 September 1997 'Quote Unquote'

5 Clement Attlee—top deity in the modern Labour Party's pantheon.

in *Independent on Sunday* 16 March 1997

William Pitt, Earl of Chatham 1708–78
British Whig statesman; he became Secretary of State (effectively Prime Minister) in 1756 and headed coalition governments 1756–61 and 1766–8; father of William **Pitt** (1759–1806)
on Pitt: see **Walpole** 374:2

6 The atrocious crime of being a young man . . . I shall neither attempt to palliate nor deny.

in the House of Commons, 2 March 1741

7 I must now address a few words to the Solicitor; they shall be few, but they shall be daggers.

to William Murray, the Attorney General, in the House of Commons, 1755

8 The poorest man may in his cottage bid defiance to all the forces of the Crown. It may be frail—its roof may shake—the wind may blow through it—the storm may enter—the rain may enter—but the King of England cannot enter!

speech, c.March 1763

9 Confidence is a plant of slow growth in an aged bosom: youth is the season of credulity.

in the House of Commons, 14 January 1766

10 Unlimited power is apt to corrupt the minds of those who possess it.

in the House of Lords, 9 January 1770; see **Acton** 1:9

11 There is something behind the throne greater than the King himself.

in the House of Lords, 2 March 1770

12 We have a Calvinistic creed, a Popish liturgy, and an Arminian clergy.

in the House of Lords, 19 May 1772

13 You cannot conquer America.

in the House of Lords, 18 November 1777

14 I invoke the genius of the Constitution!

in the House of Lords, 18 November 1777

1 Shall a people that fifteen years ago was the terror of the world now stoop so low as to tell its ancient inveterate enemy, 'Take all we have, only give us peace?'
in his last speech in the Lords, shortly before his death, opposing a surrender to the American colonists and their ally France

Basil Williams *William Pitt, Earl of Chatham* (1913)

2 Our watchword is security.

attributed

3 The parks are the lungs of London.

quoted in the House of Commons by William Windham, 30 June 1808

William Pitt 1759–1806

British statesman, Prime Minister 1783–1801 and 1804–6; second son of William **Pitt**, Earl of Chatham
on Pitt: see **Burke** 60:10, **Fox** 135:6, **Fox** 135:7, **Scott** 317:1; see also **Last words** 213:8

4 Necessity is the plea for every infringement of human freedom: it is the argument of tyrants; it is the creed of slaves.

in the House of Commons, 18 November 1783

5 We must anew commence the salvation of Europe.

in 1795; in *Dictionary of National Biography* (1917–)

6 We must recollect . . . what it is we have at stake, what it is we have to contend for. It is for our property, it is for our liberty, it is for our independence, nay, for our existence as a nation; it is for our character, it is for our very name as Englishmen, it is for everything dear and valuable to man on this side of the grave.
on the rupture of the Peace of Amiens and the resumption of war with Napoleon, 22 July 1803

Speeches of the Rt. Hon. William Pitt (1806)

7 England has saved herself by her exertions, and will, as I trust, save Europe by her example.
replying to a toast in which he had been described as the saviour of his country in the wars with France

R. Coupland *War Speeches of William Pitt* (1915)

8 Roll up that map; it will not be wanted these ten years.
*of a map of Europe, on hearing of **Napoleon**'s victory at Austerlitz, December 1805*

Earl Stanhope *Life of the Rt. Hon. William Pitt* (1862)

Pius VII 1742–1823

Pope from 1800

9 We are prepared to go to the gates of Hell—but no further.
*attempting to reach an agreement with **Napoleon**, c.1800–1*

J. M. Robinson *Cardinal Consalvi* (1987)

Pius XII 1876–1958

Italian cleric; Pope from 1939

10 One Galileo in two thousand years is enough.
on being asked to proscribe the works of Teilhard de Chardin

attributed; Stafford Beer *Platform for Change* (1975)

Plato 429–347 BC

Greek philosopher

11 What I say is that 'just' or 'right' means nothing but what is in the interest of the stronger party.

spoken by Thrasymachus in *The Republic*

12 One of the penalties for refusing to participate in politics is that you end up being governed by your inferiors.

The Republic

1 When the tyrant has disposed of foreign enemies by
conquest or treaty, and there is nothing to fear from them,
then he is always stirring up some war or other, in order
that the people may require a leader.

    'foreign enemies' here means 'exiled opponents'

The Republic

Pliny the Elder AD 23–79

Roman statesman and scholar

2 *Ex Africa semper aliquid novi.*
Always something new out of Africa.

traditional form of *Semper aliquid novi Africam adferre*; *Historia Naturalis*

Plutarch AD c.46–c.120

Greek philosopher and biographer

3 For we are told that when a certain man was accusing both
of them to him, he [Caesar] said that he had no fear of those
fat and long-haired fellows, but rather of those pale and thin
ones.

Parallel Lives 'Anthony'

4 The man who is thought to have been the first to see
beneath the surface of Caesar's public policy and to fear it,
as one might fear the smiling surface of the sea.

    of **Cicero**

Parallel Lives 'Julius Caesar'

Harry Pollitt 1890–1960

British Communist politician

on being asked by Stephen **Spender** *in the 1930s how best a poet
could serve the Communist cause:*

5 Go to Spain and get killed. The movement needs a Byron.

attributed, perhaps apocryphal

Polybius c.200 c.118 BC

Greek historian

6 Those who know how to win are much more numerous
than those who know how to make proper use of their
victories.

History bk 10

Madame de Pompadour (Antoinette Poisson, Marquise de Pompadour) 1721–64

favourite of Louis XV of France

7 *Après nous le déluge.*
After us the deluge.

Madame du Hausset *Mémoires* (1824)

Georges Pompidou 1911–74

French statesman, Prime Minister 1962–8 and President 1969–74

8 A statesman is a politician who places himself at the service
of the nation. A politician is a statesman who places the
nation at his service.

in 1973, attributed

Alexander Pope 1688–1744

English poet

1 Lo! thy dread empire, Chaos! is restored;
Light dies before thy uncreating word:
Thy hand, great Anarch! lets the curtain fall;
And universal darkness buries all.

The Dunciad (1742)

2 Old politicians chew on wisdom past,
And totter on in business to the last.

Epistles to Several Persons 'To Lord Cobham' (1734)

3 Statesman, yet friend to Truth! of soul sincere,
In action faithful, and in honour clear;
Who broke no promise, served no private end,
Who gained no title, and who lost no friend.

Epistles to Several Persons 'To Mr Addison' (1720)

4 For forms of government let fools contest;
Whate'er is best administered is best.

An Essay on Man Epistle 3 (1733)

5 If parts allure thee, think how Bacon shined,
The wisest, brightest, meanest of mankind:
Or ravished with the whistling of a name,
See Cromwell, damned to everlasting fame!

An Essay on Man Epistle 4 (1734)

6 Get place and wealth, if possible, with grace;
If not, by any means get wealth and place.

Imitations of Horace Horace bk. 1, Epistle 1 (1738); see **Horace** 176:9

7 Here thou, great Anna! whom three realms obey,
Dost sometimes counsel take—and sometimes tea.

The Rape of the Lock (1714)

Karl Popper 1902–95

Austrian-born philosopher

8 We may become the makers of our fate when we have ceased to pose as its prophets.

The Open Society and its Enemies (1945) introduction

9 We must plan for freedom, and not only for security, if for no other reason than that only freedom can make security secure.

The Open Society and its Enemies (1945)

10 There is no history of mankind, there are only many histories of all kinds of aspects of human life. And one of these is the history of political power. This is elevated into the history of the world.

The Open Society and its Enemies (1945)

11 Marxism is only an episode—one of the many mistakes we have made in the perennial and dangerous struggle for building a better and a freer world.

The Open Society and its Enemies (rev. ed., 1952)

12 Piecemeal social engineering resembles physical engineering in regarding the *ends* as beyond the province of technology.

The Poverty of Historicism (1957)

Michael Portillo 1953–

British Conservative politician
on Portillo: see **Heseltine** 171:6

13 A truly terrible night for the Conservatives.
after losing Enfield South to Labour in the General Election of 1997

comment, 2 May 1997; Brian Cathcart *Were You Still Up for Portillo?* (1997)

14 You cannot ditch policies that succeeded so convincingly that they were adopted by our opponents.

in *Independent* 27 April 1999

Eugène Pottier see Songs 341:5

Colin Powell 1937–
American general

1 Some in our party miss no opportunity to roundly and loudly condemn affirmative action that helped a few thousand black kids get an education, but hardly a whimper is heard from them over affirmative action for lobbyists who load our federal tax codes with preferences for special interest.

speech at the Republican Convention, 31 August 2000

Enoch Powell 1912–98
British Conservative politician

2 History is littered with the wars which everybody knew would never happen.

speech to the Conservative Party Conference, 19 October 1967

3 Those whom the gods wish to destroy, they first make mad. We must be mad, literally mad, as a nation to be permitting the annual inflow of some 50,000 dependents, who are for the most part the material of the future growth of the immigrant descended population. It is like watching a nation busily engaged in heaping up its own funeral pyre.

speech at Birmingham, 20 April 1968

4 As I look ahead, I am filled with foreboding. Like the Roman, I seem to see 'the River Tiber foaming with much blood'.

speech at Birmingham, 20 April 1968; see **Virgil** 371:9

5 No one is forced to be a politician. It can only compare with fox-hunting and writing poetry. These are two things that men do for sheer enjoyment too.

attributed, 1973

6 Judas was paid! I am sacrificing my whole political life.
response to a heckler's call of 'Judas', having advised Conservatives to vote Labour at the coming general election

speech at Bull Ring, Birmingham, 23 February 1974

7 There is a mania in legislation in detecting discrimination. But all life is about discrimination.

attributed, 1975

8 A party . . . is not a faction or club of individuals who associate for mutual assistance in acquiring and retaining office. It is a body of persons who hold, advocate and desire to bring into effect certain political principles and policies.

speech 30 September 1976

9 Office before honour was the password of Conservative government.
of the 1970–4 Conservative administration

in *Spectator* 15 October 1977

10 For a politician to complain about the press is like a ship's captain complaining about the sea.

in *Guardian* 3 December 1984

11 A Tory is someone who thinks institutions are wiser than those who operate them.

in *Daily Telegraph* 31 March 1986

12 ANNE BROWN: How would you like to be remembered?
ENOCH POWELL: I should like to have been killed in the war.

in a radio interview, 13 April 1986

13 To pretend that you cannot exchange goods and services freely with a Frenchman or an Italian, unless there is an identical standard of bathing beaches or tap water in the different countries is not logic. It is naked aggression.

in *Guardian* 22 May 1990

14 What is history except a nation's collective memory?

on BBC Radio 4 10 February 1991

1 All political lives, unless they are cut off in midstream at a happy juncture, end in failure, because that is the nature of politics and of human affairs.

Joseph Chamberlain (1977); epilogue

2 To be and to remain a member of the House of Commons was the overriding and undiscussable motivation of my life as a politician.

'Theory and Practice' 1990

3 Lift the curtain and 'the State' reveals itself as a little group of fallible men in Whitehall, making guesses about the future, influenced by political prejudices and partisan prejudices, and working on projections drawn from the past by a staff of economists.

attributed

John O'Connor Power 1848–1919

Irish lawyer and politician

of the Liberal Unionists:
4 The mules of politics: without pride of ancestry, or hope of posterity.

H. H. Asquith *Memories and Reflections* (1928); see **Disraeli** 113:19, **Donnelly** 117:2

John Prescott 1938–

British Labour politician; Deputy Leader of the Labour Party from 1994
on Prescott: see **Hague** 156:8

on the contest for the Labour leadership, during a debate between himself, Tony **Blair***, and Margaret* **Beckett***:*
5 We're in danger of loving ourselves to death.

in *Observer* 19 June 1994 'Sayings of the Week'

6 People like me were branded, pigeon-holed, a ceiling put on our ambitions.
on failing his 11-plus

speech at Ruskin College, Oxford, 13 June 1996; in *Guardian* 14 June 1996

7 We did it! Let's wallow in our victory!
on Tony **Blair***'s warning that the Labour Party should not be triumphalist in victory*

speech to the Labour Party Conference, 29 September 1997

8 The wife does not like her hair blown about.
explaining why he had driven from his hotel to the conference centre at the Labour Party Conference

in *Daily Telegraph* 1 October 1999

9 All that glitters isn't Gould.
after the publication of Philip **Gould***'s leaked memo*

on *Today* programme (BBC Radio Four) 21 July 2000

Richard Price 1723–91

English nonconformist minister

10 Now, methinks, I see the ardour for liberty catching and spreading; a general amendment beginning in human affairs; the dominion of kings changed for the dominion of laws, and the dominion of priests giving way to the dominion of reason and conscience.

A Discourse on the Love of our Country (1790)

Matthew Prior 1664–1721

English poet

11 What is a King?—a man condemned to bear
The public burden of the nation's care.

Solomon (1718)

Romano Prodi 1939-

Italian statesman, President of the European Commission

1 The pillars of the nation state are the sword and the currency, and we changed that. The euro-decision changed the concept of the nation state.

in *Daily Telegraph* 7 April 1999

Pierre-Joseph Proudhon 1809-65

French social reformer

2 Property is theft.

Qu'est-ce que la propriété? (1840)

■ Proverbs and sayings *see box overleaf*

Joseph Pulitzer 1847-1911

Hungarian-born American newspaper proprietor and editor

3 A cynical, mercenary, demagogic, corrupt press will produce in time a people as base as itself.
    inscribed on the gateway to the Columbia School of Journalism in New York

W. J. Granberg *The World of Joseph Pulitzer* (1965)

Pu Yi 1906-67

Emperor of China 1908-12; Japan's puppet emperor of Manchuria 1934-45

4 For the past 40 years I had never folded my own quilt, made my own bed, or poured out my own washing. I had never even washed my own feet or tied my shoes.

From Emperor to Citizen (1964)

John Pym 1584-1643

English Parliamentary leader

5 To have granted liberties, and not to have liberties in truth and realities, is but to mock the kingdom.
    *after the battle of Edgehill, in a speech at Guildhall to the citizens of London pointing out the illusory nature of **Charles I**'s promises*

in *Dictionary of National Biography* (1917-)

Pyrrhus 319-272 BC

King of Epirus from 306 BC

6 One more such victory and we are lost.
    on defeating the Romans at Asculum, 279 BC; origin of the phrase 'Pyrrhic victory'

Plutarch *Parallel Lives* 'Pyrrhus'

François Quesnay 1694-1774

French political economist

7 *Vous ne connaissez qu'une seule règle du commerce; c'est (pour me servir de vos propres termes) de laisser passer et de laisser faire tous les acheteurs et tous les vendeurs quelconques.*

You recognize but one rule of commerce; that is (to avail myself of your own terms) to allow free passage and freedom of action to all buyers and sellers whoever they may be.

letter from M. Alpha to de Quesnay, 1767, in L. Salleron *François Quesnay et la Physiocratie* (1958) vol. 2, but not found in de Quesnay's writings; see **Argenson** 13:4

Proverbs and sayings

1 A conservative is a liberal who's been mugged.

American saying, 1980s; see **Wolfe** 387:7

2 As Maine goes, so goes the nation.

American political saying, c.1840; see **Farley** 130:6

3 Bad money drives out good.

proverbial expression of a principle attributed to Sir Thomas Gresham (c.1519–79), founder of the Royal Exchange

4 Don't sell America short.

popular version of saying attributed, c.1890s, to John Pierpont Morgan (1837–1913)

5 England's difficulty is Ireland's opportunity.

proverbial from mid 19th century

6 An Englishman's home is his castle.

proverbial from late 16th century

7 Every bullet has its billet.

proverbial from late 16th century; attributed to **William III** in John Wesley *Journal* (1827) 6 June 1765

8 The higher the monkey climbs the more he shows his tail.

proverbial from late 14th century

9 If you don't like the heat, get out of the kitchen.
*associated with Harry S **Truman**, but attributed by him to Harry Vaughan, his 'military jester'*

mid 20th century saying; in *Time* 28 April 1952

10 *Il ne faut pas être plus royaliste que le roi.*
You mustn't be more of a royalist than the king.
noted as a current catch-phrase which was not in fact new; 'it was coined under Louis XVI: it chained up the hands of the loyal, leaving free only the arm of the hangman'

François René, Vicomte de Chateaubriand *De la monarchie selon la charte* (1816)

11 It'll play in Peoria.
*catchphrase of the **Nixon** administration (early 1970s) meaning 'it will be acceptable to middle America'*

originating in a standard music hall joke of the 1930s

12 Let's run it up the flagpole and see if anyone salutes it.

Reginald Rose *Twelve Angry Men* (1955); recorded as an established advertising expression in the 1960s

13 Members [of civil service orders] rise from CMG (known sometimes in Whitehall as 'Call Me God') to the KCMG ('Kindly Call Me God') to—for a select few governors and super-ambassadors—the GCMG ('God Calls Me God').

Anthony Sampson *Anatomy of Britain* (1962)

14 One man plus the truth makes a majority.

traditional saying; see **Knox** 208:1

15 Politics makes strange bedfellows.

proverbial from mid 19th century

16 Revolutions are not made with rose-water.

proverbial from early 19th century

17 A rising tide lifts all boats.

mid 20th century saying; principally known in the United States and associated with the **Kennedy** family

Proverbs and sayings *continued*

1 There's no such thing as a free lunch.
*colloquial axiom in US economics from the 1960s, much associated with Milton **Friedman***

first found in printed form in Robert Heinlein *The Moon is a Harsh Mistress* (1966)

2 To succeed in public life you have to be sincere. Once you can fake that, you've got it made.

traditional saying

3 What Manchester says today, the rest of England says tomorrow.

late 19th century saying

4 When the going gets tough, the tough get going.

proverbial from mid 20th century; widely associated with Joseph P. **Kennedy**, J. H. Cutler *Honey Fitz* (1962); also attributed to Knute Rockne

5 When war is declared, Truth is the first casualty.

attributed to Hiram Johnson, speaking in the US Senate, 1918, but not recorded in his speech; the first recorded use is as epigraph to Arthur Ponsonby's *Falsehood in Wartime* (1928); see **Johnson** 190:14

Josiah Quincy 1772–1864
American Federalist politician

6 As it will be the right of all, so it will be the duty of some, definitely to prepare for a separation, amicably if they can, violently if they must.

in Abridgement of Debates of Congress 14 January 1811

Yitzhak Rabin 1922–95
Israeli statesman and military leader, Prime Minister 1974–7 and 1992–5

7 We say to you today in a loud and a clear voice: enough of blood and tears. Enough.
to the Palestinians, at the signing of the Israel–Palestine Declaration

in Washington, 13 September, 1993

Lord Radcliffe 1899–1977
British lawyer and public servant

8 Society has become used to the standing armies of power—the permanent Civil Service, the police force, the tax-gatherer—organized on a scale which was unknown to earlier centuries.

Power and the State (BBC Reith Lectures, 1951)

9 Governments always tend to want not really a free press but a managed or well-conducted one.

in 1967; Peter Hennessy *What the Papers Never Said* (1985)

Thomas Rainborowe d. 1648
English soldier and parliamentarian

10 The poorest he that is in England hath a life to live as the greatest he.
during the Army debates at Putney, 29 October 1647

C. H. Firth (ed.) *The Clarke Papers* vol. 1 (1891)

Milton Rakove 1918–83

1 The second law, Rakove's law of principle and politics,   in *Virginia Quarterly Review* (1965)
states that the citizen is influenced by principle in direct
proportion to his distance from the political situation.

Walter Ralegh c.1552–1618

English explorer and courtier
see also **Last words** 212:11

2 Say to the court, it glows   'The Lie' (1608)
And shines like rotten wood;
Say to the church, it shows
What's good, and doth no good:
If church and court reply,
Then give them both the lie.

3 Fain would I climb, yet fear I to fall.   Thomas Fuller *History of the*
    line written on a window-pane; see **Elizabeth I** 124:10   *Worthies of England* (1662)
     'Devonshire'

4 'Tis a sharp remedy, but a sure one for all ills.   D. Hume *History of Great Britain*
    on feeling the edge of the axe prior to his execution   (1754)

5 So the heart be right, it is no matter which way the head   W. Stebbing *Sir Walter Raleigh*
lies.   (1891)
    at his execution, on being asked which way he preferred to lay his
    head

John Randolph 1773–1833

American politician

6 God has given us Missouri, and the devil shall not take it   Robert V. Remini *Henry Clay* (1991)
from us.
    in the debate in the US Senate in 1820 on the admission of
    Missouri to the Union as a slave state

7 Never were abilities so much below mediocrity so well   speech 1 February 1828
rewarded; no, not when Caligula's horse was made Consul.
    on John Quincy **Adams**'s *appointment of Richard Rush as*
    Secretary of the Treasury

8 He is a man of splendid abilities but utterly corrupt. He   W. Cabell Bruce *John Randolph of*
shines and stinks like rotten mackerel by moonlight.   *Roanoke* (1923) vol. 2
    of Edward Livingston

9 He rowed to his object with muffled oars.   W. Cabell Bruce *John Randolph of*
    of Martin Van Buren   *Roanoke* (1923) vol. 2

10 That most delicious of all privileges—spending other   William Cabell Bruce *John Randolph*
people's money.   *of Roanoke* (1923) vol. 2

Irina Ratushinskaya 1954–

Russian poet

11 Russian literature saved my soul. When I was a young girl   in *Observer* 15 October 1989
in school and I asked what is good and what is evil, no one   'Sayings of the Week'
in that corrupt system could show me.

Sam Rayburn 1882–1961

American politician

1 If you want to get along, go along.

Neil MacNeil *Forge of Democracy* (1963)

Nancy Reagan 1923–

American actress and wife of Ronald **Reagan**, First Lady of the US, 1981–9

2 If the President has a bully pulpit, then the First Lady has a white glove pulpit . . . more refined, restricted, ceremonial, but it's a pulpit all the same.

in *New York Times* 10 March 1988; see **Roosevelt** 308:1

Ronald Reagan 1911–

American Republican statesman, 40th President of the US 1981–9; former Hollywood actor
on Reagan: see **Keillor** 197:7, **Noonan** 271:1, **Schroeder** 316:2, **Vidal** 371:5; see also **Dempsey** 106:3, **Gipp** 147:1

3 Government is like a big baby—an alimentary canal with a big appetite at one end and no responsibility at the other.
campaigning for the governorship of California, 1965

attributed

4 Politics is just like show business, you have a hell of an opening, coast for a while and then have a hell of a close.

in 1966; Mark Green and Gail MacColl (eds.) *There He Goes Again* (1983)

5 Politics is supposed to be the second oldest profession. I have come to realize that it bears a very close resemblance to the first.

at a conference in Los Angeles, 2 March 1977

6 I've noticed that everybody who is for abortion has already been born.

presidential campaign debate, 21 September 1980

7 You can tell a lot about a fellow's character by his way of eating jellybeans.

in *New York Times* 15 January 1981

8 We're the party that wants to see an America in which people can still get rich.

at a Republican congressional dinner, 4 May 1982

9 So in your discussions of the nuclear freeze proposals, I urge you to beware the temptation of pride—the temptation blithely to declare yourselves above it all and label both sides equally at fault, to ignore the facts of history and the aggressive impulses of an evil empire.

speech to the National Association of Evangelicals, 8 March 1983

10 My fellow Americans, I am pleased to tell you I just signed legislation which outlaws Russia forever. The bombing begins in five minutes.
said during radio microphone test, 11 August 1984

in *New York Times* 13 August 1984

11 The taxpayer—that's someone who works for the federal government but doesn't have to take a Civil Service examination.

attributed, 1985

12 We are especially not going to tolerate these attacks from outlaw states run by the strangest collection of misfits, Looney Tunes, and squalid criminals since the advent of the Third Reich.
speech following the hijack of a US plane, 8 July 1985

in *New York Times* 9 July 1985

1 We will never forget them, nor the last time we saw them this morning, as they prepared for the journey and waved goodbye and 'slipped the surly bonds of earth' to 'touch the face of God.'
after the loss of the space shuttle Challenger *with all its crew*

broadcast from the Oval Office, 28 January 1986, quoting from 'High Flight' by the American airman John Gillespie Magee (1922–41)

2 The nine most terrifying words in the English language are, 'I'm from the government and I'm here to help.'
on assistance to farmers

at a press conference in Chicago, 2 August 1986

3 To grasp and hold a vision, that is the very essence of successful leadership—not only on the movie set where I learned it, but everywhere.

in *The Wilson Quarterly* Winter 1994; attributed

4 I now begin the journey that will lead me into the sunset of my life.
statement to the American people revealing that he had Alzheimer's disease, 1994

in *Daily Telegraph* 5 January 1995

Red Cloud (Mahpiua Luta) 1822–1909
Oglala Sioux leader

5 You have heard the sound of the white soldier's axe upon the Little Piney. His presence here is . . . an insult to the spirits of our ancestors. Are we then to give up their sacred graves to be ploughed for corn? Dakotas, I am for war!

speech at council at Fort Laramie, 1866

John Redmond 1856–1918
Irish politician and nationalist leader

in the Spring of 1914 Redmond was asked by a friend, a priest from Tipperary, if anything could now rob them of Home Rule:
6 A European war might do it.

in *Dictionary of National Biography* (1917–)

Joseph Reed 1741–85
American Revolutionary politician

7 I am not worth purchasing, but such as I am, the King of Great Britain is not rich enough to do it.
replying to an offer from Governor George Johnstone of £10,000, and any office in the Colonies in the King's gift, if he were able successfully to promote a Union between the United Kingdom and the American Colonies

W. B. Read *Life and Correspondence of Joseph Reed* (1847)

Montague John Rendall 1862–1950
member of the first BBC Board of Governors

8 Nation shall speak peace unto nation.

motto of the BBC; see **Bible** 39:13

Walter Reuther 1907–70
American labour leader

9 If it looks like a duck, walks like a duck and quacks like a duck, then it just may be a duck.
as a test, during the McCarthy era, of Communist affiliations

attributed

10 Injustice was as common as streetcars. When men walked into their jobs, they left their dignity, their citizenship and their humanity outside.
on working life in America before the Wagner Act

attributed

Paul Revere 1735–1818

American patriot

1 To the memory of the glorious Ninety-two: members of the *attributed*
Honorable House of Representatives of the Massachusetts
Bay who, undaunted by the insolent menaces of villains in
power, from a strict regard to conscience and the liberties of
their constituents on the 30th June 1768 voted NOT TO
RESCIND.
inscription on Revere's silver 'Liberty' bowl, 1768

2 [We agreed] that if the British went out by water, we would *arrangements agreed with the*
show two lanterns in the North Church steeple; and if by *Charlestown Committee of Safety*
land, one as a signal; for we were apprehensive it would be *on 16 April, 1775*
difficult to cross the Charles River or get over Boston Neck.
signals to be used if the British troops moved out of Boston

Cecil Rhodes 1853–1902

British-born South African diamond prospector and statesman,
Prime Minister of Cape Colony 1890–6
see also **Last words** 213:10

3 Being an Englishman is the greatest prize in the lottery of *A. W. Jarvis Jottings from an Active*
life. *Life (1928)*

David Ricardo 1772–1823

British economist

4 Rent is that portion of the earth, which is paid to the *On the Principles of Political*
landlord for the use of the original and indestructible powers *Economy and Taxation (1817)*
of the soil.

Grantland Rice 1880–1954

American sportswriter

5 All wars are planned by old men *'The Two Sides of War' (1955)*
In council rooms apart.

Stephen Rice 1637–1715

Irish lawyer

6 I will drive a coach and six horses through the Act of *W. King State of the Protestants of*
Settlement. *Ireland (1672)*

Tim Rice 1944–

English lyricist

7 Don't cry for me, Argentina. *title of song (1976)*
from the musical Evita, *based on the life of Eva Perón*

Mandy Rice-Davies 1944–

English model and showgirl

*at the trial of Stephen Ward, 29 June 1963, on being told that Lord
Astor claimed that her allegations, concerning himself and his house
parties at Cliveden, were untrue:*
8 He would, wouldn't he? *in Guardian 1 July 1963*

Ann Richards 1933–

American Democratic politician; State Treasurer, and later
Governor, of Texas

1 That dog won't hunt.
  of Republican policies

keynote speech at the Democratic
convention, 1988

2 Poor George, he can't help it—he was born with a silver
foot in his mouth.
  of George Bush

keynote speech at the Democratic
convention, 1988

Johann Paul Friedrich Richter ('Jean Paul')
1763–1825

German novelist

3 Providence has given to the French the empire of the land,
to the English that of the sea, and to the Germans that
of—the air!

Thomas Carlyle 'Jean Paul Friedrich
Richter' in *Edinburgh Review* no. 91
(1827)

Adam Ridley 1942–

British economist, former Director of the Conservative Research
Department

4 Parties come to power with silly, inconsistent and
impossible policies because they have spent their whole
period in opposition forgetting about the real world,
destroying the lessons they learnt in government and
clambering slowly back on to the ideological plain where
they feel happiest.

in *RIPA Report* Winter 1985

Nicholas Ridley 1929–93

British Conservative politician

of the European monetary union:
5 This is all a German racket designed to take over the whole
of Europe.
  *in an interview with Dominic Lawson, in the aftermath of which
  Ridley resigned from the Government*

in *Spectator* 14 July 1990

6 Seventeen unelected reject politicians with no accountability
to anybody, who are not responsible for raising taxes, just
spending money, who are pandered to by a supine
parliament which also is not responsible for raising taxes.
  of the European Commission

in *Spectator* 14 July 1990

Frank Roberts 1907–98

British diplomat

7 Eden . . . was rather like an Arab horse. He used to get
terribly het up and excited and he had to be sort of kept
down.

in *What Has Become of Us* Wide
Vision Productions/Channel 4
television series, 29 March 1994

8 He just didn't understand Hitler or his ruthlessness. We in
the Foreign Office kept telling him it was all in *Mein Kampf*,
but he wouldn't believe it.
  on Neville Chamberlain

in *Daily Telegraph* 10 January 1998;
obituary

George Robertson 1946–
British Labour politician

1 Serbs out, Nato in, refugees back.

summing up the Nato objective in Kosovo, 7 June 1999

Maximilien Robespierre 1758–94
French revolutionary
on Robespierre: see **Carlyle** 69:13

2 I am no courtesan, nor moderator, nor Tribune, nor defender of the people: I am myself the people.

speech at the Jacobin Club, 27 April 1792

3 The general will rules in society as the private will governs each separate individual.

Lettres à ses commettans (2nd series) 5 January 1793

4 Any law which violates the inalienable rights of man is essentially unjust and tyrannical; it is not a law at all.

Déclaration des droits de l'homme 24 April 1793, article 6; this article, in slightly different form, is recorded as having figured in Robespierre's Projet of 21 April 1793

5 Any institution which does not suppose the people good, and the magistrate corruptible, is evil.

Déclaration des droits de l'homme 24 April 1793, article 25

6 The revolutionary government is the despotism of liberty against tyranny.

speech, 5 February 1794

7 Wickedness is the root of despotism as virtue is the essence of the Republic.

in the Convention, 7 May 1794

8 One single will is necessary.

private note; S. A. Berville and J. F. Barrière Papiers inédits trouvés chez Robespierre vol. 2 (1828)

9 Intimidation without virtue is disastrous; virtue without intimidation is powerless.

J. M. Thompson The French Revolution; attributed

Mary Robinson 1944–
Irish Labour stateswoman; President from 1990

10 Instead of rocking the cradle, they rocked the system.
 in her victory speech, paying tribute to the women of Ireland

in The Times 10 November 1990

11 There are 70 million people living on this globe who claim Irish descent. I will be proud to represent them.

inaugural speech as President, 1990

12 May it be a presidency where I the President can sing to you, citizens of Ireland, the joyous refrain of the 14th century Irish poet as recalled by W. B. Yeats: 'I am of Ireland . . . come dance with me in Ireland.'

inaugural speech as President, 1990

13 As a native of Ballina, one of the most western towns in the most western province of the most western nation in Europe, I want to say—'the West's awake.'

inaugural speech as President, 1990; see **Davis** 102:10

14 Now the time has arrived to give thought to the future, to consider how best the Office of President can serve the Irish people as the new millennium approaches.
 announcing that she would not seek a second term of office

in Irish Times 13 March 1997

Boyle Roche 1743–1807

Irish politician

1 Mr Speaker, I smell a rat; I see him forming in the air and darkening the sky; but I'll nip him in the bud.

attributed

Lord Rochester 1647–80

English poet
see also **Epitaphs** 128:3

2 A merry monarch, scandalous and poor.

'A Satire on King Charles II' (1697)

Sue Rodriguez 1951–94

Canadian activist for the legalization of assisted suicide

3 If I cannot give consent to my own death, then whose body is this? Who owns my life?
appealing to a subcommittee of the Canadian Commons, November 1992, as the victim of a terminal illness

in *Globe and Mail* 5 December 1992

Will Rogers 1879–1935 ✓

American humorist

4 Politics has got so expensive that it takes a lot of money to even get beat with nowadays.

Daily Telegrams 28 June 1931

5 The more you read and observe about this Politics thing, you got to admit that each party is worse than the other. The one that's out always looks the best.

Illiterate Digest (1924)

6 A conservative is a man who has plenty of money and doesn't see why he shouldn't always have plenty of money . . . A Democrat is a fellow who never had any money but doesn't see why he shouldn't have some money.

Alex Ayres (ed.) *The Wit and Wisdom of Will Rogers* (1993)

7 I am not a member of any organized political party—I am a Democrat.

P. J. O'Brien *Will Rogers* (1935)

8 I don't know jokes—I just watch the government and report the facts.

'A Rogers Thesaurus' in *Saturday Review* 25 August 1962

9 Communism is like prohibition, it's a good idea but it won't work.

in 1927; *Weekly Articles* (1981) vol. 3

Mme Roland 1754–93 see **Last words** 213:7

Oscar Romero 1917–80

Salvadorean Roman Catholic priest, Archbishop of San Salvador

10 When a dictatorship seriously violates human rights and attacks the common good of the nation, when it becomes unbearable and closes all channels of dialogue, of understanding, of rationality, when this happens, the Church speaks of the legitimate right of insurrectional violence.

Alan Riding 'The Cross and the Sword in Latin America' (1981)

Eleanor Roosevelt 1884–1962

American humanitarian and diplomat, wife of Franklin **Roosevelt**
on Roosevelt: see **Stevenson** 347:10

1 I cannot believe that war is the best solution. No one won the last war, and no one will win the next war.

letter to Harry Truman, 22 March 1948

2 I have always felt that anyone who wanted an election so much that they would use those methods did not have the character that I really admired in public life.
   *on the tactics used by Richard **Nixon** in his 1950 Senatorial campaign against the actress and politician Helen Gahagan Douglas*

on 'Meet the Press' (NBC TV), 16 September 1956

3 No one can make you feel inferior without your consent.

in *Catholic Digest* August 1960

Franklin D. Roosevelt 1882–1945

American Democratic statesman, 32nd President of the US 1933–45
on Roosevelt: see **Churchill** 83:3, **Holmes** 175:6, **Truman** 366:1

4 These unhappy times call for the building of plans that . . . build from the bottom up and not from the top down, that put their faith once more in the forgotten man at the bottom of the economic pyramid.

radio address, 7 April 1932

5 I pledge you, I pledge myself, to a new deal for the American people.
   accepting the presidential nomination

speech to the Democratic Convention in Chicago, 2 July 1932

6 The only thing we have to fear is fear itself.

inaugural address, 4 March 1933

7 In the field of world policy I would dedicate this Nation to the policy of the good neighbour.

inaugural address, 4 March 1933

8 This generation of Americans has a rendezvous with destiny.

speech accepting renomination as President, 27 June 1936

9 I have seen war. I have seen war on land and sea. I have seen blood running from the wounded. I have seen men coughing out their gassed lungs. I have seen the dead in the mud. I have seen cities destroyed. I have seen 200 limping, exhausted men come out of line—the survivors of a regiment of 1,000 that went forward 48 hours before. I have seen children starving. I have seen the agony of mothers and wives. I hate war.

speech at Chautauqua, NY, 14 August 1936

10 I see one-third of a nation ill-housed, ill-clad, ill-nourished.

second inaugural address, 20 January 1937

11 The only sure bulwark of continuing liberty is a government strong enough to protect the interests of the people, and a people strong enough and well enough informed to maintain its sovereign control over its government.

'Fireside Chat' radio broadcast, 14 April 1938

12 When peace has been broken anywhere, the peace of all countries everywhere is in danger.

'Fireside Chat' radio broadcast, 3 September 1939

13 I am reminded of four definitions: A Radical is a man with both feet firmly planted—in the air. A Conservative is a man with two perfectly good legs who, however, has never learned to walk forward. A Reactionary is a somnambulist walking backwards. A Liberal is a man who uses his legs and his hands at the behest—at the command—of his head.

radio address to *New York Herald Tribune* Forum, 26 October 1939

1 On this tenth day of June 1940 the hand that held the dagger has struck it into the back of its neighbour.
on hearing that Italy had declared war on France

address at the University of Virginia, Charlottesville, 10 June 1940

2 I have said this before, but I shall say it again and again and again: Your boys are not going to be sent into any foreign wars.

speech in Boston, 30 October 1940

3 We have the men—the skill—the wealth—and above all, the will . . . We must be the great arsenal of democracy.

'Fireside Chat' radio broadcast, 29 December 1940

4 We, too, born to freedom, and believing in freedom, are willing to fight to maintain freedom. We, and all others who believe as deeply as we do, would rather die on our feet than live on our knees.
on receiving the degree of Doctor of Civil Law from Oxford

on 19 June 1941; see **Ibarruri** 180:9

5 We look forward to a world founded upon four essential human freedoms. The first is freedom of speech and expression—everywhere in the world. The second is freedom of every person to worship God in his own way—everywhere in the world. The third is freedom from want . . . everywhere in the world. The fourth is freedom from fear . . . anywhere in the world.

message to Congress, 6 January 1941

6 Yesterday, December 7, 1941—a date which will live in infamy—the United States of America was suddenly and deliberately attacked by naval and air forces of the Empire of Japan.

address to Congress, 8 December 1941

7 Books can not be killed by fire. People die, but books never die. No man and no force can abolish memory . . . In this war, we know, books are weapons. And it is a part of your dedication always to make them weapons for man's freedom.

'Message to the Booksellers of America' 6 May 1942

8 The American people are quite competent to judge a political party that works both sides of the street.

campaign speech in Boston, 4 November 1944

9 We have learned that we cannot live alone, at peace; that our own well-being is dependent on the well-being of other nations, far away. We have learned that we must live as men, and not as ostriches, nor as dogs in the manger. We have learned to be citizens of the world, members of the human community.

fourth inaugural address, 20 January 1945

10 It is fun to be in the same decade with you.
cabled reply to Winston Churchill, acknowledging congratulations on his 60th birthday

W. S. Churchill *The Hinge of Fate* (1950)

11 You've convinced me. Now go out and put pressure on me.

attributed; Peter Hennessy *Whitehall* (1990)

12 The work, my friend, is peace. More than an end of this war—an end to the beginnings of all wars.
undelivered address for Jefferson Day, 13 April 1945, the day after Roosevelt died

Public Papers (1950) vol. 13

13 The only limit to our realization of tomorrow will be our doubts of today. Let us move forward with strong and active faith.
undelivered address for Jefferson Day, 13 April 1945, final lines

Public Papers (1950) vol. 13

Theodore Roosevelt 1858–1919 ✓

American Republican statesman, 26th President of the US 1901–9
on Roosevelt: see **Hanna** 161:1, **Knox** 208:2; *see also* **Last words**
213:9

1 I wish to preach, not the doctrine of ignoble ease, but the
doctrine of the strenuous life.

speech to the Hamilton Club,
Chicago, 10 April 1899

2 I am as strong as a bull moose and you can use me to the
limit.
'*Bull Moose*' *subsequently became the popular name of the
Progressive Party*

letter to Mark **Hanna**, 27 June
1900

3 McKinley has no more backbone than a chocolate éclair!
*of William McKinley (1843–1901), Republican statesman and
25th President of the US, whose assassination brought about the
accession of Roosevelt*

H. T. Peck *Twenty Years of the
Republic* (1906)

4 The first requisite of a good citizen in this Republic of ours is
that he shall be able and willing to pull his weight.

speech in New York, 11 November
1902

5 There is a homely old adage which runs: 'Speak softly and
carry a big stick; you will go far.' If the American nation
will speak softly, and yet build and keep at a pitch of the
highest training a thoroughly efficient navy, the Monroe
Doctrine will go far.

speech in Chicago, 3 April 1903

6 A man who is good enough to shed his blood for the
country is good enough to be given a square deal
afterwards. More than that no man is entitled to, and less
than that no man shall have.

speech at the Lincoln Monument,
Springfield, Illinois, 4 June 1903;
see **Slogans** 336:11

7 Far and away the best prize that life offers is the chance to
work hard at work worth doing.

address at the State Fair, Syracuse,
New York Labour Day, 7
September 1903

8 The men with the muckrakes are often indispensable to the
well-being of society; but only if they know when to stop
raking the muck.

speech in Washington, 14 April
1906

9 It is not the critic who counts; not the man who points out
how the strong man stumbles, or where the doer of deeds
could have done better. The credit belongs to the man who
is actually in the arena.

'Citizenship in a Republic', speech
at the Sorbonne, Paris, 23 April
1910

10 We stand at Armageddon and we battle for the Lord.

speech at Progressive Party
Convention, Chicago, 17 June 1912

11 There is no room in this country for hyphenated
Americanism . . . The one absolutely certain way of bringing
this nation to ruin, of preventing all possibility of its
continuing to be a nation at all, would be to permit it to
become a tangle of squabbling nationalities.

speech in New York, 12 October
1915

12 One of our defects as a nation is a tendency to use what
have been called 'weasel words'. When a weasel sucks eggs
the meat is sucked out of the egg. If you use a 'weasel word'
after another, there is nothing left of the other.

speech in St Louis, 31 May 1916

13 Foolish fanatics . . . the men who form the lunatic fringe in
all reform movements.

Autobiography (1913)

14 No man is justified in doing evil on the ground of
expediency.

Works (1925) vol. 15 'Latitude and
Longitude among Reformers'

1 I have got such a bully pulpit!
his personal view of the presidency

in *Outlook* (New York) 27 February 1909; see **Reagan** 299:2

Lord Rosebery 1847–1929
British Liberal statesman, Prime Minister 1894–5

2 There is no need for any nation, however great, leaving the Empire, because the Empire is a commonwealth of nations.

speech in Adelaide, Australia, 18 January 1884

3 I have never known the sweets of place with power, but of place without power, of place with the minimum of power—that is a purgatory, and if not a purgatory it is a hell.

in *The Spectator* 6 July 1895

4 Imperialism, sane Imperialism, as distinguished from what I may call wild-cat Imperialism, is nothing but this—a larger patriotism.

speech, City of London Liberal Club, 5 May 1899

5 It is beginning to be hinted that we are a nation of amateurs.

Rectorial address at Glasgow University, 16 November 1900

6 No one outside an asylum wishes to be rid of it.
of the British Empire

Rectorial address at Glasgow University, 16 November 1900

7 I must plough my furrow alone.
speech on remaining outside the Liberal Party leadership, 19 July 1901

in *The Times* 20 July 1901

8 There are two supreme pleasures in life. One is ideal, the other real. The ideal is when a man receives the seals of office from his Sovereign. The real pleasure comes when he hands them back.

Sir Robert Peel (1899)

Ethel Rosenberg 1916–53
and Julius Rosenberg 1918–53
American husband and wife; convicted of spying for the Russians and executed

9 We are innocent . . . To forsake this truth is to pay too high a price even for the priceless gift of life.
petition for executive clemency, filed 9 January 1953

Ethel Rosenberg *Death House Letters* (1953)

10 We are the first victims of American Fascism.
letter from Julius to Emanuel Bloch before the Rosenbergs' execution, 19 June 1953

Testament of Ethel and Julius Rosenberg (1954)

Dick Ross
British economist, former Deputy Director of the Central Policy Review Staff

11 You must think the unthinkable, but always wear a dark suit when presenting the results.

in the early 1970s; Peter Hennessy *Whitehall* (1990)

Christina Rossetti 1830–94
English poet; sister of D. G. Rossetti

12 Our Indian Crown is in great measure the trapping of a splendid misery.
on the siege of Kandahar

letter to Amelia Heimann, 29 July 1880

Jean Rostand 1894–1977
French biologist

1 Stupidity, outrage, vanity, cruelty, iniquity, bad faith, falsehood—we fail to see the whole array when it is facing in the same direction as we.

Pensées d'un biologiste (1939)

Lord Rothschild 1910–90
British administrator and scientist, first Director of the Central Policy Review Staff
on Rothschild: see **Hurd** 179:8

2 Politicians often believe that their world is the real one. Officials sometimes take a different view.
on resigning as Director of the Central Policy Review Staff

in *The Times* 13 October 1974

3 The promises and panaceas that gleam like false teeth in the party manifestoes.

Meditations of a Broomstick (1977)

Jean-Jacques Rousseau 1712–78
French philosopher and novelist

4 The social contract

title of book, 1762

5 Man was born free, and everywhere he is in chains.

The Social Contract (1762)

6 Slaves become so debased by their chains as to lose even the desire of breaking from them.

The Social Contract (1762)

Maude Royden 1876–1956
English religious writer, social reformer, and preacher

7 The Church should go forward along the path of progress and be no longer satisfied only to represent the Conservative Party at prayer.

address at Queen's Hall, London, 16 July 1917

Richard Rumbold c.1622–85
English republican conspirator

8 I never could believe that Providence had sent a few men into the world, ready booted and spurred to ride, and millions ready saddled and bridled to be ridden.
on the scaffold

T. B. Macaulay *History of England* vol. 1 (1849)

Robert Runcie 1921–2000
English Protestant clergyman; Archbishop of Canterbury

9 People are mourning on both sides of this conflict. In our prayers we shall quite rightly remember those who are bereaved in our own country and the relations of the young Argentinian soldiers who were killed. Common sorrow could do something to reunite those who were engaged in this struggle. A shared anguish can be a bridge of reconciliation. Our neighbours are indeed like us.

service of thanksgiving at the end of the Falklands war, St. Paul's Cathedral, London, 26 July 1982

Dean Rusk 1909–94
US politician; Secretary of State, 1961–9

10 We're eyeball to eyeball, and I think the other fellow just blinked.
on the Cuban missile crisis, 24 October 1962

in *Saturday Evening Post* 8 December 1962

1 Only one-third of human beings are asleep at one time, and the other two-thirds are awake and up to some mischief somewhere.

attributed, 1966

2 Scratch any American and underneath you'll find an isolationist.

to the British Foreign Secretary, George Brown; Tony Benn diary 12 January 1968

3 It has been said that power tends to corrupt, but that loss of power tends to corrupt absolutely.

attributed, 1968; see **Acton** *1:9*

John Ruskin 1819–1900

English art and social critic

4 We Communists of the old school think that our property belongs to everybody, and everybody's property to us; so of course I thought the Louvre belonged to me as much as to the Parisians, and expected they would have sent word over to me, being an Art Professor, to ask whether I wanted it burnt down. But no message or intimation to that effect ever reached me.

Fors Clavigera (1871)

5 You have founded an entire Science of Political Economy, on what you have stated to be the constant instinct of man—the desire to defraud his neighbour.

Fors Clavigera (1871)

6 Visible governments are the toys of some nations, the diseases of others, the harness of some, the burdens of more, the necessity of all.

Fors Clavigera (1871)

7 I am, and my father was before me, a violent Tory of the old school; Walter Scott's school, that is to say, and Homer's.

Praeterita (1885)

8 The first duty of a State is to see that every child born therein shall be well housed, clothed, fed and educated, till it attain years of discretion.

Time and Tide (1867)

9 All mastership is not alike in principle; there are just and unjust masterships.

Time and Tide (1867)

10 You want to have voices in Parliament! Your voices are not worth a rat's squeak, either in Parliament or out of it, till you have some ideas to utter with them.

Time and Tide (1867)

11 It ought to be quite as natural and straightforward a matter for a labourer to take his pension from his parish, because he has deserved well of his parish, as for a man in higher rank to take his pension from his country, because he has deserved well of his country.

Unto this Last (1862) preface

12 The force of the guinea you have in your pocket depends wholly on the default of a guinea in your neighbour's pocket. If he did not want it, it would be of no use to you.

Unto this Last (1862)

13 Government and co-operation are in all things the laws of life; anarchy and competition the laws of death.

Unto this Last (1862)

14 Whereas it has long been known and declared that the poor have no right to the property of the rich, I wish it also to be known and declared that the rich have no right to the property of the poor.

Unto this Last (1862)

Bertrand Russell 1872–1970

British philosopher and mathematician

1 Envy is the basis of democracy.

The Conquest of Happiness (1930)

2 One should as a rule respect public opinion in so far as is necessary to avoid starvation and to keep out of prison, but anything that goes beyond this is voluntary submission to an unnecessary tyranny.

The Conquest of Happiness (1930)

3 Next to enjoying ourselves, the next greatest pleasure consists in preventing others from enjoying themselves, or, more generally, in the acquisition of power.

Sceptical Essays (1928)

4 The opinions that are held with passion are always those for which no good ground exists; indeed the passion is the measure of the holder's lack of rational conviction.

Sceptical Essays (1928)

5 If the Communists conquered the world it would be very unpleasant for a while, but not for ever.

attributed, 1958

6 Few people can be happy unless they hate some other person, nation, or creed.

attributed

7 Religion may in most of its forms be defined as the belief that the gods are on the side of the Government.

attributed

8 The trouble with the world is that the stupid are cocksure and the intelligent are full of doubt.

attributed

Lord John Russell 1792–1878

British Whig statesman, Prime Minister 1846–52 and 1865–6
on Russell: see **Derby** 107:2, **Smith** 339:3

9 It is impossible that the whisper of a faction should prevail against the voice of a nation.
    reply to an Address from a meeting of 150,000 persons at Birmingham on the defeat of the second Reform Bill, October 1831

S. Walpole *Life of Lord John Russell* (1889)

10 If peace cannot be maintained with honour, it is no longer peace.

speech at Greenock, 19 September 1853; see **Disraeli** 113:5

11 Among the defects of the Bill, which were numerous, one provision was conspicuous by its presence and another by its absence.

speech to the electors of the City of London, April 1859

Anwar al-Sadat 1918–81

Egyptian statesman, President 1970–81

12 Peace is much more precious than a piece of land.

speech in Cairo, 8 March 1978

Lord St John of Fawsley 1929–

British Conservative politician and author

13 The monarchy has become our only truly popular institution at a time when the House of Commons has declined in public esteem and the Lords is a matter of controversy. The monarchy is, in a real sense, underpinning the other two estates of the realm.

in *The Times* 1 February 1982

Andrei Sakharov 1921–89
Russian nuclear physicist

1 Every day I saw the huge material, intellectual and nervous resources of thousands of people being poured into the creation of a means of total destruction, something capable of annihilating all human civilization. I noticed that the control levers were in the hands of people who, though talented in their own ways, were cynical.

Sakharov Speaks (1974)

Saki (Hector Hugh Munro) 1870–1916
British writer

2 We all know that Prime Ministers are wedded to the truth, but like other married couples they sometimes live apart.

The Unbearable Bassington (1912)

Lord Salisbury 1830–1903
British Conservative statesman, Prime Minister 1885–6, 1886–92, and 1895–1902
on Salisbury: see **Bismarck** 42:3, **Disraeli** 113:1, **Goschen** 152:1, **Hennessy** 168:6

3 Too clever by half.
   of **Disraeli**'*s amendment on Disestablishment*

speech, House of Commons, 30 March 1868; see **Salisbury** 313:8

4 English policy is to float lazily downstream, occasionally putting out a diplomatic boathook to avoid collisions.

letter to Lord Lytton, 9 March 1877

5 No lesson seems to be so deeply inculcated by the experience of life as that you never should trust experts. If you believe the doctors, nothing is wholesome: if you believe the theologians, nothing is innocent: if you believe the soldiers, nothing is safe. They all require to have their strong wine diluted by a very large admixture of insipid common sense.

letter to Lord Lytton, 15 June 1877

6 The agonies of a man who has to finish a difficult negotiation, and at the same time to entertain four royalties at a country house can be better imagined than described.

letter to Lord Lyons, 5 June 1878

7 What with deafness, ignorance of French, and Bismarck's extraordinary mode of speech, Beaconsfield has the dimmest idea of what is going on—understands everything crossways—and imagines a perpetual conspiracy.
   letter to Lady Salisbury from the Congress of Berlin, 23 June 1878

Lady Gwendolen Cecil *Life of Robert, Marquis of Salisbury* (1921–32)

8 A party whose mission it is to live entirely upon the discovery of grievances are apt to manufacture the element upon which they subsist.

speech at Edinburgh, 24 November 1882

9 They who have the absolute power of preventing lamentable events, and knowing what is taking place, refuse to exercise that power, are responsible for what happens.

in the House of Lords, 12 February 1884

10 We are part of the community of Europe and we must do our duty as such.

speech at Caernarvon, 10 April 1888

11 Where property is in question I am guilty . . . of erecting individual liberty as an idol, and of resenting all attempts to destroy or fetter it; but when you pass from liberty to life, in no well-governed State, in no State governed according to the principles of common humanity, are the claims of mere liberty allowed to endanger the lives of the citizens.

in the House of Lords, 29 July 1897

1 Horny-handed sons of toil.

in *Quarterly Review* October 1873; later popularized in the US by Denis Kearney (1847–1907)

2 By office boys for office boys.
    of the Daily Mail

H. Hamilton Fyfe *Northcliffe, an Intimate Biography* (1930)

3 If these gentlemen had their way, they would soon be asking me to defend the moon against a possible attack from Mars.
    of his senior military advisers, and their tendency to see threats which did not exist

Robert Taylor *Lord Salisbury* (1975)

4 I rank myself no higher in the scheme of things than a policeman—whose utility would disappear if there were no criminals.
    comparing his role in the Conservative Party with that of **Gladstone**

Lady Gwendolen Cecil *Biographical Studies . . . of Robert, Third Marquess of Salisbury* (1962)

5 To defend a bad policy as an 'error of judgement' does not excuse it—the right functioning of a man's judgement is his most fundamental responsibility.

Gwendolen Cecil *Life of Robert, Marquis of Salisbury* (1921–32) vol. 3

6 Too much poring over maps drives men mad.

Peter Hennessy *Never Again* (1992)

Lord Salisbury 1893–1972
British Conservative politician

7 I never shared the optimistic views of some of our friends that the old gentleman would be willing to retire gracefully into the background.
    of Winston Churchill in 1946

John Ramsden *The Age of Churchill and Eden, 1940–1957* (1995)

8 Too clever by half.
    of Iain **Macleod**, *Colonial Secretary, 'in his relationship to the white communities of Africa'*

in the House of Lords, 7 March 1961; see **Salisbury** 312:3

Sallust 86–35 BC
Roman historian

9 *Alieni appetens, sui profusus.*
    Greedy for the property of others, extravagant with his own.

Catiline

10 *Quieta movere magna merces videbatur.*
    To stir up undisputed matters seemed a great reward in itself.

Catiline

11 *Esse quam videri bonus malebat.*
    He preferred to be rather than to seem good.
    of Cato

Catiline

12 *Urbem venalem et mature perituram, si emptorem invenerit.*
    A venal city ripe to perish, if a buyer can be found.
    of Rome

Jugurtha

13 *Punica fide.*
    With Carthaginian trustworthiness.
    meaning treachery

Jugurtha

Alex Salmond 1954–

Scottish Nationalist politician
on *Salmond: see* **Steel** 345:11

1 Nobody ever celebrated Devolution Day.
  asserting his belief in full independence

in Independent 2 April 1992

2 I do not want to be separate from anything. I want for my
country to be joined in co-operation and mutual respect—
on a footing of equality—with all the nations of Europe.

in Scotsman 27 November 1998

Anthony Sampson 1926–

British author and journalist

3 A secret tome of *The Great and the Good* is kept, listing
everyone who has the right, safe qualifications of
worthiness, soundness and discretion; and from this tome
came the stage army of committee people.

Anatomy of Britain Today (1965)

Lord Sandwich 1718–92

British politician and diplomat; First Lord of the Admiralty

4 If any man will draw up his case, and put his name at the
foot of the first page, I will give him an immediate reply.
Where he compels me to turn over the sheet, he must wait
my leisure.
  on appeals made by officers to the Navy Board

N. W. Wraxall *Memoirs* (1884)
vol. 1

George Santayana 1863–1962

Spanish-born philosopher and critic

5 Fanaticism consists in redoubling your effort when you have
forgotten your aim.

The Life of Reason (1905);
introduction

6 Those who cannot remember the past are condemned to
repeat it.

The Life of Reason (1905)

Jacques Santer 1937–

Luxembourgeois politician, former head of the European
Commission

7 I note with considerable satisfaction that I am whiter than
white.
  of the inquiry into fraud at the European Commission

at a news conference, 16 March
1999

Patrick Sarsfield c.1655–93

Irish Jacobite
see also **Last words** 214:3

8 As low as we now are, change kings with us, and we will
fight it over again with you.
  *to English officers during negotiations for the Treaty of Limerick,
  1690*

in *Dictionary of National Biography*
(1917–)

Jean-Paul Sartre 1905–80

French philosopher, novelist, playwright, and critic

9 When the rich wage war it's the poor who die.

Le Diable et le bon Dieu (1951)

Sayings see Proverbs and sayings

Hugh Scanlon 1913–

British trade union leader

1 Of course liberty is not licence. Liberty in my view is conforming to majority opinion.

television interview, 9 August 1977

Arthur Scargill 1938–

British trade union leader

2 Parliament itself would not exist in its present form had people not defied the law.

evidence to House of Commons Select Committee on Employment, 2 April 1980

3 I wouldn't vote for Ken Livingstone if he were running for mayor of Toytown.

in *Guardian* 3 May 2000

Lord Scarman 1911–

British judge

4 The people as a source of sovereign power are in truth only occasional partners in the constitutional minuet danced for most of the time by Parliament and the political party in power.

The Shape of Things to Come (1989)

5 A government above the law is a menace to be defeated.

Why Britain Needs a Written Constitution 1992

6 Men still feel the need to keep the government in order. The feeling is deep, and as old as man.

Why Britain Needs a Written Constitution 1992

on the need for a written constitution:
7 No bevy of men, not even parliament, could always be trusted to safeguard human rights.

in conversation, 1982; Anthony Sampson *The Essential Anatomy of Britain* (1992)

8 When times are abnormally alive with fear and prejudice, the common law is at a disadvantage: it cannot resist the will, however frightened and prejudiced it may be, of parliament.
  after delivering a lecture advocating the establishment of a Bill of Rights

in conversation, 20 July 1992; Anthony Sampson *The Essential Anatomy of Britain* (1992)

Arthur M. Schlesinger Jr. 1917–

American historian

9 The answer to the runaway Presidency is not the messenger-boy Presidency. The American democracy must discover a middle way between making the President a czar and making him a puppet.

The Imperial Presidency (1973) preface

10 Suppose . . . that Lenin had died of typhus in Siberia in 1895 and Hitler had been killed on the western front in 1916. What would the twentieth century have looked like now?

The Cycles of American History (1986)

Caroline Kennedy Schlossberg 1958–
American writer, daughter of John F. **Kennedy**

1 Now it is our turn to prove that the New Frontier was not a place in time but a timeless call.

speech at the Democratic Convention, 15 August 2000; see **Kennedy** 198:2

Patricia Schroeder 1940–
American Democratic politician; Congresswoman

2 Ronald Reagan . . . is attempting a great breakthrough in political technology—he has been perfecting the Teflon-coated Presidency. He sees to it that nothing sticks to him.

speech in the US House of Representatives, 2 August 1983

E. F. Schumacher 1911–77
German-born economist

3 It was not the power of the Spaniards that destroyed the Aztec Empire but the disbelief of the Aztecs in themselves.

Roots of Economic Growth (1962)

4 Small is beautiful. A study of economics as if people mattered.

title of book, 1973

Carl Schurz 1829–1906
American soldier and politician

5 My country, right or wrong; if right, to be kept right; and if wrong, to be set right!

speech, US Senate, 29 February 1872

Claud Schuster 1869–1956
British civil servant

of the relationship between the Prime Minister and the Cabinet:
6 Like the procreation of eels, [it] is slippery and mysterious.

G. H. L. Le May *The Victorian Constitution* (1979)

H. Norman Schwarzkopf III 1934–
American general, Commander of US forces in the Gulf War

7 Seven months ago I could give a single command and 541,000 people would immediately obey it. Today I can't get a plumber to come to my house.

in Newsweek 11 November 1991; see **Truman** 366:7

C. P. Scott 1846–1932
British journalist; editor of the Manchester Guardian, 1872–1929

8 Comment is free, but facts are sacred.

in Manchester Guardian 5 May 1921; see **Stoppard** 348:9

Sir Walter Scott 1771–1832
Scottish novelist and poet

9 Breathes there the man, with soul so dead,
Who never to himself hath said,
This is my own, my native land!
Whose heart hath ne'er within him burned,
As home his footsteps he hath turned
From wandering on a foreign strand!

The Lay of the Last Minstrel (1805)

1 Now is the stately column broke,
The beacon-light is quench'd in smoke,
The trumpet's silver sound is still,
The warder silent on the hill!
   on the death of Pitt

Marmion (1808); introduction to canto 1

John Seeley 1834–95
English historian

2 We [the English] seem, as it were, to have conquered and peopled half the world in a fit of absence of mind.

The Expansion of England (1883); see **Hailsham** 157:8

John Selden 1584–1654
English historian and antiquary

3 Ignorance of the law excuses no man; not that all men know the law, but because 'tis an excuse every man will plead, and no man can tell how to confute him.

Table Talk (1689) 'Law'

4 A king is a thing men have made for their own sakes, for quietness' sake. Just as in a family one man is appointed to buy the meat.

Table Talk (1689) 'Of a King'

5 There is not anything in the world so much abused as this sentence, *Salus populi suprema lex esto.*

Table Talk (1689) 'People'; see **Cicero** 86:15

Arthur Seldon 1916–
British economist

6 Government of the busy by the bossy for the bully.
   subheading on over-government

Capitalism (1990)

W. C. Sellar 1898–1951
and R. J. Yeatman 1898–1968
British writers

7 The Cavaliers (Wrong but Wromantic) and the Roundheads (Right but Repulsive).

1066 and All That (1930)

8 The Rump Parliament—so called because it had been sitting for such a long time.

1066 and All That (1930)

9 Charles II was always very merry and was therefore not so much a king as a Monarch.

1066 and All That (1930)

10 The National Debt is a very Good Thing and it would be dangerous to pay it off, for fear of Political Economy.

1066 and All That (1930)

11 Most memorable . . . was the discovery (made by all the rich men in England at once) that women and children could work twenty-five hours a day in factories without many of them dying or becoming excessively deformed. This was known as the Industrial Revelation.

1066 and All That (1930)

12 Gladstone . . . spent his declining years trying to guess the answer to the Irish Question; unfortunately whenever he was getting warm, the Irish secretly changed the Question.

1066 and All That (1930)

13 AMERICA was thus clearly top nation, and History came to a .

1066 and All That (1930)

Gitta Sereny 1923–

Hungarian-born British writer and journalist

*to Albert Speer, who having always denied knowledge of the
Holocaust had said that he was at fault in having 'looked away':*

1 You cannot look away from something you don't know. If
you looked away, then you knew.

recalled on BBC2 *Reputations*, 2
May 1996

William Seward 1801–72

American politician

2 I know, and all the world knows, that revolutions never go
backward.

speech at Rochester, 25 October
1858

Edward Sexby d. 1658

English conspirator

3 Killing no murder briefly discourst in three questions.

title of pamphlet (an apology for
tyrannicide, 1657)

Anthony Ashley Cooper, Lord Shaftesbury 1621–83

in the English Civil War, adherent first of the royalist and then
(from 1644) of the Parliamentary cause; in the reign of **Charles
II**, supporter of **Monmouth**'s claim to the succession
on Shaftesbury: see **Cromwell** 98:13, **Dryden** 118:7

refusing the claims of Cromwell's House of Lords:
4 Admit lords, and you admit all.

in *Dictionary of National Biography*
(1917–)

William Shakespeare 1564–1616

English playwright

5 What's the matter, you dissentious rogues,
That, rubbing the poor itch of your opinion,
Make yourselves scabs?

Coriolanus (1608)

6   He that depends
Upon your favours swims with fins of lead,
And hews down oaks with rushes.

Coriolanus (1608)

7 Hear you this Triton of the minnows? mark you
His absolute 'shall'?

Coriolanus (1608)

8 What is the city but the people?

Coriolanus (1608)

9 You common cry of curs! whose breath I hate
As reek o' the rotten fens, whose loves I prize
As the dead carcases of unburied men
That do corrupt my air,—I banish you.

Coriolanus (1608)

10   Despising,
For you, the city, thus I turn my back:
There is a world elsewhere.

Coriolanus (1608)

11   The beast
With many heads butts me away.

Coriolanus (1608)

1 Let me have war, say I; it exceeds peace as far as day does   *Coriolanus* (1608)
night; it's spritely, waking, audible, and full of vent. Peace is
a very apoplexy, lethargy: mulled, deaf, sleepy, insensible; a
getter of more bastard children than war's a destroyer of
men.

2   I think he'll be to Rome   *Coriolanus* (1608)
As is the osprey to the fish, who takes it
By sovereignty of nature.

3 Why should we pay tribute? If Caesar can hide the sun from   *Cymbeline* (1609–10)
us with a blanket, or put the moon in his pocket, we will
pay him tribute for light; else, sir, no more tribute.

4   The art o' th' court,   *Cymbeline* (1609–10)
As hard to leave as keep, whose top to climb
Is certain falling, or so slipp'ry that
The fear's as bad as falling.

5 But in the gross and scope of my opinion,   *Hamlet* (1601)
This bodes some strange eruption to our state.

6 His greatness weighed, his will is not his own,   *Hamlet* (1601)
For he himself is subject to his birth.
He may not, as unvalued persons do,
Carve for himself, for on his choice depends
The sanity and health of the whole state;
And therefore must his choice be circumscribed
Unto the voice and yielding of that body
Whereof he is the head.

7 Something is rotten in the state of Denmark.   *Hamlet* (1601)

8 The time is out of joint; O cursèd spite,   *Hamlet* (1601)
That ever I was born to set it right!

9 For who would bear the whips and scorns of time,   *Hamlet* (1601)
The oppressor's wrong, the proud man's contumely,
The pangs of disprized love, the law's delay,
The insolence of office, and the spurns
That patient merit of the unworthy takes,
When he himself might his quietus make
With a bare bodkin? . . .
Thus conscience doth make cowards of us all.

10 Madness in great ones must not unwatched go.   *Hamlet* (1601)

11   Indeed this counsellor   *Hamlet* (1601)
Is now most still, most secret, and most grave,
Who was in life a foolish prating knave.

12 And where the offence is let the great axe fall.   *Hamlet* (1601)

13 The great man down, you mark his favourite flies;   *Hamlet* (1601)
The poor advanced makes friends of enemies.

14   Diseases desperate grown,   *Hamlet* (1601)
By desperate appliances are relieved,
Or not at all.

15 We go to gain a little patch of ground,   *Hamlet* (1601)
That hath in it no profit but the name.

16   Rightly to be great   *Hamlet* (1601)
Is not to stir without great argument,
But greatly to find quarrel in a straw
When honour's at the stake.

1 There's such divinity doth hedge a king,
That treason can but peep to what it would.

Hamlet (1601)

2 Rebellion lay in his way, and he found it.

Henry IV, Part 1 (1597)

3 It was always yet the trick of our English nation, if they
have a good thing, to make it too common.

Henry IV, Part 2 (1597)

4 Uneasy lies the head that wears a crown.

Henry IV, Part 2 (1597)

5 O England! model to thy inward greatness,
Like little body with a mighty heart,
What might'st thou do, that honour would thee do,
Were all thy children kind and natural!
But see thy fault!

Henry V (1599)

6 A little touch of Harry in the night.

Henry V (1599)

7 Discuss unto me; art thou officer?
Or art thou base, common and popular?

Henry V (1599)

8 I think the king is but a man, as I am: the violet smells to
him as it doth to me.

Henry V (1599)

9 I am afeard there are few die well that die in a battle; for
how can they charitably dispose of any thing when blood is
their argument?

Henry V (1599)

10 Every subject's duty is the king's; but every subject's soul is
his own.

Henry V (1599)

11 Upon the king! let us our lives, our souls,
Our debts, our careful wives,
Our children, and our sins lay on the king!
We must bear all. O hard condition!

Henry V (1599)

12   What infinite heart's ease
Must kings neglect, that private men enjoy!
And what have kings that privates have not too,
Save ceremony, save general ceremony?

Henry V (1599)

13 Put forth thy hand, reach at the glorious gold.

Henry VI, Part 2 (1592)

14 Is this the fashion of the court of England?
Is this the government of Britain's isle,
And this the royalty of Albion's king?

Henry VI, Part 2 (1592)

15 I say it was never merry world in England since gentlemen
came up.

Henry VI, Part 2 (1592)

16 The first thing we do, let's kill all the lawyers.

Henry VI, Part 2 (1592)

17 Is not this a lamentable thing, that of the skin of an
innocent lamb should be made parchment? that parchment,
being scribbled o'er, should undo a man?

Henry VI, Part 2 (1592)

18 Thou hast most traitorously corrupted the youth of the
realm in erecting a grammar school: and whereas, before,
our forefathers had no other books but the score and the
tally, thou hast caused printing to be used; and, contrary to
the king, his crown and dignity, thou hast built a paper-
mill.

Henry VI, Part 2 (1592)

19 Peace! impudent and shameless Warwick, peace;
Proud setter up and puller down of kings.

Henry VI, Part 3 (1592)

20 Farewell! a long farewell, to all my greatness!

Henry VIII (1613)

1   I have ventured,   *Henry VIII* (1613)
 Like little wanton boys that swim on bladders,
 This many summers in a sea of glory,
 But far beyond my depth . . .
 Vain pomp and glory of this world, I hate ye:
 I feel my heart new opened. O how wretched
 Is that poor man that hangs on princes' favours!
 There is, betwixt that smile we would aspire to,
 That sweet aspect of princes, and their ruin,
 More pangs and fears than wars or women have;
 And when he falls, he falls like Lucifer,
 Never to hope again.

2 Cromwell, I charge thee, fling away ambition: *Henry VIII* (1613)
 By that sin fell the angels; how can man then,
 The image of his Maker, hope to win by't?
 Love thyself last: cherish those hearts that hate thee;
 Corruption wins not more than honesty.
 Still in thy right hand carry gentle peace,
 To silence envious tongues: be just, and fear not.
 Let all the ends thou aim'st at be thy country's,
 Thy God's, and truth's: then if thou fall'st, O Cromwell!
 Thou fall'st a blessed martyr.

3 Had I but served my God with half the zeal   *Henry VIII* (1613)
 I served my king, he would not in mine age
 Have left me naked to mine enemies.

4 In her days every man shall eat in safety   *Henry VIII* (1613)
 Under his own vine what he plants; and sing
 The merry songs of peace to all his neighbours.

5 You blocks, you stones, you worse than senseless things!   *Julius Caesar* (1599)
 O you hard hearts, you cruel men of Rome,
 Knew you not Pompey?

6 CAESAR: Speak; Caesar is turned to hear.   *Julius Caesar* (1599)
 SOOTHSAYER: Beware the ides of March.

7   Ye gods, it doth amaze me,   *Julius Caesar* (1599)
 A man of such a feeble temper should
 So get the start of the majestic world,
 And bear the palm alone.

8 Why, man, he doth bestride the narrow world   *Julius Caesar* (1599)
 Like a Colossus; and we petty men
 Walk under his huge legs, and peep about
 To find ourselves dishonourable graves.
 Men at some time are masters of their fates:
 The fault, dear Brutus, is not in our stars,
 But in ourselves, that we are underlings.

9 'Brutus' will start a spirit as soon as 'Caesar'.   *Julius Caesar* (1599)
 Now in the names of all the gods at once,
 Upon what meat doth this our Caesar feed,
 That he is grown so great?

10 When could they say, till now, that talked of Rome,   *Julius Caesar* (1599)
 That her wide walls encompassed but one man?
 Now is it Rome indeed and room enough,
 When there is in it but one only man.

1 Let me have men about me that are fat;   *Julius Caesar* (1599)
Sleek-headed men and such as sleep o' nights;
Yond' Cassius has a lean and hungry look;
He thinks too much: such men are dangerous.

2 Such men as he be never at heart's ease,   *Julius Caesar* (1599)
Whiles they behold a greater than themselves,
And therefore are they very dangerous.

3 Th' abuse of greatness is, when it disjoins   *Julius Caesar* (1599)
Remorse from power.

4   'Tis a common proof,   *Julius Caesar* (1599)
That lowliness is young ambition's ladder,
Whereto the climber-upward turns his face;
But when he once attains the upmost round,
He then unto the ladder turns his back,
Looks in the clouds, scorning the base degrees
By which he did ascend.

5   O conspiracy!   *Julius Caesar* (1599)
Sham'st thou to show thy dangerous brow by night,
When evils are most free?

6 Let us be sacrificers, but not butchers, Caius.   *Julius Caesar* (1599)

7 But when I tell him he hates flatterers,   *Julius Caesar* (1599)
He says he does, being then most flattered.

8 CAESAR: The ides of March are come.   *Julius Caesar* (1599)
SOOTHSAYER: Ay, Caesar; but not gone.

9 If I could pray to move, prayers would move me;   *Julius Caesar* (1599)
But I am constant as the northern star,
Of whose true-fixed and resting
There is no fellow in the firmament.
The skies are painted with unnumbered sparks,
They are all fire and every one doth shine,
But there's but one in all doth hold his place:
So, in the world; 'tis furnished well with men,
And men are flesh and blood, and apprehensive;
Yet in the number I do know but one
That unassailable holds on his rank,
Unshaked of motion: and that I am he.

10 *Et tu, Brute?* Then fall, Caesar!   *Julius Caesar* (1599)

11 Ambition's debt is paid.   *Julius Caesar* (1599)

12 CASSIUS: How many ages hence   *Julius Caesar* (1599)
Shall this our lofty scene be acted o'er,
In states unborn, and accents yet unknown!
BRUTUS: How many times shall Caesar bleed in sport.

13 Waving our red weapons o'er our heads   *Julius Caesar* (1599)
Let's all cry 'Peace, freedom, and liberty!'

14 O mighty Caesar! dost thou lie so low?   *Julius Caesar* (1599)
Are all thy conquests, glories, triumphs, spoils,
Shrunk to this little measure?

1   Caesar's spirit, ranging for revenge,   *Julius Caesar* (1599)
With Ate by his side, come hot from hell,
Shall in these confines, with a monarch's voice
Cry, 'Havoc!' and let slip the dogs of war;
That this foul deed shall smell above the earth
With carrion men, groaning for burial.

2 Not that I loved Caesar less, but that I loved Rome more.   *Julius Caesar* (1599)

3 As he was valiant, I honour him: but, as he was ambitious,   *Julius Caesar* (1599)
I slew him.

4 Friends, Romans, countrymen, lend me your ears;   *Julius Caesar* (1599)
I come to bury Caesar, not to praise him.
The evil that men do lives after them,
The good is oft interrèd with their bones;
So let it be with Caesar. The noble Brutus
Hath told you Caesar was ambitious;
If it were so, it was a grievous fault;
And grievously hath Caesar answered it.

5 He was my friend, faithful and just to me: *Julius Caesar* (1599)
But Brutus says he was ambitious;
And Brutus is an honourable man.

6 When that the poor have cried, Caesar hath wept;   *Julius Caesar* (1599)
Ambition should be made of sterner stuff.

7   On the Lupercal   *Julius Caesar* (1599)
I thrice presented him a kingly crown
Which he did thrice refuse: was this ambition?

8 You all did love him once, not without cause.   *Julius Caesar* (1599)

9 But yesterday the word of Caesar might   *Julius Caesar* (1599)
Have stood against the world; now lies he there,
And none so poor to do him reverence.

10 This was the most unkindest cut of all.   *Julius Caesar* (1599)

11 O! what a fall was there, my countrymen;   *Julius Caesar* (1599)
Then I, and you, and all of us fell down,
Whilst bloody treason flourished over us.

12 I come not, friends, to steal away your hearts: *Julius Caesar* (1599)
I am no orator, as Brutus is;
But, as you know me all, a plain, blunt man,
That love my friend.

13 For I have neither wit, nor words, nor worth,   *Julius Caesar* (1599)
Action, nor utterance, nor power of speech,
To stir men's blood; I only speak right on;
I tell you that which you yourselves do know.

14   But were I Brutus,   *Julius Caesar* (1599)
And Brutus Antony, there were an Antony
Would ruffle up your spirits, and put a tongue
In every wound of Caesar, that should move
The stones of Rome to rise and mutiny.

15 Now let it work; mischief, thou art afoot,   *Julius Caesar* (1599)
Take thou what course thou wilt!

16 He shall not live; look, with a spot I damn him.   *Julius Caesar* (1599)

17 This is a slight unmeritable man,   *Julius Caesar* (1599)
Meet to be sent on errands.

1 There is a tide in the affairs of men, *Julius Caesar* (1599)
Which, taken at the flood, leads on to fortune;
Omitted, all the voyage of their life
Is bound in shallows and in miseries.
On such a full sea are we now afloat,
And we must take the current when it serves,
Or lose our ventures.

2 O Julius Caesar! thou art mighty yet! *Julius Caesar* (1599)
Thy spirit walks abroad, and turns our swords
In our own proper entrails.

3 This was the noblest Roman of them all; *Julius Caesar* (1599)
All the conspirators save only he
Did that they did in envy of great Caesar;
He, only, in a general honest thought
And common good to all, made one of them.
His life was gentle, and the elements
So mixed in him that Nature might stand up
And say to all the world, 'This was a man!'

4 This England never did, nor never shall, *King John* (1591–8)
Lie at the proud foot of a conqueror,
But when it first did help to wound itself.
Now these her princes are come home again,
Come the three corners of the world in arms,
And we shall shock them: nought shall make us rue,
If England to itself do rest but true.

5 Let go thy hold when a great wheel runs down a hill, lest it *King Lear* (1605–6)
break thy neck with following; but the great one that goes
upward, let him draw thee after.

6 A dog's obeyed in office. *King Lear* (1605–6)

7   Get thee glass eyes; *King Lear* (1605–6)
And, like a scurvy politician, seem
To see the things thou dost not.

8 MALCOLM: Nothing in his life *Macbeth* (1606)
Became him like the leaving it: he died
As one that had been studied in his death
To throw away the dearest thing he owed
As 'twere a careless trifle.
DUNCAN: There's no art
To find the mind's construction in the face;
He was a gentleman on whom I built
An absolute trust.

9   Thou wouldst be great; *Macbeth* (1606)
Art not without ambition, but without
The illness should attend it. What thou wouldst highly,
That wouldst thou holily; wouldst not play false,
And yet wouldst wrongly win.

10   Besides, this Duncan *Macbeth* (1606)
Hath borne his faculties so meek, hath been
So clear in his great office, that his virtues
Will plead like angels trumpet-tongued, against
The deep damnation of his taking-off.

1   I have no spur   *Macbeth* (1606)
To prick the sides of my intent, but only
Vaulting ambition, which o'erleaps itself,
And falls on the other.

2 Confusion now hath made his masterpiece!   *Macbeth* (1606)

3 Thou hast it now: King, Cawdor, Glamis, all,   *Macbeth* (1606)
As the weird women promised; and, I fear,
Thou play'dst most foully for't.

4 LADY MACBETH: Things without all remedy   *Macbeth* (1606)
Should be without regard: what's done is done.
MACBETH: We have scotched the snake, not killed it:
She'll close and be herself.

5   Duncan is in his grave;   *Macbeth* (1606)
After life's fitful fever he sleeps well;
Treason has done his worst: nor steel, nor poison,
Malice domestic, foreign levy, nothing,
Can touch him further.

6 Stands Scotland where it did?   *Macbeth* (1606)

7   Liberty plucks justice by the nose;   *Measure for Measure* (1604)
The baby beats the nurse, and quite athwart
Goes all decorum.

8 We must not make a scarecrow of the law,   *Measure for Measure* (1604)
Setting it up to fear the birds of prey,
And let it keep one shape, till custom make it
Their perch and not their terror.

9 'Tis one thing to be tempted, Escalus,   *Measure for Measure* (1604)
Another thing to fall. I not deny,
The jury, passing on the prisoner's life,
May in the sworn twelve have a thief or two
Guiltier than him they try.

10 No ceremony that to great ones 'longs,   *Measure for Measure* (1604)
Not the king's crown, nor the deputed sword,
The marshal's truncheon, nor the judge's robe,
Become them with one half so good a grace
As mercy does.

11   O! it is excellent   *Measure for Measure* (1604)
To have a giant's strength, but it is tyrannous
To use it like a giant.

12   Man, proud man,   *Measure for Measure* (1604)
Drest in a little brief authority,
Most ignorant of what he's most assured,
His glassy essence, like an angry ape,
Plays such fantastic tricks before high heaven,
As make the angels weep.

13 The quality of mercy is not strained,   *The Merchant of Venice* (1596–8)
It droppeth as the gentle rain from heaven
Upon the place beneath.

14 A substitute shines brightly as a king   *The Merchant of Venice* (1596–8)
Until a king be by, and then his state
Empties itself, as doth an inland brook
Into the main of waters.

15 We were not born to sue, but to command.   *Richard II* (1595)

1 How long a time lies in one little word!   *Richard II* (1595)
Four lagging winters and four wanton springs
End in a word; such is the breath of kings.

2 This royal throne of kings, this sceptered isle,   *Richard II* (1595)
This earth of majesty, this seat of Mars,
This other Eden, demi-paradise,
This fortress built by Nature for herself
Against infection and the hand of war,
This happy breed of men, this little world,
This precious stone set in the silver sea,
Which serves it in the office of a wall,
Or as a moat defensive to a house,
Against the envy of less happier lands,
This blessèd plot, this earth, this realm, this England.

3 The caterpillars of the commonwealth.   *Richard II* (1595)

4 Not all the water in the rough rude sea   *Richard II* (1595)
Can wash the balm from an anointed king;
The breath of worldly men cannot depose
The deputy elected by the Lord.

5 Is not the king's name twenty thousand names?   *Richard II* (1595)
Arm, arm, my name! A puny subject strikes
At thy great glory.

6 For God's sake, let us sit upon the ground   *Richard II* (1595)
And tell sad stories of the death of kings.

7   For within the hollow crown   *Richard II* (1595)
That rounds the mortal temples of a king
Keeps Death his court, and there the antick sits,
Scoffing his state and grinning at his pomp.

8 What must the king do now? Must he submit?   *Richard II* (1595)
The king shall do it: must he be deposed?
The king shall be contented: must he lose
The name of king? o' God's name, let it go.

9 You may my glories and my state depose,   *Richard II* (1595)
But not my griefs; still am I king of those.

10 Now mark me how I will undo myself.   *Richard II* (1595)

11 With mine own tears I wash away my balm,   *Richard II* (1595)
With mine own hands I give away my crown.

12 Mine eyes are full of tears, I cannot see: *Richard II* (1595)
And yet salt water blinds them not so much
But they can see a sort of traitors here.
Nay, if I turn my eyes upon myself,
I find myself a traitor with the rest.

13 Now is the winter of our discontent   *Richard III* (1591)
Made glorious summer by this sun of York.

14 Grim-visaged war hath smoothed his wrinkled front;   *Richard III* (1591)
And now, instead of mounting barbèd steeds,
To fright the souls of fearful adversaries,—
He capers nimbly in a lady's chamber
To the lascivious pleasing of a lute.

15 Since every Jack became a gentleman   *Richard III* (1591)
There's many a gentle person made a Jack.

16 Woe to the land that's governed by a child!   *Richard III* (1591)

1 Talk'st thou to me of 'ifs'? Thou art a traitor: *Richard III* (1591)
   Off with his head!

2 I am not in the giving vein to-day. *Richard III* (1591)

3 Men shut their doors against a setting sun. *Timon of Athens* (c.1607)

4 A stone is soft as wax, tribunes more hard than stones. *Titus Andronicus* (1590)
   A stone is silent and offendeth not,
   And tribunes with their tongues doom men to death.

5 Rome is but a wilderness of tigers. *Titus Andronicus* (1590)

6 The heavens themselves, the planets, and this centre *Troilus and Cressida* (1602)
   Observe degree, priority, and place,
   Insisture, course, proportion, season, form,
   Office, and custom, in all line of order.

7   O! when degree is shaked, *Troilus and Cressida* (1602)
   Which is the ladder to all high designs,
   The enterprise is sick.

8 Take but degree away, untune that string, *Troilus and Cressida* (1602)
   And, hark! what discord follows.

9 A plague of opinion! a man may wear it on both sides, like a *Troilus and Cressida* (1602)
   leather jerkin.

10 How my achievements mock me! *Troilus and Cressida* (1602)

Robert Shapiro 1942–

American lawyer; originally leader of the defence team at the trial
of O. J. Simpson

*of the change of strategy embraced after Johnnie Cochran took over
from him the leadership of the defence team:*
11 Not only did we play the race card, we played it from the in *The Times* 5 October 1995; see
   bottom of the deck. **Churchill** 79:8
   *to which Cochran responded, 'We didn't play the race card, we
   played the credibility card'*

George Bernard Shaw 1856–1950 ✓

Irish playwright
see also **Misquotations** 254:5

12 All great truths begin as blasphemies. *Annajanska* (1919)

13 What Englishman will give his mind to politics as long as he *The Apple Cart* (1930)
   can afford to keep a motor car?

14 He [the Briton] is a barbarian, and thinks that the customs *Caesar and Cleopatra* (1901)
   of his tribe and island are the laws of nature.

15 SWINDON: What will history say? *The Devil's Disciple* (1901)
   BURGOYNE: History, sir, will tell lies as usual.

16 Your friend the British soldier can stand up to anything *The Devil's Disciple* (1901)
   except the British War Office.

17 A government which robs Peter to pay Paul can always *Everybody's Political What's What?*
   depend on the support of Paul. (1944)

18 Go anywhere in England where there are natural, *Heartbreak House* (1919)
   wholesome, contented, and really nice English people; and
   what do you always find? That the stables are the real
   centre of the household.

1 The captain is in his bunk, drinking bottled ditch-water; and the crew is gambling in the forecastle. She will strike and sink and split. Do you think the laws of God will be suspended in favour of England because you were born in it?

Heartbreak House (1919)

2 It is evident that if the incomes of the rich were taken from them and divided among the poor as we stand at present, the poor would be very little less poor; the supply of capital would cease because nobody could afford to save; the country houses would fall into ruins; and learning and science and art and literature and all the rest of what we call culture would perish.

The Intelligent Woman's Guide to Socialism and Capitalism (1928)

3 Money is indeed the most important thing in the world; and all sound and successful personal and national morality should have this fact for its basis.

The Irrational Knot (1905) preface

4 An Irishman's heart is nothing but his imagination.

John Bull's Other Island (1907)

5 He knows nothing; and he thinks he knows everything. That points clearly to a political career.

Major Barbara (1907)

6 Nothing is ever done in this world until men are prepared to kill one another if it is not done.

Major Barbara (1907)

7 Englishmen never will be slaves: they are free to do whatever the Government and public opinion allow them to do.

Man and Superman (1903)

8 In the arts of peace Man is a bungler.

Man and Superman (1903)

9 Revolutions have never lightened the burden of tyranny: they have only shifted it to another shoulder.

Man and Superman (1903) 'The Revolutionist's Handbook' foreword

10 Democracy substitutes election by the incompetent many for appointment by the corrupt few.

Man and Superman (1903) 'Maxims: Democracy'

11 Liberty means responsibility. That is why most men dread it.

Man and Superman (1903) 'Maxims: Liberty and Equality'

12 The art of government is the organization of idolatry.

Man and Superman (1903) 'Maxims: Idolatry'

13 The reasonable man adapts himself to the world: the unreasonable one persists in trying to adapt the world to himself. Therefore all progress depends on the unreasonable man.

Man and Superman (1903) 'Maxims: Reason'

14 Titles distinguish the mediocre, embarrass the superior, and are disgraced by the inferior.

Man and Superman (1903) 'Maxims for Revolutionists: Titles'

15 Anarchism is a game at which the police can beat you.

Misalliance (1914)

16 You'll never have a quiet world till you knock the patriotism out of the human race.

O'Flaherty V.C. (1919)

17 Assassination is the extreme form of censorship.

The Showing-Up of Blanco Posnet (1911) 'Limits to Toleration'

Hartley Shawcross 1902–

British Labour politician and barrister

1 'But,' said Alice, 'the question is whether you can make a word mean different things.' 'Not so,' said Humpty-Dumpty, 'the question is which is to be the master. That's all.' We are the masters at the moment, and not only at the moment, but for a very long time to come.

in the House of Commons, 2 April 1946; see **Carroll** 70:15, **Misquotations** 255:10

2 I don't think it was right. It was victors' justice.
of the Nuremberg Trials

interviewed on his 95th birthday, in *Daily Telegraph* 10 February 1997

Charles Shaw-Lefevre 1794–1888

3 What is that fat gentleman in such a passion about?
*as a child, on hearing Charles James **Fox** speak in Parliament*

G. W. E. Russell *Collections and Recollections* (1898)

Francis Sheehy-Skeffington 1878–1916

Irish nationalist

4 A crank is a small engine that causes revolutions.
on being described as a crank

Owen Dudley Edwards and Fergus Pyle *1916: the Easter Rising* (1968)

Lord Shelburne 1737–1805

British Whig politician; Prime Minister

5 The country will neither be united at home nor respected abroad, till the reins of government are lodged with men who have some little pretensions to common sense and common honesty.

in the House of Lords, 22 November 1770

of the defence of the king's speech at the opening of the parliamentary session:
6 Nothing more than a string of sophisms, no less wretched in their texture than insolent in their tenor.

in the House of Lords, 31 October 1776

7 The sun of Great Britain will set whenever she acknowledges the independence of America . . . the independence of America would end in the ruin of England.

in the House of Lords, October 1782

Percy Bysshe Shelley 1792–1822 ✓

English poet

8 Let there be light! said Liberty,
And like sunrise from the sea,
Athens arose!

Hellas (1822)

9 I met Murder on the way—
He had a mask like Castlereagh.

'The Mask of Anarchy' (1819)

10 'My name is Ozymandias, king of kings:
Look on my works, ye Mighty, and despair!'

'Ozymandias' (1819)

11 Kingly conclaves stern and cold
Where blood with guilt is bought and sold.

Prometheus Unbound (1820)

12 Men of England, wherefore plough
For the lords who lay ye low?

'Song to the Men of England' (written 1819)

1 The seed ye sow, another reaps;
The wealth ye find, another keeps;
The robes ye weave, another wears;
The arms ye forge, another bears.

'Song to the Men of England'
(written 1819)

2 An old, mad, blind, despised, and dying king.

'Sonnet: England in 1819' (written 1819)

3 Tyranny entrenches itself within the existing interests of the most refined citizens of a nation and says 'If you dare trample upon these, be free.'

A Philosophical View of Reform (written 1819–20)

4 Monarchy is only the string that ties the robber's bundle.

A Philosophical View of Reform (written 1819–20)

William Shenstone 1714–63

English poet and essayist

5 Laws are generally found to be nets of such a texture, as the little creep through, the great break through, and the middle-sized are alone entangled in.

Works in Verse and Prose (1764)
vol. 2 'On Politics'; see **Anacharsis** 7:4, **Swift** 350:7

Gillian Shephard 1940–

British Conservative politician

6 John Major's self-control in Cabinet was rigid. The most angry thing he would ever do was to throw down his pencil.

in *Sunday Times* on 21 November 1999 'Talking Heads'

Philip Henry Sheridan 1831–88

American Union cavalry commander in the Civil War

7 The only good Indian is a dead Indian.
at Fort Cobb, January 1869

attributed; perhaps already proverbial

Richard Brinsley Sheridan 1751–1816

Anglo-Irish playwright and Whig politician

8 The newspapers! Sir, they are the most villainous— licentious—abominable—infernal—Not that I ever read them—No—I make it a rule never to look into a newspaper.

The Critic (1779)

9 The throne *we* honour is the *people's choice.*

Pizarro (1799)

10 The Right Honourable gentleman is indebted to his memory for his jests, and to his imagination for his facts.
in reply to Mr Dundas

in the House of Commons; T. Moore *Life of Sheridan* (1825) vol. 2

Tommy Sheridan

Scottish Socialist politician

11 I'm not surprised about Donald Dewar and the Labour Party being reluctant to let the photographers stay. The closer you get to Mr Dewar, the more you see what a Tory he is.
on the decision to ban photographers from the debating chamber of the Scottish Parliament

in *Scotsman* 18 March 2000

William Tecumseh Sherman 1820–91 ✔

American general; from 1864 chief Union commander in the west in succession to Ulysses S. **Grant**

1 I will never again command an army in America if we must carry along paid spies. I will banish myself to some foreign country first.
a reference to war correspondents

letter to his wife, February 1863

2 War is the remedy our *enemies* have chosen, and I say let us give them all they want.

in 1864; Geoffrey C. Ward *The Civil War* (1991)

3 [Grant] stood by me when I was crazy, and I stood by him when he was drunk; and now we stand by each other always.
of his relationship with his fellow Union commander, Ulysses S. Grant

in 1864; Geoffrey C. Ward *The Civil War* (1991)

4 I will not accept if nominated, and will not serve if elected.
on being urged to stand as Republican candidate in the 1884 presidential election

telegram to General Henderson; *Memoirs* (4th ed., 1891)

5 I think we understand what military fame is. To be killed on the field of battle and have our name spelled wrong in the newspapers.

Ken Burns *The Civil War* (documentary, 1989) episode 9

Emanuel Shinwell 1884–1986

British Labour politician

6 We know that the organised workers of the country are our friends. As for the rest, they don't matter a tinker's cuss.

speech to the Electrical Trades Union conference at Margate, 7 May 1947

Jonathan Shipley 1714–88

English clergyman, Bishop of St Asaph

7 I look upon North America as the only great nursery of freemen left on the face of the earth.
in 1774, after voting against the alteration of the constitution of Massachusetts, proposed as a punishment for the tea-ship riots at Boston

in *Dictionary of National Biography*

William Shippen 1673–1743

English Jacobite politician

8 Robin and I are two honest men: he is for King George and I for King James, but those men in long cravats [Sandys, Rushout, Pulteney, and their following] only desire places under one or the other.
view of his relationship with his political opponent Robert Walpole

in *Dictionary of National Biography* (1917–)

Clare Short 1946–

British Labour politician

contrasting Tony Blair's political advisers with elected politicians:
9 I sometimes call them the people who live in the dark. Everything they do is in hiding . . . Everything we do is in the light. They live in the dark.

in *New Statesman* 9 August 1996

1 It will be golden elephants next.

suggesting that the government of Montserrat was 'talking mad money' in claiming assistance for evacuating the island

in *Observer* 24 August 1997

Algernon Sidney 1622–83

English conspirator, executed for his alleged part in the Rye House Plot, 1683

2 Liars ought to have good memories.

Discourses concerning Government (1698)

3 Men lived like fishes; the great ones devoured the small.

Discourses concerning Government (1698)

4 'Tis not necessary to light a candle to the sun.

Discourses concerning Government (1698)

5 The law is established, which no passion can disturb. 'Tis void of desire and fear, lust and anger . . . 'Tis deaf, inexorable, inflexible.

Discourses concerning Government (1698) ch. 3, sect. 15; see **Adams** 3:1

Emmanuel Joseph Sieyès 1748–1836

French abbot and statesman

6 *La mort, sans phrases.*

Death, without rhetoric.

on voting in the French Convention for the death of **Louis XVI**, *16 January 1793*

attributed to Sieyès, but afterwards repudiated by him (*Le Moniteur* 20 January 1793 records his vote as 'La mort')

when asked what he had done during the French Revolution:

7 *J'ai vécu.*

I survived.

F. A. M. Mignet *Notice historique sur la vie et les travaux de M. le Comte de Sieyès* (1836)

Jim Sillars 1937–

Scottish Nationalist politician

8 I think the greatest problem we have is that we will sing Flower of Scotland at Hampden or Murrayfield, and that we have too many 90-minute patriots.

interview on Scottish Television, 23 April 1992

Simonides see **Epitaphs** 128:2

Kirke Simpson

American journalist

9 [Warren] Harding of Ohio was chosen by a group of men in a smoke-filled room early today as Republican candidate for President.

news report, 12 June 1920; see **Daugherty** 101:9

C. H. Sisson 1914–

English poet

10 Here lies a civil servant. He was civil To everyone, and servant to the devil.

The London Zoo (1961)

Sitting Bull (Tatanka Iyotake) c.1831–90

Hunkpapa Sioux leader

11 The Black Hills belong to me. If the whites try to take them, I will fight.

Dee Brown *Bury My Heart at Wounded Knee* (1970) ch. 12

Noel Skelton 1880–1935
British Conservative politician

1 To state as clearly as may be what means lie ready to develop a property-owning democracy, to bring the industrial and economic status of the wage-earner abreast of his political and educational, to make democracy stable and four-square.

in The Spectator 19 May 1923

■ **Slogans** *see box overleaf*

Gillian Slovo 1952–
South African writer

2 In most families it is the children who leave home. In mine it was the parents.
   of her anti-apartheid activist parents, Joe Slovo and Ruth First

Every Secret Thing (1997)

Adam Smith 1723–90
Scottish philosopher and economist

3 Little else is requisite to carry a state to the highest degree of opulence from the lowest barbarism, but peace, easy taxes, and a tolerable administration of justice; all the rest being brought about by the natural course of things.

in 1755; Essays on Philosophical Subjects (1795)

4 And thus, *Place*, that great object which divides the wives of aldermen, is the end of half the labours of human life; and is the cause of all the tumult and bustle, all the rapine and injustice, which avarice and ambition have introduced into this world.

Theory of Moral Sentiments (1759)

5 [The man of system] seems to imagine that he can arrange the different members of a great society with as much ease as the hand arranges the different pieces upon a chessboard; he does not consider that the pieces upon the chessboard have no other principle of motion besides that which the hand impresses upon them; but that, in the great chessboard of human society, every single piece has a principle of motion of its own, altogether different from that which the legislator might choose to impress upon it.

Theory of Moral Sentiments (1759)

6 It is not from the benevolence of the butcher, the brewer, or the baker, that we expect our dinner, but from their regard to their own interest. We address ourselves not to their humanity but their self love, and never talk to them of our necessities but of their advantages.

Wealth of Nations (1776)

7 People of the same trade seldom meet together, even for merriment and diversion, but the conversation ends in a conspiracy against the public, or in some contrivance to raise prices.

Wealth of Nations (1776)

8 To found a great empire for the sole purpose of raising up a people of customers, may at first sight appear a project fit only for a nation of shopkeepers. It is, however, a project altogether unfit for a nation of shopkeepers; but extremely fit for a nation whose government is influenced by shopkeepers.

Wealth of Nations (1776); see **Adams** 4:7, **Napoleon** 265:1

continued

Slogans

1 All power to the Soviets. — workers in Petrograd, 1917

2 All the way with LBJ. — in *Washington Post* 4 June 1960
*US Democratic Party campaign slogan supporting Lyndon Baines **Johnson***

3 *Arbeit macht frei.* — inscription, 1933
Work makes free.
on the gates of Dachau concentration camp, and subsequently on those of Auschwitz

4 Ban the bomb. — adopted by the Campaign for Nuclear Disarmament
US anti-nuclear slogan, 1953 onwards

5 A bayonet is a weapon with a worker at each end. — British pacifist slogan (1940)

6 Better red than dead. — slogan of nuclear disarmament campaigners, late 1950s

7 The big tent. — recorded from 1990; see also **Newspaper headlines** 267:13
slogan used by the Republican Party to denote a policy of inclusiveness

8 A bigger bang for a buck. — Charles E. **Wilson**'s defence policy, in *Newsweek* 22 March 1954

9 Black is beautiful. — slogan of American civil rights campaigners, mid-1960s

10 Burn, baby, burn. — Black extremist slogan in use during the Los Angeles riots, August 1965

11 Can't pay, won't pay. — anti-Poll Tax slogan, *c.*1990; see **Fo** 133:4

12 *Deutschland hat einen neuen Kanzler.* — in *Guardian* 29 September 1998
Germany has a new Chancellor.
added to a poster of Gerhard Schröder in West Berlin, 28 September 1998

13 *Ein Reich, ein Volk, ein Führer.* — early 1930s
One realm, one people, one leader.
Nazi Party slogan

14 Fair shares for all, is Labour's call. — Douglas Jay *Change and Fortune* (1980)
*slogan for the North Battersea by-election, 1946, coined by Douglas **Jay***

15 Fifty-four forty, or fight! — William Allen (1803–79), American Democratic politician, speech in the US Senate, 1844
slogan of expansionist Democrats in the presidential campaign of 1844, in which the Oregon boundary definition was an issue (in 1846 the new Democratic president, James K. Polk, compromised on the 49th parallel with Great Britain)

16 Free by '93. — Scottish National Party, general election campaign, 1992

17 Give us back our eleven days. — David Ewing Duncan *The Calendar* (1998)
protesting against the adoption of the Gregorian Calendar in 1752, and in this form associated with Hogarth's cartoon showing a rowdy Oxfordshire election of 1754

Slogans *continued*

1 Hey, hey, LBJ, how many kids have you killed today?
*anti-Vietnam War marching slogan during the presidency of
Lyndon **Johnson***

Jacquin Sanders *The Draft and the
Vietnam War* (1966)

2 I like Ike.
*used when General **Eisenhower** was first seen as a potential
presidential nominee*

US button badge, 1947; coined
by Henry D. Spalding (d. 1990)

3 I'm backing Britain.
*slogan coined by workers at the Colt factory, Surbiton, Surrey,
and subsequently used in a national campaign*

in *The Times* 1 January 1968

4 It's morning again in America.

slogan for Ronald **Reagan**'s
election campaign, 1984; coined
by Hal Riney (1932–); in
Newsweek 6 August 1984

5 It's Scotland's oil.

Scottish National Party, 1972

6 It's the economy, stupid.

on a sign put up at the 1992
Clinton presidential campaign
headquarters by campaign
manager James Carville

7 *Kraft durch Freude.*
Strength through joy.

German Labour Front slogan,
from 1933; coined by Robert Ley
(1890–1945)

8 Labour isn't working.
*caption to Conservative Party poster, 1978–9, showing a long
queue outside an unemployment office*

Philip Kleinman *The Saatchi and
Saatchi Story* (1987)

9 Labour's double whammy.

Conservative Party election
slogan 1992

10 The land for the people.

Communist slogan, *c.*1917

11 *Liberté! Égalité! Fraternité!*
Freedom! Equality! Brotherhood!
motto of the French Revolution (though of earlier origin)

the Club des Cordeliers passed a
motion, 30 June 1793, 'that
owners should be urged to paint
on the front of their houses, in
large letters, the words: Unity,
indivisibility of the Republic,
Liberty, Equality, Fraternity or
death'; in *Journal de Paris* no. 182
(from 1795 the words 'or death'
were dropped)

12 Life's better with the Conservatives. Don't let Labour ruin
it.

Conservative Party election
slogan, 1959

13 Lousy but loyal.

London East End slogan at
George V's Jubilee (1935)

14 Make love not war.

student slogan, 1960s

15 New Labour, new danger.

Conservative slogan, 1996

16 No crown of thorns, no cross of gold.

American Democratic party,
1900; see **Bryan** 55:7

Slogans *continued*

the defenders of the besieged city of Derry to the Jacobite army of James II, April 1689:

1 No surrender!
    adopted as a slogan of Protestant Ulster

Jonathan Bardon *A History of Ulster* (1992)

2 Power to the people.

slogan of the Black Panther movement, from *c.*1968 onwards

3 Think globally, act locally.

Friends of the Earth slogan, *c.*1985

in response to a Republican slogan, 'Thinking feller, vote for McKellar':

4 Think some more and vote for Gore.

American Democratic slogan in Senate campaign, Tennessee, 1952; coinage is attributed to Pauline LaFon **Gore** on behalf of her husband Albert Gore Sr.

5 Thirteen years of Tory misrule.

unofficial Labour party election slogan, also in the form 'Thirteen wasted years', 1964

6 Three acres and a cow.
    regarded as the requirement for self-sufficiency; associated with the radical politician Jesse Collings (1831–1920) and his land reform campaign begun in 1885

Jesse Collings in the House of Commons, 26 January 1886, although used earlier by Joseph **Chamberlain** in a speech at Evesham (in *The Times* 17 November 1885), by which time it was already proverbial

7 Tippecanoe and Tyler, too.
    *presidential campaign song for William Henry **Harrison**, 1840*

attributed to A. C. Ross (fl. 1840); see **Songs** 342:4

8 Ulster says no.
    slogan coined in response to the Anglo-Irish Agreement of 15 November 1985

in *Irish Times* 25 November 1985

9 Votes for women.
    *adopted when it proved impossible to use a banner with the longer slogan 'Will the Liberal Party Give Votes for Women?' made by Emmeline **Pankhurst** (1858–1928), Christabel **Pankhurst** (1880–1958), and Annie Kenney (1879–1953)*

slogan of the women's suffrage movement, from 13 October 1905; Emmeline Pankhurst *My Own Story* (1914)

10 War will cease when men refuse to fight.
    pacifist slogan (often quoted as 'Wars will cease . . . ')

from *c.*1936

11 We demand that big business give people a square deal.

Theodore Roosevelt, 1901; see **Roosevelt** 307:6

12 Would you buy a used car from this man?

campaign slogan directed against Richard **Nixon**, 1968

13 Yes it hurt, yes it worked.

Conservative Party slogan, 1996; see **Major** 238:11

14 Yesterday's men (they failed before!).

Labour Party slogan, referring to the Conservatives, 1970; coined by David Kingsley, Dennis Lyons, and Peter Lovell-Davis

Slogans *continued*

1 You never had it so good.

Democratic Party slogan during the 1952 US election campaign; see **Macmillan** 235:9

Adam Smith *continued*

2 Consumption is the sole end and purpose of production; and the interest of the producer ought to be attended to only so far as it may be necessary for promoting that of the consumer.

Wealth of Nations (1776)

3 There is no art which one government sooner learns of another than that of draining money from the pockets of the people.

Wealth of Nations (1776)

4 Every individual necessarily labours to render the annual revenue of society as great as he can. He generally neither intends to promote the public interest, nor knows how much he is promoting it. He intends only his own gain, and he is, in this, as in many other cases, led by an invisible hand to promote an end which was no part of his intention.

Wealth of Nations (1776)

5 Great nations are never impoverished by private, though they sometimes are by public prodigality and misconduct. The whole, or almost the whole public revenue, is in most countries employed in maintaining unproductive hands.

Wealth of Nations (1776)

6 What is prudence in the conduct of every private family, can scarce be folly in that of a great kingdom. If a foreign country can supply us with a commodity cheaper than we ourselves can make it, better buy it of them with some part of the produce of our own industry, employed in a way in which we have some advantage.

Wealth of Nations (1776)

7 That insidious and crafty animal, vulgarly called a statesman or politician, whose councils are directed by the momentary fluctuations of affairs.

Wealth of Nations (1776)

8 Those parts of education, it is to be observed, for the teaching of which there are no public institutions, are generally the best taught.

Wealth of Nations (1776)

9 The natural effort of every individual to better his own condition . . . is so powerful, that it is alone, and without any assistance, not only capable of carrying on the society to wealth and prosperity, but of surmounting a hundred impertinent obstructions with which the folly of human laws too often encumbers its operations.

Wealth of Nations (1776)

Alfred Emanuel Smith 1873-1944

American politician; presidential candidate in 1928

10 The crowning climax to the whole situation is the undisputed fact that William Randolph Hearst gave him the kiss of death.
    on **Hearst**'s support for Ogden Mills, Smith's unsuccessful opponent for the governorship of New York State

in *New York Times* 25 October 1926

11 All the ills of democracy can be cured by more democracy.

speech in Albany, 27 June 1933

1 No sane local official who has hung up an empty stocking over the municipal fireplace, is going to shoot Santa Claus just before a hard Christmas.
comment on the New Deal

in New Outlook December 1933

F. E. Smith, Lord Birkenhead 1872–1930

British Conservative politician and lawyer
on Smith: see **Asquith** 15:12

2 Does anyone suppose that any of us enjoy the prospect of playing a part for which so many of us are not obviously suited? I myself am a middle-aged lawyer, more at home, and I may perhaps add more highly remunerated, in the law courts than I am likely to be on the parade ground.
of his role in the Ulster Volunteer Force

speech to the House of Commons, 1913

3 The world continues to offer glittering prizes to those who have stout hearts and sharp swords.

Rectorial address, Glasgow University, 7 November 1923

4 We have the highest authority for believing that the meek shall inherit the earth; though I have never found any particular corroboration of this aphorism in the records of Somerset House.

Contemporary Personalities (1924) 'Marquess Curzon'

5 Nature has no cure for this sort of madness [Bolshevism], though I have known a legacy from a rich relative work wonders.

Law, Life and Letters (1927)

6 Austen [Chamberlain] always played the game, and he always lost it.

Lord Beaverbrook *Men and Power* (1956)

Ian Smith 1919–

Rhodesian politician; Prime Minister, 1964–79

7 I don't believe in black majority rule in Rhodesia—not in a thousand years.

broadcast speech, 20 March 1976

John Smith 1938–94

Scottish-born Labour politician, Leader of the Labour Party from 1992
on Smith: see **Dewar** 108:6

8 I am a doer and I want to do things, but there exists the terrible possibility in politics that you might never win.

in You 22 March 1992

9 The settled will of the Scottish people.
of the creation of a Scottish parliament

speech at the Scottish Labour Conference, 11 March 1994

Samuel Francis Smith 1808–95

American poet and divine

10 My country, 'tis of thee,
Sweet land of liberty,
Of thee I sing:
Land where my fathers died,
Land of the pilgrims' pride,
From every mountain-side
Let freedom ring.

'America' (1831)

Sydney Smith 1771–1845
English clergyman and essayist

1 The moment the very name of Ireland is mentioned, the English seem to bid adieu to common feeling, common prudence, and common sense, and to act with the barbarity of tyrants, and the fatuity of idiots.

Letters of Peter Plymley (1807)

2 Tory and Whig in turns shall be my host,
I taste no politics in boiled and roast.

letter to John Murray, November 1834

3 Lord John . . . would perform the operation for the stone— build St Peter's or assume—(with or without ten minutes notice) the command of the Channel Fleet; and no one would discover by his manner that the patient had died, the church tumbled down, and the Channel Fleet been knocked to atoms.
   of Lord John **Russell**

Letters to Archdeacon Singleton (1837–40) vol. 2

4 Daniel Webster struck me much like a steam-engine in trousers.

Lady Holland *Memoir* (1855)

5 He [Macaulay] has occasional flashes of silence, that make his conversation perfectly delightful.

Lady Holland *Memoir* (1855)

6 Minorities . . . are almost always in the right.

H. Pearson *The Smith of Smiths* (1934)

Tobias Smollett 1721–71
Scottish novelist

7 I think for my part one half of the nation is mad– and the other not very sound.

The Adventures of Sir Launcelot Greaves (1762)

8 Mourn, hapless Caledonia, mourn
Thy banished peace, thy laurels torn.

'The Tears of Scotland' (1746)

Jan Christiaan Smuts 1870–1950
South African statesman and soldier, Prime Minister 1919–24 and 1939–48

9 There is no doubt that mankind is once more on the move. The very foundations have been shaken and loosened, and things are again fluid. The tents have been struck, and the great caravan of humanity is once more on the march.
   on the League of Nations

W. K. Hancock *Smuts* (1968)

C. P. Snow 1905–80
English novelist and scientist

10 The official world, the corridors of power.

Homecomings (1956)

Philip Snowden 1864–1937
British Labour politician

11 This is not Socialism. It is Bolshevism run mad.
   on the Labour Party's 1931 election programme

radio broadcast, 17 October 1931

12 It would be desirable if every Government, when it comes to power, should have its old speeches burnt.

C. E. Bechofer Roberts ('Ephesian') *Philip Snowden* (1929)

Socrates 469–399 BC
Greek philosopher

1 Most excellent man, are you who are a citizen of Athens, the greatest of cities and the most famous for wisdom and power, not ashamed to care for the acquisition of wealth and for reputation and honour, when you neither care nor take thought for wisdom and truth and the perfection of your soul?

Plato *Apology*

2 And I tell you that virtue does not come from money, but from virtue comes money and all other good things to man, both to the individual and to the state.

Plato *Apology*

Alexander Solzhenitsyn 1918–
Russian novelist

3 You only have power over people as long as you don't take *everything* away from them. But when you've robbed a man of *everything* he's no longer in your power—he's free again.

The First Circle (1968)

4 The Gulag Archipelago.
  referring to the political prison camps dotted around the Soviet Union

title of book (1973–5)

5 The thoughts of a prisoner—they're not free either. They keep returning to the same things.

One Day in the Life of Ivan Denisovich (1962)

6 Mankind's salvation lies exclusively in everyone's making everything his business, in the people of the East being anything but indifferent to what is thought in the West, and in the people of the West being anything but indifferent to what happens in the East.

Nobel Prize Lecture, 1970

7 In our country the lie has become not just a moral category but a pillar of the State.

interview in 1974; in appendix to *The Oak and the Calf* (1975)

8 Yes, we are still the prisoners of communism, and yet, for us in Russia, Communism is a dead dog, while for many people in the West it is still a living lion.

broadcast on BBC Russian Service, in *Listener* 15 February 1979

Anastasio Somoza 1925–80
elected President of Nicaragua in 1967, he was overthrown by the Sandinistas in 1979, and assassinated while in exile in Paraguay

replying to an accusation of ballot-rigging:
9 You won the elections, but I won the count.

in *Guardian* 17 June 1977; see **Stoppard** 348:7

■ Songs and ballads *see box opposite*

Susan Sontag 1933–
American writer

10 The white race *is* the cancer of human history, it is the white race, and it alone—its ideologies and inventions—which eradicates autonomous civilizations wherever it spreads, which has upset the ecological balance of the planet, which now threatens the very existence of life itself.

in *Partisan Review* Winter 1967

Songs and ballads

1 *Allons, enfants de la patrie,*
Le jour de gloire est arrivé . . .
Aux armes, citoyens!
Formez vos battaillons!

Come, children of our country, the day of glory has arrived
. . . To arms, citizens! Form your battalions!

'La Marseillaise' (25 April 1792),
written by Claude-Joseph Rouget
de Lisle (1760–1836)

2 Among our ancient mountains,
And from our lovely vales,
Oh, let the prayer re-echo:
'God bless the Prince of Wales!'

'God Bless the Prince of Wales'
(1862 song), written by George
Linley (1798–1865)

3 Ara! but why does King James stay behind?
Lilli burlero bullen a la
Ho! by my shoul 'tis a Protestant wind
Lilli burlero bullen a la.
> *a Williamite song in mockery of Richard Talbot, newly created*
> *Earl of Tyrconnell by the Catholic James II in Dublin in 1688;*
> *the refrain parodies the Irish language*

'A New Song' (1687), written by
Thomas, Lord **Wharton**; Thomas
Kinsella *The New Oxford Book of*
Irish Verse (1986); attribution to
Wharton has been disputed

4 Belgium put the kibosh on the Kaiser.

title of song (1914), written by
Alf Ellerton

5 *Debout! les damnés de la terre!*
Debout! les forçats de la faim!
La raison tonne en son cratère,
C'est l'éruption de la fin . . .
Nous ne sommes rien, soyons tout!
C'est la lutte finale
Groupons-nous, et, demain,
L'Internationale
Sera le genre humain.

On your feet, you damned souls of the earth! On your feet,
inmates of hunger's prison! Reason is rumbling in its
crater, and its final eruption is on its way . . . We are
nothing, let us be everything! This is the final conflict: let
us form up and, tomorrow, the International will
encompass the human race.

'L'Internationale' (1871) by the
French politician Eugène Pottier
(1818–87)

6 From the halls of Montezuma,
To the shores of Tripoli,
We fight our country's battles,
On the land as on the sea.

'The Marines' Hymn' (1847)

7 God save our gracious king!
Long live our noble king!
God save the king!
Send him victorious,
Happy, and glorious,
Long to reign over us:
God save the king!

'God save the King', attributed
to various authors of the mid
eighteenth century, including
Henry **Carey**; Jacobite variants,
such as James Hogg 'The King's
Anthem' in *Jacobite Relics of*
Scotland Second Series (1821)
also exist

Songs and ballads *continued*

1 Confound their politics,
Frustrate their knavish tricks.

'God save the King', attributed to various authors; see **Songs** 341:7 above

2 I met wid Napper Tandy, and he took me by the hand,
And he said, 'How's poor ould Ireland, and how does she stand?'
She's the most disthressful country that iver yet was seen,
For they're hangin' men an' women for the wearin' o' the Green.

'The Wearin' o' the Green' (*c.*1795 ballad)

3 In good King Charles's golden days,
When loyalty no harm meant;
A furious High-Churchman I was,
And so I gained preferment.
Unto my flock I daily preached,
Kings are by God appointed,
And damned are those who dare resist,
Or touch the Lord's Anointed.
And this is law, I will maintain,
Unto my dying day, Sir,
That whatsoever King shall reign,
I will be the Vicar of Bray, sir!

'The Vicar of Bray' in *British Musical Miscellany* (1734) vol. 1

4 The iron-armed soldier, the true-hearted soldier,
The gallant old soldier of Tippecanoe.
presidential campaign song for William Henry **Harrison**, *1840*

attributed to George Pope Morris (1802–64); see **Slogans** 336:7

5 John Brown's body lies a mould'ring in the grave,
His soul is marching on.
inspired by the execution of the abolitionist John **Brown**, *after the raid on Harper's Ferry, on 2 December 1859*

song (1861), variously attributed to Charles Sprague Hall, Henry Howard Brownell, and Thomas Brigham Bishop

6 Keep the Home-fires burning,
While your hearts are yearning,
Though your lads are far away
They dream of Home.
There's a silver lining
Through the dark cloud shining;
Turn the dark cloud inside out,
Till the boys come Home.

'Till the Boys Come Home!' (1914 song by Lena Guilbert Ford); music by Ivor Novello

7 Lloyd George knew my father,
My father knew Lloyd George.

two-line comic song, sung to the tune of 'Onward, Christian Soldiers' and possibly by Tommy Rhys Roberts (1910–75)

8 Oh! we don't want to lose you but we think you ought to go
For your King and your Country both need you so;
We shall want you and miss you but with all our might and main
We shall cheer you, thank you, kiss you
When you come back again.

'Your King and Country Want You' (1914 song), written by Paul Alfred Rubens (1875–1917)

Songs and ballads *continued*

1 The people's flag is deepest red;
It shrouded oft our martyred dead,
And ere their limbs grew stiff and cold,
Their heart's blood dyed its every fold.
Then raise the scarlet standard high!
Within its shade we'll live or die.
Tho' cowards flinch and traitors sneer,
We'll keep the red flag flying here.

'The Red Flag' (1889), written by the Irish socialist songwriter James M. Connell (1852–1929)

2 Please to remember the Fifth of November,
Gunpowder Treason and Plot.
We know no reason why gunpowder treason
Should ever be forgot.

traditional rhyme on the Gunpowder Plot (1605)

3 So on the Twelfth I proudly wear the sash my father wore.

'The Sash My Father Wore', traditional Orange song

4 'Tis bad enough in man or woman
To steal a goose from off a common;
But surely he's without excuse
Who steals the common from the goose.

'On Inclosures'; in *The Oxford Book of Light Verse* (1938)

5 We don't want to fight, but, by jingo if we do,
We've got the ships, we've got the men, we've got the money too.
We've fought the Bear before, and while Britons shall be true,
The Russians shall not have Constantinople.

We Don't Want to Fight (music hall song by G. W. Hunt, 1878)

6 We shall not be moved.

title of labour and civil rights song (1931) adapted from an earlier gospel hymn

7 We shall overcome.
revived in 1946 as a protest song by Black tobacco workers, and in 1963 during the Black Civil Rights Campaign

title of song, originating from before the American Civil War, adapted as a Baptist hymn ('I'll Overcome Some Day', 1901) by C. Albert Tindley

Lord Soper 1903–98

British Methodist minister

of the quality of debate in the House of Lords:
8 It is, I think, good evidence of life after death.

in *Listener* 17 August 1978

Robert Southey 1774–1843

English poet and writer

9 Now tell us all about the war,
And what they fought each other for.

'The Battle of Blenheim' (1800)

10 'And everybody praised the Duke,
Who this great fight did win.'
'But what good came of it at last?'
Quoth little Peterkin.
'Why that I cannot tell,' said he,
'But 'twas a famous victory.'

'The Battle of Blenheim' (1800)

1 The death of Nelson was felt in England as something more than a public calamity; men started at the intelligence, and turned pale, as if they had heard of the loss of a dear friend.

The Life of Nelson (1813)

Lord Spencer 1964–
English peer

2 She needed no royal title to continue to generate her particular brand of magic.
> *tribute at the funeral of his sister,* **Diana***, Princess of Wales, 7 September 1997*

in *Guardian* 8 September 1997

3 We, your blood family, will do all we can to continue the imaginative way in which you were steering these two exceptional young men so that their souls are not simply immersed by duty and tradition but can sing openly as you planned.
> *referring to his nephews, Prince William and Prince Harry*

in *Guardian* 8 September 1997

Oswald Spengler 1880–1936
German historian

4 Socialism is nothing but the capitalism of the working class.

The Hour of Decision (1933)

Edmund Spenser c.1552–99
English poet

5 Ill can he rule the great, that cannot reach the small.

The Faerie Queen (1596)

Steven Spielberg 1947–
American film director and producer

6 I think that today's youth have a tendency to live in the present and work for the future—and to be totally ignorant of the past.

in *Independent on Sunday* 22 August 1999

Benjamin Spock 1903–
American paediatrician

7 To win in Vietnam, we will have to exterminate a nation.

Dr Spock on Vietnam (1968)

Cecil Spring-Rice 1859–1918
British diplomat; Ambassador to Washington from 1912

8 I vow to thee, my country—all earthly things above—
Entire and whole and perfect, the service of my love,
The love that asks no question: the love that stands the test,
That lays upon the altar the dearest and the best:
The love that never falters, the love that pays the price,
The love that makes undaunted the final sacrifice.

'I Vow to Thee, My Country' (written on the eve of his departure from Washington, 12 January 1918)

9 Wilson is the nation's shepherd and McAdoo his crook.
> *of President Woodrow* **Wilson** *and his secretary of the treasury, a remark considered unfortunate in the light of British attempts to draw the US into the First World War*

Robert Skidelsky *John Maynard Keynes* vol. 1 (1983)

Joseph Stalin 1879–1953

Soviet dictator

1 The State is an instrument in the hands of the ruling class, used to break the resistance of the adversaries of that class.

Foundations of Leninism (1924)

2 There is the question: Can Socialism *possibly* be established in one country alone by that country's unaided strength? The question must be answered in the affirmative.

Problems of Leninism (1926)

3 There are various forms of production: artillery, automobiles, lorries. You also produce 'commodities', 'works', 'products'. Such things are highly necessary. Engineering things. For people's souls. 'Products' are highly necessary too. 'Products' are very important for people's souls. You are engineers of human souls.

speech to writers at **Gorky**'s house, 26 October 1932; A. Kemp-Welch *Stalin and the Literary Intelligentsia, 1928–39* (1991); see **Gorky** 151:8, **Kennedy** 199:7

4 The Pope! How many divisions has *he* got?
on being asked to encourage Catholicism in Russia by way of conciliating the Pope

on 13 May 1935; W. S. Churchill *The Gathering Storm* (1948)

5 There is one eternally true legend—that of Judas.
at the trial of Radek in 1937

Robert Payne *The Rise and Fall of Stalin* (1966)

6 One death is a tragedy, one million is a statistic.

attributed

Charles E. Stanton 1859–1933

American soldier

7 *Lafayette, nous voilà!*
Lafayette, we are here.
at the tomb of Lafayette in Paris, 4 July 1917

in *New York Tribune* 6 September 1917

Edwin McMasters Stanton 1814–69

American lawyer

8 Now he belongs to the ages.
*of Abraham **Lincoln**, following his assassination, 15 April 1865*

I. M. Tarbell *Life of Abraham Lincoln* (1900)

David Steel 1938–

British Liberal politician; Leader of the Liberal Party 1976–88
on Steel: see **Foot** 134:3

9 I have the good fortune to be the first Liberal leader for over half a century who is able to say to you at the end of our annual assembly: go back to your constituencies and prepare for government.

speech to the Liberal Party Assembly, 18 September 1981

10 It is the settled will of the majority of people in Scotland that they want not just the symbol, but the substance of the return of democratic control over internal affairs.
on the announcement that the Stone of Destiny would be returned to Scotland

in *Scotsman* 4 July 1996

11 Mr Salmond is looking increasingly like a maiden in distress waiting to be rescued by James Bond. I do not think it is going to happen.
referring to Sean Connery's support for the Scottish National Party

in *Daily Telegraph* 27 April 1999

Lincoln Steffens 1866–1936

American journalist

1 I have seen the future; and it works.
following a visit to the Soviet Union in 1919

Letters (1938) vol. 1; see J. M. Thompson *Russia, Bolshevism and the Versailles Treaty* (1954), where it is recalled that Steffens had composed the expression before he had even arrived in Russia

Gertrude Stein 1874–1946

American writer

2 In the United States there is more space where nobody is than where anybody is. That is what makes America what it is.

The Geographical History of America (1936)

James Fitzjames Stephen 1829–94

English lawyer

3 The way in which the man of genius rules is by persuading an efficient minority to coerce an indifferent and self-indulgent majority.

Liberty, Equality and Fraternity (1873)

James Stephens 1882–1950

Irish nationalist

4 People say: 'Of course, they will be beaten.' The statement is almost a query, and they continue, 'but they are putting up a decent fight.' For being beaten does not matter greatly in Ireland, but not fighting does matter.

The Insurrection in Dublin (1916)

5 In my definition they were good men—men, that is, who willed no evil. No person living is the worse off for having known Thomas MacDonagh.

The Insurrection in Dublin (1916)

Adlai Stevenson 1900–65 ✓

American Democratic politician

6 I am not a politician, I am a citizen.
speech during the 1948 election campaign

Bert Cochran *Adlai Stevenson* (1969)

7 We must be patient—making peace is harder than making war.

speech to Chicago Council on Foreign Relations, 21 March 1946

8 I suppose flattery hurts no one, that is, if he doesn't inhale.

television broadcast, 30 March 1952

9 Better we lose the election than mislead the people.
on accepting the Democratic nomination in 1952

Herbert Muller *Adlai Stevenson* (1968)

10 Let's talk sense to the American people. Let's tell them the truth, that there are no gains without pains.
accepting the Democratic nomination

speech at the Democratic National Convention, Chicago, Illinois, 26 July 1952

11 If they [the Republicans] will stop telling lies about the Democrats, we will stop telling the truth about them.

speech during 1952 Presidential campaign; J. B. Martin *Adlai Stevenson and Illinois* (1976)

12 A hungry man is not a free man.

speech at Kasson, Minnesota, 6 September 1952

1 There is no evil in the atom; only in men's souls.

speech at Hartford, Connecticut, 18 September 1952

2 In America any boy may become President and I suppose it's just one of the risks he takes.

speech in Indianapolis, 26 September 1952

3 A free society is a society where it is safe to be unpopular.

speech in Detroit, 7 October 1952

4 The Republican party did not have to . . . encourage the excesses of its Vice-Presidential nominee [Richard Nixon]— the young man who asks you to set him one heart-beat from the Presidency of the United States.

speech at Cleveland, Ohio, 23 October 1952; see **Misquotations** 255:3

5 A funny thing happened to me on the way to the White House.
   speech in Washington, 13 December 1952, following his defeat in the Presidential election

Alden Whitman *Portrait: Adlai E. Stevenson* (1965)

6 We hear the Secretary of State [John Foster Dulles] boasting of his brinkmanship—the art of bringing us to the edge of the abyss.

speech in Hartford, Connecticut, 25 February 1956; see **Dulles** 120:1

7 The idea that you can merchandize candidates for high office like breakfast cereal—that you can gather votes like box tops—is, I think, the ultimate indignity to the democratic process.

speech at the Democratic National Convention, 18 August 1956

8 You have taught me a lesson I should have learned long ago— to take counsel always of your courage and never of your fears.
   on losing the Presidential nomination in 1960

Herbert J. Muller *Adlai Stevenson* (1968)

9 Do you remember that in classical times when Cicero had finished speaking, the people said, 'How well he spoke', but when Demosthenes had finished speaking, they said, 'Let us march.'
   *introducing John Fitzgerald **Kennedy** in 1960*

Bert Cochran *Adlai Stevenson* (1969)

10 She would rather light a candle than curse the darkness, and her glow has warmed the world.
   *on learning of Eleanor **Roosevelt**'s death*

in *New York Times* 8 November 1962

11 Eggheads of the world unite; you have nothing to lose but your yolks.
   perhaps a reworking of 'Eggheads of the world, arise—I was even going to add that you have nothing to lose but your yolks', speech at Oakland, 1 February 1956

attributed

12 If I had any epitaph that I would rather have more than another, it would be to say that I had disturbed the sleep of my generation.

epigraph to Jack W. Germand and Jules Witcover *Wake Us When It's Over* (1985)

13 The kind of politician who would cut down a redwood tree, and then mount the stump and make a speech on conservation.
   *of Richard **Nixon***

Fawn M. Brodie *Richard Nixon* (1983)

14 A politician is a person who approaches every subject with an open mouth.

attributed

15 The sound of tireless voices is the price we pay for the right to hear the music of our own opinions.

in *The Guide to American Law* (1984)

Robert Louis Stevenson 1850–94
Scottish writer

1 Politics is perhaps the only profession for which no preparation is thought necessary.

Familiar Studies of Men and Books (1882)

Sting 1951–
English rock singer, songwriter, and actor

2 If I were a Brazilian without land or money or the means to feed my children, I would be burning the rain forest too.

in *International Herald Tribune* 14 April 1989

Caskie Stinnett 1911–

3 A diplomat . . . is a person who can tell you to go to hell in such a way that you actually look forward to the trip.

Out of the Red (1960)

Baroness Stocks 1891–1975
British educationist

4 The House of Lords is a perfect eventide home.

My Commonplace Book (1970)

Lord Stockton 1943–
British peer, grandson of Harold **Macmillan**

5 As an old man he only had nightmares about two things: the trenches in the Great War and what would have happened if the Cuban Missile Crisis had gone wrong.
   of Harold **Macmillan**

in 1998; Peter Hennessy *The Prime Minister: the Office and its Holders since 1945* (2000)

I. F. Stone 1907–89
American journalist

6 The difference between burlesque and the newspapers is that the former never pretended to be performing a public service by exposure.

I. F. Stone's Weekly 7 September 1952

Tom Stoppard 1937–
British playwright

7 It's not the voting that's democracy, it's the counting.

Jumpers (1972); see **Somoza** 340:9

8 The House of Lords, an illusion to which I have never been able to subscribe—responsibility without power, the prerogative of the eunuch throughout the ages.

Lord Malquist and Mr Moon (1966); see **Kipling** 207:1

9 Comment is free but facts are on expenses.

Night and Day (1978); see **Scott** 316:8

10 I'm with you on the free press. It's the newspapers I can't stand.

Night and Day (1978)

11 War is capitalism with the gloves off and many who go to war know it but they go to war because they don't want to be a hero.

Travesties (1975)

William Stoughton 1631–1701

12 God hath sifted a nation that he might send choice grain into this wilderness.

election sermon in Boston, 29 April 1669

Lord Stowell 1745–1836

English jurist

1 The elegant simplicity of the three per cents.

Lord Campbell *Lives of the Lord Chancellors* (1857); see **Disraeli** 114:10

2 A precedent embalms a principle.
  an opinion, while Advocate-General, 1788

quoted by Disraeli in the House of Commons, 22 February 1848

Thomas Wentworth, Lord Strafford

1593–1641

English statesman

3 The authority of a King is the keystone which closeth up the arch of order and government which, once shaken, all the frame falls together in a confused heap of foundation and battlement.

Hugh Trevor-Roper *Historical Essays* (1952)

John Whitaker ('Jack') Straw 1946–

British Labour politician

4 It's not because ageing wrinklies have tried to stop people having fun. It's because . . . these so-called soft drugs are potentially very dangerous.
  asserting his opposition to the legalization of cannabis

on *Breakfast with Frost*, BBC1 TV, 4 January 1998

5 What you have within the UK is three small nations who've been under the cosh of the English.

In *Sunday Times* 6 January 2000 'Talking Heads'

Barbra Streisand 1942–

American singer and actress

6 We elected a President, not a Pope.
  to journalists at the White House, 5 February 1998

reported by James Naughtie, BBC Radio 4, Today programme, 6 February 1998

Simeon Strunsky 1879–1948

7 People who want to understand democracy should spend less time in the library with Aristotle and more time on buses and in the subway.

No Mean City (1944)

Louis Sullivan 1933–

American Secretary of Health and Human Services

on the probable nature of a nationalized health service:
8 What we would have is a combination of the compassion of the Internal Revenue Service and the efficiency of the post office.

in *Newsweek* February 1992

Timothy Daniel Sullivan 1827–1914

Irish writer and politician

9 'God save Ireland!' said the heroes;
  'God save Ireland', say they all:
  Whether on the scaffold high
  Or the battlefield we die,
  Oh, what matter when for Erin dear we fall.

'God Save Ireland' (1867); see **Last words** 212:7

Maximilien de Béthune, Duc de Sully
1559–1641

French statesman

1 Tilling and grazing are the two breasts by which France is fed.

Mémoires (1638)

2 The English take their pleasures sadly after the fashion of their country.

attributed

Arthur Hays Sulzberger 1891–1968

American newspaper proprietor

3 We tell the public which way the cat is jumping. The public will take care of the cat.
   on journalism

in *Time* 8 May 1950

Charles Sumner 1811–74

American politician and orator
on Sumner: see **Adams** 2:11

4 Where Slavery is, there Liberty cannot be; and where Liberty is, there Slavery cannot be.

'Slavery and the Rebellion'; speech at Cooper Institute 5 November 1864

5 There is the National flag. He must be cold, indeed, who can look upon its folds rippling in the breeze without pride of country. If in a foreign land, the flag is companionship, and country itself, with all its endearments.

Are We a Nation? 19 November 1867

Hannen Swaffer 1879–1962

British journalist

6 Freedom of the press in Britain means freedom to print such of the proprietor's prejudices as the advertisers don't object to.

said to Tom Driberg c.1928; Tom Driberg *Swaff* (1974)

Jonathan Swift 1667–1745

Anglo-Irish poet, satirist, and clergyman

7 It is the folly of too many, to mistake the echo of a London coffee-house for the voice of the kingdom.

The Conduct of the Allies (1711)

8 Laws are like cobwebs, which may catch small flies, but let wasps and hornets break through.

A Critical Essay upon the Faculties of the Mind (1709); see **Anacharsis** 7:4, **Shenstone** 330:5

9 I cannot but conclude the bulk of your natives to be the most pernicious race of little odious vermin that nature ever suffered to crawl upon the surface of the earth.

Gulliver's Travels (1726) 'A Voyage to Brobdingnag'

10 And he gave it for his opinion, that whoever could make two ears of corn or two blades of grass to grow upon a spot of ground where only one grew before, would deserve better of mankind, and do more essential service to his country than the whole race of politicians put together.

Gulliver's Travels (1726) 'A Voyage to Brobdingnag'

1 I have been assured by a very knowing American of my acquaintance in London, that a young healthy child well nursed is at a year old a most delicious, nourishing, and wholesome food, whether stewed, roasted, baked, or boiled, and I make no doubt that it will equally serve in a fricassee, or a ragout.

A Modest Proposal for Preventing the Children of Ireland from being a Burden to their Parents or Country (1729)

2 Party is the madness of many for the gain of a few.

Thoughts on Various Subjects (1711)

Tacitus AD c.56–after 117
Roman senator and historian

3 *Res olim dissociabiles miscuerit, principatum ac libertatem.*
He [Nerva] has united things long incompatible, the principate and liberty.

Agricola; see **Disraeli** 113:9

4 Now the boundary of Britain is revealed, and everything unknown is held to be glorious.
    reporting the speech of a British leader, Calgacus

Agricola

5 They make a wilderness and call it peace.

Agricola

6 You were indeed fortunate, Agricola, not only in the distinction of your life, but also in the lucky timing of your death.

Agricola

7 With neither anger nor partiality.

Annals

8 The more corrupt the republic, the more numerous the laws.

Annals

9 These times having the rare good fortune that you may think what you like and say what you think.

Histories

10 He seemed much greater than a private citizen while he still was a private citizen, and by everyone's consent capable of reigning if only he had not reigned.
    of the Emperor Galba

Histories

11 The gods are on the side of the stronger.

Histories; see **Voltaire** 372:6

William Howard Taft 1857–1930
American Republican statesman, 27th President of the US 1909–13

12 Next to the right of liberty, the right of property is the most important individual right guaranteed by the Constitution and the one which, united with that of personal liberty, has contributed more to the growth of civilization than any other institution established by the human race.

Popular Government (1913)

Charles-Maurice de Talleyrand 1754–1838
French statesman
on Talleyrand: see **Louis Philippe** 225:10, **Napoleon** 265:4

of the Bourbons in exile:
13 They have learnt nothing, and forgotten nothing.
    a similar comment on the courtiers of **Louis XVIII**, *attributed to the French general Dumouriez, was quoted by* **Napoleon** *in his Declaration to the French on his return from Elba*

oral tradition, attributed to Talleyrand by the Chevalier de Panat, January 1796

on hearing of **Napoleon***'s costly victory at Borodino, 1812:*
1 This is the beginning of the end.

Sainte-Beuve *M. de Talleyrand* (1870); attributed

2 It is not an event, it is an item of news.
on hearing of the death of **Napoleon** *in 1821*

Philip Henry Stanhope *Notes of Conversations with the Duke of Wellington* (1888) 1 November 1831

3 Above all, gentlemen, not the slightest zeal.

P. Chasles *Voyages d'un critique à travers la vie et les livres* (1868) vol. 2

4 That, Sire, is a question of dates.
often quoted as, 'treason is a matter of dates'; replying to the Tsar's criticism of those who 'betrayed the cause of Europe'

Duff Cooper *Talleyrand* (1932)

5 What a sad old age you are preparing for yourself.
to a young diplomat who boasted of his ignorance of whist

J. Amédée Pichot *Souvenirs Intimes sur M. de Talleyrand* (1870) 'Le Pour et le Contre'

R. H. Tawney 1880–1962
British economic historian

6 The characteristic virtue of Englishmen is power of sustained practical activity and their characteristic vice a reluctance to test the quality of that activity by reference to principles.

The Acquisitive Society (1921)

7 Militarism . . . is fetish worship. It is the prostration of men's souls and the laceration of their bodies to appease an idol.

The Acquisitive Society (1921)

8 That seductive border region where politics grease the wheels of business and polite society smiles hopefully on both.

Business and Politics under James I (1958)

9 Those who dread a dead-level of income or wealth . . . do not dread, it seems, a dead-level of law and order, and of security for life and property.

Equality (1931)

10 Freedom for the pike is death for the minnows.

Equality (ed. 3 1938)

11 Private property is a necessary institution, at least in a fallen world; men work more and dispute less when goods are private than when they are common. But it is to be tolerated as a concession to human frailty, not applauded as desirable in itself.

Religion and the Rise of Capitalism (1926) ch. 1, sect. 1

12 Both the existing economic order, and too many of the projects advanced for reconstructing it, break down through their neglect of the truism that, since even quite common men have souls, no increase in material wealth will compensate them for arrangements which insult their self-respect and impair their freedom. A reasonable estimate of economic organisation must allow for the fact that, unless industry is to be paralysed by recurrent revolts on the part of outraged human nature, it must satisfy criteria which are not purely economic.

Religion and the Rise of Capitalism (1926) conclusion

13 Democracy a society where ordinary men exercise initiative. Dreadful respect for superiors. Mental enlargement . . . Real foe to be overcome . . . fact that large section of the public *like* plutocratic government, and are easily gullible. How shake them!

unpublished fragment of Chicago lecture (1939), read at Tawney's funeral

declining the offer of a peerage:
1 What harm have I ever done to the Labour Party?

in *Evening Standard* 18 January 1962

A. J. P. Taylor 1906–90
British historian

2 History gets thicker as it approaches recent times.

English History 1914–45 (1965) Bibliography

3 In the Second World War the British people came of age. This was a people's war . . . Few now sang *Land of Hope and Glory*. Few even sang *England Arise*. England had risen all the same.

English History, 1914–1945 (1965)

4 He aroused every feeling except trust.
    of **Lloyd George**

English History 1914–1945 (1965)

5 The politician performs upon the stage; the historian looks behind the scenery.

Englishmen and Others (1956)

6 The First World War had begun—imposed on the statesmen of Europe by railway timetables. It was an unexpected climax to the railway age.

The First World War (1963)

of the period after the First World War:
7 Civilization was held together by the civilized behaviour of ordinary people . . . In reality the masses were calmer and more sensible than those who ruled over them.

From Sarajevo to Potsdam (1966)

8 A racing tipster who only reached Hitler's level of accuracy would not do well for his clients.

The Origins of the Second World War (1961)

9 Human blunders, however, usually do more to shape history than human wickedness.

The Origins of the Second World War (1961)

10 With Hitler guilty, every other German could claim innocence.

The Origins of the Second World War (1961)

11 If men are to respect each other for what they are, they must cease to respect each other for what they own.

Politicians, Socialism and Historians (1980)

12 Crimea: The War That Would Not Boil.

Rumours of Wars (1952); originally the title of an essay in *History Today* 2 February 1951

13 Conformity may give you a quiet life; it may even bring you a University Chair. But all change in history, all advance, comes from the nonconformist. If there had been no trouble makers, no Dissenters, we should still be living in caves.

The Troublemakers (1957)

14 Without democracy socialism would be worth nothing, but democracy is worth a great deal even when it is not socialist.

in *Manchester Guardian* 7 March 1941

15 The British political system has no room for the rogue elephant.

in *History Today* July 1951 'Lord Palmerston'

16 Bismarck was a political genius of the highest rank, but he lacked one essential quality of the constructive statesman: he had no faith in the future.

in *Encyclopedia Britannica* (1954)

17 Appeasement was a sensible course, even though it was tried with the wrong man; and it remains the noblest word in the diplomatist's vocabulary.

in *Manchester Guardian* 30 September 1958

18 Like Johnson's friend Edwards, I, too have tried to be a Marxist but common sense kept breaking in.

'Accident Prone' in *Journal of Modern History* 1977

Henry Taylor 1800–86
British writer

1 It is of far greater importance to a statesman to make one friend who will hold out with him for twenty years, than to find twenty followers in each year, losing as many.

The Statesman (1836)

2 No statesman, be he as discreet as he may, will escape having ascribed to him, as the result of interviews, promises and understandings which it was not his purpose to convey; and yet in a short time he will be unable to recollect what was said with sufficient distinctness to enable him to give a confident contradiction.

The Statesman (1836)

3 The conscience of a statesman should be rather a strong conscience than a tender conscience.

The Statesman (1836)

4 It is very certain that there may be met with, in public life, a species of conscience which is all bridle and no spurs.

The Statesman (1836)

5 The hand which executes a measure should belong to the head which propounds it.

The Statesman (1836)

6 One who would thrive by seeking favours from the great, should never trouble them for small ones.

The Statesman (1836)

7 [A statesman] should steer by the compass, but he must lie with the wind.

The Statesman (1836)

8 A secret may be sometimes best kept by keeping the secret of its being a secret.

The Statesman (1836)

9 To choose that which will bring him the most credit with the least trouble, has hitherto been the sole care of the statesman in office.

The Statesman (1836)

10 Good nature and kindness towards those with whom they come in personal contact, at the expense of public interests, that is of those whom they never see, is the besetting sin of public men.

The Statesman (1836)

11 He who has once advanced by a stride will not be content to advance afterwards by steps. Public servants, therefore, like racehorses, should be well fed with reward, but not to fatness.

The Statesman (1836)

12 Men in high places, from having less personal interest in the characters of others—being safe from them—are commonly less acute observers, and with their progressive elevation in life become, as more and more indifferent to what other men are, so more and more ignorant of them.

The Statesman (1836)

Norman Tebbit 1931–
British Conservative politician
on Tebbit: see **Foot** 134:2

13 I grew up in the Thirties with our unemployed father. He did not riot, he got on his bike and looked for work.

speech at Conservative Party Conference, 15 October 1981

14 The cricket test—which side do they cheer for? . . . Are you still looking back to where you came from or where you are?
on the loyalties of Britain's immigrant population

interview in *Los Angeles Times*, reported in *Daily Telegraph* 20 April 1990

Tecumseh 1768–1813

Shawnee leader

1 Where today are the Pequot? Where are the Narragansett, the Mohican, the Pokanoket, and many other once powerful tribes of our people? They have vanished before the avarice and oppression of the white man, as snow before the summer sun.

Dee Brown *Bury My Heart at Wounded Knee* (1970) ch. 1

William Temple 1881–1944

English theologian; Archbishop of Canterbury from 1942

2 In place of the conception of the power-state we are led to that of the welfare-state.

Citizen and Churchman (1941)

John Tenniel 1820–1914

English draughtsman

3 Dropping the pilot.
   *cartoon caption, and title of poem, on **Bismarck**'s dismissal from office by Kaiser **Wilhelm II***

in *Punch* 29 March 1890

Lord Tennyson 1809–92

English poet

4 Kind hearts are more than coronets,
And simple faith than Norman blood.

'Lady Clara Vere de Vere' (1842) st. 7

5   Forward, forward let us range,
Let the great world spin for ever down the ringing grooves of change.

'Locksley Hall' (1842)

6 The last great Englishman is low.

'Ode on the Death of the Duke of Wellington' (1852)

7 O good grey head which all men knew!

'Ode on the Death of the Duke of Wellington' (1852)

8 O fall'n at length that tower of strength
Which stood four-square to all the winds that blew!

'Ode on the Death of the Duke of Wellington' (1852)

9 That world-earthquake, Waterloo!

'Ode on the Death of the Duke of Wellington' (1852)

10 Who never sold the truth to serve the hour,
Nor paltered with Eternal God for power.

'Ode on the Death of the Duke of Wellington' (1852)

11 Not once or twice in our rough island-story,
The path of duty was the way to glory.

'Ode on the Death of the Duke of Wellington' (1852)

12 Authority forgets a dying king.

'The Passing of Arthur' (1869)

13 The old order changeth, yielding place to new,
And God fulfils himself in many ways,
Lest one good custom should corrupt the world.

'The Passing of Arthur' 1869

14 A land of settled government,
A land of just and old renown,
Where Freedom slowly broadens down
From precedent to precedent.

'You ask me, why, though ill at ease' (1842)

Terence 190–159 BC

Roman comic playwright

1 *Quot homines tot sententiae: suus cuique mos.*
There are as many opinions as there are people: each has
his own correct way.

Phormio

Margaret Thatcher 1925– ✓

British Conservative stateswoman, Prime Minister 1979–90
on Thatcher: see **Anonymous** 9:8, **Biffen** 40:5, **Callaghan** 66:7,
Critchley 97:7, **Healey** 165:11, 166:2, **Healey** 166:4, **Hennessy**
168:6, **Kinnock** 204:6, **Major** 239:6, **Mitterrand** 256:8, **Parris**
284:2, **West** 380:9

2 No woman in my time will be Prime Minister or Chancellor
or Foreign Secretary—not the top jobs. Anyway I wouldn't
want to be Prime Minister. You have to give yourself 100%.
on her appointment as Shadow Education Spokesman

in *Sunday Telegraph* 26 October
1969

3 In politics if you want anything said, ask a man. If you want
anything done, ask a woman.

in *People* (New York) 15 September
1975

4 I'll always be fond of dear Ted, but there's no sympathy in
politics.
of her predecessor, Edward **Heath**

attributed, 1975

5 I stand before you tonight in my red chiffon evening gown,
my face softly made up, my fair hair gently waved . . . the
Iron Lady of the Western World! Me? A cold war warrior?
Well, yes—if that is how they wish to interpret my defence
of values and freedoms fundamental to our way of life.
*referring to 'the iron lady' as the name given to her by the Soviet
defence ministry newspaper* Red Star, *which accused her of trying
to revive the cold war*

speech at Finchley, 31 January
1976

6 Pennies don't fall from heaven. They have to be earned on
earth.

in *Observer* 18 November 1979
'Sayings of the Week'

7 I don't mind how much my Ministers talk, as long as they
do what I say.

in *Observer* 27 January 1980

8 We have to get our production and our earnings in balance.
There's no easy popularity in what we are proposing, but it
is fundamentally sound. Yet I believe people accept there is
no real alternative.
popularly encapsulated in the acronym TINA

speech at Conservative Women's
Conference, 21 May 1980

9 To those waiting with bated breath for that favourite media
catch-phrase, the U-turn, I have only this to say. 'You turn
if you want; the lady's not for turning.'

speech at Conservative Party
Conference in Brighton, 10
October 1980

10 Economics are the method; the object is to change the soul.

in *Sunday Times* 3 May 1981

11 We have to see that the spirit of the South Atlantic—the
real spirit of Britain—is kindled not only by war but can
now be fired by peace. We have the first prerequisite. We
know that we can do it—we haven't lost the ability. That is
the Falklands Factor.

speech in Cheltenham, 3 July 1982

12 Let me make one thing absolutely clear. The National
Health Service is safe with us.

speech at Conservative Party
Conference, 8 October 1982

1 Just rejoice at that news and congratulate our armed forces and the Marines. Rejoice!

on the recapture of South Georgia, usually quoted as, 'Rejoice, rejoice!'

to newsmen outside 10 Downing Street, 25 April 1982

2 It is exciting to have a real crisis on your hands, when you have spent half your political life dealing with humdrum issues like the environment.

on the Falklands campaign, 1982

speech to Scottish Conservative Party conference, 14 May 1982

3 I was asked whether I was trying to restore Victorian values. I said straight out I was. And I am.

speech to the British Jewish Community, 21 July 1983, referring to an interview with Brian Walden on 17 January 1983

4 Now it must be business as usual.

on the steps of Brighton police station a few hours after the bombing of the Grand Hotel, Brighton; often quoted as 'We shall carry on as usual'

in *The Times* 13 October 1984

5 In church on Sunday morning—it was a lovely morning and we haven't had many lovely days—the sun was coming through a stained glass window and falling on some flowers, falling right across the church. It just occurred to me that this was the day I was meant not to see. Then all of a sudden I thought, 'there are some of my dearest friends who are not seeing this day.'

after the Brighton bombing

television interview, 15 October 1984

*of Mikhail **Gorbachev**:*

6 We can do business together.

in *The Times* 18 December 1984

7 We got a really good consensus during the last election. Consensus behind my convictions.

attributed, 1984

8 We must try to find ways to starve the terrorist and the hijacker of the oxygen of publicity on which they depend.

speech to American Bar Association in London, 15 July 1985

9 I don't spend a lifetime watching which way the cat jumps. I know really which way I want the cats to go.

interview with Michael Charlton on BBC radio, 17 December 1985

10 No one would remember the Good Samaritan if he'd only had good intentions. He had money as well.

television interview, 6 January 1986

11 There is no such thing as Society. There are individual men and women, and there are families.

in *Woman's Own* 31 October 1987

12 We have become a grandmother.

in *The Times* 4 March 1989

13 Advisers advise and ministers decide.

*on the respective roles of her personal economic adviser, Alan Walters, and her Chancellor, Nigel **Lawson** (who resigned the following day)*

in the House of Commons, 26 October 1989

14 You don't reach Downing Street by pretending you've travelled the road to Damascus when you haven't even left home.

*of Neil **Kinnock***

in *Independent* 14 October 1989

15 I am naturally very sorry to see you go, but understand . . . your wish to be able to spend more time with your family.

*reply to Norman **Fowler**'s resignation letter*

in *Guardian* 4 January 1990; see **Fowler** 135:5

16 Others bring me problems, David brings me solutions.

of Lord Young

in *Observer* 1 July 1990

1 No! No! No!
making clear her opposition to a single European currency, and more centralized controls from Brussels

in the House of Commons, 30 October 1990

2 I fight on, I fight to win.
having failed to win outright in the first ballot for party leader

comment, 21 November 1990

3 It's a funny old world.
on withdrawing from the contest for leadership of the Conservative party

comment, 22 November 1990

4 I shan't be pulling the levers there but I shall be a very good back-seat driver.
*on the appointment of John **Major** as the next Prime Minister*

in *Independent* 27 November 1990

5 Every Prime Minister needs a Willie.
*at the farewell dinner for William **Whitelaw***

in *Guardian* 7 August 1991

of being told by a majority of her Cabinet that she could not continue as Prime Minister:
6 Treachery with a smile on its face.

on 'The Thatcher Years' (BBC 1), 20 October 1993

of the poll tax:
7 Given time, it would have been seen as one of the most far-reaching and beneficial reforms ever made in the working of local government.

The Downing Street Years (1993)

8 I'm worried about that young man, he's getting awfully bossy.
on Tony Blair

in *Irish Times* 6 February 1999 'This Week They Said'

9 In my lifetime all our problems have come from mainland Europe and all the solutions have come from the English-speaking nations of the world.

in *Times* 6 October 1999

William Roscoe Thayer 1859–1923
American biographer and historian

10 From log-cabin to White House.

title of biography (1910) of James **Garfield**

Themistocles c.528–c.462 BC
Athenian statesman

11 The wooden wall is your ships.
interpreting the words of the Delphic oracle to the Athenians, before the battle of Salamis in 480 BC

Plutarch *Parallel Lives* 'Themistocles' bk. 2, ch. 1; see below

Yet Zeus the all-seeing grants to Athene's prayer
That the wooden wall only shall not fall, but help you and your children.

words of the prophetess at Delphi; Herodotus *Histories* bk. 7, sect. 141

Louis Adolphe Thiers 1797–1877
French statesman and historian

12 The king reigns, and the people govern themselves.

unsigned article in *Le National*, 20 January 1830; a signed article, 4 February 1830, reads: 'The king neither administers nor governs, he reigns'

Dylan Thomas 1914–53

Welsh poet

1 The hand that signed the paper felled a city;
Five sovereign fingers taxed the breath,
Doubled the globe of death and halved a country;
These five kings did a king to death.

'The Hand That Signed the Paper
Felled a City'

2 The hand that signed the treaty bred a fever,
And famine grew, and locusts came;
Great is the hand that holds dominion over
Man by a scribbled name.

'The Hand That Signed the Paper
Felled a City'

J. H. Thomas 1874–1949

British Socialist politician

3 And now 'ere we 'ave this obstinate little man with 'is Mrs
Simpson. Hit won't do, 'arold, I tell you that straight.
    *to Harold **Nicolson** on **Edward VIII** and the Abdication crisis*

Harold Nicolson letter 26 February
1936

4 They 'ate 'aving no family life at Court.
    of the British people and the Abdication crisis

Harold Nicolson letter 26 February
1936

Norman Thomas 1884–1968

American Presbyterian minister and writer

5 I'd rather see America save her soul than her face.
    protesting against the Vietnam War

speech in Washington, DC, 27
November 1965

Julian Thompson 1934–

British soldier, second-in-command of the land forces during the
Falklands campaign.

6 You don't mind dying for Queen and country, but you
certainly don't want to die for politicians.

'The Falklands War—the Untold
Story' (Yorkshire Television) 1 April
1987

Lord Thomson of Fleet 1894–1976

Canadian-born British newspaper and television proprietor

on owning a commercial television station:
7 Like having your own licence to print money.

R. Braddon *Roy Thomson* (1965)

Henry David Thoreau 1817–62

American writer

8 I heartily accept the motto, 'That government is best which
governs least' . . . Carried out, it finally amounts to this,
which I also believe,—'That government is best which
governs not at all.'

Civil Disobedience (1849); see
O'Sullivan 277:6

9 Under a government which imprisons any unjustly, the true
place for a just man is also a prison.

Civil Disobedience (1849)

10 The oldest, wisest politician grows not more human so, but
is merely a grey wharf-rat at last.

Journal 1853

11 The government of the world I live in was not framed, like
that of Britain, in after-dinner conversations over the wine.

Walden (1854) 'Conclusion'

1 It takes two to speak the truth,—one to speak, and another to hear.

A Week on the Concord and Merrimack Rivers (1849) 'Wednesday'

Jeremy Thorpe 1929–
British Liberal politician; Liberal Party leader 1967–76

*of Harold **Macmillan**'s sacking seven of his Cabinet on 13 July 1962*
2 Greater love hath no man than this, that he lay down his friends for his life.

D. E. Butler and Anthony King *The General Election of 1964* (1965)

Thucydides c.455–c.400 BC
Greek historian

3 Happiness depends on being free, and freedom depends on being courageous.

Thucydides *History of the Peloponnesian War* bk. 2, ch. 4, sect. 43 (translated by Rex Warner)

James Thurber 1894–1961
American humorist

4 You can fool too many of the people too much of the time.

Fables for our Time (1940); see **Lincoln** 220:13

Lord Thurlow 1731–1806
English jurist; Lord Chancellor, 1778–83, 1783–92

5 Corporations have neither bodies to be punished, nor souls to be condemned, they therefore do as they like.
    usually quoted as 'Did you ever expect a corporation to have a conscience, when it has no soul to be damned, and no body to be kicked?'

John Poynder *Literary Extracts* (1844) vol. 1

Tipu Sultan c.1750–99
Indian ruler

6 In this world I would rather live two days like a tiger, than two hundred years like a sheep.

Alexander Beatson *A View of the Origin and Conduct of the War with Tippoo Sultan* (1800) ch. 10

Alexis de Tocqueville 1805–59
French historian and politician

7 Where is the man of soul so base that he would prefer to depend on the caprices of one of his fellow men rather than obey the laws which he has himself contributed to establish?

The Ancien Régime (1856)

8 Despots themselves do not deny that freedom is excellent; only they desire it for themselves alone, and they maintain that everyone else is altogether unworthy of it.

The Ancien Régime (1856)

9 The French Revolution operated in reference to this world in exactly the same manner as religious revolutions acted in view of the other world. It considered the citizen as an abstract proposition apart from any particular society, in the same way as religions considered man as man, independent of country and time.

The Ancien Régime (1856)

1 History is a gallery of pictures in which there are few originals and many copies.

The Ancien Régime (1856)

2 When a nation abolishes aristocracy, centralization follows as a matter of course.

The Ancien Régime (1856)

3 The only substantial difference between the custom of those days and our own resides in the price paid for office. Then they were sold by government, now they are bestowed; it is no longer necessary to pay money; the object can be attained by selling one's soul.

The Ancien Régime (1856)

4 Centralization and socialism are native of the same soil: one is the wild herb, the other the garden plant.

The Ancien Régime (1856)

5 What do men need in order to remain free? A taste for freedom. Do not ask me to analyze that sublime taste; it can only be felt. It has a place in every great heart which God has prepared to receive it; it fills and inflames it. To try to explain it to those inferior minds who have never felt it is to waste time.

The Ancien Régime (1856)

6 No example is so dangerous as that of violence employed by well-meaning people for beneficial objects.

The Ancien Régime (1856)

7 He who desires in liberty anything other than itself is born to be a servant.

The Ancien Régime (1856)

8 It is not always by going from bad to worse that a society falls into revolution . . . The social order destroyed by a revolution is almost always better than that which immediately preceded it, and experience shows that the most dangerous moment for a bad government is generally that in which it sets about reform.

The Ancien Régime (1856)

9 The surface of American society is covered with a layer of democratic paint, but from time to time one can see the old aristocratic colours breaking through.

Democracy in America (1835–40) vol.1

10 Americans rightly think their patriotism is a sort of religion strengthened by practical service.

Democracy in America (1835–40) vol.1

11 The President may slip without the state suffering, for his duties are limited. Congress may slip without the Union perishing, for above Congress there is the electoral body which can change its spirit by changing its membership. But if ever the Supreme Court came to be composed of rash or corrupt men, the confederation would be threatened by anarchy or civil war.

Democracy in America (1835–40) vol.1

12 Providence has not created mankind entirely independent or entirely free. It is true that around every man a fatal circle is traced, beyond which he cannot pass; but within the wide verge of that circle he is powerful and free.

Democracy in America (1835–40) vol. 1

13 Of all nations, those submit to civilization with the most difficulty which habitually live by the chase.

Democracy in America (1835–40) vol. 1

14 What is understood by republican government in the United States is the slow and quiet action of society upon itself.

Democracy in America (1835–40) vol. 1

15 On my arrival in the United States I was struck by the degree of ability among the governed and the lack of it among the governing.

Democracy in America (1835–40) vol. 2

1 The French want no-one to be their *superior*. The English want *inferiors*. The Frenchman constantly raises his eyes above him with anxiety. The Englishman lowers his beneath him with satisfaction. On either side it is pride, but understood in a different way.

Voyage en Angleterre et en Irlande de 1835 (1958) 8 May 1835

Wolfe Tone 1763–98
Irish nationalist
see also **Last words** 212:10

2 I am sorry it was necessary.
   on the execution of Louis XVI, 21 January 1793

Oliver Knox *Rebels and Informers* (1997)

3 To unite the whole people of Ireland, to abolish the memory of all past dissension and to substitute the common name of Irishman in place of the denominations of Protestant, Catholic and Dissenter.

in August 1796; Marianne Elliott *Wolfe Tone* (1989)

Robert Torrens 1780–1864
British economist

4 In the first stone which he [the savage] flings at the wild animals he pursues, in the first stick that he seizes to strike down the fruit which hangs above his reach, we see the appropriation of one article for the purpose of aiding in the acquisition of another, and thus discover the origin of capital.

An Essay on the Production of Wealth (1821) ch. 2

Arnold Toynbee 1889–1975
English historian

5 Civilization is a movement and not a condition, a voyage and not a harbour.

in *Readers Digest* October 1958

6 America is a large, friendly dog in a very small room. Every time it wags its tail it knocks over a chair.

attributed

7 The twentieth century will be remembered chiefly, not as an age of political conflicts and technical inventions, but as an age in which human society dared to think of the health of the whole human race as a practical objective.

attributed

Joseph Trapp 1679–1747
English poet and pamphleteer

8 The King, observing with judicious eyes
   The state of both his universities,
   To Oxford sent a troop of horse, and why?
   That learned body wanted loyalty;
   To Cambridge books, as very well discerning
   How much that loyal body wanted learning.
      lines written on **George I**'s *donation of the Bishop of Ely's Library to Cambridge University*

John Nichols *Literary Anecdotes* (1812–16) vol. 3; see **Browne** 54:5

Lord Trend 1914–87
British civil servant; Cabinet Secretary 1963–73

9 The acid test of any political decision is, 'What is the alternative?'

attributed, 1975

Charles Trevelyan 1807-86
British civil servant

on the organization of a new system of admission into the civil service:
1 It is proposed to invite the flower of our youth to the aid of public service.

to John Thadeus Delane, Editor of *The Times*, in 1853

G. M. Trevelyan 1876-1962
English historian

2 If the French noblesse had been capable of playing cricket with their peasants, their chateaux would never have been burnt.

English Social History (1942)

3 In a world of voluble hates, he plotted to make men like, or at least tolerate one another.
   *of Stanley **Baldwin***

in *Dictionary of National Biography 1941-50* (1959)

William Trevor 1928-
Anglo-Irish novelist and short story writer

of the troubles in Northern Ireland:
4 A disease in the family that is never mentioned.

in *Observer* 18 November 1990

Hugh Trevor-Roper 1914-
British historian

5 Those who exercise power and determine policy are generally men whose minds have been formed by events twenty or thirty years before.

From Counter-Reformation to Glorious Revolution (1992); introduction

6 How are we to disentangle religion from politics in a revolution? Religion may form the outlook of an individual. It may serve as an ideological intoxicant for a crowd. But in high politics it is a variable.

From Counter-Reformation to Glorious Revolution (1992)

7 Aristocracies . . . may preserve themselves longest, but only democracies, which refresh their ruling class, can expand.

Historical Essays (1952)

8 Historians in general are great toadies of power.

History and Imagination (1981)

9 Any reaction which is to be successful over a long period must have radical origins . . . A reaction which is to last, which is to be accepted as orthodoxy over several generations, must spring out of the same social circumstances as the progress which it resists.

The Rise of Christian Europe (1965)

David Trimble 1944-
Northern Irish politician, leader of the Ulster Unionists

10 We are not here to negotiate with them, but to confront them.
   on entering the Mitchell talks on Northern Ireland with Sinn Féin

in *Guardian* 18 September 1997

11 The fundamental Act of Union is there, intact.
   of the Northern Ireland settlement

in *Daily Telegraph* 11 April 1998

12 Once we are agreed our only weapons will be our words, then there is nothing that cannot be said, there is nothing that cannot be achieved.

in *Guardian* 4 September 1998

1 Mr Adams, it is over to you. We have jumped, you follow.
*after the Ulster Unionist Council had voted to accept the setting
up of the Northern Irish executive*

*in Sunday Telegraph 28 November
1999*

Tommy Trinder 1909–89
British comedian

of American troops in Britain during the Second World War:
2 Overpaid, overfed, oversexed, and over here.

*associated with Trinder, but
probably not his invention*

Anthony Trollope 1815–82
English novelist

3 I have hardly as yet met two Englishmen who were agreed
as to the political power of the sovereign.

The American Senator (1877)

4 A man who entertains in his mind any political doctrine,
except as a means of improving the condition of his fellows,
I regard as a political intriguer, a charlatan, and a conjuror.

Autobiography (1883)

5 When taken in the refreshing waters of office any . . . pill
can be swallowed.

The Bertrams (1859)

of political life:
6 The hatreds which sound so real when you read the mere
words, which look so true when you see their scornful
attitudes, on which for the time you are inclined to pin your
faith so implicitly, amount to nothing.

The Landleaguers (1883)

7 But in truth the capacity of a man . . . [to be Prime Minister]
does not depend on any power of intellect, or indomitable
courage, or far-seeing cunning. The man is competent
simply because he is believed to be so.

Lord Palmerston (1882)

8 To me it seems that no form of existing government—no
form of government that ever did exist, gives or has given so
large a measure of individual freedom to all who live under
it as a constitutional monarchy.

North America (1862)

9 There is nothing more tyrannical than a strong popular
feeling among a democratic people.

North America (1862)

10 I have sometimes thought that there is no being so
venomous, so bloodthirsty as a professed philanthropist.

North America (1862)

11 [Equality] is a doctrine to be forgiven when he who preaches
it is . . . striving to raise others to his own level.

North America (1862)

12 A fainéant government is not the worst government that
England can have. It has been the great fault of our
politicians that they have all wanted to do something.

Phineas Finn (1869)

of the radical politician:
13 It was his work to cut down forest-trees, and he had
nothing to do with the subsequent cultivation of the land.

Phineas Finn (1869)

14 The first necessity for good speaking is a large audience.

Phineas Finn (1869)

15 It is the necessary nature of a political party in this country
to avoid, as long as it can be avoided, the consideration of
any question which involves a great change . . . The best
carriage horses are those which can most steadily hold back
against the coach as it trundles down the hill.

Phineas Redux (1874)

1 Newspaper editors sport daily with the names of men of whom they do not hesitate to publish almost the severest words that can be uttered; but let an editor be himself attacked, even without his name, and he thinks that the thunderbolt of heaven should fall upon the offender.

Phineas Redux (1874) ch. 27

2 A man destined to sit conspicuously on our Treasury Bench, or on the seat opposite to it, should ask the Gods for a thick skin as a first gift.

Phineas Redux (1874)

3 Equality would be a heaven, if we could attain it.

The Prime Minister (1876)

4 What Good Government ever was not stingy?

South Africa (1878)

5 How seldom is it that theories stand the wear and tear of practice!

Thackeray (1879)

6 Let the Toryism of the Tory be ever so strong, it is his destiny to carry out the purposes of his opponents.

Why Frau Frohmann Raised Her Prices (1882)

Leon Trotsky 1879–1940

Russian revolutionary

7 Old age is the most unexpected of all things that happen to a man.

Diary in Exile (1959) 8 May 1935

8 Civilization has made the peasantry its pack animal. The bourgeoisie in the long run only changed the form of the pack.

History of the Russian Revolution (1933) vol. 3

9 You [the Mensheviks] are pitiful isolated individuals; you are bankrupts; your role is played out. Go where you belong from now on—into the dustbin of history!

History of the Russian Revolution (1933) vol. 3

10 Where force is necessary, there it must be applied boldly, decisively and completely. But one must know the limitations of force; one must know when to blend force with a manoeuvre, a blow with an agreement.

What Next? (1932)

11 Not believing in force is the same thing as not believing in gravitation.

G. Maximov *The Guillotine at Work* (1940)

12 In a country where the sole employer is the State, opposition means death by slow starvation. The old principle: who does not work shall not eat, has been replaced by a new one: who does not obey shall not eat.

attributed

Pierre Trudeau 1919–2000

Canadian Liberal statesman, Prime Minister, 1968–79 and 1980–4

13 The state has no place in the nation's bedrooms.

interview, Ottawa, 22 December 1967

14 The twentieth century really belongs to those who will build it. The future can be promised to no one.

in 1968; see **Laurier** 211:4

15 Living next to you is in some ways like sleeping with an elephant. No matter how friendly and even-tempered the beast, one is affected by every twitch and grunt.
on relations between Canada and the US

speech at National Press Club, Washington D. C., 25 March 1969

Harry S Truman 1884–1972

American Democratic statesman, 33rd President of the US 1945–53
on Truman: see **Mencken** 248:14, **Newspaper headlines** 267:2; see also **Mottoes** 262:2, **Proverbs** 296:9

to reporters the day after his accession to the Presidency on the death of Franklin Roosevelt:

1 When they told me yesterday what had happened, I felt like the moon, the stars and all the planets had fallen on me.

on 13 April 1945

2 Sixteen hours ago an American airplane dropped one bomb on Hiroshima . . . The force from which the sun draws its power has been loosed against those who brought war to the Far East.
first announcement of the dropping of the atomic bomb

on 6 August 1945

3 Effective, reciprocal, and enforceable safeguards acceptable to all nations.
Declaration on Atomic Energy by President Truman, Clement **Attlee,** *and W. L. Mackenzie King, Prime Minister of Canada*

on 15 November 1945

4 All the President is, is a glorified public relations man who spends his time flattering, kissing and kicking people to get them to do what they are supposed to do anyway.

letter to his sister, 14 November 1947

5 What we are doing in Korea is this: we are trying to prevent a third world war.
after the recall of **MacArthur**

address to the nation, 16 April 1951

6 Those who want the Government to regulate matters of the mind and spirit are like men who are so afraid of being murdered that they commit suicide to avoid assassination.

address at the National Archives, Washington, DC, 15 December 1952

7 He'll sit right here and he'll say do this, do that! And nothing will happen. Poor Ike—it won't be a bit like the Army.
of his successor **Eisenhower**

Harry S. Truman (1973) vol. 2; see **Schwarzkopf** 316:7

8 Once a decision was made, I did not worry about it afterward.

Memoirs (1955) vol. 2

9 I never give them [the public] hell. I just tell the truth, and they think it is hell.

in *Look* 3 April 1956

10 A politician is a man who understands government, and it takes a politician to run a government. A statesman is a politician who's been dead 10 or 15 years.

in *New York World Telegram and Sun* 12 April 1958

11 It's a recession when your neighbour loses his job; it's a depression when you lose yours.

in *Observer* 13 April 1958

12 Wherever you have an efficient government you have a dictatorship.

lecture at Columbia University, 28 April 1959

13 To me, party platforms are contracts with the people.

Memoirs (1955) vol. 2

14 If there is one basic element in our Constitution, it is civilian control of the military.

Memoirs (1955) vol. 2

15 Always be sincere, even if you don't mean it.

attributed

16 I didn't fire him [General MacArthur] because he was a dumb son of a bitch, although he was, but that's not against the law for generals. If it was, half to three-quarters of them would be in jail.

Merle Miller *Plain Speaking* (1974)

1 Secrecy and a free, democratic government don't mix.

Merle Miller *Plain Speaking* (1974)

Sojourner Truth c.1797–1883

American evangelist and reformer

2 That man . . . says that women need to be helped into carriages, and lifted over ditches, and to have the best place everywhere. Nobody ever helps me into carriages, or over mud puddles, or gives me any best place, and aren't I a woman? . . . I have ploughed, and planted, and gathered into barns, and no man could head me—and aren't I a woman? I could work as much and eat as much as a man (when I could get it), and bear the lash as well—and aren't I a woman? I have borne thirteen children and seen them most all sold off into slavery, and when I cried out with a mother's grief, none but Jesus heard—and aren't I a woman?

speech at Women's Rights Convention, Akron, Ohio, 1851

Morton Tsvangirai

Zimbabwean politician

3 This country is for blacks. But we need the knowledge of the whites to train people and create jobs.

in *Times* 15 April 2000 'Quotes of the Week'

Barbara W. Tuchman 1912–89

American historian and writer

4 Dead battles, like dead generals, hold the military mind in their dead grip and Germans, no less than other peoples, prepare for the last war.

August 1914 (1962)

5 No more distressing moment can ever face a British government than that which requires it to come to a hard, fast and specific decision.

August 1914 (1962)

6 For one August in its history Paris was French—and silent.

August 1914 (1962)

A. R. J. Turgot 1727–81

French economist and statesman

7 *Eripuit coelo fulmen, sceptrumque tyrannis.*
He snatched the lightning shaft from heaven, and the sceptre from tyrants.
  *for a bust of Benjamin **Franklin**, inventor of the lightning conductor and one of those who drafted the Declaration of Independence*

inscription

Desmond Tutu 1931–

South African Anglican clergyman, Archbishop of Cape Town

8 I have struggled against tyranny. I didn't do that in order to substitute one tyranny with another.
  on the ANC's attempt to prevent publication of the Truth Commission report

in *Irish Times* 31 October 1998 'This Week They Said'

Mark Twain 1835–1910
American writer

1 It could probably be shown by facts and figures that there is no distinctly native American criminal class except Congress.

Following the Equator (1897)

2 It is by the goodness of God in our country that we have those three unspeakably precious things: freedom of speech, freedom of conscience, and the prudence never to practise either of them.

Following the Equator (1897)

3 Get your facts first, and then you can distort them as much as you please.

Rudyard Kipling *From Sea to Sea* (1899)

4 Suppose you were an idiot. And suppose you were a member of Congress. But I repeat myself.

A. B. Paine *Mark Twain* (1912)

William Tyndale c.1494–1536
English translator of the **Bible** and Protestant martyr
see also **Last words** 213:4

5 If God spare my life, ere many years I will cause a boy that driveth the plough shall know more of the scripture than thou doest!
to an opponent

in *Dictionary of National Biography* (1917–)

Kay Ullrich 1943–
Scottish Nationalist politician

6 As a lady of a certain age, I am willing to let the photographers and their zoom lenses stay, but only if they use their Joan Collins lens on me for close-ups.
on the decision to ban photographers from the debating chamber of the Scottish Parliament

in *Scotsman* 18 March 2000

Universal Declaration of Human Rights
1948

7 All human beings are born free and equal in dignity and rights.

article 1

8 Everyone has the right to freedom of movement and residence within the borders of each State. Everyone has the right to leave any country, including his own, and to return to his country.

article 13

9 Everyone has the right to seek and to enjoy in other countries asylum from persecution.

article 14

Paul Valéry 1871–1945
French poet, critic, and man of letters

10 An attitude of permanent indignation signifies great mental poverty. Politics compels its votaries to take that line and you can see their minds growing more and more impoverished every day, from one burst of righteous anger to the next.

Tel Quel (1941–3)

11 Politics is the art of preventing people from taking part in affairs which properly concern them.

Tel Quel (1941–3)

William Henry Vanderbilt 1821–85

American railway magnate

1 The public be damned!
on whether the public should be consulted about luxury trains

A. W. Cole letter to *New York Times*
25 August 1918

Laurens van der Post 1906–96

South African explorer and writer

2 Human beings are perhaps never more frightening than when they are convinced beyond doubt that they are right.

The Lost World of the Kalahari
(1958)

Raoul Vaneigem 1934–

Belgian philosopher

3 Never before has a civilization reached such a degree of a contempt for life; never before has a generation, drowned in mortification, felt such a rage to live.
of the 1960s

The Revolution of Everyday Life
(1967) ch. 5

Robert Vansittart 1881–1957

British diplomatist

4 The soul of our service is the loyalty with which we execute ordained error.

attributed; David Butler et al.
Failure in British Government (1994)

Bartolomeo Vanzetti 1888–1927

American anarchist, born in Italy

5 Sacco's name will live in the hearts of the people and in their gratitude when Katzmann's and yours bones will be dispersed by time, when your name, his name, your laws, institutions, and your false god are but a deem rememoring of a cursed past in which man was wolf to the man.
statement disallowed at his trial, with Nicola Sacco, for murder and robbery; both were sentenced to death on 9 April 1927, and executed on 23 August 1927

M. D. Frankfurter and G. Jackson
Letters of Sacco and Vanzetti (1928)

Janet-Maria Vaughan 1899–1993

English scientist

6 I am here—trying to do science in hell.
working as a doctor in Belsen at the end of the war

letter to a friend, 12 May 1945; P. A. Adams (ed.) *Janet-Maria Vaughan* (1993)

Thorstein Veblen 1857–1929

American economist and social scientist

7 The first duty of an editor is to gauge the sentiment of his readers, and then tell them what they like to believe . . . His second duty is to see that nothing is said in the news items or editorials which may discountenance any claims made by his advertisers, discredit their standing, or expose any weakness or deception in any business venture that is or may become a valuable advertiser.

The Theory of Business Enterprise
1904

8 Conspicuous consumption of valuable goods is a means of reputability to the gentleman of leisure.

Theory of the Leisure Class (1899)

1 From the foregoing survey of conspicuous leisure and consumption, it appears that the utility of both alike for the purposes of reputability lies in the element of waste that is common to both. In the one case it is a waste of time and effort, in the other it is a waste of goods.

Theory of the Leisure Class (1899)

Vegetius fl. 4th century AD
Roman military writer

2 Let him who desires peace, prepare for war.
  usually quoted as 'If you want peace, prepare for war'

Epitoma Rei Militaris

Pierre Vergniaud 1753–93
French revolutionary; executed with other Girondists

3 There was reason to fear that the Revolution, like Saturn, might devour in turn each one of her children.

Alphonse de Lamartine *Histoire des Girondins* (1847)

Hendrik Frensch Verwoerd 1901–66
South African statesman, Prime Minister 1958–66

4 Up till now he [the Bantu] has been subjected to a school system which drew him away from his own community and practically misled him by showing him the green pastures of the European but still did not allow him to graze there . . . It is abundantly clear that unplanned education creates many problems, disrupts the communal life of the Bantu and endangers the communal life of the European.

speech in South African Senate, 7 June 1954

Vespasian AD 9–79
Roman emperor from AD 69
see also **Last words** 212:5

5 *Pecunia non olet.*
  Money has no smell.
   replying to Titus's objection to his tax on public lavatories; holding a coin to Titus's nose and being told it didn't smell, he replied, 'Atque e lotio est [Yes, that's made from urine]'

traditional summary of Suetonius *Lives of the Caesars* 'Vespasian'

6 Woe is me, I think I am becoming a god.
  when fatally ill

Suetonius *Lives of the Caesars* 'Vespasian'

Queen Victoria 1819–1901
Queen of the United Kingdom from 1837
on Victoria: see **Gladstone** 148:14

7 I will be good.
  on being shown a chart of the line of succession, 11 March 1830

Theodore Martin *The Prince Consort* (1875)

8 The Queen is most anxious to enlist every one who can speak or write to join in checking this mad, wicked folly of 'Woman's Rights', with all its attendant horrors, on which her poor feeble sex is bent, forgetting every sense of womanly feeling and propriety.

letter to Theodore Martin, 29 May 1870

on **Gladstone**'*s last appointment as Prime Minister:*
9 The danger to the country, to Europe, to her vast Empire, which is involved in having all these great interests entrusted to the shaking hand of an old, wild, and incomprehensible man of 82, is very great!

letter to Lord Lansdowne, 12 August 1892

1 The future Viceroy must . . . not be guided by the *snobbish* and vulgar, over-bearing and offensive behaviour of our Civil and Political Agents, if we are to go on peaceably and happily in India . . . not trying to trample on the people and continuously reminding them and making them feel they are a conquered people.

letter to Lord **Salisbury**, 27 May 1898

2 We are not interested in the possibilities of defeat; they do not exist.
  on the Boer War during 'Black Week', December 1899

Lady Gwendolen Cecil *Life of Robert, Marquis of Salisbury* (1931)

3 He speaks to Me as if I was a public meeting.
  of **Gladstone**

G. W. E. Russell *Collections and Recollections* (1898)

4 We are not amused.

attributed; Caroline Holland *Notebooks of a Spinster Lady* (1919), 2 January 1900

Gore Vidal 1925–
American novelist and critic

of Ronald **Reagan**:
5 A triumph of the embalmer's art.

in *Observer* 26 April 1981

José Antonio Viera Gallo 1943–
Chilean politician

6 Socialism can only arrive by bicycle.

Ivan Illich *Energy and Equity* (1974) epigraph

Virgil 70–19 BC
Roman poet

7 *Tantae molis erat Romanam condere gentem.*
  So massive was the effort to found the Roman nation.

Aeneid

8 *Equo ne credite, Teucri.*
  Quidquid id est, timeo Danaos et dona ferentes.
  Do not trust the horse, Trojans. Whatever it is, I fear the Greeks even when they bring gifts.

Aeneid

9 *Bella, horrida bella,*
  Et Thybrim multo spumantem sanguine cerno.
  I see wars, horrible wars, and the Tiber foaming with much blood.

Aeneid; see **Powell** 293:4

Voltaire 1694–1778
French writer and philosopher
see also **Misquotations** 254:9

10 These two nations have been at war over a few acres of snow near Canada, and . . . they are spending on this fine struggle more than Canada itself is worth.
  of the struggle between the French and the British for the control of colonial north Canada

Candide (1759)

11 *Dans ce pays-ci il est bon de tuer de temps en temps un amiral pour encourager les autres.*
  In this country [England] it is thought well to kill an admiral from time to time to encourage the others.

Candide (1759)

1 The art of government consists in taking as much money as possible from one class of citizens to give to the other.

Dictionnaire philosophique (1764) 'Money'

2 Superstition sets the whole world in flames; philosophy quenches them.

Dictionnaire philosophique (1764) 'Superstition'

3 This agglomeration which was called and which still calls itself the Holy Roman Empire was neither holy, nor Roman, nor an empire.

Essai sur l'histoire générale et sur les moeurs et l'esprit des nations (1756)

4 Indeed, history is nothing more than a tableau of crimes and misfortunes.

L'Ingénu (1767); see **Gibbon** 145:3

5 Governments need both shepherds and butchers.

'The Piccini Notebooks' (c.1735–50)

6 God is on the side not of the heavy battalions, but of the best shots.

'The Piccini Notebooks' (c.1735–50); see **Tacitus** 351:11

7 Whatever you do, stamp out abuses, and love those who love you.

letter to M. d'Alembert, 28 November 1762

8 If one must serve, I hold it better to serve a well-bred lion, who is naturally stronger than I am, than two hundred rats of my own breed.

letter to a friend; Alexis de Tocqueville *The Ancien Régime* (1856)

9 To succeed in chaining the crowd you just seem to wear the same fetters.

attributed

what Voltaire apparently said on the burning of De l'esprit:
10 What a fuss about an omelette!

James Parton *Life of Voltaire* (1881) vol. 2; see **Misquotations** 254:9

William Waldegrave 1946–
British Conservative politician

11 In exceptional circumstances it is necessary to say something that is untrue in the House of Commons.

to a House of Commons select committee, in *Guardian* 9 March 1994

12 It was much more what cabinet government is supposed to be like . . . the problem was that when people began to be disloyal later on, they were not very frightened of him.
of John **Major** *as Prime Minister*

on *The Major Years* pt 2, BBC1, 18 October 1999

Lech Wałęsa 1943–
Polish trade unionist and statesman, President since 1990

13 You have riches and freedom here but I feel no sense of faith or direction. You have so many computers, why don't you use them in the search for love?

in Paris, on his first journey outside the Soviet area, in *Daily Telegraph* 14 December 1988

Felix Walker fl. 1820
American politician

excusing a long, dull, irrelevant speech in the House of Representatives, c.1820 (Buncombe being his constituency):
14 I'm talking to Buncombe ['bunkum'].

W. Safire *New Language of Politics* (2nd ed., 1972); see **Carlyle** 70:3

George Wallace 1919–98
American Democratic politician; Governor of Alabama

15 Segregation now, segregation tomorrow and segregation forever!

inaugural speech as Governor of Alabama, January 1963

Henry Wallace 1888–1965

American Democratic politician

1 The century on which we are entering—the century which will come out of this war—can be and must be the century of the common man.

speech, 8 May 1942

Edmund Waller 1606–87

English poet

2 Others may use the ocean as their road,
Only the English make it their abode.

'Of a War with Spain' (1658)

3 Rome, though her eagle through the world had flown,
Could never make this island all her own.

'Panegyric to My Lord Protector' (1655)

4 Under the tropic is our language spoke,
And part of Flanders hath received our yoke.

'Upon the Late Storm, and of the Death of His Highness Ensuing the Same' (1659)

Horace Walpole 1717–97

English writer and connoisseur, son of Robert **Walpole**

5 His speeches were fine, but as much laboured as his extempore sayings.
*of Lord **Chesterfield**, 1751*

Memoirs of the Reign of King George II (1846) vol. 1

6 While he felt like a victim, he acted like a hero.
of Admiral Byng, on the day of his execution, 1757

Memoirs of the Reign of King George II (1846) vol. 2

7 Perhaps those, who, trembling most, maintain a dignity in their fate, are the bravest: resolution on reflection is real courage.

in 1757; *Memoirs of the Reign of King George II* (1846) vol. 2

8 They seem to know no medium between a mitre and a crown of martyrdom. If the clergy are not called to the latter, they never deviate from the pursuit of the former. One would think their motto was, *Canterbury or Smithfield.*

in 1758; *Memoirs of the Reign of King George II* (1846) vol. 3

9 All his passions were expressed by one livid smile.
*of George **Grenville**, 1763*

Memoirs of the Reign of King George III (1845) vol. 1

10 He lost his dominions in America, his authority over Ireland, and all influence in Europe, by aiming at despotism in England; and exposed himself to more mortifications and humiliations than can happen to a quiet Doge of Venice.
*of **George III**, 1770*

Memoirs of the Reign of King George III (1845) vol. 4

11 Our supreme governors, the mob.

letter to Horace Mann, 7 September 1743

12 Everybody talks of the constitution, but all sides forget that the constitution is extremely well, and would do very well, if they would but let it alone.

letter to Horace Mann, 18–19 January 1770

13 It was easier to conquer it [the East] than to know what to do with it.

letter to Horace Mann, 27 March 1772

14 By the waters of Babylon we sit down and weep, when we think of thee, O America!

letter to Revd William Mason, 12 June 1775

Robert Walpole 1676–1745

English Whig statesman; first British Prime Minister, 1721–42;
father of Horace **Walpole**
on Walpole: see **Peel** 286:4, **Shippen** 331:8

1 Madam, there are fifty thousand men slain this year in
Europe, and not one Englishman.
to Queen Caroline, 1734, on the war of the Polish succession, in
which the English had refused to participate

John Hervey *Memoirs* (written
1734–43, published 1848) vol. 1

2 We must muzzle this terrible young cornet of horse.
*of the elder William **Pitt**, who had held a cornetcy before his*
election to Parliament, but whose speech in support of the
congratulatory address on the Prince of Wales's marriage in
1736 was regarded as so offensive through its covert satire that
he was shortly afterwards dismissed from the army

in *Dictionary of National Biography*
(1917–)

3 They now *ring* the bells, but they will soon *wring* their
hands.
on the declaration of war with Spain, 1739

W. Coxe *Memoirs of Sir Robert
Walpole* (1798) vol. 1

4 All those men have their price.
of fellow parliamentarians

W. Coxe *Memoirs of Sir Robert
Walpole* (1798) vol. 1

5 [Gratitude of place-expectants] is a lively sense of future
favours.

W. Hazlitt *Lectures on the English
Comic Writers* (1819) 'On Wit and
Humour'

*the normally imperturbable Walpole, having lost his temper at a
Council, broke up the meeting:*
6 No man is fit for business with a ruffled temper.

Edmund Fitzmaurice *Life of
Shelburne* (1875)

7 There is enough pasture for all the sheep.
on his ability to spread round patronage satisfactorily

attributed

*on seeing Henry Fox (Lord **Holland**) reading in the library at
Houghton:*
8 You can read. It is a great happiness. I totally neglected it
while I was in business, which has been the whole of my
life, and to such a degree that I cannot now read a page—a
warning to all Ministers.

Edmund Fitzmaurice *Life of
Shelburne* (1875) vol. 1

Claire Ward 1972–

British Labour politician

9 I don't always admit to being an MP. If I'm in a bar with
people I don't know, to say you're a Labour MP isn't always
a good move. I have said I'm a solicitor.

in *Independent on Sunday* 14 March
1999 'Quotes'

Charles Dudley Warner 1829–1900

US author and editor

10 Politics makes strange bedfellows.

My Summer in a Garden (1871)

Earl Warren 1891–1974

American Chief Justice

11 In civilized life, law floats in a sea of ethics.

in *New York Times* 12 November
1962

Booker T. Washington 1856–1915

American educationist and emancipated slave

1 No race can prosper till it learns that there is as much dignity in tilling a field as in writing a poem.

Up from Slavery (1901)

2 You can't hold a man down without staying down with him.

attributed

George Washington 1732–99 ✓

American soldier and statesman, 1st President of the US 1789–97
on Washington: see **Byron** 64:5, **Franklin** 137:4, **Lee** 214:7; see also **Last words** 213:1

3 I can't tell a lie, Pa; you know I can't tell a lie. I did cut it with my hatchet.

M. L. Weems *Life of George Washington* (10th ed., 1810)

4 The time is now near at hand which must probably determine whether Americans are to be freemen or slaves; whether they are to have any property they can call their own . . . The fate of unborn millions will now depend, under God, on the courage and conduct of this army. Our cruel and unrelenting enemy leaves us only the choice of brave resistance, or the most abject submission. We have, therefore, to resolve to conquer or die.

General orders, 2 July 1776, in J. C. Fitzpatrick (ed.) *Writings of George Washington* vol. 5 (1932)

5 Few men have virtue to withstand the highest bidder.

letter 17 August 1779

6 'Tis our true policy to steer clear of permanent alliances, with any portion of the foreign world.

President's Address . . . (17 September 1796)

7 Let me . . . warn you in the most solemn manner against the baneful effects of the spirit of party.

President's Address . . . (17 September 1796)

8 The nation which indulges toward another an habitual hatred or an habitual fondness is in some degree a slave. It is a slave to its animosity or to its affection, either of which is sufficient to lead it astray from its duty and its interest.

President's Address . . . (17 September 1796)

9 Liberty, when it begins to take root, is a plant of rapid growth.

attributed

Keith Waterhouse 1929–

English writer

10 Why should it take three times longer to elect a Mayor for London as it does to set up an entire Scottish Parliament?

in *Observer* 24 October 1999 'They Said What . . . ?'

William Watson c.1559–1603

English Roman Catholic conspirator

11 *Fiat justitia et ruant coeli.*
Let justice be done even though the heavens fall.

A Decacordon of Ten Quodlibeticall Questions Concerning Religion and State (1602), being the first citation in an English work of a famous maxim; see **Adams** 4:3, **Mottoes** 262:3

Evelyn Waugh 1903–66
English novelist

1 'In a democracy,' said Mr Pinfold, with more weight than
originality, 'Men do not seek authority so that they may
impose a policy. They seek a policy so that they may achieve
authority.'

The Ordeal of Gilbert Pinfold (1957)

2 *The Beast* stands for strong mutually antagonistic
governments everywhere . . . Self-sufficiency at home, self-
assertion abroad.

Scoop (1938)

3 Remember that the Patriots are in the right and are going to
win . . . But they must win quickly. The British public has
no interest in a war that drags on indecisively. A few sharp
victories, some conspicuous acts of personal bravery on the
Patriot side and a colourful entry into the capital. That is
The Beast Policy for the war.

Scoop (1938)

4 Other nations use 'force'; we Britons alone use 'Might'.

Scoop (1938)

5 I do not aspire to advise my sovereign in her choice of
servants.
on why he did not vote

in *Spectator* 2 October 1959

*it had been announced after an operation on Randolph Churchill that
the trouble was 'not malignant':*

6 It was a typical triumph of modern science to find the only
part of Randolph that was not malignant and remove it.

Michael Davie (ed.) *Diaries of Evelyn
Waugh* (1976) 'Irregular Notes
1960–65', March 1964

7 The Conservative Party have never put the clock back a
single second.

Frances Donaldson *Evelyn Waugh*
(1967)

Beatrice Webb 1858–1943
English socialist, wife of Sidney **Webb**

8 Restless, almost intolerably so, without capacity for
sustained and unexcited labour, egotistical, bumptious,
shallow-minded and reactionary, but with a certain
personal magnetism, great pluck and some originality, not
of intellect but of character.
*in 1903, of Winston **Churchill***

Martin Gilbert *In Search of Churchill*
(1994)

9 I never visualised labour as separate men and women of
different sorts and kinds . . . labour was an abstraction,
which seemed to denote an arithmetically calculable mass of
human beings, each individual a repetition of the other.

My Apprenticeship (1926)

Sidney Webb 1859–1947
English socialist, husband of Beatrice **Webb**

10 Once we face the necessity of putting our principles first into
Bills, to be fought through committee clause by clause; and
then into the appropriate machinery for carrying them into
execution from one end of the kingdom to the other . . . the
inevitability of gradualness cannot fail to be appreciated.

presidential address to the annual
conference of the Labour Party, 26
June 1923

11 Nobody told us we could do this.
*when the new National Government came off the Gold Standard in
1931, the outgoing Labour Government not having resorted to
this tactic*

Nigel Rees *Brewer's Quotations*
(1994)

Max Weber 1864–1920
German economist

1 The Protestant ethic and the spirit of capitalism.

Archiv für Sozialwissenschaft Sozialpolitik vol. 20 (1904–5) (title of article)

2 In Baxter's view the care for external goods should only lie on the shoulders of the saint like 'a light cloak, which can be thrown aside at any moment.' But fate decreed that the cloak should become an iron cage.

Gesammelte Aufsätze zur Religionssoziologie (1920) vol. 1

3 The State is a relation of men dominating men, a relation supported by means of legitimate (i.e. considered to be legitimate) violence.

'Politik als Beruf' (1919)

4 The authority of the 'eternal yesterday'.

'Politik als Beruf' (1919)

5 The experience of the irrationality of the world has been the driving force of all religious revolution.

'Politik als Beruf' (1919)

6 The concept of the 'official secret' is its [bureaucracy's] specific invention.

'Politik als Beruf' (1919)

Daniel Webster 1782–1852
American politician
on Webster: see **Smith** 339:4

7 The people's government, made for the people, made by the people, and answerable to the people.

second speech in the Senate on Foote's Resolution, 26 January 1830; see **Lincoln** 219:9

8 Liberty *and* Union, now and forever, one and inseparable!

second speech in the Senate on Foote's Resolution, 26 January 1830

9 When my eyes shall be turned to behold for the last time the sun in heaven, may I not see him shining on the broken and dishonored fragments of a once glorious Union; on States dissevered, discordant, belligerent; on a land rent with civil feuds, or drenched, it may be, in fraternal blood.

second speech in the Senate on Foote's Resolution, 26 January 1830

10 Fearful concatenation of circumstances.
argument on the murder of Captain Joseph White

speech on 6 April 1830

11 He smote the rock of the national resources, and abundant streams of revenue gushed forth. He touched the dead corpse of the Public Credit, and it sprung upon its feet.
of Alexander **Hamilton**

speech 10 March 1831

12 Whatever government is not a government of laws, is a despotism, let it be called what it may.

at a reception in Bangor, Maine, 25 August 1835

13 One country, one constitution, one destiny.

speech 15 March 1837

14 Thank God, I—I also—am an American!
speech on the completion of Bunker Hill Monument, 17 June 1843

Writings and Speeches vol. 1 (1903)

15 The Law: It has honoured us, may we honour it.

speech at the Charleston Bar Dinner, 10 May 1847

16 I was born an American; I will live an American; I shall die an American.

speech in the Senate on 'The Compromise Bill', 17 July 1850

17 There is always room at the top.
on being advised against joining the overcrowded legal profession

attributed

Josiah Wedgwood 1730–95

English potter

1 Am I not a man and a brother.
   legend on Wedgwood cameo, depicting a kneeling Negro slave in chains

reproduced in facsimile in E. Darwin *The Botanic Garden* pt. 1 (1791)

Simone Weil 1909–43

French essayist and philosopher

2 I would suggest that barbarism be considered as a permanent and universal human characteristic which becomes more or less pronounced according to the play of circumstances.

Écrits Historiques et politiques (1960) 'Réflexions sur la barbarie' (written c.1939)

3 A right is not effectual by itself, but only in relation to the obligation to which it corresponds . . . An obligation which goes unrecognized by anybody loses none of the full force of its existence. A right which goes unrecognized by anybody is not worth very much.

L'Enracinement (1949) 'Les Besoins de l'âme'

4 What a country calls its vital economic interests are not the things which enable its citizens to live, but the things which enable it to make war.

W. H. Auden *A Certain World* (1971)

Stanley Weiser
and **Oliver Stone** 1946–

5 Greed—for lack of a better word—is good. Greed is right. Greed works.

Wall Street (1987 film); see **Boesky** 45:6

Chaim Weizmann 1874–1952

Russian-born Israeli statesman, President 1949–52

6 Something had been done for us which, after two thousand years of hope and yearning, would at last give us a resting-place in this terrible world.
   of the Balfour declaration

speech in Jerusalem, 25 November 1936; see **Balfour** 26:4

Orson Welles 1915–85

American actor and film director

7 In Italy for thirty years under the Borgias they had warfare, terror, murder, bloodshed—they produced Michelangelo, Leonardo da Vinci and the Renaissance. In Switzerland they had brotherly love, five hundred years of democracy and peace and what did that produce . . . ? The cuckoo clock.

The Third Man (1949 film); words added by Welles to Graham Greene's script

Duke of Wellington 1769–1852

British general and statesman; Prime Minister 1828–30
on Wellington: see **Tennyson** 355:6, 355:7, 355:10

8 As Lord Chesterfield said of the generals of his day, 'I only hope that when the enemy reads the list of their names, he trembles as I do.'
   usually quoted as 'I don't know what effect these men will have upon the enemy, but, by God, they frighten me'

letter, 29 August 1810

1 Trust nothing to the enthusiasm of the people. Give them a strong and a just, and, if possible, a good, government; but, above all, a strong one.

letter to Lord William Bentinck, 24 December 1811

2 Up Guards and at them!

letter from an officer in the Guards, 22 June 1815, in *The Battle of Waterloo* by a Near Observer [J. Booth] (1815); later denied by Wellington

3 Hard pounding this, gentlemen; let's see who will pound longest.
at the Battle of Waterloo

Sir Walter Scott *Paul's Letters* (1816)

4 Publish and be damned.
replying to Harriette Wilson's blackmail threat, c.1825

attributed; Elizabeth Longford *Wellington: The Years of the Sword* (1969)

of his first Cabinet meeting as Prime Minister:
5 An extraordinary affair. I gave them their orders and they wanted to stay and discuss them.

Peter Hennessy *Whitehall* (1990)

6 I used to say of him [Napoleon] that his presence on the field made the difference of forty thousand men.

Philip Henry Stanhope *Notes of Conversations with the Duke of Wellington* (1888) 2 November 1831

7 Ours [our army] is composed of the scum of the earth—the mere scum of the earth.

Philip Henry Stanhope *Notes of Conversations with the Duke of Wellington* (1888) 4 November 1831

8 I never saw so many shocking bad hats in my life.
on seeing the first Reformed Parliament

William Fraser *Words on Wellington* (1889)

9 Nothing the people of this country like so much as to see their great men take part in their amusements. The aristocracy will commit a great error if they ever fail to mix freely with their neighbours.
on foxhunting

in 1836; Philip Henry Stanhope *Notes of Conversations with the Duke of Wellington* (1888)

10 All the business of war, and indeed all the business of life, is to endeavour to find out what you don't know by what you do; that's what I called 'guessing what was at the other side of the hill'.

in *The Croker Papers* (1885) vol. 3

11 The battle of Waterloo was won on the playing fields of Eton.

oral tradition, but not found in this form of words; C. F. R. Montalembert *De l'avenir politique de l'Angleterre* (1856); see **Orwell** 275:11

to a gentleman who had accosted him in the street saying, 'Mr Jones, I believe?'
12 If you believe that, you'll believe anything.
George Jones RA (1786–1869), painter of military subjects, bore a striking resemblance to Wellington

Elizabeth Longford *Pillar of State* (1972)

13 I have no small talk and Peel has no manners.

G. W. E. Russell *Collections and Recollections* (1898)

14 Next to a battle lost, the greatest misery is a battle gained.

in *Diary of Frances, Lady Shelley 1787–1817* (ed. R. Edgcumbe); see S. Rogers *Recollections* (1859) for variations on the theme

1 There is no such thing as a little war for a great nation.
  to Fitzroy Somerset, urging military preparedness

attributed

2 You must build your House of Parliament upon the river . . . the populace cannot exact their demands by sitting down round you.

William Fraser *Words on Wellington* (1889)

H. G. Wells 1866–1946
English novelist

3 The Social Contract is nothing more or less than a vast conspiracy of human beings to lie to and humbug themselves and one another for the general Good. Lies are the mortar that bind the savage individual man into the social masonry.

Love and Mr Lewisham (1900)

4 The war that will end war.

title of book (1914); see **Lloyd George** 222:11

5 In England we have come to rely upon a comfortable time-lag of fifty years or a century intervening between the perception that something ought to be done and a serious attempt to do it.

The Work, Wealth and Happiness of Mankind (1931)

Rebecca West 1892–1983 ✓
writer, journalist, and literary critic

6 Having watched the form of our traitors for a number of years, I cannot think that espionage can be recommended as a technique for building an impressive civilization. It's a lout's game.

The Meaning of Treason (1982 ed.)

7 I myself have never been able to find out precisely what feminism is: I only know that people call me a feminist whenever I express sentiments that differentiate me from a doormat or a prostitute.

in *The Clarion* 14 November 1913

8 It was in dealing with the early feminist that the Government acquired the tact and skilfulness with which it is now handling Ireland.

in 1916; *The Young Rebecca* (1982)

9 Whatever happens, never forget that people would rather be lead to *perdition* by a man, than to *victory* by a woman.
  *in conversation in 1979, just before Margaret **Thatcher**'s first election victory*

in *Sunday Telegraph* 17 January 1988

John Fane, Lord Westmorland 1759–1841
English nobleman

10 *Merit*, indeed! . . . We are come to a pretty pass if they talk of *merit* for a bishopric.

noted in Lady Salisbury's diary, 9 December 1835

William C. Westmoreland 1914–
American general

11 Vietnam was the first war ever fought without censorship. Without censorship, things can get terribly confused in the public mind.

attributed, 1982

Charles Wetherell 1770–1846

English lawyer and politician

1 Then there is my noble and biographical friend who has added a new terror to death.
  of Lord Campbell

Lord St Leonards *Misrepresentations in Campbell's Lives of Lyndhurst and Brougham* (1869); also attributed to Lord Lyndhurst

Grover A. Whalen 1886–1962

2 There's a lot of law at the end of a nightstick.

Quentin Reynolds *Courtroom* (1950)

Thomas, Lord Wharton 1648–1715

English Whig politician

3 I sang a king out of three kingdoms.
  said to have been Wharton's boast after 'A New Song' became a propaganda weapon against James II

in *Dictionary of National Biography* (1917–); see **Songs** 341:3

E. B. White 1899–1985

American humorist

4 Democracy is the recurrent suspicion that more than half of the people are right more than half of the time.

in *New Yorker* 3 July 1944

5 The so-called science of poll-taking is not a science at all but a mere necromancy. People are unpredictable by nature, and although you can take a nation's pulse, you can't be sure that the nation hasn't just run up a flight of stairs.

in *New Yorker* 13 November 1948

Theodore H. White 1915–86 ✓

American author and journalist

6 Johnson's instinct for power is as primordial as a salmon's going upstream to spawn.
  *of Lyndon **Johnson***

The Making of the President (1964)

7 The flood of money that gushes into politics today is a pollution of democracy.

in *Time* 19 November 1984

William Allen White 1868–1944

American journalist and editor

8 Tinhorn politicians.

in *Emporia Gazette* 25 October 1901

9 Liberty is the only thing you cannot have unless you are willing to give it to others.

attributed

William Whitelaw 1918–99

British Conservative politician
*on Whitelaw: see **Thatcher** 358:5*

10 It is never wise to appear to be more clever than you are. It is sometimes wise to appear slightly less so.

attributed, 1975

11 The Labour Party is going around stirring up apathy.
  recalled by Alan Watkins as a characteristic 'Willieism'

in *Observer* 1 May 1983

Gough Whitlam 1916–

Australian Labor politician, Prime Minister 1972–5

the Governor-General, Sir John Kerr, had dismissed the Labor government headed by Gough Whitlam in November 1975:

1 Well may he say 'God Save the Queen'. But after this nothing will save the Governor-General . . . Maintain your rage and your enthusiasm through the campaign for the election now to be held and until polling day.

speech in Canberra, 11 November 1975

Walt Whitman 1819–92

American poet

2 O Captain! my Captain! our fearful trip is done,
The ship has weathered every rack, the prize we sought is won,
The port is near, the bells I hear, the people all exulting.
*allegorical poem on the death of Abraham **Lincoln***

'O Captain! My Captain!' (1871)

3 The ship is anchored safe and sound, its voyage closed and done.
From fearful trip the victor ship comes in with object won;
Exult O shores, and ring O bells! But I with mournful tread
Walk the deck my Captain lies, Fallen cold and dead.

'O Captain! My Captain!' (1871)

4 Where the populace rise at once against the never-ending audacity of elected persons.

'Song of the Broad Axe' (1881)

5 Where the city of the healthiest fathers stands,
Where the city of the best-bodied mothers stands,
There the great city stands.

'Song of the Broad Axe' (1881)

6 This dust was once the man,
Gentle, plain, just and resolute, under whose cautious hand,
Against the foulest crime in history known in any land or age,
Was saved the Union of these States.

'This dust was once the man' (1881)

7 The United States themselves are essentially the greatest poem.

Leaves of Grass (1855) preface

8 Strange, (is it not?) that battles, martyrs, blood, even assassination, should so condense—perhaps only really, lastingly condense—a Nationality.
of the American Civil War

Geoffrey C. Ward *The Civil War* (1991)

John Greenleaf Whittier 1807–92

American poet

9 'Shoot, if you must, this old grey head,
But spare your country's flag,' she said.
A shade of sadness, a blush of shame,
Over the face of the leader came.

'Barbara Frietchie' (1863)

Robert Whittington

10 As time requireth, a man of marvellous mirth and pastimes, and sometime of as sad gravity, as who say: a man for all seasons.
*of Thomas **More***

in *Vulgaria* (1521) pt. 2; Erasmus famously applied the idea to More, writing in his prefatory letter to *In Praise of Folly* (1509) that he played 'omnium horarum hominem [a man of all hours]'

Ann Widdecombe 1947–
British Conservative politician

1 He has something of the night in him.
of Michael Howard as a contender for the Conservative leadership

in *Sunday Times* 11 May 1997
(electronic edition)

Elie Wiesel 1928–
Romanian-born American writer and Nobel Prize winner;
Auschwitz survivor

2 Take sides. Neutrality helps the oppressor, never the victim.
Silence encourages the tormentor, never the tormented.
accepting the Nobel Peace Prize

in *New York Times* 11 December
1986

3 God of forgiveness, do not forgive those murderers of Jewish
children here.
at Auschwitz

in *The Times* 27 January 1995

Oscar Wilde 1854–1900
Anglo-Irish playwright and poet

4 We have really everything in common with America
nowadays except, of course, language.

The Canterville Ghost (1887); see
Misquotations 254:5

5 If the country doesn't go to the dogs or the Radicals, we
shall have you Prime Minister, some day.

An Ideal Husband (1895)

6 The English country gentleman galloping after a fox—the
unspeakable in full pursuit of the uneatable.

A Woman of No Importance (1893)
act 1; see **Zobel** 391:5

Wilhelm II 1859–1941
German Emperor and King of Prussia, 1888–1918

7 We have . . . fought for our place in the sun and have won
it. It will be my business to see that we retain this place in
the sun unchallenged, so that the rays of that sun may exert
a fructifying influence upon our foreign trade and traffic.

speech in Hamburg, 18 June 1901;
see **Bülow** 56:3

John Wilkes 1727–97
English parliamentary reformer

8 EARL OF SANDWICH: 'Pon my soul, Wilkes, I don't know
whether you'll die upon the gallows or of the pox.
WILKES: That depends, my Lord, whether I first embrace
your Lordship's principles, or your Lordship's mistresses.

Charles Petrie *The Four Georges*
(1935); probably apocryphal

9 Give me a grain of truth and I will mix it up with a great
mass of falsehood so that no chemist will ever be able to
separate them.

Adrian Hamilton *The Infamous
Essay on Women, or John Wilkes
seated between Vice and Virtue*
(1972)

William III 1650–1702
Stadtholder of the Netherlands from 1672; King of Great Britain
and Ireland from 1688
see also **Proverbs** 296:7

10 'Do you not see your country is lost?' asked the Duke of
Buckingham. 'There is one way never to see it lost' replied
William, 'and that is to die in the last ditch.'

Bishop Gilbert Burnet *History of My
Own Time* (1838 ed.)

Roy Williamson 1936–90

Scottish folksinger and musician

1 O flower of Scotland, when will we see your like again,
that fought and died for your bit hill and glen
and stood against him, proud Edward's army,
and sent him homeward tae think again.
  unofficial Scottish Nationalist anthem

'O Flower of Scotland' (1968)

Wendell Willkie 1892–1944

American lawyer and politician

2 Freedom is an indivisible word. If we want to enjoy it, and
fight for it, we must be prepared to extend it to everyone,
whether they are rich or poor, whether they agree with us
or not, no matter what their race or the colour of their skin.

One World (1943)

3 The constitution does not provide for first and second class
citizens.

An American Programme (1944)

A. N. Wilson 1950–

British novelist

4 I should prefer to have a politician who regularly went to a
massage parlour than one who promised a laptop computer
for every teacher.

in *Observer* 21 March 1999

Charles E. Wilson 1890–1961

American industrialist
see also **Slogan** 334:8

5 For years I thought what was good for our country was
good for General Motors and vice versa. The difference did
not exist. Our company is too big. It goes with the welfare of
the country.

testimony to the Senate Armed
Services Committee on his
proposed nomination to be
Secretary of Defence, 15 January
1953

Harold Wilson 1916–95

British Labour statesman, Prime Minister 1964–70 and 1974–6
on Wilson: see **Anonymous** 8:11, **Benn** 32:4, **Birch** 41:2, **Bulmer-
Thomas** 56:2, **Bush** 62:1, **Home** 175:10, **Junor** 195:8

6 All these financiers, all the little gnomes in Zurich and the
other financial centres about whom we keep on hearing.

in the House of Commons, 12
November 1956

7 I myself have always deprecated . . . in crisis after crisis,
appeals to the Dunkirk spirit as an answer to our problems.

in the House of Commons, 26 July
1961; see **Wilson** 385:1

8 This party is a moral crusade or it is nothing.

speech at the Labour Party
Conference, 1 October 1962

9 We are restating our socialism in terms of the scientific
revolution . . . the Britain that is going to be forged in the
white heat of this revolution will be no place for restrictive
practices or outdated methods on either side of industry.

speech at the Labour Party
Conference, 1 October 1963; see
Misquotations 256:2

10 What I think we are going to need is something like what
President Kennedy had when he came in after years of
stagnation in the United States. He had a programme of a
hundred days—a hundred days of dynamic action.

in a party political broadcast, 15
July 1964

1 I believe that the spirit of Dunkirk will carry us through . . . to success.

speech to the Labour Party Conference, 12 December 1964; see **Wilson** 384:7

2 The Smethwick Conservatives can have the satisfaction of having topped the poll, and of having sent here as their Member one who, until a further General Election restores him to oblivion, will serve his term here as a Parliamentary leper.
on the outcome of a by-election with racist overtones

in the House of Commons, 3 November 1964

3 A week is a long time in politics.
probably first said at a lobby briefing at the time of the 1964 sterling crisis

Nigel Rees *Sayings of the Century* (1984); see **Chamberlain** 74:4

4 [Labour is] the natural party of government.

in 1965; Anthony Sampson *The Changing Anatomy of Britain*

5 From now the pound abroad is worth 14 per cent or so less in terms of other currencies. It does not mean, of course, that the pound here in Britain, in your pocket or purse or in your bank, has been devalued.

ministerial broadcast, 19 November 1967

6 Get your tanks off my lawn, Hughie.
*to the trade union leader Hugh **Scanlon**, at Chequers in June 1969*

Peter Jenkins *The Battle of Downing Street* (1970)

7 I know what is going on. I am going on.
commenting on rumours of conspiracies against his leadership

at a May Day rally, 4 May 1969; Ben Pimlott *Harold Wilson* (1992)

8 One man's wage increase is another man's price increase.

speech at Blackburn, 8 January 1970

9 This party is a bit like an old stagecoach. If you drive along at a rapid rate, everyone aboard is either so exhilarated or so seasick that you don't have a lot of difficulty.
of the Labour Party, c.1974

Anthony Sampson *The Changing Anatomy of Britain* (1982)

10 Whichever party is in office, the Treasury is in power.
while in opposition, c.1974

Anthony Sampson *The Changing Anatomy of Britain* (1982)

11 I've buried all the hatchets. But I know where I've buried them and I can dig them up if necessary.
of the Cabinet in 1974

Lord Hunt in *Secret History. Harold Wilson: The Final Years* (Channel 4 TV) 15 August 1996

12 The trouble is when the old problems reappear I reach for the old solutions.
to his Press Secretary Joe Haines, July 1975

Peter Hennessy *The Prime Minister: the Office and its Holders since 1945* (2000)

13 The Monarchy is a labour-intensive industry.

in *Observer* 13 February 1977

14 The one thing we need to nationalize in this country is the Treasury, but no one has ever succeeded.

in 1984; Peter Hennessy *Whitehall* (1990)

Richard Wilson 1942–

British civil servant and Cabinet Secretary

15 There are occasions on which you have to say 'bollocks' to ministers.

in *Times* 10 February 2000

Woodrow Wilson 1856–1924

American Democratic statesman, 28th President of the US
1913–21
on Wilson: see **Clemenceau** 89:6, **Keynes** 200:7

1 Prosperity is necessarily the first theme of a political campaign.

speech, 4 September, 1912; see **Slogans** 335:6

2 Liberty has never come from the government. Liberty has always come from the subjects of government. The history of liberty is the history of resistance. The history of liberty is a history of the limitation of governmental power, not the increase of it.

speech to the New York Press Club, 9 September 1912

3 The United States must be neutral in fact as well as in name.
at the outbreak of the First World War

message to the Senate, 19 August 1914

4 It is like writing history with lightning. And my only regret is that it is all so terribly true.
on seeing D. W. Griffith's film The Birth of a Nation

at the White House, 18 February 1915

5 No nation is fit to sit in judgement upon any other nation.

speech in New York, 20 April 1915

6 There is such a thing as a man being too proud to fight; there is such a thing as a nation being so right that it does not need to convince others by force that it is right.

speech in Philadelphia, 10 May 1915

7 We have stood apart, studiously neutral.

speech to Congress, 7 December 1915

8 America can not be an ostrich with its head in the sand.

speech at Des Moines, 1 February 1916

9 It must be a peace without victory . . . Only a peace between equals can last.

speech to US Senate, 22 January 1917

10 Armed neutrality is ineffectual enough at best.

speech to Congress, 2 April 1917

11 The day has come when America is privileged to spend her blood and her might for the principles that gave her birth and happiness and the peace which she has treasured.

speech to Congress, 2 April 1917

12 The world must be made safe for democracy.

speech to Congress, 2 April 1917; see **Wolfe** 387:6

13 The right is more precious than peace.

speech to Congress, 2 April 1917

14 Once lead this people into war and they will forget there ever was such a thing as tolerance.

John Dos Passos *Mr Wilson's War* (1917)

15 The programme of the world's peace . . . is this:
ɪ. Open covenants of peace, openly arrived at.

speech to Congress, 8 January 1918

16 America is the only idealistic nation in the world.

speech at Sioux Falls, South Dakota, 8 September 1919

17 A general association of nations must be formed . . . for the purpose of affording mutual guarantees of political independence and territorial integrity to great and small states alike.

speech to Congress, 8 January 1918

18 If I am to speak for ten minutes, I need a week for preparation; if fifteen minutes, three days; if half an hour, two days; if an hour, I am ready now.

Josephus Daniels *The Wilson Era* (1946)

William Windham 1750–1810

English politician

1 Those entrusted with arms . . . should be persons of some substance and stake in the country.

in the House of Commons, 22 July 1807

John Winthrop 1588–1649

American settler

2 We must consider that we shall be a city upon a hill, the eyes of all people are on us; so that if we shall deal falsely with our God in this work we have undertaken, and so cause Him to withdraw His present help from us, we shall be made a story and a byword through the world.

Christian Charity, A Model Hereof (sermon, 1630)

Robert Charles Winthrop 1809–94

3 A Star for every State, and a State for every Star.

speech on Boston Common, 27 August 1862

Humbert Wolfe 1886–1940

British poet

4 You cannot hope
to bribe or twist,
thank God! the
British journalist.

But, seeing what
the man will do
unbribed, there's
no occasion to.

'Over the Fire' (1930)

James Wolfe 1727–59

British general; captor of Quebec

5 The General . . . repeated nearly the whole of Gray's Elegy . . . adding, as he concluded, that he would prefer being the author of that poem to the glory of beating the French to-morrow.

J. Playfair Biographical Account of J. Robinson in Transactions of the Royal Society of Edinburgh vol. 7 (1815)

Thomas Wolfe 1900–38

American novelist

6 'Where they got you stationed now, Luke?' said Harry Tugman peering up snoutily from a mug of coffee. 'At the p-p-p-present time in Norfolk at the Navy base,' Luke answered, 'm-m-making the world safe for hypocrisy.'

*Look Homeward, Angel (1929; see **Wilson** 386:12*

Tom Wolfe 1931–

American writer

7 A liberal is a conservative who's been arrested.

*The Bonfire of the Vanities (1987); see **Proverbs** 296:1*

8 A cult is a religion with no political power.

In Our Time (1980)

Thomas Wolsey c.1475–1530

English cardinal; Lord Chancellor, 1515–29

1 Father Abbot, I am come to lay my bones amongst you.

George Cavendish *Negotiations of Thomas Wolsey* (1641)

2 Had I but served God as diligently as I have served the King, he would not have given me over in my grey hairs.

George Cavendish *Negotiations of Thomas Wolsey* (1641)

Alexander Woollcott 1887–1943

American writer

3 I think your slogan 'Liberty or Death' is splendid, and whichever one you decide on will be all right with me.

attributed

William Wordsworth 1770–1850

English poet

4 Bliss was it in that dawn to be alive,
But to be young was very heaven!

'The French Revolution, as it Appeared to Enthusiasts' (1809); also *The Prelude* (1850)

5   In our halls is hung
Armoury of the invincible Knights of old:
We must be free or die, who speak the tongue
That Shakespeare spake; the faith and morals hold
Which Milton held. In every thing we are sprung
Of Earth's first blood, have titles manifold.

'It is not to be thought of that the Flood' (1807)

6 Once did she hold the gorgeous East in fee,
And was the safeguard of the West.

'On the Extinction of the Venetian Republic' (1807)

Henry Wotton 1568–1639

English poet and diplomat

7 Dazzled thus with height of place,
Whilst our hopes our wits beguile,
No man marks the narrow space
'Twixt a prison and a smile.

'Upon the sudden restraint of the Earl of Somerset' (1651)

8 An ambassador is an honest man sent to lie abroad for the good of his country.

written in the album of Christopher Fleckmore in 1604

Neville Wran 1926–

Australian politician

9 The average footslogger in the New South Wales Right . . . generally speaking carries a dagger in one hand and a Bible in the other and doesn't put either to really elegant use.

in 1973; Michael Gordon *A Question of Leadership* (1993)

Kenyon Wright 1932–

Scottish Methodist minister, Chairman of the Scottish Constitutional Convention

10 What if that other single voice we know so well responds by saying, 'We say No and we are the State.' Well, we say Yes and we are the People!
*of Margaret **Thatcher** as Prime Minister*

speech at the inaugural meeting of the Scottish Constitutional Convention, 30 March 1989

Harry Wu 1937–

Chinese-born American political activist

1 I want to see the word *laogai* in every dictionary in every language in the world. I want to see the laogai ended. Before 1974, the word 'gulag' did not appear in any dictionary. Today, this single word conveys the meaning of Soviet political violence and its labour camp system. 'Laogai' also deserves a place in our dictionaries.

the laogai *are Chinese labour camps*

in *Washington Post* 26 May 1996

Augustin, Marquis de Ximénèz 1726–1817

French poet

2 *Attaquons dans ses eaux*
La perfide Albion!

Let us attack in her own waters perfidious Albion!

'L'Ère des Français' (October 1793)

William Yancey 1814–63

American Confederate politician

*of Jefferson **Davis**, President-elect of the Confederacy, in 1861:*
3 The man and the hour have met.

Shelby Foote *The Civil War: Fort Sumter to Perryville* (1991)

W. B. Yeats 1865–1939

Irish poet; senator of the Irish Free State 1922–8

4 Too long a sacrifice
Can make a stone of the heart.
O when may it suffice?

'Easter, 1916' (1921)

5 I write it out in a verse—
MacDonagh and MacBride
And Connolly and Pearse
Now and in time to be,
Wherever green is worn,
Are changed, changed utterly:
A terrible beauty is born.

'Easter, 1916' (1921)

6 I think it better that at times like these
We poets keep our mouths shut, for in truth
We have no gift to set a statesman right.

'A Reason for Keeping Silent' (1916)

7 Out of Ireland have we come.
Great hatred, little room,
Maimed us at the start.
I carry from my mother's womb
A fanatic heart.

'Remorse for Intemperate Speech' (1933)

8 Turning and turning in the widening gyre
The falcon cannot hear the falconer;
Things fall apart; the centre cannot hold;
Mere anarchy is loosed upon the world,
The blood-dimmed tide is loosed, and everywhere
The ceremony of innocence is drowned;
The best lack all conviction, while the worst
Are full of passionate intensity.

'The Second Coming' (1920)

9 Romantic Ireland's dead and gone,
It's with O'Leary in the grave.

'September, 1913' (1914)

1 Cast your mind on other days
That we in coming days may be
Still the indomitable Irishry.

'Under Ben Bulben' (1939)

of the Anglo-Irish:
2 We . . . are no petty people. We are one of the great stocks of
Europe. We are the people of Burke; we are the people of
Swift, the people of Emmet, the people of Parnell. We have
created most of the modern literature of this country. We
have created the best of its political intelligence.

speech in the Irish Senate, 11 June
1925, in the debate on divorce

David Yelland
British journalist, Editor of the *Sun*

3 I don't think the Blairs are *Sun* readers.

on *News from Number Ten* (BBC2
documentary), 15 July 2000

Boris Yeltsin 1931–
Russian statesman, President of the Russian Federation,
1991–2000

4 Today is the last day of an era past.
*at a Berlin ceremony to end the Soviet military presence in
Germany*

in *Guardian* 1 September 1994

5 Europe is in danger of plunging into a cold peace.
*at the summit meeting of the Conference on Security and
Co-operation in Europe, December 1994*

in *Newsweek* 19 December 1994

Shoichi Yokoi 1915–97
Japanese soldier

6 It is a terrible shame for me—I came back, still alive,
without having won the war.
*on returning to Japan after surviving for 28 years in the jungles of
Guam before surrendering to the Americans in 1972*

in *Independent* 26 September 1997

Andrew Young 1932–
American Democratic politician and minister

7 Nothing is illegal if one hundred well-placed business men
decide to do it.

Morris K. Udall *Too Funny to be
President* (1988)

Michael Young 1915–
British writer

8 Today we frankly recognize that democracy can be no more
than aspiration, and have rule not so much by the people as
by the cleverest people; not an aristocracy of birth, not a
plutocracy of wealth, but a true meritocracy of talent.

The Rise of the Meritocracy (1958)

Israel Zangwill 1864–1926
British author and philanthropist, son of a Russian refugee

9 America is God's Crucible, the great Melting-Pot where all
the races of Europe are melting and re-forming!

The Melting Pot (1908)

Emiliano Zapata 1879–1919

Mexican revolutionary

1 Many of them, so as to curry favour with tyrants, for a fistful of coins, or through bribery or corruption, are shedding the blood of their brothers.
   on the maderistas *who, in Zapata's view, had betrayed the revolutionary cause*

Plan de Ayala 28 November 1911

Mikhail Zhvanetsky 1934–

Russian writer

2 We enjoyed . . . his slyness. He mastered the art of walking backward into the future. He would say 'After me'. And some people went ahead, and some went behind, and he would go backward.
   of Mikhail **Gorbachev**

in *Time* 12 September 1994; attributed

Ronald L. Ziegler 1939–

American government spokesman

reminded of the President's previous statements that the White House was not involved in the Watergate affair:
3 [Mr Nixon's latest statement] is the Operative White House Position . . . and all previous statements are inoperative.

in *Boston Globe* 18 April 1973

Grigori Zinoviev 1883–1936

Soviet politician

4 Armed warfare must be preceded by a struggle against the inclinations to compromise which are embedded among the majority of British workmen, against the ideas of evolution and peaceful extermination of capitalism. Only then will it be possible to count upon complete success of an armed insurrection.

letter to the British Communist Party, 15 September 1924, in *The Times* 25 October 1924 (the 'Zinoviev Letter', said by some to be a forgery)

Hiller B. Zobel 1932–

American judge

5 Asking the ignorant to use the incomprehensible to decide the unknowable.

'The Jury on Trial' in *American Heritage* July–August 1995; see **Wilde** 383:6

6 Judges must follow their oaths and do their duty, heedless of editorials, letters, telegrams, threats, petitions, panellists and talk shows.

judicial ruling reducing the conviction of Louise Woodward from murder to manslaughter, 10 November 1997

Émile Zola 1840–1902

French novelist

7 *J'accuse.*
   I accuse.
   title of an open letter to the President of the French Republic, in connection with the Dreyfus affair

in *L'Aurore* 13 January 1898

Keyword Index

affluent a. society   GALB 139:8
afraid feel somewhat a.   DE V 108:3
  not a. to go   LAST 213:1
afresh begins the world a.   MONN 257:8
Africa deported A.   GENE 142:5
  new out of A.   PLIN 291:2
  shape of A.   FANO 130:4
  white man in A.   LESS 216:5
African A. is conditioned   KENY 200:4
  [A.] national consciousness   MACM 236:2
  A. people   MAND 240:6
against a. everything   KENN 199:13
  He was a. it   COOL 96:1
  never met anyone who wasn't a. war

                              LOW 226:1
  not with me is a. me   BIBL 39:20
  people vote a. somebody   ADAM 2:5
  those that work a. them   HALI 158:5
age a. fatal to Revolutionists   DESM 107:4
  a. going to the workhouse   PAIN 280:12
  a. is a dream that is dying   O'SH 277:5
  a. of chivalry   BURK 58:14
  a. we live in   BURK 59:9
  Old a.   TROT 365:7
agenda any item of the a.   PARK 283:5
agents Civil and Political A.   VICT 371:1
ages belongs to the a.   STAN 345:8
aggression It is naked a.   POWE 293:13
aggressive being a.   HARN 162:7
agitation than to excite a.   PALM 281:11
agonizing a. reappraisal   DULL 119:17
agony a. is abated   MACA 230:13
agree appear to a.   PAIN 280:14
  both a. is wrong   CECI 73:7
  colours will a. in the dark   BACO 19:17
agreement a. between two men   CECI 73:7
  a. with hell   GARR 141:11
  blow with an a.   TROT 365:10
  have reached a.   MITC 256:3
agriculture taxes must fall upon a.   GIBB 145:6
ahead a. of your time   MCGO 232:10
aid Foreign a.   NIXO 270:11
  Foreign a. is a system   BAUE 28:7
aids seventeen-year-olds dying of A.   GING 146:11
aim when you have forgotten your a.   SANT 314:5
aimez a. qui vous aime   VOLT 372:7
air a. power has prevailed   KEEG 197:4
  to the Germans that of—the a.   RICH 302:3
aitches nothing to lose but our a.   ORWE 276:11
Alamein Before A.   CHUR 85:8
Albert take a message to A.   LAST 213:6
Albion perfidious A.   XIMÉ 389:2
alcohol more out of a.   CHUR 86:4
aldermen divides the wives of a.   SMIT 333:4
alien damned if I'm an a.   GEOR 144:2
  quick to blame the a.   AESC 5:4
alieni A. appetens   SALL 313:9
alive a. I shall be delighted   HOLL 175:2
  came back, still a.   YOKO 390:6
  Not while I'm a. 'e ain't   BEVI 38:12

alive (cont.):
  what keeps you a.   CAST 72:3
all a. men are evil   MACH 233:5
  Fair shares for a.   SLOG 334:14
  man for a. seasons   WHIT 382:10
allegiance flag to which you have pledged a.

                              BALD 24:7
alliance morganatic a.   HARD 161:5
alliances entangling a. with none   JEFF 186:3
  permanent a.   WASH 375:6
allies no a. to be polite to   GEOR 144:4
  no eternal a.   PALM 281:8
allons A., enfants de la patrie   SONG 341:1
allow Government and public opinion a.

                              SHAW 328:7
almighty A. had placed it there   LABO 208:9
  A. took seven   CHUR 83:2
alone a. in the room   KEYN 201:12
  cannot live a.   ROOS 306:9
  plough my furrow a.   ROSE 308:7
  right to be let a.   BRAN 50:5
  would but let it a.   WALP 373:12
altar lays upon the a.   SPRI 344:8
altars a. to the ground   JORD 193:5
alteration A. though it be   HOOK 176:2
alternative a. to war   KING 203:9
  no real a.   THAT 356:8
  What is the a.   TREN 362:9
alternatives decide between a.   BONH 47:2
  exhausted all other a.   EBAN 121:2
always a. in the majority   KNOX 208:1
Alzheimer he had A.'s disease   REAG 300:4
amateurs nation of a.   ROSE 308:5
  we prefer rule by a.   ATTL 17:7
ambassador a. is an honest man   WOTT 388:8
ambition A. can creep   BURK 59:7
  A., in a private man a vice   MASS 245:11
  A.'s debt is paid   SHAK 322:11
  A. should be made   SHAK 323:6
  fling away a.   SHAK 321:2
  not without a.   SHAK 324:9
  Vaulting a.   SHAK 325:1
  young a.'s ladder   SHAK 322:4
ambitions ceiling put on our a.   PRES 294:6
ambitious as he was a., I slew him   SHAK 323:3
  says he was a.   SHAK 323:5
amendment Fifth A.   DOUG 117:4
  First A. has erected a wall   BLAC 43:1
America A. is God's Crucible   ZANG 390:9
  A. is just ourselves   ARNO 14:7
  A. is the only idealistic   WILS 386:16
  A. our nation   DOS 117:3
  A.'s present need   HARD 161:2
  A., the land   GOLD 150:2
  A. thus top nation   SELL 317:13
  born in A.   MALC 239:9
  cannot conquer A.   PITT 289:13
  Don't seel A. short   PROV 296:4
  England and A. divided   MISQ 254:5
  glorious morning for A.   MISQ 256:1
  God bless A.   BERL 34:4

America (*cont.*):

I look upon North A.	SHIP 331:7
in common with A.	WILD 383:4
independence of A.	SHEL 329:7
in the living rooms of A.	MCLU 235:1
I, too, sing A.	HUGH 178:1
loss of A.	FREE 138:2
lost his dominions in A.	WALP 373:10
makes A. what it is	STEI 346:2
morning again in A.	SLOG 335:4
primitive North A.	BROG 52:7
see A. save her soul	THOM 359:5
think of thee, O A.	WALP 373:14
United States of A.	PAGE 278:6
whole A.	BURK 57:16

American A. as cherry pie

	BROW 54:1
A. culture	COLO 93:4
A. dream is	BYWA 64:8
A. government	JEFF 187:9
A., this new man	CEÈV 97:2
bad news to the A. people	KEIL 197:7
chief business of the A. people	COOL 95:9
free man, an A.	JOHN 189:4
Greeks in this A. empire	MACM 235:5
I also—am an A.	WEBS 377:14
I am A. bred	MILL 251:9
in A. politics	MITC 253:9
I shall die an A.	WEBS 377:16
knocking the A. system	CAPO 69:5
not a Virginian, but an A.	HENR 169:8
Scratch any A.	RUSK 310:2
send A. boys	JOHN 190:1

Americanism A. with its sleeves rolled

	MCCA 231:7
hyphenated A.	ROOS 307:11

Americans A. are to be freemen

	WASH 375:4
A. in and the Germans down	ISMA 182:5
for A. it is just beyond	KISS 207:9
let A. disdain	HAMI 160:8
my fellow A.	KENN 198:8
passed to new generation of A.	KENN 198:3

amicably a. if they can	QUIN 297:6
ammunition pass the a.	FORG 134:9
amused We are not a.	VICT 371:4
amusements part in their a.	WELL 379:9
anarch Thy hand, great A.	POPE 292:1
anarchism A. is a game	SHAW 328:15
A. stands for the liberation	GOLD 150:3
anarchy a. and competition	RUSK 310:13
cure of a.	BURK 57:19
democracy, call it a.	HOBB 173:15
Mere a. is loosed	YEAT 389:8
anatomist am but a bad a.	LAST 212:10
ancestors look backward to their a.	BURK 58:8
look backward to their a.	BURK 58:9
ancestry pride of a.	POWE 294:4
anchor firm a. in nonsense	GALB 139:10
anchored a. safe and sound	WHIT 382:3
angel a. of death	BRIG 51:5
ape or an a.	DISR 112:7
angels better a. of our nature	LINC 219:2

angels (*cont.*):

By that sin fell the a.	SHAK 321:2
make the a. weep	SHAK 325:12
plead like a.	SHAK 324:10
anger a. of the sovereign	MORE 259:9
neither a. nor partiality	TACI 351:7
Anglicization demon of A.	HYDE 180:6
Anglo-Irishman He was an A.	BEHA 30:7
Anglo-Saxon natural idol of the A.	BAGE 21:14
anguish howls of a.	HEAL 165:8
animal by nature a political a.	ARIS 13:11
insidious and crafty a.	SMIT 337:7
animals All a. are equal	ORWE 275:7
ankle chain about the a.	DOUG 117:9
Anna Here thou, great A.	POPE 292:7
annihilating a. all civilization	SAKH 312:1
a. nations	MONT 258:5
annus a. horribilis	ELIZ 125:6
anointed balm from an a. king	SHAK 326:4
answer a. is yes	DOLE 116:8
a. to the Irish Question	SELL 317:12
answering about not a.	LYNN 227:6
antiblack a. laws	FRIE 138:6
Antichrist against the a. of Communism	
	BUCH 55:9
anticipate What we a.	DISR 114:12
antique traveller from an a. land	SHEL 329:10
anti-Semitic stupid as the a.	LLOY 223:13
antiwar ecology and a.	HUNT 179:7
Antony A. Would ruffle up	SHAK 323:14
anybody no one's a.	GILB 146:2
anywhere a. I damn well please	BEVI 38:9
apart have stood a.	WILS 386:7
apathy stirring up a.	WHIT 381:11
ape Is man a.	DISR 112:7
aphrodisiac Power is the great a.	KISS 207:3
apologize Never a.	FISH 132:2
apology defence or a.	CHAR 75:8
apostles A. of freedom	CONN 94:4
true a. of equality	ARNO 14:8
appeasement A. was a sensible	TAYL 353:17
appeaser a. is one who	CHUR 81:8
appeasers A. believe	BROU 53:5
appetite no a. for truth	PEEL 285:7
appetites chains upon their own a.	BURK 57:2
applause everyone is forced to a.	MILL 252:3
appointment a. by the corrupt few	SHAW 328:10
create an a.	LOUI 225:6
apprenticeship a. for freedom	BARA 27:9
approbation a. of all their actions	HOBB 173:14
appropriate that was not a.	CLIN 91:3
après A. nous le déluge	POMP 291:7
Arab like an A. horse	ROBE 302:7
Arabs seven hundred thousand A.	BALF 26:5
Arbeicht A. macht frei	SLOG 334:3
arbiter a. of others' fate	BYRO 64:6
arbitrary a. government	CHAR 76:9
supreme power must be a.	HALI 158:10
arch a. of order	STRA 349:3
triumphant a.	COMM 93:5
archbishop My Lord A.	BULL 56:1

archer attack Jeffrey A.   HUMP 179:5
archipelago Gulag a.   SOLZ 340:4
architecture What has happened to a.   LEVI 217:5
are We a. what we are   DAVI 102:5
arena actually in the a.   ROOS 307:9
Argentina Don't cry for me, A.   RICE 301:7
Argentinian young A. soldiers   RUNC 309:9
argument a. for fisticuffs   CHUR 84:5
   a. of tyrants   PITT 290:4
   no a. but force   BROW 54:5
   no force but a.   BROW 54:5
   once in the use of an a.   BENN 33:1
   stir without great a.   SHAK 319:16
aristocracies A. . . . . may   TREV 363:7
aristocracy abolishes a.   TOCQ 361:2
   a. glean honour   MACD 232:5
   a. is rather apt   DISR 114:13
   a. means government by   CHES 78:4
   a. of Great Britain   BRIG 51:6
   A. of the Moneybag   CARL 70:2
   a. the most democratic   MACA 229:15
   a. will commit   WELL 379:9
   called a.   PAIN 280:2
   displeased with *a.*   HOBB 173:15
   love of a.   GLAD 148:2
   natural a. among men   JEFF 186:11
   not an a. of birth   YOUN 390:8
aristocrat A. who cleans   GILB 146:1
aristocratic distinguish clearly the a. class   ARNO 14:9
arithmetical a. ratio   MALT 240:1
armadillos dead a.   HIGH 172:2
Armageddon We stand at A.   ROOS 307:10
armaments bloated a.   DISR 112:2
   not a. that cause wars   MADA 237:5
armed a. conflict   EDEN 121:5
   A. neutrality is ineffectual   WILS 386:10
   A. warfare must be preceded   ZINO 391:4
armes Aux a., citoyens   SONG 341:1
armies interested in a. and fleets   AUDE 17:12
   standing a. of power   RADC 297:8
   stronger than all the a.   ANON 11:5
Arminian A. clergy   PITT 289:12
armistice It is an a. for twenty years   FOCH 133:6
armour a. of a righteous cause   BRYA 55:5
arms a. ye forge   SHEL 330:1
   it hath very long a.   HALI 159:5
   keep and bear a.   CONS 95:2
   This world in a.   EISE 122:6
   Those entrusted with a.   WIND 387:1
   world in a.   SHAK 324:4
army a. marches on its stomach   NAPO 264:12
   a. would be a base rabble   BURK 58:2
   command an a.   SHER 331:1
   Forgotten A.   MOUN 261:6
   formation of an Irish a.   GRIF 155:3
   French's contemptible little a.   ANON 8:4
   invasion by an a.   HUGO 178:3
   Irish Citizen a.   CONN 94:7
   won't be a bit like the A.   TRUM 366:7
   Your poor a.   CROM 98:9

aroused a. every feeling   TAYL 353:4
arrange French a.   CATH 72:6
arrested who's been a.   WOLF 387:7
arrive barbarians are to a.   CAVA 73:2
arse politician is an a. upon   CUMM 99:7
arsenal great a. of democracy   ROOS 306:3
art a. establishes   KENN 199:6
   a. of government   PEEL 286:11
   a. which one government sooner   SMIT 337:3
   great a. lies   MILT 252:10
   Minister that meddles with a.   MELB 247:6
   necessary a.   DULL 120:1
   Politics is not the a.   GALB 140:13
   Politics is the a.   GAND 140:16
   Politics is the a. of the possible   BISM 41:7
article first a. of my faith   GAND 141:3
artificial but an a. man   HOBB 173:5
artists A. are not engineers   KENN 199:7
arts France, mother of a.   DU B 119:14
   No a.; no letters   HOBB 173:10
ascendancy a. of the Whig party   MACA 229:11
ascent a. to greatness   GIBB 145:2
ascertainable a. facts   PEEL 286:16
Asian A. boys ought to be   JOHN 190:1
ask a. not what your country   KENN 198:8
   Don't a., don't tell   NUNN 271:10
askance looking a., other nations   GOGO 149:9
asking a. too much   CANN 69:2
asleep a. at one time   RUSK 310:1
   a. on the same benches   ONSL 274:11
aspirant a. under democracy   MENC 248:12
ass kiss my a. in Macy's window   JOHN 190:8
   on his unwashed a.   PARS 284:6
assassination A. has never changed   DISR 112:8
   A. is the extreme form   SHAW 328:17
   avoid a.   TRUM 366:6
assassins professional a.   LIVI 221:12
assembly games down at the A.   BLAI 44:7
   majority of a popular a.   ADAM 3:10
assent rash and precipitate a.   PEEL 285:10
asserted boldly a.   BURR 61:8
association a. of nations   WILS 386:17
asteroid a. hitting the planet   KING 203:1
astonished a. at my own moderation   CLIV 91:7
asylum a. from persecution   UNIV 368:9
   lunatic a. run by lunatics   LLOY 223:6
   No one outside an a.   ROSE 308:6
   was in an a.   PALM 282:1
ate With A. by his side   SHAK 323:1
atheist town a.   BROG 52:8
Athens A. arose   SHEL 329:8
   citizen of A.   SOCR 340:1
Atlanta A. is gone   CHES 77:2
atom best defence against the a. bomb   ANON 7:8
   grasped the mystery of the a.   BRAD 49:8
   no evil in the a.   STEV 347:1
atomic win an a. war   BRAD 49:7
atoms concurrence of a.   PALM 281:10
atrocities a. however horrible   NAMI 264:3
attack a. from Mars   SALI 313:3
   a. the Government   CHUR 84:1

attacking I am a.	FOCH 133:5
attacks a. on government	BREN 51:2
attempt never to a. a measure	BURK 60:3
attentive a. and favourable hearers	HOOK 176:1
Attlee A. got out	CHUR 85:15
audace *toujours de l'a.*	DANT 101:5
audacity a. of elected persons	WHIT 382:4
audience is a large a.	TROL 364:14
unwilling a.	O'CO 272:6
August traps shut in A.	DEED 104:4
Auschwitz year spent in A.	LEVI 216:7
Austen resort to Jane A.	MACM 236:13
Australia take A. right back	KEAT 196:9
author a. who speaks	DISR 112:20
authority A. doesn't work	DE G 105:11
A. forgets a dying king	TENN 355:12
a. of the eternal yesterday	WEBE 377:4
by 'lawful a.'	MACD 232:6
cede to lawful a.	GIUL 147:2
little brief a.	SHAK 325:12
Madmen in a.	KEYN 201:8
no a. from God to do mischief	MAYH 246:5
peculiar a.	MORL 260:9
Royal a.	MONT 258:15
seek a.	WAUG 376:1
authors We a., ma'am	DISR 112:12
autocracy Russian a.	HERZ 170:11
autocrat a.: that's my trade	CATH 72:7
autograph signed an a.	DE V 107:8
autonomy political a.	GRAY 153:9
autres *encourager les a.*	VOLT 371:11
avalanche perseverance of a mighty a.	
	HOUS 177:3
avenge a. even a look	BURK 58:13
avoided a. simply by	CHUR 86:8
awake a. and up to some mischief	RUSK 310:1
West's a.	DAVI 102:10
West's a.	ROBI 303:13
away WHEN I'M A.	BONH 47:1
axe a.'s edge did try	MARV 244:1
a. to the root	PAIN 280:1
let the great a. fall	SHAK 319:12
axis sword the a. of the world	DE G 105:12
underbelly of the A.	CHUR 82:12
Aztec destroyed the A. Empire	SCHU 316:3
babble Coffee house b.	DISR 113:3
babes one of Blair's b.	JACK 183:8
babies putting milk into b.	CHUR 82:14
twelve-year-olds having b.	GING 146:11
baby b. beats the nurse	SHAK 325:7
Burn, b., burn	SLOG 334:10
like a big b.	REAG 299:3
Babylon By the waters of B.	WALP 373:14
London is a modern B.	DISR 114:22
back b. him to the full	HAGU 156:6
b.-seat driver	THAT 358:4
boys in the b. rooms	BEAV 29:6
counted them all b.	HANR 161:2
have to watch his b.	HESE 171:6

back (*cont.*):	
time to get b. to basics	MAJO 239:3
backbone no more b.	ROOS 307:3
backed never so perfectly b.	HALI 158:11
backing I'm b. Britain	SLOG 335:3
backs With our b. to the wall	HAIG 157:2
backward look b. to their ancestors	BURK 58:8
look b. to their ancestors	BURK 58:9
never go b.	SEWA 318:2
walking b. into future	ZHVA 391:2
bad almost always b. men	ACTO 1:10
B. laws	BURK 60:8
B. money drives out good	PROV 296:3
brave b. man	CLAR 87:8
from b. to worse	TOCQ 361:8
shocking b. hats	WELL 379:8
things were just as b.	KENN 198:10
When b. men combine	BURK 59:14
bag b. and baggage	GLAD 148:3
baggage bag and b.	GLAD 148:3
take some b. in	CALL 66:4
baked b. cookies and had teas	CLIN 90:6
balance b. of our population	JOSE 194:1
b. of power	KISS 207:7
b. of power	NICO 266:6
b. of the Old	CANN 69:3
tongue in the b.	BISM 42:13
balanced b. spirit	GEOR 143:7
balancing B. the budget	GRAM 152:5
bald b. eagle had not been chosen	FRAN 137:1
fight between two b. men	BORG 48:9
young, b. Leader	KINN 204:12
Baldwin sandhills of the B. Cabinet	ASQU 15:6
Balfour of the B. declaration	WEIZ 378:6
Balkans prevailed in the B.	KEEG 197:4
silly thing in the B.	BISM 42:8
trouble in the B. in the spring	KIPL 206:9
ballads permitted to make all the b.	FLET 133:1
ballot b. box in one hand	BRUT 55:4
b. is stronger than	MISQ 254:2
rap at the b. box	CHIL 78:6
right of all to the b.	ANTH 12:12
Vote by b.	CARL 70:11
ballots peaceful b.	LINC 218:5
balm wash the b.	SHAK 326:4
ban B. the bomb	SLOG 334:4
bang bigger b. for a buck	SLOG 334:8
If the big b. does come	OSBO 277:1
Not with a b. but a whimper	ELIO 123:4
banish I b. you	SHAK 318:9
will b. myself	SHER 331:1
bank tyrannize over his b. balance	KEYN 201:6
banker as a Scotch b.	DAVI 102:3
bankrupts need more b.	JOSE 194:2
banner Freedom's b.	DRAK 118:4
star-spangled b.	KEY 200:5
Bantu [B.] has been subjected	VERW 370:4
banyan like the great b. tree	PATI 284:8
bar judge is a member of the B.	BOK 45:8
barbarian He is a b.	SHAW 327:14
barbarians b. are to arrive	CAVA 73:2

barbarians (*cont.*):
  B., Philistines, and Populace ARNO 14:7
  name the former *the B*. ARNO 14:9
  without the b. CAVA 73:3
barbarism b. be considered WEIL 378:2
  lowest b. SMIT 333:3
  methods of b. CAMP 68:1
barbarity b. of tyrants SMIT 339:1
bard goat-footed b. KEYN 201:4
barefoot I was born b. LONG 224:12
bark you don't b. yourself ATTL 17:8
barrel grows out of the b. of a gun MAO 242:3
barren I am but a b. stock ELIZ 123:7
  such b. terrain NOON 271:1
base art thou b. SHAK 320:7
  man of soul so b. TOCQ 360:7
  people as b. as itself PULI 295:3
baseball got a b. cap ELTO 126:3
basics time to get back to b. MAJO 239:3
basket come from the same b. CONR 94:9
bastard b. who gets the mail KEAT 197:2
  more b. children SHAK 319:1
Bastille Voltaire in the B. DE G 105:15
bathing caught the Whigs b. DISR 111:7
bathroom can't feel revolutionary in a b.
                                LINK 221:1
baton marshal's b. LOUI 225:8
bats b. have been broken HOWE 177:4
  b. will squeak and wheel NICO 266:6
  like b. amongst birds BACO 19:13
batsmen opening b. to the crease HOWE 177:4
battalions not of the heavy b. VOLT 372:6
battle b. for the mind NOON 271:1
  b. to the strong BIBL 39:11
  defeated in a great b. LIVY 222:4
  die in a b. SHAK 320:9
  France has lost a b. DE G 105:1
  in the B. of Britain BEVI 38:6
  Ireland's b. CONN 94:6
  Next to a b. lost WELL 379:14
  we b. for the Lord ROOS 307:10
battles b., martyrs WHIT 382:8
  Dead b., like dead generals TUCH 367:4
  forced marches, b. and death GARI 141:8
  mother of all b. HUSS 180:1
  opening b. of subsequent wars ORWE 275:11
baubles Take away these b. MISQ 255:8
bayonet b. is a weapon SLOG 334:5
bayonets throne of b. INGE 181:11
beaches fight on the b. CHUR 81:12
beacon b.-light is quenched SCOT 317:1
bear b. those ills we have SHAK 319:9
  embrace the Russian b. CHAN 75:7
  Puritan hated b.-baiting MACA 230:5
  so b. ourselves that CHUR 81:13
beard King of Spain's B. DRAK 118:2
bears b. the marks of the last person HAIG 157:1
beast b. With many heads SHAK 318:11
  blond b. NIET 269:5
  either a b. or a god ARIS 13:12
beat if the king b. us MANC 240:4

beat (*cont.*):
  money to even get b. ROGE 304:4
beaten b. by strangers DOS 117:3
  being b. does not matter STEP 346:4
beating glory of b. the French WOLF 387:5
beaut it's a b. LA G 209:1
beautiful all that was b. NEHR 265:12
  b. country LAST 213:13
  Black is b. SLOG 334:9
  Small is b. SCHU 316:4
beauty b. of the mountain rose BEAV 29:11
bed never made my own b. PU Y 295:4
bedfellows makes strange b. WARN 374:10
  strange b. PROV 296:15
bedrooms in the nation's b. TRUD 365:13
bee b. on royal jelly CHUR 86:1
beef roast b. of old England BURK 59:13
  Where's the b. MOND 257:1
beer b. of a man in Klondike CHES 78:3
  warm b., invincible suburbs MAJO 239:2
beg b. in the streets FRAN 136:4
began believe that the world b. CHUR 84:7
beggar b. would recognise guilt PARS 284:6
begin b. the world over PAIN 279:7
  But let us b. KENN 198:3
  Wars b. when you will MACH 233:7
beginning b. of the end TALL 352:1
  end of the b. CHUR 82:11
  In my end is my b. MARY 245:9
beginnings All b. are small JOUB 194:5
  time the b. and endings BACO 19:3
begins b. the world afresh MONN 257:8
begun b. to fight JONE 192:6
behaviour b. was intolerable MAJO 239:6
behind b. the throne PITT 289:11
Belgium B. put the kibosh on the Kaiser
                                SONG 341:4
  until B. recovers in full ASQU 15:3
Belgrano sinking of the B. DALY 101:2
belief attacks my b. JOHN 191:14
believe B. nothing until COCK 92:2
  b. what they wish CAES 64:10
  professing to b. PAIN 278:7
  you'll b. anything WELL 379:12
believed b. to be so TROL 364:7
  if b. during three days MEDI 246:7
believes politician never b. what he says
                                DE G 105:7
believing Not b. in force TROT 365:11
bella B., *horrida bella* VIRG 371:9
bells b. I hear WHIT 382:2
  now ring the b. WALP 374:3
belong To betray, you must first b. PHIL 288:5
belt no b. to tighten PANK 282:8
  see a b. without hitting ASQU 15:13
bench only a simply b. GARF 141:7
benches along Labour back b. EWIN 129:6
  asleep on the same b. ONSL 274:11
beneficial b. reforms THAT 358:7
benevolence b. of the butcher SMIT 333:6
Berliner *Ich bin ein B*. KENN 199:5

best b. is like the worst	KIPL 206:1
b. lack all conviction	YEAT 389:8
b. man among them	CAST 72:1
b. Prime Minister we have	BUTL 63:4
b. rulers	LAO- 210:4
It was the b. of times	DICK 109:9
Send forth the b.	KIPL 206:8
we will do our b.	CHUR 82:6
Whate'er is b. administered	POPE 292:4
bestow b. on every airth a limb	MONT 259:6
bestride b. the narrow world	SHAK 321:8
betray guts to b. my country	FORS 134:10
To b., you must first belong	PHIL 288:5
better b. angels of our nature	LINC 219:2
b. his own condition	SMIT 337:9
b. if he had never lived	CHUR 83:11
b. job on my son	GORE 151:7
B. red than dead	SLOG 334:6
from worse to b.	HOOK 176:2
illusion that times were b.	GREE 154:3
people can be b. off	DISR 114:16
see the b. things	OVID 277:10
We had b. wait and see	ASQU 15:2
beware B. the ides of March	SHAK 321:6
bible B. in the other	WRAN 388:9
by B. readers *for* Bible readers	BAIN 24:1
bicycle arrive by b.	VIER 371:6
bicycling old maids b.	MAJO 239:2
bidder highest b.	WASH 375:5
big b. enough to take away everything	
	FORD 134:5
b. tent	SLOG 334:7
fall victim to a b. lie	HITL 172:8
G.O.P.'s b. tent	NEWS 267:13
too b. for them	BULM 56:2
too b. to cry	LINC 219:6
bigger b. bang for a buck	SLOG 334:8
bigot mind of a b.	HOLM 175:7
bigotries b. that savage	LLOY 223:13
bike got on his b.	TEBB 354:13
biking Old maids b.	ORWE 275:12
bill B. of Rights was not	JORD 193:4
called upon to pay the b.	HARD 161:5
billet bullet has its b.	PROV 296:7
billion b. dollar country	FOST 135:2
bills pay my tax b.	HOLM 175:5
bind b. your sons to exile	KIPL 206:8
Obadiah B.-their-kings	MACA 230:7
biographical noble and b. friend	WETH 381:1
biography B. should be written	BALF 26:9
nothing but b.	DISR 114:4
bird catch the b. of paradise	KHRU 202:4
forgets the dying b.	PAIN 279:14
birds b. are flown	CHAR 75:9
for the high b.	HALI 160:2
like small b.	DISR 113:2
Birmingham B. Six released	DENN 106:9
birth disqualified by the accident of b.	CHES 77:8
one that is coming to b.	O'SH 277:5
bishop Another B. dead	MELB 247:5
B. of Rome	BOOK 47:4

bishop (*cont.*):	
hitting the niece of a b.	ORWE 276:8
No b., no King	JAME 184:1
bishopric *merit* for a b.	WEST 380:10
bite b. the hand that fed them	BURK 59:8
bites dead woman b. not	GRAY 153:10
bitterness fuelled by b.	BHUT 38:14
bizarre b. happening	HAUG 163:7
black b. domination	MAND 240:6
B. Hills belong to me	SITT 332:11
B. is beautiful	SLOG 334:9
b. kids get an education	POWE 293:1
b. majority rule	SMIT 338:7
b. men fought	MACA 228:10
B. Panther Party	NEWT 266:2
B. Power	CARM 70:12
B.'s not so black	CANN 68:9
not have the colour b.	MAND 241:4
one drop of b. blood	HUGH 178:2
with a b. skin	MALC 239:9
Blackpool this B. hot-house	HOME 175:8
blacks between whites and b.	LINC 218:8
country is for b.	TSVA 367:3
bladders boys that swim on b.	SHAK 321:1
Blair one of B.'s babes	JACK 183:8
Sun backs B.	NEWS 267:15
Blairs don't think the B.	YELL 390:3
blame quick to b. the alien	AESC 5:4
blaming b. it on you	KIPL 205:7
blancmange multi-hued b.	MITC 253:8
blank political b. cheque	GOSC 152:1
blanket with the b. over his head	BABE 18:8
blasphemies truths begin as b.	SHAW 327:12
bleed b. in sport	SHAK 322:12
bleeper do not wear a b.	CLAR 88:4
Blenheim fighting B. all over again	BEVA 36:6
blessed This b. plot	SHAK 326:7
blesseth b. him that gives	SHAK 325:13
blessing b. to the country	RISM 41:4
national b.	HAMI 160:5
blind country of the b.	ERAS 127:2
old, mad, b.	SHEL 330:2
blinked other fellow just b.	RUSK 309:10
bliss B. was it in that dawn	WORD 388:4
bloated b. armaments	DISR 112:2
block old b. itself	BURK 60:10
blocks he had b. to cut	PEEL 286:4
You b., you stones	SHAK 321:5
blond b. beast	NIET 269:5
blood b. be the price	KIPL 206:6
b.-dimmed tide is loosed	YEAT 389:8
b. drawn with the lash	LINC 220:6
b. is their argument	SHAK 320:9
b. of patriots	JEFF 185:5
b. of the socialist	CROS 99:3
B. sport brought	INGH 182:1
B. sport brought	INGH 182:2
B., sweat, and tear-wrung	BYRO 64:3
b., toil, tears and sweat	CHUR 81:10
b. with guilt is bought	SHEL 329:11
defeated in b.	O'CO 272:8

blood (*cont.*):
enough of b. and tears | RABI 297:7
foaming with much b. | POWE 293:4
fraternal b. | WEBS 377:9
guiltless of his country's b. | GRAY 154:2
Here lies b. | EPIT 128:7
Man of B. was there | MACA 230:9
mingle my b. | BROW 54:3
one drop of black b. | HUGH 178:2
rivers of b. | JEFF 187:2
seas of b. | COBB 91:9
spend her b. | WILS 386:11
through b. and iron | BISM 42:5
Tiber foaming with much b. | VIRG 371:9
tincture in the b. | DEFO 104:6
watching a stream of b. | ANON 9:13
We, your b. family | SPEN 344:3
bloodhounds Seven b. followed | SHEL 329:9
bloodshed war without b. | MAO 242:2
bloodthirsty so venomous, so b. | TROL 364:10
bloody b. curtain | ELIS 123:5
no right in the b. circus | MAXT 246:3
blossom hundred flowers b. | MAO 242:5
blot b. on the escutcheon | GRAY 153:8
blow b. at the very principles | LINC 218:2
b. with an agreement | TROT 365:10
blubbering b. Cabinet | GLAD 148:13
blue True b. and Mrs Crewe | GEOR 143:2
blunder it is a b. | BOUL 49:4
wonder at so grotesque a b. | BENT 33:11
Youth is a b. | DISR 113:18
blunders Human b. | TAYL 353:9
blunt plain, b. man | SHAK 323:12
board carried on b. | HUME 178:7
There wasn't any B. | HERB 170:2
boast b. of heraldry | GRAY 154:1
may that country b. | PAIN 281:2
Such is the patriot's b. | GOLD 150:6
boat if men are together in a b. | HALI 158:4
They sank my b. | KENN 199:8
boathook diplomatic b. | SALI 312:4
bodes b. some strange eruption | SHAK 319:5
bodies B. tied together | BURK 57:5
bodkin With a bare b. | SHAK 319:9
body b. of a weak and feeble woman | ELIZ 124:2
John Brown's b. | SONG 342:5
liberation of the human b. | GOLD 150:3
no b. to be kicked | THUR 360:5
whose b. is this | RODR 304:3
Bognor Bugger B. | LAST 212:8
bogy man Tories must have a b. | BEVA 36:7
boil war that would not b. | TAYL 353:12
boiled in b. and roast | SMIT 339:2
boldness B., and again boldness | DANT 101:5
what first? b. | BACO 18:12
bollocks 'b.' to ministers | WILS 385:15
bolshevism B. run mad | SNOW 339:11
bomb atom b. is a paper tiger | MAO 242:4
Ban the b. | SLOG 334:4
best defence against the atom b. | ANON 7:8
b. on Hiroshima | TRUM 366:2

bomb (*cont.*):
b. them back into the Stone Age | LEMA 215:4
bombed glad we've been b. | ELIZ 125:10
protect him from being b. | BALD 25:5
bombing b. begins | REAG 299:10
bondman b.'s two hundred and fifty years | LINC 220:6
bonds b. of civil b. | LOCK 224:8
surly b. of earth | REAG 300:1
boneless b. wonder | CHUR 81:1
bones b. of one British Grenadier | HARR 162:9
lay my b. amongst you | WOLS 388:1
Not worth the healthy b. | BISM 42:10
bonus *videri b. malebat* | SALL 313:11
book wrote the b. | LINC 220:11
bookie b. or a clergyman | MUGG 263:1
books b. are weapons | ROOS 306:7
b. of law | JOHN 189:7
Keeping b. on charity | PERÓ 287:10
learn men from b. | DISR 115:4
speaks about his own b. | DISR 112:20
to Cambridge b. he sent | BROW 54:5
Wherever b. will be burned | HEIN 167:10
boomerangs they pick b. | MACL 234:11
boot b. stamping on a human face | ORWE 276:7
order of the b. | CHUR 83:4
booted b. and spurred | RUMB 309:8
boots to the top of his b. | LLOY 223:15
went to school without any b. | BULM 56:2
border across the B. | O'HI 273:5
seductive b. | TAWN 352:8
bore b. people at dinner parties | KISS 207:10
would be a terrible b. | GLAD 147:4
bored b. for England | MUGG 263:2
I am b. | BISM 42:6
boredom b. makes you old | CAST 72:2
b. on a large scale | INGE 181:8
boring b. kind of guy | BUSH 62:4
born because you were b. in it | SHAW 328:1
b. free | UNIV 368:7
b. into the world alive | GILB 146:4
b. to set it right | SHAK 319:8
has already been b. | REAG 299:6
I was b. barefoot | LONG 224:12
Man was b. free | ROUS 309:5
naturally were b. free | MILT 253:3
not been b. Perón | PERÓ 287:11
those who are to be b. | BURK 59:1
We were not b. to sue | SHAK 325:15
bosom b. of a single state | DURH 120:6
bossing end to b. | LENI 215:13
nobody b. you | ORWE 276:10
bossy by the b. for the bully | SELD 317:6
getting awfully b. | THAT 358:8
Boston long way from East B. | KENN 199:1
Botany Bay New colonies seek for at B. | FREE 138:2
both wear it on b. sides | SHAK 327:9
bother Sufficient conscience to b. him | LLOY 224:2
bottom forgotten man at the b. | ROOS 305:4
from the b. of the deck | SHAP 327:11

bottom (cont.):
on our own b. — MONT 258:4
bought one who stays b. — CAME 67:2
with guilt is b. and sold — SHEL 329:11
boundary b. of Britain — TACI 351:4
right to fix the b. — PARN 283:13
bounded b. on the north — FISK 132:3
bourgeois old b. society — MARX 245:3
bourn country from whose b. — SHAK 319:9
bowels in the b. of Christ — CROM 98:3
box If you open that Pandora's B. — BEVI 38:11
boy any b. may become President — STEV 347:2
b. will ruin himself — GEOR 144:1
boys b. in the back rooms — BEAV 29:6
b. not going to be sent — ROOS 306:2
for office b. — SALI 313:2
Like little wanton b. — SHAK 321:1
rent b. of politics — FOLL 133:7
send American b. — JOHN 190:1
Till the b. come home — SONG 342:6
brain leave that b. outside — GILB 146:6
brains his b. go to his head — ASQU 15:12
brand New Labour b. — GOUL 152:2
brave b. bad man — CLAR 87:8
b. man inattentive — JACK 183:2
b. new world — KIPL 205:6
home of the b. — KEY 200:5
bravery acts of personal b. — WAUG 376:3
bray Vicar of B. — SONG 342:3
Brazilian If I were a B. — STIN 348:2
bread b. and circuses — JUVE 195:12
b. which it has earned — JEFF 185:14
looked to government for b. — BURK 59:8
should soon want b. — JEFF 187:3
took the b. and brake it — ELIZ 125:3
break b. his spirit — HOLL 175:1
b. your party — HEAD 165:7
breast with dauntless b. — GRAY 154:2
breasts b. by which France is fed — SULL 350:1
breath b. can make them — GOLD 150:4
b. of worldly men — SHAK 326:4
taxed the b. — THOM 359:1
breathe yearning to b. free — LAZA 214:4
breathes B. there the man — SCOT 316:9
brewsters b. and baksters — LANG 210:3
bribe b. or gratuity — PENN 287:2
cannot hope to b. or twist — WOLF 387:4
bribes asked Bacon how many b. — BENT 33:10
brick hardly throw a b. — ORWE 276:8
inherited it b. — AUGU 18:3
bridge going a b. too far — BROW 54:6
man on the b. — BALD 25:11
promise to build a b. — KHRU 202:5
to the b.-builders — MCAL 228:3
Women, and Champagne, and B. — BELL 31:5
bridle b. and no spurs — TAYL 354:4
brief b. as I can be — O'CO 272:6
little b. authority — SHAK 325:12
briefing b. is what *I* do — CALL 65:7
brigade of the Irish B. — DAVI 102:7
Viva la the New B. — DAVI 102:8

brilliant B.—to the top of his boots — LLOY 223:15
brink walked to the b. — DULL 120:1
brinkmanship boasting of his b. — STEV 347:6
Britain boundary of B. — TACI 351:4
B. a fit country — LLOY 222:12
B. has lost an empire — ACHE 1:5
B.'s stand alone — DE V 108:2
B. will be honoured by historians — HARL 162:6
B. will still be — MAJO 239:2
dangerous man in B. — NEWS 267:6
government of B.'s isle — SHAK 330:14
Great B. has — CURZ 99:11
I'm backing B. — SLOG 335:3
speak for B. — BOOT 48:3
Without B., Europe — ERHA 127:3
Britannia When I think of Cool B. — BENN 32:13
British as the B. public — MACA 229:5
bones of one B. Grenadier — HARR 162:9
B. government — HAMI 160:6
B. is unique — CHUR 82:5
B. king — MARK 243:4
B. Minister sneezed — LEVI 217:4
B. political system — TAYL 353:15
B. pound — DYSO 120:8
destinies of the B. Empire — DISR 112:4
from the B. government — MCAL 228:5
immobility of B. institutions — ASQU 15:4
of the B. Empire — CHUR 82:10
shield of B. fair play — AITK 6:1
so also a B. subject — PALM 281:9
thank God! the B. journalist — WOLF 387:4
Briton B., Saxon — HEWI 171:10
glory in the name of B. — GEOR 142:8
Britons B. alone use 'Might' — WAUG 376:4
broadcasters b. should be more confident — CAMP 67:3
broccoli eat any more b. — BUSH 62:2
broke If it ain't b. — LANC 209:8
broken bats have been b. — HOWE 177:4
b. window pane — PANK 282:7
Can it be b. — JENK 187:11
made to be b. — NORT 271:4
taken up the b. blade — DE G 105:3
broker more that of an honest b. — BISM 42:2
bronze noontide was b. — CHUR 84:15
broomstick tether a b. — KEYN 201:5
brother BIG B. IS WATCHING YOU — ORWE 275:13
Had it been his b. — EPIT 128:5
man and a b. — WEDG 378:1
want to be the white man's b. — KING 203:2
what my b. will do — CHAR 76:8
brotherhood table of b. — KING 203:5
brothers live together as b. — KING 203:7
brow b. of labour — BRYA 55:7
brown John B.'s body — SONG 342:5
Browning safety-catch of my B. — JOHS 192:5
bruiser piratical old b. — HAIL 157:7
brute *Et tu, B.?* — SHAK 322:10
finest b. votes in Europe — ANON 8:5
brutish nasty, b., and short — HOBB 173:10
Brutus B. is an honourable man — SHAK 323:5

Brutus (*cont.*):
'B.' will start a spirit   SHAK 321:9
You too, B.   CAES 65:2
buck bigger bang for a b.   SLOG 334:8
   b. stops here   MOTT 262:2
bud nip him in the b.   ROCH 304:1
budget Balancing the b.   GRAM 152:5
bug thinks there'a b.   BUSH 62:1
bugger B. Bognor   LAST 212:8
build those who will b. it   TRUD 365:14
builds b. on mud   MACH 233:10
   something that b. up a man   BENN 32:4
bullet b. has its billet   PROV 296:7
   stronger than the b.   MISQ 254:2
bullets bloody b.   LINC 218:5
bully by the bossy for the b.   SELD 317:6
   such a b. pulpit   ROOS 308:1
bulwark b. of continuing liberty   ROOS 305:11
   floating b. of the island   BLAC 43:4
bump b. in the road   BUSH 62:9
Buncombe talking to B.   WALK 372:14
   through reporters to B.   CARL 70:3
bungler good nature is a b.   HALI 159:15
   Man is a b.   SHAW 328:8
burden bear any b.   KENN 198:4
   b. of the nation's care   PRIO 294:11
   impossible to carry the heavy b.   EDWA 121:10
   White Man's B.   KIPL 206:8
bureaucracy and the vast b.   DOUG 117:5
   [b.'s] specific invention   WEBE 377:6
   B., the rule of no one   MCCA 231:8
bureaucrats b. will care more for routine
            BAGE 22:5
   Guidelines for b.   BORE 48:8
burglar honest b.   MENC 248:10
burial any part, in its b.   MACM 236:5
buried b. all the hatchets   WILS 385:11
   b. at midnight   O'BR 272:5
   b. in the rain   MILL 251:8
burlesque b. and the newspapers   STON 348:6
burn B., baby, burn   SLOG 334:10
   b. its children to save   MEYE 249:9
burned b. women   BRAN 50:4
   men also, in the end, are b.   HEIN 167:10
burning b. the rain forest   STIN 348:2
   by b. him   CEAU 73:6
   Keep the Home-fires b.   SONG 342:6
burnt b., tortured, fined   JEFF 187:4
bury children b. their parents   HERO 170:7
   I come to b. Caesar   SHAK 323:4
   We will b. you   KHRU 202:3
bus missed the b.   CHAM 75:4
   stepping in front of a b.   OSBO 277:1
buses more time on b.   STRU 349:7
business big b. give people   SLOG 336:11
   b. as usual   THAT 357:4
   B. carried on as usual   CHUR 80:4
   do b. together   JEFF 187:1
   do b. together   THAT 357:6
   doing b.   HEAL 166:6
   fit for b.   WALP 374:6

business (*cont.*):
   government of b.   LAWS 211:8
   Liberty is always unfinished b.   ANON 9:12
   neither b. nor rest   MORL 260:7
   of the American people is b.   COOL 95:9
   totter on in b.   POPE 292:2
   Treasury is the spring of b.   BAGE 20:9
   wheels of b.   TAWN 352:8
businessman b. has trampled   NICO 266:10
businessmen well-placed b. decide   YOUN 390:7
busy Government of the b.   SELD 317:6
butcher benevolence of the b.   SMIT 333:6
   Prime Minister has to be a b.   BUTL 63:6
   way to the b.   CHUR 81:2
butchers sacrificers, but not b.   SHAK 322:6
   shepherds and b.   VOLT 372:5
butter manage without b.   GOEB 149:5
   rather have b. or guns   GOER 149:7
butts b. me away   SHAK 318:11
buy b. a used car   SLOG 336:12
   b. it like an honest man   NORT 271:9
   Don't b. a single vote more   KENN 198:1
buyer b. can be found   SALL 313:12
Byron movement needs a B.   POLL 291:5
byword story and a b.   WINT 387:2

cabinet blubbering C.   GLAD 148:13
   C. does not propose, it decides   ATTL 17:1
   c. government   WALD 372:12
   c. is a combining committee   BAGE 20:10
   C. meeting   LAWS 211:11
   C. ministers are educated   BENN 33:3
   C. minutes are studied   KAUF 196:6
   C.'s gone to its dinner   ANON 10:5
   consequence of c. government   BAGE 20:11
   group of C. Ministers   CURZ 100:1
   head of the C.   MORL 260:9
   mislead the C.   ASQU 15:8
   self-control in C.   SHEP 330:6
   ways of getting into the C.   BEVA 37:9
Caesar always I am C.   SHAK 322:2
   Aut C., aut nihil   MOTT 262:1
   C. bleed in sport   SHAK 322:12
   C. hath wept   SHAK 323:6
   C.'s laurel crown   BLAK 44:9
   C.'s public policy   PLUT 291:4
   C.'s wife   CAES 64:11
   doth this our C. feed   SHAK 321:9
   I come to bury C.   SHAK 323:4
   in envy of great C.   SHAK 324:3
   loved C. less   SHAK 323:2
   O mighty C.   SHAK 322:14
   Render therefore unto C.   BIBL 39:21
   that C. might be great   CAMP 67:7
   Then fall, C.   SHAK 322:10
   unto C. shalt thou go   BIBL 39:26
   word of C.   SHAK 323:9
Caesars C. and Napoleons   HUXL 180:2
cage become an iron c.   WEBE 377:2
Caitlin C. Ni Uallachain   MACN 237:3

cake Let them eat c.	MARI 242:9	**capitalists** c. will sell us	MISQ 254:3
Calais 'C.' lying in my heart	MARY 245:10	**capitals** series of c.	CURZ 99:11
Caledonia Mourn, hapless C.	SMOL 339:8	**Capri** letter came from C.	JUVE 195:11
Caligula C.'s horse was made Consul	RAND 298:7	**caprices** depend on the c.	TOCQ 360:7
eyes of C.	MITT 256:8	**captain** broken by the team c.	HOWE 177:4
call Labour's c.	SLOG 334:14	c. is in his bunk	SHAW 328:1
timeless c.	SCHL 316:1	my C. lies, Fallen	WHIT 382:3
calling Germany c.	JOYC 194:9	O C.! my Captain	WHIT 382:2
calm c., rather than to excite	PALM 281:11	plain russet-coated c.	CROM 97:11
Calvinist Papist, yet a C.	EPIT 128:7	ship's c. complaining	POWE 293:10
Calvinistic C. creed	PITT 289:12	**captains** c. and the kings	KIPL 206:3
Cambridge To C. books	TRAP 362:8	**car** afford to keep a motor c.	SHAW 327:13
to C. books he sent	BROW 54:5	buy a used c.	SLOG 336:12
came c. first for the Communists	NIEM 269:1	c. in every garage	HOOV 176:5
I c., I saw, I conquered	CAES 65:1	whisky and c. keys	O'RO 275:2
I c. through	MACA 228:7	**caravan** great c. of humanity	SMUT 339:9
Camelot known As C.	LERN 216:3	**carcases** c. of unburied men	SHAK 318:9
never be another C.	ONAS 274:9	**card** c. up his sleeve	LABO 208:9
campaign c. in poetry	CUOM 99:8	Orange c.	CHUR 79:8
political c.	WILS 386:1	play the race c.	SHAP 327:11
Canada C. could have enjoyed	COLO 93:4	**care** c. of human life	JEFF 186:9
C. that shall fill	LAUR 211:4	**career** C. open to the talents	CARL 69:10
I see C.	DAVI 102:3	c. open to the talents	NAPO 264:14
more than C. itself is worth	VOLT 371:10	loyal to his own c.	DALT 100:8
cancer c. close to the Presidency	DEAN 103:4	nothing in his long c.	NEWS 268:3
white race *is* the c.	SONT 340:10	**careless** C. talk costs lives	OFFI 274:1
candid c. friend	CANN 68:10	c. trifle	SHAK 324:8
candidate c. of probity	HAGU 156:6	have been a little c.	CRES 97:1
candidates c. for power	PAIN 280:16	**cares** c. and pleasures	GIBB 145:4
c. were not men	PAIN 280:8	**caricatured** c. by our enemies	BROW 53:6
candle c. in that great turnip	CHUR 84:4	**carnivorous** sheep born c.	FAGU 130:1
c. in the wind	JOHN 189:1	**carpenter** Between them, Walrus and C.	
c. to the sun	SIDN 332:4		LEVI 217:2
light such a c.	LAST 212:2	**carry** c. a big stick	ROOS 307:5
rather light a c.	STEV 347:10	**Carthage** C. must be destroyed	CATO 72:9
candles carry c. and set chairs	HERV 170:10	**Carthaginian** C. trustworthiness	SALL 313:13
cannibals body of c.	MENC 248:14	**cartoonist** life as a c. wonderful	PETE 288:1
Canossa not go to C.	BISM 41:10	**cash** c. payment	CARL 69:9
cant c. of *Not men*	BURK 59:15	pay you c. to go away	KIPL 206:7
Canterbury C. or Smithfield	WALP 373:8	**cast** C. your mind on other days	YEAT 390:1
Cantuar how full of C.	BULL 56:1	die is c.	CAES 64:13
capable c. of reigning	TACI 351:10	**castle** C. of lies	BOOK 47:8
capers He c. nimbly	SHAK 326:14	home is his c.	PROV 296:6
capital C. must be propelled	BAGE 20:5	**Castlereagh** had a mask like C.	SHEL 329:9
destroy c.	MACA 230:6	**casualty** is the first c.	PROV 297:5
intellectual c.	CALL 66:4	**cat** big c. in a poodle parlour	PARR 284:2
interests of c. and labour	ATKI 16:4	c.'s-paw must expect	COCK 92:1
origin of c.	TORR 362:4	if a c. is black or white	DENG 106:4
capitalism C. has been singularly devoid		Like a powerful graceful c.	CHUR 84:14
	BERG 34:2	way the c. jumps	THAT 357:9
C. is using its money	CAST 72:5	which way the c. is jumping	SULZ 350:3
c. of the working class	SPEN 344:4	**catalogue** c. of human crime	CHUR 81:11
C., wisely managed	KEYN 200:10	**catch** c. the weak and poor	ANAC 7:4
c. with the gloves off	STOP 348:11	**catched** and not be c.	PEPY 287:6
extermination of c.	ZINO 391:4	**categorical** c. imperative	KANT 197:6
monopoly stage of c.	LENI 215:5	**caterpillars** c. of the commonwealth	SHAK 326:3
spirit of c.	WEBE 377:1	**catholic** Gentlemen, I am a C.	BELL 31:6
unacceptable face of c.	HEAT 167:5	Roman C. Church	MACM 236:10
Under c. man exploits man	ANON 11:12	**Catholics** When Hitler attacked the C.	NIEM 269:1
capitalist c. system	MACM 236:5	**Cato** losing one pleased C.	LUCA 226:7
slave of the c. society	CONN 94:5	Voice of C.	JONS 193:2

cats C. look down	CHUR 86:3	**change** (*cont.*):	
cattle thousands of great c.	BURK 58:18	involves a great c.	TROL 364:15
cause armour of a righteous c.	BRYA 55:5	make c. our friend	CLIN 90:11
good old C.	MILT 252:12	means of some c.	BURK 58:7
his c. being good	MORE 259:8	necessary not to c.	FALK 130:3
Our c. is just	DICK 110:3	point is to c. it	MARX 244:9
winning c. pleased the gods	LUCA 226:7	things will have to c.	LAMP 209:7
causes aren't any good, brave c.	OSBO 277:1	time for a c.	DEWE 108:10
tough on the c. of crime	BLAI 43:8	Times c., and we change	ANON 11:4
caution Speaking with that c.	PEEL 286:9	torrent of c.	CHES 77:9
cavaliers C. (Wrong but Wromantic)	SELL 317:7	wind of c. is blowing	MACM 236:2
will not do with the c.	LAMB 209:3	**changed** changed, c. utterly	YEAT 389:5
cave political C. of Adullam	BRIG 51:9	If voting c. anything	LIVI 221:8
Ceauşescus C.' execution	O'DO 273:1	until I c. myself	MAND 241:2
cede c. to lawful authority	GIUL 147:2	**changes** c. we fear be thus irresistible	
celebrated Revolutions are c.	BOUL 49:5		JOHN 190:12
Celt C., Briton, Saxon	HEWI 171:10	**channel** [C.] is a mere ditch	NAPO 264:5
Celtic C. Tiger	MCAL 228:2	Fog in C.	BROC 52:4
woods of C. antiquity	KEYN 201:4	Government . . . is simply not the c.	KENN 197:9
cement like mixing c.	MOND 257:2	**chaos** dread empire, C.	POPE 292:1
censorship extreme form of c.	SHAW 328:17	grotesque c.	KINN 204:7
fought without c.	WEST 380:11	**chaps** clever c. like you	BEVI 38:8
centralization C. and socialism	TOCQ 361:4	**chapter** write the next c.	JOHN 189:7
c. follows	TOCQ 361:2	**character** about a fellow's c.	REAG 299:7
centre c. cannot hold	YEAT 389:8	by the content of their c.	KING 203:5
c. has always melted	HAIL 157:6	did not have the c.	ROOS 305:2
in the c. of politics	MOSL 261:4	excellence in our national c.	BAGE 23:4
My c. is giving way	FOCH 133:5	**characteristic** c. vice	TAWN 352:6
cents simplicity of the three per c.	DISR 114:10	**characters** great c. are formed	ADAM 2:1
centuries All c. but this	GILB 146:8	**charitably** c. dispose of any thing	SHAK 320:9
forty c. look down	NAPO 264:4	**charity** c. for all	LINC 220:7
century c. of the common man	WALL 373:1	Keeping books on c.	PERÓ 287:10
close the c.	MAND 241:1	**charlatan** c., and a conjuror	TROL 364:4
cereal like breakfast c.	STEV 347:7	**Charles** C. II was always very merry	SELL 317:9
cerebellum If they've a brain and c.	GILB 146:6	King C.'s golden days	SONG 342:3
ceremony c. of innocence is drowned	YEAT 389:8	**charm** northern c.	KENN 199:9
c. that to great ones 'longs	SHAK 325:10	**chase** live by the c.	TOCQ 361:13
general c.	SHAK 320:12	**chatter** hare-brained c.	DISR 113:8
certain four things c.	KIPL 205:5	**cheap** done as c. as other men	PEPY 287:5
chain c. about the ankle	DOUG 117:9	obtain too c.	PAIN 279:10
chaining c. the crowd	VOLT 372:9	**cheaper** c. than we can	SMIT 337:6
chains better to be in c.	KAFK 196:1	**cheating** period of c.	BIER 40:4
c. upon their own appetites	BURK 57:2	**check** form a mutual c.	BLAC 43:7
deliverance from c.	DOUG 117:6	**checkers** spaniel, named C.	NIXO 269:7
everywhere he is in c.	ROUS 309:5	**cheeks** c. are drawn	PARR 284:5
lose but their c.	MARX 245:4	**cheer** which side do they c. for	TEBB 354:14
so debased by their c.	ROUS 309:6	**cheerful** as c. as any man could	PEPY 287:3
chairs carry candles and set c.	HERV 170:10	**cheers** Two c. for Democracy	FORS 134:11
challenge times of c.	KING 203:11	**cheese** varieties of c.	DE G 105:5
Chamberlain Listening to a speech by C.		**chemist** no c. will ever	WILK 383:5
	BEVA 37:8	**cheque** political blank c.	GOSC 152:1
chambers enchanted c. of Power	LAND 209:9	**Chequers** invited me down to C.	LIVI 222:1
chameleon paint the c.	KEYN 201:5	**cherish** c. those hearts	SHAK 321:2
champagne Women, and C.	BELL 31:5	**cherry** American as c. pie	BROW 54:1
chance c. to work hard	ROOS 307:7	**chess** high c.-game	CARL 70:8
in the last c. saloon	MELL 248:2	**chessboard** upon a c.	SMIT 333:5
chancellor C. of the Exchequer	LOWE 226:3	**chew** can't fart and c. gum	JOHN 190:9
Germany has a new C.	SLOG 334:12	**chicken** c. in every pot	HOOV 176:5
change C. is constant	DISR 112:10	c. in his pot	HENR 168:9
c. of persons	PAIN 280:9	c. shit	JOHN 189:3
c. their minds	HATT 163:5	Some c.! Some neck	CHUR 82:8

chief C. Justice was rich   MACA 229:14
   Cromwell, our c. of men   MILT 252:6
child every c. born therein   RUSK 310:8
   give a c. a weapon   BOGD 45:7
   governed by a c.   SHAK 326:16
   healthy c. well nursed   SWIF 351:1
childhood From his c. onward   HARD 161:5
children bring c. into the world   JOSE 194:1
   burn its c. to save   MEYE 249:9
   c. bury their parents   HERO 170:7
   c. died in the streets   AUDE 17:12
   c. of a larger growth   CHES 77:3
   c. were lost sight of   MOYN 262:10
   c. who leave home   SLOV 333:2
   each one of her c.   VERG 370:3
   labouring c.   CLEG 89:4
   little c. cried   MOTL 261:5
   my c. are frightened of me   GEOR 144:3
   pictures of their c.   BUSH 62:12
   women and c. could work   SELL 317:11
chill c. ran along   EWIN 129:6
china Hong Kong's return to C.   DENG 106:5
   land armies in C.   MONT 259:4
chinless c. wonders   MAND 241:9
chip c. of the old 'block'   BURK 60:10
chips tossed around like poker c.   ALBR 6:2
chivalry age of c.   BURK 58:14
chocolate c. éclair   ROOS 307:3
choice c. of working or starving   JOHN 190:11
   is the *people's c.*   SHER 330:9
   old guy drove the c.   BUSH 62:8
choisir *Gouverner, c'est c.*   LÉVI 217:8
choose to govern is to c.   LÉVI 217:8
choosing C. each stone   MARV 243:11
Christ C. and His saints slept   ANON 9:16
   C. were coming   CART 71:4
Christian die a C.   CHAR 76:3
Christianity C. is part of the laws   HALE 158:3
   C., of course   BALF 26:7
   local thing called C.   HARD 162:1
Christians generations of C.   MACA 230:4
Christmas before a hard C.   SMIT 338:1
   turkeys vote for C.   CALL 66:3
chuck C. it, Smith   CHES 77:10
church c. and state   MITC 256:7
   c. and state forever separate   GRAN 153:5
   C. of England   CHAR 76:3
   C. of [England] should   ROYD 309:7
   C. shall be free   MAGN 238:3
   C. speaks   ROME 304:10
   free c.   CAVO 73:5
   Say to the c., it shows   RALE 298:2
   spoliation of the c.   DISR 113:15
   wall between c. and state   BLAC 43:1
churches C. built to please   BURN 61:4
Churchill C. on top of the wave   BEAV 30:2
   never was a C.   GLAD 148:7
   voice was that of Mr C.   ATTL 16:7
ciel *montez au c.*   FIRM 131:5
cigar really good 5-cent c.   MARS 243:9
Cinncinnatus C. of the West   BYRO 64:5

circenses *Panem et c.*   JUVE 195:12
circle fatal c. is traced   TOCQ 361:12
   tightness of the magic c.   MACL 234:7
circumstances concatenation of c.   WEBS 377:10
   play of c.   WEIL 378:2
circus no right in the c.   MAXT 246:3
   proceedings into a c.   MURR 263:8
circuses bread and c.   JUVE 195:12
cities streets of a hundred c.   HOOV 176:6
citizen c. as an abstract proposition   TOCQ 360:9
   c., first in war   LEE 214:7
   c. in this world city   AURE 18:6
   c. is influenced   RAKO 298:1
   c. of no mean city   BIBL 39:25
   greater than a private c.   TACI 351:10
   I am a c.   STEV 346:6
   I am a Roman c.   CICE 87:1
   requisite of a good c.   ROOS 307:4
   zealous c.   BURK 59:4
citizens c. of the world   ROOS 306:9
   first and second class c.   WILL 384:3
   leave their c. free   JEFF 187:9
   refined c.   SHEL 330:3
   rights of c.   HAMI 160:10
citizenship representing the c.   MACD 232:9
city citizen in this world c.   AURE 18:6
   citizen of no mean c.   BIBL 39:25
   c. consists in men   NICI 266:5
   c. of southern efficiency   KENN 199:9
   c. of the healthiest   WHIT 382:5
   c. upon a hill   WINT 387:2
   Despising, For you, the c.   SHAK 318:10
   Happy is that c.   ANON 8:9
   if you've seen one c. slum   AGNE 5:6
   peper felled a c.   THOM 359:1
   What is the c. but the people   SHAK 318:8
civil c. to everyone   SISS 332:10
   dire effects from c. discord   ADDI 4:11
   Pray, good people, be c.   GWYN 156:3
civilian c. control   TRUM 366:14
civilization annihilating all c.   SAKH 312:1
   C. a movement   TOYN 362:5
   C. and profits   COOL 95:8
   c. of the Fabians   INGE 181:8
   C. was held together   TAYL 353:7
   elements of modern c.   CARL 69:11
   in a state of c.   JEFF 186:13
   pillars of c.   MONN 257:9
   submit to c.   TOCQ 361:13
   test of c.   JOHN 191:7
   thought of modern c.   GAND 141:5
civilizations eradicates autonomous c.
         SONT 340:10
civilized c. community   MILL 250:8
   c. society   HOLM 175:5
   force another to be c.   MILL 250:10
   that are called c.   PAIN 280:12
civilizers two c. of man   DISR 112:17
civilizes Cricket c. people   MUGA 262:11
civil servant c. doesn't make jokes   IONE 182:4
   Give a c. a good case   CLAR 87:10

civil servant (*cont.*):
  Here lies a c.   SISS 332:10
  ideal c.   PEYR 288:2
civil servants conviction c.   BANC 27:8
  of c.   BRID 51:4
Civil Service business of the C.   ARMS 14:6
  C. is a bit like   BUTL 63:5
  C. is deferential   CROS 99:5
  C. is like a rusty weathercock   BENN 32:10
  Reorganizing the C.   ANON 10:11
  Thank God for the C.   GEOR 144:6
civis *C. Romanus sum*   CICE 87:1
  C. Romanus sum   PALM 281:9
claim last territorial c.   HITL 173:2
clamour c. for war   PEEL 286:2
  those who c. most   PEEL 286:5
clan c. and race   MILL 252:1
Clapham man on the C. omnibus   BOWE 49:6
clapped-out c., post-imperial   DRAB 118:1
class c. struggle   MARX 244:10
  first and second c. citizens   WILL 384:3
  hands of the ruling c.   STAL 345:1
  history of c. struggles   MARX 245:2
  use of *force* by one c.   LENI 215:7
  While there is a lower c.   DEBS 103:8
classes All c. of society   JEVO 188:5
  Clashing of C.   CONN 94:3
  c. and class antagonists   MARX 245:3
  lower c. had such white   CURZ 100:4
  masses against the c.   GLAD 148:10
classify Germans c.   CATH 72:6
cleaning c. the streets   LA G 209:2
clear c. in his great office   SHAK 324:10
clearing c.-house of the world   CHAM 74:6
Cleopatra C.'s nose been shorter   PASC 284:7
clergy Arminian c.   PITT 289:12
  c. are not called   WALP 373:8
  Established C.   GLAD 148:5
clergyman bookie or a c.   MUGG 263:1
clerks statesmen or of c.   DISR 113:14
clever Lord Birkenhead is very c.   ASQU 15:12
  lot of c. people   ATTL 17:10
  more c. than you are   WHIT 381:10
  to appear c.   HILL 172:3
  Too c. by half   SALI 312:3
  Too c. by half   SALI 313:8
cliché c. and an indiscretion   MACM 235:8
  used every c.   CHUR 82:2
clichés wreck it with c.   CLAR 87:10
cliffs white c. I never more must see   MACA 230:11
climax end a sentence with a c.   LASK 211:2
climb c. not at all   ELIZ 124:10
  Fain would I c.   RALE 298:3
climbs None c. so high   CROM 98:12
cloak c. become an iron cage   WEBE 377:2
clock never put the c. back   WAUG 376:7
cloistered fugitive and c. virtue   MILT 252:9
cloned successfully c. a lamb   MARC 242:7
close c. my military career   MACA 228:9
  peacefully towards its c.   DAWS 103:3
  will not c. my politics   FOX 136:2

closed greatest c. shop   HOSK 177:1
closer Come c., boys   LAST 212:3
cloth Republican c. coat   NIXO 269:6
cloud c. in the west   GLAD 147:5
  in C.-cuckoo-land   HEAL 166:1
cloudcuckooland How about 'C.'   ARIS 13:5
CMG C. (Call Me God)   PROV 296:13
coach c. and six horses   RICE 301:6
  like being a football c.   MCCA 231:5
coal like miners' c. dust   BOOT 48:4
  shortage of c. and fish   BEVA 36:2
coalition rainbow c.   JACK 183:10
coalitions England does not love c.   DISR 111:14
coals c. to Newcastle   GEOR 143:9
coat doesn't have a mink c.   NIXO 269:6
  stick in his c.   BROW 54:7
cobwebs Laws are like c.   SWIF 350:8
cock Nationalism is a silly c.   ALDI 6:4
  Our c. won't fight   BEAV 29:4
cocksure c. of anything   MELB 247:7
  stupid are c.   RUSS 311:8
coercion effect of c.   JEFF 187:4
coexistence peaceful c.   FULB 139:2
coffee c.-house   SWIF 350:7
  C. house babble   DISR 113:3
  put poison in your c.   ASTO 16:1
coffin silver plate on a c.   CURR 99:10
coins for a fistful of c.   ZAPA 391:1
cold c. relation   BURK 59:4
  c. war warrior   THAT 356:5
  Fallen c. and dead   WHIT 382:3
  midst of a c. war   BARU 28:3
  offspring of c. hearts   BURK 58:15
  plunging into a c. peace   YELT 390:5
colleagues fidelity to c.   LASK 211:1
  collects beautiful c.   MACA 230:4
collects beautiful c.   MACA 230:4
collision avoid foreign c.   CLAY 88:7
colonies commerce with our c.   BURK 57:14
  New c. seek   FREE 138:2
  not cease to be c.   DISR 112:3
  These wretched c.   DISR 111:13
  united c.   LEE 214:8
colony fuzzy wuzzy c.   CAIR 65:3
colossus Like a C.   SHAK 321:8
colour by the c. of their skin   KING 203:5
  c. of their skin   WILL 384:2
  met by the c. line   DOUG 117:8
  problem of the c. line   DU B 119:16
coloured best c. man   JOHN 189:5
  no 'white' or 'c.' signs   KENN 199:4
colourless always be c.   PEYR 288:2
column stately c. broke   SCOT 317:1
columnists political c. say   ADAM 2:3
comb two bald men over a c.   BORG 48:9
combination call it c.   PALM 281:10
combine When bad men c.   BURK 59:14
comeback c. kid   CLIN 90:10
comfort a' the c. we're to get   BURN 61:6
  c. for civilization   DISR 114:21
  c. in my people's happiness   ELIZ 124:6
  good c., Master Ridley   LAST 212:2

comical I often think it's c.   GILB 146:4

coming my c. down   MORE 259:11
     Yanks are c.   COHA 92:3

command c. the rain   PEPY 287:4
     give a single c.   SCHW 316:7
     not born to sue, but to c.   SHAK 325:15

commander C. of the American Armies
     FRAN 137:4

comment C. is free   SCOT 316:8
     C. is free   STOP 348:9
     couldn't possibly c.   DOBB 116:4

commerce c. with our colonies   BURK 57:14
     In matters of c.   CANN 69:2
     Peace, c.   JEFF 186:3

commercial of the c. world   BURK 60:7

commission anyone in the C.   ANON 9:10
     C. has an established culture   GREE 154:5
     resigned c.   ANON 8:6

commissions royal c.   FRAN 137:8

committee c. divided   MCEW 233:2
     c. is organic   PARK 283:4

commodity with some c.   SMIT 337:6

common according to the c. weal   JAME 184:5
     century of the c. man   WALL 373:1
     C. Law of England   HERB 170:5
     c. market is a process   MONN 257:5
     happiness of the c. man   BEVE 38:1
     make it too c.   SHAK 320:3
     man of c. opinion   BAGE 22:14
     nor lose the c. touch   KIPL 205:8
     nothing c. did or mean   MARV 244:1
     of a c. law   JEFF 185:13
     prefers c.-looking people   LINC 220:1
     steals a c.   SONG 343:4

commoner persistent c.   BENN 32:1

commonplace c. mind   HARD 162:4

Common Prayer they hated C.   JORD 193:5

commons C., faithful to their system   MACK 234:5
     C. has declined   ST J 311:13
     C. is absolute   DISR 113:12
     C. is the most   BEVA 37:6
     English House of C.   MACA 228:6
     House of Commons   HOSK 177:1
     in the House of C.   CHUR 80:1
     in the House of C.   DISR 114:9
     in the House of C.   HAZL 165:4
     in the House of C.   WALD 372:11
     libraries of the C.   CHAN 75:6
     member of the House of C.   POWE 294:2
     than the House of C.   HAZL 165:3

common sense c. and common honesty
     SHEL 329:5
     c. kept breaking in   TAYL 353:18
     insipid c.   SALI 312:5

commonwealth caterpillars of the c.   SHAK 326:3
     Empire is a c.   ROSE 308:2

commonwealths raise up c.   DRYD 118:6
     uniting into c.   LOCK 224:7

communion biking to Holy C.   ORWE 275:12
     plucked c. tables   JORD 193:5

communism against the anti-Christ of C.
     BUCH 55:9
     caused the fall of c.   JOHN 189:2
     C. is like prohibition   ROGE 304:9
     C. is Russian autocracy   HERZ 170:11
     C. is Soviet power   LENI 215:11
     prisoners of C.   SOLZ 340:8
     Russian C.   ATTL 17:4
     spectre of C.   MARX 245:1
     trouble with C.   LAWR 211:6

communist call me a c.   CAMA 66:12
     I wasn't a C.   NIEM 269:1
     members of the C. Party   MCCA 231:6
     What is a c.   ELLI 126:1

communists C. of the old school   RUSK 310:4
     'C.' to include Fascists   ANON 8:7
     If the C. conquered   RUSS 311:5

community most perfect political c.   ARIS 14:3
     part of the c. of Europe   SALI 312:10

compact c. which exists   GARR 141:11

compass steer by the c.   TAYL 354:7

compassion C. is not weakness   HUMP 179:4
     c. of the Internal   SULL 349:8

competence question of c. and good sense
     BIRC 41:1

competent man is c.   TROL 364:7

competition anarchy and c.   RUSK 310:13
     rigour of c.   ANON 7:10

complain c. of the age   BURK 59:9
     Never c. and never explain   BALD 25:12
     Never c. and never explain   DISR 115:11

complainers c. for the public   BURK 57:8

complaints c. of ill-usage   MELB 247:2

compliance c. with my wishes   CHUR 85:9

computers so many c.   WAŁĘ 372:13

concatenation c. of circumstances   WEBS 377:10

conceal c. a fact with words   MACH 233:4

concentrate unable to c.   LAST 212:8

concentration c. of talent   KENN 199:7

concept Europe is a geographical c.   BISM 41:11

concern indifference to c.   HYDE 180:7

concerned nobody left to be c.   NIEM 269:1

concessions c. of the weak   BURK 57:13
     what c. to make   METT 249:7

conciliation not a policy of c.   PARN 283:1

conclaves Kingly c. stern   SHEL 329:11

conclusive c. judgement   GLAD 149:1

condemn c. a little more   MAJO 239:1

condition c. upon which God   CURR 99:9
     could do in that c.   PEPY 287:3

conditions better living c.   BARU 28:5

condottiere roamed like a c.   HURD 179:8

conduct c. of their rulers   ADAM 3:12
     rottenness begins in his c.   JEFF 185:11

cones eat the c. under his pines   FROS 138:10

confederacy C. has been done to death
     CHES 77:1
     if the C. fails   DAVI 102:6

conference naked into the c. chamber
     BEVA 36:11

confidence C. is a plant   PITT 289:9

confident men begin to feel c. ARIS 14:4
  Never glad c. morning BROW 54:8
confiscation legalized c. DISR 112:13
conflict armed c. EDEN 121:5
  end of the c. of centuries GRIF 155:2
  Never in the field of human c. CHUR 81:14
  tragic c. of loyalties HOWE 177:5
conflicts all disputes or c. BRIA 51:3
conform c., or be more wise PEPY 287:6
conforming c. to the times MACH 233:6
conformity C. may give you TAYL 353:13
confound C. their politics SONG 342:1
confront to c. them TRIM 363:10
confronting c. political dragons MAJO 239:7
confused anyone who isn't c. MURR 263:9
confusion C. now hath made SHAK 325:2
confute tell how to c. him SELD 317:3
congratulatory c. regrets DISR 113:6
congress C. makes no progress LIGN 218:1
  criminal class except C. TWAI 368:1
  member of C. TWAI 368:4
coniunx C. Est mihi LUCA 226:9
conjuror charlatan, and a c. TROL 364:4
  Hebrew c. CARL 70:9
Connaught Hell or C. CROM 98:11
  peasant from C. BUTT 63:8
conquer c. or die WASH 375:4
  easier to c. it WALP 373:13
conquered c. and peopled SEEL 317:2
  I came, I saw, I c. CAES 65:1
  perpetually to be c. BURK 57:15
  they are a c. people VICT 371:1
conquering c. one's enemies GENG 142:6
conqueror proud foot of a c. SHAK 324:4
conquerors c. and prophets DISR 115:1
conquests c., glories, triumphs SHAK 322:14
conscience c. doth make cowards SHAK 319:9
  c. is a still small voice ATTL 17:2
  c. of a statesman TAYL 354:3
  c. well under control LLOY 223:2
  corporation to have a c. THUR 360:5
  cut my c. HELL 168:1
  freedom of c. TWAI 368:2
  Hawking his c. MISQ 254:8
  reason and c. PRIC 294:10
  species of c. TAYL 354:4
  Sufficient c. to bother him LLOY 224:2
  taking your c. round BEVI 38:5
  with any man's c. CROM 98:2
consciences binding on the c. JOHN 188:6
  Look to your c. MARY 245:8
consciousness determines their c. MARX 244:5
conscription Not necessarily c. KING 204:2
consecrated c. by the experience of mankind
    GIBB 145:13
consensus I chose c. MAJO 239:7
  really good c. THAT 357:7
consent c. of heaven JONS 193:2
  demand not his free c. CHAR 76:1
  without his c. CAMD 67:1
  without that other's c. LINC 218:4

consent (cont.):
  without your c. ROOS 305:3
consequences damn the c. MILN 252:5
  political c. GALB 140:9
  political c. MANS 241:11
conservation make a speech on c. STEV 347:13
  means of its c. BURK 58:7
conservatism C. discards Prescription
    DISR 113:16
  c. is based upon the idea CHES 77:9
  forces of c. BLAI 44:5
  modern C. HENN 168:8
  party of C. EMER 126:4
  What is c. LINC 218:10
conservative become a c. on the day after
    AREN 13:2
  C. Government DISR 111:9
  c. is a liberal PROV 296:1
  C. is a man ROGE 304:6
  C. is a man ROOS 305:13
  C. Party WAUG 376:7
  C. Party always MACL 234:8
  C. Party at prayer ROYD 309:7
  c. who's been arrested WOLF 387:7
  it is really c. FISH 131:8
  make me c. when old FROS 138:9
  makes a man more c. KEYN 201:2
  most c. man in this world BEVI 38:4
  Or else a little C. GILB 146:4
  sound C. government DISR 113:17
conservatives better with the C. SLOG 335:12
  C. . . . being by the law MILL 250:3
  C. do not believe HAIL 157:9
  more formalistic than c. CALV 66:11
  night for the C. PORT 292:13
  trouble with c. CARV 71:7
consistency I have no c. BYRO 64:7
conspicuous c. by its presence RUSS 311:11
  C. consumption VEBL 369:8
conspiracy c. against the public SMIT 333:7
  O c. SHAK 322:5
  party is but a kind of c. HALI 159:7
  perpetual c. SALI 312:7
  vast right-wing c. CLIN 90:7
conspirators All the c. save only he SHAK 324:3
constant c. as the northern star SHAK 322:9
constellation bright c. JEFF 186:4
constituencies go back to your c. STEE 345:9
constitution boast of its c. PAIN 281:2
  British C. ELIZ 125:7
  C. between friends CAMP 67:8
  c. does not provide WILL 384:3
  C., in all its provisions CHAS 76:12
  c. is extremely well WALP 373:12
  construe the C. LINC 218:13
  essence of the c. JUNI 195:1
  genius of the C. PITT 289:14
  one c. WEBS 377:13
  people made the C. MARS 243:8
  principle of the English c. BLAC 43:5
  spirit of our c. GEOR 143:7

country (*cont.*):

c. needs good farmers	NIXO 270:8
c. takes her place	EMME 126:7
c. will be called upon	HARD 161:5
die but once to serve our c.	ADDI 4:10
died to save their c.	CHES 77:11
die for my c.	KINN 204:8
every c. but his own	GILB 146:8
fate of this c.	DISR 112:21
fight for its King and C.	GRAH 152:4
first, best c.	GOLD 150:6
friend of every c.	CANN 68:8
friends of every c.	DISR 113:4
good of his c.	WOTT 388:8
How can you govern a c.	DE G 105:6
how I leave my c.	LAST 213:8
how to run the c.	BURN 61:1
I pray for the c.	HALE 158:2
King and c. need you	MILI 251:5
leave his c. as good	COBB 91:11
let the c. down	CALL 66:5
lose for my c.	LAST 212:13
Love thy c.	DODI 116:7
love to serve my c.	GIBR 145:16
Merchants have no c.	JEFF 186:12
My c. has in its wisdom	ADAM 3:8
My c., right or wrong	CHES 77:6
My c., right or wrong	SCHU 316:5
My c., 'tis of thee	SMIT 338:10
our c., right or wrong	DECA 103:9
peace of each c.	JOHN 188:7
quarrel in a far away c.	CHAM 74:10
Queen and c.	THOM 359:6
rather than a c.	PILG 289:3
see much of the c.	GLAD 147:12
service of their c.	PAIN 279:9
there is my c.	OTIS 277:9
there is my c.	PAIN 281:1
tremble for my c.	JEFF 187:5
trouble with this c.	ADAM 2:4
understand the c.	LESS 216:4
Union, sir, is my c.	CLAY 88:13
vow to thee, my c.	SPRI 344:8
what was good for our c.	WILS 384:5
When war enters a c.	ANON 12:6
your King and your C.	SONG 342:8

countrymen advice to my c. O'CO 272:9

Friends, Romans, c.	SHAK 323:4
hearts of his c.	LEE 214:7
rebels are our c.	GRAN 153:2

countymen fellow-c. won't kill me COLL 93:3

courage accuse himself of c. BIRC 41:2

counsel of your c.	STEV 347:8
C. and faith	MACA 230:10
c. is the rarest	DISR 116:2
It takes c.	MOWL 261:8
One man with c.	JACK 183:6
on reflection is real c.	WALP 373:7
proud of their c.	DILL 110:8
test of c.	HAZL 165:4
two o'clock in the morning c.	NAPO 264:11

courageous describe it as c. LYNN 227:8

freedom depends on being c.	THUC 360:3

course what c. thou wilt SHAK 323:15

court arguments for having a mean C. BAGE 21:9

art o' the c.	SHAK 319:4
bright lustre of a c.	CECI 74:1
no family life at C.	THOM 359:4
Say to the c., it glows	RALE 298:2

courtesy women with perfect c. KITC 207:11

courtier Here lies a noble c. EPIT 128:4

courts C. for cowards were erected BURN 61:4

Coutts banks with C. GILB 146:1

covenant c. with death GARR 141:11

covenants Open c. of peace WILS 386:15

Covent Garden committee on C. KAUF 196:5

cow three acres and a c. SLOG 336:6

cowards make c. of us all SHAK 319:9

cowboy that damned c. HANN 161:1

cozenage greatest c. CROM 98:8

cradle from the c. to the grave CHUR 82:13

rocking the c.	ROBI 303:10

crank c. is a small engine SHEE 329:4

crash c. will come twenty years after BISM 42:7

crazy Is that man c. BUSH 62:1

should they go c.	PHOC 289:2
when I was c.	SHER 331:3

create c. the current of events BISM 42:9

genuinely c. Europe	MONN 257:4

created men are c. equal JEFF 185:1

creation since the C. NIXO 270:3

credit most c. TAYL 354:9

credulity craving c. DISR 112:6

season of c.	PITT 289:9
soften into a c.	BURK 59:12

creed article of my political c. ADAM 3:10

Calvinistic c.	PITT 289:12
c. of slaves	PITT 290:4
fear their c.	HEWI 171:9
last article of my c.	GAND 141:3

creep Ambition can c. BURK 59:7

Crewe True blue and Mrs C. GEOR 143:2

cricket C.—a game which the English

MANC 240:5

C. civilizes people	MUGA 262:11
c. test	TEBB 354:14
c. with their peasants	TREV 363:2

cried little children c. MOTL 261:5

poor have c.	SHAK 323:6

Crillon Hang yourself, brave C. HENR 169:1

crime catalogue of human c. CHUR 81:11

C. is crime	DYSO 120:7
c. of being a young man	PITT 289:6
foulest c. in history	WHIT 382:6
parent of revolution and c.	ARIS 14:1
prevent c.	MELB 247:15
today's alarming c. rates	BOAZ 45:3
tough on the causes of c.	BLAI 43:8
worse than a c.	BOUL 49:4

crimes c. are committed in thy name LAST 213:7

c., follies, and misfortunes	GIBB 145:3
Successful c. alone	DRYD 119:9

crimes (*cont.*):
teems with c.   ANON 9:14
criminal American c. class   TWAI 368:1
c. it deserves   KENN 200:1
ends I think c.   KEYN 200:6
while there is a c. element   DEBS 103:8
criminals if there were no c.   SALI 313:4
Looney Tunes, and squalid c.   REAG 299:12
crimson c. thread of kinship   PARK 283:1
cringe to the cultural c.   KEAT 196:9
crises every age had consisted of c.   ATKI 16:3
crisis cannot be a c.   KISS 207:2
c. in American leadership   BALT 27:5
C.? What Crisis?   MISQ 254:4
C.? What crisis   NEWS 267:1
except in a c.   HOSK 177:2
fit for a great c.   BAGE 21:1
real c. on your hands   THAT 357:2
critic not the c. who counts   ROOS 307:9
critical at a c. moment   HARD 162:4
criticism c. of administration   BAGE 20:11
criticized to be c. is not always   EDEN 121:6
critics listen to their c.   GALB 140:10
crocodile feeds a c.   CHUR 81:8
Cromwell C., I charge thee   SHAK 321:2
C. said to the Long Parliament   AMER 7:2
Some C. guiltless   GRAY 154:2
cronies money-grabbing c.   HAGU 156:5
crony government by c.   ICKE 181:5
crook McAdoo his c.   SPRI 344:9
President is a c.   NIXO 270:7
crooked c. timber of humanity   KANT 196:3
crop c. failure   BLAI 43:12
crops experimental c.   HURD 179:10
cross c. of gold   BRYA 55:7
I am c. with Jeffrey   ARCH 13:1
crosses tumbled down the c.   JORD 193:5
crossways understands everything c.   SALI 312:7
crowd chaining the c.   VOLT 377:9
riotousness of the c.   ALCU 6:3
crowds talk with c.   KIPL 205:8
crown better than his c.   SHAK 325:13
Caesar's laurel c.   BLAK 44:9
conquer a c.   O'SH 277:4
c. in possession   PAIN 278:8
c. in possession   PAIN 279:2
c. of thorns   BRYA 55:7
C., the symbol of permanence   JUAN 194:10
glory of my c.   ELIZ 124:7
head that wears a c.   SHAK 320:4
I give away my c.   SHAK 326:11
Indian C.   ROSS 308:12
influence of the C.   DUNN 120:3
king's c.   SHAK 325:10
neither abdicate the C.   JUAN 194:11
never wears the c.   HESE 171:1
No c. of thorns   SLOG 335:16
power of the c.   BURK 59:11
presented him a kingly c.   SHAK 323:7
wished to restore the c.   JOHN 191:11
Within the hollow c.   SHAK 326:7

crowned c. ruffians   PAIN 279:3
sitting c. upon the grave   HOBB 174:1
crowning c. mercy   CROM 98:4
crowns c. are empty things   DEFO 104:13
crucible America is God's C.   ZANG 390:9
crucified c. when alive   CONN 94:4
crucify c. mankind   BRYA 55:7
cruel c. and unusual punishment   CONS 95:3
c. men of Rome   SHAK 321:5
C. necessity   CROM 98:1
State business is a c. trade   HALI 159:15
crusade party is a moral c.   WILS 384:8
crush c. people to the earth   CHIL 78:5
cry Don't c. for me   RICE 301:7
rallied to that c.   BALD 25:9
Speechless still, and never c.   EPIT 128:7
too big to c.   LINC 219:6
crystal Why read the c.   BEVA 36:5
Cuban C. Missile Crisis   STOC 348:5
cuckoo c. clock   WELL 378:7
culling c. of First Secretaries   MORG 260:3
cult c. is a religion   WOLF 387:8
c. of the individual   KHRU 202:2
cultivation subsequent c.   TROL 364:13
cultural c. autonomy   GRAY 153:9
culture has an established c.   GREE 154:5
hears the word c.   GLEN 149:4
hear the word 'c.'   ESHE 127:5
hear the word c.   JOHS 192:5
men of c.   ARNO 14:8
cunctando c. restituit rem   ENNI 127:1
cunning c. men pass for wise   BACO 19:2
cure palliate what we cannot c.   JOHN 190:12
cured c. by more democracy   SMIT 337:11
curiosity You're a c.   KEEL 197:5
currency attitude to single c.   CLAR 88:3
debauch the c.   KEYN 200:9
single c.   NAPO 264:8
curs You common cry of c.   SHAK 318:9
curse is to me a c.   MASS 246:1
curst to all succeeding ages c.   DRYD 118:7
curtain bloody c.   ELIS 123:5
final c. comes down   MAJO 239:5
iron c.   CHUR 83:7
kept behind a c.   PAIN 280:11
lets the c. fall   POPE 292:1
curtains keep their c. up   DYSO 120:7
cuss don't matter a tinker's c.   SHIN 331:6
custodes quis custodiet ipsos C.   JUVE 195:10
custodiet quis c. ipsos Custodes   JUVE 195:10
custom C., that unwritten law   D'AV 102:1
Lest one good c.   TENN 355:13
Office, and c.   SHAK 327:6
customers people of c.   SMIT 333:8
customs ancient c. and its manhood   ENNI 126:10
c. of his tribe   SHAW 327:14
cut c. his throat at last   BYRO 64:4
c. my conscience to fit   HELL 168:1
c. off my head   CHAR 75:10
most unkindest c. of all   SHAK 323:10
cute c. to have the British c.   DYSO 120:8

death (*cont.*):

forced marches, battles and d.	GARI 141:8
go on living even after d.	FRAN 136:6
I am become d.	OPPE 274:12
I signed my d. warrant	COLL 92:8
Keeps D. his court	SHAK 326:7
kiss of d.	SMIT 337:10
laws of d.	RUSK 310:13
Liberty or D.	WOOL 388:3
liberty, or give me d.	HENR 169:9
nearest thing to d. in life	ANON 10:2
new terror to d.	WETH 381:1
of the sovereign is d.	MORE 259:9
reaction to her d.	ELIZ 125:8
seeds of the d. of any state	HOBB 173:14
sentence of d.	CARS 71:1
sign her own d.-warrant	BAGE 21:10
studied in his d.	SHAK 324:8
suicide 25 years after his d.	BEAV 30:1
Those by d. are few	JEFF 186:6
timing of your d.	TACI 351:6
While there is d.	CROS 99:4

deaths million d. a statistic — STAL 345:6

debate daughter of d. — ELIZ 124:3

d. a question	JOUB 194:6
Rupert of D.	BULW 56:4

debout *D.! les damnés* — SONG 341:5

debt Ambition's d. is paid — SHAK 322:11

national d.	HAMI 160:5
National D. is a very Good Thing	SELL 317:10
war, an' a d.	LOWE 226:4

debts so we can pay our d. — NYER 271:11

decade fun to be in the same d. — ROOS 306:10

deceitful inconsequential, and d. — HELL 167:11

deceiving nearly d. your friends — CORN 96:4

decency d. to shoot me — MARK 243:2

decide Ministers d. — THAT 357:13

moment to d. — LOWE 226:5

decides Cabinet does not propose, it d. — ATTL 17:1

decision d. was made — TRUM 366:8

monologue is not a d.	AI IL 16.6
specific d.	TUCH 367:5

decisions make important d. — ATTL 17:9

regard as important the d. — PARK 283:6

deck from the bottom of the d. — SHAP 327:11

Walk the d. my Captain lies — WHIT 382:3

declaration no d. of war — EDEN 121:5

decline orderly management of d. — ARMS 14:6

decorated d., and got rid of — CICE 87:3

decorum athwart Goes all d. — SHAK 325:7

decree O king, establish the d. — BIBL 39:15

deeds d. of the past — DAVI 103:1

deep d. sleep of England — ORWE 275:8

defeat D. doesn't finish a man — NIXO 270:13

d. is an orphan	CIAN 86:13
In d.; defiance	CHUR 85:6
in D., Malice	LYNN 227:7
In d. unbeatable	CHUR 84:13
never had a d.	CHUR 85:8
possibilities of d.	VICT 371:2

defeated d. in a great battle — LIVY 222:4

defeated (*cont.*):

Down with the d. — LIVY 222:3

defeats Dewey d. Truman — NEWS 267:2

defence d. of the indefensible — ORWE 276:13

greatest d. and ornament	BLAC 43:4
Never make a d.	CHAR 75:8
think of the d. of England	BALD 25:6

defend d. ourselves with guns — GOEB 149:5

d. to the death your right	MISQ 254:9
refuses to d. his rights	JACK 183:1

defiance In defeat; d. — CHUR 85:6

defined d. by our friends — BROW 53:6

definition d. of the best government — HALI 159:3

deflation or d. — HOME 175:12

defraud d. his neighbour — RUSK 310:5

defrauding d. of the State — PENN 287:2

degree d. is shaked — SHAK 327:7

dehumanizing d. the Negro — LINC 218:9

deity top d. — PIML 289:5

delay deny, or d. — MAGN 238:5

delaying One man by d. — ENNI 127:1

delays worst is that which d. — LLOY 223:3

delegate When in trouble, d. — BORE 48:8

delenda *D. est Carthago* — CATO 72:9

deleted Expletive d. — ANON 8:3

deliver d. a pizza — ANON 12:4

deliverance d. from chains — DOUG 117:6

delivered God hath d. him — BIBL 39:5

deluge *Après nous le d.* — POMP 291:7

delusion under some d. — BURK 60:12

demands cannot exact their d. — WELL 380:2

demi-paradise other Eden, d. — SHAK 326:2

democracies d. against despots — DEMO 106:1

d., which refresh	TREV 363:7
in d. it is the only sacred	FRAN 136:3

democracy aspirant under d. — MENC 248:12

basis of d.	RUSS 311:1
before D. go	CARL 69:12
cured by more d.	SMIT 337:11
d. and proper drains	BETJ 36:1
D. and socialism	NEHR 265:8
D. a society	TAWN 352:13
D. is the current suspicion	WHIT 381:4
D. is the name we give	FLER 132:8
D. is the theory	MENC 248:6
D. is the worst form	CHUR 83:13
D. means government by	CHES 78:4
d. never lasts long	ADAM 3:9
D. *not* identical with majority rule	LENI 215:7
d. of the dead	CHES 77:7
D. resumed her reign	BELL 31:5
D. substitutes election	SHAW 328:10
d. unbearable	PERE 287:8
d. was renewed	DEWA 108:8
D., which means despair	CARL 70:10
extreme d. or absolute oligarchy	ARIS 14:2
great arsenal of d.	ROOS 306:3
grieved under a *d.*	HOBB 173:15
justice makes d. possible	NIEB 268:4
less d. to save	ATKI 16:2
made safe for d.	WILS 386:12

democracy (*cont.*):
myth of d.   CROS 99:6
not the voting that's d.   STOP 348:7
pollution of d.   WHIT 381:7
principle of d.   MONT 258:9
property-owning d.   SKEL 333:1
Russia an empire or d.   BRZE 55:8
triumph for d.   HOPE 176:8
Two cheers for D.   FORS 134:11
Under d.   MENC 248:8
understand d.   STRU 349:7
Without d.   TAYL 353:14
democrat D. is a fellow   ROGE 304:6
I am a D.   ROGE 304:7
Senator, and a D.   JOHN 189:4
democratic among a d. people   TROL 364:9
aristocracy the most d.   MACA 229:15
D. or Republican way   LA G 209:2
d. paint   TOCQ 361:9
D. Party is like a mule   DONN 117:2
democratically d. governed   HAIL 157:10
democrats and a few D.   BROG 52:8
D. object to men being disqualified   CHES 77:8
saloon keepers were D.   GREE 154:4
demolition d. of a man   LEVI 216:7
demon d. of Anglicization   HYDE 180:6
d. you have roused   LINC 218:9
denied Justice d.   MILL 251:7
officially d.   COCK 92:2
Denmark in the state of D.   SHAK 319:7
deny d., or delay   MAGN 238:5
I never d.   DISR 115:10
departure point of d.   METT 249:8
deported would be d.   DE R 107:3
depose my state d.   SHAK 326:9
depositary d. of power   DISR 114:1
depression D. is when there is   PANK 282:8
d. when you lose yours   TRUM 366:11
deprivation cycle of d.   JOSE 193:8
depth far beyond my d.   SHAK 321:1
depths unfathomable d. of insincerity   ANON 11:7
deputy d. elected by the Lord   SHAK 326:4
Derry oak would sprout in D.   HEAN 166:11
descent Irish d.   ROBI 303:11
desert Stand in the d.   SHEL 329:10
deserve and d. to get it   MENC 248:6
desire d. for honour   CICE 86:17
d. of power   HOBB 173:6
desires doing what one d.   MILL 250:13
desk modern man's subservience to the d.
                                              FRAN 137:7
desolated province they have d.   GLAD 148:3
desolation years of d.   JEFF 187:2
desperate Diseases d. grown   SHAK 319:14
despise work for a Government I d.   KEYN 200:6
despot wise d.   HERB 170:6
despotism absolute oligarchy, or d.   ARIS 14:2
D. accomplishes great things   BALZ 27:6
d. in England   WALP 373:10
D. is essential   CARL 70:7
d., let it be called   WEBS 377:12

despotism (*cont.*):
d., or unlimited sovereignty   ADAM 3:10
d. tempered by epigrams   CARL 70:1
modern form of d.   MCCA 231:8
present d.   HERZ 170:12
root of d.   ROBE 303:7
despots against d.—suspicion   DEMO 106:1
D. themselves do not deny   TOCQ 360:8
destiny manifest d.   O'SU 277:7
one d.   WEBS 377:13
rendezvous with d.   ROOS 305:8
destroy d. the town to save it   ANON 9:9
my hand to d.   BURK 60:11
power to d.   MARS 243:7
Whom the mad would d.   LEVI 217:3
destroyed Carthage must be d.   CATO 72:9
Prussia is wholly and finally d.   ASQU 15:3
treated generously or d.   MACH 233:8
destroyer d. of worlds   OPPE 274:12
destruction means of total d.   SAKH 312:1
whether the mad d. is wrought   GAND 141:1
destructive simply d.   MELB 247:3
deteriora D. sequor   OVID 277:10
detest d. him more   MACA 231:2
detestation D. of the high   DICK 110:1
Deutschland D. über alles   HOFF 174:4
developed have a d. society   NYER 272:1
devil d. shall not take it from us   RAND 298:6
D. should have right   MORE 259:8
first Whig was the D.   JOHN 191:17
synonym for the D.   MACA 229:2
devils d. would set on me   LUTH 227:2
devolution D. Day   SALM 314:1
d. takes longer   BAIN 23:15
devour d. in turn each one   VERG 370:3
devourers become so great d.   MORE 259:7
diaper d. into the ring   ICKE 181:4
diaries I've kept political d.   GEOG 142:7
dictator Every d. uses religion   BHUT 38:13
dictators D. ride to and fro   CHUR 81:4
dictatorship d. impossible   PERE 287:8
d. of the proletariat   MARX 244:10
d. seriously violates   ROME 304:10
elective d.   HAIL 157:5
establish a d.   ORWE 276:6
have a d.   TRUM 366:12
inefficiencies of d.   GALB 140:11
risk the d.   LINC 220:2
dictionary search for a d.   GLEN 149:4
die And shall Trelawny d.   HAWK 164:2
better to d. on your feet   IBAR 180:9
conquer or d.   WASH 375:4
d. a Christian   CHAR 76:3
d. for my country   KINN 204:8
d. for politicians   THOM 359:6
d. in my week   JOPL 193:3
d. in the last ditch   WILL 383:10
d. is cast   CAES 64:13
d. like a true-blue rebel   LAST 213:2
D., my dear Doctor   LAST 212:4
d. to make men free   HOWE 177:7

die (cont.):

d. to vex me	MELB 247:5
Don't d. of ignorance	OFFI 274:3
Few d. and none resign	MISQ 254:6
few d. well	SHAK 320:9
he must d.	NICH 266:3
I d. happy	LAST 212:9
I d. hard	LAST 213:1
I shall d. today	MORE 259:9
I would rather d.	LEE 215:2
last Jews to d.	MEIR 247:1
Let us do—or d.	BURN 61:5
love one another or d.	AUDE 17:15
ought to d. standing	LAST 212:5
something he will d. for	KING 203:4
we can d. but once	ADDI 4:10
when you d.	HILL 172:4
you asked this man to d.	AUDE 17:11

died Alan d. suddenly CLAR 88:1
D., has he	LOUI 225:10
d. to save their country	CHES 77:11
'I never d.,' says he	HAYE 165:2
Suppose Lenin had d.	SCHL 315:10
What millions d.	CAMP 67:7

dies king never d. BLAC 43:3
diet wholesome d. CHUR 86:7
difference d. of forty thousand WELL 379:6
| tough-minded . . . respect d. | BENF 31:8 |
| What d. does it make | GAND 141:1 |

differences end now our d. KENN 199:3
| world made safe for d. | BENE 31:8 |

differently freedom for the one who thinks d.
LUXE 227:3

difficult d. to speak BURK 60:14
difficulties d. in princes' business BACO 19:4
| little local d. | MACM 236:1 |

difficulty d. is often in their own mind BACO 19:4
| England's d. | PROV 296:5 |
| solving every d. | PEEL 286:6 |

dig D. for victory OFFI 274:2
| I could not d. | KIPL 205:4 |

digging stop d. HEAL 166:3
dignity added to his d. CHUR 86:5
conciliate with d.	GREN 154:7
d. and competence	CLAR 87:16
d. in tilling a field	WASH 375:1
d. of the office	GEOR 143:6
d. which His Majesty	BALD 25:10
maintain a d. in their fate	WALP 373:7
no d. in persevering in error	PEEL 286:3

diminished ought to be d. DUNN 120:3
diminishes d. my confidence JOHN 191:14
dimming d. of the lights NICO 266:8
dinner after-d. conversations THOR 359:11
asking it to d.	HALS 160:4
bore people at d. parties	KISS 207:10
we expect our d.	SMIT 333:6

dinosaurs day of the d. MCAL 228:3
diplomacy d. backed up by fairness ANNA 7:5
| D. is about surviving | LYNN 227:10 |
| D. is saying | CATL 72:8 |

diplomacy (cont.):

D. is to do and say	GOLD 150:1

diplomas d. they can't read GING 146:11
diplomat d. . . . is a person STIN 348:3
| distinction of a d. | PEAR 285:5 |

diplomatic d. boathook SALI 312:4
diplomatist d.'s vocabulary TAYL 353:17
direction move in a given d. HOUS 177:3
dirt D. is only matter GRAY 153:8
| thicker will be the d. | GALB 139:12 |

disapprove d. of what you say MISQ 254:9
disaster Press lives on d. ATTL 17:5
| triumph and d. | KIPL 205:7 |

disastrous d. and the unpalatable GALB 140:13
discipline under such a d. HALI 159:9
discontent fund of d. PEEL 286:1
winter of d.	CALL 66:2
Winter of d.	NEWS 268:5
winter of our d.	SHAK 326:13

discord d. doth sow ELIZ 124:3
| hark! what d. follows | SHAK 327:8 |

discover d. by his manner SMIT 339:3
discretion genius for d. BAGE 21:13
| inform their d. | JEFF 186:16 |
| their happiness in thy d. | ELIZ 124:6 |

discrimination acquiesce in the face of d.
BETH 35:8
| detecting d. | POWE 293:7 |

discuss stay and d. them WELL 379:5
discussion government by d. ATTL 17:6
| reasonable d. | CHUR 85:9 |

disease desperate d. FAWK 131:1
D., Ignorance, Squalor	BEVE 38:2
d. in the family	TREV 363:4
d. of opposition	GALB 140:12

diseases D. desperate grown SHAK 319:14
dishonesty allegation of d. LEVE 216:6
disjoins d. Remorse from power SHAK 322:3
dislike enough for me to d. MCCO 231:10
disloyal began to be d. WALD 372:12
disloyalty D. is the secret CRIT 97:8
dismal D. Science CARL 70:4
Disney Walt D. Corporation ANON 9:1
disobliging d. the few MACA 230:3
disorder to preserve d. DALE 100:7
dispossessed imprisoned or d. MAGN 238:4
Disraeli D. school of Prime Ministers BLAI 44:2
dissatisfaction discontent and d. PEEL 286:1
dissent is called 'd.' HAVE 163:8
dissentious you d. rogues SHAK 318:5
dissimulation one word—d. DISR 114:5
dissolve d. the people BREC 51:1
distance proportion to his d. RAKO 298:1
distant relation of d. misery GIBB 145:10
distort then you can d. them TWAI 368:3
distress maiden in d. STEE 345:11
distressful most d. country SONG 342:2
distribute d. as fairly as he can LOWE 226:3
distribution most equitable d. ANON 11:11
disturbed d. the sleep STEV 347:12
ditch cannot d. policies PORT 292:14

ditch (*cont.*):
  [Channel] is a mere d.   NAPO 264:5
  die in the last d.   WILL 383:10
  environed with a great d.   CROM 98:10
diversity safe for d.   KENN 199:3
divided d. by a common language   MISQ 254:5
  d. into three parts   CAES 64:9
dividing by d. we fall   DICK 110:4
divine government by d. right   HARR 163:1
  indefeasible, d. right   ADAM 3:12
  say that D. providence   JOHN 189:2
divinity d. doth hedge a king   SHAK 320:1
division d. in the House   CHUR 80:1
  d. of Europe   GIBB 144:10
  old wall of d.   GORE 151:6
divisions How many d. has *he* got   STAL 345:4
divorce grounds for d.   DOWD 117:10
do d. for the nation   HARD 161:7
  d. something about it   CHOD 79:1
  d. what I please   FRED 137:12
  he'll say d. this   TRUM 366:7
  I can d. no other   LUTH 227:1
  Let us d.—or die   BURN 61:5
  so much to d.   LAST 213:10
  supposed to d. anyway   TRUM 366:4
  we could d. this   WEBB 376:11
  We must d. something   LYNN 227:11
  what can I d. for myself   NIXO 270:5
doctrine d. is something you kill for   BENN 32:8
  d. of ignoble ease   ROOS 307:1
doer I am a d.   SMIT 338:8
doffed d. their lids   KEAT 197:1
dog Black d. is back   CHUR 85:14
  D. returns to his Vomit   KIPL 205:5
  d.'s obeyed in office   SHAK 324:6
  d.'s walking on his hinder legs   JOHN 191:4
  drover's d. could   HAYD 164:6
  get your d. back   LIEB 217:11
  good d. in Mr Ernest Bevin   ATTL 17:8
  hard d. to keep   CLIN 90:8
  I must love the d.   GIBB 145:15
  kids love that d.   NIXO 269:7
  large, friendly d.   TOYN 362:6
  That d. won't hunt   RICH 302:1
Doge quiet D. of Venice   WALP 373:10
doggie saying 'Nice d.'   CATL 72:8
dogma no d., no Dean   DISR 115:15
dogs all their running d.   MAO 242:6
  D. look up   CHUR 86:3
  d. of Europe bark   AUDE 17:13
  d. or the Radicals   WILD 383:5
  let slip the d. of war   SHAK 323:1
  Tom and the other d.   CLAR 88:1
doing d. business   HEAL 166:6
  necessity of d. something   JOHN 191:6
dollar billion d. country   FOST 135:2
dome critics of the D.   HESE 171:7
  Millennium D.   MAND 241:6
domestic d. business   MONT 258:2
  Malice d.   SHAK 325:5
  pleasures of d. life   GIBB 145:4

domination d. and equilibrium   KISS 207:6
domineered You d. too much   MELB 247:4
dominion d. of kings changed   PRIC 294:10
  d. of religion   GOLD 150:3
  d. of the English   DECL 104:2
  d. of the master   HUME 178:7
  d. of the world   MAHA 238:6
  hand that holds d.   THOM 359:2
dominions His Majesty's d.   NORT 271:3
domino 'falling d.' principle   EISE 122:7
dona *timeo Danaos et d. ferentes*   VIRG 371:8
done great things are d.   BISM 42:6
  If you want anything d.   THAT 356:3
  surprised to find it d.   JOHN 191:4
  What is to be d.   LENI 215:9
  what's d. is done   SHAK 325:4
  what should be d.   MELB 247:14
donkeys Lions led by d.   MILI 251:4
doom tongues d. men   SHAK 327:4
door open d.   HAY 164:5
  prejudices through the d.   FRED 137:11
doormat d. or a prostitute   WEST 380:7
doors Men shut their d.   SHAK 327:3
doorstep do this on the d.   JUNO 195:8
dots damned d. meant   CHUR 79:12
double Labour's d. whammy   SLOG 335:9
doublethink D. means the power   ORWE 276:5
doubt in d. what should be done   MELB 247:14
  intelligent full of d.   RUSS 311:8
down born with D.'s syndrome   DE G 105:13
  kicked d. stairs   HALI 160:1
  let the country d.   CALL 66:5
  staying d. with him   WASH 375:2
downhearted We are not d.   CHAM 74:9
Downing reach D. Street   THAT 357:14
dragons political d.   MAJO 239:7
drains democracy and proper d.   BETJ 36:1
drawers hewers of wood and d. of water
     BIBL 39:2
drawing-room same men in the d.   HALI 158:8
  through my d.   EDEN 121:7
drawn died with their d. salaries   LLOY 224:4
dreadful d. human beings sitting   NORR 271:2
dreadnoughts as much to keep up as two D.
     LLOY 222:7
dream d. that is dying   O'SH 277:5
  I have a d.   KING 203:5
  no longer a d.   CLIN 91:2
  old men's d.   DRYD 118:10
  One man with a d.   O'SH 277:4
dreamed d. I saw Joe Hill   HAYE 165:2
dreams d. of being Taoiseach   HAUG 163:6
dregs d. are often filthy   CHUR 85:5
  d. of Romulus   CICE 86:14
  You would get the d.   LONG 225:1
drest D. in a little brief authority   SHAK 325:12
drift adamant for d.   CHUR 81:3
drinking d. is to continue   DEED 104:3
drive difficult to d.   BROU 53:3
  told they cannot d.   HAGU 156:8
driver back-seat d.   THAT 358:4

Eden other E. | SHAK 326:2
editor duty of an e. | VEBL 369:7
  e. himself be attacked | TROL 365:1
  News E. | ANON 8:11
educate e. our masters | LOWE 226:2
  e. our masters | MISQ 255:11
  e. our party | DISR 112:9
educated clothed, fed, and e. | RUSK 310:8
  government by the badly e. | CHES 78:4
education black kids get an e. | POWE 293:1
  discretion by e. | JEFF 186:16
  e., education, and education | BLAI 43:10
  E. makes a people | BROU 53:3
  e. of a politician | CHUR 84:16
  e. of the people | DISR 112:21
  first part of politics? E. | MICH 249:10
  parts of e. | SMIT 337:8
  unplanned e. creates | VERW 370:4
EEC E. is a horse and carriage | DE G 105:14
eels procreation of e. | SCHU 316:6
effective Being e. | BECK 30:5
efficiency e. of the post office | SULL 349:8
  southern e. | KENN 199:9
  where there is no e. | DISR 112:11
efficient have an e. government | TRUM 366:12
effort last e. of the patriots | ADAM 3:3
  redoubling your e. | SANT 314:5
effusive don't be too e. | ELIZ 125:9
égalité É.! Fraternité | SLOG 335:11
egg lays an e. | NEWS 268:2
eggheads E. of the world | STEV 347:11
ego e. has landed | DOBS 116:6
eight We want e., and we won't wait | ANON 12:3
elder to e. statesman | FOOT 134:3
elect dissolve the people and e. | BREC 51:1
  e., and to reject | PAIN 280:15
  e. the second chamber | JAY 184:11
elected audacity of e. persons | WHIT 382:4
  e. by the manhood | ELLI 126:2
  will not serve if e. | SHER 331:4
election Better lose the e. | STEV 346:9
  e. by the incompetent many | SHAW 328:10
  e. is coming | ELIO 123:3
  good e. can't fix | NIXO 270:1
  I've won the e. | GEOR 144:5
  right of e. | JUNI 195:1
  wanted an e. | ROOS 305:2
elections e. are won | ADAM 2:5
  fighting of e. | CHUR 84:16
  I do not like e. | CHUR 85:10
  You won the e. | SOMO 340:9
elective e. dictatorship | HAIL 157:5
electricity moral e. | O'CO 272:10
  must use less e. | JENK 187:10
  usefulness of e. | FARA 130:5
electrification e. of the whole country | LENI 215:11
elegant e. simplicity | STOW 349:1
elegy whole of Gray's E. | WOLF 387:5
elements e. So mixed in him | SHAK 324:3
elephant rogue e. | TAYL 353:15

elephant (cont.):
  sleeping with an e. | TRUD 365:15
elephants golden e. next | SHOR 332:1
eleven failing his e.-plus | PRES 294:6
  our e. days | SLOG 334:17
elite power e. | MILL 252:4
eloquence finest e. | LLOY 223:3
  I admire his e. | GIBB 145:14
  parliamentary e. | CARL 70:5
eloquent e. in a more sublime language | MACA 229:4
elsewhere There is a world e. | SHAK 318:10
Elysian in the E. fields | DISR 115:9
embalmer triumph of the e.'s art | VIDA 371:5
embarrassment financial e. | DISR 112:2
emblem e. of mortality | DISR 113:10
embrace e. your Lordship's principles | WILK 383:8
emergency one e. following upon another | FISH 131:6
emigration e. system | JOHN 192:3
emotion dependable international e. | ALSO 6:7
emotional of being e. | HARN 162:7
emotions e. were riveted | FOOT 134:4
  underlying e. | NAMI 264:2
emperor e. holds the key | CUST 100:5
  E. is everything | METT 249:6
  e. to die standing | LAST 212:5
emperors E. can do nothing | BREC 50:10
empire All e. is no more | DRYD 119:1
  Britain has lost an e. | ACHE 1:5
  destinies of the British E. | DISR 112:4
  E. is a commonwealth | ROSE 308:2
  e., vast as it is | CUST 100:5
  e. walking very slowly | FITZ 132:6
  evil e. | REAG 299:9
  found a great e. | SMIT 333:8
  great e. and little minds | BURK 58:3
  great Mother E. | FOST 135:3
  Greeks in this American e. | MACM 235:5
  How's the E. | LAST 212:8
  meaning of E. Day | CHES 78:3
  metropolis of the e. | COBB 91:12
  nor Roman, nor an e. | VOLT 372:3
  of the British E. | CHUR 82:10
  Russia an e. or democracy | BRZE 55:8
  strength of the E. | GLAD 148:6
  this E. will perish | DISR 115:20
  trample an e. | O'SH 277:4
  unity of the e. | BURK 58:1
  way she disposed of an e. | HARL 162:6
  westward the course of e. | BERK 34:3
  wilderness into a glorious e. | BURK 58:4
empires day of E. | CHAM 74:8
  drizzle of E. | CHUR 80:5
  e. of the future | CHUR 82:15
employed innocently e. | JOHN 191:10
employer sole e. is the State | TROT 365:12
employers e. of past generations | BALD 25:4
employment happily known as gainful e. | ACHE 1:4
empty e. taxi arrived | CHUR 85:15

empty (*cont.*):
from an e. chair	HESE 171:5
on an e. stomach	BRAN 50:7
party in an e. room	DEWA 108:6

enamoured So e. on peace — CLAR 87:7

encompassed e. but one man — SHAK 321:10

encourage right to e. — BAGE 21:12
to e. the others — VOLT 371:11

encourager *e. les autres* — VOLT 371:11

encourages never vote. It only e. them — ANON 9:7

end ane e. of ane old song — OGIL 273:4
beginning of the e.	TALL 352:1
came to an e. all wars	LLOY 222:11
do not e. when you please	MACH 233:7
e. is not yet	BIBL 39:22
e. of a thousand years of history	GAIT 139:7
e. of earth	LAST 214:1
e. of history	FUKU 138:11
e. of the beginning	CHUR 82:11
e. to bossing	LENI 215:13
e. to the beginnings of all wars	ROOS 306:12
e. to the old Britain	BROW 53:8
In my e. is my beginning	MARY 245:9
reserved for some e.	CLIV 91:8
sole e. for which mankind	MILL 250:6
war that will e. war	WELL 380:4

ended Georges e. — LAND 210:1

ending way of e. a war — ORWE 276:16

endings time the beginnings and e. — BACO 19:3

endogenous neoclassical e. growth — BROW 53:7

endure human hearts e. — JOHN 190:16

enemies conquering one's e. — GENG 142:6
e. are on your own side	ANON 11:9
e. he has made	BRAG 50:3
e. of Freedom do not argue	INGE 181:7
e. of liberty	HUME 178:8
e. to laws	BURK 60:6
left me naked to mine e.	SHAK 321:3
no perpetual e.	PALM 281:8
those e. they killed	PEEL 285:11
you are now our e.	MUGA 262:12

enemy E. ears are listening — OFFI 274:7
inveterate e.	PITT 290:1
quieten your e. by talking	CEAU 73:6
will have upon the e.	WELL 378:8
worst e. Ireland ever had	MITC 253:7
written by an acute e.	BALF 26:9

enfants *e. de la patrie* — SONG 341:1

enforceable e. safeguards — TRUM 366:3

engine crank is a small e. — SHEE 329:4
not connected to the e. — GOOD 151:2

engineering social e. — POPP 292:12

engineers age of the e. — HOGB 174:5
Artists are not e.	KENN 199:7
e. of human souls	STAL 345:3
e. of the soul	GORK 151:8

engines e. to play a little — BURK 58:6

England Church of E. — CHAR 76:3
damn you E.	OSBO 277:3
deep sleep of E.	ORWE 275:8
end in the ruin of E.	SHEL 329:7

England (*cont.*):
E. and America divided	MISQ 254:5
E. has saved herself	PITT 290:7
E. is a disguised republic	BAGE 22:9
E. is a nation of shopkeepers	NAPO 265:1
E. not the jewelled isle	ORWE 275:10
E.'s difficulty	PROV 296:5
E. shall perish	ELIZ 124:11
E.'s native people	BURN 61:7
E.'s not a bad country	DRAB 118:1
E. to be the workshop	DISR 111:4
E. was too pure an Air	ANON 10:6
E. will have her neck wrung	CHUR 82:8
God punish e.	FUNK 139:4
Goodbye, E.'s rose	JOHN 188:9
Gott strafe E.	FUNK 139:4
history of E.	MACA 229:10
last King of E.	EDWA 121:8
Let not E. forget	MILT 252:11
never have seen E. more	CROM 97:9
O E.! model	SHAK 320:5
old E.'s winding sheet	BLAK 44:10
roast beef of old E.	BURK 59:13
royal navy of E.	BLAC 43:4
speak for E.	AMER 7:1
strong arm of E.	PALM 281:9
suspended in favour of E.	SHAW 328:1
This E. never did	SHAK 324:4
this Realm of E.	BOOK 47:4
this realm, this E.	SHAK 326:2
Wake up, E.	GEOR 143:3
we are the people of E.	CHES 77:12
who only E. know	KIPL 205:3
world where E. is finished	MILL 251:9

English cosh of the E. — STRA 349:5
Cricket—a game which the E.	MANC 240:5
dominion of the E.	DECI 104:2
E. Church shall be free	MAGN 238:3
E. have taken their idea	MONT 258:13
E. House of Commons	MACA 228:6
E. in Ireland	MARK 243:1
E. in taste	MACA 231:3
E. know-how	COLO 93:4
E. make it their abode	WALL 373:2
E. never smash in a face	HALS 160:4
E.-speaking nations	THAT 358:9
E. subject's sole prerogative	DRYD 119:11
E. take their pleasures	SULL 350:2
E. up with which I will not put	CHUR 84:2
E. want *inferiors*	TOCQ 362:1
excellence of the E. government	BLAC 43:7
Exterminate . . . the treacherous E.	ANON 8:4
impulse of the E. people	BAGE 22:10
miracle if the E. people	BAGE 22:7
mobilized the E. language	MURR 263:7
really nice E. people	SHAW 327:18
Saxon-Danish-Norman E.	DEFO 104:9
seven feet of E. ground	HARO 162:8
shed one E. tear	MACA 230:11
talent of our E. nation	DRYD 119:10
to the E. that of the sea	RICH 302:3

English (*cont.*):
trick of our E. nation	SHAK 320:3

Englishman Being an E. | RHOD 301:3
E. of the strongest	DAVI 103:2
E.'s home	PROV 296:6
E. will give his mind	SHAW 327:13
last E. to rule	NEHR 265:13
last great E.	TENN 355:6
makes an E. convinced	DISR 112:18
not one E.	WALP 374:1
rights of an E.	JUNI 195:7
thing, an E.	DEFO 104:8

Englishmen E. never will be slaves | SHAW 328:7
| very name as E. | PITT 290:6 |
| virtue of E. | TAWN 352:6 |

Englishwoman Princess leave the E. | BISM 41:4
enigma mystery inside an e. | CHUR 81:6
enjoying from e. themselves | RUSS 311:3
enough e. of blood and tears | RABI 297:7
| Patriotism is not e. | CAVE 73:4 |
| two thousand years is e. | PIUS 290:10 |

enslave impossible to e. | BROU 53:3
entangled middle-sized are alone e. | SHEN 330:5
enter King of England cannot e. | PITT 289:8
enterprise e. is sick | SHAK 327:7
enthusiasm e. moves the world | BALF 26:1
| e. of the people | WELL 379:1 |

entire E. and whole and perfect | SPRI 344:8
| e. surrender | BELH 30:9 |

entrails swords In our own proper e. | SHAK 324:2
entreat e. heaven daily | ELIZ 124:6
entrusted Those e. with arms | WIND 387:1
environed e. with a great ditch | CROM 98:10
environment humdrum issues like the e.

THAT 357:2

environmental any e. group | BRUN 55:2
envy E. is the basis | RUSS 311:1
| in e. of great Caesar | SHAK 324:3 |
| prisoners of e. | ILLI 181:6 |

epigrams despotism tempered by e. | CARL 70:1
episode Marxism is only an e. | POPP 292:11
epistula *Verbosa et grandis e.* | JUVE 195:11
epitaph no man write my e. | EMME 126:7
equal all men are created e. | ANON 11:13
all men are created e.	LINC 219:9
All shall e. be	GILB 146:1
both free and e.	BAGE 23:5
e. division of unequal earnings	ELLI 126:1
e. in dignity and rights	UNIV 368:7
E. *Pay for Equal Work*	ANTH 12:11
men are created e.	JEFF 185:1
more e. than others	ORWE 275:7
talked about e. rights	JOHN 189:7
we are all e.	JUNI 195:4

equality e. such a difficult business | BECQ 30:6
E. would be heaven	TROL 364:11
E. would be heaven	TROL 365:3
majestic e. of the law	FRAN 136:4
neither e. nor freedom	FRIE 138:5
political and social e.	LINC 218:8
spirit of e. is lost	MONT 258:9

equality (*cont.*):
true apostles of e.	ARNO 14:8
We wish, in a word, e.	BAKU 24:4

equalize never e. | BURK 58:10
equals peace between e. | WILS 386:9
equanimity face with e. | GILB 146:7
equations politics and e. | EINS 122:4
equilibrium domination and e. | KISS 207:6
equivocate I will not e. | GARR 141:10
equo E. *ne credite* | VIRG 371:8
Erin for E. dear we fall | SULL 349:9
eripuit E. *coelo fulmen* | TURG 367:7
err most may e. | DRYD 119:3
errands Meet to be sent on e. | SHAK 323:17
error as an 'e. of judgement' | SALI 313:5
e. and oppression	JEFF 187:6
E. has never approached	METT 249:5
no dignity in persevering in e.	PEEL 286:3
ordained e.	VANS 369:4

eruption bodes some strange e. | SHAK 319:5
escutcheon blot on the e. | GRAY 153:6
Eskimo E. forgets his language | OKPI 273:6
espionage e. can be recommended | WEST 380:6
esse E. *quam videri bonus* | SALL 313:11
essenced long e. hair | MACA 230:9
essential Despotism is e. | CARL 70:7
| give up e. liberty | FRAN 137:5 |

established E. Clergy | GLAD 148:5
estate fourth e. of the realm | MACA 228:11
| ordered their e. | ALEX 6:5 |

esteem e. too lightly | PAIN 279:10
état *L'É. c'est moi* | LOUI 225:3
eternal authority of the e. yesterday | WEBE 377:4
eternity some conception of e. | MANC 240:5
ethic protestant e. | WEBE 377:1
ethical e. dimension | COOK 95:6
| nuclear giants and e. infants | BRAD 49:9 |

ethics law floats in a sea of e. | WARR 374:11
Eton decry E. and Harrow | BEVI 38:6
| playing-fields of E. | ORWE 275:11 |
| playing fields of E. | WELL 379:11 |

eunuch prerogative of the e. | STOP 348:8
eunuchs seraglio of e. | FOOT 133:9
Europe all the nations of E. | SALM 314:2
create a nation E.	MONN 257:10
division of E.	GIBB 144:10
dogs of E. bark	AUDE 17:13
E. a continent of energetic mongrels	FISH 131:7
E. by her example	PITT 290:7
E. has never existed	MONN 257:4
E. in danger of plunging	YELT 390:5
E. is a geographical concept	BISM 41:11
E. of nations	DE G 105:8
E. on the lips of politicians	BISM 42:1
E. will decide	DE G 105:4
from mainland E.	THAT 358:9
get out of E.	BOOK 47:8
glory of E.	BURK 58:14
great stocks of E.	YEAT 390:2
lamps are going out all over E.	GREY 155:1
liberation of E.	EISE 122:5

Europe (*cont.*):
map of E. has been changed — CHUR 80:7
part of the community of E. — SALI 312:10
revival of E. — CHUR 83:8
salvation of E. — PITT 290:5
security of E. — MITC 256:6
smaller nationalities of E. — ASQU 15:3
spectre is haunting E. — MARX 245:1
take over the whole of E. — RIDL 302:5
United States of E. — CHUR 83:9
welfare of E. — PEEL 286:8
whole of E. — NAPO 264:8
Without Britain, E. — ERHA 127:3
European e. integration — KOHL 208:6
E. talks of progress — DISR 114:21
E. war might do it — REDM 300:6
E. wars — PAIN 279:5
green pastures of the E. — VERW 370:4
I'm E. — HEWI 171:11
involved in a E. war — BEAV 29:5
on E. Monetary Union — CHIR 78:8
event greatest e. it is — FOX 136:1
not an e. — TALL 352:2
pseudo e. — BOOR 48:1
eventide perfect e. home — STOC 348:4
events create the current of e. — BISM 42:9
e. have controlled me — LINC 220:3
train of e. has carried him — AMER 6:8
We cannot make e. — ADAM 4:8
Everest He is a Chimborazo or E. — ASQU 15:6
evermore name liveth for e. — EPIT 129:3
everyone like e. else — DE G 105:13
everything against e. — KENN 199:13
knowledge of e. — HERO 170:8
Macaulay is of e. — MELB 247:7
robbed a man of e. — SOLZ 340:3
evidence e. against their own understanding
— HALI 158:9
evil all government is e. — O'SU 277:6
all men are e. — MACH 233:5
doing e. — ROOS 307:14
E. be to him who evil thinks — MOTT 262:4
e. effects are gradual — DICE 109:5
e. empire — REAG 299:9
e. that men do lives — SHAK 323:4
for e. to triumph — MISQ 255:2
meet e.-willers — ELIZ 123:9
necessary e. — PAIN 279:1
no e. in the atom — STEV 347:1
respond to e. — HAVE 164:1
willed no e. — STEP 346:5
evils enamoured of existing e. — BIER 40:3
no necessary e. — JACK 183:4
evolution progress of e. — ADAM 2:12
exact not to be e. — BURK 57:10
Politics is not an e. science — BISM 41:6
exactitude *L'e. est la politesse* — LOUI 225:9
examination e. of the acts — HARR 163:2
examiners than my e. — KEYN 201:10
example Europe by her e. — PITT 290:7
No e. is so dangerous — TOCQ 361:6

excellence e. of the English government
— BLAC 43:7
excess poverty and e. — PENN 287:1
excite e. those feelings — ADAM 4:8
excited populace is e. — LA B 208:10
excitement no e. like a big division — CHUR 80:1
exclusion cannot be built on e. — ADAM 2:7
excuse e. every man will plead — SELD 317:3
I will not e. — GARR 141:10
excuses e. for our failures — FULB 139:1
execution Ceaușescus' e. — O'DO 273:1
fascination of a public e. — FOOT 134:4
imminent e. — CLAR 87:12
stringent e. — GRAN 153:4
executioners shouting at her e. — O'DO 273:2
executive e. expression — BRIT 52:3
e. of this country — ACHE 1:8
hold the e. to account — BOOT 48:6
legislative and e. — ADAM 4:1
more corrupt than e. — MONT 258:14
new powers of the e. — DENN 106:10
nominated by the e. — GIBB 145:1
exercise desire to e. it — LEVI 217:6
exertions e. of private citizens — MACA 230:6
saved herself by her e. — PITT 290:7
exigency to the e. of the moment — PEEL 285:8
exile die in e. — LAST 212:12
exiled outlawed or e. — MAGN 238:4
exiles Politicians are e. — GRIG 155:7
existence e. as a nation — PITT 290:6
threatens the e. of life — SONT 340:10
existing enamoured of e. evils — BIER 40:3
paid for e. — KIPL 205:6
exit Such a graceful e. — JUNO 195:8
expectation E. of good news — MCAL 228:5
public e. — GALB 140:5
expectations revolution of rising e. — CLEV 90:4
expediency E. is everything — DEAN 103:5
ground of e. — ROOS 307:14
expedient not a principle, but an e. — DISR 111:8
not only necessary but e. — ARIS 13:13
expenditure annual e. nineteen — DICK 109:7
E. rises to meet income — PARK 283:2
particular e. — EDEN 121:4
tried to get e. under control — BIRC 40:11
expense regardless of e. — PEEL 286:13
expenses facts are on e. — STOP 348:9
expensive got so e. — ROGE 304:4
experience benefit of much e. — BENN 32:3
e. has taught me — EDEN 121:6
E. is the child of Thought — DISR 115:4
man of no e. — CURZ 100:2
experiment social and economic e. — HOOV 176:3
tide of successful e. — JEFF 186:2
experimental e. crops — HURD 179:10
expert e. in being a minority — EWIN 129:8
experts never trust e. — SALI 312:5
explain e. why it didn't happen — CHUR 85:12
Never complain and never e. — BALD 25:12
Never complain and never e. — DISR 115:11
Never e. — FISH 132:2

explained uneasiness when being e. — BALF 27:2
expletive E. deleted — ANON 8:3
explicit Frank and e. — DISR 114:17
exposure public e. — STON 348:6
extempore as his e. sayings — WALP 373:5
extend attempt to e. their system — MONR 258:1
exterminate e. a nation — SPOC 344:7
extermination e. of capitalism — ZINO 391:4
extraordinary e. man — JOHN 191:19
extravagant e. with his own — SALL 313:9
extreme e. equality is taken up — MONT 258:9
extremism e. in the defence of liberty — GOLD 150:9
  E. in the pursuit — JOHN 190:2
extremists dangerous about e. — KENN 199:14
extremity daring pilot in e. — DRYD 118:8
exulting people all e. — WHIT 382:2
eye cast a longing e. — JEFF 185:11
  e.-catching initiatives — BLAI 44:8
  e. to the main chance — CECI 73:8
  neither e. to see — LENT 216:2
  spoils one's e. — HALI 160:2
eyeball e. to eyeball — RUSK 309:10
eyes constitutional e. — LINC 220:9
  e. are full of tears — SHAK 326:12
  e. of Caligula — MITT 256:8
  King of England's e. — LAST 213:4
  Mine e. have seen — HOWE 177:6
  sun in his e. — CHUR 81:7

Fabians civilization of the F. — INGE 181:8
  F. . . . found socialism — HEAL 166:1
  good man fallen among F. — LENI 215:14
face construction in the f. — SHAK 324:8
  f. neither East nor West — NKRU 270:16
  socialism would not lose its human f. — DUBČ 119:13
  stamping on a human f. — ORWE 276:7
  than her f. — THOM 359:5
  unacceptable f. of capitalism — HEAT 167:5
faction Liberty is to f. — MADI 237:6
  made them a f. — MACA 230:1
  party . . . is not a f. — POWE 293:8
  shine in a f. — HALI 159:8
  whisper of a f. — RUSS 311:9
factions good in canvasses and f. — BACO 19:1
factor Falklands F. — THAT 356:11
facts f. are on expenses — STOP 348:9
  f. are sacred — SCOT 316:8
  Get your f. first — TWAI 368:3
  imagination for his f. — SHER 330:10
  politics consists in ignoring f. — ADAM 2:13
  report the f. — ROGE 304:8
  very few f. — PEEL 286:16
faculties borne his f. so meek — SHAK 324:10
  f. of men — MADI 237:7
  From each according to his f. — BAKU 24:4
fade just f. away — MACA 228:9
fail shall not flag or f. — CHUR 81:12
failed they f. before — SLOG 336:14
failing from f. hands — MCCR 232:1

failure crop f. — BLAI 43:12
  political lives end in f. — POWE 294:1
  Success or f. — MACH 233:6
fain F. would I climb — RALE 298:3
fair F. shares for all — SLOG 334:14
fairness excellence as well as f. — ANON 12:2
faith f. and morals hold — WORD 388:5
  f. in a nation of sectaries — DISR 114:2
  f. in The People — DICK 110:2
  f. is something you die for — BENN 32:8
  first article of my f. — GAND 141:3
  good sense and the good f. — GLAD 148:4
  if ye break f. — MCCR 232:1
  Marxism is now a world f. — BENN 32:5
faithful mentally f. to himself — PAIN 278:7
fake one you can f. that — PROV 297:2
Falklands F. Factor — THAT 356:11
  F. thing was a fight — BORG 48:9
fall Another thing to f. — SHAK 325:9
  by dividing we f. — DICK 110:4
  O! what a f. was there — SHAK 323:11
  Then f., Caesar — SHAK 322:10
  yet I fear to f. — RALE 298:3
fallen F. cold and dead — WHIT 382:3
  good man f. among Fabians — LENI 215:14
  planets had f. on me — TRUM 366:1
fallible f. men in Whitehall — POWE 294:3
falling 'f. domino' principle — EISE 122:7
false f. report, if believed — MEDI 246:7
  philosopher, as equally f. — GIBB 144:12
falsehood mass of f. — WILK 383:9
  strife of Truth with F. — LOWE 226:5
falsehoods f. which interest dictates — JOHN 190:14
falters love that never f. — SPRI 344:8
fame came here for f. — DISR 115:19
  damned to everlasting f. — POPE 292:5
  F. and tranquillity — MONT 258:3
  military f. — SHER 331:5
families Great f. of yesterday — DEFO 104:11
family disease in the f. — TREV 363:4
  f. with the wrong members — ORWE 275:10
  have a young f. — FOWL 135:5
  no f. life at Court — THOM 359:4
  running of a f. — MONT 258:2
  Selling off the f. silver — MISQ 255:5
  spend more time with f. — THAT 357:15
  We, your blood f. — SPEN 344:3
famine F. Queen — GONN 150:10
famous advantage of being f. — KISS 207:10
  f. men have the whole earth — PERI 287:9
  Let us now praise f. men — BIBL 39:17
  'twas a f. victory — SOUT 343:10
fanatic f. is a great leader — BROU 53:4
fanaticism f. consists in — SANT 314:5
fanatics Foolish f. — ROOS 307:13
far going a bridge too f. — BROW 54:6
  Mexico, so f. from God — DIAZ 109:4
  quarrel in a f. away country — CHAM 74:10
farce second as f. — MARX 244:7
fardels Who would f. bear — SHAK 319:9
farewell bid the company f. — LAST 212:11

farewell (*cont.*):
    F.! a long farewell   SHAK 320:20
fart can't f. and chew gum   JOHN 190:9
    forgot the f.   ELIZ 125:2
fascination subject myself to his f.   GLAS 149:3
Fascism victims of American F.   ROSE 308:10
fascists 'Communists' to include F.   ANON 8:7
fashion f. in these things   FRAN 137:8
fashions fit this year's f.   HELL 168:1
fastidiousness f. a quality   LEVI 216:8
fat Butter merely makes us f.   GOER 149:7
    f. and long-haired   PLUT 291:3
    men about me that are f.   SHAK 322:1
    that f. gentleman   SHAW 329:3
fate arbiter of others' f.   BYRO 64:6
    decide the f. of the world   DE G 105:4
    f. of Abraham Lincoln   GRIG 155:6
    f. of this country   DISR 112:21
    F., thou art defied   MITC 253:6
    makers of our f.   POPP 292:8
    thy too rigid f.   MONT 259:5
father cut off thy f.'s head   CHAR 75:10
    f. was frightened of his mother   GEOR 144:3
    Had it been his f.   EPIT 128:5
    Lloyd George knew my f.   SONG 342:7
    politique f.   JAME 184:3
    sash my f. wore   SONG 343:3
fatherland unity of our f.   KOHL 208:5
fathers healthiest f.   WHIT 382:5
    Victory has a hundred f.   CIAN 86:13
    years ago our f. brought forth   LINC 219:9
fatness but not to f.   TAYL 354:11
fault f., dear Brutus   SHAK 321:8
Faust behind this shabby F.   HEAL 165:11
favour Fools out of f.   DEFO 104:7
    in f. of the people   BURK 59:10
favourite his f. flies   SHAK 319:13
favours depends Upon your f.   SHAK 318:6
    f. from the great   TAYL 354:6
    sense of future f.   WALP 374:5
fear alive with f.   SCAR 315:8
    begins in f.   COLE 92:6
    concessions of f.   BURK 57:13
    eventide of f.   MORR 260:10
    F. God. Honour the King   KITC 207:11
    f. is the foundation   ADAM 3:14
    f. to negotiate   KENN 198:6
    fourth is freedom from f.   ROOS 306:5
    only thing we have to f.   ROOS 305:6
    Severity breedeth f.   BACO 19:7
    so long as they f.   ACCI 1:3
    try to have no f.   CHES 77:2
    what man living, freed from f.   AESC 5:3
feared neither f. nor flattered   EPIT 128:6
    prince to be f.   MACH 233:9
fearful f. trip is done   WHIT 382:2
fears never of your f.   STEV 347:8
feast Nature's mighty f.   MALT 240:3
feature to be the striking f.   GEOR 143:1
fed clothed, f., and educated   RUSK 310:8
federal Our F. Union   JACK 183:3

fee gorgeous East in f.   WORD 388:6
feeble f. can seldom persuade   GIBB 145:11
    f. government   BURK 59:6
    man of such a f. temper   SHAK 321:7
feed doth this our Caesar f.   SHAK 321:9
feeling appeals to diffused f.   BAGE 21:7
feelings governed more by their f.   ADAM 4:8
feet better to die on your f.   IBAR 180:9
    hotbed of cold f.   EBAN 121:3
    seven f. of English ground   HARO 162:8
    where he put his f.   NICO 266:10
fell It f. by itself   JOHN 189:2
female f. worker slave of that slave   CONN 94:5
    patriotic virtue in the f.   ADAM 2:2
feminist call me a f.   WEST 380:7
    dealing with the early f.   WEST 380:8
fence sat on the f. so long   LLOY 223:17
fences barbed wire f.   JOHN 192:4
    Good f. make good neighbours   FROS 138:10
Fenian grave of a dead F.   COLL 92:7
    left us our F. dead   PEAR 285:1
fens reek o' the rotten f.   SHAK 318:9
Fermanagh dreary steeples of f.   CHUR 80:7
fermenting speech f. in me   GLAD 148:17
fertility by reason of their f.   MONT 259:2
fetish Militarism . . . is f. worship   TAWN 352:7
fetters f. rent in twain   DAVI 102:9
    wear the same f.   VOLT 372:9
fever life's fitful f.   SHAK 325:5
    treaty bred a f.   THOM 359:2
Février Janvier and F.   NICH 266:4
few as grossly as the f.   DRYD 119:3
    disobliging the f.   MACA 230:3
    so much owed by so many to so f.   CHUR 81:14
    they shall be f.   PITT 289:7
fewer one man f.   METT 249:4
fiat *f. justitia*   MANS 241:11
    F. justitia   MOTT 262:3
    F. justitia   WATS 375:11
fiction f. lags after truth   BURK 57:14
    one form of continuous f.   BEVA 37:4
fiddler f. after Paganini   NICO 266:9
fide *Punica f.*   SALL 313:13
fidelity f. to colleagues   LASK 211:1
    pursues us with malignant f.   BALF 27:1
field only inhabitants of the f.   BURK 58:18
    presence on the f.   WELL 379:6
fields In Flanders f.   MCCR 232:1
fiery f. trial through which we pass   LINC 219:7
fifth F. Amendment   DOUG 117:4
fifty F.-four forty   SLOG 334:15
fig f. for those by law protected   BURN 61:4
fight begun to f.   JONE 192:6
    Citizen Army will f.   CONN 94:7
    deadliness to f. Germany   CHUR 79:5
    don't want to f.   SONG 343:5
    Fifty-four forty, or f.   SLOG 334:15
    f. against the future   GLAD 147:10
    f. and fight again   GAIT 139:6
    f. for freedom   PANK 282:5
    f. for freedom and truth   IBSE 181:2

fight (*cont.*):

f. for its King and Country	GRAH 152:4
f. for the living	JONE 192:7
f. for what I believe	CAST 72:3
f. it out on this line	GRAN 153:1
f. no more	JOSE 193:6
f. on the beaches	CHUR 81:12
f. on to the end	HAIG 157:2
f. our country's battles	SONG 341:6
f. to maintain freedom	ROOS 306:4
I f. on	THAT 358:2
I will f.	SITT 332:11
I will not cease from mental f.	BLAK 44:13
put up as good a f.	DILL 110:8
refuse to f.	SLOG 336:10
those who bade me f.	EWER 129:5
too proud to f.	WILS 386:6
Ulster will f.	CHUR 79:9

fighting not f. does matter — STEP 346:4
two periods of f. — BIER 40:4

figures prove anything by f. — CARL 69:7
three sets of f. — ASQU 15:8

fils *F. de Saint Louis* — FIRM 131:5

final f. curtain comes down — MAJO 239:5
f. solution — HEYD 171:12

finality F. is not the language — DISR 112:1

finance F. is the stomach — GLAD 147:7

financial unsordid f. act — CHUR 83:3
with f. acumen — KAUF 196:5

finest f. hour — CHUR 81:13

finger burnt Fool's bandaged f. — KIPL 205:5
f. on the trigger — MACM 236:3
Whose f. — NEWS 268:4

fingers Five sovereign f. — THOM 359:1
pulled our f. out — PHIL 288:6

finish didn't let me f. — BABE 18:9
f. the job — CHUR 82:7

finished f. in the first 100 days — KENN 198:7
f. when he quits — NIXO 270:13
world where England is f. — MILL 251:9

finita f. la commedia — MACM 236:12

fins swims with f. of lead — SHAK 318:6

fire f. brigade and the fire — CHUR 80:10
have kindled a f. — COBB 91:9
neighbour's house is on f. — BURK 58:6
shouting f. in a theatre — HOLM 175:3
take a walk into the f. — ENGE 126:9
wabbling back to the F. — KIPL 205:5

firebell f. in the night — JEFF 186:14

firmament fellow in the f. — SHAK 322:9

first culling of F. Secretaries — MORG 260:3
f. in a village — CAES 64:12
f. in the hearts — LEE 214:7
f. Kinnock in a thousand — KINN 204:9
nothing should be done for the f. time — CORN 96:3
to be called F. Lady — ONAS 274:8

fish pretty kettle of f. — MARY 245:5
shortage of coal and f. — BEVA 36:2

fishes f. in a saucepan — KHRU 202:6
Men lived like f. — SIDN 332:3

fistful for a f. of coins — ZAPA 391:1

fisticuffs argument for f. — CHUR 84:5

fit I am f. for nothing — HERV 170:10

fitful life's f. fever — SHAK 325:5

Fitzdotterel F.'s eldest son — BROU 53:1

five f. per cent — MACA 229:6

fix don't f. it — LANC 209:8
good election can't f. — NIXO 270:1

flag brought back the f. — GRIF 155:3
carry the f. — CHOA 78:9
f. of the United States — BELL 31:1
keep the red f. flying — SONG 343:1
national f. — SUMN 350:5
people's f. is deepest red — SONG 343:1
shall not f. or fail — CHUR 81:12
spare your country's f. — WHIT 382:9

flagpole run it up the f. — PROV 296:12

Flanders part of F. — WALL 373:4

flashes f. of silence — SMIT 339:5

flashing f. out beams of light — JENK 188:2

flat debt, an' a f. — LOWE 226:4

flattered being then most f. — SHAK 322:7
neither feared nor f. — EPIT 128:6

flatterer hypocrite and f. — BLAK 44:11

flatterers sycophants and f. — HARD 161:5
tell him he hates f. — SHAK 322:7
within a week the same f. — HALI 158:8

flatteries against f. — MACH 234:1

flattering f., kissing and kicking — TRUM 366:4

flattery Everyone likes f. — DISR 115:7
f. corrupts — BURK 58:12
f. hurts no one — STEV 346:8

flaws Psychological f. — ANON 10:10

flesh flattered any f. — EPIT 128:6

flies catch small f. — SWIF 350:8
f. off the meat — CHUR 82:3

float f. lazily downstream — SALI 312:4

flog f. the rank and file — ARNO 14:11

flood just cause reaches its f.-tide — CATT 72:10
return it as a f. — GLAD 148:16
taken at the f. — SHAK 324:1

floor I could f. them all — DISR 111:1

flourish Princes and lords may f. — GOLD 150:4

flow blood must yet f. — JEFF 187:2

flower f. of our youth — TREV 363:1
f. of Scotland — WILL 384:1

flowers hundred f. blossom — MAO 242:5

flown birds are f. — CHAR 75:9

foaming f. with much blood — POWE 293:4

focus renewed f. of politics — HAVE 163:9

foe erect and manly f. — CANN 68:10
Where breathes the f. — DRAK 118:4
willing f. and sea room — ANON 12:8

fog F. in Channel — BROC 52:4
sheep scattered in a f. — BRUT 55:3

fogies same old f. — KEAT 197:1

fogs insular country, subject to f. — DISR 114:7

folds f. rippling — SUMN 350:5

follies crimes, f., and misfortunes — GIBB 145:3

follow f. the worse — OVID 277:10
had to f. them — LEDR 214:5

fourth f. estate of the realm   MACA 228:11
   This is the F.   LAST 213:14
   your F. of July   DOUG 117:7
fox compared with f.-hunting   POWE 293:5
   f.-hunting—the wisest religion   HAIL 157:9
   galloping after a f.   WILD 383:6
   My God! They've shot our f.   BIRC 40:10
   Pitt as opposed to F.   BUTL 63:3
   prince must be a f.   MACH 233:11
foxes f. have a sincere interest   ELIO 123:3
foxholes signs on the f.   KENN 199:4
fracture f. the Labour party   KINN 204:10
fragment not a geographical f.   PARN 283:9
fragrance Has she f.   CAUL 73:1
frailty concession to human f.   TAWN 352:11
France by which F. is fed   SULL 350:1
   F. and England   PEEL 286:8
   F. and Germany   CHUR 83:8
   F. has lost a battle   DE G 105:1
   F. is adequately secured   ASQU 15:3
   F. is the coachman   DE G 105:14
   F., mother of arts   DU B 119:14
   F. wants you to take part   CHIR 78:8
   F. was long a despotism   CARL 70:1
   I now speak for F.   DE G 105:2
   one illusion—F.   KEYN 200:7
   safeguard against F.   ADEN 5:1
   wield the sword of F.   DE G 105:3
frank F. and explicit   DISR 114:17
   many f. words   COOK 95:5
fraternal f. blood   WEBS 377:9
fraternité Égalité F.   SLOG 335:11
fraud Force, and f.   HOBB 173:11
   f. and a liar   CONN 94:8
frauds all great men are f.   BONA 46:11
freak grotesque composite f.   HENN 168:6
Fred Here lies F.   EPIT 128:5
Frederick death of F. the Great   BISM 42:7
   F. the Great lost   ANON 8:8
free as a f. lunch   PROV 297:1
   be f.   SHEL 330:3
   born f.   UNIV 368:7
   both f. and equal   BAGE 23:5
   Church shall be f.   MAGN 238:3
   Comment is f.   SCOT 316:8
   died that we might be f.   LARK 210:5
   die to make men f.   HOWE 177:7
   essence of f. government   CALH 65:4
   forever f.   LINC 219:5
   f. again   SOLZ 340:3
   F. at last   EPIT 128:1
   F. at last   KING 203:6
   F. by '93   SLOG 334:16
   f. church   CAVO 73:5
   f., democratic government   TRUM 367:1
   f. development   MARX 245:3
   freedom to the f.   LINC 219:8
   f. man, an American   JOHN 189:4
   f. press not a privilege   LIPP 221:5
   f. society is a society where   STEV 347:3
   half f.   LINC 218:6

free (*cont.*):
   I am not f.   DEBS 103:8
   If a f. society cannot help   KENN 198:5
   ignorant and f.   JEFF 186:13
   in a f. country   BURK 57:21
   in chains than to be f.   KAFK 196:1
   land of the f.   KEY 200:5
   leave their citizens f.   JEFF 187:9
   man is either f. or he is not   BARA 27:9
   Man was born f.   ROUS 309:5
   men everywhere could be f.   LINC 219:4
   Mother of the F.   BENS 33:4
   naturally men born f.   MILT 253:3
   No f. man shall be taken   MAGN 238:4
   not a f. man   STEV 346:12
   not a f. press but a managed   RADC 297:9
   not f. either   SOLZ 340:5
   not only to be f.   PANK 282:5
   people are as f. as they want   BALD 24:5
   prerogative of a f. people   PAIN 280:15
   press is f.   JEFF 185:9
   protection of f. speech   HOLM 175:3
   should themselves be f.   BROO 52:9
   so far kept us f.   JEFF 186:2
   through f. trade   CHOD 79:2
   to be f. to choose   BERL 34:7
   truth which makes men f.   AGAR 5:5
   unless he is f.   CUST 100:6
   Was he f.? Was he happy   AUDE 18:1
   We must be f. or die   WORD 388:5
   wholly slaves or wholly f.   DRYD 119:6
   will to be f.   LIPP 221:6
   Work makes f.   SLOG 334:3
freed not be many f. men   HALI 159:12
freedom abridging the f. of speech   CONS 95:1
   Apostles of f.   CONN 94:4
   better organised than f.   PÉGU 286:18
   conditioned to a f.   KENY 200:4
   destroy the f. of thinking   ADAM 3:11
   efficiencies of f.   GALB 140:11
   enemies of f. do not argue   INGE 181:7
   fight for f. and truth   IBSE 181:2
   fight to maintain f.   ROOS 306:4
   first is f. of speech   ROOS 306:5
   for f. alone   DECL 104:2
   f., and liberty   SHAK 322:13
   F. and not servitude   BURK 57:19
   F. and slavery are mental states   GAND 141:2
   F. an English subject's   DRYD 119:11
   F. cannot exist   METT 249:8
   f. depends on being courageous   THUC 360:3
   f. for the one who thinks differently   LUXE 227:3
   f. for the pike   TAWN 352:10
   F. hunted   PAIN 279:6
   F. is about   GIUL 147:2
   F. is an indivisible   WILL 384:2
   f. is excellent   TOCQ 360:8
   F. is not a gift   NKRU 270:15
   F. is slavery   ORWE 275:14
   f. is something people take   BALD 24:5
   F. is the freedom to say   ORWE 276:3

good (*cont.*):

G. government	CAMP 68:2
G. Government	TROL 365:4
g. is oft interrèd	SHAK 323:4
g. man to do nothing	MISQ 255:2
g. of subjects	DEFO 104:13
g. of the people	CICE 86:15
g. old Cause	MILT 252:12
G. words do not last long	JOSE 193:7
Great and the G.	SAMP 314:3
have a g. thing	SHAK 320:3
I will be g.	VICT 370:7
never had it so g.	MACM 235:9
never had it so g.	SLOG 337:1
never so g. or so bad	MACK 234:4
only g. Indians	SHER 330:7
policy of the g. neighbour	ROOS 305:7
pursuing our own g.	MILL 250:7
than to seem g.	SALL 313:11
they were g. men	STEP 346:5
twelve g. men	BROU 53:2
what g. came of it	SOUT 343:10
what was g. for our country	WILS 384:5
would be a g. idea	GAND 141:5
would do g. to another	BLAK 44:11
goods care for external g.	WEBE 377:2
when g. are private	TAWN 352:11
goodwill In peace; g.	CHUR 85:6
goose on the ground at G. Green	KINN 204:5
steals a g.	SONG 343:4
Gore Vote for G.	SLOG 336:4
gorgeous g. East in fee	WORD 388:6
Goschen forgot G.	CHUR 79:11
gossip I admit there is g.	DISR 113:8
in the g. columns	INGH 182:1
in the g. columns	INGH 182:2
gotcha G.	NEWS 267:3
Götterdämmerung G. without the gods	
	MACD 232:4
Gotto name is Ainsley G.	ERWI 127:4
Gould glitters isn't G.	PRES 294:9
gouverner G. *c'est choisir*	LÉVI 217:8
govern easy to g.	BROU 53:3
good enough to g. another	LINC 218:4
g. according to the common	JAME 184:5
g. in prose	CUOM 99:8
No man is fit to g.	MACA 230:3
not to g.	GLAD 147:8
people g. themselves	THIE 358:12
right to g.	HARR 163:1
to g. is to choose	LÉVI 217:8
governed ability among the g.	TOCQ 361:15
g. by your inferiors	PLAT 290:12
g. in London	BLAI 43:12
kings g. their rude age	BAGE 21:5
nation is not g.	BURK 57:15
not so well g.	HOOK 176:1
governing incapable of g.	CHES 77:5
in the people g.	DICK 110:2
right of g.	FOX 135:7
government abandon a g.	JEFF 186:2

government (*cont.*):

acts of g.	HARR 163:2
all g. is evil	O'SU 277:6
arbitrary g.	CHAR 76:9
art of g.	PEEL 286:11
art of g.	VOLT 372:1
art of g. is	SHAW 328:12
as well be in g.	HELL 167:11
attacks on g.	BREN 51:2
attack the G.	CHUR 84:1
become the most corrupt g.	JEFF 185:13
British g.	HAMI 160:6
business of g.	LAWS 211:8
constitution and its g.	PAIN 281:2
corruption of each g.	MONT 258:8
deal with the g.	HOLM 175:4
definition of the best g.	HALI 159:3
duty of g.	PAIN 279:8
enable the g. to control	MADI 238:1
end of g.	ADAM 3:13
essence of free g.	CALH 65:4
Every g. will do	LEWI 217:9
excellence of the English g.	BLAC 43:7
feeble g.	BURK 59:6
for a bad g.	TOCQ 361:12
forms of g.	POPE 292:4
for the federal g.	REAG 299:11
four pillars of g.	BACO 19:11
function of a g.	PALM 281:11
get all of the g.	FRIE 138:8
Good G.	TROL 365:4
g. above the law	SCAR 315:5
G. acquired the tact	WEST 380:8
G. and co-operation	RUSK 310:13
G. and public opinion	SHAW 328:7
g. as an adversary	BRUN 55:2
G. at Washington lives	GARF 141:6
g. been instituted	HAMI 160:9
g. by crony	ICKE 181:5
g. by the people	CAMP 68:2
g. by the uneducated	CHES 78:4
G., even in its best state	PAIN 279:1
G. is a contrivance	BURK 58:11
g. is best	THOR 359:8
G. is dangerously ill	BENN 33:2
g. is influenced by	SMIT 333:8
G. is like a big baby	REAG 299:3
G. . . . is simply not the channel	KENN 197:9
g. it deserves	MAIS 238:9
g. of Britain's isle	SHAK 320:14
g. of laws, and not of men	ADAM 3:4
G. of laws and not of men	FORD 134:7
g. of statesmen	DISR 113:14
G. of the busy	SELD 317:6
g. of the people	LINC 219:9
g. of the people	PAGE 278:6
g. of the world	DISR 113:8
g. was a practical thing	BURK 57:6
g. which imprisons	THOR 359:9
g. which robs Peter	SHAW 327:17
g. will do for me	NIXO 270:5

great (*cont.*):

G. and the Good	SAMP 314:3
g. break through	SHEN 330:5
G. is the hand	THOM 359:2
g. man down	SHAK 319:13
g. man helped the poor	MACA 230:12
g. men	ACTO 1:10
G. men are not always	BIBL 39:9
g. men make mistakes	CHUR 79:11
g. ones devoured the small	SIDN 332:3
g. qualities, the imperious will	BAGE 21:1
G. Society	JOHN 189:10
g. things are done	BISM 42:6
grown so g.	SHAK 321:9
Ill can he rule the g.	SPEN 344:5
Madness in g. ones	SHAK 319:10
Men in g. place	BACO 19:5
Rightly to be g.	SHAK 319:16
weren't such a g. man	GLAD 147:4
with small men no g. thing	MILL 250:14
greater g. than a private citizen	TACI 351:10
they behold a g.	SHAK 322:2
greatest g. event it is	FOX 136:1
g. week	NIXO 270:3
life to live as the g. he	RAIN 297:10
greatness abuse of g.	SHAK 322:3
ascent to g.	GIBB 145:2
farewell, to all my g.	SHAK 320:20
G., with private men	MASS 246:1
His g. weighed	SHAK 319:6
nature of all g.	BURK 57:10
Grecian G. horse	HAMI 160:10
greed G. is healthy	BOES 45:6
G. works	WEIS 378:5
greedy G. for the property	SALL 313:9
Greek G. as a treat	CHUR 85:3
Greeks G. in this American empire	MACM 235:5
I fear the G.	VIRG 371:8
green England's g. and pleasant land	BLAK 44:13
g. pastures of the European	VERW 370:4
g. shoots of economic spring	LAMO 209:5
g. shoots of recovery	MISQ 254:7
Make it a g. peace	DARN 101:7
My passport's g.	HEAN 166:9
wearin' o' the G.	SONG 342:2
Wherever g. is worn	YEAT 389:5
greenest g. political party	JONE 192:8
Greenpeace G. had a ring to it	HUNT 179:7
grenadier single Pomeranian g.	BISM 42:10
grey good g. head	TENN 355:7
in my g. hairs	WOLS 388:2
this old g. head	WHIT 382:9
grief could I but rate My g.	MONT 259:5
griefs But not my g.	SHAK 326:9
soothed the g.	MACA 230:4
grievance deep-rooted g.	CRIL 97:4
desire to have a g.	PEEL 286:12
grievances discovery of g.	SALI 312:8
grind Laws g. the poor	GOLD 150:7
grooves ringing g. of time	TENN 355:5
grotesque g. chaos	KINN 204:7

grotesque (*cont.*):

g. situation	HAUG 163:7
ground gain a little patch of g.	SHAK 319:15
let us sit upon the g.	SHAK 326:6
grovelling g. tyranny	DISR 115:2
groves g. of *their* academy	BURK 58:16
growth children of a larger g.	CHES 77:3
neoclassical endogenous g.	BROW 53:7
guard Be on your g.	OFFI 274:7
guards Brigade of G.	MACM 236:10
Up G. and at them	WELL 379:2
who is to guard the g.	JUVE 195:10
gubu *acronym* G.	HAUG 163:7
Gucci G. shoes	MURD 263:3
guessing g. what was at the other side	
	WELL 379:10
guided g. missiles	KING 203:12
guiding g.-star of a whole brave nation	
	MOTL 261:5
guilt beggar would recognise g.	PARS 284:6
blood with g. is bought	SHEL 329:11
g. of Stalin	GORB 151:3
guilty with Hitler g.	TAYL 353:10
guinea but the g.'s stamp	BURN 61:1
g. you have in your pocket	RUSK 310:12
Guinness pint of G.	MALL 239:12
gulag G. archipelago	SOLZ 340:4
word 'g.' did not appear	WU 389:1
gum can't fart and chew g.	JOHN 190:9
gun grows out of the barrel of a g.	MAO 242:3
g. in the other	BRUT 55:4
we have got the Maxim G.	BELL 31:4
gunfire towards the sound of g.	GRIM 155:8
gunpowder G., Printing	CARL 69:11
G. Treason and Plot	SONG 343:2
invention of g.	MONT 258:5
printing, g., and the magnet	BACO 20:1
guns rather have butter or g.	GOER 149:7
with g. not with butter	GOEB 149:5
guts g. of the last priest	DIDE 110:5
Mrs Thatcher 'showed g.'	KINN 204:5
strangled with the g.	MESL 249:2

habeas corpus protection of *h.*	JEFF 186:4
habits prejudices and h.	GIBB 145:13
habitual h. hatred	WASH 375:8
hack Do not h. me	MONM 257:3
hair cutting h.	BURN 61:1
h. blown about	PRES 294:8
long essenced h.	MACA 230:9
half h. slave	LINC 218:6
Too clever by h.	SALI 312:3
Too clever by h.	SALI 313:8
halitosis h. of the intellect	ICKE 181:3
Hallelujah H. . . . Never again	ALBR 6:2
hallow cannot h. this ground	LINC 219:9
halls h. of Montezuma	SONG 341:6
Hamlet putting on H.	MACL 234:6
hamsters tigress surrounded by h.	BIFF 40:5
hand bite the h. that fed them	BURK 59:8

hand (*cont.*):
  h. impresses upon them — SMIT 333:5
  h. into the Hand of God — HASK 163:3
  h. that signed the paper — THOM 359:1
  h. that signed the treaty — THOM 359:2
  h. to execute — CLAR 87:5
  h. to execute — GIBB 145:9
  h.-up not a hand-out — BLAI 44:4
  h. which executes — TAYL 354:5
  invisible h. in politics — FRIE 138:3
  led by an invisible h. — SMIT 337:4
  lifted h. between — HEWI 171:9
  Thy h., great Anarch — POPE 292:1
handbag hitting it with her h. — CRIT 97:7
  wield a h. — HESE 171:5
handkerchief lady's pocket h. — LLOY 223:5
hands Look, Daddy, no h. — HOGG 174:6
  pair of h. — BAUE 28:8
  unproductive h. — SMIT 337:5
  With mine own h. — SHAK 326:11
hang all h. together — FRAN 136:9
  didn't h. John C. Calhoun — JACK 183:7
  H. yourself, brave Crillon — HENR 169:1
  let him h. there — EHRL 122:1
  with which to h. them — MISQ 254:3
hanged h., drawn, and quartered — PEPY 287:3
  h. for stealing horses — HALI 159:13
  if they'd been h. — DENN 106:9
hanging h. men an' women — SONG 342:2
hangman fit for the h. — LASK 211:1
happen fools said would h. — MELB 247:12
happiness H. depends on being free — THUC 360:3
  H. lies in conquering — GENG 142:6
  h. of an individual — JOHN 191:8
  h. of society — ADAM 3:13
  h. of the greatest number — BENT 33:7
  h. of the human race — BURK 58:4
  human life and h. — JEFF 186:9
  liberty and the pursuit of h. — ANON 11:13
  my people's h. — ELIZ 124:6
  no h. exists — CUST 100:6
  pursuit of h. — JEFF 185:1
  result h. — DICK 109:7
happy Be h. for me — BOOT 48:5
  Few people can be h. — RUSS 311:6
  I die h. — LAST 212:9
  none should be h. — JOHN 191:15
  someone, somewhere, may be h. — MENC 248:4
  splendid and a h. land — GOLD 150:5
  Was he free? Was he h. — AUDE 18:1
harbour voyage not a h. — TOYN 362:5
hard h. dog to keep — CLIN 90:8
  h. on soft drugs — FLYN 133:3
hare usually beat the h. — MAJO 238:10
harlot prerogative of the h. — KIPL 207:1
harm as much h. as it can — LEWI 217:9
  h. wercheth To the povere — LANG 210:3
  prevent h. to others — MILL 250:8
  What h. have I ever done — TAWN 353:1
Harold H. knows best — CROS 98:15
Harry little touch of H. — SHAK 320:6

harvest h. in England — BUTT 63:8
haste what h. I can to be gone — LAST 213:5
hat man who doesn't wear a h. — BEAV 30:3
hatchet cut it with my h. — WASH 375:3
hatchets buried all the h. — WILS 385:11
hate h. some other person — RUSS 311:6
  hearts that h. thee — SHAK 321:2
  I h. war — ROOS 305:9
  letter of h. — OSBO 277:3
  Let them h. — ACCI 1:3
  People must learn to h. — MAND 240:10
  roughness breedeth h. — BACO 19:7
  seen much to h. here — MILL 251:9
hated rather h. the ruling few — BENT 33:9
hates just heaven now h. — EPIT 128:4
  world of voluble h. — TREV 363:3
hating By h. vices too much — BURK 59:3
hatred Great h., little room — YEAT 389:7
  habitual h. — WASH 375:8
  mutual h. — BURK 57:5
  What we need is h. — GENE 142:4
hatreds h. which sounded — TROL 364:6
  organization of h. — ADAM 2:9
hats shocking bad h. — WELL 379:8
Haughey H. buried at midnight — O'BR 272:5
havoc Cry, 'H.!' and let slip — SHAK 323:1
hawk h. is in the air — DISR 113:2
hawking H. his conscience — MISQ 254:8
hay live on h. — HILL 172:4
he H. would, wouldn't he — RICE 301:8
head admirable h. of state — HAIL 157:10
  good grey h. — TENN 355:7
  h. beneath the feet — OVID 278:1
  h. in the sand — WILS 386:8
  h. of the Cabinet — MORL 260:9
  h. that wears a crown — SHAK 320:4
  h. to contrive — CLAR 87:5
  h. to contrive — GIBB 145:9
  h. which propounds — TAYL 354:5
  his brains go to his h. — ASQU 15:12
  ideas of its "h." — DISR 111:9
  If you can keep your h. — KIPL 205:7
  On my h. — DISR 111:2
  shorter by the h. — ELIZ 124:1
  show my h. to the people — DANT 101:6
  strike at the h. — BURK 60:13
  which way the h. lies — RALE 298:5
  your good h. — ELIZ 124:5
headmasters H. have powers — CHUR 85:2
healing not heroics, but h. — HARD 161:8
health h. of the whole human race — TOYN 362:7
  National H. Service — MACL 234:6
  National H. Service — THAT 356:12
  seriously damage your h. — OFFI 274:6
healthy Greed is h. — BOES 45:6
  h. state of political life — MILL 250:10
hear H. ye! Hear ye — ANON 8:14
  prefer not to h. — AGAR 5:5
  you will h. me — DISR 111:3
heard I will be h. — GARR 141:10
  right to be h. — HUMP 179:2

hearers attentive and favourable h.   HOOK 176:1
heart broken h. lies here   MACA 230:11
  committed adultery in my h.   CART 71:5
  examine my own h.   DE V 107:6
  Fourteen h. attacks   JOPL 193:3
  h. and stomach of a king   ELIZ 124:2
  h. to resolve   GIBB 145:9
  If thy h. fails thee   ELIZ 124:10
  Irishman's h.   SHAW 328:4
  its h. should be   HUME 178:11
  just a h.-beat away   MISQ 255:3
  key of my h.   CLAY 88:11
  lying in my h.   MARY 245:10
  make a stone of the h.   YEAT 389:4
  So the h. be right   RALE 298:5
  with a mighty h.   SHAK 320:5
heartbeat h. from the Presidency   STEV 347:4
hearth skeletons on their own h.   MITC 253:5
hearts all that human h. endure   GOLD 150:8
  h. of his countrymen   LEE 214:7
  Kind h. are more than coronets   TENN 355:4
  offspring of cold h.   BURK 58:15
  O you hard h.   SHAK 321:5
  queen in people's h.   DIAN 109:1
heat don't like the h.   PROV 296:9
  not without dust and h.   MILT 252:9
  white h. of revolution   WILS 384:9
  white h. of technology   MISQ 256:2
heather cries 'Nothing but h.'   MACD 232:3
heaven absolute h.   CALL 66:8
  ascend to h.   FIRM 131:5
  consent of h.   JONS 193:2
  Equality would be h.   TROL 364:11
  Equality would be h.   TROL 365:3
  house as nigh h.   MORE 259:10
  just h. now hates   EPIT 128:4
  looketh this way to H.   CECI 74:1
  not go to H.   JEFF 185:7
  Pennies don't fall from h.   THAT 356:6
  sudden journey to h.   BEAV 29:10
  though h. perish   ADAM 4:3
  young was very h.   WORD 388:4
Hebrew H. conjuror   CARL 70:9
hedge divinity doth h. a king   SHAK 320:1
hedgehogs throwing h. under me   KHRU 202:7
heights commanding h. of the economy
    BEVA 37:2
hell agreement with h.   GARR 141:11
  come hot from h.   SHAK 323:1
  do science in h.   VAUG 369:6
  H. has no terror for me   LARK 210:6
  H. of not making money   CARL 70:6
  H. or Connaught   CROM 98:11
  tell you to go to h.   STIN 348:3
  they think it is h.   TRUM 366:9
  to the gates of H.   PIUS 290:9
  War is h., and all that   HAY 164:3
helmsman change the h.   BAGE 21:2
help God h. me   LUTH 227:1
  h. and support of the woman   EDWA 121:10
  I'm here to h.   REAG 300:2

helped shall have h. it   DICK 109:10
helpless h. and ineffectual   HERB 170:6
helps Nobody ever h. me   TRUT 367:2
hemisphere portion of this h.   MONR 258:1
hen h.-roost to rob   LLOY 222:6
  take a wet h.   KHRU 202:4
heraldry boast of h.   GRAY 154:1
herd Morality is the h.-instinct   NIET 269:3
here H. I am   MACM 235:2
hereditary h. government   PAIN 280:6
  idea of h. legislators   PAIN 280:4
heresy mislike it, h.   HOBB 173:7
hero acted like a h.   WALP 373:6
  don't want to be a h.   STOP 348:11
  may be the H. of a novel   MACA 231:1
heroes fit country for h.   LLOY 222:12
  h. to govern you   CARL 70:10
  Unhappy the land that needs h.   BREC 50:8
heroics not h., but healing   HARD 161:8
Herr H. and there   COOK 95:5
hewers h. of wood and drawers of water
    BIBL 39:2
hiding bloody good h.   GRAN 152:7
high Be ye never so h.   DENN 106:7
  Detestation of the h.   DICK 110:1
  Men in h. places   TAYL 354:12
  taking the h. ground   MAND 241:5
higher h. the monkey climbs   PROV 296:8
  not taking a h. road   NIXO 270:12
highest h. bidder   WASH 375:5
  to the h. office   MCCA 231:4
hill city upon a h.   WINT 387:2
hills Black H. belong to me   SITT 332:11
  red h. of Georgia   KING 203:5
hinterland She has no h.   HEAL 166:4
hip smote them h. and thigh   BIBL 39:3
hired They h. the money   COOL 95:10
hireling Pay given to a state h.   JOHN 190:13
Hiroshima bomb on H.   TRUM 366:2
historian h. looks behind   TAYL 353:5
historians H. in general   TREV 363:8
history admired your h.   MURR 263:4
  cancer of human h.   SONT 340:10
  cannot escape h.   LINC 219:7
  discerned in h. a plot   FISH 131:6
  dustbin of h.   TROT 365:9
  end of h.   FUKU 138:11
  fair summary of h.   FRAN 136:7
  hand of h.   BLAI 44:3
  H. came to a .   SELL 317:13
  H. gets thicker   TAYL 353:2
  H. is a gallery of pictures   TOCQ 361:1
  H. is almost always   NEHR 265:10
  H. . . . is, indeed, little more   GIBB 145:3
  h. is nothing more   VOLT 372:4
  h. is on our side   KHRU 202:3
  H. is past politics   FREE 138:1
  H. littered with the wars   POWE 293:2
  h. of class struggles   MARX 245:2
  h. of progress   MACA 229:10
  h. of the world   DISR 112:8

Ill (*cont.*):

i.-trained spaniel — CRAN 96:7
one-third of a nation i.-housed — ROOS 305:10
vain, i.-natured — DEFO 104:8
warn you not to fall i. — KINN 204:6
illegal i. we do immediately — KISS 207:4
it is not i. — NIXO 270:14
Nothing is i. if — YOUN 390:7
illegally accomplishes great things i. — BALZ 27:6
illegitimate i. parents — JOSE 194:3
illness i. should attend — SHAK 324:9
ills i. of democracy — SMIT 337:11
illusion one i.—France — KEYN 200:7
illusionist i. without ideals — MACL 234:9
illusions human i. — LYND 227:5
idealist without i. — KENN 199:10
image Political i. — MOND 257:2
spelling the word i. — PEYT 288:3
imagination i. cold and barren — BURK 57:14
i. for his facts — SHER 330:10
nothing but his i. — SHAW 328:4
Wanting i. — DISR 114:14
immaturity expression of human i. — BRIT 52:3
immobility i. of British institutions — ASQU 15:4
immoral good and i. — CHUR 80:6
impartial decline utterly to be i. — CHUR 80:7
impeachment articles of i. — ANON 8:14
not grounds for i. — DOWD 117:10
impediments i.—in common times — BAGE 21:1
imperative categorical i. — KANT 196:2
imperfect i. man — JEFF 186:5
imperial our great I. family — ELIZ 125:4
imperialism I. is the monopoly stage — LENI 215:5
wild-cat I. — ROSE 308:4
imperialisms prey of rival i. — KENY 200:4
imperialist i. system — MAND 240:8
imperialists make the i. dance — KHRU 202:6
imperially Learn to think I. — CHAM 74:7
imperium I. *et Libertas* — DISR 113:9
implacable i. in hate — DRYD 118:9
importance taking decisions of i. — PARK 283:6
important being less i. — MONT 258:2
no longer i. enough — MCCO 231:10
importunate no less i. — MONT 258:2
impossible i. to be silent — BURK 60:14
i. to carry the heavy burden — EDWA 121:10
impostors treat those two i. — KIPL 205:7
imprisoned taken or i. — MAGN 238:4
improvement schemes of political i. — JOHN 191:5
improvements no great i. — MILL 250:2
impulses man's noblest i. — KENN 197:9
impunity provokes me with i. — MOTT 262:5
inactivity genius for i. — LIPP 221:3
masterly i. — MACK 234:5
inadvertence chance or i. — HAIL 157:8
inattentive i. to his duty — JACK 183:2
incapable i. of governing — CHES 77:5
income Annual i. twenty pounds — DICK 109:7
dread a dead-level of i. — TAWN 352:9
Expenditure rises to meet i. — PARK 283:2
moderate i. — DURH 120:5

Income (*cont.*):

real i. is increased — KEYN 201:7
incomes i. of the rich — SHAW 328:2
incompatible united things long i. — TACI 351:3
incomprehensible use the i. — ZOBE 391:5
inconceivable not totally i. — HEAT 167:8
inconsistency little i. at times — OWEN 278:3
inconveniences i., and those weighty — HOOK 176:2
i. there must be — HALI 159:3
incorruptible seagreen I. — CARL 69:13
increase another man's price i. — WILS 385:8
increasing has increased, is i. — DUNN 120:3
indefensible defence of the i. — ORWE 276:13
indemnity BILL OF I. . . . . FOR RAID — KRUG 208:7
independence i. as dearly — ANON 12:2
i. of America — SHEL 329:7
i. of judges — DENN 106:8
right to i. — NAMI 264:3
war for i. — MCAL 228:4
independent colonies will all be i. — DISR 111:13
entirely i. — TOCQ 361:12
free and i. States — ADAM 3:6
free and i. states — LEE 214:8
to be i. — LOWE 226:4
when they are i. — DISR 112:3
indestructible i. Union — CHAS 76:12
India I. adds nothing — GLAD 148:6
I. will awake to life — NEHR 265:5
peaceably and happily in I. — VICT 371:1
to rule in I. — NEHR 265:13
Indian I. Affairs are concerned — ACHE 1:8
I. Crown — ROSS 308:12
I. in blood and colour — MACA 231:3
Indiana I. were running it — DELO 105:16
Indians I. are you — BALD 24:7
I. have the most — GALB 140:8
like the I. — PEEL 285:11
only good I. — SHER 330:7
indictment i. against an whole people — BURK 57:17
indifference from total i. — HYDE 180:7
Indignatio I. *principis mors est* — MORE 259:9
indignation permanent i. — VALÉ 368:10
indiscretion cliché and an i. — MACM 235:8
individual cult of the i. — KHRU 202:2
each separate i. — ROBE 303:3
injustice done to an i. — JUNI 195:5
liberty of the i. — MILL 250:11
individualism system of rugged i. — HOOV 176:4
individuals things which i. are doing — KEYN 201:3
indivisible i. word — WILL 384:2
Peace is i. — LITV 221:7
indomitable i. Irishry — YEAT 390:1
indoors i. and no heavy lifting — ABBO 1:1
industrial developing our i. strategy — BENN 32:3
I. Revelation — SELL 317:11
military-i. complex — EISE 123:1
industry i. is to be paralysed — TAWN 352:12
national i. of Prussia — MIRA 253:4
not his i. only — BURK 60:5

industry (*cont.*):
permit a cottage i.   MARC 242:7
ineffectual i. liberal   FRAY 137:10
inefficiencies i. of dictatorship   GALB 140:11
inequality i. and subordination   JOHN 192:2
inevitability i. of gradualness   WEBB 376:10
inevitable i. the Titanic   HAGU 156:4
war regarded as i.   KENN 197:10
inexactitude terminological i.   CHUR 80:2
inexorable deaf, i.   SIDN 332:5
infâme *écrasez l'i.*   VOLT 372:7
infamous rich, quiet, and i.   MACA 229:14
infamy date which will live in i.   ROOS 306:6
infancy Nations have their i.   BOLI 46:4
infection Against i.   SHAK 326:2
inferior disgraced by the i.   SHAW 328:14
make you feel i.   ROOS 305:3
inferiority acknowledgement of i.   CALH 65:5
inferiors English want *i.*   TOCQ 362:1
governed by your i.   PLAT 290:12
infidelity I. does not consist   PAIN 278:7
inflation about i.   HOME 175:12
little i.   HEND 168:5
place where i. is made   FRIE 138:7
inflexible we must be i.   CHUR 82:1
influence exercise i. and not authority   ACTO 1:10
i. into affluence   JOHN 190:10
i. of the Crown   DUNN 120:3
under the name of I.   BURK 59:11
inform i. the reader   ACHE 1:7
ingeminate i. the word *Peace*   CLAR 87:6
inhale didn't i.   CLIN 90:9
if he doesn't i.   STEV 346:8
inherit i. the people   PAIN 280:6
inhumanity insufficient i.   ANON 9:6
iniquity hated i.   LAST 212:12
initiatives eye-catching i.   BLAI 44:8
injuries i. and attempts of other men   LOCK 224:5
i. which it is necessary   MACH 234:2
revenge for slight i.   MACH 233:8
injustice I. anywhere   KING 203:3
i. done to an individual   JUNI 195:5
i. makes democracy necessary   NIEB 268:10
I. was as common   REUT 300:10
protect him against i.   PALM 281:9
innocence badge of lost i.   PAIN 279:1
ceremony of i. is drowned   YEAT 389:8
could claim i.   TAYL 353:10
innocent i. men, women, and children   JEFF 187:4
sweat of the i.   JACK 183:9
We are i.   ROSE 308:9
innovate i. is not to reform   BURK 57:4
innovation i. can only be occasional   BAGE 20:4
that of I.   EMER 126:4
inoperative all previous statements i.   ZIEG 391:3
inquisition before the I.   LIVI 221:11
less than an i.   HALI 159:9
insane every hereditary monarch was i.
                                                      BAGE 22:8
inseparable one and i.   WEBS 377:8
inside i. the tent pissing out   JOHN 190:5

insidious i. and crafty animal   SMIT 337:7
insignificance of the utmost i.   CURZ 100:2
insignificant most i. office   ADAM 3:8
insincerity enemy of clear language i.
                                                      ORWE 276:12
unfathomable depths of i.   ANON 11:7
insolent i. in their tenor   SHEL 329:6
insoluble political ones are i.   HOME 175:11
instantaneous i. courage   NAPO 264:11
institution i. of government   BURK 60:11
i. which does not suppose   ROBE 303:5
institutions acquiring their i.   HAIL 157:8
comprehending the great i.   BAGE 23:13
critic of our i.   BAGE 21:15
immobility of British i.   ASQU 15:4
I. govern relationships   MONN 257:9
no public i.   SMIT 337:8
thinks i. are wiser   POWE 293:11
instrument State is an i.   STAL 345:1
instruments work by such i.   PEEL 286:11
insular i. both in situation and in mind   BAGE 22:7
i. country, subject to fogs   DISR 114:7
insult threatened her with i.   BURK 58:13
insurance National compulsory i.   CHUR 82:13
insurrection involving i.   MACN 237:4
intact is there, i.   TRIM 363:11
integration not fighting for i.   MALC 239:10
intellect halitosis of the i.   ICKE 181:3
second-class i.   HOLM 175:6
subtlety of i.   MORL 260:5
intellectual i. capital   CALL 66:4
i. resistance   O'BR 272:4
intellectuals characterize themselves as i.
                                                      AGNE 5:7
treachery of the i.   BEND 31:7
intelligence in charge of the I. Service
                                                      FORS 134:12
so little i.   JENK 188:4
started at the i.   SOUT 344:1
underestimating the i.   MENC 248:11
intelligent honest and i.   ORWE 276:15
intelligible i. government   BAGE 21:4
intensity full of passionate i.   YEAT 389:8
intent sides of my i.   SHAK 325:1
intention i. to keep my counsel   GLAD 148:8
intentions i. of a government   GALB 140:2
only had good i.   THAT 357:10
interest I., not sentiment   CHES 77:4
i. that keeps peace   CROM 98:7
its duty and its i.   WASH 375:8
natural i. of money   MACA 229:6
regard to their own i.   SMIT 333:6
interests consult the i.   PEEL 285:12
Our i. are eternal   PALM 281:8
pursue their respective i.   JEVO 188:5
interfered i. too much   MELB 247:4
interference No i.   ARGE 13:4
internal destroyed by an i. vice   MONT 258:10
international i. finance system   LIVI 222:2
Internationale L'I.   SONG 341:5

interpreted i. the world   MARX 244:9
interpreters i. between us and the millions
    MACA 231:3
interrèd good is oft i.   SHAK 323:4
intervention state i.   DICE 109:5
interview but an i.   BOOR 48:1
interviews result of i.   TAYL 354:2
intimacy avoid any i.   KITC 207:11
intimidation without i.   ROBE 303:9
intolerable behaviour was i.   MAJO 239:6
intolerant they are i.   KENN 199:14
intoxicated i. with power   BURK 56:7
invasion i. by an idea   HUGO 178:3
invention [bureaucracy's] specific i.   WEBE 377:6
    i. is unfruitful   BURK 57:14
inverse i. proportion to the sum   PARK 283:5
inverted like i. Micawbers   GUED 156:1
investigation i. and thought   HALD 157:12
invisible i. hand in politics   FRIE 138:3
    led by an i. hand   SMIT 337:4
involuntary It was i.   KENN 199:8
IRA deal with the I.   PAIS 281:4
Ireland affection for 'I.'   CONN 94:8
    bound to lose I.   GLAD 149:2
    coming to I. today   GEOR 143:4
    dance with me in I.   ROBI 303:12
    dying for I.   HUME 178:10
    evacuation of I.   GRIF 155:3
    God save I.   LAST 212:7
    God save I.   SULL 349:9
    have a united I.   DE V 107:9
    how's poor ould I.   SONG 342:2
    inhabiting island of I.   O'BR 272:3
    I. bound to England   PARN 283:12
    I., Ireland!   GLAD 147:5
    I., Ireland, Ireland   GLAD 148:11
    I. is mentioned   SMIT 339:1
    I. is not a geographical   PARN 283:9
    I., long a province   DAVI 102:9
    I.'s battle   CONN 94:6
    I.'s opportunity   PROV 296:5
    I. unfree shall never be at peace   PEAR 285:1
    I. we dreamed of   DE V 108:1
    I. where people are not   MCAL 227:12
    jurisdiction in I.   ADAM 2:6
    knew I. too little   MACA 228:6
    many parties in I.   PEEL 286:12
    my love for I.   CARS 70:17
    now handling I.   WEST 380:8
    Out of I. have we come   YEAT 389:7
    pacify I.   GLAD 147:11
    parties in Northern I.   MITC 256:3
    people of I.   TONE 362:3
    Romantic I.'s dead and gone   YEAT 389:9
    split I.   BRUG 55:1
    what I have got for I.   COLL 92:8
    worst enemy I. ever had   MITC 253:7
    would had been for I.   LAST 214:3
Irish answer to the I. Question   SELL 317:12
    for an I. purpose   DAVI 103:2
    I. are ashamed   MARV 244:2

Irish (*cont.*):
    I. Citizen Army   CONN 94:7
    I. descent   ROBI 303:11
    I. Question   DISR 111:5
    of the I. Brigade   DAVI 102:7
    serve the I. people   ROBI 303:14
    what the I. people wanted   DE V 107:6
Irishman common name of I.   TONE 362:3
    I'm an I.   HEWI 171:11
    I. has no sense of   PEEL 286:15
    I.'s heart   SHAW 328:4
Irishmen appeal to all I.   GEOR 143:4
    I. in her Parliament   BALF 26:3
Irishry indomitable I.   YEAT 390:1
iron become an i. cage   WEBE 377:2
    he's got i. teeth   GROM 155:10
    i.-armed soldier   SONG 342:4
    i. curtain   CHUR 83:7
    i. curtain   CRIL 97:4
    i. has entered into his soul   LLOY 223:17
    i. lady   ANON 9:8
    I. Lady   THAT 356:5
    through blood and i.   BISM 42:5
    wood painted to look like i.   BISM 42:3
irrationality i. of the world   WEBE 377:5
is what the meaning of 'i.' is   CLIN 91:4
Islam I. has established them   KHOM 201:13
island everyone on this i.   AHER 5:10
    never make this i. all her own   WALL 373:3
    rough i.-story   TENN 355:11
isle sceptered i.   SHAK 326:2
isms All the i. are wasms   ANON 7:6
isolated Continent i.   BROC 52:4
    splendidly i.   FOST 135:3
isolation Splendid i.   NEWS 267:14
isolationist find an i.   RUSK 310:2
Israel glory is departed from I.   BIBL 39:4
    prophet in I.   BIBL 39:6
Italy in I. for thirty years   WELL 378:7
    I. is a geographical expression   METT 249:3
itch poor i. of your opinion   SHAK 318:5
itself contained nothing but i.   ADAM 2:11

jack J. became a gentleman   SHAK 326:15
jaguar park one J.   HAGU 156:8
jails not enough j.   HUMP 179:1
jam j. to-morrow   CARR 70:14
    j. we thought was for tomorrow   BENN 32:2
James King J. stay behind   SONG 341:3
Jameson RAID BY DR J.   KRUG 208:7
Janvier J. and Février   NICH 266:4
Japan J.'s advantage   HIRO 172:6
jaw j.-jaw is always better   CHUR 84:10
jeers flouts and j.   DISR 113:1
Jeffrey I am cross with J.   ARCH 13:1
jellybeans way of eating j.   REAG 299:7
Jena lost the battle of J.   ANON 8:8
Jerusalem was J. builded here   BLAK 44:12
jests to his memory for his j.   SHER 330:10
Jesus *bon Sansculotte J.*   DESM 107:4

Jesus (*cont.*):
 thinks he is J. Christ   CLEM 89:6
Jew especially a J.   MALA 239:8
 J. and the language   CELA 74:3
 J. of Tarsus   BIBL 39:25
 old J.! That is the man   BISM 42:4
jewel j. in the crown   GRAY 153:8
Jewish murderers of J. children   WIES 383:3
 national home for the J. people   BALF 26:4
 total solution of J. question   GOER 149:8
Jews last J. to die   MEIR 247:1
 When Hitler attacked the J.   NIEM 269:1
jingo Be a little J. if you can   CHAM 74:5
 by j. if we do   SONG 343:5
job finish the j.   CHUR 82:7
 hold down his j.   NICO 268:8
 j. creation scheme   HENN 168:7
 MP is the sort of j.   ABBO 1:1
 neighbour loses his j.   TRUM 366:11
 politician who has lost his j.   MENC 248:3
jobbing j., speculating   JEFF 185:12
jobs create j.   TSVA 367:3
jog as a man *might j. on with*   DURH 120:5
jogging alternative to j.   FITT 132:4
John more MPs called J.   JOWE 194:7
joint time is out of j.   SHAK 319:8
joints know the j.   BUTL 63:6
jokes civil servant doesn't make j.   IONE 182:4
 don't know about j.   ROGE 304:8
 good at telling j.   BLAI 44:6
Josephine Not tonight, J.   NAPO 265:3
Joshua like J. of old   FRAN 137:4
journalism but why j.   BALF 26:7
 cancer of bent and twisted j.   AITK 6:1
journalist thank God! the British j.   WOLF 387:4
journalists j. dabbling   MCGR 233:1
journey j. *really* necessary   OFFI 274:4
 long j. to take   LAST 212:11
 now begin the j.   REAG 300:4
joy politics of j.   HUMP 179:3
 Strength through j.   SLOG 335:7
Judas J. was paid   POWE 293:6
 that of J.   STAL 345:5
judge j. is a member of the Bar   BOK 45:8
 J. not, that ye be not judged   BIBL 39:18
 j.'s robe   SHAK 325:10
 Justly to j.   BROO 52:9
judged Judge not, that ye be not j.   BIBL 39:18
judgement conclusive j.   GLAD 149:1
 everything except j.   ATTL 17:10
 fit to sit in j.   WILS 386:5
 functioning of a man's j.   SALI 313:5
 j. is a mere lottery   DRYD 119:12
 j. of his peers   MAGN 238:4
 j. was faultless   DISR 114:14
 j. will probably   MANS 242:1
 owes you his j.   BURK 60:5
 people's j.   DRYD 119:3
 question of j.   BLAI 44:6
judges independence of j.   DENN 106:8
 j. can tap   MARS 243:10

judges (*cont.*):
 J. must follow their oaths   ZOBE 391:6
judicial j. power   ADAM 4:1
jumped We have j.   TRIM 364:1
jumps way the cat j.   THAT 357:9
jungle Law of the J.   KIPL 205:9
junto oligarchical j.   ADAM 3:10
jurisdiction j. in Ireland   ADAM 2:6
 j. in this Realm   BOOK 47:4
just God is j.   JEFF 187:5
 j. and old renown   TENN 355:14
 j. cause reaches its flood-tide   CATT 72:10
 'j.' or 'right'   PLAT 290:11
 may not be a j. peace   IZET 182:8
 Our cause is j.   DICK 110:3
 place for a j. man   THOR 359:9
justice call for j.   MORE 259:8
 J. denied   MILL 251:7
 j. is ever lagging   GLAD 148:1
 J. is in one scale   JEFF 186:15
 J. is truth   DISR 111:11
 j. makes democracy possible   NIEB 268:10
 J. should not only be done   HEWA 171:8
 let j. be done   ADAM 4:3
 Let j. be done   MOTT 262:3
 Let j. be done   WATS 375:11
 liberty plucks j.   SHAK 325:7
 loved j.   LAST 212:12
 miracle of social j.   HAYE 164:7
 moderation in the pursuit of j.   GOLD 150:9
 moral good and of j.   JOHN 188:8
 reason, and j.   BURK 57:18
 right or j.   MAGN 238:5
 think j. requires   MANS 242:1
 threat to j. everywhere   KING 203:3
 truth, j., and humanity   GLAD 148:10
 victors' j.   SHAW 329:2
justifiable not a j. act of war   BELL 30:10
justitia *Fiat j.*   MOTT 262:3
 fiat j., pereat coelum   ADAM 4:3

Kaiser put the kibosh on the K.   SONG 341:4
Kalashnikovs didn't have K.   BONO 47:3
keener with his k. eye   MARV 244:1
keep If you can k. your head   KIPL 205:7
 intention to k. my counsel   GLAD 148:8
Kennedy Senator, you're no Jack K.   BENT 34:1
kettle back to the tea-k.   DISR 111:10
 pretty k. of fish   MARY 245:5
key k. of the Union   CLAY 88:11
 possession of the k.   PAIN 278:8
 possession of the k.   PAIN 279:2
keyholes screaming through the k.   LLOY 223:1
keystone k. which closeth   STRA 349:3
kibosh put the k. on the Kaiser   SONG 341:4
kick Nixon to k. around   NIXO 269:9
 will k. and fling   HALI 158:11
kicked k. up stairs   HALI 160:1
 no body to be k.   THUR 360:5

kicking flattering, kissing and k.   TRUM 366:4
kid comeback k.   CLIN 90:10
kids how many k. did you kill   SLOG 335:1
kill Athenians will k. thee   PHOC 289:2
   how many kids did you k.   SLOG 335:1
   k. all the lawyers   SHAK 320:16
   k. animals and stick in stamps   NICO 268:6
   k. the world   MILL 252:1
   prepared to k. one another   SHAW 328:6
   won't k. me   COLL 93:3
   you must k. him   EMER 126:6
killed don't mind your being k.   KITC 207:12
   Go to Spain and get k.   POLL 291:5
   I have k. my mother   ASQU 15:10
   k. in the war   POWE 293:12
   Suppose Hitler had been k.   SCHL 315:10
killers serial k.   LIVI 221:12
killing k. for Ireland   HUME 178:10
   K. no murder   SEXB 318:3
kills k. more people   LIVI 222:2
kind K. hearts are more than coronets   TENN 355:4

king As to the K.   CHAR 76:2
   authority forgets a dying k.   TENN 355:12
   authority of a K.   STRA 349:3
   brightly as a k.   SHAK 325:14
   British k.   MARK 243:4
   Cotton is K.   CHRI 79:4
   despised and dying k.   SHEL 330:2
   divinity doth hedge a k.   SHAK 320:1
   duty is the k.'s   SHAK 320:10
   fight for its K. and Country   GRAH 152:4
   five kings did a k. to death   THOM 359:1
   God bless the K.   BYRO 64:1
   God save our gracious k.   SONG 341:7
   God save the k.   SONG 341:7
   great and mighty k.   EPIT 128:3
   greater than the K.   PITT 289:11
   have served the K.   WOLS 388:2
   If we beat the K.   MANC 240:4
   K. and country need you   MILI 251:5
   K. asks you to form a Government   ATTL 16:9
   k. can do no wrong   BLAC 43:5
   k. delighteth to honour   BIBL 39:8
   K. enjoys his own again   PARK 282:10
   k. is a thing men have made   SELD 317:4
   k. is but a man   SHAK 320:8
   k. is truly *parens patriae*   JAME 184:3
   k. may make a nobleman   BURK 60:16
   k. never dies   BLAC 43:3
   K., observing with judicious   TRAP 362:8
   K. of England cannot enter   PITT 289:8
   K. of England's eyes   LAST 213:4
   K. of Great Britain   REED 300:7
   K. over the Water   ANON 9:11
   K. refused a lesser sacrifice   MARY 245:7
   k. reigns   THIE 358:12
   K.'s life moving peacefully   DAWS 103:3
   K.'s Moll Reno'd   NEWS 267:10
   k.'s name   SHAK 326:5
   K. to have things done as cheap   PEPY 287:5

king (*cont.*):
   K. to Oxford sent   BROW 54:5
   K. will get away with it   CHAN 75:5
   last K. of England   EDWA 121:8
   lay on the k.   SHAK 320:11
   leave without the k.   ELIZ 125:11
   lessened my esteem of a k.   PEPY 287:4
   loses the k. in the tyrant   MAYH 246:6
   material for a constitutional k.   BAGE 21:13
   Mrs Simpson's pinched our k.   ANON 8:10
   My dead k.   JOYC 194:8
   my life to make you K.   CHAR 76:7
   mystery of the k.'s power   JAME 184:4
   my true k.   MACA 230:3
   neck of the last k.   DIDE 110:5
   No bishop, no K.   JAME 184:1
   Northcliffe has sent for the K.   ANON 8:13
   not offended the k.   LAST 213:12
   not so much a k.   SELL 317:9
   O k., establish the decree   BIBL 39:15
   sang a k. out of three kingdoms   WHAR 381:3
   self-dedication of the King   BLUN 45:2
   still am I k. of those   SHAK 326:9
   stomach of a k.   ELIZ 124:2
   strike at a k.   EMER 126:6
   What is a k.   PRIO 294:11
   What must the k. do   SHAK 326:8
   whatsoever K. shall reign   SONG 342:3
   when thy k. is a child   BIBL 39:12
   you must not be a k.   CHAR 75:10
   your K. and your Country   SONG 342:8
   zeal I served my k.   SHAK 321:3
kingdom but to mock the k.   PYM 295:5
   k. against kingdom   BIBL 39:23
   voice of the k.   SWIF 350:7
kingdoms out of three k.   WHAR 381:3
kingfish call me the K.   LONG 224:11
   call me the K.   LONG 224:13
kingly K. conclaves stern   SHEL 329:11
kings captains and the k.   KIPL 206:3
   change k. with us   SARS 314:8
   death of k.   SHAK 326:6
   dominion of k. changed   PRIC 294:10
   end of k.   DEFO 104:13
   five K. left   FARO 130:7
   keep even k. in awe   D'AV 102:1
   k. and parliaments   FRAN 136:8
   k. are not only God's lieutenants   JAME 184:2
   K. will be tyrants   BURK 58:17
   last of the k. strangled   MESL 249:2
   laws or k.   JOHN 190:16
   laws or k. can cause   GOLD 150:8
   politeness of k.   LOUI 225:9
   puller down of k.   SHAK 320:19
   ruin k.   DRYD 118:6
   Through talk, we tamed k.   BENN 32:6
   walk with K.   KIPL 205:8
   War is the trade of k.   DRYD 119:8
Kinnock If K. wins   NEWS 267:5
kinship crimson thread of k.   PARK 283:1
kiss k. my ass in Macy's window   JOHN 190:8

language (*cont.*):

except, of course, l.	WILD 383:4
l. of the unheard	KING 203:13
laogai in every l.	WU 389:1
learning the l.	CLIN 91:6
mobilized the English l.	MURR 263:7
national l.	DE V 107:9
Political l. . . . is designed	ORWE 276:14
Under the tropic is our l.	WALL 373:4

lanterns show two l. — REVE 301:2

laogai want to see *l.* ended — WU 389:1

laptop promised a l. computer — WILS 384:4

lascivious long, l. reign — DEFO 104:10

lash blood drawn with the l. — LINC 220:6

rum, sodomy, prayers, and the l. — CHUR 84:3

lass It came with a l. — JAME 184:6

last Free at l. — EPIT 128:1

l. day of an era past	YELT 390:4
l. great Englishman	TENN 355:6
l. King of England	EDWA 121:8
l. person who has sat on him	HAIG 157:1
l. thing I shall do	LAST 212:4
l. while they last	DE G 105:9
won the l. war	ROOS 305:1

late offering even that too l. — NEVI 266:1

later I'll let you know l. — ATTL 16:9

Latin L. as an honour — CHUR 85:3

laugh too badly hurt to l. — LINC 219:6

laughable very l. things — JOHN 191:5

laughed honest man is l. at — HALI 159:14

l. at in the second — NAPO 264:6

laurels l. to paeans — CICE 86:16

l. torn	SMOL 339:8
Northern l.	LEE 214:6

law against the l. for generals — TRUM 366:16

books of l.	JOHN 189:7
chief l.	CICE 86:15
Common L. of England	HERB 170:5
Custom, that unwritten l.	D'AV 102:1
dead-level of l. and order	TAWN 352:9
economic l.	MARX 244:8
enforce a l.	HUMP 179:1
first is l.	DRYD 119:5
government above the l.	SCAR 315:5
had people not defied the l.	SCAR 315:2
have a l.	DYSO 120:7
Ignorance of the l.	SELD 317:3
judgement of the l.	JACK 183:12
keystone of the rule of l.	DENN 106:8
l. at the end	WHAL 381:2
l. enforcement	KENN 200:1
l. floats in a sea of ethics	WARR 374:11
l. is above you	DENN 106:7
L. is boldly	BURR 61:8
l. is contrary to liberty	BENT 33:8
l. is established	SIDN 332:5
L.: It has honoured us	WEBS 377:15
l. is at a disadvantage	SCAR 315:8
L. of the Jungle	KIPL 205:9
l.'s delay	SHAK 319:9
lesser breeds without the L.	KIPL 206:5

law (*cont.*):

liberty under the l.	HAIL 157:4
majestic equality of the l.	FRAN 136:4
make a scarecrow of the l.	SHAK 325:8
Necessity hath no l.	CROM 98:8
not a l. at all	ROBE 303:4
of a common l.	JEFF 185:13
People crushed by l.	BURK 60:6
respect for the l.	CHUR 86:6
Right . . . is the child of l.	BENT 33:5
this is the royal l.	CORO 96:5
those by l. protected	BURN 61:4
where no l. is	BIBL 39:27

lawful by 'l. authority' — MACD 232:6

lawn Get your tanks off my l. — WILS 385:6

scooters off my l. — CLAR 88:2

laws are the l. of nature — SHAW 327:14

arranges l.	MACH 233:5
Bad l.	BURK 60:8
bad or obnoxious l.	GRAN 153:4
care who should make the l.	FLET 133:1
country's planted thick with l.	BOLT 46:6
dominion of l.	PRIC 294:10
do with the l.	HORS 176:10
everything the l. permit	MONT 258:11
folly of human l.	SMIT 337:9
government of l., and not of men	ADAM 3:4
Government of l. and not of men	FORD 134:7
If l. are needed	KHOM 201:13
If the l. could speak	HALI 159:4
l. and learning	MANN 241:10
L. are generally found to be nets	SHEN 330:5
L. are like cobwebs	SWIF 350:8
l. are like spider's webs	ANAC 7:4
L. are silent	CICE 87:2
l. are their enemies	BURK 60:6
L. grind the poor	GOLD 150:7
L., like houses	BURK 59:16
l. of God will be suspended	SHAW 328:1
l. of the land	CHAR 76:2
l. or kings	JOHN 190:16
l. or kings can cause	GOLD 150:8
L. were made to be broken	NORT 271:4
l. which cannot be enforced	EINS 122:2
more numerous the l.	TACI 351:8
neither l. made	JOHN 188:6
new code of l.	ADAM 1:11
not a government of l.	WEBS 377:12
part of the l. of England	HALE 158:3
politics and our l.	DEWA 108:9
rather than obey the l.	TOCQ 360:7
taint pure l.	AESC 5:3
their l. approve	DRYD 119:7
trample bad l.	PHIL 288:9
world abounds with l.	ANON 9:14

lawyer l. tells me I may — BURK 57:18

middle-aged l.	SMIT 338:2
to a corporate l.	COMM 93:5

lawyers complain of the l. — HALI 159:4

kill all the l.	SHAK 320:16
l. should do business	JEFF 187:1

lazy l., long, lascivious — DEFO 104:10
LBJ All the way with L. — SLOG 334:2
  Hey, L., how many kids — SLOG 335:1
lead cold l. and steel — O'DO 273:3
  easy to l. — BROU 53:3
  evening l. — CHUR 84:15
leader fanatic is a great l. — BROU 53:4
  great and wonderful l. — LLOY 223:9
  I am their l. — LEDR 214:5
  l. of the Labour party — KINN 204:11
  no longer a political l. — BARU 28:6
  one people, one l. — SLOG 334:13
  right l. for the Labour Party — BEVA 37:1
  test of a l. — LIPP 221:4
leaders l. and their wives — HEAD 165:6
  l. Labour loves — HARR 162:10
  l. of a revolution — CONR 94:10
leadership L. is not about being nice — KEAT 197:3
  successful l. — REAG 300:3
leaking L. is what you do — CALL 65:7
lean l. and hungry look — SHAK 322:1
  l. as much to the contrary — HALI 158:4
  l. on one another — BURK 59:16
leap l. into the ocean — HUME 178:7
  l. to a hasty opinion — BAGE 23:10
learn l. men from books — DISR 115:4
  People must l. to hate — MAND 240:10
learned l. anything from history — HEGE 167:9
learners slow l. — MALL 239:13
learning loyal body wanted l. — TRAP 362:8
  of liberty, and of l. — DISR 112:19
learnt They have l. nothing — TALL 351:13
least l. government was the best — FEIN 131:3
  what we l. expected — DISR 114:12
leave dying to l. — MITC 256:4
  l. the country — NEWS 267:5
  l. things alone you leave them — CHES 77:9
  l. without the King — ELIZ 125:11
  Once I l. — BALD 25:11
leaving like the l. it — SHAK 324:8
left l. out would be dangerous — MELB 247:3
  l.-wing, like humanity — DEBR 103:6
  No L. — MITC 253:8
  nothing l. for me — LEE 215:2
leg nor breaks my l. — JEFF 187:8
legacy l. from a rich relative — SMIT 338:5
legality any taint of l. — KNOX 208:2
legally accomplishing small things l. — BALZ 27:6
legend true l. — STAL 345:5
  Your l. ever will — JOHN 189:1
legions give me back my l. — AUGU 18:2
legislation foundation of morals and l. — BENT 33:7
legislative l. and executive — ADAM 4:1
  l. power — GIBB 145:1
  l. power — MONT 258:14
legislator people is the true l. — BURK 59:17
legislators idea of hereditary l. — PAIN 280:4
legislature no l. can manufacture — BAGE 20:6
  safe while the l. is in session — ANON 10:4
  work for a L. — ELLI 126:2
legitimate l. self-interest — BAST 28:9

legs dog's walking on his hinder l. — JOHN 191:4
  Four l. good — ORWE 275:6
  not for your bad l. — ELIZ 124:5
  vast and trunkless l. — SHEL 329:10
  Walk under his huge l. — SHAK 321:8
Leicester Here lies the Earl of L. — EPIT 128:4
leisure conspicuous l. — VEBL 370:1
  increased l. — DISR 112:17
lend called L.-Lease — CHUR 83:3
  l. me your ears — SHAK 323:4
lenses zoom l. — ULLR 368:6
leper Parliamentary l. — WILS 385:2
lesser l. breeds — KIPL 206:5
lessons l. to be drawn — ELIZ 125:8
lest L. we forget — KIPL 206:3
let L. my people go — BIBL 39:1
  l. the country down — CALL 66:5
letter huge wordy l. — JUVE 195:11
letters No arts; no l. — HOBB 173:10
level Those who attempt to l. — BURK 58:10
levellers l. wish to level *down* — JOHN 191:3
levelling cannot bear l. *up* — JOHN 191:3
Leviathan L., called a commonwealth — HOBB 173:5
lex *Salus populi suprema l.* — SELD 317:5
  suprema est l. — CICE 86:15
liar l. should be outlawed — HALI 158:7
  proved l. — HAIL 157:3
liars L. ought to have good memories — SIDN 332:2
liberal between l. concessions — BOOK 47:6
  either a little L. — GILB 146:4
  first L. leader — STEE 345:9
  harm to the l. cause — HAYE 164:9
  ineffectual l. — FRAY 137:10
  l. is a conservative — WOLF 387:7
  L. is a man — ROOS 305:13
  l. who has been mugged — PROV 296:1
  particular L. Party — HERB 170:3
liberals Attacking the L. — PATT 284:9
liberation 'L.' in its title — LEVI 217:7
  l. of Europe — EISE 122:5
  l. of the human mind — GOLD 150:3
libertas *Imperium et L.* — DISR 113:9
liberté *L.! Égalité* — SLOG 335:11
liberties give up their l. — BURK 60:12
  L. . . . . depend on the silence — HOBB 173:12
  not to have l. — PYM 295:5
liberty ardour for l. — PRIC 294:10
  be light! said L. — SHEL 329:8
  bulwark of continuing l. — ROOS 305:11
  by reason of the l. — MONT 259:2
  conceived in all l. — LINC 219:9
  contend for their l. — HALI 159:10
  cost of l. — DU B 119:15
  dangers to l. lurk — BRAN 50:6
  desires in l. — TOCQ 361:7
  endanger the public l. — ADAM 3:2
  enemies of l. — HUME 178:8
  equivalent for l. — MONT 259:1
  extremism in the defence of l. — GOLD 150:9
  freedom, and l. — SHAK 322:13
  given l. to man — CURR 99:5

lords (*cont.*):
l. who lay ye low — SHEL 329:12
l. whose parents were — DEFO 104:11
new unhappy l. — CHES 78:2
reform the House of L. — DANG 101:3
wit among L. — JOHN 191:2
lordships good enough for their l. — ANON 11:8
lose Better l. the election — STEV 346:9
hurts to l. — DOLE 117:1
is to l. it — ORWE 276:16
l. her as a friend — GLAD 149:2
nothing to l. — MARX 245:4
nothing to l. but our aitches — ORWE 276:11
not to l. wars — CHUR 83:10
on the right side and lose — GALB 140:14
we don't want to l. you — SONG 342:8
loser It is a l. politically — NIXO 270:11
losing l. one pleased Cato — LUCA 226:7
loss l. of power — RUSK 310:3
lost All is l. save honour — MISQ 254:1
always l. it — SMIT 338:6
and we are l. — PYRR 295:6
Britain has l. an empire — ACHE 1:5
France has not l. the war — DE G 105:1
friend in power is a friend l. — ADAM 2:10
Next to a battle l. — WELL 379:14
OK. We l. — MAJO 239:4
Vietnam was l. in — MCLU 235:1
Lothian West L. — DALY 100:9
West-L. — DALY 101:1
lottery genetic l. comes up with — PIML 289:4
judgement is a mere l. — DRYD 119:12
l. of life — RHOD 301:3
louder l. he talked of his honour — EMER 126:5
lousy L. but loyal — SLOG 335:13
lout l.'s game — WEST 380:6
love all did l. him once — SHAK 323:8
earth could never living l. — EPIT 128:4
Gratitude, like l. — ALSO 6:7
greater l. hath no man — THOR 360:2
how I l. my country — LAST 213:8
I must l. the dog — GIBB 145:15
l. him most — BRAG 50:3
l. men too little — BURK 59:3
l. of freedom — GLAD 148:2
l. of the people — BURK 58:2
l. one another or die — AUDE 17:15
l. that asks no question — SPRI 344:8
L. the Beloved Republic — FORS 134:11
l. those who love you — VOLT 372:7
L. thyself last — SHAK 321:2
Make l. not war — SLOG 335:14
man, That l. my friend — SHAK 323:12
my l. for Ireland — CARS 70:17
pangs of disprized l. — SHAK 319:9
party I l. — LIVI 221:13
search for l. — WAŁĘ 372:13
support of the woman I l. — EDWA 121:10
You can only l. one war — GELL 142:3
loved come to Washington to be l. — GRAM 152:6
feared than l. — MACH 233:9

loved (*cont.*):
l. Caesar less — SHAK 323:2
l. the suffering many — BENT 33:9
loves reigned with your l. — ELIZ 124:7
loving l. ourselves to death — PRES 294:5
low dost thou lie so l. — SHAK 322:14
l. road to the highest — MCCA 231:4
Malice is of a l. stature — HALI 159:5
lower call the L. House — DISR 113:13
l. classes had such white — CURZ 100:4
While there is a l. class — DEBS 103:8
lowliness l. is young ambition's — SHAK 322:4
loyal Lousy but l. — SLOG 335:13
l. to his own career — DALT 100:8
loyalties l. which centre upon number one — CHUR 85:7
tragic conflict of l. — HOWE 177:5
loyalty constitute l. — BOSW 49:3
I want l. — JOHN 190:8
learned body wanted l. — TRAP 362:8
L. is a fine quality — KINN 204:4
L. the Tory's secret weapon — KILM 202:11
Lucifer falls like L. — SHAK 321:1
Luddite That's L. — HURD 179:10
luggage flamboyant labels on empty l. — BEVA 37:3
lunatic l. fringe — ROOS 307:13
lunatics lunatic asylum run by l. — LLOY 223:6
lunch as a free l. — PROV 297:1
luncheon take soup at l. — CURZ 100:3
lungs l. of London — PITT 290:3
Lupercal on the L. I thrice — SHAK 323:7
lurk dangers to liberty l. — BRAN 50:6
lurks l. a politician — ARIS 13:7
lustre bright l. of a court — CECI 74:1
lute pleasing of a l. — SHAK 326:14
luxury Republics end in l. — MONT 258:7
lying branch of the art of l. — CORN 96:4

Macaulay as Tom M. — MELB 247:7
mace fool's bauble, the m. — CROM 98:6
mackerel like rotten m. — RAND 298:8
mad half of the nation is m. — SMOL 339:7
old, m., blind — SHEL 330:2
We must be m. — POWE 293:3
Whom the m. would destroy — LEVI 217:3
madam M. I may not call you — ELIZ 125:1
madame misunderstood M. — DE V 108:4
madmen M. in authority — KEYN 201:8
madness M. in great ones — SHAK 319:10
m. of many — SWIF 351:2
moment of m. — DAVI 102:4
no cure for this sort of m. — SMIT 338:5
magic let in daylight upon m. — BAGE 21:11
tightness of the m. circle — MACL 234:7
magistrate m. corruptible — ROBE 303:5
magna M. Charta is such a fellow — COKE 92:4
magnanimity M. in politics — BURK 58:3
magnet printing, gunpowder, and the m. — BACO 20:1
magnetism personal m. — WEBB 376:8

maiden m. in distress　STEE 345:11
maidens laughter of comely m.　DE V 108:1
maids Old m. biking　ORWE 275:12
mail gets the m. through　KEAT 197:2
maimed M. us at the start　YEAT 389:7
Maine As M. goes　FARL 130:6
　　As M. goes　PROV 296:2
majestic m. equality of the law　FRAN 136:4
majesty earth of m.　SHAK 326:2
majorities parliamentary m.　BONA 46:8
majority always in the m.　KNOX 208:1
　　black m. rule　SMIT 338:7
　　however safe its m.　BOOK 47:5
　　is a m.　PHIL 288:10
　　large parliamentary m.　BUTL 63:2
　　m. are wrong　DEBS 103:7
　　m. in a small part　LYNC 227:4
　　m. is always the best repartee　DISR 114:20
　　m. never has right　IBSE 181:1
　　m. . . . one is enough　DISR 114:8
　　makes a m.　JACK 183:6
　　makes a m.　PROV 296:14
　　opinions of the m.　PEEL 285:13
　　silent m.　NIXO 270:4
　　tyrannical m.　BALF 26:2
　　untutored m.　HEAD 165:5
　　will of the m.　JEFF 186:1
make does not usually m. anything　PHEL 288:4
　　M. do and mend　OFFI 274:5
　　M. love not war　SLOG 335:14
maker to meet my M.　CHUR 84:9
malice M. domestic　SHAK 325:5
　　M. is of a low stature　HALI 159:5
　　m. toward none　LINC 220:7
malignant part of Randolph that was not m.　WAUG 376:6
malignity m. truly diabolical　BURK 59:12
man best m. among them　CAST 72:1
　　century of the common m.　WALL 373:1
　　demolition of a m.　LEVI 216:7
　　encompassed but one m.　SHAK 321:10
　　every m. against every man　HOBB 173:8
　　every m. and nation　LOWE 226:5
　　everyone has sat except a m.　CUMM 99:7
　　extraordinary m.　JOHN 191:19
　　for the sake of the m.　HALI 159:1
　　God has more right than m.　JOHN 188:6
　　good of m. must be the objective　ARIS 13:8
　　happiness of the common m.　BEVE 38:1
　　It's that m. again　NEWS 267:8
　　led to *perdition* by a m.　WEST 380:9
　　make a m. a woman　PEMB 286:19
　　m. and a brother　WEDG 378:1
　　m. and the hour　YANC 389:3
　　m. at the gate of the year　HASK 163:3
　　M. being . . . by nature all free　LOCK 224:6
　　m. for all seasons　WHIT 382:10
　　m. in the street　BALD 25:5
　　M. is something to be surpassed　NIET 269:2
　　m. is the only animal　JEFF 185:3
　　M. is the only creature　ORWE 275:5

man (*cont.*):
　　M., proud man　SHAK 325:12
　　M.'s laws, not God's　BOLT 46:6
　　m.'s the gowd　BURN 61:3
　　old Jew! That is the m.　BISM 42:4
　　plain, blunt m.　SHAK 323:12
　　right m. in the right place　JEFF 187:7
　　said, ask a m.　THAT 356:3
　　standing by my m.　CLIN 90:5
　　This was a m.　SHAK 324:3
manage m. without butter　GOEB 149:5
managed not a free press but a m.　RADC 297:9
management m. of a balance　KISS 207:7
　　orderly m. of decline　ARMS 14:6
Manchester committed at M.　PARN 283:10
　　school of M.　DISR 115:17
　　What M. says today　PROV 297:3
Mandy name is M.　PARR 284:5
manhood ancient customs and its m.　ENNI 126:10
　　M. a struggle　DISR 113:18
manifesto m. written by Dr Mori　BENN 32:7
manifestoes in the party m.　ROTH 309:3
mankind has not created m.　TOCQ 361:12
　　leave free the energies of m.　BAGE 22:6
　　M. always sets itself　MARX 244:4
　　M. is on the move　SMUT 339:9
　　M. must put an end to war　KENN 198:11
　　no history of m.　POPP 292:10
　　one disillusion—m.　KEYN 200:7
manner discover by his m.　SMIT 339:3
manners Oh, the m.　CICE 86:19
　　Peel has no m.　WELL 379:13
manoeuvre force with a m.　TROT 365:10
mansion in a shuttered m.　FITZ 132:7
manufacture content to m. life　BERN 35:3
　　m. the element　SALI 312:8
manufacturing m. the plausible　BALD 25:14
manure natural m.　JEFF 185:5
many fool too m.　THUR 360:4
　　makes so m. of them　LINC 220:1
　　so much owed by so m. to so few　CHUR 81:14
map Roll up that m.　PITT 290:8
maps poring over m.　SALI 313:6
marathon Politics is a m.　LIVI 221:10
marble left it m.　AUGU 18:3
march Beware the ides of M.　SHAK 321:6
　　boundary of the m. of a nation　PARN 283:13
　　do not m. on Moscow　MONT 259:4
　　ides of M. are come　SHAK 322:8
　　Let us m.　STEV 347:9
　　m. as an alternative　FITT 132:4
　　m. my troops towards　GRIM 155:8
　　m. towards it　CALL 66:1
marche *congrès ne m. pas*　LIGN 218:1
marches forced m., battles and death　GARI 141:8
marching m. where it likes　ARNO 14:10
　　people m. on　MORR 260:10
　　soul m. on　SONG 342:5
　　truth is m. on　HOWE 177:6
marijuana experimented with m.　CLIN 90:9
market common m. is a process　MONN 257:5

market (*cont.*):
  enterprise of the m.   ANON 7:10
  gathered in the m.-place   CAVA 73:2
  m. economy   JOSP 194:4
  m. has no morality   HESE 171:2
marquis there is the noble M.   HEAL 166:8
marriage for a m. than a ministry BAGE 21:6
married like other m. couples   SAKI 312:2
  time we got m.   CALL 66:10
  unhappily m.   PARK 283:7
Mars attack from M.   SALI 313:3
marshal m.'s baton   LOUI 225:8
martyr soul of a m.   BAGE 23:2
martyrdom crown of m.   WALP 373:8
  torches of m.   JEFF 186:10
martyred shrouded oft our m. dead SONG 343:1
martyrs battles, m.   WHIT 382:8
Marx Karl M. and Catherine the Great ATTL 17:4
  M is for M.   CONN 94:3
Marxian M. Socialism   KEYN 201:1
Marxism M. is now a world faith BENN 32:5
  M. is only an episode   POPP 292:11
  monetarism, like M.   GILM 146:10
  more to Methodism than to M. PHIL 288:7
Marxist I am not a M.   MARX 244:11
  tried to be a M.   TAYL 353:18
mask had a m. like Castlereagh SHEL 329:9
masochism spirit of national m. AGNE 5:7
mass Paris is well worth a m. HENR 169:2
  two thousand years of m.   HARD 162:3
Massachusetts denied in M. MILL 251:7
massage to a m. parlour   WILS 384:4
masses huddled m. yearning LAZA 214:4
  m. against the classes   GLAD 148:10
  Movement of M.   CONN 94:3
master and no M.   ELIZ 124:4
  Death is a m. from Germany CELA 74:2
  dominion of the m.   HUME 178:7
  I would not be a *m*.   LINC 218:7
  M. and Servant   CHUR 80:9
  M.-morality   NIET 269:4
  m. of the Party   HEAL 166:5
  slew his m.   BIBL 39:7
masterly m. inactivity   MACK 234:5
masters anything but new m. HALI 159:10
  educate our m.   LOWE 226:2
  educate our m.   MISQ 255:11
  I have had two m.   BEAV 30:4
  people are the m.   BLAI 43:11
  people are the m.   BURK 60:9
  We are the m.   SHAW 329:1
  We are the m. now   MISQ 255:10
mastership All m. is not alike RUSK 310:9
mastiff m.? the right hon. Gentleman's poodle
                  LLOY 222:5
matches have a box of m. HOME 175:9
  with that stick of m.   MAND 241:3
mateship as dearly as m. ANON 12:2
matter m. out of place   GRAY 153:8
  not fighting does m.   STEP 346:4

maxim just political m.   HUME 178:9
  m. of a free government   ADAM 3:2
mayor as his 'night m.'   HAGU 156:9
  if I was elected m.   LIVI 222:1
  M. for London   WATE 375:10
  running for m. of Toytown SCAR 315:3
  tart who has married the M. BAXT 29:1
maypole organ and the m. JORD 193:5
MBEs M. and your knighthoods KEAT 196:9
McCarthyism M. is Americanism with
                  MCCA 231:7
McNamara M.'s War   MCNA 237:1
me save thee and m.   OWEN 278:2
mean Happy the golden m. MASS 246:1
  nothing common did or m. MARV 244:1
meanest m. of mankind   POPE 292:5
means Increased m.   DISR 112:17
  m. just what I choose   CARR 70:15
  m. of rising   JOHN 191:13
  politics by other m.   CLAU 88:5
meant damned dots m.   CHUR 79:12
  what he m. by that   LOUI 225:10
measles m. of the human race EINS 122:3
measure Shrunk to this little m. SHAK 322:14
  ultimate m.   KING 203:11
measures Great public m. PEEL 286:17
  M. not men   CANN 69:1
  Not men, but m.   BURK 59:15
  weights and m.   NAPO 265:2
meat appointed to buy the m. SELD 317:4
  flies off the m.   CHUR 82:3
  teeth are in the real m. GRIM 155:9
  Upon what m.   SHAK 321:9
Meath member from M.   BUTT 63:9
mechanical m. arts and merchandise BACO 19:18
medal m. glitters   CHUR 82:9
meddle I m. not   CROM 98:2
  M. and muddle   DERB 107:2
meddles Minister that m. with art MELB 247:6
meddling m. government MACA 230:15
media Live m. is where it's at CAMP 67:3
  not m. driven   PEYT 288:3
medicine rotational m.   MORG 260:1
mediocre Titles distinguish the m. SHAW 328:14
meek borne his faculties so m. SHAK 324:10
  m. shall inherit   SMIT 338:4
meet to m. my Maker   CHUR 84:9
meeting *loves* m. people LLOY 223:10
méfiez-vous *Taisez-vous! M.* OFFI 274:7
Mein Kampf all in *M.*   ROBE 302:8
meliora *Video m.*   OVID 277:10
mellow ability to m.   MARG 242:8
melted centre has always m. HAIL 157:6
melting M.-Pot where all the races ZANG 390:9
member responsible for the m. BUTT 63:9
memoirs write one's m. is to speak ill
                  PÉTA 287:12
memorable that m. scene MARV 244:1
memorandum m. is written ACHE 1:7
memorial whole earth as their m. PERI 287:9
memories ought to have good m. SIDN 332:2

memory m. for a politician — MORL 260:8
my name and m. — LAST 212:6
mystic chords of m. — LINC 219:2
nation's collective m. — POWE 293:14
no force can abolish m. — ROOS 306:7
to his m. for his jests — SHER 330:10
men 200,000 m. — NAPO 264:13
all m. would be tyrants — ADAM 1:11
government of laws, and not of m. — ADAM 3:4
Great m. are not always — BIBL 39:9
innocent m., women, and children — JEFF 187:4
learn m. from books — DISR 115:4
Measures not m. — CANN 69:1
m. and nations behave wisely — EBAN 121:2
m. are created equal — JEFF 185:1
M. lived like fishes — SIDN 332:3
m. naturally were born free — MILT 253:3
m. who will support me — MELB 247:13
m. with the muck-rakes — ROOS 307:8
Not m., but measures — BURK 59:15
State is a relation of m. — WEBE 377:3
twelve good m. — BROU 53:2
wealth accumulates, and m. decay — GOLD 150:4
menace m. to be defeated — SCAR 315:5
mend Make do and m. — OFFI 274:5
mental Freedom and slavery are m. states — GAND 141:2
m. decay — NICO 266:8
Mephistopheles who is the M. — HEAL 165:11
merchandise mechanical arts and m. — BACO 19:18
merchandize m. candidates — STEV 347:7
merchants M. have no country — JEFF 186:12
mercury pick up m. with a fork — LLOY 224:1
mercy crowning m. — CROM 98:4
m. on my poor country — LAST 213:3
m. to forgive — DRYD 119:5
quality of m. — SHAK 325:13
shut the gates of m. — GRAY 154:2
so good a grace As m. — SHAK 325:10
merit *m.* for a bishopric — WEST 380:10
What is m. — PALM 282:2
meritocracy m. of talent — YOUN 390:8
merry always very m. — SELL 317:9
m. monarch — ROCH 304:2
never m. world in England — SHAK 320:15
message ask me to take a m. — LAST 213:6
if there is a m. — PAXM 284:10
messenger m.-boy Presidency — SCHL 315:9
Methodism more to M. than to Marxism — PHIL 288:7
metropolis m. of the empire — COBB 91:12
Mexico M., so far from God — DIAZ 109:4
MI5 head of M. — ANON 8:11
M. is a job creation — HENN 168:7
Micawbers like inverted M. — GUED 156:1
mice as long as it catches m. — DENG 106:4
Mickey Mouse M. project — MAND 241:7
middle m. of the road — HIGH 172:2
m.-sized are alone entangled — SHEN 330:5
m. way is none at all — ADAM 3:5
middle class m. is in control — ARIS 14:3

middle class (*cont.*):
M. was quite prepared — BELL 31:2
Philistines proper, or m. — ARNO 14:9
sinking m. — ORWE 276:11
Middlesex acre in M. — MACA 229:8
midnight stroke of the m. hour — NEHR 265:5
might Britons alone use 'M.' — WAUG 376:4
mightiest m. in the mightiest — SHAK 325:13
mighty thou art m. yet — SHAK 324:2
militarism M. . . . is fetish worship — TAWN 352:7
military control of the m. — TRUM 366:14
entrust to m. men — CLEM 89:8
m. fame — SHER 331:5
m.-industrial complex — EISE 123:1
milk putting m. into babies — CHUR 82:14
mill lie so near the m. — CLEG 89:4
millennium m. is going to present us — DEED 104:3
new m. approaches — ROBI 303:14
million m. deaths a statistic — STAL 345:6
millionaire m. has just as good a chance — HOPE 176:8
millionaires need more m. — JOSE 194:2
millions I will be m. — EPIT 128:8
multiplying m. — O'SU 277:7
What m. died — CAMP 67:7
millstone m. round our necks — DISR 111:13
Milton morals hold Which M. held — WORD 388:5
mute inglorious M. — GRAY 154:2
mind absence of m. — SEEL 317:2
battle for the m. — NOON 271:1
Cast your m. on other days — YEAT 390:1
[Charles] Sumner's m. — ADAM 2:11
commonplace m. — HARD 162:4
depth and compass of his m. — ADAM 4:4
empires of the m. — CHUR 82:15
liberation of the human m. — GOLD 150:3
m. and truth — HEWI 171:9
m. of the oppressed — BIKO 40:8
m.'s construction — SHAK 324:8
prepare the m. of the country — DISR 112:9
retail mind — LLOY 223:8
minds great empire and little m. — BURK 58:3
miners like m.' coal dust — BOOT 48:4
mineworkers National Union of M. — MACM 236:10
minister As m. of the Crown — PEEL 285:8
cheer the m. — CANN 69:4
God help the M. — MELB 247:6
last m. is strangled — NAIR 264:1
m. going to run — HEND 168:4
M., whoever he at any time — PAIN 280:7
m. who moves about — CHOI 79:3
M. whose stubbornness — JENK 187:12
wisdom of a great m. — JUNI 195:2
Yes, M.! No, Minister — CROS 99:5
ministers 'bollocks' to m. — WILS 385:15
group of Cabinet M. — CURZ 100:1
how much my M. talk — THAT 356:7
m. are behaving — BRUT 55:3
M. decide — THAT 357:13
M. say — HOGG 174:6
my actions are my m.' — CHAR 76:5

money (*cont.*):

make as much m.	FRIE 138:4
m. and power	O'RO 275:2
m.-grabbing cronies	HAGU 156:5
m. gushes into politics	WHIT 381:7
M. has no smell	VESP 370:5
M. is indeed the most important	SHAW 328:3
M. . . . is none of the wheels	HUME 178:5
m. the sinews of war	BACO 19:14
m. to even get beat	ROGE 304:4
natural interest of m.	MACA 229:6
nobody ever lost m.	DEED 104:5
not spending m. alone	EISE 122:6
other people's m.	RAND 298:10
plenty of m.	ROGE 304:6
spending the public m.	COOL 96:2
state is or can be master of m.	BEVE 38:3
They hired the m.	COOL 95:10
unlimited m.	CICE 86:18
use the m. for the poor	PERÓ 287:10
virtue does not come from m.	SOCR 340:2

moneybag Aristocracy of the M. — CARL 70:2
mongrels continent of energetic m. — FISH 131:7
monk political old m. — MURD 263:3
monkey higher the m. climbs — PROV 296:8

m. looking for fleas	LASK 211:2
no reason to attack the m.	BEVA 36:10

monologue m. is not a decision — ATTL 16:6
monopolies only one M. Commission — ANON 12:7
monopoly best of all m. profits — HICK 172:1

m. stage of capitalism	LENI 215:5

Monroe M. Doctrine — MONR 258:1
monsters bastard brood of m. — BENT 33:5
monstrous m. regiment of women — KNOX 207:13
Montezuma halls of M. — SONG 341:6

who imprisoned M.	MACA 229:13

moon defend the m. — SALI 313:3

man on the M.	KENN 198:9
m. the stars	TRUM 366:1
Rising of the M.	LARK 210:5

moor in the middle of a m. — HUXL 180:5
moose strong as a bull m. — ROOS 307:2
moral attainment of m. good — JOHN 188:8

It *is* a m. issue	NEWS 267:7
m. electricity	O'CO 272:10
m. imperative	DIDI 110:6
most m.	MENC 248:9
party is a m. crusade	WILS 384:8
single m. action	GLAD 149:1

morality damned m. — MELB 247:11

fits of m.	MACA 229:5
market has no m.	HESE 171:2
M. is the herd-instinct	NIET 269:3
national m. should have this	SHAW 328:3
slave-m.	NIET 269:4

morals either m. or principles — GLAD 148:7

faith and m. hold	WORD 388:5
m. and legislation	BENT 33:7

more m. equal than others — ORWE 275:7
mores *O tempora, O m.* — CICE 86:19

morganatic m. alliance — HARD 161:5
Mori manifesto written by Dr M. — BENN 32:7
moribus *M. antiquis res* — ENNI 126:10
morning m. again in America — SLOG 335:4

m. had been golden	CHUR 84:15
Never glad confident m.	BROW 54:8
What a glorious m.	ADAM 4:6
What a glorious m.	MISQ 256:1

mors *Indignatio principis m. est* — MORE 259:9
mort *La m., sans phrases* — SIEY 332:6
mortality emblem of m. — DISR 113:10
mortar Lies are the m. — WELL 380:3
mortifications m. and humiliations — WALP 373:10
Moscow do not march on M. — MONT 259:4
Mosley Why does M. always speak — ATTL 16:5
mosquito just another m. — OKPI 273:6
mother father was frightened of his m. — GEOR 144:3

France, m. of arts	DU B 119:14
I have been a m. to you	O'DO 273:2
m. of all battles	HUSS 180:1
m. of all treachery	PAIS 281:5
m. of Parliaments	BRIG 51:8
M. of the Free	BENS 33:4
m. who talks about her own	DISR 112:20
My m., drunk or sober	CHES 77:6
skin of his m.	LLOY 223:18

mothers best-bodied m. — WHIT 382:5

m.-in-law and Wigan Pier	BRID 51:4

motion m. of the wheels — HUME 178:5
motives sooner will the m. prevail — BAGE 23:14
mould frozen in an out-of-date m. — JENK 187:11
mountain go up to the m. — KING 203:8
mourn M., hapless Caledonia — SMOL 339:8
mourning Don't waste time in m. — LAST 213:2
mouth Keep your m. shut — OFFI 274:7

m. of Marilyn Monroe	MITT 256:8
not take from the m.	JEFF 185:14
silver foot in his m.	RICH 302:2
with an open m.	STEV 347:14
With every m.	BAUE 28:8

mouthful gold filling in a m. of decay — OSBO 277:2
mouths poet's m. be shut — YEAT 389:6

stuffed their m. with gold	BEVA 37:7

moved m. about like the wind — GERO 144:9

We shall not be m.	SONG 343:6

movement freedom of m. — UNIV 368:8

right of free m.	JOHN 188:8

movere *Quieta m.* — SALL 313:10
movie on the m. set — REAG 300:3
Mowlam of Ms Mo M. — CLAR 87:16
MP Being an M. — PARR 284:3

M. is the sort of job	ABBO 1:1
say you're a Labour M.	WARD 374:9

MPs dull M. in close proximity — GILB 146:7

healthy cynicism of M.	CREW 97:3
many M. never see	LIVI 221:9
more M. called John	JOWE 194:7
When in that House M. divide	GILB 146:6

much so m. owed by so many to so few | CHUR 81:14
so m. to do | LAST 213:10
muckrakes men with the m. | ROOS 307:8
mud builds on m. | MACH 233:10
muddle Meddle and m. | DERB 107:2
muddy m. understandings | BURK 58:15
mudging fudging and m. | OWEN 278:4
muffled with m. oars | RAND 298:9
mugged liberal who has been m. | PROV 296:1
mule is like a m. | DONN 117:2
m. of politics | DISR 113:19
Sicilian m. was to me | GLAD 148:14
mules m. of politics | POWE 294:4
multitude m., the *hoi polloi* | DRYD 119:12
mumble When in doubt, m. | BORE 48:8
murder believe that any m. | PARN 283:10
I met M. on the way | SHEL 329:9
Killing no m. | SEXB 318:3
m. by the throat | LLOY 223:4
m. respectable | ORWE 276:14
We hear war called m. | MACD 232:7
murderers m. of Jewish children | WIES 383:3
murders exhausts, and m. itself | ADAM 3:9
muse talked shop like a tenth m. | ANON 9:2
mush m. and slush | OWEN 278:4
mushroom supramundane m. | LAUR 211:3
music M. means everything | HEAT 167:3
m. of the Union | CHOA 78:9
must Must! Is *m.* a word | ELIZ 124:9
mute except that of m. | MACM 236:5
mutiny rise and m. | SHAK 323:14
mystery grasped the m. of the atom | BRAD 49:8
m. of the king's power | JAME 184:4
riddle wrapped in a m. | CHUR 81:6
myth 'good old days' were a m. | ATKI 16:3
m. of democracy | CROS 99:6
myths devoid of plausible m. | BERG 34:2
m. of the British Parliament | MAYB 246:4

nabobs nattering n. of negativism | AGNE 5:8
naked It is n. aggression | POWE 293:13
left me n. to mine enemies | SHAK 321:3
n. into the conference chamber | BEVA 36:11
name Arm, arm, my n. | SHAK 326:5
ghost of a great n. | LUCA 226:8
glory in the n. of Briton | GEOR 142:8
I do not see your n. | NORT 271:6
In the n. of God, go | CROM 98:5
my n. and memory | LAST 212:6
n. is Mandy | PARR 284:5
n. is neither one thing | CHUR 86:12
n. liveth for evermore | EPIT 129:3
n. spelled wrong | SHER 331:5
n. things after you | BUSH 61:10
n. to all succeeding ages curst | DRYD 118:7
n. we give the people | FLER 132:8
no profit but the n. | SHAK 319:15
whistling of a n. | POPE 292:5
names man with three n. | CROM 98:13

names (*cont.*):
n. of men | TROL 365:1
Napoleon thinks he is N. | CLEM 89:6
Napoleons Caesars and N. | HUXL 180:2
Narragansett Where are the N. | TECU 355:1
nastiest n. thing in the nicest way | GOLD 150:1
nasty n., brutish, and short | HOBB 173:10
nation AMERICA thus top n. | SELL 317:13
boundary of the march of a n. | PARN 283:13
broad mass of a n. | HITL 172:8
can deprive a n. | NAMI 264:3
conduct the affairs of the n. | AMER 7:2
create a n. Europe | MONN 257:10
every man and a n. | LOWE 226:5
existence as a n. | PITT 290:6
exterminate a n. | SPOC 344:7
ghosts of a n. | PEAR 285:2
great n. | WELL 380:1
lift up sword against n. | BIBL 39:13
n. a le gouvernment | MAIS 238:9
n. at his service | POMP 291:8
n. expects to be ignorant | JEFF 186:13
n. grieve | DRYD 119:2
n. is not governed | BURK 57:15
N. is starving | O'CO 272:7
n. of amateurs | ROSE 308:5
n. of shopkeepers | ADAM 4:7
n. of shopkeepers | NAPO 265:1
n. of shopkeepers | SMIT 333:8
N. once again | DAVI 102:9
n. shall rise against nation | BIBL 39:23
N. shall speak peace | REND 300:8
N. spoke to a Nation | KIPL 206:2
n. talking to itself | MILL 252:2
n. that had lion's heart | CHUR 84:11
n. which indulges toward another | WASH 375:8
new n. | LINC 219:9
No n. is fit | WILS 386:5
No n. was ever ruined | FRAN 137:6
no rainbow n. | MAND 241:4
of the n.'s care | PRIO 294:11
of the whole n. | MACD 232:9
one n. under God | BELL 31:1
one-third of a n. ill-housed | ROOS 305:10
opt out of a n. | LYNC 227:4
pillars of the n. state | PROD 295:1
rich and lazy n. | KIPL 206:7
small n. that stood alone | DE V 108:2
so goes the n. | PROV 296:2
Still better for the n. | EPIT 128:5
terrorize a whole n. | MURR 263:6
things which make a n. great | BACO 20:2
unity of the n. | KOHL 208:4
voice of a n. | RUSS 311:9
what our N. stands for | BETJ 36:1
national n. debt | HAMI 160:5
N. Debt is a very Good Thing | SELL 317:10
n. flag | SUMN 350:5
n. language | DE V 107:9
n. morality should have this | SHAW 328:3
nationalism N. is an infantile sickness | EINS 122:3

nationalism (*cont.*):
  N. is a silly cock   ALDI 6:4
  Scottish and Welsh n.   BAKE 24:2
nationalist good N.   MARK 243:1
nationality condense—a N.   WHIT 382:8
  Welsh n.   GLAD 148:12
nationalize need to n.   WILS 385:14
nations association of n.   WILS 386:17
  commonwealth of n.   ROSE 308:2
  danger of great n.   BAGE 23:13
  day of small n.   CHAM 74:8
  Europe of n.   DE G 105:8
  friendship with all n.   JEFF 186:3
  great n. acted like gangsters   KUBR 208:8
  let fierce contending n. know   ADDI 4:11
  N. have their infancy   BOLI 46:4
  n. how to live   MILT 252:11
  N. touch at their summits   BAGE 22:2
  n. which have put mankind   INGE 181:10
  other n. and states draw aside   GOGO 149:9
  Other n. use 'force'   WAUG 376:4
  place among the n.   EMME 126:7
  three small n.   STRA 349:5
  Two n.   DISR 114:15
  two n. have been at war   VOLT 371:10
  two n. warring   DURH 120:6
native England's n. people   BURN 61:7
  my n. land   SCOT 316:9
  our ideas about the n.   LESS 216:4
NATO N. exists for three reasons   ISMA 182:5
  N. in   ROBE 303:1
natural n. party of government   WILS 385:4
  n. propensities   BURK 60:2
  N. rights is simple nonsense   BENT 33:6
nature better angels of our n.   LINC 219:2
  How N. always does contrive   GILB 146:4
  N. has not cure   SMIT 338:5
  n. of war   HOBB 173:9
  N.'s mighty feast   MALT 240:3
  simply follow N.   LAO- 210:4
  violates the order of n.   HERO 170:7
naval N. tradition   CHUR 84:3
navies our n. melt away   KIPL 206:4
navy head of the N.   CARS 71:3
  n. nothing but rotten timber   BURK 58:2
  royal n. of England   BLAC 43:4
  upon the n.   CHAR 76:4
Nazis N. were great believers   JONE 192:8
  originated by the N.   BRUT 55:4
nearly n. kept waiting   LOUI 225:5
necessarily Not n. conscription   KING 204:2
necessary became n. to destroy the town   ANON 9:9
  if it is deemed n.   BROW 54:3
  journey *really* n.   OFFI 274:4
  n. evil   PAIN 279:1
  n. not to change   FALK 130:3
  no n. evils   JACK 183:4
  not only n. but expedient   ARIS 13:13
  sorry it was n.   TONE 362:2
necessities great n. call out   ADAM 2:1

necessity Cruel n.   CROM 98:1
  N. hath no law   CROM 98:8
  N. is the plea   PITT 290:4
  n. of being *ready*   LINC 219:3
  n. of doing something   JOHN 191:6
  pragmatic n.   DIDI 110:6
neck break thy n.   SHAK 324:5
  had but one n.   CALI 65:6
  Some chicken! Some n.   CHUR 82:8
necklace with our n.   MAND 241:3
necromancy mere n.   WHIT 381:5
needs according to his n.   MARX 244:6
  to each according to his n.   BAKU 24:4
negation n. of God   GLAD 147:6
negativism nattering nabobs of n.   AGNE 5:8
negotiate n. out of fear   KENN 198:6
  not here to n.   TRIM 363:10
negotiating N. with de Valera   LLOY 224:1
  when I was n.   MAND 241:2
negotiation difficult n.   SALI 312:6
Negro one drop of N. blood   HUGH 178:2
  root of the American N. problem   BALD 24:6
Negroes drivers of n.   JOHN 190:15
neighbour make war upon a n. nation   FAIR 130:2
  n.'s house is on fire   BURK 58:6
  policy of the good n.   ROOS 305:7
  rob a n.   MACA 228:10
neighbours Good fences make good n.   FROS 138:10
  happening to our n.   CHAM 74:9
  have good n.   ELIZ 123:9
Nell Pretty witty N.   PEPY 287:7
Nemo *N. me impune lacessit*   MOTT 262:5
neoclassical n. endogenous growth   BROW 53:7
nephews Priests have n.   PEEL 286:14
Nero N. fiddled   MENC 248:13
nerve do not lose my n.   NEHR 265:7
nest I have no n.-eggs   LLOY 222:6
nets Laws are generally found to be n.   SHEN 330:5
neutral studiously n.   WILS 386:7
  United States must be n.   WILS 386:3
neutrality Armed n. is ineffectual   WILS 386:10
  Just for a word 'n.'   BETH 35:7
  N. helps the oppressor   WIES 383:2
never N. explain   FISH 132:2
  n. had it so good   MACM 235:9
  n. had it so good   SLOG 337:1
  N. in the field of human conflict   CHUR 81:14
  n. surrender   PAIS 281:3
  n. thought of thinking   GILB 146:3
new believes that n. Labour   DAVI 102:2
  called the N. World   CANN 69:3
  n. and untried   LINC 218:10
  n. deal for the American people   ROOS 305:5
  n. frontier   KENN 198:2
  N. Frontier was not   SCHL 316:1
  N. Hampshire has long   BUSH 62:9
  N. Labour brand   GOUL 152:2
  New Labour, n. danger   SLOG 335:15

obedience (*cont.*):
  reluctant o.   MACA 229:12
obedient o. to their laws we lie   EPIT 128:2
obey not o. shall not eat   TROT 365:12
  not o. the will   PEEL 285:12
  o. them   HORS 176:10
obeyed right to be o.   JOHN 188:6
object o. of oratory   MACA 230:14
objections o. may be made   JOHN 191:6
objective o. of the science of politics   ARIS 13:8
obligation o. which goes unrecognized
                                                  WEIL 378:3
obliteration policy is o.   BELL 30:10
obstinate o. little man   THOM 359:3
obstruction kind of 'consecrated o.'   BAGE 21:8
obstructions impertinent o.   SMIT 337:9
occasion never lose an o.   DISR 115:1
occupations let us love our o.   DICK 109:6
occupy o. himself more intensively   NICO 268:8
ocean abandon the o.   CLAY 88:7
  billowy o.   BARR 28:2
  leap into the o.   HUME 178:7
  o. as their road   WALL 373:2
  rolling on of o.   MORR 260:10
Odysseus Like O., the President   KEYN 200:8
  O. was a bastard   CROS 98:15
off I want to be o. it   PAXM 284:10
  O. with his head   SHAK 327:1
offence o. inspires less horror   GIBB 145:7
  only defence is in o.   BALD 25:5
  where the o. is   SHAK 319:12
offended not o. the king   LAST 213:12
offering o. too little   CANN 69:2
office dignity of the o.   GEOR 143:6
  dog's obeyed in o.   SHAK 324:6
  for o. boys   SALI 313:2
  got into o.   CHUR 84:7
  got into o.   KENN 198:10
  holding public o.   ACHE 1:4
  if in o.   PEEL 285:11
  in o. but not in power   LAMO 209:6
  insolence of o.   SHAK 319:9
  man unfit for o.   FABI 129:9
  most insignificant o.   ADAM 3:8
  not to be trusted with the o.   BROD 52:6
  O., and custom   SHAK 327:6
  O. before honour   POWE 293:9
  o.-building   JEFF 185:12
  o. going to run him   HEND 168:4
  o. of the Prime Minister   ASQU 15:5
  O. tends to confer   LAWS 211:7
  o. you refer to   BROW 53:9
  ousted from o.   LIEB 217:10
  price paid for o.   TOCQ 361:3
  receives the seals of o.   ROSE 308:8
  statesman in o.   TAYL 354:9
  trying to get into o.   MCMA 235:3
  waters of o.   TROL 364:5
  when o. is in question   PEEL 286:15
  Whichever party is in o.   WILS 385:10
  without an o.   CHUR 85:11

officer art thou o.   SHAK 320:7
offices o. as public trusts   CALH 65:4
official concept of the o. secret   WEBE 377:6
  This high o., all allow   HERB 170:2
officially o. denied   COCK 92:2
officials o. are the servants   GOWE 152:3
  O. take different view   ROTH 309:2
  to protect o.   LYNN 227:9
offspring Time's noblest o.   BERK 34:3
often Vote early and vote o.   MILE 250:1
oil o. which renders   HUME 178:5
  Scotland's o.   SLOG 335:5
OK O. We lost   MAJO 239:4
old adherence to the o.   LINC 218:10
  balance of the O.   CANN 69:3
  good o. Cause   MILT 252:12
  instead of o. ones   PEEL 285:9
  make me conservative when o.   FROS 138:9
  name thee O. Glory   DRIV 118:5
  O. age   TROT 365:7
  O. Age a regret   DISR 113:18
  o. gentleman would be willing   SALI 313:7
  o. guy drove the choice   BUSH 62:8
  o., mad, blind   SHEL 330:2
  o. man in a hurry   CHUR 79:10
  o. order changeth   TENN 355:13
  o. people are ostracized   MONB 256:9
  o. problems   WILS 385:12
  o., wild, and incomprehensible man   VICT 370:9
  planned by o. men   RICE 301:5
  sad o. age   TALL 352:5
  warn you not to grow o.   KINN 204:4
older O. men declare war   HOOV 176:7
oldest o., wisest politician   THOR 359:10
olet *Pecunia non o.*   VESP 370:5
oligarchy *aristocracy*, call it o.   HOBB 173:15
  extreme democracy or absolute o.   ARIS 14:2
Olympian O. bolts   DISR 111:12
omelette fuss about an o.   VOLT 372:10
omitted O., all the voyage   SHAK 324:1
omnibus man on the Clapham o.   BOWE 49:6
omnipotent land of the o. No   BOLD 46:1
once O. is more than enough   BIRC 40:11
  O. to every man   LOWE 226:5
one encompassed but o. man   SHAK 321:10
  loyalties which centre upon number o.
                                                  CHUR 85:7
  o.-eyed man is king   ERAS 127:2
  o. man fewer   METT 249:4
  O. man plus the truth   PROV 296:14
  O. man shall have one vote   CART 71:6
  O. step forward   LENI 215:6
open enter the o. society   CARM 70:13
  O. covenants of peace   WILS 386:15
  o. door   HAY 164:5
  with an o. mouth   STEV 347:14
opinion being without an o.   BAGE 23:10
  call it o.   HOBB 173:7
  form a clear o.   BONH 47:2
  Government and public o.   SHAW 328:7

opinion (*cont.*):
moves with o. then it stays | BENN 32:10
o. is truth filtered | PHIL 289:1
o. of the people | JEFF 185:2
o. one man entertains | PALM 282:2
Party is organized o. | DISR 112:5
plague of o. | SHAK 327:9
poor itch of your o. | SHAK 318:5
Public o. | BAGE 23:1
were of one o. | MILL 250:9
opinions as many o. as people | TERE 356:1
by men's o. | FABI 129:9
delivers his o. | CICE 86:14
music of our own o. | STEV 347:15
o. of the majority | PEEL 285:13
o. that are held | RUSS 311:4
so bad as their o. | MACK 234:4
opium o. of the people | MARX 244:3
with an o. wand | PAIN 280:7
opponent o. cannot be | ORWE 276:15
opponents adopted by our o. | PORT 292:14
purpose of his o. | TROL 365:6
opportunism principally o. | CHUR 79:6
opportunities one of those o. | GLAD 148:9
opportunity gates of o. | JOHN 190:4
greatest o. | DISR 114:9
Ireland's o. | PROV 296:5
O. is more powerful | DISR 115:1
oppose o. everything | DERR 107:1
opposed o. to any proposal | MACN 237:4
opposite on the o. side | ANON 11:9
opposition capacity in the Leader of the O.
| BAGE 23:7
disease of o. | GALB 140:12
duty of an O. | DERB 107:1
effective means of o. | GOEB 149:6
figure by o. | HALI 159:8
Her Majesty's O. | BAGE 20:11
His Majesty's O. | HOBH 174:2
Leader of the O. | KINN 204:12
O. is four or five | HATT 163:4
O., on coming into power | BAGE 22:4
O.'s about asking | LYNN 227:6
period in o. | RIDL 302:4
pleasure of the O. | MACL 234:10
without a formidable O. | DISR 114:3
oppressed barbarously o. | LAST 213:3
mind of the o. | BIKO 40:8
oppression violate would be o. | JEFF 186:1
war against o. | MCAL 228:4
oppressive o. and unjust | BURK 59:6
oppressor Neutrality helps the o. | WIES 383:2
o.'s wrong | SHAK 319:9
opprobrium term of o. | MOYN 262:10
opt o. out of a nation | LYNC 227:4
opulence degree of o. | SMIT 333:3
oracles lively O. of God | CORO 96:5
orange O. card | CHUR 79:8
Orangemen why the O. are not | O'HI 273:5
orator I am no o., as Brutus is | SHAK 323:12
No o. ever made an impression | BAGE 20:8

orators greatest living o. | LLOY 223:3
oratory appetite for o. | GALB 140:8
first in o. | DEMO 106:2
object of o. | MACA 230:14
ordained not o. by nature | JORD 193:4
o. error | VANS 369:4
ordeal fourteen years' o. | MITC 253:6
order defined by the word 'o.' | METT 249:8
Good o. is the foundation | BURK 59:5
keep the government in o. | SCAR 315:6
new world o. | BUSH 62:7
old o. changeth | TENN 355:13
o. of the boot | CHUR 83:4
O. reigns in Warsaw | ANON 10:7
party of o. or stability | MILL 250:10
renovation of the natural o. | PAIN 280:9
social o. destroyed | TOCQ 361:8
violates the o. of nature | HERO 170:7
war creates o. | BREC 50:9
orders gave them their o. | WELL 379:5
ordinary behaviour of o. people | TAYL 353:7
o. men exercise initiative | TAWN 352:13
warn you not to be o. | KINN 204:6
organ o. and the maypole | JORD 193:5
o. of public opinion | DISR 111:12
organic committee is o. | PARK 283:4
organization o. of idolatry | SHAW 328:12
organize Don't waste time mourning—o.
| LAST 213:2
organized o. hypocrisy | DISR 111:9
o. political party | ROGE 304:7
Party is o. opinion | DISR 112:5
organs other o. take their tone | GLAD 147:7
original sound and o. ideas | MACM 236:4
originality some o. | WEBB 376:8
originals few o. and many copies | TOCQ 361:1
ornament Nobility is a graceful o. | BURK 59:2
orphan defeat is an o. | CIAN 86:13
osprey o. to the fish | SHAK 319:2
ostracized old people are o. | MONB 256:9
ostrich can not be an o. | WILS 386:8
other o. Eden | SHAK 326:2
Prudence is the o. woman | ANON 10:9
otherwise would wish o. | NEWS 268:3
ought didn't o. never to have done it | BEVI 38:10
out cannot o.-vote them | JOHN 191:16
counted them all o. | HANR 161:2
o. with the Stuarts | DISR 114:11
will o.-argue them | JOHN 191:16
outdated o. methods | WILS 384:9
outdoor system of o. relief | BRIG 51:6
outlaw attacks from o. states | REAG 299:12
outlawed liar should be o. | HALI 158:7
o. or exiled | MAGN 238:4
outlaws o. Russia | REAG 299:10
outrage Stupidity, o. | ROST 309:1
outside o. pissing in | JOHN 190:5
over it is all o. | NORT 271:7
oversexed, and o. here | TRIN 364:2
O. there | COHA 92:3
overbearing o. and offensive | VICT 371:1

overcome We shall o.   SONG 343:7
overpaid grossly o.   HERB 170:2
   O., overfed, oversexed   TRIN 364:2
oversexed o., and over here   TRIN 364:2
owed so much o. by so many to so few
                                                   CHUR 81:14
own my words are my o.   CHAR 76:5
   only to those who o. one   LIEB 217:12
owner I am the o.   MAND 241:6
ownership o. of the means of production
                                                   ANON 11:11
Oxford academia in O.   AUNG 18:4
   King to O. sent   BROW 54:5
   secret in the O. sense   FRAN 137:9
   To O. sent a troop   TRAP 362:8
oxygen o. of publicity   THAT 357:8

pacify p. Ireland   GLAD 147:11
pack running with the p.   BUTL 63:7
Paddington London is to P.   CANN 68:11
paeans laurels to p.   CICE 86:16
Paganini fiddler after P.   NICO 266:9
page foot of the first p.   SAND 314:4
paid Judas was p.   POWE 293:6
   we ha' p. in full   KIPL 206:6
pain p. to the bear   MACA 230:5
pains no gains without p.   STEV 346:10
paint democratic p.   TOCQ 361:9
   p. the chameleon   KEYN 201:5
painted wood p. to look like iron   BISM 42:3
palace p. is not safe   DISR 115:12
pale turned p.   SOUT 344:1
Palladium P. of all the civil   JUNI 195:7
palm bear the p. alone   SHAK 321:7
Pandora If you open that P.'s Box   BEVI 38:11
panem P. et circenses   JUVE 195:12
panics Tory party never p.   HOSK 177:2
pantheon Labour Party's p.   PIML 289:5
panther Black P. Party   NEWT 266:2
papacy p. is not other   HOBB 174:1
paper All reactionaries are p. tigers   MAO 242:4
   built a p.-mill   SHAK 320:18
   here is the p.   CHAM 75:1
   virtue of p. government   BURK 57:12
Papist P., yet a Calvinist   EPIT 128:7
parade on the p. ground   SMIT 338:2
parades produce victory p.   HOBS 174:3
paradise catch the bird of p.   KHRU 202:4
parapet could not see a p.   CRIT 97:5
parchment should be made p.   SHAK 320:17
pardon God may p. you   ELIZ 124:8
parens king is truly p. patriae   JAME 184:3
parents all working-class p.   ABBO 1:1
   children bury their p.   HERO 170:7
   illegitimate p.   JOSE 194:3
   In mine it was the p.   SLOV 333:2
   p. were the Lord knows who   DEFO 104:11
   produce bad p.   MORS 261:2
Paris Hoares to P.   GEOR 143:9
   P. is well worth a mass   HENR 169:2

Paris (*cont.*):
   P. was French—and silent   TUCH 367:6
parish pension from his p.   RUSK 310:11
park p. one Jaguar   HAGU 156:8
parks p. are the lungs of London   PITT 290:3
parliament build your House of P.   WELL 380:2
   function of P.   BOOT 48:6
   in a 21st-century p.   ASHD 15:1
   Irishmen in her P.   BALF 26:3
   let alone a P.   ANON 12:4
   look on the proceedings of P.   BAGE 23:3
   minuet danced by P.   SCAR 315:4
   modern P.   CONN 94:1
   myths of the British P.   MAYB 246:4
   not even p.   SCAR 315:7
   object of P.   CHUR 84:5
   of [P.]   BOOT 48:4
   p. are a lot of hard-faced men   BALD 24:9
   p. can do any thing   PEMB 286:19
   P. itself would not exist   SCAR 315:2
   p. of whores   O'RO 275:4
   P., Rabble   COBB 91:10
   P. speaking through reporters   CARL 70:3
   returned to P.   DISR 115:20
   Rump P.   SELL 317:8
   Scots p.   JOHN 192:3
   Scottish P.   EWIN 129:7
   shall be a Scottish p.   ANON 11:6
   shall be a Scottish p.   DEWA 108:7
   three years in P.   BROC 52:5
   united P.   FLET 133:2
   voices in P.   RUSK 310:10
parliamentarian safe pleasure for a p.   CRIT 97:6
parliamentary large p. majority   BUTL 63:2
   old P. hand   GLAD 148:8
   p. eloquence   CARL 70:5
   P. Government   DISR 112:14
   P. leper   WILS 385:2
   p. majorities   BONA 46:8
parliaments In p., men   HALI 159:6
   mother of P.   BRIG 51:8
Parnell Poor P.   JOYC 194:8
parrot has become a p.   PAIS 281:7
parson Whig in a p.'s gown   JOHN 191:1
   world's p.   HEAL 165:9
partiality neither anger nor p.   TACI 351:7
participate refusing to p.   PLAT 290:12
particular Did nothing in p.   GILB 146:5
particulars in minute p.   BLAK 44:11
parties P. come to power   RIDL 302:4
   P. must ever exist   BURK 57:21
   p. which divide the state   EMER 126:4
   that there are three p.   MAYB 246:4
party break your p.   HEAD 165:7
   but with a p.   JEFF 185:7
   each p. is worse than   ROGE 304:5
   educate our p.   DISR 112:9
   extreme p. is most irritated   BAGE 23:11
   greenest political p.   JONE 192:8
   I believe that without p.   DISR 112:15
   in the p. manifestoes   ROTH 309:3

peace (*cont.*):

in time of p. thinks of war	ANON 8:9
just and lasting p.	LINC 220:7
Let us have p.	GRAN 153:3
Let war yield to p.	CICE 86:16
live alone, at p.	ROOS 306:9
Make it a *green* p.	DARN 101:7
making p.	HEAL 166:6
making p. is harder	STEV 346:7
man of p.	DE V 107:5
may not be a just p.	IZET 182:8
more precious than p.	WILS 386:15
nation is only at p.	KING 204:3
not a p. treaty	FOCH 133:6
only give us p.	PITT 290:1
Open covenants of p.	WILS 386:15
p. and welfare of Europe	PEEL 286:8
p. between equals	WILS 386:9
P. cannot be built	ADAM 2:7
p. cannot be maintained	RUSS 311:10
P., commerce	JEFF 186:3
p., easy taxes	SMIT 333:3
p. for our time	CHAM 75:2
P., freedom	SHAK 322:13
p. from freedom	MALC 239:11
p. has been broken	ROOS 305:12
P. hath her victories	MILT 252:7
p. I hope with honour	DISR 113:5
p. is a modern invention	MAIN 238:8
P. is a very apoplexy	SHAK 319:1
P. is indivisible	LITV 221:7
P. is much more precious	SADA 311:12
P. is no longer a dream	CLIN 91:2
P. is poor reading	HARD 162:2
P. nothing but slovenliness	BREC 50:9
P., political p.	MITC 256:5
P., retrenchment, and reform	BRIG 51:7
'P. upon earth!' was said	HARD 162:3
p. which she has treasured	WILS 386:11
p. with honour	CHAM 75:2
people want p. so much	EISE 122:9
plunging into a cold p.	YELT 390:5
potent advocates of p.	GEOR 143:5
sing The merry songs of p.	SHAK 321:4
So enamoured on p.	CLAR 87:7
solution for world p.	MARS 243:5
speak p. unto nation	REND 300:8
tell me p. has broken out	BREC 50:12
than to make p.	CLEM 89:7
war and p. in the 21st century	KOHL 208:6
War is p.	ORWE 275:14
war that we may live in p.	ARIS 13:9

peaceably p. if we can | CLAY 88:8

peaceful p. coexistence | FULB 139:2

p. revolution | KENN 199:1

peacefully p. towards its close | DAWS 103:3

Pearsean P. ghost in the eye | O'BR 272:3

peasant cross woman's p. origins | O'DO 273:2

peasantry p. its pack animal | TROT 365:8

p., their country's pride | GOLD 150:4

peasants cricket with their p. | TREV 363:2

pecker p. in my pocket	JOHN 190:8
pecunia *P. non olet*	VESP 370:5
peer Not a reluctant p.	BENN 32:1
p. is exalted	PAIN 280:2
peerage owe the English p.	DISR 113:15
When I want a p.	NORT 271:9
peers House of P.	GILB 146:5
in the P. will take his place	BROU 53:1
judgement of his p.	MAGN 238:4
love our House of P.	GILB 146:9
pen mightier than the p.	HOGB 174:5
pencil throw down his p.	SHEP 330:6
pencils feel for their blue p.	ESHE 127:5
pendulum vibration of a p.	JUNI 195:2
pennies P. don't fall from heaven	THAT 356:6
penny Not a p. off the pay	COOK 95:4
pension labourer to take his p.	RUSK 310:11
p. list of the republic	CLEV 90:2
P. Pay given	JOHN 190:13
pentagon P., that immense monument	
	FRAN 137:7

people as if p. mattered	SCHU 316:4
as many opinions as p.	TERE 356:1
belongs to the p.	LINC 219:1
builds on the p.	MACH 233:10
by the p.	PAGE 278:6
enthusiasm of the p.	WELL 379:1
faith in The P.	DICK 110:2
fiery, impulsive p.	HOUS 177:3
fool all of the p.	ADAM 2:4
fool all the p.	LINC 220:13
good of the p.	CICE 86:15
I am myself the p.	ROBE 303:2
impulse of the English p.	BAGE 22:10
indictment against an whole p.	BURK 57:17
in favour of the p.	BURK 59:10
is the *p.'s choice*	SHER 330:9
knowledge among the p.	ADAM 3:12
labours of the p.	JEFF 186:7
Let my p. go	BIBL 39:1
love of the p.	BURK 58:2
made for the p.	WEBS 377:7
more than half the p. are right	WHIT 381:4
my p.'s happiness	ELIZ 124:6
new p. takes the land	CHES 78:1
no petty p.	YEAT 390:2
one p., one leader	SLOG 334:13
opinion of the p.	JEFF 185:2
opium of the p.	MARX 244:3
p. are the masters	BURK 60:9
p. as a source of power	SCAR 315:4
p. as base as itself	PULI 295:3
p. govern themselves	THIE 358:12
p. have spoken	FITT 132:5
p. is the true legislator	BURK 59:17
p. made the Constitution	MARS 243:8
p. marching on	MORR 260:10
People p., but books never die	ROOS 306:7
p.'s prayer	DRYD 118:10
Power to the p.	SLOG 336:2
same as if they was p.	DURE 120:4

people (*cont.*):
servants of the p.	BLAI 43:11
She was the P.'s Princess	BLAI 44:1
support of the p.	CLEV 90:3
suppose the p. good	ROBE 303:5
This was a p.'s war	TAYL 353:3
voice of the p.	ALCU 6:3
we are the p. of England	CHES 77:12
What is the city but the p.	SHAK 318:8
What kind of a p.	CHUR 82:4
worship the p.	BACO 18:10

peopled conquered and p.	SEEL 317:2
Peoria play in P.	PROV 296:11
perdition led to *p.* by a man	WEST 380:9
perestroika restructuring [p.]	GORB 151:4
started the process of p.	GORB 151:5
perfect Entire and whole and p.	SPRI 344:8
most p. political community	ARIS 14:3
perfidious p. Albion	XIMÉ 389:2
performers no all the p.	MURR 263:8
perish England shall p.	ELIZ 124:11
p. together as fools	KING 203:7
though the world p.	MOTT 262:3
venal city ripe to p.	SALL 313:12
permanent p. alliances	WASH 375:6
p. indignation	VALÉ 368:10
p. officials	HARC 161:4
permitted all is p.	MEGA 246:8
p. to make all the ballads	FLET 133:1
pernicious most p. race	SWIF 350:9
Perón have liked to be P.	PERÓ 287:11
perpetual p. quarrel	BURK 57:20
persecution asylum from p.	UNIV 368:9
P. is not an original feature	PAIN 280:5
P. produced its natural effect	MACA 230:1
persevering no dignity in p. in error	PEEL 286:3
person most superior p.	ANON 10:1
personality political p.	JENK 188:4
rocks of mere p.	ANON 11:1
personally should be p. associated	BLAI 44:8
perspire Gladstone may p.	CHUR 79:7
persuade p. a multitude	HOOK 176:1
persuading By p. others	JUNI 195:3
persuasion P. is the resource	GIBB 145:11
p. only	MILT 252:10
Peter government which robs P.	SHAW 327:17
petticoat out of the Realm in my p.	ELIZ 123:8
petty no p. people	YEAT 390:2
we p. men	SHAK 321:8
phantom embarrassed p.	DISR 114:6
pheasant make room for the p.	JOHN 192:4
philanthropist as a professed p.	TROL 364:10
Philistine run by a p.	KAUF 196:5
Philistines Barbarians, P., and Populace	ARNO 14:7
P. proper, or middle class	ARNO 14:9
philosopher p. may preach	GIBB 145:13
philosophers P. are very regardless	PEEL 286:13
philosophy p. quenches them	VOLT 372:2
study mathematics and p.	ADAM 3:7

photographers let the P. stay	SHER 330:11
p. and their zoom	ULLR 368:6
phrases *La mort, sans p.*	SIEY 332:6
P. make history here	MAFF 238:2
pickle weaned on a p.	ANON 11:10
pictures behind all the p.	BUSH 62:1
furnish the p.	HEAR 167:2
p. of their children	BUSH 62:12
pie p. in the sky	HILL 172:4
pies Bellamy's veal p.	LAST 213:8
piety bear witness to his p.	ADAM 4:4
pig wrestling with a greased p.	PATT 284:9
pigeon branded, p.-holed	PRES 294:6
pigs I am fond of p.	CHUR 86:3
pike freedom for the p.	TAWN 352:10
p. at the bottom	HEAL 166:8
p. in the thatch	DE C 104:1
Pilate What is truth? said jesting P.	BACO 19:16
pilgrims Land of the p.' pride	SMIT 338:10
pill any p. can be swallowed	TROL 364:5
pillar p. of the State	SOLZ 340:7
pillars four p. of government	BACO 19:11
p. of civilization	MONN 257:9
p. of the nation state	PROD 295:1
pillow like the feather p.	HAIG 157:1
pilot daring p. in extremity	DRYD 118:8
Dropping the p.	TENN 355:3
p. of the storm	BAGE 21:2
pink p., quivering Ted	ANON 7:7
pinstripe come in a p. suit	FEIN 131:2
pips until the p. squeak	GEDD 142:2
piratical p. old bruiser	HAIL 157:7
piss pitcher of warm p.	GARN 141:9
pissing inside the tent p. out	JOHN 190:5
like p. down your leg	JOHN 190:7
pistol found the smoking p.	CONA 93:6
I reach for my p.	JOHS 192:5
pitcher p. of warm piss	GARN 141:9
Pitt P. as opposed to Fox	BUTL 63:3
pity Scots deserve no p.	FLET 133:2
pixie some vanilla-flavoured p.	PARR 284:4
pizza deliver a p.	ANON 12:4
place All rising to great p.	BACO 19:8
for the sake of the p.	HALI 159:1
Get p. and wealth	POPE 292:6
Gratitude of p.-expectants	WALP 374:5
In p. of strife	CAST 72:4
p. in the sun	BÜLO 56:3
p. in the sun	WILH 383:7
P., that great object	SMIT 333:4
p. without power	ROSE 308:3
right man in the right p.	JEFF 187:7
rising unto p. is laborious	BACO 19:6
thus with height of p.	WOTT 388:7
plagues of all p.	DEFO 104:12
plain p., blunt man	SHAK 323:12
plaintive p. treble	DISR 111:12
plan p. the future by the past	BURK 57:1
planets stars and all the p.	TRUM 366:1
planning resist all p.	OAKE 272:2
plant not a structure, but a p.	PARK 283:4

plant (*cont.*):
p. of rapid growth — WASH 375:9
p. of slow growth — PITT 289:9
planter of p. stock — HEWI 171:11
platitude p. is simply a truth repeated — BALD 25:1
plausibility confer a dreadful p. — LAWS 211:7
plausible manufacturing the p. — BALD 25:14
plausibly p. maintained — BURR 61:8
play Better than a p. — CHAR 76:6
only to p. fair — LABO 208:9
p. in Peoria — PROV 296:11
played p. the game — SMIT 338:6
playedst p. most foully for't — SHAK 325:3
playing won on the p. fields — WELL 379:11
pleasant England's green and p. land — BLAK 44:13
please do what I p. — FRED 137:12
not here to p. myself — HEND 168:3
To tax and to p. — BURK 57:11
pleasure p. to the spectators — MACA 230:5
pleasures English take their p. — SULL 350:2
two supreme p. — ROSE 308:8
plebeian of a p. leader — DISR 114:13
plebiscite justice by p. — ZOBE 391:6
plot discerned in history a p. — FISH 131:6
Gunpowder Treason and P. — SONG 343:2
This blessèd p. — SHAK 326:2
plots P., true or false — DRYD 118:6
plotting p., and playing — CARL 70:8
plough boy that driveth the p. — TYND 368:5
p. my furrow alone — ROSE 308:7
wherefore p. — SHEL 329:12
ploughman wrong even the poorest p. — CHAR 76:1
plowshares beat their swords into p. — BIBL 39:13
pluck great p. — WEBB 376:8
plumage pities the p. — PAIN 279:14
plumber can't get a p. to come — SCHW 316:7
plumbers good p. — NIXO 270:8
plus *Il n'y a p. de Pyrénées* — LOUI 225:4
I think that's a p. — DOLE 116:9
Plymouth pious ones of P. — EVAR 127:7
PM he ended P. CH and OM — ATTL 17:3
pocket guinea you have in your p. — RUSK 310:12
in Britain, in your p. — WILS 385:5
neither picks my p. — JEFF 187:8
pecker in my p. — JOHN 190:8
picking his p. — JOHN 189:5
pockets fructify in the p. — GLAD 148:19
poem being the author of that p. — WOLF 387:5
essentially the greatest p. — WHIT 382:7
poet p.'s mouth be shut — YEAT 389:6
p. will give up writing — CELA 74:3
poetical p. abstractions — MACN 237:3
poetry campaign in p. — CUOM 99:8
writing p. — POWE 293:5
poets P. hope too much — LAWR 211:5
point different p. of view — NAPO 264:7
points thousand p. of light — BUSH 62:5
poising p. every weight — MARV 243:11
poison food only a cover for p. — BURK 59:13
got as far as p.-gas — HARD 162:3
put p. in your coffee — ASTO 16:1

poison (*cont.*):
strongest p. ever known — BLAK 44:9
poker tossed around like p. chips — ALBR 6:2
pole top of the greasy p. — DISR 115:8
polecat semi-house-trained p. — FOOT 134:2
police p. can beat you — SHAW 328:15
p. were to blame — GRAN 152:7
policeman p. is there — DALE 100:7
terrorist and the p. — CONR 94:9
than a p. — SALI 313:4
world's p. — HEAL 165:9
policemen p. of the world — BONA 46:10
policies but rarely p. — HURD 179:8
P. must 'grow' — BAGE 23:8
policy defend a bad p. — SALI 313:5
determine p. — TREV 363:5
English p. is to float — SALI 312:4
foreign p. — COOK 95:6
home p.: I wage war — CLEM 89:5
If the p. isn't hurting — MAJO 238:11
impose a p. — WAUG 376:1
My [foreign] p. — BEVI 38:9
national p. — BRIA 51:3
on foreign p. — GALB 140:9
p. of retaliation — PARN 283:11
p. of the good neighbour — ROOS 305:7
tyrants from p. — BURK 58:17
polite no allies to be p. to — GEOR 144:4
politeness p. of kings — LOUI 225:9
politic unavoidably be p. — PEEL 285:6
political by nature a p. animal — ARIS 13:11
fear of P. Economy — SELL 317:10
feature of p. life — KILM 202:10
fills p. graveyards — KINN 204:4
half your p. life — THAT 357:2
healthy state of p. life — MILL 250:10
hold of the p. machinery — CHOD 79:1
I've kept p. diaries — GEOG 142:7
nature of a p. party — TROL 364:15
no p. power — WOLF 387:8
not a p. figure — DIAN 109:2
points to a p. career — SHAW 328:5
p. advancement — LEVI 216:8
p. aspirant — MENC 248:12
p. autonomy — GRAY 153:9
p. Cave of Adullam — BRIG 51:9
p. consequences — MANS 241:11
p. decision — TREN 362:9
P. Economy — RUSK 310:5
p. genius — TAYL 353:16
p. heads — HARC 161:4
p. intriguer — TROL 364:4
P. language . . . is designed — ORWE 276:14
p. lives end in failure — POWE 294:1
p. old monk — MURD 263:3
p. party is not capable — DISR 115:3
p. power — TROL 364:3
p. power of another — LOCK 224:6
p. speech and writing — ORWE 276:13
schemes of p. improvement — JOHN 191:5
something beyond p. life — ARIS 13:10

politician education of a p.   CHUR 84:16
    forced to be a p.   POWE 293:5
    generosity of the p.   MAUG 246:2
    good p.   MENC 248:10
    greatest art of a p.   BOLI 46:3
    honest p.   CAME 67:2
    I'm not a p.   DOLE 116:9
    judge a p.   IVIN 182:6
    lurks a p.   ARIS 13:7
    memory for a p.   MORL 260:8
    my life as a p.   POWE 294:2
    not a p.   STEV 346:6
    oldest, wisest p.   THOR 359:10
    p. is a man   TRUM 366:10
    p. is an arse upon   CUMM 99:7
    p. is a person   STEV 347:14
    p. is a statesman who   POMP 291:8
    p. never believes what he says   DE G 105:7
    p. performs upon   TAYL 353:5
    P.'s corpse was laid away   BELL 31:3
    p. to complain about   POWE 293:10
    p. was a person   LLOY 223:7
    p. who has lost his job   MENC 248:3
    popular p.   ARIS 13:6
    scurvy p.   SHAK 324:7
politicians Conviction p.   BANC 27:8
    die for p.   THOM 359:6
    done to death by p.   CHES 77:1
    Europe on the lips of p.   BISM 42:1
    fault of our p.   TROL 364:12
    Ninety percent of the p.   KISS 207:5
    Old p. chew   POPE 292:2
    P. also have no leisure   ARIS 13:10
    P. are entitled   HATT 163:5
    P. are exiles   GRIG 155:7
    P. are the same   KHRU 202:5
    p. have had to listen   FITT 132:5
    P. hear the word 'culture'   ESHE 127:5
    P. neither love nor hate   CHES 77:4
    p. of our time   MACA 229:3
    P. often believe   ROTH 309:2
    Tinhorn p.   WHIT 381:8
    too serious to be left to p.   DE G 105:5
    unelected reject p.   RIDL 302:6
    visionary p.   BURK 57:6
    whole race of p.   SWIF 350:10
politics aim of practical p.   MENC 248:5
    by the rules of p.   NIXO 270:12
    Confound their p.   SONG 342:1
    continuation of p.   CLAU 88:5
    except in p.   BYRO 64:7
    first part of p.   MICH 249:10
    give his mind to p.   SHAW 327:13
    In p., if you want anything   THAT 356:3
    in p. the middle way   ADAM 3:5
    In p., there is no use   CHAM 74:4
    In p., what begins   COLE 92:6
    invariably of the p.   BORR 49:2
    invisible hand in p.   FRIE 138:3
    In well-framed p.   BAGE 20:4
    I taste no p.   SMIT 339:2

politics (*cont.*):
    language of p.   DISR 112:1
    Magnanimity in p.   BURK 58:3
    mule of p.   DISR 113:19
    no true friends in p.   CLAR 87:13
    objective of the science of p.   ARIS 13:8
    people in p.   DEED 104:4
    p. and equations   EINS 122:4
    p. and our laws   DEWA 108:9
    P. and the fate   CAMU 68:3
    P. are now nothing more   JOHN 191:13
    p., as a practice   ADAM 2:9
    p. as a profession   HOWE 177:8
    P. can only be   KEEN 197:6
    P. comes at least second   GIUL 147:3
    P., executive expression   BRIT 52:3
    p. grease   TAWN 352:8
    P. has got so expensive   ROGE 304:4
    P. has got to be fun   CLAR 87:15
    P. is a marathon   LIVI 221:10
    P. is a very long-run game   MAJO 238:10
    P. is just like   REAG 299:4
    p. is local   O'NE 274:10
    P. is not the art   GALB 140:13
    p. is present history   FREE 138:1
    P. is the art   GAND 140:16
    P. is the art of preventing   VALÉ 368:11
    P. is the only profession   STEV 348:1
    P. is war without bloodshed   MAO 242:2
    P. is worse   MONT 259:3
    P. makes strange   PROV 296:15
    P. makes strange   WARN 374:10
    P. make you think   CAST 72:2
    p. of purpose   HUMP 179:3
    p. of the left   JENK 187:11
    P. supposed to be   REAG 299:5
    P. too serious a matter   DE G 105:5
    practical p.   ADAM 2:13
    practice of p.   DISR 114:5
    religion from p.   TREV 363:6
    renewed focus of p.   HAVE 163:9
    speak from above p.   MCAL 227:12
    succeed in p.   LLOY 223:2
    their p. usually stink   LAWR 211:5
    this P. thing   ROGE 304:5
    times in p.   GALB 140:14
    week is a long time in p.   WILS 385:3
    will not close my p.   FOX 136:2
    zeal in p.   JUNI 195:3
politique p. father   JAME 184:3
poll of the p. tax   THAT 358:7
    science of p.-taking   WHIT 381:5
pollute p. now   HOLD 174:8
pollution p. of democracy   WHIT 381:7
Pomeranian single P. grenadier   BISM 42:10
pomp grinning at his p.   SHAK 326:7
    p. of pow'r   GRAY 154:1
    p. of yesterday   KIPL 206:4
Pompey Knew you not P.   SHAK 321:5
poodle in a p. parlour   PARR 284:2
    right hon. Gentleman's p.   LLOY 222:5

pool at the bottom of a p. — HEAL 166:8
poor better to be p. than rich — CECI 73:9
cannot help the p. — LINC 220:12
divided among the p. — SHAW 328:2
faces of the p. — NICO 266:10
give food to the p. — CAMA 66:12
Laws grind the p. — GOLD 150:7
make the p. poorer — NEHR 265:9
many who are p. — KENN 198:5
no peasant in my kingdom so p. — HENR 168:9
p. did not — DE V 108:4
p. have cried — SHAK 323:6
p. have no right — RUSK 310:14
p. man at his gate — ALEX 6:5
p. man loved the great — MACA 230:12
p. people in rich countries — BAUE 28:7
p. who die — SART 314:9
provision for the p. — JOHN 191:7
RICH AND THE P. — DISR 114:15
rich as well as the p. — FRAN 136:4
rich on the p. — JEFF 185:3
so p. to do him reverence — SHAK 323:9
To the p. people — LANG 210:3
your tired, your p. — LAZA 214:4
poorest p. he that is in England — RAIN 297:10
p. man may in his cottage — PITT 289:8
pope against the P. or the NUM — BALD 25:13
P.! How many divisions — STAL 345:4
President, not a P. — STRE 349:6
popish P. liturgy — PITT 289:12
poppy not to wear a p. — MCAL 228:1
populace Barbarians, Philistines, and P. — ARNO 14:7
clamours of the p. — ADAM 3:1
give the name of P. — ARNO 14:10
p. is excited — LA B 208:10
p. rise at once — WHIT 382:4
popular p. in Scotland — DAVI 102:2
p. institution — ST J 311:13
p. politician — ARIS 13:6
p. sentiments — PEEL 285:14
strong p. feeling — TROL 364:9
population balance of our p. — JOSE 194:1
p., when unchecked — MALT 240:1
populi Salus p. — CICE 86:15
Salus p. suprema lex — SELD 317:5
porch keep on the p. — CLIN 90:8
porcupines throw p. under you — KHRU 202:7
poring p. over maps — SALI 313:6
port p. is near — WHIT 382:2
Portillo P. comes back — HESE 171:6
position p. must be held to the last man — HAIG 157:2
possessed world already p. — MALT 240:3
possessions All my p. — LAST 212:1
possibilities p. possibilities — GOLD 150:2
possible knowledge of the p. — BEVA 37:5
Politics is the art of the p. — BISM 41:7
p. you may be mistaken — CROM 98:3
poster Kitchener is a great p. — ASQU 15:9
posterity go down to p. — DISR 113:11

posterity (*cont.*):
hope of p. — POWE 294:4
look forward to p. — BURK 58:9
P. will do justice — DISR 115:14
think of your p. — ADAM 4:2
trustees of P. — DISR 114:18
postindustrial to the p. — MCEW 233:3
postmaster make him a p. — HIND 172:5
postponing simply by p. them — CHUR 86:8
pot chicken in every p. — HOOV 176:5
chicken in his p. — HENR 168:9
potency evidence of his p. — DISR 115:13
potential p. you actually have — BROW 53:8
Potomac quiet along the P. — MCCL 231:9
poultry lives of the p. — ELIO 123:3
pound British p. — DYSO 120:8
p. here in Britain — WILS 385:5
pounding Hard p. this — WELL 379:3
poverty against hunger, p. — MARS 243:6
amidst its p. and squalor — ARNO 14:10
conquer p. — JOHN 189:9
cost of setting him up in p. — NAID 263:11
hunger and p. — LARK 210:6
languishing in p. — MAND 241:1
mental p. — VALÉ 368:10
p. and excess — PENN 287:1
P. is the parent of revolution — ARIS 14:1
p. of individuals — HUME 178:6
war on p. — JOHN 189:8
power absolute p. corrupts — ACTO 1:9
acquisition of p. — RUSS 311:3
All p. to the Soviets — SLOG 334:1
any man who has p. — MONT 258:12
arts of p. — CLAY 88:10
balance of p. — KISS 207:7
balance of p. — NICO 266:6
Black P. — CARM 70:12
conception of the p. state — TEMP 355:2
considerable p. — BUTL 63:2
corridors of p. — SNOW 339:10
depositary of p. — DISR 114:1
desire of p. — HOBB 173:6
duty is to augment official p. — BAGE 22:6
enchanted chambers of P. — LAND 209:9
Everyone who desires p. — MILL 251:6
exercise p. — TREV 363:5
friend in p. is a friend lost — ADAM 2:10
greater the p. — BURK 60:4
greed for p. — LEVI 216:9
honour, command, p. — CICE 86:17
immense p. — DE V 108:3
in office but not in p. — LAMO 209:6
intoxicated with p. — BURK 56:7
jaws of p. are always opened — ADAM 3:11
Johnson's instinct for p. — WHIT 381:6
knowledge itself is p. — BACO 19:19
lay down the reins of p. — LINC 220:5
legislative p. — MONT 258:14
less the p. — LEVI 217:6
live without a common p. — HOBB 173:8

power (*cont.*):

loss of p.	RUSK 310:3
mystery of the king's p.	JAME 184:4
no hopes but from p.	BURK 60:6
only have p. over people	SOLZ 340:3
outrun our spiritual p.	KING 203:12
Parties come to p.	RIDL 302:4
place without p.	ROSE 308:3
political p. of another	LOCK 224:6
politics of p.	HAIL 157:6
p. and glory, or happiness	ARIS 13:10
p. can be rightfully exercised	MILL 250:8
p. elite	MILL 252:4
p. grows out of the barrel of a gun	MAO 242:3
p. in trust	DRYD 119:1
p. is a trust	DISR 115:5
P. is not a means	ORWE 276:6
P. is so apt to be insolent	HALI 159:11
P. is the great aphrodisiac	KISS 207:3
P.? It's like Dead Sea fruit	MACM 236:8
p. of preventing	SALI 312:9
p. of suppress	NORT 271:8
p. of the crown	BURK 59:11
p. over nothing	HERO 170:8
p. should always be distrusted	JONE 193:1
p. to act	LOCK 224:9
p. to tax	MARS 243:7
P. to the people	SLOG 336:2
P., which has the ability	MARG 242:8
p. which stands on Privilege	BELL 31:5
P. without responsibility	KIPL 207:1
responsibility without p.	STOP 348:8
source of p.	MARS 243:10
Sovereign state p.	KEAN 196:7
standing armies of p.	RADC 297:8
supreme p. must be arbitrary	HALI 158:10
toadies of p.	TREV 363:8
Treasury is in p.	WILS 385:10
Unlimited p.	PITT 289:10
utility of monarchical p.	BOSW 49:3
What p. have you got	BENN 32:9
when it comes to p.	SNOW 339:12
wielding p.	GAND 140:16
with Eternal God for p.	TENN 355:10
powerful p. and free	TOCQ 361:12
powers accumulation of all p.	MADI 237:8
Headmasters have p.	CHUR 85:2
high contracting p.	BRIA 51:3
non-resistance to the higher p.	MAYH 246:6
real separation of p.	DENN 106:8
ultimate p. of the society	JEFF 186:16
pox or of the p.	WILK 383:8
practical aim of p. politics	MENC 248:5
p. politics	ADAM 2:13
p. service	TOCQ 361:10
practice intention of putting it into p.	BISM 42:14
politics, as a p.	ADAM 2:9
wear and tear of p.	TROL 365:5
practise never to p. either	TWAI 368:2
pragmatists p., who hoped	MCEW 233:2
praise Let us now p. famous men	BIBL 39:17

praise (*cont.*):

lived on p.	HEAT 167:6
P. the Lord	FORG 134:9
praised everybody p. the Duke	SOUT 343:10
happy when being p.	BALF 27:2
p., and got rid of	CICE 87:3
pray fervently do we p.	LINC 220:6
I p. for the country	HALE 158:2
P. for the dead	JONE 192:7
p. for them	LEE 215:3
p. you, master Lieutenant	MORE 259:11
Work and p.	HILL 172:4
prayer Conservative Party at p.	ROYD 309:7
One p. absorbs all others	GLAD 148:11
people's p.	DRYD 118:10
preaching woman's p.	JOHN 191:4
precedent is a dangerous p.	CORN 96:3
p. embalms a principle	STOW 349:2
p. to precedent	TENN 355:14
precious so p. it must be rationed	LENI 216:1
This p. stone	SHAK 326:2
predicament not a position, it is a p.	BENN 32:14
pregnant being a little p.	HEND 168:5
prejudices Drive out p.	FRED 137:11
p. and habits	GIBB 145:13
proprietor's p.	SWAF 350:6
prelaty yoke of p.	MILT 253:1
preparation no p. is thought necessary	STEV 348:1
p. for this hour	CHUR 81:9
week for p.	WILS 386:18
prerogative English subject's sole p.	DRYD 119:11
last p.	DRYD 119:5
p. of the eunuch	STOP 348:8
p. of the harlot	KIPL 207:1
rotten as P.	BURK 59:11
that which is called p.	LOCK 224·9
prescience lacked p.	DISR 114:14
presence conspicuous by its p.	RUSS 311:11
p. on the field	WELL 379:6
present characteristic of the p. age	DISR 112:6
live in the p.	SPIF 344:6
no redress for the p.	DISR 113:16
nothing but the p.	KEYN 201:2
who controls the p.	ORWE 276:1
preservation p. of their property	LOCK 224:7
preserved Union: it must be p.	JACK 183:3
presidency away from the P.	MISQ 255:3
cancer close to the P.	DEAN 103:4
heart-beat from the P. '	STEV 347:4
I will seek the p.	DOLE 116:10
messenger-boy P.	SCHL 315:9
pursuit of the P.	JOHN 190:2
Teflon-coated P.	SCHR 316:2
US p. a Tudor monarchy	BURG 56:6
wants the p. that much	BROD 52:6
want the p.	MCCA 231:4
president All the P. is	TRUM 366:4
All the P.'s men	BERN 35:5
anybody could become P.	DARR 101:8
any boy may become P.	STEV 347:2

president (*cont.*):

around the American P.	MAIL 238:7
As P., I have no eyes	LINC 220:9
come to the p.	EISE 123:2
cowboy is P.	HANN 161:1
first p. to be ousted	LIEB 217:10
more than any other P.	MENC 248:13
nothing to hide from the P.	CHUR 83:6
Office of P.	ROBI 303:14
powers of P.	GALB 140:10
P. can sing to you	ROBI 303:12
P. is a crook	NIXO 270:7
P. may slip	TOCQ 361:11
P., not a Pope	STRE 349:6
P. of the United States	ANON 11:3
P.'s hardest task	JOHN 190:3
P. should not wear	MCAL 228:1
P.'s spouse	BUSH 61:9
p. who can speak	MCAL 227:12
rather be right than be P.	CLAY 88:12
respect the p.	BUSH 62:12
vote for the best P.	PETE 288:1
We are the P.'s men	KISS 207:8
What did the P. know	ANON 12:5
When the P. does it	NIXO 270:14

press as I believe, with the P.

	MELB 247:4
complain about the p.	POWE 293:10
demagogic, corrupt p.	PULI 295:3
freedom of the p.	CHUR 85:13
freedom of the p.	JEFF 186:4
Freedom of the p. guaranteed	LIEB 217:12
Freedom of the p. in Britain	SWAF 350:6
free p. not a privilege	LIPP 221:5
liberty of the p.	JUNI 195:7
lose your temper with the P.	PANK 282:4
not a free p. but a managed	RADC 297:9
popular p. is drinking	MELL 248:2
power of the p.	NORT 271:8
p. is ferocious	DIAN 109:3
p. is free	JEFF 185:9
P. lives on disaster	ATTL 17:5
to the p. alone	JEFF 187:6
Viewed by the p.	CHIL 78:7
with you on the free p.	STOP 348:10

pressure put p. on me — ROOS 306:11

prestige p. of government — EINS 122:2

p. without distance — DE G 105:11

presumes p. more boldly — GLAD 148:4

pretender blessing—the P. — BYRO 64:1

pretexts Tyrants seldom want p. — BURK 56:8

pretty P. witty Nell — PEPY 287:7

prevarication last dyke of p. — BURK 60:15

prevent try to p. it — MILN 252:5

preventing power of p. — SALI 312:9

p. people from taking part — VALÉ 368:11

prey p. of the rich — JEFF 185:3

to hast'ning ills a p. — GOLD 150:4

price another man's p. increase — WILS 385:8

bought it at any p. — CLAR 87:7

love that pays the p. — SPRI 344:8

pay any p. — KENN 198:4

price (*cont.*):

p. of admiralty	KIPL 206:6
p. of championing human	OWEN 278:3
p. paid for office	TOCQ 361:3
p. well worth paying	LAMO 209:4
those men have their p.	WALP 374:4

prices contrivance to raise p. — SMIT 333:7

rise in p. — HEAT 167:4

prick spur To p. the sides — SHAK 325:1

pride save its p. — MEYE 249:9

priest guts of the last p. — DIDE 110:5

rid me of this turbulent p. — HENR 169:4

priests dominion of p. — PRIC 294:10

p. by the imposition	MACA 229:4
p. have been enemies	HUME 178:8
P. have nephews	PEEL 286:14
with the guts of p.	MESL 249:2

priggish p. schoolgirl — GRIG 155:5

prigs p. and pedants — DISR 112:4

p. who attack — HUMP 179:5

Prime Minister best P. we have — BUTL 63:4

buried the Unknown P.	ASQU 15:7
fresh to be our war P.	BALD 25:7
have you P.	WILD 383:5
HOW DARE YOU BECOME P.	BONH 47:1
known every P.	HAIL 157:11
last British P.	ADAM 2:6
model of a modern P.	HENN 168:6
next P. but three	BELL 31:2
No woman will be P.	THAT 356:2
office of the P.	ASQU 15:5
P. has had a very difficult	GEOR 144:6
P. has nothing to hide	CHUR 83:6
P. has to be a butcher	BUTL 63:6
P. is like the banyan	PATI 284:8
P. needs a Willie	THAT 358:5
P.'s advisers	FOLL 133:8
to become P.	CALL 66:8
to be P.	TROL 364:7
turned-out P.	MELB 247:2
want to be p.	BROW 53:9
When P. he became	MARG 242:8
woman becoming a P.	ASQU 15:11

Prime Ministers birds, wild flowers, and P.

	BALD 25:2
Disraeli school of P.	BLAI 44:2
Former P.	GLAD 148:15
like my P. to be	ANON 9:6
limpet-like P.	JENK 188:1
P. are wedded	SAKI 312:2
P. dissatisfied	JENK 188:3
P. have never yet been	CHUR 85:2

primitive call it a 'p. society' — GREG 154:6

prince bless the P. of Wales — SONG 341:2

dominion of a p.	HUME 178:7
in a p. the virtue	MASS 245:11
p. must be a fox	MACH 233:11
p. sets himself up above the law	MAYH 246:6
p. who gets a reputation	NAPO 264:6
safer for a p.	MACH 233:9

princes P. and lords may flourish — GOLD 150:4

princes (*cont.*):
  p. are come home again   SHAK 324:4
princess P. leave the Englishwoman   BISM 41:4
  She was the People's P.   BLAI 44:1
principate p. and liberty   TACI 351:3
principis *Indignatio p. mors est*   MORE 259:9
principle approves of something in p.   BISM 42:14
  compass of p.   ANON 11:1
  except from some strong p.   MELB 247:8
  influenced by p.   RAKO 298:1
  matter of p.   HEAD 165:7
  precedent embalms a p.   STOW 349:2
  p. of all social progress   FOUR 135:4
  p. of the English constitution   BLAC 43:5
  Protection is not a p.   DISR 111:8
  rebels from p.   BURK 58:17
  rise above p.   LONG 224:14
principles adjust their p.   HATT 163:5
  begins with that of its p.   MONT 258:8
  Damn your p.   DISR 115:6
  either morals or p.   GLAD 148:7
  embrace your Lordship's p.   WILK 383:8
  need good p.   HAYE 164:10
  no retreat from the p.   MURR 263:5
  not men but p.   PAIN 280:8
  p. are the same   JOHN 191:18
  p., rather than persons   PAIN 280:16
  p. that gave her   WILS 386:11
print licence to p. money   THOM 359:7
printing caused p. to be used   SHAK 320:18
  Gunpowder, P.   CARL 69:11
  p., gunpowder, and the magnet   BACO 20:1
prison born in p.   MALC 239:9
  is also a p.   THOR 359:9
  only a p.   CUST 100:5
  p. and a smile   WOTT 388:7
  three years in p.   BROC 52:5
  while there is a soul in p.   DEBS 103:8
prisoner object to your being taken p.
    KITC 207:12
  thoughts of a p.   SOLZ 340:5
prisoners p. of addiction   ILLI 181:6
  p. of Communism   SOLZ 340:8
private my p. will   ELIZ 123:6
  P. faces in public places   AUDE 17:14
  p. family   SMIT 337:6
  p. opulence   GALB 139:11
  P. property   LIPP 221:2
  P. property is a necessary   TAWN 352:11
  p. will governs   ROBE 303:3
  sphere of p. life   MELB 247:10
  system of p. property   HAYE 164:8
privilege Englishman's heaven-born p.
    ARNO 14:10
  free press not a p.   LIPP 221:5
  power which stands on P.   BELL 31:5
privileges p. you were born with   BROW 53:8
prize p. in the lottery   RHOD 301:3
prizes glittering p.   SMIT 338:3
probabilities Human p. are not sufficient
    FAIR 130:2

probity p. and integrity   HAGU 156:6
problem p. of the colour line   DU B 119:16
  you're part of the p.   CLEA 89:2
problems all our p.   THAT 358:9
  No *easy* p.   EISE 123:2
  old p.   WILS 385:12
  Others bring me p.   THAT 357:16
  p. as it can solve   MARX 244:4
  two p. in my life   HOME 175:11
process common market is a p.   MONN 257:5
procreation p. of eels   SCHU 316:6
produce more than they p.   HAYE 165:1
producing consumes without p.   ORWE 275:5
production purpose of p.   SMIT 337:2
profaned desolated and p.   GLAD 148:3
profession politics as a p.   HOWE 177:8
  second oldest p.   REAG 299:5
professor p. of rotational medicine   MORG 260:1
profit no p. but the name   SHAK 319:15
profits best of all monopoly p.   HICK 172:1
  Civilization and p.   COOL 95:8
profusus *sui p.*   SALL 313:9
progress Congress makes no p.   LIGN 218:1
  history of p.   MACA 229:10
  illusion of p.   ANON 12:1
  party of p. or reform   MILL 250:10
  principle of all social p.   FOUR 135:4
  p. depends on unreasonable man   SHAW 328:13
  P. to what   DISR 114:21
  Social P. began   KIPL 205:5
  social p., order, security   JOHN 188:7
progressive in a p. country   DISR 112:10
prohibited not expressly p.   MEGA 246:8
prohibition by the P. laws   EINS 122:2
  Communism is like p.   ROGE 304:9
  drug p.   BOAZ 45:3
  enacting P.   HOOV 176:3
  more successful than P. was   BOAZ 45:4
  P. law strikes a blow   LINC 218:2
proletarian p. socialist state   LENI 215:10
proletariat dictatorship of the p.   MARX 244:10
promise broke no p.   POPE 292:3
  Whose p. none relies on   EPIT 128:3
promised reach the p. land   CALL 66:1
  seen the p. land   KING 203:8
  weird women p.   SHAK 325:3
promises he is a young man of p.   BALF 27:4
  make good their p.   BAGE 22:4
  p. and panaceas   ROTH 309:3
  p. and understandings   TAYL 354:2
  p. nothing   ANON 9:5
  Vote for the man who p. least   BARU 28:4
propaganda on p.   CORN 96:4
  ran the paper purely for p.   BEAV 29:7
propagandist p.'s purpose   HUXL 180:4
propensities natural p.   BURK 60:2
proper know our p. stations   DICK 109:6
property degrees and kinds of p.   MADI 237:7
  dominion of p.   GOLD 150:3
  not p. but a trust   FOX 135:7
  preservation of their p.   LOCK 224:7

property (*cont.*):

preserve his p.	LOCK 224:5
Private p.	LIPP 221:2
Private p. is a necessary	TAWN 352:11
P. is theft	PROU 295:2
p. of others	SALL 313:9
p. of the rich	RUSK 310:14
p. or honour	MACH 233:12
p.-owning democracy	SKEL 333:1
public p.	JEFF 186:8
rank or p.	JUNI 195:4
right of p.	TAFT 351:12
system of private p.	HAYE 164:8
through p. that we shall strike	PANK 282:6
Where p. is in question	SALI 312:11
prophet not as a p.	MAND 240:7
p. in Israel	BIBL 39:6
prophets ceased to pose as its p.	POPP 292:8
proportions by p. true	MARV 243:11
proprietor p.'s prejudices	SWAF 350:6
prose govern in p.	CUOM 99:8
prosper Treason doth never p.	HARI 162:5
prosperity p. and salvation	CARD 69:6
P. is necessarily	WILS 386:1
prosperous p. or caring	HESE 171:3
prostitute doormat or a p.	WEST 380:7
prostitutes small nations like p.	KUBR 208:8
protect p. the writer	ACHE 1:7
protection great p. against war	BEVI 38:7
P. is not a principle	DISR 111:8
P. is not only dead	DISR 115:16
Protestant attacked the P. church	NIEM 269:1
I am the P. whore	GWYN 156:3
p. ethic	WEBE 377:1
P. Province of Ulster	CARS 70:16
P. Religion	CARL 69:11
P. with a horse	BEHA 30:7
'tis a P. wind	SONG 341:3
proud p. of their courage	DILL 110:8
too p. to fight	WILS 386:6
prove p. anything by figures	CARL 69:7
providence P. had sent a few men	RUMB 309:8
P. has not created	TOCQ 361:12
p. that protects idiots, drunkards	BISM 42:12
way that P. dictates	HITL 173:1
province p. they have desolated	GLAD 148:3
provision p. for the poor	JOHN 191:7
provokes No one p. me	MOTT 262:5
prudence P. is the other woman	ANON 10:9
What is p.	SMIT 337:6
Prussia military domination of P.	ASQU 15:3
national industry of P.	MIRA 253:4
put P. on the Rhine	ADEN 5:1
pseudo p. event	BOOR 48:1
psychological P. flaws	ANON 10:10
p. rule	KEYN 201:7
public admired in p. life	ROOS 305:2
aggrandizes the p.	HUME 178:6
aid of p. service	TREV 363:1
as if I was a p. meeting	VICT 371:3
assumes a p. trust	JEFF 186:8

public (*cont.*):

burn your fingers in p. life	BEAV 29:3
complainers for the p.	BURK 57:8
Debate on p. issues	BREN 51:2
exercises a p. trust	CLEV 90:1
expense of p. interests	TAYL 354:10
for the p. good	LOCK 224:9
glorified p. relations man	TRUM 366:4
Great p. measures	PEEL 286:17
hand into the p. purse	PEEL 286:6
holding p. office	ACHE 1:4
in p. administration	GALB 140:5
lifetime in p. office	GALB 140:6
portion of the p. business	MILL 250:4
Private faces in p. places	AUDE 17:14
p. be damned	VAND 369:1
p. liberty	HENR 170:1
p. opinion concentrated	O'CO 272:10
p. squalor	GALB 139:11
p. will not stand	HARC 161:4
researchers into P. Opinion	AUDE 17:16
respect p. opinion	RUSS 311:2
servants of p. 6	GOWE 152:3
tell the p. which way	SULZ 350:3
publicity oxygen of p.	THAT 357:8
qualities which create p.	ATTL 16:11
publish P. and be damned	WELL 379:4
pudding Take away the p.	CHUR 86:10
pugna P. *magna victi sumus*	LIVY 222:4
Pulitzer as a P. Prize	CHIL 78:7
puller p. down of kings	SHAK 320:19
pulling Here p. down	MARV 243:11
pulpit such a bully p.	ROOS 308:1
white glove p.	REAG 299:2
punch p. above its weight	HURD 179:9
punctuality P. is the politeness	LOUI 225:9
Punica P. *fide*	SALL 313:13
punish God p. England	FUNK 139:4
punishment cruel and unusual p.	CONS 95:3
less horror than the p.	GIBB 145:7
punishments sanguinary p.	PAIN 280:1
pupil p. of the eye	HOLM 175:7
puppets not party p.	CANA 68:7
purchasing not worth p.	REED 300:7
puritan P. and Presbyterian	GALB 140:7
P. hated bear-baiting	MACA 230:5
puritanism P. The haunting fear	MENC 248:4
Puritans P. from England	KEIL 197:8
purpose for an Irish p.	DAVI 103:2
politics of p.	HUMP 179:3
purse hand into the public p.	PEEL 286:6
pursuing p. our own good	MILL 250:7
pursuit p. of happiness	JEFF 185:1
p. of the uneatable	WILD 383:6
push p. something	HARN 162:7
put up with which I will not p.	CHUR 84:2
puzzling has always been p.	ELIZ 125:7
pyramid bottom of the economic p.	ROOS 305:4
pyramids summit of these p.	NAPO 264:4
pyre own funeral p.	POWE 293:3
Pyrenees P. are no more	LOUI 225:4

reasonable R. Man   HERB 170:5
  r. man adapts   SHAW 328:13
  will must be r.   JEFF 186:1
reasons R. are not like garments   ESSE 127:6
  r. will certainly   MANS 242:1
  twenty good r. why I can   BEVI 38:8
rebel die like a true-blue r.   LAST 213:2
  I am *still* a r.   BROW 54:4
  starve or r.   DUND 120:2
  What is a r.   CAMU 68:4
rebelled have already r.   GIBB 145:5
rebellion little r. now and then   JEFF 185:4
  R. lay in his way   SHAK 320:2
  R. to tyrants   BRAD 50:2
  R. to tyrants   MOTT 262:6
  r. was the certain consequence   MANS 241:11
  rum, Romanism, and r.   BURC 56:5
rebels r. are our countrymen   GRAN 153:2
  subjects are r.   BURK 58:17
  tip to r.   NICO 268:9
rebuilt requires to be r.   MILL 250:5
receiver r. and the giver   BURK 58:12
recession R. is when you have to   PANK 282:8
  r. when your neighbour   TRUM 366:11
  spend way out of a r.   CALL 65:9
recognized being r.   BECK 30:5
reconciliation bridge of r.   RUNC 309:9
  stability and r.   MITC 256:5
  True r. does not   MAND 240:9
reconvened hereby r.   EWIN 129:7
record look at the r.   IVIN 182:6
  reversal of his r.   MARS 243:5
red Better r. than dead   SLOG 334:6
  get very r. in the face   BENT 33:10
  keep the r. flag flying   SONG 343:1
  people's flag is deepest r.   SONG 343:1
  raiment all r.   MACA 230:8
  r. men scalped each other   MACA 228:10
redtape r. talking-machine   CARL 70:5
refined ruled in more r. ages   BAGE 21:5
reform innovate is not to r.   BURK 57:4
  party of progress or r.   MILL 250:10
  Peace, retrenchment, and r.   BRIG 51:7
  sets about r.   TOCQ 361:8
  thunder for r.   NEWS 268:1
reformation plotting some new r.   DRYD 119:10
  total r.   PAIN 279:12
reforms beneficial r.   THAT 358:7
refuge Patriotism is the last r.   JOHN 191:12
refugees r. back   ROBE 303:1
refuse r. of your teeming tents   LAZA 214:4
  r. to fight   SLOG 336:10
  Which he did thrice r.   SHAK 323:7
regiment r. of women   KNOX 207:13
register r. of the crimes, follies   GIBB 145:3
regret Old Age a r.   DISR 113:18
  spoken with greater r.   BALD 25:8
regrets congratulatory r.   DISR 113:6
  I have no r.   CRES 96:10
regrette *Je ne r. rien*   CRES 96:10
regulations avalance of r.   BOOK 47:7

regulations (*cont.*):
  ten thousand r.   CHUR 86:6
Reich *Ein R.*   SLOG 334:13
reign Long to r. over us   SONG 341:7
reigned if he had not r.   TACI 351:10
  r. with your loves   ELIZ 124:7
reigns king r.   THIE 358:12
reinvent r. ourselves   HUMP 179:5
reject elect, and to r.   PAIN 280:15
  Minister will r. it   LYNN 227:8
  unelected r. politicians   RIDL 302:6
rejoice r. at that news   THAT 357:1
  r., rejoice   HEAT 167:7
relation cold r.   BURK 59:4
  State is a r. of men   WEBE 377:3
relations not have sexual r.   CLIN 91:1
  r. of life and death   DOUG 117:8
relationship r. that was not   CLIN 91:3
relief system of outdoor r.   BRIG 51:6
relieve chance to r. yourself   ANON 10:3
relieved By desperate appliances are r.
    SHAK 319:14
religion As to r.   PAIN 279:8
  dominion of r.   GOLD 150:3
  establishment of r.   CONS 95:1
  Every dictator uses r.   BHUT 38:13
  feature of *any* r.   PAIN 280:5
  fox-hunting—the wisest r.   HAIL 157:9
  Freedom of r.   JEFF 186:4
  Leave the matter of r.   GRAN 153:5
  Not a r. for gentlemen   CHAR 76:10
  on account of my r.   BELL 31:6
  politics as well as in r.   JUNI 195:3
  Politics, like r.   JEFF 186:10
  r. from politics   TREV 363:6
  r. is allowed to invade   MELB 247:10
  R. is the sigh   MARX 244:3
  r. is to do good   PAIN 280:13
  R. may in most   RUSS 311:7
  r. of humanity   PAIN 279:11
  r. of Socialism   BEVA 36:4
  r. without a prelate   BANC 27:7
  reproach to r.   PENN 287:1
  sort of r.   TOCQ 361:10
religions r. considered man as man   TOCQ 360:9
religious all r. revolution   WEBE 377:5
  r. observance   DEED 104:3
reluctant r. obedience   MACA 229:12
remedy applying the wrong r.   BENN 31:9
  dangerous r.   FAWK 131:1
  Force is not a r.   BRIG 52:2
  grievance to the r.   PEEL 286:12
  r. our *enemies* have chosen   SHER 331:2
  Things without all r.   SHAK 325:4
  'Tis a sharp r.   RALE 298:4
remember cannot r. the past   SANT 314:6
  knows what to r.   MORL 260:8
  r. the Fifth of November   SONG 343:2
  r. what is past   HALI 158:6
remembered like to be r.   POWE 293:12
remorse disjoins R. from power   SHAK 322:3

remunerated more highly r.	SMIT 338:2	**resolution** r. on reflection	WALP 373:7
render R. therefore unto Caesar	BIBL 39:21	**respect** destroy all r.	CHUR 86:6
rendezvous r. with destiny	ROOS 305:8	fail to get r.	MACH 234:1
Reno King's Moll R.'d	NEWS 267:10	r. each other	TAYL 353:11
renounce I r. war	FOSD 135:1	r. of the people	MARS 243:10
rent r. boys of politics	FOLL 133:7	**respected** r. persons occasionally	HURD 179:8
R. is that portion	RICA 301:4	**respecter** r. of persons	BROW 54:2
r. we pay for our room	CLAY 89:1	**responsibility** Liberty means r.	SHAW 328:11
reorganized we would be r.	ANON 12:1	Power without r.	KIPL 207:1
repartee always the best r.	DISR 114:20	r. without power	STOP 348:8
repeal r. of bad or obnoxious laws	GRAN 153:4	slightest sense of r.	ANON 9:10
repeat condemned to r. it	SANT 314:6	**responsible** personally r.	HIRO 172:7
I r. myself	TWAI 368:4	**rest** neither business nor r.	MORL 260:7
repeated mistake shall not be r.	EPIT 129:1	period of real r.	LAWS 211:11
reporters speaking through r.	CARL 70:3	r. were little ones	ELIZ 124:13
representation Taxation and r.	CAMD 67:1	**resting** give us a r.-place	WFIZ 378:6
Taxation without r.	OTIS 277:8	**restituit** *cunctando r. rem*	ENNI 127:1
representative r. assemblies	BEVA 37:6	**restored** r. all that was beautiful	NEHR 265:12
r. government	DISR 114:19	**restrain** r. the popular sentiments	PEEL 285:14
Your r. owes you	BURK 60:5	**restraint** r. and punishment	MILT 252:10
repression price of r.	DU B 119:15	**restrictions** finding greater r.	KEIL 197:8
reproach leave affairs of r.	MACH 234:3	**restructuring** r. [perestroika]	GORB 151:4
reproofs r. from authority	BACO 19:7	**result** r. happiness	DICK 109:7
republic destroyed the R.	DE V 107:7	**retail** r. mind	LLOY 223:8
England is a disguised r.	BAGE 22:9	**retaliation** policy of r.	PARN 283:11
essence of the R.	ROBE 303:7	**retard** r. what we cannot repel	JOHN 190:12
If a r. is small	MONT 258:10	**reticence** It is a R.	GLAD 148:18
Love the Beloved R.	FORS 134:11	Northern r.	HFAN 167:1
r., if you can keep it	FRAN 137:2	**retire** r. from this station	JEFF 186:5
R. is a government	BAGE 21:7	r. gracefully	SALI 313:7
r. is a raft	AMES 7:3	**retirement** r. from the stage	MACM 236:12
r. with a wholly	HAIL 157:10	there must be no r.	HAIG 157:2
republican Democratic or R. way	LA G 209:2	**retiring** r. at high speed toward	HALS 160:3
R. cloth coat	NIXO 269:6	**retreat** no r. from the principles	MURR 263:5
r. government	HAMI 160:7	not r. a single inch	GARR 141:10
r. is the only form	JEFF 185:8	**retreating** my right is r.	FOCH 133:5
understood by r. government	TOCQ 361:14	**retrenchment** Peace, r., and reform	BRIG 51:7
republics R. end in luxury	MONT 258:7	**retrograde** r. if it does not advance	GIBB 145:12
repulsive Right but R.	SELL 317:7	**retrospective** r. or utopian	ARON 14:12
reputation r. and the favour	JEFF 186:5	**return** I shall r.	MACA 228:7
requirement r. of a statesman	ACHE 1:6	I will r.	EPIT 128:8
rerat ingenuity to r.	CHUR 80:8	r. of democratic control	STEE 345:10
rescind NOT TO R.	REVE 301:1	**revenge** Gerald Ford as his r.	ABZU 1:2
rescued waiting to be r.	STEE 345:11	in Victory, R.	LYNN 227:7
researchers Our r. into Public Opinion		ranging for r.	SHAK 323:1
	AUDE 17:16	r. for slight injuries	MACH 233:8
reservations no mental r.	LINC 218:13	r. what has happened	BISM 41:9
reserve second profession in r.	NICO 268:9	tribal, intimate r.	HEAN 166:10
reserved r. for some end	CLIV 91:8	**revenue** Internal R. Service	SULL 349:8
resign Few die and none r.	MISQ 254:6	standing r.	BURK 57:20
says he won't r.	GALB 140:15	**reverence** mystic r.	BAGE 20:6
resignation Always threatening r.	BEAV 29:9	so poor to do him r.	SHAK 323:9
by r. none	JEFF 186:6	**revolt** It is a big r.	LA R 210:7
r. in him	BUTL 63:1	**revolution** After a r.	HALI 158:8
resigned r. commission	ANON 8:6	age of r.	JEFF 186:4
resistance break the r.	STAL 345:1	destroyed by a r.	TOCQ 361:8
history of r.	WILS 386:2	entered into this R.	BROW 54:4
intellectual r.	O'BR 272:4	French R. operated	TOCQ 360:9
line of least r.	AMER 6:8	it is a big r.	LA R 210:7
r. by the *sword*	CLAY 88:6	leaders of a r.	CONR 94:10
r. of established ideas	BERL 35:2	parent of r. and crime	ARIS 14:1

revolution (*cont.*):

peaceful r.	KENN 199:1
restrained tyrants, averted r.	BENN 32:6
R. a parent of settlement	BURK 58:8
R., like Saturn	VERG 370:3
r. of rising expectations	CLEV 90:4
safeguard a r.	ORWE 276:6
served the cause of the r.	BOLÍ 46:5
You've had a r.	GEOR 144:7

revolutionaries R. more formalistic   CALV 66:11

r. potential Tories	ORWE 275:9
unmanageable r.	DE V 108:5

revolutionary can't feel r. in a bathroom

	LINK 221:1
Every r. ends as	CAMU 68:6
fine r. phrases	KHRU 202:8
forge his r. spirit	GUEV 156:2
most radical r.	AREN 13:2
r. government	ROBE 303:6
r. right	LINC 219:1

revolutionists age fatal to R.   DESM 107:4

revolutions All modern r.   CAMU 68:5

causes r.	SHEE 329:4
formerly called r.	PAIN 280:9
main cause of r.	INGE 181:8
R. are celebrated	BOUL 49:5
R. are not made	PHIL 288:8
R. are not made	PROV 296:16
R. have never lightened	SHAW 328:9
r. never go backward	SEWA 318:2
r. with rosewater	HEAL 166:7
share in two r.	PAIN 280:17

revolver reaches for a r.   GLEN 149:4

resembles a r.	FANO 130:4

reward fed with r.   TAYL 354:11

rhetoric Death, without r.   SIEY 332:6

rhetorician sophistical r.   DISR 113:7

Rhine R. is where our frontier lies   BALD 25:6

Rhodesia black majority rule in R.   SMIT 338:7

riband Just for a r.   BROW 54:7

rich better to be r. than poor   CECI 73:9

by destroying the r.	LINC 220:12
few who are r.	KENN 198:5
incomes of the r.	SHAW 328:2
make the r. richer	NEHR 265:9
not r. enough	REED 300:7
people can still get r.	REAG 299:8
poor people in r. countries	BAUE 28:7
R. AND THE POOR	DISR 114:15
r. as well as the poor	FRAN 136:4
r. enough to pay	HEAL 165:8
r. have no right	RUSK 310:14
r. in a more precious treasure	MACA 229:4
r. man in his castle	ALEX 6:5
r. men rule the law	GOLD 150:7
r. on the poor	JEFF 185:3
r., quiet, and infamous	MACA 229:14
r. wage war	SART 314:9
tax r. people	LLOY 223:16

rid decorated, and got r. of   CICE 87:3

How do we get r. of you	BENN 32:9

rid (*cont.*):

wishes to be r. of it	ROSE 308:6

riddle r. wrapped in a mystery   CHUR 81:6

riddles R. lie here   EPIT 128:7

ride if you cannot r. two horses   MAXT 246:3

ridiculous no sense of the r.   PEEL 286:15

no spectacle so r.	MACA 229:5
sublime to the r.	NAPO 264:10

Ridley good comfort, Master R.   LAST 212:2

rien R.   LOUI 225:7

right almost always in the r.   SMIT 339:6

be on the r. side	GALB 140:14
convinced that they are r.	VAN 369:2
defend to the death your r.	MISQ 254:9
firmness in the r.	LINC 220:7
forgive those who were r.	MACL 234:8
if r., to be kept right	SCHU 316:5
I had rather be r.	CLAY 88:12
individual r.	TAFT 351:12
just not r.	PARK 283:8
'just' or 'r.'	PLAT 290:11
know what is r.	JOHN 190:3
Liberty is the r.	MONT 258:11
majority never has r.	IBSE 181:1
man of the r.	MOSL 261:4
more than half the people are r.	WHIT 381:4
my r. is retreating	FOCH 133:5
No R.	MITC 253:8
no r. in the circus	MAXT 246:3
not r. now	JAY 184:9
our country, r. or wrong	DECA 103:9
R. but Repulsive	SELL 317:7
r. is more precious	WILS 386:13
r. man in the right place	JEFF 187:7
r. of the ignorant man	CARL 69:8
r. of trampling on them	CHIL 78:5
r. to be heard	HUMP 179:2
r. to be let alone	BRAN 50:5
r. to be obeyed	JOHN 188:6
r. to govern	HARR 163:1
r. to rise up	LINC 218:3
r. to vote	ANTH 12:12
r. which goes unrecognized	WEIL 378:3
r.-wing, like nature	DEBR 103:6
Self-government is our r.	CASE 71:8
vast r.-wing conspiracy	CLIN 90:7
What is r.	PEEL 285:6

righteous armour of a r. cause   BRYA 55:5

rightful will to be r.   JEFF 186:1

rights all your r. become   CASE 71:9

Bill of R. seems	COMM 93:5
certain unalienable r.	ANON 11:13
championing human r.	OWEN 278:3
equal in dignity and r.	UNIV 368:7
extension of women's r.	FOUR 135:4
from the South its dearest r.	LEE 215:3
imaginary r., a bastard brood	BENT 33:5
inalienable r.	ROBE 303:4
respect for the r. of all	BAGE 23:12
r. are disregarded	BROW 54:3
r. bequeathed to us	ADAM 4:5

rights (*cont.*):
r. inherent and inalienable — JEFF 185:1
r. of an Englishman — JUNI 195:7
r. of mankind — JEFF 185:8
Sovereign has three r. — BAGE 21:12
talked about equal r. — JOHN 189:7
rigid thy too r. fate — MONT 259:5
ring diaper into the r. — ICKE 181:4
now r. the bells — WALP 374:3
ringleaders r. from the Tarpeian rock
— ARNO 14:11
riot r. is at bottom — KING 203:13
rise people should never r. — ADAM 3:3
right to r. up — LINC 218:3
rising from r. hope — FOOT 134:3
means of r. — JOHN 191:13
revolution of r. expectations — CLEV 90:4
r. hope — MACA 229:9
R. of the Moon — LARK 210:5
r. tide lifts all boats — PROV 296:17
risks just one of the r. he takes — STEV 347:2
rivalry dead there is no r. — MACA 229:7
river as in a r. — HALI 159:2
Fame is like a r. — BACO 19:10
House of Parliament upon the r. — WELL 380:2
where there is no r. — KHRU 202:5
rivers r. of blood — JEFF 187:2
road in the middle of the r. — BEVA 36:8
r. to Damascus — THAT 357:14
roar called upon to give the r. — CHUR 84:11
roast in boiled and r. — SMIT 339:2
robber r.'s bundle — SHEL 330:4
robe judge's r. — SHAK 325:10
robes r. ye weave — SHEL 330:1
robin R. and I are two honest men — SHIP 331:8
robs government which r. Peter — SHAW 327:17
rock smote the r. — WEBS 377:11
until you find a r. — CATL 72:8
rocked r. the system — ROBI 303:10
rocket rose like a r. — PAIN 279:13
rogue r. elephant — TAYL 353:15
roi *que le roi* — PROV 296:10
Roisin R. Dubh — MACN 237:3
roll R. up that map — PITT 290:8
Rolls like a R. Royce — BUTL 63:5
Roman deceased R. Empire — HOBB 174:1
found the R. nation — VIRG 371:7
I am a R. citizen — CICE 87:1
neither holy, nor R. — VOLT 372:3
noblest R. of them all — SHAK 324:3
R. people — CALI 65:6
R.-Saxon-Danish-Norman — DEFO 104:9
Romana *stat R. virisque* — ENNI 126:10
Romanism rum, R., and rebellion — BURC 56:5
Romans Friends, R., countrymen — SHAK 323:4
R. were like brothers — MACA 230:12
romantic R. Ireland's dead and gone — YEAT 389:9
Wrong but R. — SELL 317:7
Romanus *Civis R. sum* — CICE 87:1
Civis R. sum — PALM 281:9
Rome Bishop of R. — BOOK 47:4

Rome (*cont.*):
cruel men of R. — SHAK 321:5
loved R. more — SHAK 323:2
Men, I'm getting out of R. — GARI 141:8
Now is it R. indeed — SHAK 321:10
R., though her eagle — WALL 373:3
R. under Sulla was like a bus — ADCO 4:9
second at R. — CAES 64:12
Treaty [of R.] — DENN 106:6
voice of R. — JONS 193:2
romping r. of sturdy children — DE V 108:1
Romulus dregs of R. — CICE 86:14
roof beneath whose r. I sleep — BORR 49:2
roofs tiles on the r. — LUTH 227:2
room always r. at the top — WEBS 377:17
Great hatred, little r. — YEAT 389:7
just entering the r. — BROU 53:4
smoke-filled r. — SIMP 332:9
struggle for r. — MALT 240:2
rooms boys in the back r. — BEAV 29:6
root axe to the r. — PAIN 280:1
begins to take r. — WASH 375:9
r., hog, or die — BROG 52:7
roots lay bare its r. — JOUB 194:5
party comes from the grass r. — BEVE 37:10
rope sell us the r. — MISQ 254:3
rose Goodbye, England's r. — JOHN 188:9
R. shall fade — DAVI 102:8
white r. of Scotland — MACD 232:2
roses smells like r. — JOHN 190:8
Treaties like girls and r. — DE G 105:9
rosewater made with r. — PROV 296:16
revolutions with r. — HEAL 166:7
rotational r. medicine — MORG 260:1
rotten like r. mackerel — RAND 298:8
shines like r. wood — RALE 298:2
Something is r. — SHAK 319:7
rottenness r. begins in his conduct — JEFF 185:11
Roundheads R. (Right but Repulsive) — SELL 317:7
rout r. send forth a joyous shout — MACA 230:8
routine care more for r. — BAGE 22:5
royal bee on r. jelly — CHUR 86:1
If you have a R. Family — PIML 289:4
needed no r. title — SPEN 344:2
R. authority — MONT 258:15
r. throne of kings — SHAK 326:2
this is the r. Law — CORO 96:5
royalist more of a r. — PROV 296:10
royalties entertain four r. — SALI 312:6
royalty our r. is to be reverenced — BAGE 21:11
R. is a government — BAGE 21:7
r. of Albion's king — SHAK 320:14
R. the gold filling — OSBO 277:2
when you come to R. — DISR 115:7
rue nought shall make us r. — SHAK 324:4
ruffians crowned r. — PAIN 279:3
ruffle r. up your spirits — SHAK 323:14
rugged system of r. individualism — HOOV 176:4
rugs like a million bloody r. — FITZ 132:6
ruin its r. didst not share — DODI 116:7
Resolved to r. — DRYD 118:9

ruin (*cont.*):
r. himself in twelve months	GEOR 144:1
ruined ever r. by trade	FRAN 137:6
men that are r.	BURK 60:2
rule Ill can he r. the great	SPEN 344:5
last Englishman to r.	NEHR 265:13
Reason to r.	DRYD 119:5
rich men r. the law	GOLD 150:7
R. I, on page I	MONT 259:4
r. o'er freemen	BROO 52:9
r. out indefinitely	BROW 53:9
r. that is fundamental	BURK 60:3
r. the state	DRYD 118:9
ruler choose a r. and dismiss a ruler	BAGE 22:3
rulers best r.	LAO- 210:4
conduct of their r.	ADAM 3:12
R. have no authority	MAYH 246:5
rules break known r.	CROM 98:8
man of genius r.	STEP 346:3
need fixed r.	HAYE 164:10
played by the r.	NIXO 270:12
ruling refresh their r. class	TREV 363:7
rum r., Romanism, and rebellion	BURC 56:5
r., sodomy, prayers, and the lash	CHUR 84:3
rumour sound and r.	MORR 260:10
rump R. Parliament	SELL 317:8
run *In the long r.*	KEYN 201:9
Now Teddy must r.	KENN 200:3
runaway r. Presidency	SCHL 315:9
runner prize for the r.-up	BRAD 49:10
running all their r. dogs	MAO 242:6
can't keep on r. from	JACK 183:11
r. with the pack	BUTL 63:7
Rupert Prince R.	DISR 111:6
R. of Debate	BULW 56:4
R. of the Rhine	MACA 230:9
russet plain r.-coated captain	CROM 97:11
Russia forecast the action of R.	CHUR 81:6
good treaty with r.	BISM 41:5
misfortune for R.	HERZ 170:12
power of R.	MITC 256:6
really seen r.	CUST 100:6
R. an empire or democracy	BRZE 55:8
R. has two generals	NICH 266:4
Russian embrace the R. bear	CHAN 75:7
R. autocracy	HERZ 170:11
R. Communism	ATTL 17:4
R. literature saved	RATU 298:11
Russians keep the R. out	ISMA 182:5

Sacco S.'s name will live	VANZ 369:5
sack S. the lot	FISH 132:1
sacked we are all s.	CLAR 87:9
sacred only s. thing	FRAN 136:3
reserved for s. texts	KAUF 196:6
sacrifice final s.	SPRI 344:8
Further s. of life	DE V 107:7
great pinnacle of S.	LLOY 222:8
King refused a lesser s.	MARY 245:7
penchant to s.	GING 146:12

sacrifice (*cont.*):
s. the seals	LLOY 223:11
Thine ancient S.	KIPL 206:3
Too long a s.	YEAT 389:4
sacrificers s., but not butchers	SHAK 322:6
sacrilege consecrated s.	DISR 112:13
sad s. old age	TALL 352:5
tell s. stories	SHAK 326:6
saddle put Germany in the s.	BISM 41:8
saddled s. and bridled	RUMB 309:8
sadly take their pleasures s.	SULL 350:2
safe made s. for democracy	WILS 386:12
S. is spelled D-U-L-L	CLAR 87:15
s. to be unpopular	STEV 347:3
s. with us	THAT 356:12
see me s. up	MORE 259:11
Whips want the s. men	MACM 235:6
world s. for hypocrisy	WOLF 387:6
safeguard s. of the West	WORD 388:6
safeguards enforceable s.	TRUM 366:3
safer s. for a prince	MACH 233:9
s. than a known way	HASK 163:3
safety every man shall eat in s.	SHAK 321:4
S. first	BALD 25:3
s., honour, and welfare	CHAR 76:4
strike against public s.	COOL 95:7
temporary s.	FRAN 137:5
said if you want anything s.	THAT 356:3
not know what they have s.	CHUR 80:3
s. something foolish	ANON 8:12
sailed you never s. with *me*	JACK 183:5
saint call me a s.	CAMA 66:12
saints Christ and His s. slept	ANON 9:16
salad chicken s.	JOHN 189:3
salaries died with the drawn s.	LLOY 224:4
salmon primordial as a s.	WHIT 381:6
saloon in the last chance s.	MELL 248:2
s. keepers were Democrats	GREE 154:4
salt s. water blinds them not	SHAK 326:12
salus S. populi	CICE 86:15
S. populi *suprema lex*	SELD 317:5
salutes see if anyone s.	PROV 296:12
salvation Mankind's s.	SOLZ 340:6
prosperity and s.	CARD 69:6
s. of Europe	PITT 290:5
Samaritan Good S.	THAT 357:10
same all say *the s.*	MELB 247:9
Ever the s.	MOTT 262:7
sanctuary three classes which need s.	BALD 25:2
sandhills s. of the Baldwin Cabinet	ASQU 15:6
sang s. a king out of three kingdoms	WHAR 381:3
sansculotte *bon S. Jésus*	DESM 107:4
Santa Claus shoot S.	SMIT 338:1
sash s. my father wore	SONG 343:3
sat everyone has s. except a man	CUMM 99:7
s. too long here	CROM 98:5
Satanic dark S. mills	BLAK 44:12
satellite With s. TV	O'DO 273:1
satirist s. may laugh	GIBB 145:13
Saturn Revolution, like S.	VERG 370:3
saucepan fishes in a s.	KHRU 202:6

savaged s. by a dead sheep HEAL 165:10
save God s. the king SONG 341:7
 helped s. the world KEYN 201:11
 less democracy to s. ATKI 16:2
 Save me, oh, s. me CANN 68:10
 s. the Governor-General WHIT 382:1
 s. the Union LINC 219:4
saved be s. in this World HALI 159:16
 only s. the world CHES 77:11
saw I came, I s., I conquered CAES 65:1
Saxon S. will ever relax O'DO 273:3
say all s.*the same* MELB 247:9
 do as I s. THAT 356:7
 just on our s.-so KILF 202:9
 s. nothing HEAN 167:1
 s. what they please FRED 137:12
 s. what you think TACI 351:9
says What Manchester s. today PROV 297:3
scabbard threw away the s. CLAR 87:4
scabs Make yourselves s. SHAK 318:5
scaffold forever on the s. LOWE 226:6
scandal s. by a woman of easy virtue HAIL 157:3
scandalous s. and poor ROCH 304:2
scarecrow make a s. of the law SHAK 325:8
scarlet raise the s. standard SONG 343:1
scent whiff of s. LLOY 223:5
sceptered s. isle SHAK 326:2
sceptre s. of George III JOHN 192:1
schedule my s. is already full KISS 207:2
schemes s. of political improvement JOHN 191:5
Schleswig-Holstein S. question PALM 282:1
scholarship indications of s. CHUR 85:1
school destroy every grammar s. CROS 99:1
 erecting a grammar s. SHAK 320:18
 s. of Manchester DISR 115:17
 went to s. without any boots BULM 56:2
schoolboy Every s. knows MACA 229:13
schoolgirl priggish s. GRIG 155:5
schools hundred s. of thought contend
 MAO 242:5
science Dismal S. CARL 70:4
 do s. in hell VAUG 369:6
 Politics is not an exact s. BISM 41:6
 separation of state and s. FEYE 131:4
 triumph of modern s. WAUG 376:6
scientific s. power has outrun KING 203:12
scoffing S. his state SHAK 326:7
scold what a s. you are BULL 56:1
scooters s. off my lawn CLAR 88:2
scorn think foul s. ELIZ 124:2
Scotch as a S. banker DAVI 102:3
 like the S. terrier BRIG 52:1
scotched s. the snake SHAK 325:4
Scotland flower of S. WILL 384:1
 new voice of S. CONN 94:2
 our infinite S. MACD 232:3
 popular in S. DAVI 102:2
 renewed in S. DEWA 108:8
 S., land of omnipotent No BOLD 46:1
 S.'s oil SLOG 335:5
 S.'s rightful heritage CONN 94:1

Scotland (*cont.*):
 S. will be reborn NAIR 264:1
 sing Flower of S. SILL 332:8
 Stands S. SHAK 325:6
 white rose of S. MACD 232:2
Scots S. deserve no pity FLET 133:2
Scottish S. and Welsh nationalism BAKE 24:2
 S. Parliament EWIN 129:7
 S. Parliament WATE 375:10
 shall be a S. parliament ANON 11:6
 shall be a S. parliament DEWA 108:7
 will of the S. people SMIT 338:9
scoundrel plea of the s. BLAK 44:11
 refuge of a s. JOHN 191:12
scoundrels ten obvious s. MENC 248:7
scout newly enrolled Boy S. LEVI 217:1
scratch S. any American RUSK 310:2
screaming s. through the keyholes LLOY 223:1
scribbled by a s. name THOM 359:2
scribbler academic s. KEYN 201:8
scribblers Teenage s. LAWS 211:9
scripture know more of the s. TYND 368:5
scum glittering s. CHUR 80:11
 s. of the earth WELL 379:7
scurvy s. politician SHAK 324:7
sea complaining about the s. POWE 293:10
 dominion of the s. COVE 96:6
 in a s. of glory SHAK 321:1
 s.-change in politics CALL 66:6
 s., which seems to want MONT 258:6
 set in the silver s. SHAK 326:2
 slowly towards the s. CHES 78:1
 smiling surface of the s. PLUT 291:4
 to the English that of the s. RICH 302:3
 very much at s. CARS 71:3
 water in the rough rude s. SHAK 326:4
 willing foe and s. room ANON 12:8
seagreen s. Incorruptible CARL 69:13
sealed My lips are s. MISQ 255:4
seals receives the s. of office ROSE 308:8
 sacrifice the s. LLOY 223:11
seasons man for all s. WHIT 382:10
seat in the driver's s. BEAV 29:8
 s. in the House DISR 114:9
 s. of Mars SHAK 326:2
 without a s. CHUR 85:11
seated looked wiser when he was s. KEYN 200:8
second elect the s. chamber JAY 184:11
 In war there is no s. prize BRAD 49:10
 not a s. on the day COOK 95:4
 Politics comes at least s. GIUL 147:3
 s. at Rome CAES 64:12
 s.-class intellect HOLM 175:6
 s. oldest profession REAG 299:5
 s. profession in reserve NICO 268:9
 You would get s. raters LONG 225:1
secrecy S., and a free TRUM 367:1
secret concept of the official s. WEBE 377:6
 is the s. weapon CRIT 97:8
 keeping the s. TAYL 354:8
 measly affair s. FORS 134:12

shake How s. them	TAWN 352:13	shopkeepers nation of s.	ADAM 4:7
shaking entrusted to the s. hand	VICT 370:9	nation of s.	NAPO 265:1
shall mark you His absolute 's.'	SHAK 318:7	nation of s.	SMIT 333:8
shallows in s. and in miseries	SHAK 324:1	shopocracy abuse the s.	NORT 271:5
sham celebration is a s.	DOUG 117:7	short Don't sell America s.	PROV 296:4
shambles accountable s.	HUNT 179:6	nasty, brutish, and s.	HOBB 173:10
shame terrible s. for me	YOKO 390:6	s. decisive war	LYND 227:5
shamrock Apart from the s.	MCAL 228:1	shorter s. by the head	ELIZ 124:1
s. shine for ever	DAVI 102:8	shots of the best s.	VOLT 372:6
shape dwellings s. us	CHUR 83:1	shoulder hifted it to another s.	SHAW 328:9
shapely It wiggles, it's s.	ERWI 127:4	keep looking over his s.	BARU 28:6
share its ruin didst not s.	DODI 116:7	shout S. with the largest	DICK 109:8
shareholder sole s.	MAND 241:6	they s. and they shoot	INGE 181:7
shares Fair s. for all	SLOG 334:14	shouting tumult and the s.	KIPL 206:3
sharks s. circling, and waiting	CLAR 87:13	show just like s. business	REAG 299:4
sharp 'Tis a s. remedy	RALE 298:4	s. business right	BERN 35:4
shed Burke under a s.	JOHN 191:19	showing worth s.	DANT 101:6
sheep in s.'s clothing	CHUR 86:9	shrimp s. learns to whistle	KHRU 202:1
pasture for all the s.	WALP 374:7	shrunk S. to this little measure	SHAK 322:14
savaged by a dead s.	HEAL 165:10	shut Men s. their doors	SHAK 327:3
s. born carnivorous	FAGU 130:1	shuttered in a s. mansion	FITZ 132:7
s. on the way	CHUR 81:2	side on the opposite s.	ANON 11:9
s. scattered in a fog	BRUT 55:3	other s. of the hill	WELL 379:10
s., that were wont to be	MORE 259:7	which s. do they cheer for	TEBB 354:14
s. to pass resolutions	INGE 181:9	sides both s. of the street	ROOS 306:8
two hundred years like a s.	TIPU 360:6	God does not take s.	MITC 253:9
sheet old England's winding s.	BLAK 44:10	sifted s. a nation	STOU 348:12
turn over the s.	SAND 314:4	sight safely out of s.	GALB 140:7
shell s. with a hole	HUME 178:11	sign if you s. this	BRUG 55:1
shepherd nation's s.	SPRI 344:9	signed hand that s. the paper	THOM 359:1
shepherds s. and butchers	VOLT 372:5	I s. my death warrant	COLL 92:8
shift let me s. for myself	MORE 259:11	s. an autograph	DE V 107:8
s. in what the public wants	CALL 66:6	What I have s.	GRIF 155:2
shines s. and stinks	RAND 298:8	signposts s. to socialist Utopia	CROS 98:14
shining one brief s. moment	LERN 216:3	signs no 'white' or 'coloured' s.	KENN 199:4
ship desert a sinking s.	BEAV 29:12	read s. of the times	CHOI 79:3
s. has weathered every rack	WHIT 382:2	silence flashes of s.	SMIT 339:5
S. me somewheres	KIPL 206:1	Gospel of S.	MORL 260:4
s. of the Union	LINC 218:11	Go to where the s. is	GOOD 151:1
ships s. empty of men	NICI 266:5	it was an easy step to s.	AUST 18:7
s. have been salvaged	HALS 160:3	my day of s.	GAND 141:4
storm-beaten ships	MAHA 238:6	period of s. on your part	ATTL 16:8
we've got the s.	SONG 343:5	s. of the law	HOBB 173:12
wooden wall is your s.	THEM 358:11	silenced because you have s. him	MORL 260:6
shirt in his s.	HUXL 180:5	silencing justified in s.	MILL 250:9
shit chicken s.	JOHN 189:3	silent impossible to be s.	BURK 60:14
s. in a silk stocking	NAPO 265:4	Laws are s.	CICE 87:2
shits knew who the s. were	CLAR 87:11	Paris was French—and s.	TUCH 367:6
shock we shall s. them	SHAK 324:4	s. majority	NIXO 270:4
shoes never tied my s.	PU Y 295:4	strong, s. man	MORL 260:4
shoot decency to s. me	MARK 243:2	silk shit in a s. stocking	NAPO 265:4
didn't s. Henry Clay	JACK 183:7	silly s. thing in the Balkans	BISM 42:8
S., if you must	WHIT 382:9	silver all the Georgian s.	MACM 236:11
s. me in my absence	BEHA 30:8	for a handful of s.	BROW 54:7
s. Santa Claus	SMIT 338:1	Selling off the family s.	MISQ 255:5
they shout and they s.	INGE 181:7	s. foot in his mouth	RICH 302:2
shoots green s. of economic spring	LAMO 209:5	s. plate on a coffin	CURR 99:10
green s. of recovery	MISQ 254:7	There's a s. lining	SONG 342:6
if he s. you	BOGD 45:7	simplicity elegant s.	STOW 349:1
man who s. him gets caught	MAIL 238:7	Lost is our old s.	ANON 9:14
shop talked s. like a tenth muse	ANON 9:2	S. of character	MORL 260:5

snatching s. his victuals — CHUR 81:5
sneezed British Minister s. — LEVI 217:4
snobbish s. and vulgar — VICT 371:1
snobs effete corps of impudent s. — AGNE 5:7
snow few acres of s. — VOLT 371:10
  like the s. geese — OKPI 273:6
  s. before the summer sun — TECU 355:1
snows our Lady of the S. — KIPL 206:2
soapflakes sell Jack like s. — KENN 199:12
soar creep as well as s. — BURK 59:7
social new s. contract — CALL 65:8
  s. and economic experiment — HOOV 176:3
  s. being that determines — MARX 244:5
  s. contract — ROUS 309:4
  S. Contract is nothing more — WELL 380:3
  s. engineering — POPP 292:12
  s. progress, order, security — JOHN 188:7
  with a s. position — ORWE 276:9
socialism Centralization and s. — TOCQ 361:4
  Democracy and s. — NEHR 265:8
  Marxian S. — KEYN 201:1
  paternal s. — MACM 235:4
  religion of S. — BEVA 36:4
  S. can only arrive — VIER 371:6
  S. does not mean — ORWE 276:10
  s. has been singularly blessed — BERG 34:2
  S. is an ideology — BROW 53:6
  S. *possibly* be — STAL 345:2
  s. wandering — HEAL 166:1
  s. would be worth — TAYL 353:14
  s. would not lose its human face — DUBČ 119:13
  This is not S. — SNOW 339:11
  trying to get s. — KINN 204:10
socialist blood of the s. — CROS 99:3
  build a s. society — NYER 272:1
  proletarian s. state — LENI 215:10
  signposts to s. Utopia — CROS 98:14
  typical S. — ORWE 276:9
socialists s. throw it away — CAST 72:5
  We are all s. now — HARC 161:3
society action of s. upon itself — TOCQ 361:14
  affluent s. — GALB 139:8
  bonds of civil s. — LOCK 224:8
  call it a 'primitive s.' — GREG 154:6
  capital of polished s. — BURK 59:2
  dyspepsia of s. — CARL 70:11
  Every s. gets — KENN 200:1
  Great S. — JOHN 189:10
  happiness of s. — ADAM 3:13
  market s. — JOSP 194:4
  modern s. — MARX 244:8
  moves about in s. — CHOI 79:3
  No human s. — MCEW 233:3
  no letters; no s. — HOBB 173:10
  No s. can survive — GING 146:11
  no such thing as S. — THAT 357:11
  of a great s. — SMIT 333:5
  shape of s. — ORWE 275:9
  s. begins to act — PAIN 280:10
  S. is indeed a contract — BURK 59:1
  S. needs to condemn — MAJO 239:1

society (*cont.*):
  s. requires to be s. — MILL 250:5
  s. where it is safe to be — STEV 347:3
  unable to live in s. — ARIS 13:12
sodomy rum, s., prayers, and the lash — CHUR 84:3
soft hard on s. drugs — FLYN 133:3
  s. under-belly of Europe — MISQ 255:6
soil Freedom's s. beneath our feet — DRAK 118:4
  grows in every s. — BURK 57:22
  powers of the s. — RICA 301:4
sold Never s. the truth — TENN 355:10
  what cannot be s.—liberty — GRAT 153:7
  would have s. all I had — CROM 97:9
soldier British s. can stand up to — SHAW 327:16
  iron-armed s. — SONG 342:4
  side of the Unknown S. — ASQU 15:7
  s. of the Great War — EPIT 129:2
soldiers old s. never die — MACA 228:9
  young Argentinian s. — RUNC 309:9
solicitor said I'm a s. — WARD 374:9
solidity appearance of s. to pure wind
   — ORWE 276:14
solution conditions for its s. — MARX 244:4
  either part of the s. — CLEA 89:2
  final s. — HEYD 171:12
  kind of s. — CAVA 73:3
  s. for world peace — MARS 243:5
  total s. — GOFR 149:8
solutions all the s. — THAT 358:9
  David brings me s. — THAT 357:16
  old s. — WILS 385:12
solve easy to s. — EISE 123:2
some fool s. of the people — LINC 220:13
somebody s. in his own right — BENN 32:4
  When every one is s. — GILB 146:2
someone s., somewhere, may be happy
   — MENC 248:4
something S. must be done — MISQ 255:7
  S. of the night — WIDD 383:1
  S. should be done — EDWA 121:9
Somme S. is like the Holocaust — BARK 28:1
son better job on my s. — GORE 151:7
  leichter of a fair s. — ELIZ 123:7
  S. of Saint Louis — FIRM 131:5
song ane end of ane old s. — OGIL 273:4
songs Gaelic s., and argument — DEWA 108:6
  they know no s. — CHES 78:2
soon leave five minutes too s. — BIFF 40:6
sophisms string of s. — SHEL 329:6
sordid this s. saga — LIEB 217:10
soul change the s. — THAT 356:10
  engineers of the s. — GORK 151:8
  engineers of the s. — KENN 199:7
  every subject's s. — SHAK 320:10
  iron has entered into his s. — LLOY 223:17
  literature saved my s. — RATU 298:11
  no s. to be damned — THUR 360:5
  perfection of your s. — SOCR 340:1
  save her s. — THOM 359:5
  s. is marching on — SONG 342:5
  with s. so dead — SCOT 316:9

souls common men have s. TAWN 352:12
engineers of human s. STAL 345:3
only in men's s. STEV 347:1
open windows into men's s. ELIZ 124:12
stuff of other people's s. MCGR 233:1
times that try men's s. PAIN 279:9
sound other half is not very s. SMOL 339:7
s. and original ideas MACM 236:4
s. and rumour MORR 260:10
soundbite trade the s. DOBS 116:5
soundbites can't speak in s. CLAR 88:4
not a time for s. BLAI 44:3
soup take s. at luncheon CURZ 100:3
south S. is avenged BOOT 48:2
wrest from the S. LEE 215:3
sovereign advise my s. WAUG 376:5
Here lies our s. lord EPIT 128:3
he will have no s. COKE 92:4
power of the s. TROL 364:3
s. Nation PAGE 278:6
S. state power KEAN 196:7
subject and a s. CHAR 76:2
subjects to the s. HOBB 173:13
to be a S. ELIZ 123:9
sovereigns what s. are doing NAPO 264:9
sovereignties addition of s. MONN 257:4
sovereignty s. is an artificial soul HOBB 173:5
S. is unlimited BARK 27:10
s. of nature SHAK 319:2
soviet Communism is S. power LENI 215:11
S. Union has indeed FULB 139:1
soviets All power to the S. SLOG 334:1
sow hath the s. by the right ear HENR 169:5
hath the s. by the right ear HENR 169:6
S. returns to her Mire KIPL 205:5
when to s. JEFF 187:3
sown They have s. the wind BIBL 39:16
space more s. where nobody is STEI 346:2
Spain Go to S. and get killed POLL 291:5
nor leave S. JUAN 194:11
permanence and unity of S. JUAN 194:10
Spaniards not the power of the S. SCHU 316:3
thrash the S. too DRAK 118:3
spaniel ill-trained s. CRAN 96:7
little cocker-s. NIXO 269:7
spare s. your country's flag WHIT 382:9
spark s.-gap is mightier HOGB 174:5
sparrows pass through for the s. GALB 140:1
Spartans Go, tell the S. EPIT 128:2
spasm I call it an emotional s. BEVA 36:12
speak didn't s. up NIEM 269:1
difficult to s. BURK 60:14
I now s. for France DE G 105:2
I only s. right on SHAK 323:13
one to s. THOR 360:1
s. for Britain BOOT 48:3
s. for England AMER 7:1
s. for ten minutes WILS 386:18
s. ill of everybody except oneself PÉTA 287:12
S. softly ROOS 307:5
speaking necessity for good s. TROL 364:14

speaks He s. to Me VICT 371:3
specific s. decision TUCH 367:5
spectacle no s. so ridiculous MACA 229:5
spectator disposition of the s. PHIL 289:1
s. sport GALB 140:3
spectre s. is haunting HAVE 163:8
s. of Communism MARX 245:1
speech abridging the freedom of s. CONS 95:1
freedom of s. TWAI 368:2
function of s. to free BRAN 50:4
little other use of their s. HALI 158:9
make a s. on conservation STEV 347:13
nonpolitical s. NIXO 269:8
s. fermenting in me GLAD 148:17
s. from Ernest Bevin FOOT 134:4
s. on economics JOHN 190:7
utterance, nor power of s. SHAK 323:13
speeches old s. burnt SNOW 339:12
s. were fine WALP 373:5
speechless let it lie S. still EPIT 128:7
spend If you have money you s. it KENN 200:2
s. more time with my family FOWL 135:5
s. your way out CALL 65:9
spending s. other people's money RAND 298:10
s. the public money COOL 96:2
spies paid s. SHER 331:1
spin great world s. for ever TENN 355:5
Labour s. doctors CAMP 67:4
s.-doctors in spin clinics BENN 32:12
spine s. to run up EWIN 129:6
spirit break his s. HOLL 175:1
'Brutus' will start a s. SHAK 321:9
forge his s. spirit GUEV 156:2
never approached my s. METT 249:5
s. of Dunkirk WILS 385:1
s. of party WASH 375:7
Thy s. walks abroad SHAK 324:2
spirits insult to the s. RED 300:5
ruffle up your s. SHAK 323:14
spiritual not being a s. people MANC 240:5
outrun our s. power KING 203:12
spit s. on the deck BALD 25:11
splendid s. and a happy land GOLD 150:5
S. isolation NEWS 267:14
s. little war HAY 164:4
s. misery JEFF 185:10
splendidly s. isolated FOST 135:3
splendour s. of hawthorn buds in spring BEAV 29:11
split s. Ireland BRUG 55:1
spoke How well he s. STEV 347:9
s. for an hour GARV 142:1
spoken never have s. yet CHES 77:12
spoons counted our s. EMER 126:5
sport bleed in s. SHAK 322:12
spectator s. GALB 140:3
spot with a s. I damn him SHAK 323:16
spouse President's s. BUSH 61:9
spread be made to s. CHUR 83:12
spring s. that should move easily MONT 258:15
trouble in the Balkans in the s. KIPL 206:9

steaks s. to a tiger	BROU 53:5
steal s. bread	FRAN 136:4
stealing hanged for s. horses	HALI 159:13
steam s.-engine in trousers	SMIT 339:4
traces the s.-engine	DISR 111:10
steeds mounting barbèd s.	SHAK 326:14
steel cold lead and s.	O'DO 273:3
steeple North Church s.	REVE 301:2
steeples dreary S. of Fermanagh	CHUR 80:7
steer s. by the compass	TAYL 354:7
steering s. wheel that's not	GOOD 151:2
step One s. forward	LENI 215:6
steps hears the s. of God	BISM 42:11
sterner made of s. stuff	SHAK 323:6
stick carry a big s.	ROOS 307:5
fell like the s.	PAIN 279:13
s. that he seizes	TORR 362:4
still s. it is not we	CHES 78:1
stingy was not s.	TROL 365:4
stink their politics usually s.	LAWR 211:5
stir s. men's blood	SHAK 323:13
s. up undisputed matters	SALL 313:10
s. without great argument	SHAK 319:16
stirring s. up apathy	WHIT 381:11
stock Woman s. is rising	CHIL 78:6
stockholders money for their s.	FRIE 138:4
stomach army marches on its s.	NAPO 264:12
on an empty s.	BRAN 50:7
s. of a king	ELIZ 124:2
s. of the country	GLAD 147:7
stone bomb them back into the S. Age	
	LEMA 215:4
make a s. of the heart	YEAT 389:4
s. which he flings	TORR 362:4
This precious s.	SHAK 326:2
Under every s.	ARIS 13:7
stones move The s. of Rome	SHAK 323:14
stood s. against the world	SHAK 323:9
s. four-square to all the winds	TENN 355:8
stories tell sad s.	SHAK 326:6
storm coming s.	GLAD 147:5
Stormont Ulster Parliament at S.	GEOR 143:4
storms He sought the s.	DRYD 118:8
story s. and a byword	WINT 387:2
Strafford S., who was hurried hence	EPIT 128:7
straight no s. thing	KANT 196:3
strain s. is awful	MACM 236:13
strangers beaten by s.	DOS 117:3
strangled last minister is s.	NAIR 264:1
s. with the guts	MESL 249:2
strategy developing our industrial s.	BENN 32:3
strawberry Like s. wives	ELIZ 124:13
stream watching a s. of blood	ANON 9:13
street both sides of the s.	ROOS 306:8
in a good s.	MAND 241:8
streetcars common as s.	REUT 300:10
streets grass will grow in the s.	BRYA 55:6
grass will grow in the s.	HOOV 176:6
strength giant's s.	SHAK 325:11
S. through joy	SLOG 335:7
that tower of s.	TENN 355:8

strenuous s. life	ROOS 307:1
strife In place of s.	CAST 72:4
step towards an end of s.	GEOR 143:4
strike s. against public safety	COOL 95:7
s. at a king	EMER 126:6
s. at the head	BURK 60:13
S. the tent	LAST 213:11
string s. of sophisms	SHEL 329:6
s. that ties	SHEL 330:4
untune that s.	SHAK 327:8
stringent s. execution	GRAN 153:4
stroke at a s.	HEAT 167:4
stroked if not s.	HALI 158:11
stroll s. round Walton Heath	LLOY 222:10
strong nature of s. people	BONH 47:2
not to the s. alone	HENR 169:10
people s. enough	ROOS 305:11
s. as a bull moose	ROOS 307:2
s., silent man	MORL 260:4
stronger interest of the s.	PLAT 290:11
on the side of the s.	TACI 351:1
struggle class s.	MARX 244:10
Manhood a s.	DISR 113:18
s. for room	MALT 240:2
s. of the African	MAND 240:6
s. was of blood	O'CO 272:8
struggled s. against tyranny	TUTU 367:8
struggles history of class s.	MARX 245:2
Stuarts out with the S.	DISR 114:11
stubbornness self-righteous s.	JENK 187:12
stud retired s.-horse	MENC 248:3
students S. accept	JONE 192:9
studiously s. neutral	WILS 386:7
stuff made of sterner s.	SHAK 323:6
stumbled s. over the truth	CHUR 86:2
stumbles how the strong man s.	ROOS 307:9
stump mount the s.	STEV 347:13
stupid It's the economy, s.	SLOG 335:6
more s. than their people	EISE 122:8
s. are cocksure	RUSS 311:8
stupidest s. party	MILL 250:3
stupidity alcoholic s.	HILL 172:3
conscientious s.	KING 203:10
explanation of s.	LEVE 216:6
S., outrage	ROST 309:1
subject Every s.'s duty	SHAK 320:10
s. and a sovereign	CHAR 76:2
what it is to be a s.	ELIZ 123:9
subjection some are marked for s.	ARIS 13:13
subjects among his s.	HERB 170:6
good of s.	DEFO 104:13
obligation of s.	HOBB 173:13
s. are rebels	BURK 58:17
sublime s. to the ridiculous	NAPO 264:10
submission s. of men's actions	HOBB 173:14
submit Must he s.	SHAK 326:8
subordination inequality and s.	JOHN 192:2
s. of one sex	MILL 250:15
subsistence S. only increases	MALT 240:1
substance persons of some s.	WIND 387:1
substitute no s. for victory	MACA 228:8

substitute (*cont.*):
s. shines brightly | SHAK 325:14
subtlety s. of intellect | MORL 260:5
subversion Gracchi complaining about s. |
 | JUVE 195:9
succeed s. in politics | LLOY 223:2
success ask of you is military s. | LINC 220:2
 S. or failure | MACH 233:6
successful S. crimes alone | DRYD 119:9
successors dissatisfield with s. | JENK 188:3
 none of my s. | MAJO 239:6
Sudeten problem of the S. Germans | HITL 173:3
Suez East of S. | KIPL 206:1
 S.—a smash and grab raid | NICO 268:7
 S. Canal | EDEN 121:7
suffer Better one s. | DRYD 119:2
 not s. fools gladly | PEAR 285:4
 s. most | PEEL 286:5
suffering sorrow and s. | CONN 94:8
 untold s. | MAND 240:8
sufficient S. conscience to bother him | LLOY 224:2
suffrage Women's s. | DILL 110:7
suicide commit s. | TRUM 366:6
 democracy that did not commit s. | ADAM 3:9
 it is s. | MACD 232:7
 longest s. note | KAUF 196:4
 s. 25 years after his death | BEAV 30:1
suis *J'y* s. | MACM 235:2
suit wear a dark s. | ROSS 308:11
summer if it takes all s. | GRAN 153:1
summits Nations touch at their s. | BAGF 22:2
sun against a setting s. | SHAK 327:3
 candle to the s. | SIDN 332:4
 commanded the s. | FRAN 137:4
 place in the s. | BÜLO 56:3
 place in the s. | WILH 383:7
 S. backs Blair | NEWS 267:15
 s. doesn't revolve | LIVI 221:11
 s. in his eyes | CHUR 81:7
 s. never sets | NORT 271:3
 s. now stands | JOSE 193:6
 s. of York | SHAK 326:13
 S. readers | YELL 390:3
 S. wot won it | NEWS 267:9
Sunningdale S. for slow | MALL 239:13
sunset s. of my life | REAG 300:4
superior embarrass the s. | SHAW 328:14
 most s. person | ANON 10:1
 no-one to be their s. | TOCQ 362:1
superiors want it with our s. | BECQ 30:6
superman I teach you the s. | NIET 269:2
superstition s. sets the whole world | VOLT 372:2
suppliant s. for his own | BYRO 64:6
supplies just bought fresh s. | BREC 50:12
support depend on the s. of Paul | SHAW 327:17
 help and s. of the woman | EDWA 121:10
 s. me when I am in the wrong | MELB 247:13
 s. of the people | CLEV 90:3
supported not s. by the people | HUMP 179:1
suppress power of s. | NORT 271:8
supreme if ever the S. Court | TOCQ 361:11

supreme (*cont.*):
 s. *power must be arbitrary* | HALI 158:10
surrender entire s. | BELH 30:9
 I s. to you | GERO 144:9
 never s. | PAIS 281:3
 No s. | SLOG 336:1
 we shall never s. | CHUR 81:12
surrendered never s. her soul | DE V 108:2
survived I s. | SIEY 332:7
survives still s. | LAST 214:2
surviving s. till the next century | LYNN 227:10
suspicion above s. | CAES 64:11
 against despots—s. | DEMO 106:1
 s. that more than half | WHIT 381:4
suspicions S. amongst thoughts | BACO 19:13
swap s. horses when crossing | LINC 220:4
swayed s. by the basest men | CLAY 88:9
sweat Blood, s., and tear-wrung | BYRO 64:3
 blood, toil, tears and s. | CHUR 81:10
 s. of its labourers | EISE 122:6
sweep he'd s. the country | DISR 115:13
sweet technically s. | OPPE 275:1
sweets bag of boiled s. | CRIT 97:6
 s. of place with power | ROSE 308:3
swift race is not to the s. | BIBL 39:11
swimming S. for his life | GLAD 147:12
Switzerland in S. they had | WELL 378:7
sword first drew the s. | CLAR 87:4
 I gave them a s. | NIXO 270:10
 lift up s. against nation | BIBL 39:13
 not to send peace, but a s. | BIBL 39:19
 resistance by the *s.* | CLAY 88:6
 s. and the currency | PROD 295:1
 s. the axis of the world | DE G 105:12
 terrible swift s. | HOWE 177:6
 We shall never sheath the s. | ASQU 15:3
 wield the s. of France | DE G 105:3
swords s. In our own proper entrails | SHAK 324:2
 s. into plowshares | BIBL 39:13
 ten thousand s. leapt | BURK 58:13
sycophants s. and flatterers | HARD 161:5
syllable never used one s. | JAY 184:8
sympathy just enough s. | GAIB 140:10
 no s. in politics | THAT 356:4
 s. is cold | GIBB 145:10
system rocked the s. | ROBI 303:10
 s. of Government | GLAD 147:6
 s. of outdoor relief | BRIG 51:6

table at whose t. I sit | BORR 49:2
tableau t. of crimes | VOLT 372:4
tail more he shows his t. | PROV 296:8
 sensations of its "t." | DISR 111:9
 wags its t. | TOYN 362:6
taint any t. of legality | KNOX 208:2
taisez-vous *T.! Méfiez-vous* | OFFI 274:7
take big enough to t. away everything |
 | FORD 134:5
 T. up the White Man's Burden | KIPL 206:1
 t. you in the morning | BALD 24:8

takes if it t. all summer   GRAN 153:1
talent concentration of t.   KENN 199:2
  t. of choosing his servants   MACA 230:2
talents career open to the t.   NAPO 264:14
  ministry of all the t.   ANON 9:17
  virtue and t.   JEFF 186:11
talk Careless t. costs lives   OFFI 274:1
  how much my Ministers t.   THAT 356:7
  I have no small t.   WELL 379:13
  t. to your dad   BUSH 62:10
talking if you can stop people t.   ATTL 17:6
  nation t. to itself   MILL 252:2
  quieten your enemy by t.   CEAU 73:6
  redtape t.-machine   CARL 70:5
talks t. frankly only with his wife   BABE 18:8
tamed in one year t.   MARV 244:2
Tandy met wid Napper T.   SONG 342:2
tanks Get your t. off my lawn   WILS 385:6
tantae T. molis erat   VIRG 371:7
taoiseach dreams of being T.   HAUG 163:6
taping t. of conversations   NIXO 270:9
Tarsus Jew of T.   BIBL 39:25
tart t. who has married the Mayor   BAXT 29:1
tarts action of two t.   MACM 236:6
taste t. for freedom   TOCQ 361:5
  underrating public t.   DEED 104:5
tasteless odourless and t.   PEYR 288:2
tax pay my t. bills   HOLM 175:5
  power to t.   MARS 243:7
  soon be able to t. it   FARA 130:5
  t.-paying Americans   GING 146:12
  t. rich people   LLOY 223:16
  t. with a heavier hand   FRAN 136:8
  To t. and to please   BURK 57:11
taxation heavy t.   MACA 230:6
  modes of t.   PEEL 286:10
  T. and representation   CAMD 67:1
  T. without representation   OTIS 277:8
taxes compensation for heavy t.   MONT 259:1
  death and t.   FRAN 137:3
  little people pay t.   HELM 168:2
  no new t.   BUSH 62:6
  peace, easy t.   SMIT 333:3
  people overlaid with t.   BACO 19:15
  t. must fall upon agriculture   GIBB 145:6
taxi driving t. cabs   BURN 61:1
  empty t. arrived   CHUR 85:15
taxidermist veterinarian and the t.   LIEB 217:11
taxing t. machine   LOWE 226:3
taxpayer at the t.'s expense   MENC 248:14
  t.—that's someone   REAG 299:11
tea and sometimes t.   POPE 292:7
  damned t. parties   LODG 224:10
  Queen drops in for t.   BYWA 64:8
teaching for the t. of which   SMIT 337:8
  t. nations how to live   MILT 252:11
tearing t. down an old wall   GORE 151:6
tears blood, toil, t. and sweat   CHUR 81:10
  enough of blood and t.   RABI 297:7
  With mine own t.   SHAK 326:11
technically t. sweet   OPPE 275:1

technology Sixties t.   LEVI 217:1
  white heat of t.   MISQ 256:2
Ted pink, quivering T.   ANON 7:7
teddy Now T. must run   KENN 200:3
teenage T. scribblers   LAWS 211:9
teenagers unemployment among t.   FRIE 138:6
teeth clean their t. in the dark   JENK 187:10
  he's got iron t.   GROM 155:10
  kick them in the t.   BEVA 37:9
  t. are in the real meat   GRIM 155:9
  t. taken out   HITL 173:4
teetotaller secret t.   ORWE 276:9
Teflon T.-coated Presidency   SCHR 316:2
telephones Tudor monarchy with t.   BURG 56:6
television accomplishments of t.   GALB 140:3
  t. and radio   DE V 108:3
  T. brought brutality   MCLU 235:1
  T. has made dictatorship   PERE 287:8
tell Don't ask, don't t.   NUNN 271:10
  Go, t. the Spartans   EPIT 128:2
  t. sad stories   SHAK 326:6
  t. them of us and say   EPIT 129:4
temper enforce with t.   GREN 154:7
  including my t.   NEHR 265:7
  lose your t. with the Press   PANK 282:4
  with a ruffled t.   WALP 374:6
temperament first-class t.   HOLM 175:6
tempest occurrence of a grave t.   BAGE 21:2
tempora O t., O mores   CICE 86:19
temporary force alone is but t.   BURK 57:15
temptation t. to a rich and lazy nation   KIPL 206:7
temptations t. both in wine and women   KITC 207:11
tempted one thing to be t.   SHAK 325:9
ten amend the T. Commandments   BIGG 40:7
  aren't no T. Commandments   KIPL 206:1
  t. minutes notice   SMIT 339:3
tenants feudal landlord abusing t.   ATTL 16:5
tent big t.   SLOG 334:7
  G.O.P.'s big t.   NEWS 267:13
  inside the t. pissing out   JOHN 190:5
  Strike the t.   LAST 213:11
tents t. have been struck   SMUT 339:9
termination law for its own t.   LINC 218:12
terminological t. inexactitude   CHUR 80:2
terrible t. night   PORT 292:13
terrier like the Scotch t.   BRIG 52:1
territorial last t. claim   HITL 173:2
terror new t. to death   WETH 381:1
  t. instituted   MACD 232:6
  t. of the world   PITT 290:1
terrorism subtle t. of words   GAIT 139:5
terrorist t. and the hijacker   THAT 357:8
  t. and the policeman   CONR 94:9
terrorize t. a whole nation   MURR 263:6
test cricket t.   TEBB 354:14
testators T. would do well   HERB 170:3
testimony t. against slavery   DOUG 117:6
Thames T. is liquid history   BURN 61:2
thatch pike in the t.   DE C 104:1

Thatcher it is for Mrs T. — CALL 66:6
theatre shouting fire in a t. — HOLM 175:3
  t. of the world — MARY 245:8
  t. where no-one allowed — MILL 252:3
  This House today is a t. — BALD 25:10
thee save t. and me — OWEN 278:2
theft Property is t. — PROU 295:2
theme first t. — WILS 386:1
  it has no t. — CHUR 86:10
themselves thinking about t. — MACM 236:7
theories t. stand the wear — TROL 365:5
theorists divided between the t. — MCEW 233:2
theory *Died of a T.* — DAVI 102:6
there Over t. — COHA 92:3
  you were not t. — HENR 169:1
thick ask the Gods for a t. skin — TROL 365:2
  t. skin is a gift from God — ADEN 5:2
thicker History gets t. — TAYL 353:2
thigh smote them hip and t. — BIBL 39:3
thin pale and t. ones — PLUT 291:3
thing sort of t. they like — LINC 220:10
things T. fall apart — YEAT 389:8
think easier to act than to t. — AREN 13:3
  might very well t. that — DOBB 116:4
  t. alike who think at all — PAIN 280:14
  t. globally — SLOG 336:3
  t. of your forefathers — ADAM 4:2
  t. other men's thoughts — BAGE 23:1
  T. some more — SLOG 336:4
  t. what you like — TACI 351:9
thinking Áll t. for themselves — GILB 146:7
  every t. man — ADAM 2:3
  modes of t. are different — JOHN 191:18
  own way of t. — NAPO 264:7
  t., speaking, and writing — ADAM 3:11
thinks He t. too much — SHAK 322:1
  t. he knows everything — SHAW 328:5
third t. way — HAGU 156:7
thirst man can raise a t. — KIPL 206:1
  offer you hunger, t. — GARI 141:8
thirteen t. States — HAMI 160:8
  T. years of Tory misrule — SLOG 336:5
this T. was a man — SHAK 324:3
thorn t. in Charles's side — FOX 135:6
thorns can't have the crown of t. — BEVA 36:9
  crown of t. — BRYA 55:7
  No crown of t. — SLOG 335:16
thought investigation and t. — HALD 157:12
  modes of t. — MILL 250:2
  never t. of thinking — GILB 146:3
  Political t., in France — ARON 14:12
  put t. in a concentration camp — ROOS 306:7
  T. is the child of Action — DISR 115:4
  troubled seas of t. — GALB 139:10
thoughtcrime t. literally impossible — ORWE 276:2
thoughts t. of a prisoner — SOLZ 340:5
thousand Empire lasts for a t. years — CHUR 81:13
  first t. days — KENN 198:7
  not in a t. years — SMIT 338:7
  t. points of light — BUSH 62:5
  t. years of history — GAIT 139:7

thread crimson t. of kinship — PARK 283:1
three divided into t. parts — CAES 64:9
  T. acres and a cow — SLOG 336:6
  t. corners of the world — SHAK 324:4
  T. Wise Men — DE R 107:3
thriftless t. and hopeless — DAVI 103:1
throat cut his t. at last — BYRO 64:4
  murder by the t. — LLOY 223:4
throne behind the t. — PITT 289:11
  On the highest t. — MONT 258:4
  royal t. of kings — SHAK 326:2
  t. of bayonets — INGE 181:11
  T. sent word to a Throne — KIPL 206:2
  t. *we* honour — SHER 330:9
  T. will sway a little — CHAN 75:5
  through slaughter to a t. — GRAY 154:2
  vacancy of the t. — GIBB 144:11
  worthy of the t. — GIBB 145:5
throw t. away — SHAK 324:8
throwing t. themselves off it — MAND 241:5
thrown All *this* t. away — MARY 245:6
thunder t. for reform — NEWS 268:1
  voice like t. — DAVI 102:10
Tiber River T. foaming — POWE 293:4
  T. foaming with much blood — VIRG 371:9
tickets t. in their hands — BONO 47:3
tide rising t. lifts all boats — PROV 296:17
  t. in the affairs — SHAK 324:1
  Treaty like an incoming t. — DENN 106:6
tiger atom bomb is a paper t. — MAO 242:4
  Celtic T. — MCAL 228:2
  steaks to a t. — BROU 53:5
  two days like a t. — TIPU 360:6
tigers t. are getting hungry — CHUR 81:4
  wilderness of t. — SHAK 327:5
tight t. gag of place — HEAN 167:1
tigress t. surrounded by hamsters — BIFF 40:5
tiles t. on the roofs — LUTH 227:2
timber crooked t. of humanity — KANT 196:3
  navy nothing but rotten t. — BURK 58:2
time devote more t. — FOWL 135:5
  for a moment of t. — LAST 212:1
  idea whose t. has come — ANON 11:5
  in a limited t. — ATTL 17:9
  leave exactly on t. — MUSS 263:10
  peace for our t. — CHAM 75:2
  ringing grooves of t. — TENN 355:5
  spend more t. with family — THAT 357:15
  that it will be on t. — CONN 94:7
  t. for a change — DEWE 108:10
  t. has come — LONG 224:14
  t. is money — HUGO 178:4
  T. is on our side — GLAD 147:10
  t. is out of joint — SHAK 319:8
  t.-lag of fifty years — WELL 380:5
  T. spent on any item — PARK 283:5
  T.'s up — BOOT 48:7
  t. to win this game — DRAK 118:3
  t. will come — DISR 111:1
  to fill the t. available — PARK 283:3
  unconscionable t. dying — CHAR 76:11

time (*cont.*):

waste of t. and effort	VEBL 370:1
well to t. the beginnings	BACO 19:3
whips and scorns of t.	SHAK 319:9

timeless t. call — SCHL 316:1

timeo t. *Danaos et dona ferentes* — VIRG 371:8

times illusion that t. were better — GREE 154:3

It was the best of t.	DICK 109:9
Oh, the t.	CICE 86:19
T. change, and we change	ANON 11:4
t. that try men's souls	PAIN 279:9
t. will not mend	PARK 282:10

timetables by railway t. — TAYL 353:6

timing real bad sense of t. — MCGO 232:10

t. of your death — TACI 351:6

tincture t. in the blood — DEFO 104:6

tinhorn T. politicians — WHIT 381:8

tinker don't matter a t.'s cuss — SHIN 331:6

Tippecanoe soldier of T. — SONG 342:4

T. and Tyler, too — SLOG 336:7

tipster racing t. — TAYL 353:8

tired Give me your t., your poor — LAZA 214:4

I was t. of it — PARK 283:8

tireless sound of t. voices — STEV 347:15

titanic furniture on the deck of the T. — MORT 261:3

inevitable the T. — HAGU 156:4

title gained no t. — POPE 292:3

needed no royal t. — SPEN 344:2

titles T. are but nick-namess — PAIN 280:3

T. are shadows	DEFO 104:13
T. distinguish the mediocre	SHAW 328:14
with 15th-century t.	ASHD 15:1

toadies t. of power — TREV 363:8

today doubts of t. — ROOS 306:13

never jam t.	CARR 70:14
standing here t.	JOHN 189:6
T. is the last day	YELT 390:4
we gave our t.	EPIT 129:4
What Manchester says t.	PROV 297:3

toga Idealism is the noble t. — HUXL 180:3

toil blood, t., tears and sweat — CHUR 81:10

Horny-handed sons of t.	SALI 313:1
unrequited t.	LINC 220:6

told Nobody t. us — WEBB 376:11

tolerance such a thing as t. — WILS 386:14

tolerate like, or at least t. — TREV 363:3

tolerated women not merely t. — AUNG 18:5

toleration t. produced mutual indulgence — GIBB 144:12

tombstone written on its t. — DAVI 102:6

Tomnoddy My Lord T. — BROU 53:1

tomorrow For your t. we gave — EPIT 129:4

jam t.	CARR 70:14
jam we thought was for t.	BENN 32:2
realization of t.	ROOS 306:13

tongue nor t. to speak — LENT 216:2

t. In every wound	SHAK 323:14
t. in the balance	BISM 42:13
t. of Fox	JOHN 192:1
t. That Shakespeare spake	WORD 388:5
t. to persuade	CLAR 87:5

tongue (*cont.*):

yield to the t. — BIER 40:2

tongues t. doom men — SHAK 327:4

tonight Not t., Josephine — NAPO 265:3

Tony straight from T. — PARR 284:5

tools Give us the t. — CHUR 82:7

t. to him that can handle them — CARL 69:10

tooth danger of her former t. — SHAK 325:4

toothpaste t. is out of the tube — HALD 158:1

top always room at the t. — WEBS 377:17

no friendship at the t. — LLOY 224:3

torch t. passed to a new generation — KENN 198:3

we throw The t. — MCCR 232:1

torches t. of martyrdom — JEFF 186:10

Tories both T. — BOSW 49:3

Mamma, are T. born wicked	ANON 9:15
revolutionaries potential T.	ORWE 275:9
T. must have a bogy man	BEVA 36:7
T. own no argument	BROW 54:5
unbending T.	MACA 229:9

torment most hateful t. for men — HERO 170:2

torrent t. of gin — GLAD 147:13

torso remain only a t. — ERHA 127:3

tortoise t. will usually beat — MAJO 238:10

Tory burning hatred for the T. Party — BEVA 36:3

Loyalty the T.'s secret weapon	KILM 202:11
my favourite T.	FOOT 134:1
Thirteen years of T. misrule	SLOG 336:5
to like T. MPs	CAMP 67:4
T. and Whig in turns	SMIT 339:2
T. Corps d'Armée	GLAD 148:5
Toryism of the T.	TROL 365:6
T. is someone who	POWE 293:11
T. men and Whig measures	DISR 113:17
T. party never panics	HOSK 177:2
t. recognizes	HESE 171:4
violent T.	RUSK 310:7
weapon of the T. Party	CRIT 97:8
what a T. he is	SHER 330:11
what T. Democracy is	CHUR 79:6
wise T.	JOHN 191:18

Toryism T. has always been — MACM 235:4

T. of the Tory — TROL 365:6

total t. reformation — PAIN 279:12

t. solution — GOER 149:8

totalitarian lead to the t. state — DENN 106:10

t. innovation — O'BR 272:4

totalitarianism under the name of t. — GAND 141:1

touch nothing, Can t. him further — SHAK 325:5

touchstone t. of our judgement — KENN 199:6

tough t. on the causes of crime — BLAI 43:8

When the going gets t. — PROV 297:4

toughness T. doesn't have to come — FEIN 131:2

tower fall'n at length that t. — TENN 355:8

town destroy the t. to save it — ANON 9:9

Toytown running for mayor of T. — SCAR 315:3

trade autocrat: that's my t. — CATH 72:7

ever ruined by t.	FRAN 137:6
great t.	BURK 57:10
People of the same t.	SMIT 333:7
There isn't any T.	HERB 170:2

trade (*cont.*):
War is the t. of kings	DRYD 119:8
wheels of t.	HUME 178:5
tradition T. means giving votes to	CHES 77:7
t. objects to their being disqualified	CHES 77:8
tragedy first time as t.	MARX 244:7
trahison *La t. des clercs*	BEND 31:7
train like a runaway t.	CONL 93:7
trained t. them both	GORE 151:7
We t. hard	ANON 12:1
traitor hate the t.	DANI 101:4
t. to myself	SHAK 326:12
traitors form of our t.	WEST 380:6
hate t. and the treason love	DRYD 119:7
trample t. bad laws	PHIL 288:9
trampling right of t. on them	CHIL 78:5
tranquillity Fame and t.	MONT 258:3
transgression where no law is, there is no t.	
	BIBL 39:27
transient t. and embarrassed	DISR 114:6
traps recognize the t.	MACH 233:11
travel obliged to t. again	CHAR 76:8
traveller No t. returns	SHAK 319:9
t. from an antique land	SHEL 329:10
treacherous Exterminate . . . the t. English	
	ANON 8:4
treachery mother of all t.	PAIS 281:5
t. cannot trust	JUNI 195:6
t. of the intellectuals	BEND 31:7
t. or meanness	DISR 115:3
T. with a smile	THAT 358:6
treason bloody t. flourished	SHAK 323:11
condoned high t.	DISR 112:13
Gunpowder T. and Plot	SONG 343:2
hate traitors and the t. love	DRYD 119:7
In trust I have found t.	MISQ 255:1
love the t.	DANI 101:4
none dare call it t.	HARI 162:5
t. a matter	TALL 352:4
t. can but peep	SHAK 320:1
T. has done his worst	SHAK 325:5
t. is not owned	DRYD 119:9
t., make the most of it	HENR 169:7
t. to his country	JOHN 190:13
'Twixt t. and convenience	EPIT 128:7
treasure day we should t.	AHER 5:9
treasury nationalize is the T.	WILS 385:14
our T. Bench	TROL 365:2
T. is in power	WILS 385:10
T. is the spring of business	BAGE 20:9
treble of the T. Bench	DISR 111:12
treaties T. like girls and roses	DE G 105:9
treaty against this T.	DE V 107:5
good t. with Russia	BISM 41:5
hand that signed the t.	THOM 359:2
not a peace t.	FOCH 133:6
T. like an incoming tide	DENN 106:6
tree cut down a redwood t.	STEV 347:13
killing a t.	JOUB 194:5
t. of liberty	JEFF 185:5
trees apple t. will never get across	FROS 138:10

trees (*cont.*):
cut down forest-t.	TROL 364:13
Trelawny And shall T. die	HAWK 164:2
tremble t. for my country	JEFF 187:5
trembles t. as I do	WELL 378:8
trembling t. most, maintain a dignity	
	WALP 373:7
trenches t. in the Great War	STOC 348:5
trial t. by juries	JEFF 186:4
t. is by what is contrary	MILT 252:9
tribal t., intimate revenge	HEAN 166:10
tribalism pure t.	FITT 132:4
tribunes t. with their tongues	SHAK 327:4
tribute Why should we pay t.	SHAK 319:3
trick to win the t.	LABO 208:9
trickle T.-down theory	GALB 140:1
tricks Frustrate their knavish t.	SONG 342:1
trifle careless t.	SHAK 324:8
trigger finger on the t.	MACM 236:3
want on the t.	NEWS 268:4
trimmer innocent word T.	HALI 158:4
trinity God also is a T. man	BIRR 41:3
trip forward to the t.	STIN 348:3
from fearful t.	WHIT 382:3
triple t. cord	BURK 57:3
Triton T. of the minnows	SHAK 318:7
triumph for evil to t.	MISQ 255:2
shall not see the t.	DICK 109:10
t. and disaster	KIPL 205:7
t. from the north	MACA 230:8
t. of modern science	WAUG 376:6
t. of the embalmer's art	VIDA 371:5
trivial t., inconsequential	HELL 167:11
troika like a spirited *t.*	GOGO 149:9
Trojan what T. 'orses will jump out	BEVI 38:11
troops t. towards the sound	GRIM 155:8
tropic Under the t. is our language	WALL 373:4
trouble art of looking for t.	BENN 31:9
T. in the Balkans in the spring	KIPL 206:9
t. with 'the vision thing'	IVIN 182:7
When in t., delegate	BORE 48:8
with the least t.	TAYL 354:9
trousers have your best t. on	IBSE 181:2
steam-engine in t.	SMIT 339:4
trowel lay it on with a t.	DISR 115:7
true by the people as equally t.	GIBB 144:12
my t. king	MACA 230:10
to itself do rest but t.	SHAK 324:4
T. blue and Mrs Crewe	GEOR 143:2
t. legend	STAL 345:5
Truman T.'s integrity	BUSH 62:11
trumpet t.'s silver sound	SCOT 317:1
trunkless vast and t. legs	SHEL 329:10
trust assumes a public t.	JEFF 186:8
built An absolute t.	SHAK 324:8
except t.	TAYL 353:4
In t. I have found treason	MISQ 255:1
never t. experts	SALI 312:5
not property but a t.	FOX 135:7
power in t.	DRYD 119:1
power is a t.	DISR 115:5

trust (*cont.*):

treachery cannot t.	JUNI 195:6
trusted not to be t. with the office	BROD 52:6
unfit to be t.	CHES 77:5
trustworthiness Carthaginian t.	SALL 313:13
truth can tell you the t.	MACH 234:1
diminution of the love of t.	JOHN 190:14
economical with the t.	ARMS 14:5
economy of t.	BURK 60:1
fiction lags after t.	BURK 57:14
fight for freedom and t.	IBSE 181:2
forsake this t.	ROSE 308:9
grain of t.	WILK 383:9
just tell the t.	TRUM 366:9
Never sold the t.	TENN 355:10
no appetite for t.	PEEL 285:7
One man plus the t.	PROV 296:14
opinion is t. filtered	PHIL 289:1
simple sword of t.	AITK 6:1
speak the t.	HAZL 165:4
Statesman, yet friend to T.	POPE 292:3
stop telling the t.	STEV 346:11
strife of T. with Falsehood	LOWE 226:5
stumbled over the t.	CHUR 86:2
there *is* such a thing as t.	BAGE 23:2
to speak the t.	NIXO 270:2
T. against the world	LLOY 223:12
T. forever on the scaffold	LOWE 226:6
t. in action	DISR 111:11
t. is marching on	HOWE 177:6
t. is the first	PROV 297:5
t. is the glue	FORD 134:8
t., justice, and humanity	GLAD 148:10
t. which makes men free	AGAR 5:5
two to speak the t.	THOR 360:1
wedded to the t.	SAKI 312:2
truths basic human t.	KENN 199:6
these t. to be self-evident	ANON 11:13
t. begin as blasphemies	SHAW 327:12
We hold these t.	JEFF 185:1
try here to t.	BLAI 44:3
Nice t.	MORG 260:2
tu *Et t., Brute?*	SHAK 322:10
tube toothpaste is out of the t.	HALD 158:1
Tudor US presidency a T. monarchy	BURG 56:6
tumult t. and the shouting	KIPL 206:3
tunnel back down the time t.	KEAT 196:9
turbulent rid me of this t. priest	HENR 169:4
turkey T. is a dying man	NICH 266:3
turkeys t. vote for Christmas	CALL 66:3
Turks Let the T. now carry	GLAD 148:3
turn t. over the sheet	SAND 314:4
turned t. from one's course	FABI 129:9
t. out of the Realm	ELIZ 123:8
turning lady's not for t.	THAT 356:9
turnip in that great t.	CHUR 84:4
TV T. has merely demonstrated	MURR 263:8
twelve ruin himself in t. months	GEOR 144:1
t. good men	BROU 53:2
twentieth fill the twentieth t.	LAUR 211:4
t. century belongs to those	TRUD 365:14

twentieth (*cont.*):

t. century have looked	SCHL 315:10
t. century will be	TOYN 362:7
twice it is t. blessed	SHAK 325:13
twist t. slowly in the wind	EHRL 122:1
two say that t. plus two make four	ORWE 276:3
t. ears of corn	SWIF 350:10
t. hundred thousand men	NAPO 264:13
T. nations	DISR 114:15
t. o'clock in the morning	NAPO 264:11
t. to speak the truth	THOR 360:1
you did in t. minutes	EVER 127:8
you the t. fingers	HAGU 156:7
Tyler Tippecanoe and T., too	SLOG 336:7
tyrannical In all t. governments	BLAC 43:6
nothing more t.	TROL 364:9
t. majority	BALF 26:2
tyrannis *Sic semper t.*	BOOT 48:2
Sic semper t.	MOTT 262:8
tyrannize t. over his bank balance	KEYN 201:6
tyrannous t. To use it like a giant	SHAK 325:11
tyranny burden of t.	SHAW 328:9
call it t.	HOBB 173:15
caused by some one's t.	BAGE 20:8
definition of t.	MADI 237:8
Ecclesiastic t.	DEFO 104:12
grovelling t.	DISR 115:2
liberty against t.	ROBE 303:6
specious disguise for brutal t.	BERL 35:1
struggled against t.	TUTU 367:8
T. entrenches	SHEL 330:3
T. is always better organized	PÉGU 286:18
Under conditions of t.	AREN 13:3
unnecessary t.	RUSS 311:2
wage war against a monstrous t.	CHUR 81:11
without representation is t.	OTIS 277:8
worst sort of t.	BURK 60:8
tyrant each T., every Mob	KIPL 205:2
loses the king in the t.	MAYH 246:6
No t. need fear	ARIS 14:4
t. has disposed	PLAT 291:1
t. of his fields withstood	GRAY 154:2
tyrants all men would be t.	ADAM 1:11
all men would be t.	DEFO 104:6
argument of t.	PITT 290:4
barbarity of t.	SMIT 339:1
Kings will be t.	BURK 58:17
patriots and t.	JEFF 185:5
reasoning of t.	GIBB 145:5
Rebellion to t.	BRAD 50:2
Rebellion to t.	MOTT 262:6
restrained t., averted revolution	BENN 32:6
sceptre from t.	TURG 367:7
stuff of which t. are made	BEAV 30:2
T. seldom want pretexts	BURK 56:8
Tyre Nineveh and T.	KIPL 206:4

UK within the U.	STRA 349:5
ulcer 8 U. Man	EARL 121:1
Ulster betrayal of U.	CAIR 65:3

Ulster (*cont.*):

Province of U.	CARS 70:16
title deeds of U.	PAIS 281:6
to which U. will not go	BONA 46:8
U. says no	SLOG 336:8
U.'s honoured dead	PAIS 281:4
U. will fight	CHUR 79:9

Ulsterman I'm an U. — HEWI 171:11

umbra *magni nominis u.* — LUCA 226:8

unacceptable u. face of capitalism — HEAT 167:5

unaided country's u. strength — STAL 345:2

unbearable in victory u. — CHUR 84:13

unbeatable In defeat u. — CHUR 84:13

unconscionable u. time dying — CHAR 76:11

unconstitutional u. takes a little longer

    KISS 207:4

uncreating U. word — POPE 292:1

undaunted we must be u. — CHUR 82:1

under those that work u. them — HALI 158:5

underbelly soft u. of Europe — MISQ 255:6

    u. of the Axis — CHUR 82:12

underestimated u. for decades — KOHL 208:3

underestimating lost money by u. — MENC 248:11

underlings ourselves, that we are u. — SHAK 321:8

underrating u. public taste — DEED 104:5

understand doesn't u. the situation — MURR 263:9

u. a little less	MAJO 239:1
u. the country	LESS 216:4
u. what is happening	CHAM 74:9
u. what it is	HALI 159:12

understanding evidence against their own u.

    HALI 158:9

understandings muddy u. — BURK 58:15

understatement that was an u. — MITC 253:10

undertaking no such u. has been received

    CHAM 75:3

    u. of Great Advantage — ANON 8:1

undiscovered death, The u. country — SHAK 319:9

undo will u. myself — SHAK 326:10

uneasy makes me u. — JOHN 191:14

    U. lies the head — SHAK 320:4

    You are u. — JACK 183:5

uneatable pursuit of the u. — WILD 383:6

uneducated government by the u. — CHES 78:4

unelected u. reject politicians — RIDL 302:6

unemployed from among the u. — LLOY 222:9

unemployment u. among teenagers — FRIE 138:6

unequal equal division of u. earnings — ELLI 126:1

unexpected age is the most u. — TROT 365:7

unfinished Liberty is always u. business

    ANON 9:12

unfit u. to be trusted — CHES 77:5

    u. to rule — MENC 248:8

unforeseen situations as yet u. — MONN 257:7

ungraceful no more u. figure — CECI 73:8

unhappily u. married — PARK 283:7

unhappy have died u. — HAIL 157:11

    some should be u. — JOHN 191:15

    U. the land that needs heroes — BREC 50:8

unheard language of the u. — KING 203:13

uniformity u. [of opinion] — JEFF 187:4

uninspiring may be u. — GEOR 144:2

union Act of U. is there — TRIM 363:11

    destroyed the Act of U. — PAIS 281:6

    determined to preserve this U. — HOUS 177:3

    devotion to the u. — CARS 71:2

    England to carry the U. — O'CO 272:8

    indestructible U. — CHAS 76:12

    Join the u., girls — ANTH 12:11

    key of the U. — CLAY 88:11

    knell of the u. — JEFF 186:14

    Liberty *and* U. — WEBS 377:8

    music of the U. — CHOA 78:9

    once glorious U. — WEBS 377:9

    Our Federal U. — JACK 183:3

    our u. is perfect — DICK 110:3

    save the U. — LINC 219:4

    ship of the U. — LINC 218:11

    U. of these States — WHIT 382:6

    U., sir, is my country — CLAY 88:13

    U. will be dissolved — COBB 91:9

    unnatural a bond of u. — BURK 57:5

unionist British Trade U. — BEVI 38:4

unionists trades u. at heart — JEVO 188:5

unions when Hitler attacked the u. — NIEM 269:1

unite u. the whole people — TONE 362:3

    Workers of the world, u. — MARX 245:4

united u. colonies — LEE 214:8

    U. States of Europe — CHUR 83:9

    We must be u. — CHUR 82:1

United Kingdom in this our U. — DEWA 108:8

United States believe in the U. — PAGE 278:6

    close to the U. — DIAZ 109:4

    drunkards, children, and the U. — BISM 42:12

    In the U. today — AGNE 5:8

    U.—bounded — FISK 132:3

    U. themselves — WHIT 382:7

    U. to be a democracy — BEAR 29:2

uniting By u. we stand — DICK 110:4

unity u. of our fatherland — KOHL 208:5

    u. of the empire — BURK 58:1

    u. of the nation — KOHL 208:4

universities from ancient u. — HENN 168:7

university able to get to a u. — KINN 204:9

    U. should be — DISR 112:19

unjoined u. system — ANON 9:4

unkindest most u. cut of all — SHAK 323:10

unking u. himself — MAYH 246:6

unknowable decide on the u. — ZOBE 391:5

unknown side of the U. Soldier — ASQU 15:7

    tread safely into the u. — HASK 163:3

    u. is held to be glorious — TACI 351:4

    Woman is the great u. — HARD 161:6

unlimited u. possibilities — GOLD 150:2

unmanageable u. revolutionaries — DE V 108:5

unmeritable slight u. man — SHAK 323:17

unmuzzled come among you 'u.' — GLAD 147:9

unperson abolished, an u. — ORWE 276:4

unpleasant u. for a while — RUSS 311:5

unpleasantness put up with u. — NAPO 264:7

unpolitical no such thing as an u. man
MALA 239:8
unpopular safe to be u.   STEV 347:3
unpredictable aim to be u.   JAY 184:10
unproductive u. hands   SMIT 337:5
unreasonable progress depends on u. man
SHAW 328:13
unrepresentative most u.   BEVA 37:6
unsoiled delicately and u.   CHUR 84:14
unspeakable u. in full pursuit   WILD 383:6
unspun I am u.   DOBS 116:5
unstable English call u.   MACM 236:9
unthinkable think the u.   ROSS 308:11
  'u.' thoughts   FULB 139:3
untried new and u.   LINC 218:10
untrue something that is u.   WALD 372:11
untying u. with the teeth   BIER 40:2
unusual cruel and u. punishment   CONS 95:3
unwilling u. audience   O'CO 272:6
unwritten Custom, that u. law   D'AV 102:1
up U. Guards and at them   WELL 379:2
upstairs kicked u.   HALI 160:1
urge u. for destruction   BAKU 24:3
used buy a u. car   SLOG 336:12
useful magistrate, as equally u.   GIBB 144:12
usual Business carried on as u.   CHUR 80:4
usurper u. ought to examine   MACH 234:2
Utopia principality in U.   MACA 229:8
  signposts to socialist U.   CROS 98:14
  U. is a blessed past   KISS 207:9
utopian retrospective or u.   ARON 14:12
Utopias all the static U.   INGE 181:8
utterances silly, flat, dishwatery u.   ANON 11:3
U-turn media catchphrase, the U.   THAT 356:9

vacancies v. to be obtained   JEFF 186:6
vae V. victis   LIVY 222:3
vain v., ill-natured   DEFO 104:8
valiant As he was v., I honour him   SHAK 323:3
values Victorian v.   THAT 357:3
vanilla some v.-flavoured pixie   PARR 284:4
vanished v. before the white man   TECU 355:1
vanity feeds your v.   PARR 284:3
vapour I absorb the v.   GLAD 148:16
vast v. right-wing conspiracy   CLIN 90:7
vaulting V. ambition   SHAK 325:1
veal Bellamy's v. pies   LAST 213:8
  cold boiled v.   MACA 231:2
vécu J'ai v.   SIEY 332:7
vegetarian v. leanings   ORWE 276:9
vein not in the giving v.   SHAK 327:2
venal v. city ripe to perish   SALL 313:12
vengeance gods forbade v.   CHUR 85:5
  stay the hands of v.   JACK 183:12
veni V., vidi, vici   CAES 65:1
venomous no being so v.   TROL 364:10
verbosa V. et grandis epistula   JUVE 195:11
verbosity exuberance of his own v.   DISR 113:7
verdict v. can be favourable   BIRC 41:1
verge get to the v.   DULL 120:1

vermin little odious v.   SWIF 350:9
  Tory Party are lower than v.   BEVA 36:3
Vermont so goes V.   FARL 130:6
Versailles politics of V.   MONN 257:6
verse write it out in a v.   YEAT 389:5
vessel remaining in a v.   HUME 178:7
veterinarian v. and the taxidermist   LIEB 217:11
vex die to v. me   MELB 247:5
vibration v. of a pendulum   JUNI 195:2
vicar V. of Bray   SONG 342:3
vice defence of liberty is no v.   GOLD 150:9
  in a private man a v.   MASS 245:11
  render v. serviceable   BOLI 46:3
vice-presidency v. isn't worth   GARN 141:9
viceroy every other V.   NEHR 265:12
  future V. must . . . not be   VICT 371:1
vices By hating v. too much   BURK 59:3
vicious didn't know what v. was   AUNG 18:4
victa sed v. Catoni   LUCA 226:7
victi Pugna magna v. sumus   LIVY 222:4
victim felt like a v.   WALP 373:6
  oppressor, never the v.   WIES 383:2
victims They are its v.   CONR 94:10
  v. of American Fascism   ROSE 308:10
victis Vae v.   LIVY 222:3
Victorian stuffy V. family   ORWE 275:10
  V. values   THAT 357:3
victories few sharp v.   WAUG 376:3
  Peace hath her v.   MILT 252:7
  proper use of v.   POLY 291:6
victorious Send him v.   SONG 341:7
victors v.' justice   SHAW 329:2
  written by the v.   NEHR 265:10
victory Dig for v.   OFFI 274:2
  In v.; magnanimity   CHUR 85:6
  in V., Revenge   LYNN 227:7
  in v. unbearable   CHUR 84:13
  Labor Party to v.   HAYD 164:6
  never had a v.   CHUR 85:8
  no substitute for v.   MACA 228:8
  One more such v.   PYRR 295:6
  peace without v.   WILS 386:9
  produce v. parades   HOBS 174:3
  'twas a famous v.   SOUT 343:10
  v. by a woman   WEST 380:9
  V. has a hundred fathers   CIAN 86:13
  v. in war   KEEG 197:4
  wallow in our v.   PRES 294:7
victrix V. causa deis placuit   LUCA 226:7
vidi Veni, v., vici   CAES 65:1
Vienna at the Congress of V.   ADEN 5:1
  V. is nothing   METT 249:6
Vietnam led to the V. War   BLAC 43:2
  To win in V.   SPOC 344:7
  V. as a war   PILG 289:3
  V. was lost in   MCLU 235:1
  V. was the first   WEST 380:11
vigilance eternal v.   CURR 99:9
vigilant v., the active   HENR 169:10
vile V., but viler George the Second   LAND 210:1
  you are a v. Whig   JOHN 191:9

village first in a v.   CAES 64:12
   Like a v. fiddler   NICO 266:9
   Some v.-Hampden   GRAY 154:2
vine Under his own v.   SHAK 321:4
vintage trampling out the v.   HOWE 177:6
violate v. would be oppression   JEFF 186:1
violence legitimate v.   WEBE 377:3
   v. employed   TOCQ 361:6
   v. is necessary   BROW 54:1
violent policy is v.   HUME 178:6
   v. revolution   KENN 199:1
   v. Tory   RUSK 310:7
violently v. if they must   QUIN 297:6
violet v. smells to him   SHAK 320:8
Virginian I am not a V.   HENR 169:8
virisque stat Romana v.   ENNI 126:10
virtue in a prince the v.   MASS 245:11
   practise v. afterwards   HORA 176:9
   serviceable to the cause of v.   BOLI 46:3
   v. and talents   JEFF 186:11
   v. does not come from money   SOCR 340:2
   v. is the essence   ROBE 303:7
   v. of Englishmen   TAWN 352:6
   without v.   ROBE 303:9
   woman of easy v.   HAIL 157:3
virtues v. Will plead   SHAK 324:10
virtuous looking upon men as v.   BOLI 46:2
visible V. governments   RUSK 310:6
vision hold a v.   REAG 300:3
   trouble with 'the v. thing'   IVIN 182:7
   v. thing   BUSH 62:3
   Where there is no v.   BIBL 39:10
   young men's v.   DRYD 118:10
visionary v. politicians   BURK 57:6
vocabulary diplomatist's v.   TAYL 353:17
voice horrible v.   ARIS 13:6
   new v. of Scotland   CONN 94:2
   v. of a nation   RUSS 311:9
   v. of Rome   JONS 193:2
   v. of the kingdom   SWIF 350:7
   v. was that of Mr Churchill   ATTL 16:7
   v. we know so well   WRIG 388:10
voices sound of tireless v.   STEV 347:15
   v. in Parliament   RUSK 310:10
volcanoes range of exhausted v.   DISR 112:16
Volk ein V.   SLOG 334:13
volley v. we have just heard   COLL 92:7
Voltaire V. in the Bastille   DE G 105:15
volumes thirty fine v.   MORL 260:4
vomit Dog returns to his V.   KIPL 205:5
vote did not v. Labour because   ELTO 126:3
   Don't buy a single v. more   KENN 198:1
   I never v.   ANON 9:7
   inspire them to v.   JACK 183:11
   One man shall have one v.   CART 71:6
   people v. against somebody   ADAM 2:5
   right to v.   ANTH 12:12
   turkeys v. for Christmas   CALL 66:3
   V. early and vote often   MILE 250:1
   V. for Gore   SLOG 336:4
   v. for the best President   PETE 288:1

vote (cont.):
   V. for the man who promises least   BARU 28:4
   v. for us   KILF 202:9
   v. is to perform   PAIN 280:16
   v. just as their leaders tell 'em   GILB 146:6
voted v. at my party's call   GILB 146:3
   v. cent per cent   BYRO 64:3
voter every intelligent v.   ADAM 2:3
   every v.   CLEV 90:1
votes finest brute v. in Europe   ANON 8:5
   gather v. like box tops   STEV 347:7
   V. for women   SLOG 336:9
voting If v. changed anything   LIVI 221:8
   not the v. that's democracy   STOP 348:7
vow v. to thee, my country   SPRI 344:8
vox V. populi, vox Dei   ALCU 6:3
voyage v. not a harbour   TOYN 362:5
   v. of their life   SHAK 324:1

wage home policy: I w. war   CLEM 89:5
   One man's w. increase   WILS 385:8
wages better w. and shorter hours   ORWE 276:10
   neither honours nor w.   GARI 141:8
wags w. its tail   TOYN 362:6
wait may indeed w. for ever   MACA 229:3
   We had better w. and see   ASQU 15:2
   We want eight, and we won't w.   ANON 12:3
   who only stand and w.   MILT 252:8
waited w. nearly 300 years   CONN 94:2
waiting keeping you w.   LAST 212:8
   nearly kept w.   LOUI 225:5
   w. seven hundred years   COLL 93:1
   What are we w. for   CAVA 73:2
wake W. up, England   GEOR 143:3
Wales bless the Prince of W.   SONG 341:2
   W.'s own annual blood sport   MORG 260:3
   womanhood of W.   LLLI 126:2
walk no easy w.-over   NEHR 265:11
   upon which the people w.   CRAZ 96:9
   W. under his huge legs   SHAK 321:8
walking empire w. very slowly   FITZ 132:6
wall w. of division   GORE 151:6
   W. Street lays an egg   NEWS 268:2
   w. to a layman   COMM 93:5
   With our backs to the w.   HAIG 157:2
   wooden w. is your ships   THEM 358:11
wallow w. in our victory   PRES 294:3
walls not in w.   NICI 266:5
   wooden w. are the best   COVE 96:6
walrus Between them, W. and Carpenter
                                                              LEVI 217:2
want that people know what they w.   MENC 248:6
   third is freedom from w.   ROOS 306:5
wants provide for human w.   BURK 58:11
war ain't gonna be no w.   MACM 235:7
   alternative to w.   KING 203:9
   at w. with Germany   CHAM 75:3
   better than to w.-war   CHUR 84:10
   business of w.   WELL 379:10
   calamities of w.   JOHN 190:14

war (*cont.*):

clamour for w.	PEEL 286:2
cold w. warrior	THAT 356:5
condition which is called w.	HOBB 173:8
cruellest and most terrible w.	LLOY 222:11
desolation of w.	GEOR 143:5
done very well out of the w.	BALD 24:9
Don't mention the w.	CLEE 89:3
easier to make w.	CLEM 89:7
enable it to make w.	WEIL 378:4
essence of w. is violence	MACA 229:1
European w. might do it	REDM 300:6
ever another w. in Europe	BISM 42:8
except the British W. Office	SHAW 327:16
first w. fought without	WEST 380:11
First World W. had begun	TAYL 353:6
France has not lost the w.	DE G 105:1
furnish the w.	HEAR 167:2
great protection against w.	BEVI 38:7
Grim-visaged w.	SHAK 326:14
hand of w.	SHAK 326:2
harder than making w.	STEV 346:7
home policy: I wage w.	CLEM 89:5
I am for w.	RED 300:5
If w. should ever come	BONA 46:7
I hate w.	ROOS 305:9
I have seen w.	ROOS 305:9
in peace and w.	CHUR 84:6
in time of peace thinks of w.	ANON 8:9
involved in a European w.	BEAV 29:5
involve us in the wrong w.	BRAD 50:1
In w. it is necessary	BONA 46:9
In w.; resolution	CHUR 85:6
In w. there is no second prize	BRAD 49:10
in w. the two cardinal virtues	HOBB 173:11
I renounce w.	FOSD 135:1
killed in the w.	POWE 293:12
lead this people into w.	WILS 386:14
Let me have w.	SHAK 319:1
let slip the dogs of w.	SHAK 323:1
Let w. yield to peace	CICE 86:16
made this great w.	LINC 220:11
Make love not w.	SLOG 335:14
make w. on a kindred nation	BETH 35:7
Mankind must put an end to w.	KENN 198:11
man of w.	DE V 107:5
McNamara's W.	MCNA 237:1
midst of a cold w.	BARU 28:3
money the sinews of w.	BACO 19:14
nature of w.	HOBB 173:9
never met anyone who wasn't against w.	
	LOW 226:1
never to go to w.	CHAM 75:1
never was a good w.	FRAN 136:10
no declaration of w.	EDEN 121:5
not a justifiable act of w.	BELL 30:10
Older men declare w.	HOOV 176:7
open or secret w.	JEFF 185:8
page 1 of the book of w.	MONT 259:4
prepare for w.	VEGE 370:2
recourse to w.	BRIA 51:3

war (*cont.*):

rich wage w.	SART 314:9
seek no wider w.	JOHN 189:11
short decisive w.	LYND 227:5
silent in time of w.	CICE 87:2
sinews of w.	CICE 86:18
splendid little w.	HAY 164:4
stirring up some w.	PLAT 291:1
study politics and w.	ADAM 3:7
tell us all about the w.	SOUT 343:9
tempered by w.	KENN 198:3
third world w.	TRUM 366:5
This was a people's w.	TAYL 353:3
two nations have been at w.	VOLT 371:10
Vietnam as a w.	PILG 289:3
wage w. against a monstrous tyranny	
	CHUR 81:11
W. always finds a way	BREC 50:11
w., an' a debt	LOWE 226:4
w. and peace in the 21st century	KOHL 208:6
W. appears to be	MAIN 238:8
w. creates order	BREC 50:9
w. for independence	MCAL 228:4
W. is a very rough game	MONT 259:3
W. is capitalism with	STOP 348:11
W. is continuation of politics	CLAU 88:5
W. is hell, and all that	HAY 164:3
w. is over	GRAN 153:2
W. is peace	ORWE 275:14
w. is politics with bloodshed	MAO 242:2
w. is so terrible	LEE 215:1
W. is the national industry	MIRA 253:4
W. is the remedy	SHER 331:2
W. is the trade of kings	DRYD 119:8
W. is too serious	CLEM 89:8
W. makes good history	HARD 162:2
W. Office kept three sets	ASQU 15:8
w. of words	CAMP 67:5
w. on 23 million Americans	BOAZ 45:4
w. on poverty	JOHN 189:8
w. regarded as inevitable	KENN 197:10
w. run to show the world	BERR 35:6
w. situation	HIRO 172:6
w. that drags on	WAUG 376:3
w. that we may live in peace	ARIS 13:9
w. that will end war	WELL 380:4
w. that would not boil	TAYL 353:12
w. war	WELL 380:1
w. which existed to produce	HOBS 174:3
W. will cease	SLOG 336:10
way of ending a w.	ORWE 276:16
We hear w. called murder	MACD 232:7
we prepare for w.	PEAR 285:3
what did you do in the W.	MILI 251:2
When is a w. not a war	CAMP 68:1
when it's at w.	KING 204:3
when there was w., he went	AUDE 17:16
When w. enters a country	ANON 12:6
When w. is declared	PROV 297:5
will not have another w.	GEOR 143:8
win an atomic w.	BRAD 49:7

west (*cont.*):

face neither East nor W.	NKRU 270:16
Go W., young man	NEWS 267:4
safeguard of the W.	WORD 388:6
thought in the W.	SOLZ 340:6
W. is West	KIPL 205:1
W. Lothian	DALY 100:9
W.-Lothian	DALY 101:1
W.'s awake	DAVI 102:10
W.'s awake	ROBI 303:13
western W. civilization	DILL 110:7
Westminster bars and brothels of W.	LIVI 221:9
w. sent to W.	CANA 68:7
whale decent w.	HENN 168:8
whammy Labour's double w.	SLOG 335:9
wharf sit on the w. for a day	BEAV 29:12
what W. is to be done	LENI 215:9
wheel w. runs down	SHAK 324:5
wheels w. of trade	HUME 178:5
where fixed the w. and when	HAWK 164:2
Whig ascendancy of the W. party	MACA 229:11
first W. was the Devil	JOHN 191:17
Tory and W. in turns	SMIT 339:2
Tory men and W. measures	DISR 113:17
W. in any dress	JOHN 191:1
wise W.	JOHN 191:18
you are a vile W.	JOHN 191:9
Whigs caught the W. bathing	DISR 111:7
W. admit no force	BROW 54:5
whimper Not with a bang but a w.	ELIO 123:4
whine thin w. of hysteria	DIDI 110:6
whip W.'s duty is	CANN 69:4
whips Like most Chief W.	CLAR 87:11
w. and scorns of time	SHAK 319:9
W. want the safe men	MACM 235:6
whirlwind they shall reap the w.	BIBL 39:16
whisky large w.	MALL 239:12
w. and car keys	O'RO 275:2
whisper w. of a faction	RUSS 311:9
whist ignorance of w.	TALL 352:5
whistle shrimp learns to w.	KHRU 202:1
white acceptance of w. people	BOES 45:5
best friends are w.	DURE 120:4
lowest w. man	JOHN 189:5
nor w. so very white	CANN 68:9
no 'w.' or 'coloured' signs	KENN 199:4
say this for the w. race	GREG 154:6
want to be the w. man's brother	KING 203:2
w. cliffs I never more must see	MACA 230:11
w. domination	MAND 240:6
w. heat of technology	MISQ 256:2
w. man in Africa	LESS 216:5
W. Man's Burden	KIPL 206:8
w. race *is* the cancer	SONT 340:10
Whitehall condottiere through W.	HURD 179:8
fallible men in W.	POWE 294:3
gentleman in W.	JAY 184:7
White House imported the W.	ANON 9:4
Log-cabin to W.	THAY 358:10
no whitewash at the W.	NIXO 270:6
way to the W.	STEV 347:5

White House (*cont.*):

W. is another world	DEAN 103:5
W. or home	DOLE 116:10
whiter w. than white	SANT 314:7
whites between w. and blacks	LINC 218:8
need the knowledge of w.	TSVA 367:3
whitewash no w. at the White House	NIXO 270:6
who W.? Whom	LENI 215:12
whom Who? W.	LENI 215:12
whore I am the Protestant w.	GWYN 156:3
whores parliament of w.	O'RO 275:4
whose W. finger	NEWS 268:4
WI war of words with the W.	CAMP 67:5
wicked all the world w.	BURK 59:12
Mamma, are Tories born w.	ANON 9:15
w. and moral	CHUR 80:6
wickedness than human w.	TAYL 353:9
W. is the root	ROBE 303:7
wider seek no w. war	JOHN 189:11
widow actions of a retired w.	BAGE 21:3
wields he who w. the knife	HESE 171:1
wife Caesar's w.	CAES 64:11
I have a w.	LUCA 226:9
joined me as my w.	HEAT 167:8
talks frankly only with his w.	BABE 18:8
w. does not like	PRES 294:8
Wigan mothers-in-law and W. Pier	BRID 51:4
wiggles It w., it's shapely	ERWI 127:4
wild one is the w. herb	TOCQ 361:4
w. geese	BARR 28:2
W. Geese fly	DAVI 102:11
W. men screaming	LLOY 223:1
wilderness grain into the w.	STOU 348:12
They make a w.	TACI 351:5
w. into a glorious empire	BURK 58:4
w. of tigers	SHAK 327:5
will according to the common w.	JAME 184:5
cannot resist the w.	SCAR 315:8
general w. rules	ROBE 303:3
not obey the w.	PEEL 285:12
One single w.	ROBE 303:8
settled w.	SMIT 338:9
settled w.	STEE 345:10
w. is not his own	SHAK 319:6
w. of the majority	JEFF 186:1
w. o' the wisp	MARK 243:3
w. to be free	LIPP 221:6
w. to carry on	LIPP 221:4
Willie needs a W.	THAT 358:5
willows Southern w.	LEE 214:6
win know how to w.	POLY 291:6
might never w.	SMIT 338:8
spend it, and w.	KENN 200:2
To w. in Vietnam	SPOC 344:7
w. an atomic war	BRAD 49:7
W. just one for the Gipper	GIPP 147:1
wind appearance of solidity to pure w.	
	ORWE 276:14
lie with the w.	TAYL 354:7
moved about like the w.	GERO 144:9
They have sown the w.	BIBL 39:16

worker (*cont.*):
w. can be lulled — KHRU 202:8
w. slave of capitalist society — CONN 94:5
workers organized w. of the country — SHIN 331:6
secure for the w. — ANON 11:11
w. are perfectly free — ENGE 126:9
W. of the world — MARX 245:4
working choice of w. or starving — JOHN 190:11
it isn't w. — MAJO 238:11
Labour isn't w. — SLOG 335:8
working class capitalism of the w. — SPEN 344:4
into the w. — ORWE 276:11
vast portion . . . of the w. — ARNO 14:10
works it w., doesn't it — CALL 66:9
seen the future and it w. — STEF 346:1
workshop nation may be its w. — CHAM 74:6
w. of the world — DISR 111:4
world begins the w. afresh — MONN 257:8
begin the w. over — PAIN 279:7
believe that the w. began — CHUR 84:7
bestride the narrow w. — SHAK 321:8
country is the w. — PAIN 280:13
decide the fate of the w. — DE G 105:4
enthusiasm moves the w. — BALF 26:1
funny old w. — THAT 358:3
governs the whole w. — OXEN 278:5
great w. spin for ever — TENN 355:5
interpreted the w. — MARX 244:9
loosed upon the w. — YEAT 389:8
new w. order — BUSH 62:7
one half the w. fools — JEFF 187:4
only saved the w. — CHES 77:11
start of the majestic w. — SHAK 321:7
There is a w. elsewhere — SHAK 318:10
third w. war — TRUM 366:5
though the w. perish — MOTT 262:3
three corners of the w. — SHAK 324:4
Thus passes the glory of the w. — ANON 11:2
Truth against the w. — LLOY 223:12
turned the w. upside down — BIBL 39:24
way the w. ends — ELIO 123:4
way to a w. society — CHOD 79:2
Winds of the W. — KIPL 205:3
workshop of the w. — DISR 111:4
w. becoming like a lunatic asylum — LLOY 223:6
w. must be made safe — WILS 386:12
w. safe for hypocrisy — WOLF 387:6
w.'s policeman — HEAL 165:9
written for the w. of 1918 — BLAI 43:9
worldly breath of w. men — SHAK 326:4
worlds destroyer of w. — OPPE 274:12
worms set on me in W. — LUTH 227:2
worry did not w. about it — TRUM 366:8
Don't W. Me — EARL 121:1
worse follow the w. — OVID 277:10
from w. to better — HOOK 176:2
w. off for having known — STEP 346:5
w. than a crime — BOUL 49:4
worship second is freedom to w. — ROOS 306:5
various modes of w. — GIBB 144:12
w. the people — BACO 18:10

worst be told the w. — CHUR 82:5
it was the w. of times — DICK 109:9
While the w. are full — YEAT 389:8
w. form of Government — CHUR 83:13
You do your w. — CHUR 82:6
worth confident of their own w. — AUNG 18:5
nor words, nor w. — SHAK 323:13
would He w., wouldn't he — RICE 301:8
wound help to w. itself — SHAK 324:4
tongue In every w. — SHAK 323:14
w. had been for Ireland — LAST 214:3
wounds bind up the nation's w. — LINC 220:7
wrangle men w. — HALI 159:6
wrath grapes of w. — HOWE 177:6
wreckers not the w. — MCAL 228:3
wrestled w. for perhaps too long — HOWE 177:5
wring soon w. their hands — WALP 374:3
wrinklies not because ageing w. — STRA 349:4
write I w. one — DISR 116:1
written w. by the victors — NEHR 265:10
wrong both agree is w. — CECI 73:7
disastrously w. — GALB 140:4
if w., to be set right — SCHU 316:5
involve us in the w. war — BRAD 50:1
majority are w. — DEBS 103:7
never in the w. — BURK 59:10
not always to be w. — EDEN 121:6
only an accumulated w. — CASE 71:9
our country, right or w. — DECA 103:9
We were w. — MCNA 237:2
when I am in the w. — MELB 247:13
W. but Wromantic — SELL 317:7
w. even the poorest ploughman — CHAR 76:1
W. forever on the throne — LOWE 226:6
w. members in control — ORWE 275:10

Yanks Y. are coming — COHA 92:3
year man at the gate of the y. — HASK 163:3
years two hundred y. like a sheep — TIPU 360:6
two thousand y. of hope — WEIZ 378:6
y. of desolation — JEFF 187:2
yellow y. stripes — HIGH 172:2
yelps loudest y. for liberty — JOHN 190:15
yes answer is y. — DOLE 116:8
We say Y. — WRIG 388:10
Y. it hurt — SLOG 336:13
Y., Minister! No, Minister — CROS 99:5
yesterday authority of the eternal y. — WEBE 377:4
Y.'s men — SLOG 336:14
yoke hath received our y. — WALL 373:4
y. of prelaty — MILT 253:1
yolks lose but your y. — STEV 347:11
you Y. too, Brutus — CAES 65:2
young crime of being a y. man — PITT 289:6
defrauded y. — KIPL 205:4
too y. to understand — BROW 54:2
what the world would call y. men — PEEL 285:9
y., bald Leader — KINN 204:12
y. men's vision — DRYD 118:10
y. was very heaven — WORD 388:4

younger curse of the y. generation   MACM 236:7
youth flower of our y.   TREV 363:1
  In the y. of a state   BACO 19:18
  it is y. who must fight   HOOV 176:7
  today's y.   SPIE 344:6
  widow and an unemployed y.   BAGE 21:3
  Y. is a blunder   DISR 113:18
  y. is the season of credulity   PITT 289:9
  Y. of a Nation   DISR 114:18
  y. of the realm   SHAK 320:18
  y. to the gallows   PAIN 280:12

Zaire Z. is the trigger   FANO 130:4
Zane works by Mr Z. Grey   ACHE 1:8
zeal by men of z.   BRAN 50:6
  holy mistaken z.   JUNI 195:3
  not the slightest z.   TALL 352:3
zealous z. citizen   BURK 59:4
Zionism Z. is rooted in traditions   BALF 26:5
zoom z. lenses   ULLR 368:6
Zurich gnomes in Z.   WILS 384:6